THE WESTMINSTER GUIDE TO THE
BOOKS OF THE BIBLE

THE WESTMINSTER GUIDE TO THE

BOOKS OF THE BIBLE

WILLIAM M. RAMSAY

WESTMINSTER JOHN KNOX PRESS
Louisville, Kentucky

© 1994 William M. Ramsay

Book design by Publishers' WorkGroup
Cover design by Kevin Darst, KDEE Design Inc.

First edition
Published by Westminster John Knox Press
Louisville, Kentucky

This book is printed on acid-free paper that meets the American National Standards Institute Z39.48 standard. ∞

PRINTED IN THE UNITED STATES OF AMERICA

00 01 02 03 — 10 9 8 7 6 5 4 3

Library of Congress Cataloging-in-Publication Data

Ramsay, William M., date.
    The Westminster guide to the books of the Bible / William M. Ramsay. — 1st ed.
        p.   cm.
    Includes a rev. ed. of the author's The layman's guide to the New Testament.
    Includes bibliographical references (p.   ).
    ISBN 0-664-22061-4
    1. Bible—Introductions.   I. Ramsay, William M. Layman's guide to the New Testament.   II. Title.
BS475.2.R36   1994
220.6'1—dc20
                                                94-2706

CONTENTS

Part Two
The New Testament

PREFACE

When Dr. Richard Ray, then editor of the John Knox Press, was editing my book *The Layman's Guide to the New Testament* for its 1981 publication, he suggested to me that I write a companion volume introducing the Old Testament. I declined. At that time I had not had enough experience teaching Old Testament at the college level. After thirteen years of teaching Old Testament at Bethel College in McKenzie, Tennessee, I informed Dr. Walter Sutton of Westminster John Knox Press that I was now willing. He suggested that I revise *The Layman's Guide to the New Testament* and that a new book be published to include both the Old and the New Testament. Thus the present volume was begun.

Most of the New Testament section of this book is a republication of *The Layman's Guide to the New Testament*. I have, however, made three kinds of revisions in it. First, I have made some use of newly developed techniques of biblical interpretation and new insights that have come about since the earlier publication. Second, I have used more inclusive language, and third, the New Revised Standard Version of the Bible has been used throughout, except where otherwise noted.

Sales of *The Layman's Guide to the New Testament* suggest that it has had some success in reaching the two groups of readers for whom it was intended. It has been adopted as a text for courses in biblical literature on several college campuses, and it has been on the reading list in a number of seminaries and graduate schools of religion. Sunday school teachers, directors of Christian education, pastors, and interested lay people have reported that they have found it useful. *The Westminster Guide to the Books of the Bible* is intended for those same readers. It is written with the same goals:

1. This book is intended to be an introduction. It does not assume that the reader has a great deal of prior knowledge of biblical criticism. Technical terms are avoided or, where they are especially useful, explained. Views of some scholars that may be upsetting to beginners have been introduced gently.

2. The approach is ecumenical. My own point of view is, I believe, generally in the mainstream of present-day biblical scholarship. But this volume is written with respect for the scholarship and integrity of those in the very conservative camp and for those of the opposite extreme. At most points where I have taken a position on a controversial issue, I have at least footnoted to the work of scholars on the other side.

3. I have tried to allow the challenge of the scripture itself to come through. For many centuries, readers have found the Bible to be fascinating literature. No volume that is lifeless and dull, therefore, can be a completely valid introduction. Too often I have read works on the Bible that have somehow managed to conceal why it is that people have been ready to live and even die for the Bible's truths. I have not preached in this *Guide*. I have made some effort to be "objective." But I hope that I have helped my readers to stand imaginatively with the ancient Hebrews and the earliest Christians as they read these sacred words. I hope that through this *Guide*, modern readers will hear the ancient call to decision. I am writing to present an avowedly Christian understanding of the scripture.

4. *The Westminster Guide to the Books of the Bible* undertakes to relate Old Testament and New Testament in a way that separate introductions cannot do so easily. A chapter on the Apocrypha has also been included, partly for the value of these books in their own right but partly because they help to link the two Testaments.

My deepest gratitude goes to my wife, DeVere Maxwell Ramsay, for help in countless ways. I am grateful to Professor Gilbert Carp of the University of Tennessee at Martin for his help in matters relating to Judaism and to Mitzi Minor of Bethel College, who helped bring my biblical criticism up to date. And I will always be grateful to my former teachers, including James Stewart and William Manson of Edinburgh and John Bright, Balmer Kelly, Donald George Miller, and others of Union Theological Seminary in Virginia, and to many under whom I have had a chance to study more recently at the Bible and Theology Conference each summer at Montreat, North Carolina. My Bethel colleague Melanie Young helped make my writing clear. Harold Kelly of the Bethel College library and Dale Bilbrey of the library at Memphis Theological Seminary have always been helpful. I must also express thanks to colleague Bill King and the staff of the Bethel College Writing Center, including student Randi Gardner and others, who patiently taught me to use their word-processing system, and to Greg Herr for many hours of wise help in the preparation of the manuscript.

W.M.R.

INTRODUCTION:
INTERPRETING THE BIBLE

Whatever his or her view about religion, any student of literature would agree that the Bible has been the most influential book in the history of the Western hemisphere.

Any student of world religions will list the Bible among the great classics of religious literature.

Traditionally, Christians have agreed in going much further, speaking of their holy book as the inspired word of God, the message on which they base their claim to salvation.

The problem that makes helps such as this *Westminster Guide to the Books of the Bible* necessary, however, is the difficulty of understanding what the Bible means. Christians in the United States are split into more than three hundred different denominations, in part because they cannot agree in their interpretations of scripture. Different understandings of the Bible have led to religious wars: Christians slaughtering Christians. Even now, people are known to begin reading the Bible, full of high expectations for finding inspiration and guidance, only to give up the study after a few pages out of confusion—even boredom.

Dogmatic partisans of particular religious or social ideologies, from the Ku Klux Klan and Adolf Hitler's Nazis to radicals of the Left, have twisted the Bible to support their own prejudices. In cynical despair, others have joked that "you can prove anything by the Bible" and have given up trying to understand it.

Those who take the trouble really to study it, however, find the Bible no harder to understand than many other works of ancient literature. Even little children find many of its stories immediately intelligible. Analyses of vocabulary and sentence structure have shown many passages to be comprehensible when read by the average fifth-grader. More difficult passages become clearer as they are analyzed and set in historical context.

This chapter, therefore, presents certain principles of interpretation that students of the Bible have found helpful as they have sought to understand the scripture. Perhaps it is true that, in a sense, "you can prove anything by the Bible," but you cannot prove "just anything" if you follow the principles that are proposed here.[1]

THREE TRADITIONAL
BUT LESS HELPFUL APPROACHES

Naive literalists have sometimes suggested that the Bible really needs no interpretation. Let the believer simply read in faith, ready to obey, and the Holy Spirit will make clear the meaning of the scripture.

Most Christians agree that nothing is more important in receiving a divine message from scripture than a heart open to spiritual truth. It is quite another matter, however, to go from the recognition of the proper role of faith in religion to the assumption that study and interpretation of the Bible are not necessary.

"Believe, obey, and don't ask all those questions," the naive literalist piously proposes.

"But exactly what am I to believe and obey?" a student must reply. As soon as that is asked, the question of interpretation is inevitably confronted. Because the Old Testament was originally written in Hebrew and the New Testament in Greek, one might argue that the naive literalist, to be perfectly consistent, ought only to recite the scripture using the original languages.

To the religious believer, the attitude of the heart is important to understanding. People of equally good will, however, have differed and do differ as to the meaning of the Bible. It is not simply lack of "faith" but also failure to study carefully, using sound principles of interpretation, that is the cause of much misunderstanding.

From very early on, *allegorizing interpreters* have proposed that each item in a biblical account of an earthly event stood for some hidden heavenly reality. Rabbis pioneered this method. Paul used allegory to find new meaning in the story of Hagar and Sarah (Gal. 4:21–24). Clement of Alexandria, a Christian scholar and writer near the end of the second century, excelled in this technique. For example, Joshua 2—6 relates the story of how the Israelites slaughtered every man, every woman, and even every baby in Jericho. They spared only the family of one whore, with whom the Israelite spies had spent a night. Her protection of those spies was rewarded. A red cord suspended from her window marked her home, the only one not destroyed. Literally interpreted, and in the light of the New Testament, the story might not seem uplifting. Clement, however, claimed to find a truly spiritual meaning. The red cord, he said, was really the blood of Christ. That scarlet thread of saving grace, said Clement, by allegory runs all through scripture, to be climaxed on the cross.

Another example of allegorical interpretation involves the sensual love songs of the Song of Solomon. These probably would not have been included in the canon had they not been interpreted allegorically to refer to the love of Christ for the church.

Although Martin Luther did occasionally use allegory, he, John Calvin, and other scholars at the time of the Reformation demanded that we turn to what the original writers actually said and meant. Allegory, many Reformers warned, can allow us to impose our own fanciful meanings on scripture. Many contemporary preachers, however, have allegorized scripture and some even preach sermons that echo Clement's "scarlet thread."

Authoritarian interpretation was also attacked by the Reformers, though again, not always consistently. In the Middle Ages, people who could read were rare, and copies of the Bible were rarer. The masses had to turn to their priests to tell them what the Bible said and what it meant. The church was the authority, and the Latin Vulgate was the authoritative version of scripture, rather than the original Hebrew of the Old Testament and the Greek of the New Testament. When Galileo defended the idea that the earth moves around the sun, the authority of the church forced him to recant on his knees. The Reformers, too, could at times be authoritarian, but they did insist on translating from the original languages into the languages of the people. Thus individuals could do their own interpreting of the Bible.

Most of us, it should be said, are still grateful for the guidance of the church's scholars, trained by those who teach with the wisdom of lifetimes of study. These "authorities" do help us understand the scripture. *The Westminster Guide to the Books of the Bible* is written to help you use what scholars have taught us. But no one else's authority can substitute fully for your own study of the Bible.

SOME "SCIENTIFIC" APPROACHES

Interpretation can never be an exact science, but many kinds of science have been enlisted to help us understand the Bible. Here are three examples.

Sociological criticism has helped us understand the Bible by using the insights from the social sciences. For example, sociologists have attempted to cast light on the tribal system of Israel and have compared Israelite marriage customs to those of other ancient cultures. Perhaps, one sociologist has proposed, Israel moved to a monarchy because of its increased population; a population of about two hundred thousand seems to have been the upper limit for a loosely organized government. Social scientists suggest how the development of an urban society led to the unjust economic conditions that Amos denounced. Sociologists have pointed to similarities and striking contrasts between the place of women in the Bible and their place in most ancient societies.

Archaeology has enabled us to picture the times in which biblical events occurred and the situations that caused books to be written. For example, archaeologists have helped us to see the grandeur of Egypt in the days of Moses and have uncovered ancient carvings that actually give us contemporary pictures of the Assyrian army's siege of the Judean city of Lachish at the time of the fall of Samaria, scriptures of the baals who competed with the Lord for Israel's worship, and even copies of the pagan Babylonian stories of creation and the Flood. The archaeologist Sir William Mitchell Ramsay retraced Paul's journeys and made numerous discoveries that shed light on historical details in Acts.

Chemistry and physics have been used in helping textual critics determine the age of manuscripts and thus decide which are closest to the originals. Indeed, almost every discipline has at some time contributed to our understanding of scripture.

NEW INSIGHTS FROM CONTEMPORARY MOVEMENTS FOR SOCIAL JUSTICE

Several contemporary movements for social justice could be mentioned, but two have been especially influential on biblical interpretation.

Liberation theologians have called us to read the Bible from the perspective of the poor. The story of how God liberated the slaves from Egypt, calling them to come out of bondage, sounds different when interpreted by those working among people enslaved by poverty and injustice today. The prophets' calls for justice and the hope given the exiles in Babylon take on new meaning when read as they sound to modern victims of oppression.

Feminist interpreters have pointed us to parts of the Bible that were there all along but which were overlooked in a male-dominated church. The independence and courage of Ruth, the validity of sexual passion manifest in the Song of Songs, the surprising places of the matriarchs along with the patriarchs in Genesis, and the biblical use of feminine metaphors about God, which have long been ignored, are among the lessons these thinkers teach us. Indeed, by 1992 *The Women's Bible Commentary* had been published, devoted entirely to new insights on each book of the Bible as gleaned from a feminist perspective.[2]

ANALYZING BIBLICAL LITERATURE INTO ITS PARTS

Since the middle of the nineteenth century, many scholars have painstakingly analyzed biblical literature. Disagreements have been frequent, but often such analysis has helped answer questions about the meaning of difficult passages of scripture. Here are two examples of analytical approaches.

Source criticism has undertaken the identification and division of assorted strands of literature that are found within various books. Often, puzzling features can be explained by recognizing that what we now have as one book may contain the work of more than one author. For example, Exodus contains different names for Moses' father-in-law and different names for Mount Sinai. The problem is solved if one recognizes that the person responsible for the book of Exodus in the form we now have it used different versions of the same stories, traditions that had been passed down orally by different tribes in different places before being written down for different purposes. The editor wove the traditions together to form Exodus as we have it now. Another example is Isaiah 1—39, which seems to have been written when God delivered Jerusalem in the days of King Hezekiah; but Isaiah 40—66 describes Jerusalem as in ruins and summons the Jews to leave captivity in Babylon. The problem is easily solved by recognizing that the last half of the book of Isaiah contains poems from a prophet who lived a century and a half later than the author of the first chapters.

Form criticism enables us to get behind the written documents themselves and imagine how different stories and poems were first used. For example, a careful reading of some psalms suggests that they must have been sung by pilgrims to the Temple. "Etiological" stories were told to explain the sacred origins of shrines at such places as Bethel, Shechem, and Gilgal. Around campfires, perhaps, long before our present accounts were written down, stories were told about why a rainbow appears in the sky or why Jericho was in ruins. Stories clustered around heroes of the past: Abraham, Jacob, Moses, Joshua, and the rest. New Testament form critics such as Rudolph Bultmann have sought to recover the earliest forms of the gospel stories and sayings. Calling attention to such patterns as parables, miracle stories, and stories associated with pronouncements by Jesus, they have tried to show how these may have been developed as they were handed down orally by the early Christian preachers.

MORE RECENT LITERARY CRITICISM

Many recent scholars, however, have believed that the approach of those who delight in analyzing the different literary and oral strands that make up individual books of the Bible has at times obscured the message in the scripture. While there is value in looking at its ancient parts, scripture comes to us now as a whole. What we must examine, these scholars remind us, is the text itself in its final form.

Redaction criticism, for example, has examined the purposes that seem to have guided those who composed or edited books of the Bible as we now have them. Those editors selected from the earliest campfire traditions, the stories told by the first preachers, or stories from earlier writers and put them together to form the books we now read. Later in this *Guide,* when we compare the first three Gospels, for example, we shall see that each writer may fit a given story into a different place in his account of Jesus' life, in order to bring out how that story supports his particular emphasis.

Going further, *the "new" literary criticism* has applied to the study of the Bible insights from current study of secular literature. For example, R. Alan Culpepper, in *Anatomy of the Fourth Gospel,* writes a helpful commentary on the Gospel according to John by reviewing it much as an English professor might explain a novel. He does not analyze it verse by verse; nor does he, like a form critic, attempt to get behind the written stories to their oral sources. Instead, he traces the "plot" of this Gospel's narrative, describes its characters, and discusses the "implied narrator" and that narrator's point of view.[3] Charles H. Talbert, in *Reading John,* repeatedly shows the concentric structure of a discourse and how that literary pattern focuses on the central idea of the passage.[4]

Finally, *canonical criticism* has insisted that Jews and Christians read the Bible not as a collection of ancient tales and poems but as scripture, canonized, recognized as authoritative by the people of God in the form in which it is now put together. Down through the centuries, in the books as we now have them, Christians and Jews have found a message from God, the kerygma, good news. To analyze the books into parts based on their sources may be useful but may miss the whole. The message of the whole is the reason we study them. For example, most scholars agree that the second half of Isaiah comes from a different author from that of the first half, one writing at a later time. Isaiah the son of Amoz in the first half of the book of Isaiah voices a message of coming judgment. The second half contains the words of one or more prophets emphasizing comfort and hope. Recognizing their different historical settings and sources helps us to explain the puzzling contrasts between the two halves of the book. But Isaiah comes to us now as one volume. Canonical critics suggest that the two halves are welded together for a purpose. The kerygma, the good news that people of faith find in Isaiah, includes both judgment and hope. The two belong together.[5]

UNDERSTANDING THE BIBLE:
THREE BASIC QUESTIONS

Building on what these and other scholars have taught us, here are some suggestions for studying the scripture. Think of Bible study as the effort to answer three questions.

1. *What does the book or the passage say?* There is no substitute for

reading and rereading the Bible itself. Books such as *The Westminster Guide to the Books of the Bible* are designed only to help you understand what you read for yourself.

Ideally, you should read the Old Testament in Hebrew and the New Testament in Greek, the original languages. *Textual critics* examine the oldest manuscripts to try to reconstruct as nearly as possible what the original writers actually wrote. Comparing ancient manuscripts to ascertain which is the oldest is a science that requires trained technicians. There are some two hundred thousand variations in ancient Greek manuscripts of the New Testament. Nearly one word out of every eight appears in a different form—perhaps a different tense of a verb, a different case ending, or even a different word altogether—in some ancient Greek manuscript. Fortunately, none of these variations really affects any of the major doctrines of Judaism or Christianity. Rabbis were extremely careful in copying their sacred books. Among the Dead Sea Scrolls was found a manuscript of Isaiah, probably older than the one Jesus read in the Nazareth synagogue. Amazingly, though it was perhaps a thousand years older than any previously known copy of Isaiah, there were relatively few substantive differences between it and existing modern manuscripts.

Though most readers cannot read Hebrew or Greek, anyone can compare different modern translations. Commentaries by scholars who know the original languages may help, but the most important thing is to read and reread the Bible for yourself in the best modern versions available to you. (Quotations in this *Guide* are from the New Revised Standard Version unless otherwise indicated.)

2. *What did a book or a passage mean when it was written?* There are many things we can do to help us in some sense to get back into the minds of the biblical writers and those to whom their words were addressed.

For one thing, we can read the Bible in the light of ancient history. The original readers of the Bible were familiar with the ancient world. We, however, need to study history if we are fully to stand with them and understand what they would have grasped immediately. With the help of the historians, try to imagine yourself among the Hebrew slaves who helped build great pagan temples in Egypt. Walk with the Jewish captives into Babylon as the archaeologists describe it for us. Listen with those who first heard the prophet denounce the royal "house of ivory," the palace at Samaria, whose ruins archaeologists have partially unearthed. Feel the hatred for Roman oppressors that caused the first-century Jews to long for a messiah who would deliver them. Historians produce the commentary that paints for twentieth-century readers the scenes the first readers knew all too well.

Think Hebrew! Harley Swiggum, founder of the Bethany Series of Bible Studies in Madison, Wisconsin, gets his students of the Old Testament to wear badges inscribed with this slogan. If we are to understand ancient Hebrew scriptures, it helps to remember that these people of long ago thought in patterns different from those of modern people in the Western world. We are prosaic and scientific; they loved the pictorial and symbolic. We ask how; they asked why. We deal with here and now, the immediate cause and effect; they pointed to ultimate purposes. We seek the practical and use it; they sought the meaning of events and worshiped. We distort scripture if we try to force it into twentieth-century scientific ways of thinking. The more we can understand the mind of the ancient Hebrews, the better we will understand what they have written.

Scholars who practice what is called *higher criticism* help us to answer such questions as who wrote a book of the Bible, when was it written, and in what situation its readers first read it. Remembering that the fiery warnings of Amos came from a farmer turned prophet only one generation before Assyria destroyed Israel, visualizing Jeremiah prophesying while the Babylonian army is actually advancing on Jerusalem, relating the book of Deuteronomy to the reforms under King Josiah for which it was the law, and contrasting 1 John with the Gnostic heresy that historians tell us was soon to disrupt the church are only a few illustrations of how this kind of study can help us see what some part of the Bible meant when it was written.

Unique as the Bible is, the techniques that are useful in studying any other great work of literature also help us understand the Bible. Here are a few such methods which will be used in this volume:

Set any verse in its context in scripture. To take an obvious example: "Skin for skin! All that people have they will give to save their lives" is in the Bible (Job 2:4), but is it the word of God? Hardly! Inspection of the context reveals that it is prefaced with the words "Then Satan answered." Beware of plucking a few words out of context. You may twist their meaning completely.

Similarly, look at wholes before looking at parts. This volume contains many outlines of whole books to help you set verses and chapters in their larger context.

Consider what kind of literature a passage is. The Bible contains history, poetry, liturgy for worship, census reports, letters, accounts of apocalyptic visions, and other sorts of compositions, each of which has to be understood in its own way. For example, Isaiah assures us that when Judah returns from captivity, "all the trees of the field shall clap their hands" (Isa. 55:12). A student of literature would recognize that this is joyful, delightful poetry, not a prediction in a botany laboratory. Controversies about the account of creation in the first chapter of

Genesis dissolve when one recognizes that passage is a kind of liturgy, a confession of faith about the nature of God and humankind, not a work of empirical science.

Look for repeated words and ideas. Themes such as "law," "kingdom," "land," "justice," and "love" go all through the Bible. For example, count the number of times the word "covenant" occurs at the end of the story of Noah—seven times in the ten verses of Gen. 9:8–17—and you will see clearly what a biblical writer wanted to emphasize as he retold that ancient tale.

Analyze a biblical story as you might a narrative in any other work of great literature, tracing its plot, studying its characters, noting their conflicts, and recognizing the point of view from which the story is told. How does the writer build suspense? What hints are given early in the story of how it may end?

In short, almost everything one knows about history, literature, or social sciences can be used in helping one understand the Bible.

3. *What does this passage mean to us now, today?* Ultimately, this is the most important question for believers to ask. The synagogue and the church have preserved the Bible not because it is fascinating literature or a book giving insights into ancient history; for people of faith, the Bible is scripture. The scholars like to speak of its message by using the Greek word *kerygma,* "proclamation," "good news." Christians and Jews read the scriptures, sure that in the Bible they hear God speaking to them in their own lives today.

There is a danger in rushing too quickly to the belief that one has discovered a personal message from God in some passage of scripture. Practicing the principles of interpretation described above will help to keep us from reading our own ideas into the Bible. But when you have done the kind of study we have described, the kind this *Guide* is designed to help one do, then do not fail also to ask what meaning there may be in a book or a passage for your own life. Here are just a few of the many ways that some people have found helpful in finding personal meanings in the Bible:

Ask what things in your own life or in our world are like those of the people for whom this book was originally written.

Ask what change would be made in your life if you did what a particular passage says.

Read the Bible with a newspaper in the other hand, asking what the scripture may be saying, through you, to the world that newspaper describes.

Pick out verses or ideas that especially appeal to you. Why do you like them?

See what meaning, if any, you can find by digging deeper into verses that at first do not appeal to you.

Study and discuss the meaning of scripture with others in the fellowship of believers.

Ask what the passage you are reading suggests you ought to pray about.

THE UNITY OF THE TESTAMENTS

Before we look at the different parts of the Bible, one more principle should be recalled: *Interpret the Old Testament and New Testament in the light of each other.*

Christians, it is true, have sometimes had difficulty knowing exactly what to do with the Old Testament. "Reject the Old Testament!" was the approach proposed by a second-century scholar named Marcion. Had not Jesus in the Sermon on the Mount repeatedly contrasted his teachings with the Jewish law? "You have heard that it was said [in the Old Testament] . . . But I say . . ." is a chorus running through the fifth chapter of Matthew. Paul repeatedly contrasted the law of Moses to the gospel of Christ. The God of the Jews, Marcion proposed, had made this corrupt, material earth. But the good news of the Christian scriptures, he alleged, is about the true God, too spiritual to be involved with flesh and dirt. And so Marcion drew up a canon, a list of books which he felt the church should recognize as authoritative. His was the first such list, as far as we have any record. He included no Old Testament books. He also did not include such books as Matthew and Hebrews, which apparently seemed too close to the Old Testament for Marcion. Marcion threw out the Old Testament; the church threw out Marcion! He was excommunicated as a heretic. The Old Testament, the church affirmed, is part of the written word of God.

Few Christians would join Marcion today. It must be said, however, that some have tended to treat parts of the Old Testament as relics of a primitive past, now outgrown and irrelevant for today. Harry Emerson Fosdick summarized eloquently a view of the Bible that seemed almost to reject the Old Testament:

> Beginning with a storm god on a desert mountain, [the Bible] ends with men saying, "God is a Spirit; and they that worship him must worship in spirit and truth." Beginning with a tribal war god, leading his devotees to bloody triumph over their foes, it ends with men seeing that "God is love; and he that abideth in love abideth in God, and God abideth in him."
>
> Beginning with a territorial deity who loved his clansmen and hated the remainder of mankind, it ends with a great multitude out of every tribe and tongue and people and nation, worshiping one universal Father.

Beginning with a god who walked in a garden in the cool of the day or who showed his back to Moses as a special favor, it ends with the God whom "no man hath seen . . . at any time" and in whom "we live, and move, and have our being."

Beginning with a god who commanded the slaughter of infants and sucklings without mercy, it ends with the God whose will it is that not "one of these little ones should perish."

Beginning with a god from whom at Sinai the people shrank in fear, saying, "Let not God speak with us, lest we die," it ends with the God to whom one prays in the solitary place and whose indwelling Spirit is our unseen friend.

Beginning with a god whose highest social vision was a tribal victory, it ends with the God whose worshipers pray for a world-wide kingdom of righteousness and peace.[6]

Fosdick's words serve as a useful warning that Christians must interpret the Old Testament in the light of the New Testament. Christians who, for example, have used the Old Testament's story of Joshua's slaughter of the people of Jericho to justify some modern war of conquest may need to ponder Fosdick's words and the New Testament's call to love one's enemies. There is truth in the idea that the Bible gives us a progressive revelation of God and of God's will, a revelation climaxed in the New Testament's presentation of Jesus Christ.

But Christians affirm that God speaks through the Old Testament as through the New. Few New Testament passages picture the care of God more beautifully than does the Old Testament's Twenty-third Psalm. What New Testament passage more forcefully presents God's demand for social justice than does the prophecy of Amos?

With good reason, Jews see their scriptures as a book with integrity, able to stand alone. But Christians down through the ages have read it from a special point of view. They have seen the Old Testament as a book of promise. Christians always read it in relation to what for them is the fulfillment of those promises: Jesus Christ.

The Bible is a collection of sixty-six diverse books, writings from a period of more than a thousand years. But recent scholarship has emphasized that the canon—this authoritative set of books—is also one book. Hulda Niebuhr taught us to speak of *The One Story of the Bible,* from creation to the new creation. John Bright summarized the Bible around a single theme, *The Kingdom of God,* from the call to Israel at Sinai to be God's "priestly kingdom" to Jesus' announcement that "the kingdom of God is at hand." G. Ernest Wright and A. B. Rhodes have described the unity of the Old and New Testaments around *The Mighty Acts of God,* who redeems, judges, and restores. Bernard Anderson has helped us see the Old and New Testaments together as *The Unfolding Drama of the Bible,* each act having its place. And others in various ways have developed the theme Paul expressed: "For in [Jesus Christ] every one of God's promises is a 'Yes' " (2 Cor. 1:20).

All the New Testament writers seem to have regarded the Old Testament as a gift of God, and everywhere they based their message on its foundation. They loved even passages that seem foreign to us. The New Testament book of Hebrews interprets the bloody sacrifices of Leviticus, repulsive to modern taste, as foreshadowing the sacrificial death of Christ. They are seen as witness to God's holiness and forgiveness, revealed supremely in the cross. The ethical implications of the story of the destruction of Jericho are transcended in the Sermon on the Mount, but even that story can be seen as an event that "in the fullness of time" could prepare a place for Jesus. Few modern scholars would interpret some Old Testament passages as boldly as did Matthew as he found prophecies of the coming of Christ. But Christians do see the *whole* story begun in the Old Testament as climaxed in Jesus.

Just as Christians must interpret the Old Testament in the light of the New, the New Testament must be interpreted in the light of the Old. The whole canon (the books that make up the Bible) tells one story.

To the beginning of that story, the Pentateuch, the first five books of the Bible, we turn now.

PART ONE

THE OLD TESTAMENT

1

INTRODUCING THE "FIVE BOOKS OF MOSES": THE PENTATEUCH

Go to a synagogue today and join in the worship. Your eyes are likely to focus on the "ark" at the center of what Christians would call the chancel. At the high point of the service, the leader will bring forth from behind the curtain of that ark the holiest object in the synagogue: it is the scroll of the Torah, meaning "the Law" or "the Instruction." It is also called "the Pentateuch," meaning "the five books" (of Moses), the name given to it by early Greek-speaking Jews. By its 613 laws, Orthodox Jews guide every aspect of their lives. To Jews, of the thirty-nine books of their scriptures these five are the most important. Here the faithful find their origins, the story of their redemption, and the guide for their lives.

Christians, too, love these books. Christians boast that spiritually they are adopted sons of Abraham, the father of the faithful and the central figure of Genesis (Rom. 11:17–18). The God whom Exodus describes as redeeming ancient Israel from slavery in Egypt is the God Christians worship as Redeemer still.

This *Guide* discusses each book of the Pentateuch in turn: Genesis, Exodus, Leviticus, Numbers, and Deuteronomy. Because these were, at one time, one scroll and because they tell a connected story, it is appropriate briefly to introduce them together.

THE PENTATEUCH TELLS A STORY

Though scholars find traces of multiple authorship spanning five hundred years, with traditions going back centuries further, the Pentateuch comes to us now as one story. The story begins, in the first chapter of Genesis, at the beginning of time, and it ends, in the last chapter of Deuteronomy, with the death of Moses. That ending comes at a critical moment: Moses, called by God, has led God's chosen people at last to the edge of Canaan, the Promised Land.

As the biblical writers recount the history of the world, they find everywhere the chief actor to be God. In majestic, liturgy-like prose, one writer of Genesis tells how the one God created the heavens and the earth and all that is in them. Another takes up the story to focus on the relationship that God seeks with humankind and how that relationship has been broken. Over and over that tragedy recurs, until God washes the world clean with a flood, as it were, and begins again with Noah. The covenant with all creation, however, seems fragmented once more by sin, even to the point of cosmic disorder.

And so, the Genesis narrative continues, God reveals to Abraham and Sarah a special plan. Though they are old, God promises miraculously to give them a family. Through that family, all the families of the earth will be blessed. Focusing almost exclusively on their relationship to God, Genesis traces three generations of that family, ending with the whole clan settling in Egypt.

Centuries later, now enslaved, they cry to God. Exodus, continuing the narrative, tells of how God hears their cry; prepares Moses; reveals the special, divine name, "the Lord," to this leader; and sends him to deliver the Lord's people. Neither pharaoh's magicians nor pharaoh's armies can stand against Moses' God. At the sea Egypt's forces are defeated. At Sinai the whole people Israel enter into covenant. These impotent, bricklaying slaves, now rescued by God, are called to be the Lord's "priestly kingdom." They are to do this by living, in gratitude to their Liberator, a special kind of life. That life is described in the law of God.

Leviticus describes symbols of worship divinely given to remind the Israelites of what the Lord has done for them and prescribed ceremonies to help renew their relationship to the Lord, their Savior. Though the story continued in Numbers and Deuteronomy repeatedly confesses Israel's unfaithfulness, even rebellion, toward God, the Pentateuch ends with a message of challenge and hope. Forty years have gone by and they still have not received the land God has promised. But Deuteronomy ends the Pentateuch's story with Israel poised to enter that place of destiny.

HISTORIANS CAUTION AGAINST TAKING
THE STORY AS LITERAL HISTORY

The Pentateuch tells a marvelous story—so marvelous, in fact, that many historians feel that honesty forces them to read it with skeptical eyes. Many modern scholars reject traditional literal interpretations of these books. Some, indeed, question whether we can accord the Pentateuch any value as history. Here are three of the reasons for their skepticism.

1. Modern science tells a story that seems far different from that of the first eleven chapters of Genesis. For example, computing the years listed in Genesis seems to indicate that the world was created in 4004 B.C. Most scientists, with good reason, believe that the universe is many millions of years old and that this world evolved over thousands of centuries, not in the "seven days" described in Genesis 1. Also, many cultures have stories of floods, but geologists find no trace of the flood that Genesis 6 implies covered the entire earth to wipe out humankind in somewhere around 3000 B.C. Instead, we know of civilizations continuing in unbroken development from long before that time.

2. As literal history, the stories of the exodus and the wilderness wanderings abound in difficulties. No Egyptian records make any mention of Israelite slaves, a revolt by them, or a catastrophe for pharaoh's army at the sea. The number of escaping slaves given in Ex. 12:37–38 (six hundred thousand Israelite men plus women, children, and foreigners, implying a total of more than two million) seems at best a great exaggeration. One commentator suggests that, walking four abreast, that many people would have formed a line from Egypt to Sinai and back again! On their way to Canaan, the Israelites are said to have had to contend with the kingdoms of the Edomites and the Moabites, but historians report that neither of these existed, at least as powerful nations, until centuries later.[1]

3. The traditional view that the first five books of the Bible were written by Moses, an eyewitness of the events described in four of those books, has been largely abandoned except by those who hold it on theological rather than purely historical grounds. A close reading of the Pentateuch itself shows that it cannot have come to us, in its present form at least, from Moses himself. Here are a few of the signs of later writing: First, Moses could hardly have written Deuteronomy 34; it describes his death and burial. Second, many phrases presuppose that the writers and readers are among those who live in Canaan, which Moses never reached, and look back on the events of the Pentateuch as ancient history. For example, Gen. 36:31 describes kings in Edom "before any king reigned over the Israelites," obviously implying that the writer lives in a day when the Israelites have established a monarchy. "At *that time* the Canaanites were in the land" (italics added) says the writer of Gen. 12:6, looking back long after the conquest of these Canaanites. Third, multiple authorship is suggested by numerous duplications, even apparent conflicts. For example, Moses' father-in-law is called Reuel in Ex. 2:18, Jethro in Ex. 3:1, and Hobab in Num. 10:29 and Judg. 4:11. The simplest explanation is that different tribes in different places at different times handed down the story in different forms. We have what appear to be two stories of creation (Gen. 1:1–2:4 and 2:4–25);

three very similar stories of patriarchs lying about their wives (Gen. 12:10–20; 20:1–18; 26:1–11); and two accounts, with different locations, of the change of Jacob's name to Israel (Gen. 32:28; 35:10). The sequence of events in Exodus's story of the giving of the law and the covenant ceremony is so confusing that many scholars suggest that the narrative combines different traditions from different times.

These and many other duplications have led the vast majority of scholars to adopt, though usually in modified form, the pattern proposed by the nineteenth-century scholar Julius Wellhausen.[2] He took as the key the fact that some passages in the Pentateuch refer to God as "Elohim." In others, the divine name is "Yahweh" (or Jahweh, "the Lord"). Using this and other clues, Wellhausen traced four sources in what is now woven together as our Pentateuch. Far from being the work of one eyewitness author, Moses, the Pentateuch seems to be made up of at least these four sources, all from times long after the events described:

J (for its use of "Jahweh" as the name of God), a Judean source written perhaps around 950 B.C. in the days of David and Solomon;

E (for its use of "Elohim" as God's name), a source from Ephraim and the Northern Kingdom, written perhaps around 850 B.C.;

D (for Deuteronomy), probably the law found in the days of King Josiah, which guided the reformation he led, written perhaps around 640 B.C.; and

P (for Priestly), a retelling of the stories by priests, written perhaps during the Babylonian captivity around 550 B.C. and emphasizing formal worship.

Many historians argue that the Pentateuch does not give us a documented account of events going back to the beginning of time or even to an exodus in (perhaps) 1290 B.C. The various strands of the Pentateuch often reflect not so much ancient history as the experience of God which Israel and the inspired writers continued to have many centuries later. The Pentateuch was not put together until perhaps around 450 B.C.

THE PENTATEUCH ROOTS IN HISTORICAL MEMORY

At the very least, the discoveries we have been reviewing should make us cautious about accepting as literal history every detail of the Pentateuch, however committed one is to the religious truths that its stories present. Many scholars, however, argue that there is good reason to believe that much of the Pentateuch is based on actual historical events. Granted, these historians say, the Pentateuch's stories have been expanded, developed, and interpreted in the light of centuries of experience with the God they describe. There is still evidence that many of the original stories are much, much older than the written sources we now possess. Here are three reasons for holding that the Pentateuch does contain many very ancient and genuinely historical traditions.

First, the patterns and forms of many parts of the Pentateuch suggest oral transmission dating back much earlier than their final editing. Early in the twentieth century, Hermann Gunkel, no biblical literalist, set scholarship on a new course as he examined the Pentateuch's poems, liturgies, and stories.[3] No matter how much late material may be involved in Exodus, for example, form critics note that our oldest account of the exodus is in a poem, ascribed to Moses and Miriam, in a style that might be ancient indeed (Ex. 15:1–21). Other ancient folk songs and ballads recur throughout these books (Gen. 3:14–19; 8:22; 14:19; 16:11; Ex. 32:18; Num. 10:35–36; 21:27–30; and many more). Traditional liturgical formulae are embedded in the Pentateuch; for example, the "creed" an Israelite recited when offering a sacrifice summarized the Pentateuch's story:

> A wandering Aramean was my ancestor; he went down into Egypt and lived there as an alien, few in number, and there he became a great nation, mighty and populous. When the Egyptians treated us harshly and afflicted us, by imposing hard labor on us, we cried to the Lord, the God of our ancestors; the Lord heard our voice and saw our affliction, our toil, and our oppression. The Lord brought us out of Egypt with a mighty hand and an outstretched arm, with a terrifying display of power, and with signs and wonders; and he brought us into this place and gave us this land, a land flowing with milk and honey. (Deut. 26:5–9)

Ancient monuments, shrines, and cities such as Shechem, Bethel, and Hebron came to be regarded as sacred. Stories clustered around them, purporting to explain how they became holy. Though he did not assign much value to the Pentateuch as literal history, Gunkel wrote of those who produced our written documents that they were collectors, not really authors:

> These collectors, then, are not masters, but rather servants of their subjects. We may imagine them, filled with reverence for the beautiful ancient stories and endeavoring to reproduce them as well and faithfully as they could. Fidelity was their prime quality. This explains why they accepted so many things which they but half understood and which were alien to their own taste and feeling.[4]

Second, while it is true that archaeologists find no records outside the Bible of the lives of Abraham, Isaac, or Jacob, and Egyptian records say nothing of Moses and the exodus, many students of archaeology—William Foxwell Albright, G. Ernest Wright, and John Bright, for example—argue that many stories in the Pentateuch fit far better in the historical period in which the events they describe are supposed to have taken place than they do in the time when the Pentateuch was being assembled. Here are a few examples:

> The migration of ancient peoples described by the historians parallels that of the biblical patriarchs, the ancestors of Israel.
>
> The Flood story of Genesis appears to come from ancient Mesopotamia, the culture of the patriarchs of Genesis.
>
> The great ziggurat tower of Babylon was gone long before the much later time of the writers of Genesis 11.
>
> Many of the names that occur in Genesis are characteristic of the early second millennium B.C.
>
> Later writers, who hated idolatry, would hardly have invented the story of how their ancestress Rachel stole her father's idols (Gen. 31:19).
>
> The city of Rameses, said to have been rebuilt by the Israelite slaves (Ex. 1:11), was known by a different name after the eleventh century B.C.
>
> The covenant at Sinai is much like treaties of the time of Moses, drawn up between sovereigns of great empires and small satellite nations.

Admittedly, there are details in these stories that clearly reflect later times. For example, it appears that the camel was not domesticated until long after the time of Abraham (contrast Gen. 12:16). Recently, archaeologists have argued that in the Pentateuch there are more parallels to patterns of life in later times than to those supposed to have been characteristic of the days of the patriarchs and the exodus. The best one can claim is that some stories seem to fit better with customs of the middle Bronze Age (the time of the patriarchs such as Abraham) than with those of the later Iron Age. Nevertheless, John Bright, after extensive discussion, still maintained in his 1982 edition of *A History of Israel,* "We conclude, then, that the patriarchs were historical figures, a part of that movement of Northwest-Semitic (Amorite) people which brought a new infusion to the population of Palestine toward the beginning of the second millennium B.C."[5]

Third, the strongest reason for believing that the Pentateuch does contain much that is historical is the consistent, repeated witness of the Hebrew scriptures themselves to the exodus, the major event the Pentateuch describes. Israel proclaimed as the foundation of its faith that God had rescued them from bondage. Psalmists, prophets, lawgivers, and court historians all described or assumed this event as the basis of Israel's very existence as a separate people. Its religious ceremonies celebrated it. Almost every line of the Old Testament bears witness to Israel's historic redemption. It is difficult to imagine how Israel came to be what it was apart from the event that, it was sure, so powerfully influenced its formation.

THE TRUTH OF THE PENTATEUCH IS ITS
PROCLAMATION ABOUT GOD,
NOT COMPLETE HISTORICITY

Recent scholarship has deemphasized the whole question of the extent to which the Pentateuch is based on history. Some modern scholars have gone so far as to maintain that questions about the date, the authorship, and even the intention of the original writer are irrelevant. At least two recent developments have lent support to this idea.

One is a movement in interpretation of literature quite apart from the Bible. "The new criticism" proposes that a work of art stands or falls on its own. Things external to the work of art—historical considerations, for example—are beside the point. "The text itself" is what matters, such critics maintain. Focus attention only on it, they say, and let the picture, the poem—or the passage of scripture—speak for itself. Narrative critics help us to get at the meaning of stories by studying plot, characters, and perspective, without concern for history and sources.

The other movement—this one church-oriented—is that of "canonical criticism." Scholars such as Brevard Childs have pointed out that, for people of faith, the Bible is "scripture."[6] Its message is a kerygma, a proclamation, about God. Through the centuries, the church has read the Bible not as a bit of ancient history but as contemporary good news. What the Old Testament meant to its writers or even to ancient Israel is of only secondary importance. We must ask rather what the Bible has meant and—even more—now means to us, the church.

There is much truth in these ideas. Archaeology cannot prove or disprove the spiritual truth of scripture. The authority of the Bible, Christians maintain, comes from the witness of the Holy Spirit in the heart of the believer. Long before the first scientific archaeologist turned his first spade full of dry earth, women and men were reading the scriptures with enlightened minds and hearts. A story told about Abraham a thousand years after the death of that patriarch may reflect more of what God was doing with that writer than what God did with Abraham. The important question is what God through that story is doing with us.

In this vein, recognizing the uncertainty of all historical evidence, Walter Brueggemann has written his very helpful commentary on Genesis, leaving completely aside the entire question of the relationship of the stories in that book to actual history.[7]

For reasons suggested above, however, to ignore history would be unnecessarily cautious. This *Guide* will make use of the light that history seems to shed on "the text itself." Sometimes historical information solves puzzles about what a passage means. Often it can help us visualize a scene. It can point up the contrast between biblical religion and the paganism that was its rival. Historians can supply us with information that the first writers could assume the first readers knew. The Pentateuch bases its message about God on stories of mighty acts, which, it maintains, God performed in the real world in history.

At the same time, however, we must remember that the church finds in the Bible not so much a record of the past as a living word from God for the present.

With this in mind, and using the methods of Bible study listed in the preceding chapter, we turn now to the first book of the first "Book of Moses," Genesis.

GENESIS

"In the beginning. . . ." These are the first words of the Bible. "Genesis" means "the beginning." The ancient Hebrews began their story with God.

If you want to know the direction in which you are going, it is helpful to know where you have been. The Israelites knew that and became the world's first great historians. In Genesis they professed to trace history back to the dawn of time.

They knew another fact, however: we understand history in the light of our present situation and our future hopes. Every history is interpreted history. For example, Alex Haley's *Roots* taught us that American history looks quite different when viewed from the perspective of Americans whose ancestors were slaves. The story of the American Revolution would look quite different if written by King George III. Genesis—and all other biblical history—is written from a particular perspective. Its inspired writers took ancient stories handed down at campfires, covenant ceremonies, and even pagan traditions and reinterpreted them in the light of their continued experience with God. Thus they presented truth about their day—and ours—which no other history has ever quite so fully understood.

Part of the perspective from which the Genesis narrative is written is clearly expressed near the end of its story: Joseph's brothers had kidnapped him and sold him into Egypt as a slave. By God's providence, however, he has prospered there and has become the means of saving his whole family from starvation. His brothers fear that he will avenge himself on them for their crime against him. But he reassures them: "Do not be afraid! . . . Even though you intended to do harm to me, God intended it for good, in order to preserve a numerous people, as he is doing today" (Gen. 50:19–20). From creation to their preservation in Egypt, in spite of all the sins they so faithfully recorded, Israelites saw all of history as the story of how they had been guided and protected by the providence of God.

Genesis looks to the future. Repeatedly, it points ahead of itself to the

GENESIS

The Creator's Grace with the Whole Human Family and Covenant Grace with Abraham's Family

"Now the Lord said to Abram, 'Go . . . to the land that I will show you. I will make of you a great nation, and I will bless you, . . . and in you all the families of the earth shall be blessed'" (12:1–3).

1	12	24	37
God Seeks Fellowship with the Whole Human Family	**A New Approach: God Makes a Covenant with One Family, Abraham and Sarah**	**God's Promises Continue through the Chosen Family**	**Through Joseph, God Brings the Family to Egypt**
God creates the world and humankind, 1—2	God promises them land, descendants, and blessings and, through them, blessings to all families, 12:1–3	God with Isaac and Rebekah, 24—26	Jacob's sons sell their brother into slavery, 37
But humans sin:	In spite of difficulties, the promises are repeated, 12:4–20:18	God with their son Jacob, who becomes Israel, 27—33	But God blesses Joseph in Egypt, 38—41
Adam and Eve sin, 3	One promise fulfilled: Isaac is born, 21	But family troubles continue, 34—36	The family is reunited, 42—47
Cain murders, 4	Abraham passes the test of faith; he is willing to sacrifice his son, 22		The promises are handed down to succeeding generations, 48—49
Sin multiplies into cosmic disorder, 5:1–6:8	The death of Sarah, 23		The brothers are reconciled and God's plans are being fulfilled, 50—54
God tries again, with the family of Noah, 6:9–9:19			
But Noah and his family sin, 9:20–29			
The families of humanity divide, climaxed by the tower of Babel, 10:1–11:31			

Author: Traditionally Moses, but actually probably the work of many writers, compiled perhaps in the fifth century B.C.

Purpose: To show the beginning of God's plan for the world, especially God's promises for the family of Abraham _____.

Significance in the New Testament: Genesis is quoted repeatedly and built upon in many ways. Abraham is especially cited as a model of faith. The church claims to be spiritual heirs, in a sense, of the promises that Genesis describes.

54

great acts of redemption that Exodus and subsequent books describe. Its last word is "Egypt." Thus it sets the stage for the exodus. Genesis is only the beginning.

Its writers knew that what they had become could not be understood apart from the past. And so they undertook to trace their origins back to the very beginning.

And thus it came about that our Bible begins with these words: "In the beginning . . . God" (Gen. 1:1).

God Seeks Fellowship with the Whole Human Family (Gen. 1—11)

Ever since Charles Darwin, the first chapters of Genesis have been a battleground. Parliaments, preachers, scientists, and even law courts have argued about their meaning. Here we will make obvious our use of the principles of interpretation described in the first chapter of this *Guide,* in the belief that these will enable us to discover some clear meanings in admittedly controversial verses.

God Creates the World and Humankind (Gen. 1—2)

The first chapter of this *Guide* proposed that one thing which often helps us understand a passage in the Bible is to *read it in the light of ancient history.* To do this with the first chapter of Genesis, imagine yourself a Jewish slave in Babylon. Your nation has been destroyed, and you have been kidnapped and taken to a faraway land. All day, every day, you sweat as you labor for your masters in the region that today is known as Iraq. Daily, your captors taunt you with their myths. This world, they tell you, originated in chaos, in the warfare of competing gods. At length, Tiamat (chaos) and her son Marduk battled each other, a cosmic struggle. Marduk, the god of Babylon, drew his sword and cut his mother in two. From her top he made the firmament, the vaulted sky. From her bottom half he made the earth. Now look, the Babylonians challenge you, at the greatness of Marduk. All gods worship him. He has made Babylon the greatest power on earth.[8]

On Friday night, however, you gather with other slaves, under the stars, to hear a very different version of the creation story. Assisted, perhaps, by Levites, an exiled Jewish priest chants the liturgy of Gen. 1:1–2:4. And you grasp its message. There are not many gods but one. Our world is not a place of chaos; it is the product of the plan of the one true God. That God does not have to struggle to create; the God of Israel needs only to speak. Step by step, in orderly fashion, the God of Israel worked out the divine purpose. This purpose was not the exaltation of Babylon but of humanity, man and woman. And the climax is not an empire but the Sabbath. All builds up to the cosmically ordained day of rest. In this hope, the Jews survived until God did, indeed, deliver them from their forced labor.

Another principle for interpreting the Bible that was proposed in chapter 1 of this *Guide* was to *look for repeated words and ideas*. In Genesis 1, these or similar phrases immediately stand out:

> "And God said . . . And it was so." God is so powerful that God has only to speak and everything takes form.
>
> "And there was evening and there was morning, the . . . day." All creation is orderly, according to a step-by-step plan.
>
> "And God saw that it was good." Nature, including human nature, is good. At last, when creation was completed, "God saw everything that he had made, and indeed, it was very good."
>
> "In the image of God"—three times Genesis 1 affirms this about humankind (1:26–27; cf. 5:1–2). Both sexes equally are in that image, and it is not just Babylonians but all people who reflect the divine. To emphasize the uniqueness of humanity, the story pictures God as pausing and speaking, perhaps to the heavenly court of angels or perhaps simply using the majestic plural found in royal proclamations, "Let us make humankind . . . according to our likeness."

It would have been blasphemy to the ancient Hebrews to suggest that "in the image of God" meant literally that we look like God, that God has two eyes, a nose, an appendix, and so forth. They absolutely refused to allow anyone to make an idol, an image of God in human form. Rather, by "image of God" they wanted to say that human beings are intended for a unique relationship to their Creator, able to respond to God and to take responsibility. Perhaps there is a hint in the fact that the man and the woman are specifically mentioned in the same sentence as God's image. The Bible repeatedly compares the love of husband and wife to the covenant relationship between God and God's people. Humankind is intended to love in a way that mirrors the love of God. Using another principle previously suggested, *note how the New Testament interprets* "the image of God." That image, which the Creator had intended for us all, is fully realized at last, Paul says, in Christ (Col. 1:15).

Another principle previously suggested for interpreting the Bible is to *set each verse in its context*; see how it fits with what comes before and after it. Note, then, how this whole story builds up to the creation of humankind. Everything else is important, but in a sense, the biblical writer affirms, it all exists *for us.* Humanity is given dominion over everything. We are uniquely blessed. In this good world, it is good for us to enjoy the fruits of the world and to multiply. But note, too, that the end of the story is not the creation of human beings; it is the Sabbath. The whole passage points to that day of rest and worship. The Sabbath was so important to Israel that they told this story: When Moses found a man picking up sticks on Saturday, Moses, at God's command, had him stoned to death (Num. 15:32–36). Of course, if you had asked an ancient Hebrew whether he thought that God literally was so worn out by the work of creation that the Creator was forced to rest a full day, he would have accused you of blasphemy. The point Genesis is making by setting its story in the framework of a seven-day week is that the Sabbath, still so important to Orthodox Jews today, was built into the very structure of the cosmos.

Finally, this *Guide* has suggested that you *interpret a passage in the light of the kind of literature to which that particular passage belongs: history, poetry, song, letter, and so forth*. Note, then, the orderly, stately prose of Gen. 1:1–2:4, building up to the day of rest and worship. Recall the repeated phrases noted above, recurring almost like the chorus in a gospel hymn. This is poetic prose, a kind of liturgy or responsive reading, to be read and recited, even chanted, in the synagogue. It has been called "the creed of creation." For Jews and Christians, it is true—every word true. Its truth is that there is but one God, Creator of heaven and earth, who according to plan has made us in the divine image and given us this good earth to enjoy and care for. All points to the day of rest and worship of that Creator.

The first chapter of Genesis is a kind of litany, almost a hymn, for worship. Its literary form, therefore, shows us that it is not meant as a laboratory report. The alleged conflict between a scientific account of the origins of humankind and the narrative in Genesis dissolves when one realizes that the two are different kinds of literature seeking to answer different questions. "Think Hebrew!" The modern scientist asks *how*, but the Hebrew writer tells us *why*. The writer of Genesis was attacking Babylonian paganism, not scientific evolution (of which the writer, of course, had never heard). The truth of Genesis lies in the theological affirmations listed in the preceding paragraph. Nothing in empirical science deals with these in any way.

That the compiler of Genesis was not concerned about the length of time God used in creation is confirmed by the use of another of our principles of interpretation. Often it helps to *compare scripture with scripture*, seeing how another passage on the same subject is like it and different from it.

Compare, then, the first chapter of Genesis with the second chapter. Beginning with Gen. 2:4, we seem to have a different version of the creation story, told for a different but equally important purpose. In this second story creation takes place in just one day (Gen. 2:4), not seven. In Genesis 2, man is created first, not last; then plants and animals; and only then is woman created, the climax of this story being not the Sabbath but marriage. To those who want to make Genesis a scientific account, these differences present problems. But obviously, to the inspired compiler of Genesis, the differences about the time and order of creation do not matter at all. Each story presents revealed truth, truth not about science but about God and ourselves.

As early as the time of Paul, Rabbi Philo Judaeus recognized that these are two different stories of creation. Modern scholarship has explained this as the result of the combining of two originally separate documents. Genesis 1 is from the Priestly source, emphasizing worship and ceremony, and probably was written during or soon after the Babylonian captivity. Genesis 2, however, comes from a much earlier and very different time, that of the proud empire of David and Solomon.

There may be traces of the story of the Garden of Eden in ancient paintings and carvings found in what is now Iraq and dating from even earlier than the time of Moses. One picture from ancient Mari shows four cosmic rivers (cf. Gen. 2:10–14) and two trees (cf. Gen. 2:9) but, in sharp contrast to the Bible, two goddesses. Serpents appear in pagan legends. But the biblical writer knows the truth. All creation, he tells us, is the work of only one God. All is created for humankind. Adam—the word means "man" or "humankind"—is created by a special act. It is true, as Darwin later demonstrated, that human beings are created from exactly the same source as the animals: the earth itself (Gen. 2:7, 19). Thus, according to Genesis, we have the same humble origin as apes and other lower animals. But God "breathed into his nostrils the breath of life; and the man became a living being" (2:7). Once again, the uniqueness of humanity and our special relationship to God is affirmed.

Relationships are central to this story. Humankind is not really human apart from relationships. "It is not good that the man should be alone" (2:18). The animals are not fit for the kind of relationship that God knows this creature needs. And so from Adam's rib, his side, a symbol of partnership, God creates woman. The first story of creation builds to the institution of the Sabbath. But this second story builds to the institution of marriage. Love is the proper reflection or image of God. Adam sings the first song, a love song (2:23). Thus the writer explains the meaning of the story. It is the divine purpose of marriage, permanent, intimate, loving, and exclusive (2:24–25).

The story says that there is also a proper relationship between human beings and nature. Adam is to "till [the garden] and keep it" (2:15). Nature is not God or even a part of God. But it belongs to God, and humankind is not only to enjoy it but to take care of it.

Humans Sin (Gen. 3—5)

The ancient Hebrews preferred stories to sermons or to lectures in systematic theology. Therefore they told the stories of Genesis 1 and 2 as their way of saying what God intends for us and the world. But with Genesis 3, they told how things actually are, marred by human sin. In their story of Adam (humankind) and Eve, they present the repeated and tragic history of the human race.

The "serpent" tempts Eve. Snakes were associated with several pagan goddesses. The New Testament, going beyond Old Testament theology, understands the serpent as the devil or Satan (Rev. 12:9). Either way, what happens in Genesis's pictorial language is what recurs in the lives of all human beings. The tempter begins with doubt: "Did God say . . . ?" (3:1). He moves to denial: "You will not die" (3:4). He appeals to lust: "The woman saw that . . . it was a delight to the eyes" (3:6). But probably temptation's most effective trick is the appeal to pride: "You will be like God" (3:5). And sin enters the world.

But now God comes, calling the creature that is in God's image (3:8–9). From start to finish in the Bible, God seeks humankind and calls us to fellowship. The language of Genesis 3 is "anthropomorphic," describing God as if God were a human being. But if you had asked an ancient Hebrew if this meant that God literally got so hot in the day that God needed to walk in the garden "at the time of the evening breeze," you might have been stoned for blasphemy. What the Bible does insist is that God loves and craves fellowship with us. And so God "calls."

But we sinners immediately try to hide, to avoid responsibility for what we have done (3:8). We make excuses. Adam, like men down through history, blames the sin on the woman. (In effect, he even tries to blame God, who gave him Eve.) Eve even tries to blame her sin on a snake!

The story goes on to tell of the consequences of sin. Pain enters life (3:16). The good earth is polluted (3:17). Work, intended to be a joy, becomes a burden (3:19). The sex relationship, intended to be idyllic, is messed up, with men seeking to rule women (3:7, 16). And death itself enters the picture (3:19). The world we live in, the story says, is no Garden of Eden. It is corrupted and polluted by human sin.

But the story ends with a bit of gospel. God clothes us still, a symbol of grace (3:21). God has not given up on humanity.

Read as a bit of scientific history, this story of our fall presents problems. Read as the Hebrew way of telling the continuing truth about God and about us, the story is all too evidently true!

Sin, the story continues, produces more sin. The family relationship was intended to mirror the relationship of God to humanity. Instead, Cain kills his brother (4:8). Four generations later, Lamech sings a horrid boast to his two wives that he is far more vengeful than even Cain (4:23–24). Humankind was meant to multiply, but sin, says the story, multiplies with it. Genesis 5 traces the growing human family through the generations. By Genesis 6, the corruption of the universe is described in terms of cosmic catastrophe. Nobody today is quite sure what is meant by the report that "the sons of God" took for themselves human women, but evidently it represents a tragic disorder in God's orderly creation, one so radical that it requires a radical solution.

So evil has the world become that God decides to start over again.

God Tries Again, with
the Family of Noah (Gen. 6—11)

The historians tell us that in the biblical story of the Flood, the composers of Genesis again have written the corrections on a story that is very old indeed. In the Babylonian version, the gods and goddesses become annoyed by the sin of humankind. They decide to wipe out humankind with a flood. One god, however, named Ea, has a favorite on earth, Ut-napishtim. He goes to this man, calling to the wall of his house, because Babylonian gods do not speak to humans, and warns him to build a boat. Into this boat Ut-napishtim takes two of every kind of animal. The gods work together to bring rain for seven days and seven nights. Then they weep at the sight of the deed they have done. At length, as in the story of Noah, to see how far the flood has receded, Ut-napishtim sends out a succession of birds. When one bird does not return, he knows it is safe to disembark. He immediately offers sacrifice, and the gods cluster around its sweet odor "like flies." They make Ut-napishtim an immortal.[9]

"No!" the biblical writer almost shouts. There is only one God. This God speaks to human beings. The cause of the Flood was the human sin so graphically described in Genesis 3—5. But the one God is concerned for humankind—and the preservation of other endangered species. Two of every kind of animal are preserved, but a Priestly writer adds that seven pairs of the "clean" (kosher) animals that Jews were allowed to eat were preserved (7:2). And when the flood is over, Noah's sacrifice is to the one true God, who alone enjoys the sweet savor of its smoke (8:21).

The most significant difference, however, between the pagan myth and the biblical story is in the conclusion of the stories. The biblical narrative builds to the announcement of the *covenant,* a covenant with both humanity and all nature. Note how in Gen. 9:8–17 the word "covenant" is repeated again and again. For the eyes of faith, the rainbow in the cloud after a storm becomes the symbol of the care and promise of a faithful God. We see the concept of covenant repeated over and over in the Bible until it is clear that it is at the heart of the biblical faith.

For many years, well-meaning archaeologists have attempted to find and examine a boatlike object said to be on the top of a high mountain on the border between Turkey and Russia. Some believe that mountain to be the biblical Ararat on which the ark landed and the object to be remnants of Noah's ark. Thus far, however, efforts of this kind have fallen short of success. Moreover, it would be impossible to find any historian who, apart from purely theological grounds, would affirm that there was around 3000

B.C. a flood which wiped out all human beings and animals except for one boatload. Archaeological research does shed much light on the story, but it does so by showing the contrasts between the inspired Bible story and the earlier pagan myths, rather than by confirming the story as a curious bit of science.

The truth the biblical writers wish to tell us is about God, nature, and ourselves. God, says the biblical story, will not forever tolerate sin. Sin brings dire consequences. Yet humankind is sinful. Out of pure grace, however, God saves a group and starts again with the divine goal of fellowship. And God plants in the sky a sign of God's covenant promise to and concern for both humankind and nature itself.

But sin enters again. Noah gets drunk (9:21). Shame comes upon the family, and the family begins to disintegrate. Noah even hurls curses at his own grandson (9:25), ancestor of the Canaanites whom the Jews dominated at the time the story was written. Long lists of families are recorded, for God is concerned for all the families of the earth. But once again, history is seen as a process of going from bad to worse.

Again, one thing that helps us to discover what a biblical writer wants to emphasize is to look for repeated words and ideas. One such theme in Genesis is that of the breakdown of relationships between people, even family relationships. Adam and Eve blame each other and dominance is substituted for partnership. Cain kills his own brother. Lamech multiplies vengeance. Noah's sons split apart. But the climax of this theme of the breakdown of relationships is the story of the tower of Babel.

The secular historians can also help us to understand this ancient narrative. Throughout historic Mesopotamia—now Iraq, Turkey, and Syria—there were ziggurats, pyramid towers. Their stairs reached up to a shrine on the top, a symbol of heaven, where an idol symbolized the presence of a pagan god. The largest ziggurat was in Babylon, ruler and terror of the ancient world. Historians can tell us much of the power and glory of that once-mighty empire, dominating the region in the early second millennium B.C. But Babylon was destined to fall. Surely something of this historic fact lies behind the story of the tower of Babel in Genesis 11.

The Babylonians, the story tells us, had developed new technology. They could make not only brick but a new kind of mortar that could hold the bricks together. They would build a city and engineer "a tower with its top in the heavens" (11:4). They build their city and their tower. The bricks hold together. But the people do not. People no longer understand one another. Races become segregated. Humankind, like the Babylonians' empire, falls apart. The story is a parable not only of that empire but of human achievement everywhere apart from the loving relationships God wants for humankind.

The god described by the Greek philosopher Aristotle is unchanging, "the unmoved mover"; not so the God of the Bible. This God is dynamic, always relating in new ways to new situations, though always faithful to the covenant purpose. And so, the biblical writers suggest, God tries again. But this time God concentrates on just one family, though the purpose is to bless all the families in the world.

A New Approach: God Makes a Covenant with One Family, Abraham and Sarah (Gen. 12—23)

Genesis 11 gives a lengthy genealogy. Name after name is recorded, with nothing but ages reported. Who were Arpachshad and Shelah and Eber and Peleg and Reu and Serug and Nahor and Terah? Their only function in the story is that they are family members. The genealogical listing races through generation after generation. Then, suddenly, the genealogies come to a halt and the narrative begins. With the birth of Abraham, God is about to do something new.

A close reading of the scripture shows that not all Israelites were biologically descended from Abraham (Ex. 12:38; Num. 10:29–31; etc.) But at least spiritually, Abraham was to become "the father of the faithful." The rest of the Old Testament focuses on God's providential plan, which begins to be manifested in this one family. Christians, too, claim to be spiritual descendants of that same family of faith.

Genesis really falls into two parts. The first eleven chapters are about the Creator and all the families of the earth. But chapters 12 through 50 are about God and one family, the family of Abraham and Sarah.

Abraham and History

Archaeologists have never found a single trace of Abraham. Nevertheless, from Genesis 12 on, the relationship of the biblical stories to history becomes much clearer.

Where did Cain kill Abel? Where did Lamech or Noah live? The Bible never attempts to answer these questions. But with the story of Abraham, the action is repeatedly placed in identifiable locations. Abraham is born in Ur. Stories relate him to Haran, Shechem, Bethel, and the court of the pharaoh in Egypt. With America's Operation Desert Storm and war against Iraq, many of us have become familiar with that part of the world. Scholars name it "the Fertile Crescent." The river valleys in the region curve from the Persian Gulf up through Iraq, north of the Arabian Desert, into Syria and Turkey, and south through Israel's Jordan Valley toward Egypt. If the archaeologists can tell us nothing directly about Abraham himself, they can tell us in detail about the culture of that area in which he is said to have traveled.

We have ruins, records, and monuments of great civilizations, empires that rose and fell. Court records and thousands of business memorandums have been unearthed. Museums house idols of the pagan gods and the scriptures loved by their worshipers. Genesis pictures Abraham as the head of a large, prosperous, but itinerant clan, generally peaceful but capable of making war. Records from Assyria to Babylon describe such migratory families, sometimes called *Habiru*. Though the proposal that the word "Hebrew" is derived from that term is strongly challenged, Abraham's clan does seem to fit into the *Habiru* pattern. The *Habiru* were almost like gypsies: locating on the fringes of the cities, sometimes hiring themselves out as mercenary soldiers, in hard times becoming slaves, but sometimes prospering as traveling merchants.

We can even guess what Abraham, Sarah, and their caravan may have looked like. Sometime around 1900 B.C., a wealthy Egyptian commissioned an artist to decorate his tomb. He chose for the mural one of the most exotic scenes of his life. The artist painted a picture of an itinerant band of Semites, the broad racial group of which Abraham was a part. The men wore beards but no mustaches, and their hair was of medium length but trimmed. Their knee-length, woolen robes of brightly colored patterns hung on the left shoulder to leave the right shoulder and arm free. On their feet were sandals. If the garment pictured on the tomb is typical, Sarah wore a dress with a similar bright pattern, also designed to leave the right shoulder and arm free, and had long hair hanging down the back but with a braid on each side in front, a headband, and shoes. Slaves in the caravan depicted in the mural wear only knee-length skirts. Some carry spears or bows and arrows; one carries a stringed musical instrument to entertain the clan at night. A little boy carries a toy spear, and two children are riding on a donkey. As far as we can guess, this is what Abraham, Isaac, Jacob, and their families may have looked like.

Law codes of the time seem to help explain bits of Abraham's story that otherwise might puzzle us. His expectation that a slave might become his heir, his use of his wife's maid to provide a blood descendant, and his cutting an animal in two for ceremonial covenant making are paralleled in documents of the time.

We can even hazard a guess as to Abraham's date, perhaps around 1800 B.C.[10]

Nevertheless, it is important to note that dress, customs, and the historical events of the time seem to be of no direct interest to the writers of Genesis. Events of concern to historians become enormously important to biblical writers in other books, but Genesis gives us little information of this kind. For its writers, the drama of Abraham and God can be played out on an almost empty stage. It is the relationship of Abraham to God, not to current events of his time, that is vital to their story.

To that story itself, therefore, we now turn.

God Promises Land, Descendants, and Blessings to Abraham

What do matter to the writers of Genesis are the promises of the covenant-keeping God and Abraham's response to them. That theme of promise and response is summarized as the story of Abraham begins:

> Now the Lord said to Abram, "Go from your country and your kindred and your father's house to the land that I will show you. I will make of you a great nation, and I will bless you, and make your name great, so that you will be a blessing. . . . In you all the families of the earth shall be blessed." So Abram went. (Gen. 12:1–4)

God's promises can be thought of as three: (1) land, (2) descendants, and, more broadly, (3) blessings to Abraham's family and through them to all the families of the earth. They will become a great nation, but not one like Babylon. They will bless, not conquer, the world. From the beginning, readers of the Bible are reminded, even if Israel sometimes forgot, that God's plan, though focused now on one family, is ultimately for all the peoples of the world. Almost every story in the rest of Genesis can be thought of as in one way or another related to one or more of those promises.

Being called, Abram now goes from Haran—in what is now Turkey—to the *land* of Canaan (Israel). Next a curious story tells how, in spite of weakness on the part of Abram, Sarai is saved from pharaoh. If there are to be descendants, there must be a mother as well as a father (in a culture where women were thought of as simply vessels in which a man sowed his seed to produce a child, Genesis is remarkable in the attention it gives to the matriarchs as well as the patriarchs of its people). Genesis 13 describes a discussion between Abram and his nephew Lot about *land,* but when Abram generously renounces claim to the best part, God renews the promise to give Abram the whole country.

Chapters 15 and 17 introduce a word of critical importance: "covenant" (note how often that word occurs in chapter 17). Customs of the time help explain the strange symbolism of Gen. 15:17–21. When a bargain or covenant was reached in the ancient world, an animal might be cut in two as a sacrifice to a god. The two parties to the agreement would then walk between the two halves of the animal, thus calling the god to witness to their promise. Now, in Abram's vision, God, the divine self, passes through the animals to seal the covenant promises. This covenant is sure.

The most repeated emphasis of those promises and of Genesis 16—22 is on the promise of *descendants*. The story is told with an eye for suspense. The aged couple have no child. Will perhaps a child by Sarai's maid do, as ancient Mesopotamian custom allowed? No, the heir must be legitimate. The Muslims say that Hagar's child, Abram's firstborn, became father of the Arabs.

But God's promise is for something impossible. Abraham at one hundred years old and Sarah at ninety will have a son. God's promise is so ridiculous that Abraham laughs when he hears it (17:17) and Sarah laughs when she hears it (18:12). But in the end the laughter is one of joy. With a play on words, Isaac's name is said to be derived from the Hebrew word for laughter (21:1–7).

There are so many repetitions in these stories that it seems likely that different accounts of the same events have been preserved. Not only are there repeated accounts of the promises but there are repeated stories of the rivalry between Sarah and Hagar and even two stories of Abraham lying about his wife. But the very repetition emphasizes the repeated point of the narrative: God is doing the impossible to carry out the divine purpose.

The climactic story of Abraham is his willingness to sacrifice his beloved son (chapter 22). "Take your son, your only son Isaac, whom you love," our writer reports God as saying, carefully emphasizing the pathos in the command. Movingly, suspensefully, the tale is told. Abraham draws the knife to slay Isaac and give up the hope and joy of his life at the command of God. But the gracious God provides a substitute offering, and once more the promises of *land, descendants,* and *blessings* to this family and, through it, to all the world are repeated. Israel was to encounter people of other religions who sought to win the favor of their gods through human sacrifice. They viewed that pagan practice with horror. But it was not for lack of zeal for God, Israel could affirm; their father, Abraham, had in effect offered all of them up long before. Abraham had passed the test of faith. With Isaac, the impossible promises of God were beginning to come true.

Curiously, in a narrative that gives us so few details, we have an extended account of the elaborately courteous bargain for a grave for Sarah. Perhaps its place in the story is in part to show that Abraham did in fact receive one tiny bit of the Promised Land: a cave at Hebron in which to bury the mother of the people of God.

God's Promises Continue through the Chosen Family (Gen. 24—36)

Genesis continues with one great theme repeated over and over. This family is promised *land, descendants* who will become a great nation, and *blessings,* which will reach the whole earth.

God Affects the Lives of Isaac and Rebekah (Gen. 24—26)

Genesis does not tell us much about Isaac. One story, however, is reported in great—and to us, somewhat amusing—detail: the account of the courtship of Isaac and Rebekah. We can understand it best in the light of the marriage customs of the ancient Middle East, so foreign to us. Only Abraham's most trusted servant can be commissioned to select the perfect wife for Abraham's son (24:1–9). Apparently, it would be too risky to trust such a decision to a young man like Isaac himself! The choice, however, is really made by God in answer to prayer (24:13–14). The servant showers Rebekah and her family with gifts, including a ring for her nose. In effect, the servant is bargaining for her in the ancient fashion. She herself, however, we are carefully told, makes the decision. And so she comes, veiling herself as she at last meets her husband-to-be (24:65). "And he loved her" (24:67). To this day, a blessing at Jewish weddings is the wish that the couple's marriage might be like that of Isaac and Rebekah. But why this detailed account, when so much else of Isaac's life is never told us? Apparently, it is because of the importance of the mothers as well as the fathers of the chosen people. This prominence given to women is uncharacteristic of that time and place, but for the writers of Genesis it is essential to the plans of God.

Then we have another story of a patriarch lying about his wife. Once again, God intervenes to save her—this time Rebekah from Abimelech of the Philistines (26:1–11). It would probably not have mattered to the writer that, as contemporary historians suggest, the Philistines were not in the land until several centuries later. The repeated point he is making is God's care of this mother and thus the promised descendants.

We are told of the birth of Isaac's descendants (25:19–26). The only other events depicted that relate to Isaac concern the digging of wells. In spite of opposition, Isaac at last has a well he can keep. He owns an estate in the Promised Land (26:12–22).

But the essential point in the stories of Isaac is that of the repetition of the covenant promises. The writers continue to build suspense; the promises are far from being fulfilled as yet. But the very same promises that were given to Abraham are now given to Isaac: *land, descendants,* and *blessings,* blessings that will reach the whole world (26:1–5).

God Both Reassures and Wrestles with
Their Son Jacob/Israel (Gen. 27—36)

Many cultures have a beloved scoundrel. For centuries, Germans have laughed at the merry pranks of Till Eulenspiegel. The English love tales of Robin Hood, and the Scots enjoy tales of Rob Roy. In the Southern United States, Brer Rabbit is the trickster. In the tradition of Israel, Jacob must have fulfilled something of that function. He is certainly not pictured as a saint. But once again, Genesis tells us that God does the impossible; God works out the divine purpose even through "the Supplanter."

Stories were handed down around the shrines at Bethel, Peniel, and Beersheba. Even at the moment of his birth, Jacob, they said, was trying to get ahead of his brother. His very name meant "heel grabber." He tricked his brother out of his claim to the promises. He cheated his father into bestowing them on him. He tricked his uncle Laban out of whole herds of livestock. Just in time he left Laban's house, making off with both of Laban's daughters and Laban's family idols. He even managed diplomatically to regain favor with his long estranged brother. Jacob even wrestled a blessing out of God.

Two of Jacob's experiences with God, however, are told especially to carry out the themes of Genesis. The first concerns the shrine at Bethel. Young Jacob has been forced to run for his life from the vengeance of his brother. Alone at Luz, far from home, with only a stone for a pillow, he sleeps. But that night in a dream he sees a stairway—as on a ziggurat tower?—from earth to heaven, with angels walking up and down it. And, to this unlikely candidate for blessing in this utterly unexpected place, God makes exactly the same promises that had been made to Abraham and Isaac. God promises to Jacob *descendants, land,* and *blessings* (28:13–15). And God assures him that all the families of the earth will be blessed through those descendants, the children of Jacob (later Israel). Jacob makes an altar of the stone he had used for a pillow and renames the place Bethel, "the house of God". Throughout the rest of the Old Testament, Bethel is a shrine city. (Incidentally, note how tradition can cluster around some material object. According to British tradition, that stone was subsequently brought to Scotland, Scottish kings were crowned while sitting on it, and it is the stone that now rests beneath the queen's throne in Westminster Abbey.)

There is also a detailed account of Jacob's marriages. Rachel, Leah, Zilpah, and Bilhah are also part of God's plan. Now the parents of the twelve tribes of Israel can be born (29—30). God's promise of many descendants is coming to pass.

One of the most dramatic, if puzzling, stories in Genesis reports that the trickster Jacob actually attempted to get the better of God. He has tricked his brother, his father, and his uncle. But having fled from Laban just in time, Jacob must the next day face his brother Esau, who had earlier threatened to murder him. He has tried to soften his brother by sending him lavish gifts. But the night before they meet, we are told that Jacob wrestles with God. The story at one point says he is wrestling with a man (32:25), but in the end he is sure that it is God whom he has encountered (32:30). All night long they contend, and at one point Jacob seems to be winning. In the end, however, he is crippled for life. But—the important thing to Jacob—he has won God's blessing. Jacob receives a new name, Israel (32:28). It is the symbol of his becoming a new man. Those promised descendants will be called not "the children of Jacob" but "the children of Israel," "Israelites," or, today, "Israelis." The name is interpreted to mean "one who strives with God," surely a valid name for that people throughout their long history.

Once again the family theme appears, as Jacob is reconciled with his brother (33:4). He even secures a bit of the Promised Land (33:19). Another account repeats the story of the change of Jacob's name. This version, evidently from a different source, says that the new name was given at Bethel rather than Peniel, and it gives a different story of how the shrine at Bethel got its name (35:9–15).

Again, however, there is warfare even within the clan (chapters 34, 38). The line of Edom, descendants of Esau, is traced for a chapter, but the promise is not for them. Instead, the story moves on to Jacob's son Joseph and the land of Egypt.

Through Joseph, God Brings the Family to Egypt (Gen. 37—50)

Nearly one quarter of the book of Genesis, most of Genesis 37—50, is taken up with the story of Joseph. Several reasons may be suggested: (1) the story of Joseph is in itself a delightful story; (2) Joseph is the ancestor of the dominant tribe of what became, after the civil war, the Northern Kingdom, and it was natural that they would preserve the story of their heroic ancestor; (3) Joseph is presented as a wise sage and a model Israelite, one who remains faithful in spite of trials and temptations; but most importantly, (4) this story explains how, even though it looked impossible, God carried out the divine plan, setting the stage for the great act of redemption, the rescue of the people and their exodus from Egypt.

Joseph and History

Once again, it is important to remember that the truth of Genesis lies in its affirmations about God and ourselves, not in whether it can be confirmed by secular historians. Egyptian records tell us nothing of a prime minister of Egypt named Joseph.

There are facts, however, which suggest that the story fits in certain ways into the historical background in which it is set—so well that we may use what we know of ancient Egypt to help interpret it. Egyptians loved dream interpretation and magicians. Genesis's titles for court officials are paralleled in Egyptian records. The ceremonies in which Joseph is invested with his office are appropriate for Egypt (41:37–45). At his death, Joseph is mummified (50:26). Some scholars find parallels between the story and the ancient Egyptian "Tale of Two Brothers" (Anubis and Bitis).[11]

Most interesting is the reign of the Hyksos dynasty. The Hyksos were foreigners to Egypt who managed to seize the government. They ruled Egypt and part of Palestine from about 1650 to 1542 B.C. They were Semites and thus from the same large racial group to which the Israelites belonged. They were hated by the Egyptians. The rule of Egypt by the "cousins" of the Israelites may help explain how an Israelite could gain a high position in the Egyptian court. Placing Joseph in the Hyksos dynasty suggests a date of perhaps 1630

B.C. for the move of the clan to Egypt. Whatever the historical basis for the story itself, its Egyptian elements do suggest that at least some of Israel's ancestors did indeed once live in Egypt.[12]

Joseph's Story Is Told (37—50)

The story of Joseph, like the rest of Genesis, was written in the assurance that God had predestined the future of Israel. It begins with Joseph announcing to his brothers dreams which clearly indicate that someday he will dominate them. Already envious of him because he is their father's favorite, the brothers kidnap Joseph and sell him as a slave into Egypt. When he resists the efforts of his owner's wife to seduce him, she accuses him of attempted rape, and he is thrown in jail. His ability to predict the future as God has planned it attracts attention, and eventually he becomes an adviser to the pharaoh, king of Egypt. Joseph rises at last to the position of prime minister. Aided by this ability to predict the future as revealed in dreams, he enables the pharaoh to accumulate a wealth of grain just before a famine runs up its price. Guided by Joseph, the pharaoh succeeds in dominating Egypt economically as well as politically.

Now Joseph's brothers come from Canaan, seeking grain. Joseph recognizes them, though they never suspect that the prime minster, now bearing the Egyptian name Zaphenath-paneah and married to the daughter of a pagan priest, is their long-lost brother. Joseph is thus able to test them in various ways. When, at length, Judah volunteers to give his life in exchange for that of young Benjamin, falsely accused of theft, Joseph knows that his brothers have changed. With tears he announces, "I am your brother, Joseph," and he explains how all that has happened is in accordance with the plan and purpose of God. The brothers now bring to Egypt old Israel and their wives and children. The story once more ends with the theme of family reconciliation, but it is in the faraway land of Egypt.

Joseph's Story and the Book of Genesis
Come to a Close

The ancient world took blessings and curses very seriously. The formal blessing of an old father was regarded as full of power. And so Genesis 48—49 pictures old Jacob as giving his blessings, preserved in poetry, to the different patriarchs. Crossing his hands and thus putting his right hand on Joseph's younger son's head, Jacob bestows dominance on the tribe of Ephraim rather than on that of Manasseh. God selects as God chooses. Ephraim was indeed to become the dominant tribe of the Northern Kingdom, and it preserved the story that its place was thus predestined by God. Jacob also blesses his own sons. The best blessing is given to Judah, though he is not the oldest (49:8–10). The poem reflects the subsequent power of that tribe. Judah is symbolized by a lion, and God has chosen them, says the poem, for the royal scepter. Centuries later, King David and King Solomon came from that tribe, and so did Jesus.

Genesis ends with one more affirmation that all that has happened has been in accordance with the plan of God, the divine destiny of Israel, the people of the promise. Once again, there is the theme of family reconciliation. Joseph reassures the brothers who had sold him into slavery: "Even though you intended to do harm to me, God intended it for good, in order to preserve a numerous people, as he is doing today" (50:20). In unexpected, even impossible ways, God is working out the divine promises.

It is important to remember, however, that Genesis is only the beginning. Repeatedly, it looks beyond itself to that to which it is a prelude. Its last phrase is by no means a symbol of promises fulfilled. It is rather a hint of suspense: Can fulfillment come? "And Joseph died, being one hundred ten years old; he was embalmed and placed *in a coffin in Egypt*" (50:26; italics added). To see how, against all odds, God began to fulfill those promises completely, Genesis leads us to the next book of the Pentateuch, Exodus.

EXODUS

"You have seen what I did to the Egyptians, and how I bore you on eagles' wings and brought you to myself." So, in an ancient liturgy, Israelite priests chanted the story. God had miraculously rescued them from slavery. "Now therefore," the litany continues, since God had thus liberated them, "if you obey my voice and keep my covenant, you shall be my treasured possession out of all the peoples. Indeed, the whole earth is mine, but you shall be for me a priestly kingdom and a holy nation" (Ex. 19:5–6). God set the Israelites free from slavery to Egypt. Now they are to respond by serving God.

A skeptical secular historian would probably fail to see that meaning in the story. Perhaps all that would be reported would read something like this: "In the late Bronze Age, in Egypt's Nineteenth Dynasty, probably in the reign of Rameses II, about 1290 B.C., a group of bricklaying slaves escaped from Egypt.[13] They were Semites of the kind frequently depicted in wall carvings of the era, and apparently, they adopted the life of *Habiru*, the gypsylike wanderers of the period. They were led by a man whose name, Moses, indicated that he probably had been involved with Egyptian culture (compare such Egyptian names as Thut-moses). For some reason, the name of the pagan god that must originally have been a part of Moses' name has been lost. Perhaps this loss can be related to the fact that, as an adult, Moses seems to have claimed help from a previously unknown deity called Yahweh. Apparently, a series of natural catastrophes caused confusion among the masters of these Semitic slaves and helped the slaves to escape. An east wind enabled them to ford the Sea of Reeds, while the pursuing police bogged down in that sea's mud and water. By the year 1220 B.C., these former slaves

EXODUS

The Lord Rescues Israel, Makes a Covenant with Them, and Gives Them the Law

"You have seen what I did to the Egyptians. . . . Now therefore, if you . . . keep my covenant, . . . you shall be for me a priestly kingdom" (19:4–6).

Redemption: The Lord, through Moses, Rescues Israel.			Responsibility: Israel Is to Keep the Covenant and Law.		
1	5	14	19	25	40
The Lord Prepares and Calls Moses	**The Lord, through Moses, Persuades Pharaoh to Release Israel**	**The Lord Leads Israel through the Sea to Sinai**	**The Lord Institutes the Covenant and Its Law**	**The Lord Makes Provision for Proper Worship**	
The baby Moses is rescued, 1:1–2:10	God sends plagues on Israel's masters, 5—11	The Lord rescues them from pharaoh at the sea, 14—15	The Lord speaks at Sinai, 19	God gives direction for the ark and the tabernacle, 25—31	
Moses flees to Midian, 2:11–25	The tenth plague forces their release, and the Passover is instituted, 12—13	God feeds and leads them, in spite of rebellion, 16—18	Gives the Ten Commandments, 20	Instead, the people worship the golden calf, 32	
There God reveals the sacred name and calls Moses, 3—4			The laws of the Covenant Code, 21—23	The covenant has to be renewed, 33—35	
			The covenant is ratified by the people, the elders, and Moses, 24	Now the tabernacle and the ark are made, 36—40	

Author: Traditionally Moses, but actually from various sources, spanning centuries
Theme: The Lord is the Deliverer of Israel; therefore Israel is to keep its covenant with God.
Special Significance: The themes of redemption, covenant response, and law, as introduced especially in Exodus, are basic to all the rest of the Bible.
Best-known Passage: The Ten Commandments (20:1–17)

had established themselves in Palestine, where they were soundly defeated by the Egyptian army. Subsequently, they related their elaborate law code to their escape, which they attributed to their God, Yahweh."

Thus a secular historian might, with a kind of accuracy, report the facts. But that kind of history would miss the whole point. The inspired writers of Exodus knew that the Creator of the universe had rescued them. The God of grace had liberated them. This God had called them to a special mission, to be priests to the whole world. They were to be a special kind of nation. In response to the grace of this God who had rescued them, they were covenanted to live in a certain way, according to the law of God.

Their first telling of the story, they recalled, was in song and dance. "Sing to the Lord, for he has triumphed gloriously; horse and rider he has thrown into the sea" (Ex. 15:21); thus Miriam and the women are reported to have sung at their victory celebration, and scholars suggest that the song may go back even to the time of the event itself. From that moment until the celebration of the Passover in millions of Jewish homes this year, the story has been told and retold. At every Passover, the youngest child is to ask, "What do you mean by this observance?" The parents are to reply by telling again the story of how God delivered them (12:26–27).

Literary critics trace the various strands of the telling and retelling of the story by the various biblical writers. There is Miriam's song and its expansion in the Song of Moses (15:1–18). Poets retold the story (Pss. 78; 106; 114; etc.). The prose authors of what scholars call the "J document" added details to clarify its meaning. In their captivity in Babylon, priests recalled that earlier deliverance and elaborated the story further to relate its message to their desperate situation. But the basic core of the story remained the same. God had delivered them from slavery. Now, in response, they were to live as the people of God.

This is the basis of the Jewish religion. In the context of its celebration, the Passover, the first Christians at the Lord's Supper interpreted the meaning of their new faith. To our basic account of these events, then, the book of Exodus, we now turn.

Redemption: The Lord, through Moses, Rescues Israel (Ex. 1—18)

The Lord Prepares
and Calls Moses (Ex. 1—4)

Genesis ends with the clan of Jacob prospering in Goshen, an area of the Nile Delta closest to Israel, the best grazing land in Egypt. But "now a new king arose over Egypt, who did not know Joseph" (Ex. 1:8). Perhaps this reflects the overthrow of the Hyksos dynasty, who were Semites and thus, at least broadly speaking, "cousins" of the Israelites. With the fall of their royal patrons, Jacob's descendants become slaves. Soon they are forced to build the military supply depot of Pithom and to rebuild the city of Rameses, or "The House of Rameses, the beloved of Amun," as the Egyptians called it. Archaeologists have explored its remains and can date the construction to the early thirteenth century B.C. In this situation Moses is born.

> My changeling mother conceived me, in secret she bore me.
> She set me in a basket of rushes, with bitumen she sealed my lid.
> She cast me into the river which rose not over me.
> The river bore me up and carried me to Akki, the drawer of water. . . .
> Akki, the drawer of water, took me as his son and reared me.[14]

Thus, long before Moses, the ancients told the story of the infant Sargon, king of Agade. Perhaps, some suggest, that tale influenced the story of Moses' marvelous preservation when the pharaoh had decided to kill all Hebrew boy babies. But the inspired writers knew that the honor of that story belonged properly not to Sargon but to Moses. And they attributed his deliverance not to Akki the irrigator but to five brave women.

Pharaoh was the most powerful ruler of the ancient world. But he is no match, the inspired narrator tells us, almost laughing, for two shrewd Hebrew women. These midwives cleverly foil his genocidal plot (1:15–22). Now Moses' mother defies the law and hides the baby. Pharaoh's daughter is not afraid to ignore pharaoh's decree and adopt the child she finds in the riverbank reeds. And Moses' smart sister completes the frustration of pharaoh's plans. Her bold advice results in Moses' mother actually being paid to do what she most wanted to do.

God uses five brave and resourceful women. But our writers want us to know that it is God who is at work through them. And so, by whatever human means but especially by the plan of God, "Moses was instructed in all the wisdom of the Egyptians" (Acts 7:22).

He still knows himself to be an Israelite, however. Therefore, when he is grown, he makes an abortive effort to mitigate the condition of his people. Our skilled narrator tells that story (Ex. 2:11–14) as a kind of preview of the rest of the book. Moses kills a cruel Egyptian taskmaster, but by the next day it is his own people who are disputing, and they reject his mediation. "Who made you a ruler and judge over us?" they demand (2:14). Forced to flee from pharaoh, Moses finds the answer to that question at Mount Sinai.

There, in the Sinai wilderness, he rescues seven sisters, daughters of the Kenite priest named Reuel or Jethro (2:15–22). Did Moses learn from this priest about a God named Yahweh? So some have suggested. All we are told is that he became this priest's son-in-law and that later he accepted advice from Jethro (Exodus 18). But it was while he was engaged in his father-in-law's sheep business that Moses had his first, life-changing encounter with the God with the curious name, Yahweh, the Lord.

From the midst of a burning bush, God calls Moses: "I will send you to Pharaoh to bring my people, the Israelites, out of Egypt" (3:10). But Moses recalls the challenge of the Israelites earlier, "Who made you a ruler and judge?" By what authority could he lead these people? And God answers by revealing the divine name.

> God said to Moses, "I AM WHO I AM." He said further, "Thus you shall say to the Israelites, "I AM has sent me to you." (3:14)

"I AM WHO I AM"—what kind of name is that? Some translate this mysterious phrase as "I am the One Who Causes Things to Be," that is, the Creator. Terence Fretheim seems to prefer "I Am Who I Will Be," that is, the God whose authority will be revealed in the liberation of Israel.[15] Names are often important in the Bible. If you have a person's name, you have—in the jargon of CB radios—a "handle," a way to call on someone. God reveals the name. Yet it is a mystery, too. Later Israelites would not pronounce the sacred name and substituted "The Lord." Based on the verb "to be," the name is sometimes transliterated into English as "Jehovah." When it was pronounced, it probably sounded like "Yahweh." Using the German letter "J" for the initial sound, it is often written "Jahweh." But most translations write it as Jews for centuries reading it aloud have said it: "The Lord."

"Please, oh Lord, send anybody else"; so Brevard S. Childs translates Ex. 4:13.[16] But the Lord commands, and Moses goes.

Once again, a woman saves his life. Stricken by illness or fear, Moses nearly dies. But his wife's circumcision of their son and her symbolic intercession save Moses (4:24–26). Now he is ready to confront the pharaoh.

The Lord, through Moses, Persuades Pharaoh to Release Israel (Ex. 5—13)

What an unequal contest! Rameses the Great was the most powerful ruler of his time and was worshiped as a god. A visitor to Egypt can still see his statues, sixty feet high and weighing eighty tons, towering above the Nile. His temples are marvels. His treasures enrich museums. And he commanded powerful armies, multitudes of slaves, and priests of the gods of Egypt. Except by implication (1:11), Exodus never says which pharaoh is meant. He represents all the might that, throughout Israel's history, had been arrayed against the people of God.

What an unequal contest; for against the king of Egypt come only Moses and his brother Aaron—and the invisible God with the mysterious name. This is really a battle between the gods of Egypt and the Lord. In such a contest, those pagan deities never have a chance. Recalling the humor of the situation, Israelite grandparents later told their children that Yahweh "made fools of the Egyptians" (10:2). Indeed, one senses the narrators laughing as they tell the story of how the Lord persuaded the reluctant pharaoh to give up his slaves. Already they have recalled how two Israelite women tricked the king of Egypt and how the pharaoh who sought to kill all Israelite boys ended up rearing the one who will rescue them. Now they tell how Moses and Aaron outdo all pharaoh's magicians. When pharaoh will not let the people go, the Creator of the universe attacks the Nile, the god who is the source of all Egyptian life. Step by step, as the ten plagues come and go, pharaoh yields a little more, then goes back on his word, only to confront yet another demonstration of the power of God.

According to Exodus, the technique Yahweh uses to persuade the pharaoh is a series of ten disasters. It would be a misreading of scripture to take Exodus's account as identical to that which a modern biologist or meteorologist might give. True, the plagues are all in some sense "natural" events in Egypt. Erosion does sometimes pollute the Nile, turning it red (7:14–24). Frogs have sometimes multiplied to the point of being a nuisance, and when they died, it would have been natural for gnats, flies, cattle disease, and boils to follow (8:1–9, 21). Thunder and hail (9:22–35), millions of locusts (10:12–20), and dust storms producing darkness (10:21–29) still occur. But only biblical literalists are likely to be upset by the fact that in Psalm 78, the list of plagues is rather different. The story in Exodus is told in a stylized fashion, full of delightful repetitions. It is, in fact, intended for repeating to children (10:2). And those who analyze the different literary sources that are combined in Exodus tell us that the miraculous element was heightened as the later writers retold the story. The later writers tell us how all the dust of Egypt became gnats (8:16); how the plagues came and went at the command of the rods of Moses and Aaron; how when the Egyptian magicians duplicated Aaron's signs, his rod-turned-snake ate theirs (7:8–12); and how the plagues never touched the Israelites (8:22; 9:26). One can almost hear the laughter of the Israelite parents as, through the generations, they told and retold these stories. By the end of the story, they said, pharaoh actually begged them to get out (12:31)!

We have spoken of ten "plagues," but the repeated word for them in Exodus is "signs" (4:8, 17; 7:3; 8:23; etc.). What our writers want us to know is not some catalog of catastrophes in nature. The truth lies not so much in the signs themselves as in what the signs point to: "You shall know that I am the Lord your God" (6:7). In every way they can think of, the writers seek to remind us of the power of the redeeming God. "Who is the Lord, that I should heed him and let Israel go?" (5:2), the pharaoh demands. All is told in order that we, like pharaoh, will learn the answer.

After nine signs, Exodus interrupts its story to describe the continuing memorial to these events; the Passover is instituted (11:1–12:28). As Christians converted the Roman Saturnalia into Christmas, so, some scholars suggest, Israel took an earlier festival and filled it with new meaning. To this day, devout Jews celebrate the Passover every year. Many ancient religions seem to have thought of their god as having a special claim on the firstborn male. This was reflected in the Jewish sacrificial system, with the firstborn sacrificed and the firstborn son redeemed by sacrifice (13:2, 12–15). In that context, one understands the story of the climactic plague that involved a sacrificed lamb, blood on the doorpost, and even the death of the unredeemed firstborn of the Egyptians. Retelling the story of the Exodus at the Passover feast guaranteed that no generation would ever forget: In spite of all opposition, the Lord set Israel free.

The Lord Leads Israel through the Sea
to Sinai (Ex. 14—18)

An ancient Egyptian painting shows, in full color, a pharaoh charging into battle, his chariot drawn by prancing horses. To show his power, he is painted larger than his enemies, and his bow and arrow are aimed at his hapless victims. It reminds us that the fleeing Israelites had reason to be terrified (14:10). Another picture shows us war-horses and chariots of Egypt's enemies bogged down in a flood, while their riders fall before the foe. At the exodus, it was the Egyptians' turn to be mired down and destroyed (14: 25–28).

Exodus records at least three accounts of the escape at the Sea of Reeds: there is the oldest, Miriam's song (15:21); there is the later expansion of that ballad (15:1–18); and there is a prose account, almost surely a combination of several early and later written versions, no doubt embodying various oral traditions (14:1–30). One account said that "a strong east wind all night" was the instrument by which God drove back the waters (14:21). But the final editor wants to make sure we cannot miss the marvel of God's power, the real truth of the story. That editor tells us, therefore, how the waters came and went simply at the command of Moses' hand (14:21, 27). The purpose of all this is not only the liberation of God's people; it is that the Egyptians "shall know that I am the Lord" (14:18).

And so Miriam leads the women in a victory dance: "Sing to the Lord, for he has triumphed gloriously; horse and rider he has thrown into the sea" (15:21).

But if we look in the chapters that follow for a repeated phrase or idea, one immediately strikes us: "And the people complained" (15:24; cf. 16:2, 12; 17:3; and recall 2:14). Realistically and factually, these Israelite historians make no effort to idealize their ancestors. The freed Israelites complain for lack of water, but God, through Moses, provides it. They complain for lack of bread, and God provides it. They complain for lack of meat, and God provides it. They complain again for water, and God provides it again.

Even in the desert there are oases. And still today, Arabs find what they call manna, a product of desert insects. But to make sure we understand that it is God, not just ordinary nature, that is providing manna, a later Priestly writer has included this story: manna, he tells us, spoiled overnight except on Friday, when enough could be harvested for the Sabbath (16:13–36). It is the Creator of nature, not just nature, who is caring for God's people.

It is God, too, who guides their path through the wilderness (13:21). God brings them at last to Sinai, the mountain of the Lord.

Responsibility: Israel Is to Keep the Covenant and Law (Ex. 19—40)

The Lord Institutes the Covenant and Its Law (Ex. 19—24)

The book of Exodus falls into two parts. The first eighteen chapters tell the story of how God liberated Israel. The remaining twenty-two tell how Israel is to respond to that liberation. God had delivered them; therefore, they were to live as the people of God. At Mount Sinai, described as if it were a quaking volcano or shaken by an awesome thunderstorm (19:18), the Lord makes the covenant with the chosen people. "I have rescued you," God says, in effect; "now therefore . . . you shall be for me a priestly kingdom" (19:6). Laws outline how Israel is to fulfill this destiny. In solemn assembly, with bloody ceremony, the people agree. The *covenant* is ratified (24:7–8).

Martin Noth, who is usually very cautious about ascribing historical worth to stories in the Pentateuch, writes, "There is no doubt that the Sinai tradition, the basic substance of which is quite unique and unrelated to any other phenomenon in the history of religion, derived from an actual event."[17] The inspired narrators, however, have given us a theological interpretation of that event which goes far beyond what an ordinary historian might report. At Sinai, we are told, the Lord made a covenant with Israel.

At about the time of Moses, a Hittite king laid down the terms of his covenant with one of his satellites. "I have protected you," he said in effect. "Now, in gratitude, you are to obey me. Be careful, however, that you do not disobey, as your father sometimes did. And preserve, ratify, and keep this treaty."[18] In much the same pattern, the treaty, the covenant, between the sovereign Lord and Israel is presented in Exodus. The whole Bible gets its name from this repeated idea: Old Testament (or Old Covenant) and New Testament (or New Covenant).

"You shall be for me a . . . kingdom" (19:6). If you are going to have a kingdom, you must have a king. Yahweh (the Lord) is the king. You must have citizens. Israel is to be that group of subjects, God's "treasured possession" (19:5). But you must also have laws. Therefore the basic constitution for this kingdom of God is given; it is the Ten Commandments (20:1–17). They tell Israel how it can be this curious kind of kingdom, "a holy nation" (19:6).

Several things mark the Ten Commandments as different from other laws found in the Pentateuch. They are said to be the first that were given. God, we are told, spoke them to all the people, not just to Moses (20:1). Their form is absolute and universal, not related to special cases. They are identified later as "the Ten Commandments" (34:28) and written on two tablets of stone "with the finger of God" (31:18). Apparently, these tablets were to be carried in the ark of the covenant (25:21). They are repeated in a slightly different form in Deuteronomy.

Many scholars propose that, at least in their short form, these laws are very old indeed; perhaps, some would say, going all the way back to the time of Moses himself. So Exodus tells us.

While the ancient Hebrews would probably not have made this distinction, it is often said that the first four commandments outline Israel's duties toward God.

1. You shall have no other gods before me.
2. You shall not make for yourself an idol.
3. You shall not make wrongful use of the name of the Lord your God.
4. Remember the sabbath day.

The other six are thought of as outlining duties toward one's fellow human beings.

5. Honor your father and your mother.
6. You shall not murder.
7. You shall not commit adultery.
8. You shall not steal.
9. You shall not bear false witness against your neighbor.
10. You shall not covet.

Christian writers have sometimes seen in these laws implications for a whole system of ethics. Jesus himself quoted several of the last six in summarizing God's requirements (Mark 10:19).

There follows another ancient set of laws, sometimes called "the Covenant Code" (21:1–23:33). These are quite different in form from the Ten Commandments. Instead of being universal, they relate to specific situations and cases: "When an ox gores a man . . . If someone leaves a pit open . . . If a thief is found breaking in . . ." and so forth. Later we are told that not all the laws written in the book of the law of God were actually given by Moses (Josh. 24:26). As new situations arose, additional laws were needed. But even those, like some of the Covenant Code, that seem to imply a settled community at last arrived in Canaan were revered as part of the law that God had instituted through the great lawgiver Moses.

Christians do not regard all of these laws as eternally binding. For example, some laws seek to prohibit cruelty to slaves (21:1–21), but Jesus' teachings make clear that even the most humane slavery is horrible. Jesus specifically rejects the concept of "an eye for an eye" (21:24; contrast Matt. 5:38–42). But many of these ordinances prescribe practical, commonsense rules. A thief, for example, is expected not so much to spend time in jail as to make restitution, double, for what he has stolen (22:4).

Precisely how the covenant was ratified is not quite clear. Was God physically seen by seventy-four men (24:9–10), or did only Moses have such a vision, and then only of God's "back" (33:17–23)? Was the covenant ratified by all the people (24:3–8) or primarily by the representative elders (24:9–11)? Were the priests involved (19:22) or excluded (19:24; 24:1–2)? The probable explanation of such seeming inconsistencies is that different oral and written traditions have been combined. Obviously, such differences did not matter to the inspired editor. In every way they can imagine, our writers tell us that Israel solemnly pledged, even in blood (24:8), to obey the law and keep the covenant.

The Lord Makes Provision
for Proper Worship (Ex. 25—40)

Nearly one-third of the book of Exodus is devoted to a description of the tabernacle and the ark. Careful directions are given for the building of the tabernacle and the ark and for related ceremonies (25—31). Then, after the story of Israel's false worship, the golden calf and its aftermath (32—35), the description is given all over again, as we are told how craftsmen Bezalel and Oholiab actually built this tent for worship.

Such detail is surprising. After all, our written account seems to come from the P document, written perhaps some seven centuries after the event it describes. While Israel may indeed have had a goats'-hair tent for worship during its wilderness wanderings, to many historians it seems that Exodus gives a somewhat idealized picture of the tabernacle used by these escaped slaves. Why, then, this extended account? Perhaps the idea of the tabernacle fascinated those Jews precisely because they had been carried off into captivity in Babylon. The tabernacle, they recalled, was not a temple, confined to one place. It was portable. God, therefore, was not confined to one place. God, they were affirming, was able to be with them in Babylon, even though the Temple at Jerusalem had been destroyed. And these priestly writers dreamed that someday the Temple would be rebuilt, an ideal "tabernacle" (dwelling place) for God. Their description of the tabernacle was not just a bit of nostalgia; it was an expression of hope, of faith.

The ark, too, was portable, a symbol of God's presence wherever God's people might be. Later tradition said that in it Israel carried Aaron's miraculous rod and the Ten Commandments (Heb. 9:4), and on it was God's throne, the "mercy seat" between two cherubim. Archaeologists have found thrones of ancient kings, flanked by such winged sphinxes. But the Hebrews never carved an idol to go on that throne. Symbolically, the throne was empty, for they were forbidden to carve an image of the Lord (37:8–9).

Yet in the midst of this elaborate picture of the symbols of true worship prescribed by God, Exodus tells us that Israel began worshiping an idol, a golden calf (32:1–35). In the British Museum, one may see a curious bronze bull calf. Between his horns he bears a disk, the symbol of the sun, and in front of the disk is a viper. Around his neck is carved a ribbon, and a rug is depicted as spread over his back. His sex organ is clearly visible. This image is an idol of Apis, the bull-god of Memphis in Egypt. Did a memory of that idol inspire Israel's wilderness apostasy? Archaeologists have unearthed bull idols in Israel too, symbols for Canaanite worship. Perhaps the story is recalled especially because of the calf shrines set up much later by evil King Jeroboam (1 Kings 12:28). In strong terms, Exodus warns that God does not take idolatry lightly (32:30–35).

The story of the golden calf serves as a reminder of the importance of true worship. Exodus describes something of the forms that worship was supposed to take. But more of that instruction is found in the next book, Leviticus. And so the narrative leads directly into it.

LEVITICUS

Page for page, Leviticus is for many people the least-read and least-loved book of the Bible.

There are reasons. For one thing, as James L. Mays puts it, some readers find Leviticus and Numbers "as barren and unknown as the dry, trackless wilderness in which much of their story is set."[19] Leviticus seems not only dull but irrelevant. It focuses on ceremonies to be carried out in the tabernacle, a structure that has not existed for some three thousand years. When the Temple at Jerusalem was destroyed in 70 A.D., Jews abandoned the system of sacrifices that Leviticus describes. Christians have never made the rituals of Leviticus a part of their worship.

And yet, providentially, the book remains a part of the canon, the Bible. Here are some of the things that make it still valuable. Liberation theologians and others have risked their lives for the concept of freedom and justice that finds expression in the year of jubilee (Leviticus 25). A verse from the passage about that year is inscribed on the Liberty Bell: "Proclaim liberty throughout all the land to all the inhabitants thereof" (25:10, KJV). Asked what is the greatest of all the 613 laws of the Jewish scripture, Jesus placed as second only to the command to love God (Deut. 6:5) a verse from Leviticus, "You shall love your neighbor as yourself" (Lev. 19:18; cf. Mark 12:31). Though our forms of worship today are quite different, much of the theology and its related principles that guided the worship of the biblical Hebrews still apply. And finally, New Testament writers and Christian theologians through the

LEVITICUS
Laws to Guide the Life and Especially the Worship of Israel
"You shall be holy, for I the Lord your God am holy." (19:2).

1 God Gives Laws Concerning Sacrifices	8 Priests Are Purified and Ordained to Lead the Worship	11 Laws Guide God's Holy People in Keeping Pure and Clean	16 The Annual Day of Atonement	17 The Holiness Code Gives Guidance for Holy Living	27 An Appendix about Vows
Burnt offerings, 1	Aaron and his sons are consecrated, 8—9	Clean food, 11	Purifying the nation, 16	Holiness in sacrifices, 17	
Grain offerings, 2	Aaron's sons, however, are destroyed for profaning a sacrifice, 10	Female cleanliness, 12		Family relationships, 18	
Free will offerings, 3		Cleansing and quarantine for leprosy, 13—14		Life, rituals, and festivals, 19—24	
Appropriate offerings for particular offenses, 4—7		Sex-related cleanliness, 15		The Year of Jubilee, 25	
				Promises and warnings about obedience to these laws, 26	

Author: Traditionally Moses, but actually the work of Priestly writers, compiled perhaps as late as 450 B.C.
Theme: The Lord God is holy, separate, above us, not to be approached casually but only through prescribed ceremonies led by holy priests and by holy living in obedience to God's law.
Special Significance: Of all the 613 laws of the Old Testament, Jesus called "Love your neighbor as yourself" (19:18) second only to love of God. The New Testament epistle to the Hebrews uses ideas from Leviticus to interpret the meaning of Christ's sacrifice.

centuries have turned to Leviticus to explain some of the meaning of the center of the Christian faith, the atoning death of Jesus.

To this archaic yet still relevant book we now turn.

God Gives Laws
Concerning Sacrifices (Lev. 1—7)

"The Lord summoned Moses and spoke to him from the tent of meeting" (1:1); so Leviticus begins. Because the book is so concerned with priests and the ceremonies over which they preside, and because the Levites were the tribe who were to be priests, Christians have called the book Leviticus. In Hebrew Bibles, however, it is named "Called," from that opening phrase, "The Lord summoned" (or "called").

God's call is at the tabernacle. Following the principle of interpretation that a passage should be understood in the light of its context, note that Leviticus follows directly on Exodus 25—40. Those earlier chapters described the construction of the tabernacle. Now the laws of Leviticus are given by God from its doorway. The use of the tabernacle's other name, "the tent of meeting," links Leviticus all the way back to Genesis. Once God had come calling for Adam, seeking a meeting (Gen. 3:9). Genesis describes how our sin frustrated God's efforts to meet with, to establish fellowship with, humankind. God responded with a new approach, climaxed in the covenant. At Sinai, God met with this one group, called to be a "holy nation" (Ex. 19:6). How will that fellowship, that "at-one-ment," that meeting, be continued? In Leviticus 1—7, God provides one answer: the sacrificial system.[20]

If you love someone, you want to do things for and with that person. "Burnt offerings" (Lev. 1:1–17) were Israel's way of showing gratitude to God. These offerings were to be burned up completely, a sign of complete sacrificial thanksgiving in response to God's grace. The "grain offerings" or "cereal offerings" (2:1–16), however, were eaten in part by the priests. This was God's provision for their support.

Persons who love each other want fellowship. The "sacrifice of well-being" (3:1–17), therefore, was a shared meal, a kind of communion service in which the worshiper and God were united. It is called the "peace offering" in many translations, but the Hebrew scholars insist that the Hebrew word *shalom* has broader connotations of happiness and blessing.

But suppose you have wronged your benefactor. Sin had repeatedly broken humankind's fellowship with God. Now God provides symbols of confession and repentance: guilt offerings and sin offerings (4:1–6:7). The first offerings described are for unintentional sins (4:1–35). But the next chapters give hope for those who have deliberately sinned, even for thieves and robbers (6:1–3). True, the act of sacrifice by itself is not enough. The sinner must confess (5:5) and make restitution (6:5). But a repeated phrase gives the good news of God's grace: when confession, restitution, and sacrifice are accomplished, "you shall be forgiven" (6:7; cf. 4:20, 26, 31, etc.).

This section on sacrifices concludes with a manual to tell the priests how to do these offerings (6:8–7:38).

One good guide for getting at what a passage of scripture wants to emphasize is to look for repeated words and ideas. More than twenty-five times, Israel is reminded that their offerings must be "without blemish" (1:3; 3:1, 6; 4:3; etc.). And repeatedly, they are told that it is the first fruits (2:12; 23:10; etc.) and the firstborn animals (27:26) that are to be sacrificed. God must come first, and one must offer to God only the best. More than eighty times, Leviticus uses the word "blood." The whole idea of bloody sacrifices seems repugnant to us, but Leviticus insists on it. Perhaps all this sprinkling of blood was shocking to Israelites too. It was a dramatic reminder that a right relationship with the holy God is a life-or-death matter. In a sense, these ceremonies, like most rituals, were dramas. Not simply in words but in actions, priests and people acted out the relationship of God and God's people.

Priests Are Purified and Ordained to Lead the Worship (Lev. 8—10)

Not only must the sacrifices be without blemish, but those who offer them must also be properly purified. The next section of Leviticus describes the consecration of the priests.

Though it is set in the context of the covenant at Sinai, most scholars regard Leviticus, in its present form at least, as the work of priests centuries later. Priests were the successors of Moses' brother Aaron and Aaron's descendants. Only holy people were to approach closest to the holy God. Therefore the leaders of Israel's worship were purified with special washings (8:6), sacred dress (8:7–9), anointing with holy oil (8:10–13), and elaborate sacrifices and ceremonies (8:18–9:24).

Priests are out of fashion among many Protestants today. In ancient Israel, however, their duties were essential. It was they who represented God to humanity and humanity to God. They offered sacrifices, which involved supervising the preparation of a great deal of food (17:1–7). They were also Israel's teachers (10:11). They had certain medical responsibilities (14:48), and on occasion they were even to act as judges (Numbers 5). Therefore their qualifications were more than ceremonial. They had to be physically fit (Lev. 21:16–24), careful of their appearance (21:10), sober (10:8), and with respectable families (21:12–15).

To make clear how important it was that priests not trifle with their solemn responsibilities, the authors of Leviticus retold an awe-inspiring story (10:1–7): two of Aaron's own sons broke the rules, and the Lord burned them to death with the unholy fire they had offered.

Laws Guide God's Holy People
in Keeping Pure and Clean (Lev. 11—15)

Lay people were to be holy too. Having described proper worship and a properly ordained priesthood, Leviticus now sets forth rules for all the people in their everyday life.

First, there are careful regulations about food (11:1–47). Orthodox Jews still will not eat pork or other foods that are not kosher, "clean." Some of these rules may originally have been for the prevention of disease. Some may have been related to pagan practices that Israel was to avoid. Some may have simply reflected feelings of aversion to certain foods. But probably the main reason for such food laws was to provide a daily reminder that Israel was to be different from all other people. They were to be a "holy nation," a "priestly kingdom," separate in every aspect of life from their pagan neighbors.

The next chapter deals with childbirth and cleanliness for women. Again, some of the same reasons that may have pertained to the food laws— prevention of disease, avoidance of pagan practices, and so forth—may apply here, along with a possible humanitarian concern for the comfort of women. Centuries later, after Jesus' birth, Mary and Joseph availed themselves of Leviticus's concession allowing less-expensive sacrifices for the poor (12:8; cf. Luke 2:24).

Two long chapters deal with leprosy (13—14). Again, cleanliness and holiness are related. Victims of the dread disease were quarantined, forced to wear torn clothes and disheveled hair, and required to cry a warning to any who came near (13:45). The novel and the motion picture *Ben Hur* made the plight of these afflicted people familiar to us. No modern cures were available, of course, but no doubt many skin diseases that could have been cured were classified as leprosy. When a person recovered from one of these, it was the priest who pronounced the leper clean.

Bodily impurity of men (15:1–18) is also dealt with, and other laws again discuss bodily impurity of women (15:19–33). Cleanliness, Leviticus repeatedly affirms, is necessary to holiness. It was no accident that when the plague swept Europe in the Middle Ages, often the cleanly Jews survived while their Christian neighbors perished.

The Annual Day of Atonement (Lev. 16)

Yom Kippur, the Day of Atonement, is still important to all Jews. Coming soon after the Jewish New Year, it is a solemn time of reflection, repentance, intercession, and new beginnings.

While its purpose was the same in the wilderness, its rituals were quite different from those of today. Two goats were used. With elaborate ceremonies one goat was offered to the Lord as a sin offering, but on the other, the scapegoat, were symbolically laid the sins of the people. The scapegoat was then driven into the wilderness, carrying those sins to Azazel, a wilderness demon. There is where sins belong.

The Holiness Code Gives Guidance
for Holy Living (Lev. 17—26)

The longest and probably oldest section of Leviticus is called "the Holiness Code" or "the Law of Holiness."[21]

The Holiness Code propounds food laws (17:1–17), laws about sex relations (18:1–30; 20:10–21), regulations about uncleanness related to contact with the dead (21:1–24), and further guidance for priests (22:1–33). These laws seem to have been collected and published without any order we can now discover. All, however, are related to one central theme, the basic idea of the whole book: "You shall be holy to me; for I the Lord am holy, and I have separated you from the other peoples to be mine" (20:26). The word "holy" occurs more than eighty times in Leviticus, far more than in any other book of the Bible. If some of the rules of Leviticus seem odd to us, perhaps that was part of their purpose. Israel, as the people of God, was to be so obviously different in so many ways that the Israelites could never forget their unique mission.

But not all of these rules were ceremonial, what the scholars call "cultic." Leviticus 19 is full of moral laws, which govern how people are to treat each other. Poverty-stricken Ruth would profit one day from the humane provision that at harvest some grain was to be left for the poor (Lev. 19:9–10; cf. Ruth 2:1–23). Theft, falsehood, fraud, mistreatment of the handicapped, injustice, and slander are prohibited (19:11–16). Israelites were to treat with respect people of other races among them, remembering that they themselves had once been strangers in a strange land (19:33–34). Dishonesty in business was forbidden (19:35–37).

And in the midst of this book of exotic ceremonies and cultic regulations comes the commandment that Jesus said was second only to—and really quite like—the great commandment to love the Lord: "You shall love your neighbor as yourself" (19:18; cf. Mark 12:31).

Leviticus 23 gives an account of the three great festivals that are still celebrated by Jews as instituted by God through Moses (cf. Ex. 23:14–17; 34:18–24; Deut. 16:1–17). Every spring there is the Passover, or Feast of Unleavened Bread (Lev. 23:1–14). Fifty days later there is Pentecost (23:15–22; cf. Acts 2). Originally a harvest festival, Pentecost later came to be celebrated as an anniversary of the giving of the law. Then each fall there is a series of ceremonies, beginning with the New Year (23:23–25), moving to the Day of Atonement (23:26–32) and then to the Feast of Booths (23:33–44). Orthodox Jews may still construct booths on their lawns, a memorial to the days when Israel lived in tents in the wilderness.[22]

But of Leviticus's celebrations, one that has drawn special attention in recent times is the year of jubilee (Leviticus 25). Every fiftieth year, all property was to go back to the family of its original owners (25:13–34). Slaves were to be set free, and the people were to "proclaim liberty throughout the land" (25:10). Debts were to be canceled (25:25–29). The poor were to be cared for (25:35–46). And the same passage says that every seventh year the land itself was to have "rest," apparently to avoid erosion and soil depletion (25:3, 11). This year of jubilee may not have been a practical proposal. Nowhere is it recorded that Israel ever actually observed it. But in recent years, the principles of concern for the soil, for liberation of the oppressed, and for economic justice that underlie Leviticus 25 have made this chapter perhaps the most discussed in the entire book.[23]

Originally, Leviticus probably ended with chapter 26, a series of promises and warnings concerning obedience to its rules. An appendix has been added concerning vows. Some rules allow money to be substituted for other kinds of sacrifices in specified cases (Leviticus 27).

The New Testament and Leviticus

One of our principles of interpretation has been that Christians interpret each Testament in the light of the other. For Christians, therefore, it is important to note at least three things. First, both Jesus and Paul warn against too much stress on the externals of forms and ceremonies such as Leviticus describes. Formalism and legalism may take the focus away from concern for faith and love (for example, contrast Matt. 23:23 with Lev. 27:30; and see Gal. 3:2 and 4:10). Second, it was in the great moral law of Lev. 19:18 that Paul found his summary of all God's law (Gal. 5:14) and Jesus his "second commandment" (Matt. 22:39). Finally, the ninth chapter of the New Testament letter to the Hebrews uses the concept of the blood atonement through the tabernacle sacrifices to explain the meaning of the death of Jesus. While all of that process of form and ceremony has now been transcended, it all pointed, Hebrews says, to the cross. In a divine paradox, Hebrews describes Christ as at the same time the true priest and the true sacrifice. Thus without Leviticus we could not fully understand the atonement God won for us through Jesus.

NUMBERS

Because it begins with a report of how Israel was "numbered" in a census, Christians have called the fourth book of Moses "Numbers." That title, however, does not do justice to this book, with its meaningful stories about God and God's people. More wisely, the Jews have named the book from a phrase in its opening verse, recalling the locale of the adventures it describes: "In the Wilderness."

Numbers is not the most popular book in the Bible. Foster R. McCurley has

Israel in the Wilderness: A Rebellious Generation Perishes, but God Prepares and Purifies the People

"And the Lord spoke to Moses and to Aaron, saying: How long shall this wicked congregation complain? . . . 'Not one of you shall come into the land. . . . Your children shall be . . . in the wilderness for forty years'" (14:26–33).

1	10:11	26
At Sinai: God Prepares Israel for the Journey through the Wilderness	**In the Wilderness: Israel Rebels, God Punishes; but God Still Leads the People**	**Approaching Canaan: A New Generation Prepares to Seize the New Land**
Census and ordering of the wilderness camp, 1—4	Led by God, they leave Sinai, 10:11-36	A new census for a new beginning, 26
Laws given concerning moral and ceremonial purity, 5—6	But repeatedly they are faithless: They complain about food, 11 They complain about Moses' wife, 12	Women as well as men are promised inheritance in Canaan, 27:1-11
Response: the leaders bring offerings, 7	Frightened by the spies' report, they fail to enter Canaan, 13—14	God appoints Joshua to succeed Moses, 27:12-23
The Levites are consecrated to lead worship, 8	God gives laws about worship, 15	Festivals for the Promised Land, 28—29
They celebrate Passover and prepare to leave Sinai; 9:1–10:10	Korah rebels against Moses and Aaron, 16	Laws about faithfulness to vows, 30
	But God endorses and guides Aaron's priesthood, 17—19	Early victories won, booty allotted, 31—32
	Even Moses fails in faith, 20:1-13	The stages of the journey toward Canaan, 33:1-48
	Leaving Kadesh, they battle enemies in their way, 20:14-21:35	Moses' final instructions, 33:50-36:13
	But God turns Balaam's pagan curses to blessings, 22—24	
	Even here, Baal worship threatens, 25	

Author: Traditionally Moses, but actually compiled by priests as late as 450 B.C.

Purpose: The story of Israel's wanderings in the wilderness is told to remind Israel of God's grace and God's law and to warn against repeating their pattern of faithlessness and rebellion.

Best-known Passage: The Aaronic benediction (6:22–26)

written a helpful commentary titled *Genesis, Exodus, Leviticus, Numbers,* but of his 128 pages, not more than 3 are devoted primarily to Numbers.[24]Indeed, there are long passages in Numbers that may seem valueless to the modern reader: census statistics of people long dead, rules governing ceremonies no longer practiced, laws that often seem inapplicable in urban society, and directions for the order of a march through a wilderness long left behind. Numbers purports to describe how Israel traveled from Mount Sinai to the border of the Promised Land. But many historians question the value of the book as an accurate guide to that ancient history.[25]

Modern scholars, however, like devout souls through the ages, have found in the stories included in Numbers pictures of God and God's people in every age. The cycle of people's rebellion, the inevitable judgment, and yet the patient guidance of God is the recurring pattern of Numbers. Many readers have said that it is our pattern too.

At Sinai: God Prepares Israel for the Journey through the Wilderness (Num. 1:1–10:10)

In the continuing narrative of their escape from Egypt, Exodus 19 reported the arrival of Israel at Mount Sinai. They have been at Sinai throughout the story in the rest of Exodus and the entire book of Leviticus. In the first nine chapters of Numbers, they are still at Sinai, but now the time has come for them to prepare to march to the Promised Land.

Their first act of preparation is to take a census and organize the people for an orderly journey. Immediately, the historians note a problem. The census figures total 603,550 men (Num. 2:32). Add women, children, and Gentiles who accompanied them, and Numbers seems to be saying that there were well over two million people wandering in the wilderness. Numbers does describe miraculous provision of water but never enough to take care of that many people in such a dry country. Indeed, a close reading of scripture reveals that elsewhere Israelites seem to have remembered their ancestors as totaling only forty thousand (Judg. 5:8). The tribe of Dan had only six hundred men (Judg. 18:11). Here are two of the explanations that have been proposed. First, some suggest that the word translated "thousands" really refers to much smaller military units, making the total approximately fifty-five hundred men. Second, others propose that the figures in Numbers are really from a later census, perhaps the one David took some three centuries later. Reading the figures back into the exodus was a Hebrew way of saying, "Through our ancestors, we ourselves were really all there too."

The elaborate directions for the order of march carefully stipulate the important thing: God's tabernacle, the tent of meeting, must always be at the center of their camp (Num. 2:17).

Priestly editors of the story have made sure that the prominence of priests and Levites—and hence of the worship of the Lord—is made abundantly clear. Not only moral but ceremonial laws are given (5—6), offerings are presented (7), and the Levites are consecrated to lead worship.

At last (9:1–10:10), a year after the first Passover and eleven months after they had arrived at Sinai, they celebrate their second Passover, ready to march to the Promised Land.

In the Wilderness:
Israel Rebels, God Punishes; but God
Still Leads the People (Num. 10:11–25:16)

Led by a God-given cloud (9:15–26) and the ark of the covenant (10:33) and fed by manna from heaven (11:7), the Israelites begin their journey. Yet in spite of the faithfulness of God, the story soon describes a repeated cycle of complaint, even rebellion, against God and Moses, with catastrophic consequences.

The Israelites complain about having only manna to eat, and God gives them quails. The meat, however, seems only to bring them disease (11:1–35). Aaron and Miriam complain about Moses' wife, and Miriam is afflicted briefly with leprosy (12:1–12). Of longer-lasting significance, the people lose faith in the promises of God and are afraid to enter the Promised Land. Thus they are condemned to forty years of wandering in the wilderness, and they survive only through the intercession of Moses (13—14). Though the laws about the worship they conduct are given by God (15), Moses and Aaron face a rebellion, led by a man named Korah. Again, only intercession by Moses and Aaron enables any of the rebellious people to survive (16). God now miraculously demonstrates Aaron's rightful place (17), and additional laws are given for the ceremonies he and others are to lead (18—19).

At last, even Moses loses his patient dependence on God (20:1–13). Apparently, the sinful act that Moses performed was that instead of simply commanding a rock to bring forth water, he struck it with his staff, as if he rather than God were doing the miracle. The act may seem trivial, but the basic sin is clear. God says, "You did not trust in me" (20:12).

Nearly forty years go by. At last, Israel is ready to move again. Most of this time they have been at Kadesh-Barnea, an oasis south of the Promised Land. Miriam (20:1) and Aaron (20:28) have died. Though they had failed before, Israel's warriors now succeed in approaching and battling the Canaanites from the south (21:1–3). Even so, there is another rebellion (21:4–9). But Israel is now a military force to be feared.

Three chapters (22—24) are devoted to the delightful story of Israel's invasion of Moab. Frightened by the oncoming horde of Israelites, the king of Moab employs a famous pagan seer, Balaam, to put a curse on these invaders from the desert. God, however, commands Balaam not to curse but to bless Israel. The frustrated king and the pagan prophet try and try again, but each time the words that come forth are a blessing. Israelite mothers must have laughed as they told and retold this story to their children. Even Balaam's donkey sees better than the ancient seer (22:23–25)! Incidentally, an inscription of a vision ascribed to the legendary Balaam, dating from about 700 B.C., has been unearthed in Jordan. It includes curses: "You shall be on your eternal bed of rest [the grave]. . . . Death shall take away the child who is in the womb." Evidently Balaam could curse others but not the Israelites. But though the Lord turned Balaam's curses to blessings, some Israelites turned to the worship of the baals, the pagan gods through whose lands they were now traveling (Num. 25).

The prophecies attributed to the ancient seer are important to Christians for a special reason. They include the Bible's first promise of a coming great king.

> I see him, but not now;
> I behold him, but not near—
> a star shall come out of Jacob,
> and a scepter shall rise out of Israel. (24:17)

The king is to conquer Moab and all Israel's enemies. The prediction was fulfilled in the days of David, and it may well be that David's conquests influenced the retelling of this story. But long after the death of David and even after there were no more kings at all in Israel, Israelites still recited this prophecy of a coming king, the messiah. The New Testament begins with other Eastern seers coming to Bethlehem. These Wise Men have seen a star, we are told, and they see in it a sign that the promised king has come at last (Matt. 2:1–12).

Approaching Canaan:
A New Generation Prepares to
Seize the New Land (Num. 26—36)

Poised now to invade Canaan, where they will distribute land to the different tribes, Israelites take a new census of their new generation (Numbers 26). The coming allotment of land brings up the question of the rights of women, and through Moses, God decrees that women without husbands shall have property rights in the Promised Land (27:1–11). (Here again, one notes that in Israel women have a higher place than in many societies around them.) The laws about the three annual festivals are reviewed: Passover, Pentecost, and Booths (28—29). Another set of laws asserts the priority of the marriage relationship even over vows to God taken prior to the marriage (30).

Numbers tells us that Israel, now grown powerful, with God's help wins military victories over all enemies who would block their path. Earlier they were forced to circle around Edom when threatened by that nation's large army (20:14–21). Now, however, Israel is able to annihilate the Midianites (31). At this point archaeology helps us to understand the purpose of the stories of such conquests. Archaeologists tell us that apparently Edom and Moab did not even exist, at least as powerful nations, in the thirteenth century B.C., the time of the exodus. The Bible itself subsequently makes clear that Midian was by no means completely destroyed (Judg. 6:1–2). Perhaps we should think of the Midianites and the others whom Moses' forces defeated as being still nomadic tribes, like Israel, as indeed they appear to have been in earlier times (Gen. 37:28). Most scholars suggest, indeed, that we read stories such as that in Numbers not primarily as careful records of ancient history but as expressions of the faith of inspired authors at the time when the stories were written. In David's day it was God, the writers were sure, who had given God's people victory over all the enemies that surrounded them. Even in the days of the decline and fall of Israel's empire, these stories voiced Israel's faith that God could still deliver them if they remained faithful.

In a larger sense, Numbers seems to be very accurate "history" indeed. In the form of a collection of stories about its days in the wilderness, Israel described its repeated history through the centuries. The pattern described there was not just of that little part of God's people in the thirteenth century; it was their history right down to their own time. It is a history of God's grace; of human complaint, lack of faith, and rebellion; and of subsequent disaster. But it is also a story of the Lord's continuing patient perseverance with God's people. In the same way, Christians have seen Numbers as describing the repeated history of the church.

The final editors (or "redactors") of Numbers wove together the ancient documents that the scholars call J, E, D, and P.[26] From time to time, these documents have "footnoted" to even earlier records, such as traditional ballads (Num. 21:27) and the now-lost "Book of the Wars of the Lord" (21:14). But even though these materials are interspersed with collections of laws, the editors have given us one connected narrative, from creation to the climactic moment. They pause to retrace for us the path of Israel's journey through the wilderness (33). Now their story ends with Israel at the very border of the Promised Land.

As the people prepare to invade, the writers tell us, Moses voices God's final instructions. God's people are to drive out the Canaanites but, especially, to destroy every trace of Canaan's idolatrous religion (33:50–56). The Israelites are to divide the land equitably (34). They are to provide for the Levites who help to lead their worship (35:1–5). They are to establish a criminal justice system, with cities of refuge to provide temporary shelter for those who may be unjustly accused (35:9–34). A close reading of the laws of Exodus, Leviticus, and Numbers shows that many laws really do seem to relate to times and situations much later than the wilderness wanderings. But if Moses was not the human author of all of these laws, he came to be regarded as, under God, their human authority. All God's law could be thought of as the law of Moses.

The J–E–P narrative now has led us to the edge of the Promised Land, but our canon of scripture does not quite yet permit us to enter. Our storytellers keep us in suspense. The story of the exodus, the law, and the wilderness wandering is told for us one more time. To that fifth and last "Book of Moses" we now turn, the book of Deuteronomy.

DEUTERONOMY

Leviticus and Numbers are often neglected, even sometimes thought of as irrelevant; not so Deuteronomy. Patrick D. Miller calls it "the center of Old Testament theology."[27] Few books of the Old Testament are more quoted in the New Testament. Jesus is said to have quoted Deuteronomy repeatedly as he resisted temptation (Matt. 4:4–10). Rabbis through the centuries and Jesus himself have revered Deut. 6:5 as the most important of all the 613 laws of the Jewish scriptures (Luke 10:27). And much of the book is a kind of exposition of what that great law means. Deuteronomy merits careful study.

The Setting of the Book

The background of Deuteronomy is doubly dramatic.

For one thing, it tells us that its words come from a critical moment in Israel's history. The forty years of wandering in the wilderness are over. Now God's people have come to the very edge of the Promised Land. Though Moses himself cannot enter Canaan, he gives three addresses, designed not so much for that moment alone as for the continued guidance of the nation soon to be born. The book ends, still on that border, with a brief account of the very last preparations, the very last days of Moses, and finally, the death of Israel's greatest leader, looking across toward the Promised Land. Now, guided by the principles set forth in Deuteronomy, Israel is ready to begin its new life as the people of God.

But the scholars double the dramatic impact of Deuteronomy by proposing that this edition of the law was actually drawn up in an equally critical time. It was a time of heroic martyrdom, political chaos, bloody revolution, and a last, desperate chance for Judah. For fifty-five years the evil king Manasseh had ruled in Jerusalem. A lackey of Assyria, he had erected pagan shrines even in the temple itself. He burned his own son as a sacrifice. When worshipers of the Lord protested, the cruel dictator "shed very much innocent blood, until he had filled Jerusalem from one end to another" (2 Kings 21:16). Apparently, what copies of the law already existed had to be hidden, and the party of the prophets and their followers had to go underground. At last Assyria began to weaken and the old king died, and his son lasted on the throne for only two years. A popular uprising brought his assassination, and in the end the political turmoil was calmed by a coup, which set on the throne Manasseh's eight-year-old grandson, Josiah. The

DEUTERONOMY
At the Edge of Canaan, Moses Reviews Their Redemption and Challenges Israel

"You shall love the Lord your God with all your heart" (6:5).

1 **Moses' First Address: History and Challenge**	5 **Moses' Second Address: What the Covenant Requires**		29 **Moses' Third Address: Challenge for the Future**	31 **The Last Days of Moses** 34
	The Heart of the Law, 5—13	**Miscellaneous Laws, 14—28**		
A review of God's care of Israel and their frequent rebellion, 1—3	The Ten Commandments repeated, 5	These include such diverse concerns as	God's grace in the past, 29:1—9	Moses writes the law and commissions Joshua to succeed him, 31
Therefore, the challenge: remember to keep the covenant, 4	The Shema, 6	help for the needy, 15	The covenant for future generations, 29:10—29	He sings of God's deliverance of Israel, 32
	Remember this covenant, 7—9	three annual feasts, 16	Warnings and promises, 30:1—14	He blesses each tribe, 33
	Two basic requirements of the covenant: love God, and care for the needy, 10—11	and laws about kings, sexual relationships, criminal justice, honesty, etc., 17—26	The challenge: love God; obey God's laws, 30:15—20	Then Moses dies, looking across to the Promised Land, 34
	Worship *one* God in *one* place, 12—13	Blessings for those who keep the covenant and curses for those who do not, 27—28		

Author: Traditionally Moses, but more likely it is the work of prophets and scribes in the seventh century B.C.

Theme: In spite of Israel's unfaithfulness, God has delivered them and brought them to the Promised Land; therefore, in that land they are to keep the covenant and obey the law.

Most Important Passage: The Shema (6:4–9) is basic to Judaism, and Jesus called it the greatest commandment.

party of the prophets gradually gained control; the Temple was purified and repaired; and in that Temple was found "the book of the law" (2 Kings 22:8). Advised by the high priest Hilkiah, the prophetess Huldah, and others loyal to the Lord, young King Josiah undertook to make that book the law of the land. For centuries, scholars have identified that book as at least part of our book of Deuteronomy.

It seems quite likely, therefore, that Deuteronomy was an edition of the law prepared in secret by plotters waiting for the moment when the law of God could again be taught to God's people.[28] Perhaps it would be going too far to say that it was drafted to be a written constitution by which the revolutionary party hoped to establish a constitutional monarchy.[29] But in sharp contrast to the practices of Manasseh, Deuteronomy set strict limits on the king, centralized all sacrifice on worship of the Lord in Jerusalem, and over and over called for that social justice which prophets such as Amos and Micah and Isaiah had proclaimed as the essence of the will of God.

Moses' First Address: History and Challenge (Deut. 1—4)

A brief introduction sets the stage. Moses is speaking to Israel at the edge of the Promised Land. "See, I have set the land before you; go in and take possession of the land," God challenges the Israelites through Moses (1:8).

Moses' lecture is a review of Israel's history in the wilderness. That history, as in the other books of the law, is one of repeated faithlessness. Their parents had "rebelled" (1:26), "grumbled" (1:27), failed to take the land of Canaan when they had a chance because they had "no trust in the Lord" (1:32), and "rebelled" again (1:43). That faithless generation has died in the wilderness.

Moses now recounts, however, how God has led the new generation to the border of Canaan. The Lord has given Israel victories over King Sihon the Amorite (2:24) and King Og of Bashan (3:3). Already some parts of the Promised Land on the east bank have been occupied.

The real point of the address, however, lies in Moses' exhortation in the fourth chapter. It is not military might that will establish Israel in the land. Rather, Moses says, "Give heed to the statutes and ordinances that I am teaching you" (4:1). "Take care and watch yourselves closely" (4:9, 15), "so that you do not act corruptly by making an idol for yourselves" (4:16). "Be careful not to forget the covenant" (4:23). The narrator makes no secret of the fact that he is writing from a later time and place (3:11; 4:44–46). When he writes, the battle to take the land is long over. But the issue is still the same. "If you act corruptly . . . you will soon utterly perish" (4:25–26). But remembering how God "loved your ancestors" (4:37), if they will "keep his statutes," Moses promises succeeding generations that they will "remain in the land the Lord your God is giving you for all time" (4:40).

Moses' Second Address: What the
Covenant Requires (Deut. 5—28)

What makes Deuteronomy "the center of Old Testament theology," however, is Moses' second address. Especially in the first half of that sermon (or teaching), Deuteronomy 5—13, we find the very heart of the religion of Israel.

"Hear, O Israel," Moses begins (5:1). The writer wants to make quite sure his readers will understand that what follows is not simply for a past time and place. "Not with our ancestors did the Lord make this covenant, but with us, who are all of us here alive today" (5:3). The covenant is for every generation.

God has liberated Israel and brought them to the Promised Land. "I am the Lord your God, who brought you out of the land of Egypt, out of the house of slavery" (5:6). Therefore the Israelites are to keep God's law. Now there follow, in a new edition, the basic laws of the Lord, the Ten Commandments (5:7–21).

The Ten Commandments in Deuteronomy are almost word for word the same as those in Exodus 20. But there is one significant difference: the fourth commandment is explained in quite a different way. The liberating God who freed them from slavery now commands them to liberate themselves; their families; their slaves, both Hebrew and alien; and even their livestock, at least for one day each week (5:12–15). "Remember that you were a slave in the land of Egypt" (5:15). Miller says that "the second most important word" in Deuteronomy (after the command to "love" the Lord) is "sabbath."[30] The word itself is not frequently repeated in this book. But each week the Sabbath is to remind Israel of what Deuteronomy does command over and over: the people of Israel are to treat others as those who have themselves experienced oppression and know its horror (10:19; 15:15; 24:18).

Jews call what follows the "Shema," from the Hebrew word for "hear." Through the centuries, down to our own day, Jews have revered these words so carefully that they have fulfilled literally the command to "bind them as a sign on your hand, fix them as an emblem on your forehead, and write them on the doorposts of your house" (6:9).

> Hear, O Israel: The Lord is our God, the Lord alone. You shall love the Lord your God with all your heart, and with all your soul, and with all your might. (6:4–5)

Jesus said that this is the greatest commandment.

Deuteronomy was written to ensure that Israel would never forget this command. "Just remember" (7:18), "do not forget" (8:11), "remember today" (11:2), "be careful to obey all these words" (12:28)—so, over and over, runs the appeal of this book. Israel is to "recite them to your children" (6:7). "When your children ask you in time to come," the Israelites are to tell the story of how the great God who loves them liberated them and how they are to love that God in return (6:20–25).

No other book of the Old Testament so emphasizes the command to love God. "It was because the Lord loved you" that God rescued the people of Israel. Therefore they are to love God (7:8–9). "He will love you" (7:13). "You shall love the Lord your God, therefore" (11:1). "Heed his every commandment . . . loving the Lord" (11:13). And Deuteronomy makes clear what it means to love God:

> What does the Lord your God require of you? Only to fear the Lord your God, to walk in all his ways, to love him, to serve the Lord your God with all your heart and with all your soul, and to keep the commandments of the Lord your God. (10:12–13)

With such words Deuteronomy echoes the cry of prophets such as Micah 6:8. To love the Lord is to mirror the love of God. God had liberated them. Now Israel is to liberate the oppressed. "For the Lord your God . . . executes justice for the orphan and the widow, and . . . loves the strangers, providing them food and clothing. You shall also love the stranger, for you were strangers in the land of Egypt" (Deut. 10:17–19). "Do not be hard-hearted or tight-fisted toward your needy neighbor. You should rather open your hand" (15:7–8). "Justice, and only justice, you shall pursue" (16:20). Every seven years all debts are to be forgiven and all Hebrew slaves freed (15). The social justice for which the prophets pleaded is in Deuteronomy proclaimed as law.

No proud and unjust monarch will do (17:14–20), says Deuteronomy, almost painting a portrait of Solomon and some of his successors. And as for the horror of human sacrifice as practiced by Manasseh, it is strictly forbidden (18:10).

To love the Lord is not only to mirror God's justice; it is to be faithful to the one true God. Guidance is given for proper worship. Annual feasts will remind Israel of its obligations (16). Levites and prophets will give guidance (18). If apostates propose the worship of any other god, "you shall surely kill them" (13:9). To protect the purity of worship, all sacrifices are to be offered only in the central shrine (the Temple at Jerusalem) (12). This law is found only in Deuteronomy. That King Josiah attempted to enforce it is the chief reason for believing that Deuteronomy contains the book of the law found in his reign (2 Kings 23:6–20).

Thus Deuteronomy echoes not only the prophets' concern for social justice but also their predictions about Israel's future. The future depends on Israel's single-hearted devotion to the Lord:

> See, I am setting before you today a blessing and a curse: the blessing, if you obey the commandments of the Lord your God . . . and the curse, if you do not obey . . . but turn from the way . . . to follow other gods. (11:26–28)

Moses' Third Address: Challenge for the Future (Deut. 29—30)

It is the choice for the future that is the theme of Moses' third and briefest address. Its concept of the covenant is summarized in its closing words:

> See, I have set before you today life and prosperity, death and adversity. If you obey the commandments . . . by loving the Lord your God, walking in his ways . . . then you shall live . . . and the Lord your God will bless you in the land that you are entering to possess. But if your heart turns away and you do not hear, but are led astray to bow down to other gods and serve them, I declare to you today that you shall perish. . . . Choose life. (30:15–19)

The Last Days of Moses (Deut. 31—34)

The last four chapters of Deuteronomy form a kind of appendix to the book. There are laws in Deuteronomy that reflect a time later than that of Moses, and Josh. 24:26 says clearly that the law grew as new situations arose. The editors of Deuteronomy insist, however, that the written covenant ultimately goes back to words written by Moses himself (31:9, 24). That is, the words of this book are to be the formal, authoritative, written law of Israel.

Joshua is appointed to succeed Moses (31:7–15). Moses sings a psalm of praise (32). He recites blessings on the various tribes (33). Finally, he dies on Mount Nebo, gazing across at the Promised Land into which he was not allowed to enter.

We have proposed that this edition of the law was the work of prophets and other wise leaders in a day when the warnings of Moses were being fulfilled. These editors knew and echoed the work of such prophets as Amos, Isaiah, and Micah. They were prophets themselves. But they end the book with a fitting epitaph: "Never since has there arisen a prophet in Israel like Moses" (34:10)!

2

THE FORMER PROPHETS

When it comes to naming these books, the Jews are wiser than the Christians. The books of Joshua through 2 Kings are called "the Historical Books" by many Christians, and so they are. A case can be made that it was the Jews who invented history writing, long before the first Greek historians. These books form a remarkable record of the history of Israel.

With deeper insight, however, Jews have traditionally called these books "the Former Prophets." They are different, of course, from "the Latter Prophets" (Isaiah through Malachi). "The Latter Prophets" are oracles, sermons, poems, predictions, warnings, and promises. The books to which we now turn are stories. But these stories are written to make much the same points as those the prophets were making. They recall the past in order to point to the future. They recall how, over and over, Israel suffered when it strayed from God and how God redeemed the people when they turned back to God. By presenting that pattern, these stories challenge their readers to faithfulness in the days ahead.

All written history, however much the writer intends to make it "objective," is *interpreted* history. Interpretation is most clearly evident in the case of biblical history. Here and there the modern historian may indeed question the historical accuracy of the Bible's report of a particular event. But it is the faith of Jews and Christians that the message of "the Former Prophets," as a presentation of how God has worked and continues to work in the affairs of humankind, is profoundly true.

JOSHUA

Grossly exaggerating his king's victory, like many government propaganda agencies since, the court poet of Pharaoh Merenptah sang:

JOSHUA
God Gives the Tribes of Israel the Promised Land

"So Joshua took the whole land, according to all that the Lord had spoken" (11:23).

1	6	13	23
Israel Prepares and Then Enters the Promised Land	**With God's Help, They Conquer Canaan**	**The Land Is Allotted to the Different Tribes**	**Joshua Calls Israel to Faithfulness in Their New Home**
God encourages Israel's new leader, Joshua, 1	They conquer Jericho, 6	Land east of Jordan, 13	He preaches a farewell sermon, 23 and leads Israel in renewing the covenant, 24
Spies survey Jericho, 2	They conquer the cities of central and southern Canaan, 7—10	The reward of the faithful, 14	
Israel enters the Promised Land, 3—5	They conquer the north, 11	Judah's inheritance, 15	
	A summary of their conquests, 12	Ephraim and Manasseh, 16—17	
		Seven tribes assigned territory by lot, 18—19	
		Cities of refuge, 20	
		Provision for the Levites, 21	
		Civil war started, 22	

(end at chapter **24**)

Authors: Later historians, influenced by the kind of philosophy of history expressed in Deuteronomy
Theme: God gave Israel the Promised Land and will bless them in it if they will be faithful and obedient.
Special Significance: To this day, Israelis regard their land as a gift of God, assigned forever to their nation.

Ascalon is carried captive, Gezer is conquered; Yano'am is made as though it did not exist. *The people Israel* is desolate, it has no offspring; *Palestine* [Khuru] has become a widow for Egypt. (Italics added.)[1]

Israel, of course, had not really been exterminated. But the inscription on Merenptah's stela (monument) clearly indicates that by about the year 1220 B.C. there was in the land of Palestine an identifiable group of people known as Israel. True, they are not called a nation, as are others in the inscription. Though it is debated, there is a hint that the poet thought of them as simply an ethnic group, confirming the biblical picture of Israel at this stage as only a loose collection of clans and tribes with no king or central government.[2] Merenptah's monument is our oldest record outside of the Bible of the existence of Israel.

How this "mixed multitude" began to take possession of what the Egyptians called "Khuru" and Israel believed to be "the Promised Land" is the subject of the book of Joshua.

The Conquest and History

The Israelite conquest of Canaan has been the subject of more scholarly research and more debate than almost any other event in Old Testament history. Here are some contrasting views that historians have proposed.

The book of Joshua itself depicts Israel as seizing the Promised Land in a brilliant military conquest led by Joshua. From its headquarters at Gilgal, the Israelite army is said to have overrun Canaan in three successive campaigns. First it seized the center (Joshua 6—9), then the south (10), and finally, the north (11). The writer summarizes this idealized account, "So Joshua took the whole land, according to all that the Lord had spoken to Moses; and Joshua gave it for an inheritance to Israel according to their tribal allotments" (11:23).

Fully recognizing that the actual history was more complex than the summary in Joshua, John Bright, building on the work of his teacher, the archaeologist William Foxwell Albright, maintains:

> Archeological evidence clearly shows that a major upheaval engulfed Palestine as the Late Bronze Age ended; numerous towns, a number of them said in the Bible to have been taken by Israel, were actually destroyed at this time. Many scholars (perhaps the majority?) have seen in this evidence that the Israelite conquest took place late in the thirteenth century B.C.[3]

For example, in the 1950s, Dr. Yigael Yadin, director of the Institute of Archaeology at the Hebrew University of Jerusalem, excavated Hazor. Joshua 11:10–13 tells how Joshua's army utterly destroyed this city, until "there was no one left who breathed, and he burned Hazor with fire." Yadin found that this once-great city had been razed to the ground in the late thirteenth century. Its idols were beheaded and its temples were deliberately defaced.

After its destruction, the area was occupied by squatters and tent dwellers, whom Yadin took to be the relatively primitive Israelite invaders.[4]

By contrast, Dame Kathleen Kenyon has argued that Canaan was the target of numerous raids and invasions over several centuries. Most devastating to the traditional view, her excavations at Jericho apparently proved that that city, whose conquest is so graphically described in Joshua 6, was destroyed several times but was not in existence at all in the late thirteenth century. And Ai (Joshua 7) had been a ruin for centuries before Joshua can be placed in Canaan.[5] Similarly, there are the letters of a desperate governor in Jerusalem, writing to pharaoh for help:

> The Habiru plunder all lands of the king,
> If archers are here
> this year, then the lands of the king,
> the lord, will remain; but if archers are not here,
> then the lands of the king, my lord, are lost.[6]

When those Tell El-Amarna letters were first discovered, some thought they must refer to Joshua's invasion. But it is now agreed that these tablets come from battles at least a century earlier than one can place Moses and Joshua.

As a matter of fact, a close reading of the Bible suggests that the book of Joshua's picture of a sudden and complete conquest is not the whole story. We are told of one Israelite raid into Canaan a generation prior to Joshua's (Num. 14:39–45). And the first chapter of Judges repeatedly tells us that Israel's invasion was neither complete nor unified, with the different tribes and clans occupying different areas as they were able.

Martin Noth and other scholars have proposed that there never was an invasion of Canaan by Joshua and a united Israelite army. We should think rather of a gradual infiltration by the group that had followed Moses. Indeed, most of what subsequently became Israel need not be thought of as descended from former Egyptian slaves. Genesis 25 tells us that there were many people regarded as legitimate descendants of Abraham who were not among those who went to Egypt in the days of Joseph. The covenant ceremony at Shechem included "all Israel, alien as well as citizen" (Josh. 8:33). Alliances with some people already living in Canaan are described (Josh. 2:1–14; 6:22–25; 9; Judg. 1:22–26). The covenant described in the last chapter of Joshua may be thought of as including Canaanite converts to the worship of the Lord.

Going further in this direction, George Mendenhall has proposed that the little group of slaves who escaped Egypt were soon joined in alliance by many Canaanites attracted to their religion. Guided by Marxist sociology, Mendenhall proposed that *Habiru* elements in various city-states threw off the yoke of their oppressive kings and joined the Israelites in their covenant religion, attracted by its emphasis on social justice.

There is probably some truth in all of these views.[7] The first chapter of Judges makes abundantly clear that Joshua did not conquer the whole land with a unified army. The Israelites were forced to settle down side by side with idolaters, which was to lead the Israelites into repeated apostasy (Judg. 2:1–3). In all likelihood they did find cousins in Canaan who joined them in the ceremonies of covenant with the Lord.

It is almost certainly true that thousands of people who subsequently claimed the heritage and covenant of Moses were not genetically descended from that little group of slaves who escaped from Egypt. But they allied themselves with the covenant people, attracted by the religion of this marvelous God. Thus they too became spiritual descendants of Abraham and of the followers of Moses. Few Americans are literally descendants of the pilgrims who landed at Plymouth Rock, but most Americans think of them as our pilgrim "fathers" and "mothers." So, it appears, it was with Israel.

Archaeology does make clear, however, that many Canaanite cities were violently destroyed, including several in the latter part of the thirteenth century. It seems reasonable to believe that some of these were conquered by the invading Israelites. Subsequent tradition knew that all such conquests could be described as the work of the Lord, using as God's instrument the great Hebrew hero Joshua.

The Conquest and Theology

In a sense, all of these historical accounts of the conquest are beside the point the biblical writers wanted to make. Israel received the land not by human conquest, not by human revolutions in city-states, and not by human alliances with cousins in Canaan. The land was a gift from God.

Military strategy, the book of Joshua tells us, had nothing to do with Israel's initial victory at Jericho. The army simply obeyed God and marched around the city, and its walls came tumbling down (Joshua 6). Failure of military strategy had nothing to do with their defeat at Ai (Joshua 7). Even though the story may have been poetry at first, it was subsequently said to be literally true that once the Lord even made the sun stand still to guarantee the Israelites' victory (10:12–14). At the great covenant ceremony at the end of the book, Joshua could picture God as listing all those who had opposed the invaders and then reminding them, "I handed them over to you. . . . I gave you [this] land" (24:11–13).

Centuries later, if you were to ask an Israelite, "What sign do you have that God loves you?" the first reply would be, "God gave us this land." Walter Brueggemann has shown that a whole theology of the Old Testament can be built around the concept of the land.[8] God had promised the land to the Israelites' ancestor Abraham for his descendants. In the days of Joshua, God had given it to them. Even if later they were temporarily exiled from it, God would bring them back to it. It was their "inheritance" forever.

The determination of Israelis today to hold that land is rooted in the theological conviction that it was God, the divine self, who gave them this inheritance. This theology also may help us understand the repeated word that God commanded extermination of Israel's enemies, even the women and children. This "holy" war was believed necessary if Israel was to have the Promised Land. And the land was necessary if Israel was to carry out its divine mission. Moreover, the writers of Joshua emphasize that there was to be no compromise with idolatrous religion. Pagan neighbors would bring temptations to paganism. Other passages in the Old Testament, as well as Jesus' Sermon on the Mount, make clear that a fuller understanding of God's will shows that God does not command genocide. But the writers of Joshua see the Promised Land, kept in all purity, as essential to the divine destiny of Israel to be the kingdom of God.

The Structure of Joshua

The story of the book of Joshua is framed by its first and last chapters. In the first chapter, Joshua, now the leader of Israel with the death of Moses, is instructed to cross the Jordan and to take the Promised Land. Indeed, the Lord assures Joshua that the victory is already won. "Every place that the sole of your foot will tread upon I have given to you" (1:3). Therefore Joshua is told—four times in the first chapter—to "be strong and courageous," for "the Lord . . . will give you this land" (1:13). There is, however, one repeated reminder. Joshua must be "careful to act in accordance with all the law that my servant Moses commanded you; do not turn from it to the right hand or to the left, so that you may be successful wherever you go. This book of the law [in the mind of the writers, probably Deuteronomy] shall not depart out of your mouth" (1:7–8).

The last chapter completes the story. It tells how Joshua gathers "all the tribes of Israel to Shechem" (24:1). There he reviews their whole history, from the time of the patriarchs' pagan ancestors through the call of Abraham and through Moses, on down to the present. The Lord "gave you a land on which you had not labored," Joshua reminds them (24:13). The gift promised in the first chapter of the book has now been given. The exhortation remains the same. "Choose this day whom you will serve," Joshua challenges Israel (24:15). In solemn ceremony, the people vow to keep their covenant with God. A monument is erected to commemorate that covenant, and "the book of the law of God," its expansion begun by Joshua, is established as their guide. What God promised Joshua at the beginning God has now achieved.

Framed at the beginning and the end by these two chapters, promise and fulfillment, the book tells us how the Lord enabled Israel to conquer its enemies and how the land, once it was won, was distributed equitably to the different tribes.

Israel Prepares and Then Enters
the Promised Land (Josh. 1—5)

The story of Joshua picks up precisely where Deuteronomy left off. Indeed, it is widely held that the final editors of Joshua were also the editors of Deuteronomy. History in the two books is written from the same perspective. The book does, however, contain very ancient traditions. It even "footnotes" to one of its sources, the now-lost Book of Jashar (Josh. 10:13).

From his camp on the east bank of the Jordan, Joshua sends spies across the river to the nearest town in Canaan, Jericho. Hidden in the place where the fewest questions might be asked of strangers, the home of the prostitute Rahab, they escape arrest and return to report that "the Lord has given all the land into our hands; moreover all the inhabitants of the land melt in fear before us" (2:24).

Mirroring Moses' miracle of the crossing of the sea on dry land, Joshua leads Israel across the Jordan River. The preparation they now make for combat, however, is not a military drill. Instead, we are told that they build an altar to the Lord, circumcise the men, and at Gilgal, celebrate their first Passover in the Promised Land.

With God's Help,
They Conquer Canaan (Josh. 6—12)

Obedient to God's command, they march around Jericho. God levels its fortress walls for them (6). But when one man hoards some of the booty from Jericho, the whole army fails in its next battle (7). Only when the miser has been stoned to death can Israel succeed in destroying Ai (8). Their bloody invasion now annihilates foe after foe in central and southern Canaan (9—10).

The narrative is interrupted to report a ceremony in the vicinity of Shechem in which the commands of Deuteronomy 27 are carefully carried out (Josh. 8:30–35). This story may be a duplicate account of the covenant ceremony described in the last chapter of Joshua. "Alien as well as citizen" are included, and Joshua 9 tells of an alliance made with one group of Canaanites, the people of Gibeon. Here, perhaps, are hints that the book of Judges is accurate in its picture of infiltration and only gradual conquest, rather than the sudden, complete victory the idealized story in Joshua would suggest.

Finally, Joshua turns south and brings that part of Canaan under control. "So Joshua took the whole land, according to all that the Lord had spoken to Moses; and Joshua gave it for an inheritance to Israel according to their tribal allotments. And the land had rest from war" (11:23). Thus, for the purposes of this book, the theologian-historian summarizes the story.

The Land Is Allotted to
the Different Tribes (Josh. 13—22)

Nine chapters are devoted to a detailed account of how the land is divided among the twelve tribes. Repeatedly, these allotments are called "inheritances." The designated lands are to stay forever as the property of the assigned tribes, clans, and families. Even if a property owner is forced to sell his land, it is supposed to go to a relative, and every fifty years all land is to revert back to the family that originally owned it (Leviticus 25). The land is a gift from God, to be held equitably in trust from the Lord.

Cities of refuge are designated (Joshua 20), fulfilling the command of Ex. 21:12–14. A person accused of murder could flee to these cities from the family of the alleged victim, which would have been bent on blood revenge, until guilt or innocence had been properly decided. One sees here an early effort to protect the rights of those who are accused of crimes. The tribe of Levi, designated for priestly duties, was not assigned to one section of Canaan. Instead, cities and adjacent grazing lands, scattered throughout the areas of the twelve tribes, were to be given to them, so that they might carry on their religious functions within reach of all Israel.

Again the editor summarizes, "Not one of all the good promises that the Lord had made to the house of Israel had failed; all came to pass" (21:45).

Finally, this section tells us that the command of Deuteronomy 12 was enforced (Joshua 22). The tribes of Reuben and Gad and the half-tribe of Manasseh had been allotted territory on the east side of the Jordan. There they built an altar. Only when they agreed not to offer sacrifices on it was civil war averted. The historian, following the pattern of Deuteronomy, wants it understood that worship is to be centralized in one sanctuary. Only thus, he believes, can it be kept pure.

Joshua Calls Israel to Faithfulness in
Their New Home (Josh. 23—24)

The book ends with two farewell addresses by Joshua. The first is a plea that Israel "be very steadfast to observe and do all that is written in the book of the law of Moses, turning aside from it neither to the right nor to the left" (23:6). The book began with that command to Joshua (1:7). Now Joshua gives it to all Israel.

The second address (24) is at a formal ceremony of covenant renewal in Shechem. The archaeologists have found at this ancient city the ruins of a large temple to "the Lord of the Covenant." Ancient tradition said that it was in this area that Abraham had first sojourned in the Promised Land (Gen. 12:6). Shechem was flanked by the mount of blessing and the mount of cursing (Deut. 27:11–13). It was an appropriate place for Joshua to issue his challenge.

It is widely held that the ceremony described in Joshua 24 may be given as a kind of model for what perhaps came to be an annual observance. The scattered tribes, living among idolaters and intermarrying with them, without any central government, were held together by only one thing: they all claimed a share in the covenant heritage.

The challenge Joshua issued was "Choose this day whom you will serve" (24:15). The book of Joshua was written to call Israel to remain faithful to the God they had chosen there, the Lord who had first chosen them.

JUDGES

Viewed from one perspective, Judges is not edifying reading. It tells quite frankly stories of mass murder, seduction, idolatry, civil war, deceit, and rape. It describes two hundred years of near anarchy. When the book repeatedly reminds us that "in those days there was no king in Israel; all the people did what was right in their own eyes" (21:25), it does not mean that all freely chose to obey the laws of God. It means that this was a time without law and order, and the consequences were often catastrophic.

Yet those who collected and edited the stories of this period, guided by the ideas expressed in Deuteronomy, could see theological meaning in the traditions of even such diverse characters as Deborah, Jephthah, and Samson. It was to illustrate that message of the consequences of faithfulness and unfaithfulness that they preserved the tales of these ancient heroes—and at least one notable heroine.

The Situation in the Period
of the Judges

In the period from approximately 1220 to 1020 B.C., there was indeed "no king in Israel." For centuries, Palestine had been under Egyptian domination. But in spite of Pharaoh Merenptah's boast of victory in 1220, the Egyptian Empire was declining, never fully to recover. The invading Israelites found themselves in a land of small city-states, each independent of the other.

Later historians could summarize a process of generations with a simple statement: "So Joshua took the whole land . . . and Joshua gave it for an inheritance to Israel. . . . And the land had rest from war" (Josh. 11:23). But Judges gives us detailed reports of the actual situation at the time of Joshua's death. Over and over we are told about the different tribes: that "the Benjaminites did not drive out the Jebusites" (1:21); "Manasseh did not drive out the inhabitants of Beth-shean" (1:27); "Ephraim did not drive out the Canaanites who lived in Gezer" (1:29); "Zebulun did not drive out the inhabitants of Kitron" (1:30); and so on. Instead, the "Canaanites lived among them" (1:29). True, as Joshua tells us, the invading Israelites did conquer and destroy some Canaanite cities. Others, kinspeople already in the land or

JUDGES
Stories of Spirit-filled Deliverers in a Cycle of Apostasy and Renewal

"The Israelites did what was evil in the sight of the Lord. . . . But when the Israelites cried out to the Lord, the Lord raised up a deliverer for the Israelites" (3:7–9). "In those days there was no king in Israel" (21:25).

1	3	17
Introduction	**Stories of the Judges**	**Stories of Chaotic Times**
The incompleteness of the conquest, 1	When the oppressed tribes turn to the Lord, God raises up a Spirit-filled deliverer:	The Danites set up an idolatrous shrine in the north, 17—18
The cyclic pattern of Israel's history:	Othniel against Mesopotamia, 3:7–11	The tribe of Benjamin is almost exterminated in genocidal civil war, 19—21
sin,	Ehud against Moab, 3:12–30	
oppression,	Shamgar against the Philistines, 3:31	
repentance,	Deborah against the Canaanites, 4—5	
devine deliverance,	Gideon against Midian, 6—8	
and sin again, 2	(Abimelech unsuccessfully tries to become king), 9	
	A series of judges, 10	
	Jephthah against the Ammonites, 11—12	
	Samson against the Philistines, 13—16	

Author: "The Deuteronomist," that is, a historian—or probably a group of historians—who collected and edited those stories, using the philosophy of history described in Deuteronomy

Purpose: To show how the pattern of history foretold in Deuteronomy worked out in chaotic times

Canaanites attracted by the "new" God, Yahweh (the Lord), entered into covenant with these former slaves from Egypt and with their God, as Joshua 8 and 24 suggest. But the first chapter of Judges makes very clear that Israel now found itself a weak and divided group among idolatrous and often more powerful neighbors.[9]

Those neighbors were pagans. As the memory of Moses and Joshua faded, "another generation grew up after them, who did not know the Lord" (2:10). Time after time, we are told, "the Israelites did what was evil in the sight of the Lord and worshiped the Baals [the gods of their Canaanite neighbors]" (2:11).[10] Some modern readers have wondered how it could be that, after all the Lord had done for them, Israel could so quickly and so often turn to other gods. Here are some of the reasons:

1. The Israelites were surrounded by neighbors who worshiped baals. Modern church-growth experts tell us that most Americans looking for a church select a congregation where their friends and neighbors go, and sociologists tell us that the religion and ethics of most people are likely to be similar to the beliefs of others of their race and class. For Israel as for us, conformity proved a powerful force in determining religious values.

2. Israel's pagan neighbors were far more wealthy and sophisticated than these former slaves. Archaeology reveals that Canaanites lived in finer houses. Even serfs of Canaanite city lords owned imported artworks.[11] Moreover, the economy of Canaan was based on agriculture. In the wilderness and in slavery in Egypt, Israel had not been a nation of farmers. Now the Israelites were to raise crops, and Baal was the god of agriculture and fertility. Thus Baal was the god of economic security.

3. Baalism did not have the same kind of moral restrictions that were so essential to Mosaic religion. If a farmer wanted good crops, he might go to the neighborhood shrine. There he could have sexual intercourse with a priestess-prostitute. Canaanite religion promised that as he did so, Baal would mate in heaven with his divine consort and the farmer's crops would also germinate. Baal had no Ten Commandments.

A religion of conformity, wealth, and a certain degree of moral license has appeared in many forms and many ages, and it has always had an appeal. So it was that repeatedly Israel turned to one or another of the Canaanite baals.

The Cyclic Pattern in the Book of Judges

The book of Judges is part of a continued history of Israel, which spans the time from Joshua—or even Deuteronomy—through 2 Kings and into the time of the exile, some six centuries after the events it describes. Looking back on this history, its inspired editors could see in the ancient stories a pattern. Time and again, Israel turned from the Lord to other gods, fell under the control of some oppressor, repented and turned back to God, and was then delivered by a Spirit-inspired leader. The second chapter of Judges is a sermon based on that interpretation of history. The stories which follow that sermon (3—16) are given as illustrations of that pattern.

The first such story (Judg. 3:7–11) is typical of them all:

Israel sins and turns from the Lord to baals and their consorts.
The Lord then delivers Israel to an oppressor, in this case, the otherwise
    unknown Cushan-rishathaim from somewhere in Mesopotamia.
Now the Israelites cry to the Lord for help.
The Lord raises up for them a deliverer, in this case, Othniel.
The Spirit of the Lord comes upon him, and he "judges" Israel and, with
    the Lord's help, defeats the oppressor.
Israel now has a period of peace.

But soon Israel strays once again, and the cycle repeats.

Stories of the Judges (Judg. 3—16)

The title "judge" suggests to us a robed figure, sitting gravely on a raised seat in a courtroom, perhaps even wearing a wig, like judges in Great Britain. This is not what the "judges" in this book were. Deborah, we are told, held court, such as it was, sitting under a palm tree (4:4–5). The judges did decide disputes, and perhaps that was the main work done by those whom the book names but about whom it tells no stories. Instead, the tales that have fired the imaginations of centuries of readers and, in the case of Samson, Hollywood producers are about military leaders. Through them, God "delivered" Israel. Not all of them are entirely admirable characters. A bastard hated by his own kin, Jephthah kills his own daughter as a human sacrifice. Samson is a kind of playboy, unable to resist seductive women. But of most judges we are told that, in spite of their defects, "the spirit of the Lord" came upon them. Through these very human agents, God delivered the chosen people.

Othniel's victory we have outlined. *Ehud* is praised for his trickery and assassination, graphically described, of Eglon of Moab (3:12–30). *Shamgar* is remembered for his mass slaughter of Philistines with a primitive weapon (3:31)

Deborah merits two whole chapters (4—5). The second is a poem, which many scholars suggest may go back to the time of Deborah herself. Vividly, it sings of the victory, then taunts the mother of the slain general, who is waiting nervously for his return (5:28–30). In fact, two women are the heroines of the story. Deborah defeated the enemy's army, and another woman, Jael, finished off the Canaanite general, inviting him into her tent, pretending friendship, and then driving a tent peg through his head. How startling it was for women to have so important a place is indicated by Deborah herself (4:9). But we have already noted that in Israel, women seem from the beginning to have had respect denied them in many other ancient cultures.

Gideon's story, however, is told in even more detail and hints at a special theological and political concern. A. Graeme Auld translates Gideon's name as "Hacker."[12] Gideon hacks down a (probably) phallic symbol of Baal (6:25–27) and becomes remarkably successful at hacking down Midianites, in spite of their new military technique, the use of camel cavalry (6:5; 7:12). But the story makes abundantly clear that the victory is not Gideon's but God's. The Lord instructs Gideon to cut his army of twenty-two thousand down to a mere three hundred, just to make clear when the victory is won that no human can say, "My own hand has delivered me" (7:2). Again, the story is told in a way to delight subsequent generations of readers.

Of great significance, however, is what follows Gideon's victories. Tired of anarchy and foreign oppressors, the men of Israel attempt to make Gideon king. He flatly refuses. "I will not rule over you, and my son will not rule over you; the Lord will rule over you," Gideon replies (8:23). At Sinai, God had told Israel, "You shall be for me a priestly kingdom and a holy nation" (Ex. 19:6). No human was to be Israel's king. Israel was called to be the kingdom of God. John Bright has shown how the whole of the biblical story, Old Testament and New, in a sense can be summarized around this theme.[13]

Abimelech, Gideon's son, had no such scruples. He murdered his seventy brothers, presumably lest they attempt the same kind of coup, and attempted to set himself up as an all-too-human king. The ballad-parable of one surviving brother, Jotham, ridicules the whole idea of an earthly monarchy, comparing it to the worthless bramble attempting to rule useful fruit trees (Judg. 9:7–15). Sure enough, Abimelech's abortive monarchy is only local and is short-lived. Only God is to be Israel's king.

Jephthah's rather unsavory career is climaxed by his killing his own daughter in fulfillment of a rash vow. Later readers properly react in horror. But the story does embody the conviction that one should not take the name of the Lord in vain. Jephthah fulfilled his vow no matter what the cost, and it seems implied that even his daughter understood the kind of religious devotion that motivated this violent worshiper of the Lord (11:29–40).

Samson, however, is the judge whose tragic story has most delighted readers down through history. Tales of his strength rival those later told of Hercules. But his weakness for women such as Delilah finally proved his undoing. The stories that cluster around this legendary figure were told not only to delight the reader and to exalt the power of the Spirit of the Lord, which gave Samson strength (14:6; 15:14); they remind the reader how important the vow of a Nazirite could be (13:5). When Samson breaks that vow, letting his hair be cut, he loses his strength.

In the overall narrative of Israel's history, the story of Samson performs another important function: it introduces the Philistine menace. Egyptian carvings show invading "sea peoples," armored and wearing feathered headdresses. Some were of the same people, perhaps, as those who participated in the Trojan War, of which Homer later sang. They helped drive Egypt out of Palestine. Among those sea peoples were the Philistines, from which the name Palestine is derived. They occupied the coast, preventing Israel from gaining control of parts of it for centuries. Gradually they expanded their domination eastward, threatening the more primitive Israelites. Apparently, in Samson's youth it was still possible at times to maintain friendly relationships with Philistine neighbors. But by the end of the eleventh century, they had become the greatest threat Israel faced.

Stories of
Chaotic Times (Judg. 17—21)

Rape, murder, genocide, kidnapping, civil war—these are the themes of the last five chapters of Judges. Yet even these stories have a place in the overall history of what was intended to be "the kingdom of God."

The first story (17—18) begins with theft. A man of the tribe of Ephraim confesses to his mother that he has stolen eleven hundred pieces of silver from her. When he returns the money, she makes an idol and other religious objects with it and builds a shrine, and they even succeed in persuading a Levite of Bethlehem, who has left his hometown, to become their chaplain. Now, surely, these semi-pagans think, the Lord will *have* to give them prosperity. Instead, a band of wandering men from the tribe of Dan, unable to conquer their assigned territory in the south (19:40–48), pass through the town. They steal the idol and persuade the Levite to join them. These thieves now butcher a defenseless Canaanite city in the north, rename it Dan, and set up their idol and their priest in it.

Centuries later, the kingdom of Israel split in two. The northern tribes left behind the dynasty of David, born in Bethlehem. More importantly, they set up a shrine at Dan with an image, a golden calf. Loyal to the Temple at Jerusalem, the authors of Judges want their readers to know that the rival shrine had its origin in crime and in pagan perversions of the worship of the Lord.

The second story (19—21) is one of sheer horror. In these days when there were relatively few hotels, hospitality was a sacred duty. A traveling Levite and his concubine are offered lodging by a man of Gibeah, a town in the area occupied by the tribe of Benjamin. In the middle of the night, a mob of Benjaminites storms the house and demands that the Levite be sent out so that the Benjaminites can engage in an orgy of homosexual rape. Eventually, they settle for mass rape of the Levite's concubine. Finding her dead the next morning, the Levite takes her body to his home, cuts it into twelve parts, and sends the bloody pieces of her corpse to the twelve tribes. Horrified by the crime, the tribes call an assembly of their chiefs. The tribe of Benjamin, however, refuses to deliver for punishment the men who have violated hospitality, engaged in mass rape, and murdered the woman. The result is civil war, in which the other tribes virtually exterminate the tribe of Benjamin. They even swear that they will never allow their daughters to marry the few surviving Benjaminites. (Benjamin was never again a major division within Israel.) But now these tribes begin to have qualms of conscience about this genocide. Because they cannot break their oaths and give their daughters to Benjaminites, they plot another violent solution to the problem: they agree to look the other way while the remaining Benjamites kidnap the dancing girls at a wine festival in Jabesh-gilead. Thus at least a remnant of Benjamin could survive.

The story may have been preserved in part because of later political implications. The concubine was from David's hometown. Benjamin was the tribe of David's rivals, Saul and his son Ishbaal. Jabesh-gilead was a stronghold of support for Saul. The authors of Judges are from David's tribe, Judah.

But the point the authors of Judges spell out for us—four times (17:6; 18:1; 19:1; 21:25), to make sure we don't miss it—is that "in those days there was no king in Israel." It was a time of compromise with pagan religion, violent crime, civil wars, and near anarchy. The tribes were largely independent of one another, and even the tribal organization is not clear. The number twelve seems sometimes to have been important, but what constituted the twelve tribes may have changed. At times, Ephraim and Manasseh, said to be descended from Joseph, are regarded as two tribes, with the Levites regarded as a special religious group. But in other instances Ephraim and Manasseh are grouped together, and the Levites are listed as a twelfth tribe. Few, if any, of the judges seem to have exercised control over twelve tribes. The Song of Deborah (Judges 5), for example, chides the tribes of Reuben, Gilead (Gad), and Dan for failure to join her army; lists a tribe called Machir; and never even mentions Judah, Simeon, or Levi. As we have seen, the scattered tribes and clans could butcher each other almost as quickly as they could their enemies.

The amazing thing, therefore, is that in two hundred years Israel not only survived but emerged as a nation. What was it that united and empowered this motley collection of former slaves, of many tribes and clans and several races? It was not racial unity, for "a mixed crowd" (Ex. 12:38) left Egypt, and in Canaan the covenant came to include other racial groups (Josh. 8:33–35). It was not a succession of oppressors, for those not immediately threatened often refused to help, as in the case of Deborah. What the last chapter of Joshua tells us must indeed have been the case. One thing bound this odd assortment of people together: they had united in a covenant with the Lord. If tribes failed to respond to Deborah's call, at least her song reminded them that they were obligated to do so. They were to be one people because they shared a covenant with one God. In all likelihood, they met each year for an annual ceremony of covenant renewal at the central shrine at Shiloh (1 Sam. 1:3). And though many often strayed from that covenant, those who were faithful knew that the covenant God was to be their true king. It was in faithfulness to that God that Israel found its unity and strength.

How Israelites undertook to unite their commitment to the Lord as king with the practical necessity of establishing a human monarchy is the subject to which the Jewish historians now turned. But first, our Bibles give us one delightful story from the time of the Judges: the book of Ruth.

RUTH

There is a legend that Benjamin Franklin, when he was ambassador to France, once entertained the ladies of the court of Louis XVI by reading them a story. "What a delightful rustic idyll!" they exclaimed. "Wherever did you get it?" "It is called the book of Ruth," Franklin explained to the astonished ladies of that worldly court, "and it is found in the Bible."

It is a delightful idyll, but there is much more to the story. Because it is so short and so clearly written, no outline is needed in this *Guide*.

The Story of Ruth

"In the days when the judges ruled," the story begins. But if it reflects none of the bloody battles of that period, the tale does begin with a series of tragedies. Famine forces Naomi's family to migrate from Bethlehem across the Jordan to Moab. There they find shelter, but soon tragedy strikes again. Her two sons, now married to Moabite wives, die, and so does the father of the family. Three lone and childless widows are left, the mother-in-law, Naomi, being not only widowed but in a strange land.

Perhaps a modern reader needs to be reminded that in these days there were no life insurance policies or social security programs. So Naomi, determined to return to Bethlehem, urges her daughters-in-law to seek the only security that most women of the time could find: to marry again. "The Lord grant that you may find security, each of you in the house of your husband" (1:9).

One widowed daughter-in-law, however, Ruth, resolves to leave the past behind and go with Naomi to Bethlehem. Her moving testimony of love and faith is the most quoted passage in the book.

> Where you go, I will go;
> Where you lodge, I will lodge;
>
> your people shall be my people,
> and your God my God. (1:16)

In Bethlehem, guided by her mother-in-law, Ruth makes a living in the only way available. The law of God commanded that when the grain was harvested, "you shall not reap to the very edges of your field, or gather the gleanings of your harvest. . . . You shall leave them for the poor and the alien" (Lev. 19:9–10). Seeing the beautiful young widow gleaning in his field, Boaz makes sure that plenty of grain is left for her. Again following her mother-in-law's advice, Ruth approaches Boaz in the middle of the night, uncovering him as he sleeps. He proposes marriage. Because Boaz is at least a distant cousin of Ruth's first husband, he claims the right to fulfill the law which said that in the case of a widow, "her husband's brother shall go in to her, taking her in marriage" (Deut. 25:5). There was also the law that property should stay within the clan (Lev. 25:25). A closer cousin is willing to buy Naomi's property but relinquishes his claim when he realizes this also involves marrying Ruth. And so Ruth and Boaz are married.

Their marriage, however, is not the happy ending of the story. The joyful climax comes when Ruth bears a son, a son who was to become the grandfather of David, Israel's greatest king.

The Story as Sacred History

Ruth does not seem to be a part of the monumental Deuteronomic history of Israel, which extends from Deuteronomy through 2 Kings. Nevertheless, it has its place in the centuries-long story of what was intended to be the kingdom of God. It is not simply that Ruth's story takes place near the end of the period of the judges and thus fits neatly between the books of Judges and 1 Samuel. Ruth has a place as the great-grandmother of David, the one in whose reign the kingdom of God seemed closest to fulfillment.

Thus the story affirms that great David's ancestors were people of brave faith, sexual purity, benevolence, and obedience to the laws of Moses. Long after his death, David was remembered as the ideal king. Even after the monarchy itself had perished, prophets dreamed of the day when a new David would come and the kingdom of God would at last be realized. And so stories in praise of David were told and retold down through the history of Israel. They witnessed not only to past glory but to future hope.

Two Heroic Women in a Man's World

Feminist biblical scholar Phyllis Trible has enabled us to see this book in a new light. As interpreted by Trible, Ruth is the story of two brave and independent women struggling for survival in a male-dominated world.

Naomi and Ruth know hardship, danger, insecurity, and death. No God promises them blessing; no man rushes to their rescue. They risk bold decisions and shocking acts to work out their own salvation in the midst of the alien, the hostile, and the unknown.[14]

Marveling at Ruth's decision to leave the prospect of marriage, her home, and her religion to accompany another woman, Naomi, Trible exclaims,

> In the entire epic of Israel, only Abraham matches this radicality. . . . She [Ruth] has also reversed sexual allegiance. A young woman has committed herself to the life of an old woman rather than to search for a husband. . . . One female has chosen another female in a world where life depends upon men. There is no more radical decision in all the memories of Israel.[15]

When she has completed her study of Ruth, Trible summarizes the story as suggesting

> a theological interpretation of feminism: women working out their own salvation with fear and trembling, for it is God who works in them. . . . All together they are women in culture, women against culture, and women transforming culture. What they reflect, they challenge. And that challenge is a legacy of faith to this day for all who have ears to hear the stories of women in a man's world.[16]

A Tract against Racism

It may be that Trible has seen meaning in the story even beyond that which its author realized. But it is quite possible that the writer did intend this little book to be a tract against a kind of racism.

Centuries after the time of Ruth, Jerusalem fell, its people carried into slavery in Babylon. A century after a little group of refugees returned, Ezra and Nehemiah led in rebuilding what had been intended to be the kingdom of God. Israel's undoing, they were sure, had been its compromise with paganism, its adoption of the gods of its pagan neighbors. And so they attempted to stamp out all foreign influences. Nehemiah boasts of his determined "cleansing" of the sacred race: "In those days also I saw Jews who had married women of Ashdod, Amon, and Moab. . . . And I contended with them and cursed them and beat some of them and pulled out their hair" (Neh. 13:23–25). Not only did Ezra forbid Jews to marry Gentile women, but he ordered them to divorce the Gentile wives they already had and to throw out their own half-Gentile children (Ezra 10:3). And of all races, Jews hated the Moabites most of all. It was the law that if you married a Gentile, your family could not worship in the congregation of Israel for three generations. But if one married a Moabite, "even to the tenth generation, none of their descendants shall be admitted to the assembly of the Lord" (Deut 23:3).

It is perhaps no accident, therefore, that the author of Ruth seizes every opportunity to remind us that this heroine is by birth a Moabite. We meet her as one of the "Moabite wives" of Naomi's sons (1:4). It is with "Ruth the Moabite" that Naomi returns to Bethlehem "from the country of Moab" (1:22). There the author again identifies her as "Ruth the Moabite" (2:2). "She is the Moabite . . . from . . . Moab," Boaz's servants inform him (2:6). "I am a

foreigner," she exclaims, surprised by his kindness (2:10). "Ruth the Moabite" reports events to Naomi (2:21). Their kinsman turns down the chance to
marry "Ruth the Moabite" (4:5). But in the end, Boaz announces proudly, "I
have . . . acquired Ruth the Moabite . . . to be my wife" (4:10). Over and over
the author hammers it in, so that one cannot miss it: Ruth was a Moabite.

Perhaps it was in a time when Jews were being told to divorce their
Gentile wives and expel their half-Gentile children that our unknown author
wrote this protest; for this woman, the story tells us, though a Moabite by
race, was a woman of deep faith in the God of Israel. Her race did not matter.
Far from her descendants being excluded from the assembly of the Lord for ten
generations, it was one of them, Solomon, who built the Temple itself. Far from
her son being expelled, he became the grandfather of Israel's greatest king.

Thus Naomi's friends could sing to her the praises of "your daughter-in-
law who loves you, who is more to you than seven sons" (4:15).

1 SAMUEL

When Samuel began as a judge, Israel was a loose collection of clans and
tribes, sometimes at war with each other. The Israelites were so weak that
they could not defend from their enemies even their most sacred symbol, the
ark of the covenant. Seventy years later, Israel was a united empire, a world
power, firmly astride a major trade route, extracting tribute from the peoples
who had so recently threatened its very existence. Originally parts of the
same book, 1 and 2 Samuel tell the remarkable story of this radical, rapid
transformation.

Sociologists, economists, military historians, and theologians have all
undertaken in their various ways to explain the causes of this transition.
Internationally, the eleventh century B.C., they tell us, presented a power
vacuum. Egypt, once dominant in the region, was now steadily weakening.
Assyria was still a century away from being a threat. The Philistines were
indeed threatening, but the danger they presented seems actually to have
helped unite Israel for a common defense.[17]

What welded Israel into an empire, however, was also the influence of
three charismatic men. Two books, 1 and 2 Samuel, bear the name of the
prophet-priest-judge who initiated the transition. The tragic figure of Saul,
Israel's first king, typifies the birth pangs of the Israelite kingdom. And from
the second half of 1 Samuel through the entire book of 2 Samuel, one
personality dominates this history, Israel's greatest king, David.

The inspired writers of these books, however, tell us over and over,
directly and in subtle ways, that the rise of the Israelite Empire was not really
the result of military success, power politics, or even remarkable personali-
ties. What happened was planned and purposed by the Lord, for Israel was
chosen to be the kingdom of God.

1 SAMUEL

The Last of the Judges and the Beginnings of the Earthly Monarchy in the Kingdom of God

"Samuel said to Saul, . . . 'Your kingdom will not continue; the Lord has sought out a man after his own heart; and . . . appointed him to be ruler . . . because you have not kept what the Lord commanded you'" (13:13–14).

1	9	16	28	31
Samuel: Last of the Judges	**Saul: First of the Kings**	**The Early Life of David, Israel's Greatest King**	**The Last Days of Saul**	
In answer to prayer, Samuel is born, 1	Guided by God, Samuel anoints Saul as Israel's first king, 9—10	David gains high position in Saul's court, 16—18	Through a witch, Samuel's ghost warns Saul that he will be killed, 28	
and is reared in the house of the Lord, 2—3	Saul wins battles, 11, 14	But Saul's jealously forces David to flee, 19—24	The Philistines advance on Saul, though without David, 29	
The Philistines defeat Israel and even briefly capture the ark, 4—6	Samuel gives a farewell address, 12 but now turns from Saul to David, 13, 15	David becomes leader of a guerrilla band, 25—27	(David's battle with Ziklag), 30	
Encouraged by Samuel, Israel resists the Philistines, 7			Saul kills himself after being wounded in battle by the Philistines, 31	
Reluctantly, Samuel at last agrees to appoint a human king for Israel, 8				

Sources: First and Second Samuel and 1 and 2 Kings are one continuous story and contain both contemporary court records and later tradition, completed and edited during the exile.

Purpose: First Samuel extols the glories of Samuel, Saul, and David, but it also warns that the welfare of the nation depends on its faithfulness to its true king, the Lord.

One Relationship to the New Testament: The concept of the kingdom of God is basic to the teaching of Jesus.

The Nature of 1 Samuel

First Samuel, David F. Payne writes, is "as much a sermon as a history lesson."[18] In the form in which we have it, it is the product of those historians who, during the exile, wrote to show how the promises and warnings attributed in Deuteronomy to Moses came true. Faithfulness to God was rewarded. Disobedience brought catastrophe.

First Samuel continues the history that began with Deuteronomy and ends with 2 Kings's story of the fall of Jerusalem. Everywhere the "sermon" makes clear that the force behind all this history was the plan and purpose of God.

But the story of the rise—and then fall—of the Israelite Empire is also a history lesson. The accent may be on the lesson, but these books contain a great deal of genuine history. Songs from the time, stories quite possibly by eyewitnesses, and court records are preserved and brought together to give us a vivid and basically accurate account of events. After extensive study, Baruch Halpern gave the authors of Deuteronomy and the books of Samuel and Kings the honorable title "the first historians."[19] He does not claim that they were inerrant or that they were historians in quite the modern sense, but they did intend to write history.

If anything, perhaps our historians were too eager to preserve all the stories they had learned. Scholars detect two basic sources running through the narrative, which are not always in complete agreement. Traditions clustered around the heroes of these books, especially David. Fortunately for us, many of these tales have been preserved, even if they cannot now be fitted together neatly. For example, we have two stories of how Saul became known as a prophet (1 Sam. 10:9–13; 19:23–24), two stories of why Samuel finally rejected Saul (13:2–15; 15:1–35), two stories of how David found a place in Saul's court (16:14–23; 17:1–58), two stories of Saul's throwing his spear at David (18:10–11; 19:8–10), and two stories of David's sparing Saul's life (24:1–22; 26:1–25). Perhaps the double witness to some of these events helps assure us that they do rest ultimately on genuine history.

First and Second Samuel describe, often in vivid detail, the rise of the kingdom of David. But behind those events, the writers are concerned to tell us the more significant story, the history of what was meant to be the kingdom of God.

Samuel: Last of
the Judges (1 Sam. 1—8)

One leader played so large a role in the transformation of Israel that his name is given to two books in our modern Bibles: Samuel. It was the Lord whose purpose was being worked out in the events these books describe, but the human agent by which they were initiated was this prophet, priest, and judge.

The story of Samuel's birth and childhood is so beautifully told that, centuries later, Luke used it in part as a model for describing the births of John the Baptist and Jesus. Beloved but childless, Hannah prays so hard for a child that the old priest Eli thinks she is drunk. When, as Eli promises, her son is born, Hannah sings of the God of justice and compassion:

> He raises up the poor from the dust;
>   he lifts the needy from the ash heap,
> to make them sit with princes
>   and inherit the seat of honor. (2:8)

As soon as he can leave his mother, Samuel is taken to the ark's shrine at Shiloh, the successor to the ancient tabernacle. There "the boy Samuel continued to grow both in stature and in favor with the Lord and with the people" (2:26). In that house of God, Samuel heard God's call (3:4). (Luke's story of Jesus' childhood [Luke 1—2] reflects that of Samuel, with barren Elizabeth, an old priest, promises of birth, a mother's song of God's concern for the poor, and the summary that Jesus grew in wisdom and stature and in divine and human favor [Luke 2:52; cf. 1 Sam. 2:26]. Even as a child, Jesus, too, was at home in God's house [Luke 2:41–51].)

The idyllic story of Samuel's childhood, however, is soon interrupted by all-too-real tragedy. At least for devout Israelites, there had been a fragile unity in that many, like Samuel's parents, worshiped at least once a year at the Lord's shrine in Shiloh. But ceremonies of covenant renewal proved futile against Philistine steel. Even the old order of priests had become corrupt (3:13). Wooden spears could not penetrate the iron shields of the Philistines, and Israel's trust that somehow the ark of the covenant would repel these invaders smacks more of superstition than of intelligent religion.

Samuel comes to manhood, then, when Israel's fortunes are at their lowest ebb. For a century or more, Philistines had been occupying the Palestinian coast. Israel had never gained even a foothold there. We know something of these "sea peoples" from Egyptian inscriptions. Egyptian carvings show them with feathered headdresses, carrying iron weapons, riding on war wagons. They were probably cousins of those fighters of whom Homer wrote in the *Iliad*.[20] Judges tells us that, in his day, Samson could for a while live with them in uneasy neighborliness. Now, however, the Philistines were bent on easy conquest. With superstitious hope, the Israelite army carried the ark of the covenant into battle. The Philistines not only slaughtered four thousand Israelite soldiers (4:2) but even captured the ark, the symbol of Israel's only real hope, the Lord (4:11). Old Eli fell dead at the news (4:17–18).

In Israelite history, this was a moment of abject weakness. Therefore it was precisely at that point, the inspired writers want us to understand, that God took the first steps toward building David's powerful empire. No human agency brought back the ark. Plague struck the Philistines. Relying on sympathetic magic, the Philistines put the ark in a cart along with golden models of the tumors with which they had been afflicted and of the rodents that had spread a plague among them (6:4–5). A modern diagnostician might say that the bubonic plague was the means the Lord used to strike fear into the hearts of those who had captured this covenant box. The ancient writers were interested only in the ultimate cause, the Lord. Terrified Philistines let the oxen return the holy symbol to Israel. A plague struck even Israelites who irreverently gazed too closely upon the holy object (6:19–20).

Now God's man, Samuel, begins to lead. As far as we know, he never served as a general in the field. But as he prays, God sends a storm, and at Mizpah, Israel at last defeats the Philistines (7:7–11). An uneasy truce enables this holy man to become Israel's last and greatest judge. He holds court in a circuit of traditional holy places: Bethel, Mizpah, and Gilgal. Led by Samuel, for a few years Israel enjoyed a relative and uneasy peace.

It could not last. Sociologists report that there have been cultures which have survived with something like the loose confederation of tribes that Israel had during the period of the judges. But when a people become as numerous as Israel probably was at this time, such an alliance proves no longer practical. Israel was tired, too, of being victimized by one invader after another. Reliance simply on a succession of charismatic leaders seemed to offer little security and stability; and after all, all the other nations had kings.

And so, as Samuel grew old, the demand could not be resisted. "Appoint for us . . . a king to govern us, like other nations" (8:5), demanded Israel's elders. Samuel was horrified. Their demand for an earthly king was, he told them, a rejection of the very reason for Israel's existence. They had been called at Mount Sinai to be something unique on earth, to be the kingdom of *God* (Ex. 19:5–6). Solemnly, he relayed divine warnings to them. A king would tax them, waste their money in luxury, build military power at their expense, draft them, and finally enslave them (1 Sam. 8:10–18). His prophecy of coming tyranny so perfectly describes the latter part of Solomon's reign that many scholars suggest that, in the form in which we have it, it must have been written by an angry historian who had witnessed its literal fulfillment. But even though warned in the name of God, the elders continued to insist on an earthly king. We are told that God and Samuel reluctantly gave in.

Throughout the rest of the history of the kingdom of Israel, there would continue to be a tension between Israel's ambition to be an earthly kingdom and its sense of mission to be the kingdom of God.

Saul: First of the Kings (1 Sam. 9—16)

In the memory of many in later generations, for "one brief shining moment" earthly kingdom and heavenly kingdom merged. Looking back on it centuries later, Israel could see the reign of David as almost embodying the reign of God.

But first there was the byway of the reign of Saul.

Tall, handsome, courageous, impulsive, and charismatic, Saul attracted and held the loyalty of thousands. He welded together twelve divisive tribes, fought the Philistines on even terms, and began a kingdom that lasted for centuries. But he was also moody, psychologically unstable, and given to fits of jealousy. More important to our writers, in spite of moments of religious ecstasy, he was, by Samuel's standards, unfaithful to God. A hero and a failure, Saul perhaps more than any other figure in the Bible is like a protagonist in some Greek tragedy.

The son of a wealthy livestock farmer, Saul, when we meet him, is out rounding up strays. Samuel the seer has the reputation of being able to help locate stray livestock, so Saul comes to this prophet. He finds not just donkeys but a kingdom. Samuel anoints him, and within a few hours the amazed young rancher is sharing religious ecstasies with a band of prophets.

In 1 Sam. 10:5–13, we meet these charismatic figures for the first time. Singing and dancing to the sound of their musical instruments, these early prophets were lifted out of themselves in mystic exaltation of spirit in the hope of being open to God. Joining them for at least a few moments, Saul was "turned into a different person" (10:6), given "another heart" by God (10:9), and "fell into a prophetic frenzy along with them" (10:10). The judges had received their office not by heredity but because the Spirit of the Lord came upon them. Similarly, it was said, God had anointed Saul with that Spirit.

The sense of divine empowerment did not last. When Samuel called an assembly to present to Israel its new king, Saul, terrified, was found hiding behind the baggage they had brought. No wonder many scoffed, "How can this man save us?" (10:27). Saul himself went back to farming.

It was the horror of Ammonite brutality that inflamed Saul into action. Jabesh-gilead was an Israelite city on the east side of the Jordan. Thus it was undefended by the majority of Israelites, who lived west of the river. When Nahash laid siege, the city offered to surrender. But that monster agreed to let them live only on the condition that "I gouge out everyone's right eye, and thus put disgrace upon all Israel" (11:2). Enraged by the news, Saul chopped his oxen into bits and sent bloody pieces to every part of Israel, dramatically threatening retaliation if any did not join his army. The "dread of the Lord fell upon the people" (11:7); they rallied to his call, and they rescued Jabesh-gilead. Now Saul was indeed king!

At first his was not a luxurious court. He commanded his troops from under a pomegranate tree (14:2). Archaeologists have dug up a two-story stone house in his hometown, which may have been his "palace." But probably more than any of the judges, he united the contending tribes, and thus he was able to mount a partially successful defense against the Philistines. That was no easy task. The Philistines were a "modern" people; that is, they had mastered the art of smelting, had entered what historians call the Iron Age. At the beginning of the monarchy, Israel was still a Bronze Age people, attempting to fight Philistine steel with wooden weapons (13:19–22). But empowered by the Spirit and often led by Prince Jonathan, the popular son of Saul, Saul's Israel was able to win some victories and drive the Philistines back to their cities on the coast. Samuel could feel that his life's work had been a success (12:1–25).

It was not to last. We have two stories of how the rift developed between Samuel and Saul. In each, the modern reader may feel a certain sympathy for the temperamental king. A huge Philistine army was poised for attack. Saul's troops did not want to engage them in battle without first offering to the Lord a burnt offering for victory. Samuel had promised to come within a week to preside over that ceremony. As the days dragged by, more and more of Saul's terrified troops were deserting; so Saul took matters into his own hands. Was he not the king? He offered the sacrifice. Discovering on his arrival what had happened, Samuel was enraged. "You have done foolishly; you have not kept the commandment of the Lord," he cried (13:13). Kings might lead armies, but God's laws were to rule. The Lord, Samuel was sure, limited kings to political duties; Samuel as priest was to offer sacrifices. A second story tells us that Saul disobeyed Samuel—and his God—by failing to sacrifice to God everything taken in a battle, including even the captured enemy king (15:4–35). What was meant to be the kingdom of God was becoming the kingdom of Saul.

"I regret that I made Saul king," our writer pictures God as telling Samuel, "for he has turned back from following me, and has not carried out my commands" (15:11). "Now," Samuel solemnly announced to Saul, "your kingdom will not continue; the Lord has sought out a man after his own heart" (13:14).

That man was David.

The Early Life of David,
Israel's Greatest King (1 Sam. 16—27)

To the biblical writers, the whole reign of Saul was only a kind of side road. It was to David that God's plan had pointed all along. He was handsome, strong, courageous, a shrewd politician, and an able leader, perhaps beyond any other character in the Old Testament able to win the love and loyalty of men and women. He was also a sinner, but one who could repent. He was Israel's greatest king. The biblical writers were sure that his amazing success lay not simply in those God-given talents but in the fact that "the spirit of the Lord came mightily upon David" (16:13). David was the truly charismatic hero.

The second half of 1 Samuel is devoted to the story of how, step by step, Saul's reign disintegrated and David rose to power.

We are told that when Samuel broke with Saul, he secretly anointed young

David (16:1–13). There are two quite different stories of how David got his start in court. In the first (16:14–23), he became the court minstrel. Never a stable personality, Saul, convinced by Samuel that God had rejected him, has become what modern psychologists might perhaps diagnose as a manic depressive. To soothe him in his fits of despair, David is summoned to play music. Saul finds him so attractive that he soon makes David his armor-bearer (16:21). In the second story, young David, armed only with a slingshot and faith in God, kills the Philistine giant Goliath (17:1–58). The stories do not fit together neatly, because in the second, Saul and his general have no idea who David is (17:55–58), though previously we were told that he is Saul's beloved court musician and armor-bearer. Indeed, 2 Sam. 21:19 says that Goliath was killed by one Elhanan. No matter; we can be grateful that these delightful stories have been preserved. In any event, David soon was a military hero. "The commanders of the Philistines came out to battle; and as often as they came out, David had more success than all the servants of Saul, so that his fame became very great" (18:30).

"All Israel and Judah loved David" (18:16). So widely loved was David that we are told that the popular song of the day, sung by women as they made merry, was

> Saul has killed his thousands,
> and David his ten thousands. (18:7)

The old king, deep in his depression, was doubly jealous. David's popularity exceeded his own. And David's popularity threatened the claim of Prince Jonathan, Saul's beloved son, to succeed his father as king. So magnetic was the personality of David, however, that even Jonathan swore an alliance with his rival (20:16–17). As Samuel had warned, Saul's reign was steadily decaying. God, Saul feared, had chosen David.

We have two stories of how Saul, in a fit of madness, threw his spear at David (18:10–11; 19:9–10). David, however, survived. And indeed, he was ambitious; if he was not Saul's son, he could at least hope to become the king's son-in-law. In that culture, such a marriage would have been no small help for one whose goal was to succeed to a throne. Thus two stories tell of betrothals to daughters of Saul. Saul reneged on the promise of his older daughter. When David brought as his marriage payment one hundred bloody foreskins of Philistines he had slaughtered, Saul had to give his next daughter, Michal, to the young soldier.

Saul, however, would not remain reconciled. Just in time, aided by Saul's own children—David's bride Michal and his rival Jonathan—David escaped Saul's plot to kill him. A fugitive from the king but not really trusted by the Philistines, Saul's enemies, David headed an outlaw band, patrolling the no-man's-land between the Philistines and Israel. By means of various tricks, he at least partially blinded the Philistines to the potential threat he was to pose them. He attracted a private guerrilla army, and they supported themselves by raiding Gentile villages all over the area. Two stories tell us that David had a chance to assassinate Saul even as Saul was pursuing David to kill him (24:1–22; 26:1–25). In each case, David magnanimously spared Saul. But after all, why not? By now, even Saul knew what the writers wanted the readers to know: David was God's choice, bound to succeed (26:25). He had only to wait the news of the final defeat of Saul.

The Last Days of Saul (1 Sam. 28—31)

David does not have to wait long. Saul's story hastens to its tragic end. Samuel, whose birth narrative forms the beginning of the book, though now dead, appears once more near the end of the story. Though Saul has outlawed witches, he finds one and asks this medium to contact the spirit of Samuel for guidance. And we are told in an eerie scene that the vision of the dead prophet conjured up by the witch confirms Saul's fears. The next day he will die (28:3–25).

Meanwhile, David is winning more victories and, with a mixture of threat and deliverances, more allies.

First Samuel closes with the tragic story of the death of Saul. This time the Philistines triumph. Jonathan and other sons of Saul are slain. Mortally wounded, Saul begs his armor-bearer to finish him off, but the soldier will not lift his hand against his beloved king. And so, to avoid capture and disgrace at the hands of the Philistines, Saul ends his own life, a suicide.

There were still many who loved him. When the Philistines found Saul's body, they took it and crucified his corpse on the wall of a conquered city. But the men of Jabesh-gilead could not forget how, at the beginning of his reign, Saul had rescued them. Risking their lives, they rescued his body to bury their king with honor.

The way was now clear for David to make his bid for the throne; but that is the story of 2 Samuel.

2 SAMUEL

The kingdom of God or the kingdom of a man—in the days of Gideon and Samuel, Israel had wrestled with the choice. At least in retrospect, however, there seemed to be one moment in history (1000 to 961 B.C.) when the ideal and the practical merged. David ruled, but David was "a man after God's own heart."

David was so successful that one might almost call his realm the *empire* of God. He conquered surrounding nations and exacted tribute from them. At the same time, he brought the ark of the covenant, symbol of the presence of the Lord, to his capital city, making worship of the one God the state religion. So much wealth and power flowed to Jerusalem that it must have seemed to

2 SAMUEL
The Kingdom of David and the Kingdom of God

"The Lord declares . . . your house and your kingdom . . . shall be established forever" (7:11–16).

1 **David Wins the Throne**	5:6 **Blessed by God, David Reigns**	11 **The "House" (Family) of David**	21 24 **An Appendix: Additional Stories about David**
David mourns for Saul and courts Saul's followers, 1	He seizes Jerusalem, makes alliances, and defeats the Philistines, 5:6–25	David sinfully adds Bathsheba to his harem, and judgment is announced, 11—12	He slaughters Saul's sons, 21:1–14
Anointed by his tribe, Judah, David wages civil war against Saul's son, 2—4	He brings the ark to Jerusalem, 6	His son Amnon commits incest and is murdered by another son, Absalom, 13	He wins victories over the Philistines, 21:15–22
Victorious at last, he is crowned king of all Israel, 5:1–5	God promises to establish David's "house" forever, 7	Absalom leads a rebellion against his father, 14—19	Two Songs of David, 22:1–23:7
	David builds an empire, 8—10	Sheba also attempts a revolution, 20	Lists of his mighty men, 23:8–38
			David's census and the ensuing plague, 24

Sources: First and Second Samuel were originally one book composed of many sources, some contemporary with the events described, edited after the fall of Jerusalem.
Subject: The reign of David and promises and disappointments about his "house"
One Relationship to the New Testament: Jesus Christ was hailed as the promised son of David who would be the Son of God.

many Israelites that the kind of blessings which God was said to have promised were at last being showered on them. Genesis says that God promised Abraham that his descendants would become a great and blessed nation with a large and prosperous land. Deuteronomy reports Moses as assuring Israel that if it remained faithful, it would be richly blessed. Second Samuel tells us that in the days of David, it appeared that those promises had come true.

First and Second Samuel were originally one book. Second Samuel simply picks up the story where 1 Samuel leaves off. Its one subject is the reign of David. Historians regard much of the book as of high historical value, resting in part on court records or accounts actually written in the days of David or Solomon. There are passages that reflect the idealization of David, which continued into later times. Second Samuel, however, also preserves frank, clearly historical accounts of some of David's failures, even sins.[21]

Israel preserved its stories of David for a reason far more important than mere antiquarian curiosity. David was, their prophets promised in effect, "their once and future king." Long after David's death, long after there was no throne in Jerusalem and no king reigning there, prophets still sang that a new David would come. That son of David would reign at last in the coming kingdom of God.

David Wins
the Throne (2 Sam. 1:1—5:5)

Young, handsome, winsome, devout—perhaps the best word for David is that in every way he was "charismatic." The Spirit of the Lord, which had come upon the great judges of the past, "mightily" possessed this prince (1 Sam. 16:13). He was also a shrewd politician. The first chapters of 2 Samuel describe how, step by step, this young candidate for office welded together the scattered tribes of Israel and placed himself firmly in control over them.

From the moment he heard of the death of Saul and Jonathan, David set out to win Saul's followers to his side. He executed the man who claimed to have killed the wounded Saul, even though that man had brought David the crown (2 Sam. 1:15). He composed a song of lament for Saul and Jonathan and ordered that it be sung all over Israel. Thus he dramatized how he shared the affection Saul's followers felt for the former king and for the one who, had he lived, might have succeeded to the throne (1:17–27). He sent a diplomatic delegation to Jabesh-gilead, a city so strong in support of their deliverer Saul that they had risked their lives to recover his body (2:4–7). But he made it very clear to them that he regarded himself, not Saul's surviving son, as the Lord's anointed, at least in Judah.

It was in his own tribe, Judah, that David established his base. He made his capital in the southern city of Hebron, traditional site of the tomb of Abraham.

In this decision, as in so many others, the writers of 2 Samuel assure us that David was guided by the Lord (2:1–4).

Who would reign over the other tribes, however, was an open question. There was no precedent for a son succeeding a father as a leader in Israel. Judges had gained their offices not by inheritance but by clear indications that "the Spirit of the Lord came upon" them. Would Saul's surviving son, Ishbaal (Ish-bosheth), inherit the throne, or would it go to the charismatic, Spirit-endowed David? It took not only diplomacy but war to decide.

"There was a long war between the house of Saul and the house of David; David grew stronger and stronger, while the house of Saul became weaker and weaker" (3:1). The name "Ish-bosheth" for Saul's son (used in the Hebrew and most translations) means "Man of Shame." Because few mothers would have given their sons such a name, it seems likely that the name of Saul's surviving son really was "Ishbaal," "Man of Baal" (cf. 1 Chron. 8:33). Perhaps the writer changed it in 2 Samuel to indicate his contempt for Baal worship. Apparently a weakling, Ish-bosheth (or Ishbaal) was no match for the seasoned warrior David. The real power in his reign was his captain Joab. When Joab defected to David's side, Ishbaal's cause was clearly lost. Still seeking to win followers of Saul's house by means other than military, David refused to accept Joab unless he brought with him David's former wife, Saul's daughter Michal (3:12–16).

Again using the tool of propaganda, David publicly mourned when his ever-aggressive captain Joab murdered Abner, though he did not punish Joab. Similarly, he made provision for Jonathan's crippled son Mephibosheth, though keeping this possible rival under his protective custody (4:4; 9:1–8). And when, at last, two of Ishbaal's own captains assassinated their king, bringing his head to David, David immediately executed them (4:9–12). David knew how to win over his opponents.

In fact, "everything the king did pleased all the people" (3:36). With the death of Ishbaal, all open opposition to David faded. "So all the elders of Israel came to the king at Hebron; and King David made a covenant with them at Hebron before the Lord, and they anointed David king over Israel" (5:3). "The Lord had established him king" (5:12).

Blessed by God,
David Reigns (2 Sam. 5:6—10:19)

Two more acts were designed to unite the once-warring tribes. David conquered the neutral city Jerusalem. Located near the border between the two most powerful tribes, Judah and Ephraim, Jerusalem had belonged to neither but had remained in the hands of the Jebusites. David conquered it and made it his personal capital (5:6–10). Thus he sought politically and militarily to unite previously warring factions. (Centuries later, the infant United States followed David's example by establishing its capital in a new city on the border between rival north and south.)

David also attempted to unite Israel religiously. To this end, with great fanfare, he brought to his capital the ancient symbol of God's presence, the ark of the covenant (6:1–23). "Church" and state would be one; the kingdom of David was to be the kingdom of God.

With his kingdom established, David built a small empire. By his victory at Jerusalem, he completed the conquest of the Canaanites begun by Joshua more than two centuries before. On the coast, "he struck down the Philistines from Geba all the way to Gezer" (5:25). Never again were those ancient enemies of Israel a significant threat. His army marched beyond Israel's borders, and Moab, Syria, Edom, Ammon, Amalek—nearly all of Israel's neighbors—became David's vassals. They began to pour tribute money into his treasury and to provide slave labor for his building projects (8:11–12; cf. chap. 10; 20:24). With the help of his ally King Hiram of Tyre, he built in Jerusalem a palace for himself (5:11), and in it he set up a harem of ten or more wives and concubines. There he established a full-fledged bureaucracy, military, political, and religious (8:15–18).

At one point, however, David's goal of consolidating political and religious power met an obstacle. The prophet Nathan, David's religious adviser, refused to go along with David's proposal to build a temple beside the palace. So much of the tradition from the wilderness survived that the idea of a fixed temple seemed almost as foreign as the idea of an earthly kingdom had seemed a generation earlier. Nathan the prophet announced that God demanded, "I have not lived in a house since the day I brought up the people of Israel from Egypt to this day, but I have been moving about in a tent and a tabernacle. . . . Did I ever speak . . . saying, 'Why have you not built me a house of cedar?' " (7:6–8). Such a God could not be confined to one place, even by an ambitious king. David was not to build a house for the Lord.

Second Samuel 7, which reports the conversation between David and Nathan, is one of the most important chapters in the entire Old Testament. It is also one of the most ambiguous. There is a deliberate ambiguity there, a play on the double meaning of the word "house." David proposes to build a "house" for God, meaning literally a building for God to live in. But even though God rejects this offer, the Lord replies, "The Lord will make *you* a house" (7:11; italics added). Here "house" means "family" or "dynasty." The next king in David's dynasty, his "house," will indeed build a house, a temple, for God: David's son Solomon.

Nathan's puzzling prophecy, however, seems to describe more than Solomon. David is to have a son; God says, "He shall build a house for my name" (7:13). That seems clear enough. But then God says, "I will be a father to him, and he shall be a son to me" (7:14). David's son is to be a son of God.

Solomon fell far short of fulfilling that prophecy. We are not told that this promised king is to be perfect. "When he commits iniquity, I will punish him" (7:14). But of this son, God makes remarkable promises. "I will not take my steadfast love from him" (7:15). "Your house and your kingdom shall be made sure forever" (7:16). Is God through Nathan speaking of Solomon, or of the whole dynasty of David, or of some future, ideal king who will be son of David and son of God? So much in the chapter is so puzzling that many scholars believe that it combines the work of different writers or editors. In subsequent generations, two things are clear: Jews believed that God had made a "covenant" with David, eternally to bless his dynasty (23:5; cf. Ps. 89:3–4); and even when that dynasty fell and there were no more kings, they still looked with hope to the day when a son of David, a new David, the messiah, would reign in the kingdom of God (Ezek. 34:20–24). That son of David would be the son of God.

The "House" (Family)
of David (2 Sam. 11—20)

Much of the rest of 2 Samuel focuses on the subject of the sons of David and which son would become heir to the throne and this promise.

Already our writers have told us that David would have no heir by his first wife, Michal. Had she borne him a son, that child would have been both son of David and grandson of Saul, thus further uniting to David's house the tribes that had favored Saul's dynasty. Separated for years, some time after their reunion Michal and David had an angry quarrel. Apparently, David had little to do with her after that (6:20–23).

It was a child of Bathsheba who did succeed to David's throne. Hollywood has glamorized the sordid story. David seduced and impregnated Bathsheba, the wife of Uriah, one of his army officers. When he could not get loyal Uriah to return home to sleep with Bathsheba, thus concealing David's adultery, David had Uriah murdered. He then added Bathsheba to his own harem (11:1–27). Why not? Was David not king and thus lord of all? "Not so!" cried Nathan, in effect. "The thing that David had done displeased the Lord" (11:27), Israel's true king. With the clever use of a parable, the prophet Nathan tricked David into condemning himself. In the story of David's adultery, one senses the contrast between the kingdom of God and the tyranny of David. Nevertheless, it is recorded that this "man after God's own heart" repented. "I have sinned against the Lord," David confessed (12:13). The first son of David and Bathsheba, born of their sin, died.

"I will raise up trouble against you from within your own house," God warned sinful David through Nathan (12:11). The next chapters tell how this warning of judgment came true. David's son Amnon raped and then abandoned David's beautiful daughter Tamar. The next son, Absalom, gained revenge by murdering his incestuous brother Amnon. The handsome and politically cunning Absalom was now the heir apparent.

David had been a popular hero in his youth. Now, however, with his palace and his harem and his bureaucracy, some Israelites regarded David as a tyrant. Remember that many had not wanted a king at all. Chapters 14 through 19 tell how, playing on this discontent, Absalom gathered supporters and how, impatient for the throne, which presumably he would have inherited at David's death, he instigated a revolution. So widespread had the dissatisfaction become that David was forced to flee Jerusalem and to rely especially on his own hired Philistine bodyguard. Few passages in scripture are more moving than the account of how this torn father sought to keep his throne but save the life of his rebellious son, and how he wept when the news came to him that his beloved Absalom had been killed (2 Samuel 18).

In the minds of many, loyalty to their own tribes was stronger than loyalty to this monarch from the tribe of Judah. "A scoundrel named Sheba" was able, therefore, to instigate yet another a rebellion, almost splitting the nation in two. But with his captain Joab and his private army of Philistine "Cherethites and Pelethites," David crushed all opposition. In the end, his developing bureaucracy flourished (20:23–26).

Clearly, however, the kingdom of David was turning out to be something less than the kingdom of God.

An Appendix: Additional Stories about David (2 Sam. 21—24)

The last four chapters of 2 Samuel appear to be a loose collection of stories handed down about David. Our writers did not fit them into the connected history they have given us, but an editor wanted to make sure they were not lost. The editor therefore appended them to the end of this book.

The first story (21:1–14) describes David's slaughter of some of Saul's sons. This mass murder is said to be at God's command and at the request of some Gibeonites, who had demanded revenge on the house of Saul for something Saul had done to them. The slaughter also eliminated some potential rivals to David's kingship.

Another story describes previously unreported victories over the Philistines. Interestingly, here we are told that one Elhanan of Bethlehem, not David of Bethlehem, killed Goliath (21:19; contrast 1 Sam. 17:49). Such differences suggest that the writers carefully preserved stories from ancient sources from different clans and times, rather than always trying to twist the stories to fit together neatly.

Two beautiful songs attributed to David, famous for his music, are reported in 2 Sam. 22:1–23:7. The first is a celebration of deliverance by God, and it is also preserved as Psalm 18. The second celebrates the covenant God made with David.

Into a list of David's chief warriors (23:8–38) has been inserted a moving tale of their devotion to David and his to them. Three men risked their lives to break through Philistine lines to bring him a drink from the well of his hometown, Bethlehem. He poured out the water as an offering to the Lord, unwilling to drink what might have brought the death of his friends. Such stories explain in part why "everything the king did pleased the people."

The final story in 2 Samuel 24 tells how David took a census and God sent a plague on Israel in judgment. A census is especially useful for two purposes: taxation and a military draft. Long before, Samuel had warned that a king would tax and draft the people until they were virtual slaves (1 Sam. 8:10–18). Already one can see the beginnings of the fulfillment of that grim prophecy.

But how Samuel's warning was completely fulfilled in the days of Solomon, with catastrophic consequences, is the subject of the next book, 1 Kings.

1 KINGS

The "golden age"—every great empire has one. In Athens it was the age of Pericles. In Rome it was the reign of Caesar Augustus. For England it was the era of Elizabeth I. In Israel it was the age of Solomon.

With 1 Kings's account of that marvelous era, the narrative that began in Deuteronomy reaches its happy climax. But then it points toward its tragic conclusion. Picking up where 2 Samuel leaves off, 1 Kings tells with joy the glory of Solomon's reign. But it tells also how he strayed from true loyalty to the Lord. What was meant to be the kingdom of God became an Oriental despotism. It tells how, with his oppressive policies made even worse by his son and successor, his empire fell apart. The book ends with prophets such as Elijah risking their lives in a vain effort to call Israel back to worship only the Lord.

The Sources, Background, and Purpose of First Kings

The reader of 1 Kings is expected to know the story told in 1 and 2 Samuel. Indeed, the books of Samuel and Kings were originally one "history." They were written in more or less the form in which we we have them, probably in the reign of Josiah, the last good king of Judah before the exile. Because 2 Kings includes an account of the Babylonian captivity itself, the final edition of the book cannot have been completed before the middle of the sixth century B.C.

Repeatedly, however, the writers "footnote" to sources that presumably come from the time of the events themselves: for example, the Book of the Acts of Solomon (1 Kings 11:41), the Book of the Annals of the Kings of Israel

1 KINGS

"Apostate Kings and Warning Prophets"

"The prophet . . . said: . . . Thus says the Lord, . . . 'I am about to tear the kingdom from the hand of Solomon . . . because he has forsaken me. . . . Yet to [David's] son I will give one tribe' " (11:29–36).

1 **Solomon Reigns in Wealth and Glory**	12 **Apostasy Brings Civil War and Splits the Nation**	17 **Elijah and Other Prophets Defy Ahab and Jezebel**
Solomon secures the throne, 1—2	Jeroboam leads a revolution, which splits the nation, 12	Through Elijah, God announces famine as punishment on Israel, 17
He displays great wisdom, 3 and reorganizes the nation, 4	But prophets now condemn Jeroboam as apostate, 13:1–14:20	The famine ends when Baal is defeated in a contest at Mount Carmel, 18
Solomon's greatest act: he builds and dedicates the Temple, 5—9	Egypt raids Judah, 14:21–31	But Elijah flees for his life; he encounters God at Mount Horeb, 19
He grows richer and richer, 10	Revolutions, assassinations, and wars devastate Israel, 15—16	When guided by prophets, Ahab wins a victory, 20
But Solomon sins, and encouraged by a prophet, Jeroboam plots secession, 11		But Jezebel's cruelty brings utter condemnation from Elijah, 21
		And Ahab dies, as foretold by a prophet, 22

Sources: Edited by the Deuteronomic historians centuries later, the book incorporates many sources, some contemporary with the events described, as interpreted from the point of view of the prophets.

Subject: Picking up where 2 Samuel leaves off, 1 Kings describes the reign of Solomon, its tragic aftermath, and the witness of prophets, especially Elijah.

Theme: Faithfulness to the one true God brings blessing, but apostasy, as the prophets warn, leads to disaster.

(14:19), and the Book of the Kings of Judah (14:29), each probably based on court records. In general, our writers tell their story in chronological sequence and tell about events that usually fit well with the findings of archaeological research. In this sense, 1 and 2 Kings are books of history.[22]

The modern reader, however, finds it a strange kind of history writing. We are told that Baasha reigned for twenty-four years and that he was a powerful king (15:27–16:7). But all we are told about those twenty-four years is how he got the throne by assassinating King Nadab and his family, how prophets denounced him, and how "he did what was evil in the sight of the Lord, walking in the way of Jeroboam and in the sin that he caused Israel to commit" (15:34). The reader who is curious about Baasha's deeds of power (16:5) is simply referred to "the Book of the Annals of the Kings of Israel" (16:5). We know from secular history that Omri was a powerful ruler, but his twelve years get only ten verses in biblical history (16:16–17, 21–28). It is their religious faithfulness and the interactions of the kings with God's prophets that really matter to the writers of 1 Kings. These writers have selected and shaped their account of events for a special purpose.

To understand that purpose, review Deuteronomy. Much of its message is summarized in these words, attributed to Moses at the time when people are about to enter the Promised Land:

> See, I am setting before you today a blessing and a curse: the blessing, if you obey the commandments of the Lord your God that I am commanding you today; and the curse, if you do not obey the commandments of the Lord your God, but turn from the way that I am commanding you today, to follow other gods that you have not known. (Deut. 11:26–28)

Israel is to worship *one* God, with worship centralized in one place:

> You shall bring everything that I command you to the place that the Lord your God will choose as a dwelling for his name: your burnt offerings and your sacrifices, your tithes and your donations. (Deut. 12:11)

Israel is authorized to anoint kings, but those kings are to be strictly limited in what they do. It is the Lord who is to be sovereign; God's laws are to be the laws of the land:

> [The king] must not acquire horses for himself. . . . He must not acquire many wives for himself, or else his heart will turn away; also silver and gold he must not acquire in great quantity for himself. . . . He shall have a copy of this law written for him in the presence of the levitical priests. It shall remain with him . . . so that he may learn to fear the Lord his God, diligently observing all the words of this law . . . neither exalting himself above other members of the community nor turning aside from the commandment, . . . so that he and his descendants may reign long over his kingdom in Israel. (Deut. 17:16–20)

A similar passage from 1 Samuel underlines this concern. It reports that when the people demanded a king, Samuel prophetically warned them:

> These will be the ways of the king who will reign over you: he will take your sons and appoint them to his chariots and to be his horsemen . . . and he will appoint for himself commanders of thousands and commanders of fifties, and some to plow his ground and to reap his harvest, and to make his implements of war. . . . He will take the best of your fields and vineyards . . . one-tenth of your grain . . . and give it to his officers and his courtiers . . . and the best of your cattle . . . one-tenth of your flocks, and you shall be his slaves. (1 Sam. 8:11–18)

Those words sound so much like a description of Solomon that many scholars suggest that his reign helped shape the memory of Samuel's warning.

One other passage from Deuteronomy is especially relevant. In God's name, Moses promised that there would always be a prophet to guide Israel:

> Anyone who does not heed the words that the prophet shall speak in my name, I myself will hold accountable. But any prophet who speaks in the name of other gods, or who presumes to speak in my name a word that I have not commanded the prophet to speak—that prophet shall die. (Deut. 18:19–20)

What the writers of 1 and 2 Kings have done is to tell stories from Israel's history that illustrate promises and warnings such as those here quoted. These books tell how blessings came with faithfulness but tragedy resulted when Israel turned to other gods. They also tell how kings obeyed or—more often—disobeyed Israel's true Lord, and how prophets stood for the law of the one true God against the tyranny of apostate monarchs.

Solomon Reigns in
Wealth and Glory (1 Kings 1—11)

The first half of 1 Kings is the story of the reign of Solomon, and ten of its eleven chapters focus on the glories of that golden age. A thousand years later, one of Solomon's descendants still spoke of "Solomon in all his glory" (Matt. 6:29). Though the writers of these chapters know that not everything was ideal during the early years of Solomon's reign, no negative criticism is made of Solomon until the account of Solomon's old age (1 Kings 11). The narrative seeks first to show how faithfulness to God can bring all the blessings Deuteronomy promised.

First, we are to understand that it was the Lord who, through a prophet, chose Solomon to be king. Adonijah was older and, like his father in his youth, a very handsome man. Moreover, Adonijah had the support of General Joab and the priest Zadok. But Nathan the prophet, with the help of the queen mother, Bathsheba, persuaded the dying David to endorse

Solomon. The prophet's choice won, albeit with the help of David's private army.

Solomon's ways of cementing his power seem cruel to us, but by ancient standards they were justified, even required. He executed General Joab, but this was to remove from the dynasty the blood guilt of Joab's murders of Abner and Amasa (2 Sam. 3:26–30; 20:8–10). Solomon exiled the priest Abiathar, but this was justified by an ancient curse concerning that priestly family (1 Sam. 2:27–36). And he executed his brother Adonijah but only after that brother had asked for Abishag, the newest beauty in their father's harem, thus making a veiled claim to a share in Solomon's kingdom. "So the kingdom was established in the hand of Solomon" (1 Kings 2:46). And we are told that "Solomon loved the Lord, walking in the statutes of his father David" (3:3).

The narrative of the glories of Solomon's reign is framed by two encounters with the Lord (3:5–15; 9:1–9). The first occurs as the young king— perhaps in his teens—sacrifices at the shrine at Gibeon. In a dream, God offers him his choice of gifts. Solomon asks for "an understanding mind . . . to discern between good and evil" (3:9). God is so pleased that he promises Solomon also things for which he did not ask, riches and honor and long life. But even this promise is conditional; Solomon must keep God's law (3:10–14).

God, we are told, does give Solomon wisdom. The story of how he settled the question of which woman was really the mother of a disputed child illustrates his shrewdness (3:16–28). "All Israel . . . perceived that the wisdom of God was in him" (3:28). "He composed three thousand proverbs, and his songs numbered a thousand and five" (4:32). He became internationally famous for his wisdom, and subsequently, most of Israel's wisdom books were referred to as works of Solomon.[23]

The narrative presents Solomon's vast bureaucracy and military organization as signs also of his wisdom. He replaces the old, awkward tribal system with twelve administrative districts, each yielding taxes for one month each year. His foreign policy brings a marriage alliance with Egypt in the south (3:1) and a trade alliance with Tyre in the north (5:12). The latter is a bargain in which Solomon cunningly gets the better of Hiram of Tyre (9:11–14).

As far as our writers are concerned, however, Solomon's greatest achievement was that he built the Temple. Long after it was destroyed, Jews gloried in the memory of this magnificent complex. Carefully dressed, costly stones and imported cedar were covered with gleaming gold. Carvings of cherubim, palm trees, and open flowers, overlaid with gold, decorated the Temple's doors and the entrance to its nave. Great winged sphinxes guarded the ark of the covenant. After a joyful parade, the king himself led the seven-petition dedicatory prayer. "The glory of the Lord filled the house" so completely that the priests were overwhelmed (8:11).

Yet even in the midst of this joyful moment, there is another *if* clause: "There shall never fail you a successor before me to sit on the throne of Israel, *if* only your children look to their way, to walk before me as you have walked before me" (8:25; italics added). First Kings is written not simply to remind its readers of the glories of the past; like Deuteronomy, it is a call to faithfulness in the future. And the story of Solomon's greatest accomplishment is closed with another appearance of God to the king. As at Gibeon (3:3–14), God makes Solomon conditional promises. This time, however, as the story of Solomon nears its tragic conclusion, the warnings are longer than the promises (9:1–9).

See what blessings flowed to Israel and its faithful king! Solomon's house was so grand that it took twice as long to build as did God's house (6:38–7:1). Remember how the gold was showered upon Solomon (10:14). Even that did not include his income from foreign trade and the tariff placed on merchants who had to go through Israel to get to and from Egypt and the empires to the north. His huge army, equipped with thousands of horses, guaranteed his power. In his court as remembered years later, "all King Solomon's drinking vessels were of gold, . . . none were of silver—it was not considered as anything in the days of Solomon" (10:21). If courtiers tired of drinking from those golden goblets, they could repair to the royal zoo and admire the royal peacocks and laugh at the royal apes (10:22). "The king made silver as common in Jerusalem as stones" (10:27). "Judah and Israel," the later writers could exult, "were as numerous as the sand by the sea" (4:20); the promise to Abraham had come true (Gen. 22:17). "They ate and drank and were happy" (1 Kings 4:20). The blessings promised in Deuteronomy had arrived.

This glory, however, was not the whole story. The narrative reserves its criticisms of Solomon until chapter 11, but it has already been full of hints of troubles to come. The great judges, Saul, and David all had gained their office as "the Spirit of the Lord came upon them." Solomon gained the throne instead through a palace plot, stimulated by the sexual impotence of David (1:1–4) and ensured by executions (2:5–6, 24–25). Not only did Solomon demand loyalty to his throne above loyalty to the ancient tribes, but his twelve administrative districts often ignored tribal boundaries. Only huge taxes could support his vast army and his thousand-woman harem (4:22–28). Solomon's treaty with Hiram of Tyre was purchased by his gift to that pagan king of twenty cities of what was supposed to be God's Promised Land (9:10–14). Later writers might speak of Solomon's reign as one of glory, but the common people of Israel had a different evaluation. To Solomon's son Rehoboam they summarized it: "Your father made our yoke heavy" (12:4).

Most hated, surely, was the forced labor. David had enslaved conquered peoples, and at first Solomon's work gangs were made up of foreigners (9:21–22). Eventually, however, he drafted every Israelite man to work in his labor battalions for one month out of every three (5:13–14). Already Samuel's worst prediction had come true: the king had made slaves of God's people.

Subsequently, prophets such as Amos would denounce the social injustice that characterized the reigns of most of Israel's kings. But the writers of 1 Kings point to the sin that lies behind that injustice: religious unfaithfulness. "King Solomon loved many foreign women" (11:1), cementing alliances by marrying foreign princesses. He even married a daughter of the pharaoh of Egypt, and the mother of Prince Rehoboam was from a pagan neighbor state. For these women Solomon built shrines to their gods, as indeed the custom of the times seemed to demand. As the writers of 1 Kings penned these words, the warnings of Deuteronomy must have resounded in their minds: "the curse, if you . . . follow other gods." With the death of Solomon, that curse began.

Apostasy Brings Civil War and Splits the Nation (1 Kings 12—16)

This book of the Bible is properly called 1 Kings, but remember that, in Hebrew Bibles, 1 Kings is one of those books called "the Former Prophets." From chapter 11 on, prophets are perhaps even more important to the narrative than are monarchs. First Kings names Nathan, Ahijah, Shemaiah, Elijah, Elisha, and Micaiah, and other unnamed prophets appear frequently in its pages. It is through them that God reveals the divine will.

It is a prophet who incites Jeroboam to rebellion. Ahijah was a prophet from Shiloh, the place where the ark had stood for centuries. He has no great love for Jerusalem and its Temple. At his urging (11:29–39), Jeroboam, who controlled the work gangs of Ephraim, the tribe best able to rival Judah, attempts a revolt. He fails, but supported by Egypt, he tries again when Solomon dies. When Solomon's son Rehoboam stupidly rejects the just demands of the people, civil war explodes. The union of the northern tribes to Judah was always fragile. Led by Jeroboam, the northern tribes secede. The nation was never united again. Only the intervention of another prophet, Shemaiah, prevented the whole thing from becoming a bloodbath (12:21–24). Even so, sporadic civil war continued for years.

Capable and hard-working, Jeroboam reigned for twenty-two years. He quickly recognized that if he was to destroy the political unity of Solomon's empire, he had to destroy its religious unity. And so he committed the sin for which the writers of 1 and 2 Kings cannot forgive him: in Dan in the north and Bethel in the south, he set up shrines with golden bull-calf images. No one needed now to go to Jerusalem to worship. Quite likely, these were not intended to be pagan shrines. The ark had included the "mercy seat," an empty throne on which the invisible God could be thought to sit. Perhaps in the same way, the archaeologists tell us, God could be imagined as enthroned on the back of each bull. But even if this was so, the distinction between worship using those bulls and idolatry was too subtle for many. The scripture sees these shrines as the first step toward the very polytheism against which Deuteronomy warned. Jeroboam was politically and militarily successful, but Ahijah and other prophets soon denounced him (13—14).

The situation, we are told, was little better in the Southern Kingdom, Judah. "They also built for themselves high places, pillars, and sacred poles. . . . There were also male temple prostitutes" (14:23). Shishak of Egypt, who had sheltered Jeroboam after his first rebellion failed, now availed himself of the opportunity presented by the civil war. He invaded Judah and carried off all the gold that Solomon had amassed (14:25–28). The archaeologists have unearthed remnants of a victory monument that Shishak erected at Meggido.[24]

The second half of 1 Kings and all of 2 Kings repeatedly give their story in a set formula. Each king of Israel (the ten northern tribes) is dated by reference to the king of Judah, and each king of Judah is dated by reference to the contemporaneous king of Israel. The king's mother is named, the length of the reign is given, a brief evaluation related to exclusive worship of the Lord is made, and the king's death is reported. Readers wanting more details are referred to the appropriate—now long lost—Book of Annals. Because the writers still think of the twelve tribes as one nation, the narrative alternates from Israel to Judah and back again.

The situation in Israel (the northern tribes) became chaotic. Jeroboam's son Nadab was assassinated after reigning for only two years. The assassin's son Elah was murdered after a two-year reign, and his assassin, Zimri, lasted on the throne only one week!

Now, however, an able general, Omri, seized—and held—the throne. He built his own capital, Samaria, easily defended on its high hill. A Moabite inscription admits that Omri "humbled Moab for many years,"[25] but the writers of 1 Kings have no interest in Omri's triumphs. What they are interested in is the contest between Omri's son and successor, Ahab, together with his queen, Jezebel, and that prototype of the prophets, Elijah.

Elijah and Other Prophets Defy Ahab and Jezebel (1 Kings 17—22)

Ahab had married Jezebel, the daughter of the king of Tyre (part of modern Lebanon). Perhaps determined to bring Israel "up" to the cultural standards of her more cosmopolitan home, Jezebel seems to have resolved to make the worship of Tyrian Baal the state religion of Israel. If they resisted, prophets of the Lord could be executed.

Suddenly, dramatically, there appears on the scene the prophet Elijah. With hair and beard uncut, wearing rough clothes, at home in the wilderness, Elijah is the embodiment of the Mosaic tradition, in contrast to the life of the ivory-inlaid palace of Ahab. In solemn, dogmatic pronouncement, the prophet declares that the Lord would attack Baal right in that fertility god's pretended stronghold, rain and sunshine: "As the Lord the God of Israel lives, before whom I stand, there shall be neither dew nor rain these years, except by my word" (17:1). Far more than any king, Elijah dominates the rest of 1 Kings (his successor, Elisha, dominates the first half of 2 Kings).

Having delivered this ultimatum, Elijah flees for his life, surviving by the kindness of a foreign woman. But eventually he returns to renew his challenge. Chapter 18 tells how Elijah leads the contest between Baal and the Lord. Two altars are erected, two sacrifices prepared, but no fire is kindled. The deity who can provide fire without human aid is to be worshiped. Baal's priests dance, chant, and pray to no avail, while Elijah mocks them. Then, pouring water over his sacrifice to make the contrast all the clearer, Elijah takes his turn. When Elijah prays, the Lord's lightning strikes. (One can imagine the impact of the retelling of this story among the captive Jews in pagan Babylon.)

Determined to stamp out Baal worship, Elijah presides over the execution of the prophets of Baal. But a threat from Jezebel forces him to flee for his life. Like Moses, he encounters God at Mount Sinai. There God addresses him not in powerful forces of nature, which Baal falsely has claimed as his own, but in "a sound of sheer silence" (19:12), that inner, quiet voice that commands him to go back to work.

For at least this one time, Ahab is guided by a prophet, and he wins a victory over Ben-hadad of Aram (1 Kings 20). But Jezebel now commits a crime so heinous that it brings the ultimate condemnation from Elijah. When a man named Naboth refuses to sell his vineyard, part of his ancestral inheritance, to the king, Jezebel murders him by arranging for his execution on trumped up charges. Forgetting the danger, Elijah solemnly pronounces the curse of horrible death on both Ahab and Jezebel (21:19, 23). Dogs shall lick Ahab's blood and devour Jezebel's corpse.

The last chapter of 1 Kings tells how the prophet's words concerning Ahab came true. This time, however, the focus is not on Elijah but on a prophet named Micaiah. As he prepares for war, Ahab has dozens of hired prophets willing to predict falsely that he will win the victory. Only one, whom he hates so much that he has put him in prison, tells Ahab the truth. But as that one, Micaiah, has predicted, Ahab dies in battle, and the horrible prophecy of Elijah and Micaiah comes true.

By the end of 1 Kings, the reader has been shown how the worst fears expressed in Deuteronomy have been fulfilled. Kings have amassed wealth for themselves. False prophets have arisen. The central shrine has been abandoned. Every commandment of God has been broken. The people have been oppressed. And most important, kings and people have tolerated, even turned to, the worship of other gods.

The tragic consequences of this apostasy, including the destruction of what had been meant to be the kingdom of God, are the subject of the next book, the sad end of the Deuteronomic history, 2 Kings.

2 KINGS

"Sargon . . . king of Assyria . . . conqueror of Samaria and the whole of the land of Israel"—so, among other titles, the emperor of Assyria styled himself. "I surrounded and captured the city of Samaria," he boasted, "27,290 of the people who dwelt in it I took away as prisoners." "I clashed with them in the power of the great gods, my lords, and counted as spoil 27,280 people, together with their chariots."[26] So ended forever the ten northern tribes, the nation then known as Israel.

The fate of Judah (the Southern Kingdom) at the hands of Babylon seemed almost as tragic. Around 587 B.C., Jerusalem fell and its people were carried into slavery in that foreign land.

Perhaps at only one point in their descriptions of these catastrophes do the biblical writers completely differ from the proud boasts of the pagan conquerors. They were sure that it was not because of Ashur, "the great Lord" of Assyria, or Marduk, god of Babylon, that Samaria and Jerusalem fell. It was "because the people of Israel had sinned against the Lord" (2 Kings 17:7).

The sad story of that fall is the subject of 2 Kings.

The Sources, Background, and Purpose of 2 Kings

Second Kings is simply a continuation of 1 Kings; originally, the two were one book (see the comments on 1 Kings in this *Guide* for fuller discussion of its sources and purpose). Probably at some time during the reign of good King Josiah (ca. 640–609 B.C.), prophets and Levites edited the records of the history of the kingdoms of Israel and Judah. They wrote to show how the promises and the warnings described in Deuteronomy had come true. Thus they called Judah to repentance and faithfulness.

Second Kings, however, does add one further purpose. While most of this history was composed before the fall of Jerusalem (587 or 586 B.C.), 2 Kings as we now have it describes that fall and ends with Judah captive in Babylon. What the final editors of this history wanted the exiles in Babylon to understand was that it was not the fault of the Lord God that Jerusalem fell; it was the fault of God's people. From Moses (as shown in Deuteronomy) on, God through the prophets had warned Israel of the fate to which their faithlessness might lead. Thus 2 Kings implied a kind of hope, even in exile, for nothing had defeated or ever could defeat the Lord.

Commentaries on the books of Kings tend to opposite emphases. Archae-

2 KINGS
The Story of the Decline and Fall of Israel and Judah

"This occurred because the people of Israel had sinned against the Lord" (17:7).

1 **Elisha Does Marvels and Instigates a Revolution in Israel**	10 **In Spite of Efforts at Reform, Judah Becomes a Vassal of Assyria, and Israel Falls**	18 **King Hezekiah Brings Reform and Judah Survives**	21 **Despite Josiah's Reforms, Judah Falls at Last to Babylon** 25
Elisha succeeds the prophet Elijah, 1—2	Jehu violently purges out baalism from Israel, 10	Assyria forces Judah to pay tribute, 18	King Manasseh's sins bring God's condemnation of Judah, 21
He guides Israel's king to victory, 3 Performs miracles, 4—8	Jehoiada the priest attempts reforms in Judah, 11—12	Guided by the prophet Isaiah, Hezekiah refuses to surrender, and God saves Jerusalem, 19	Josiah, however, instigates one last effort at reform, 22—23
Incites Jehu to bloody revolution, 9	But Syria oppresses Israel, 13	Isaiah, however, warns that someday Babylon will enslave Judah, 20	His successors are corrupt, and Babylon invades, dominates, and at last enslaves Judah, 24—25
	Under Jeroboam II, Israel has its last days of power, 14		
	Then falls into anarchy, 15		
	Judah becomes a vassal of Assyria, 16		
	Israel is carried off captive, 17		

Sources: Annals, some contemporary with the events described, edited by the Deuteronomic historians and completed after the Babylonian captivity

Subject: Taking up where 1 Kings left off, it tells the tragic story of the decline and fall of Israel and Judah in spite of prophetic calls for reform.

Purpose: To interpret theologically the tragic events of Israel's history and to call for faithfulness in the future

ology has shed much light on this period of world history, in which the conquests by Assyria and Babylon played so large a part. Some commentaries written in the middle of the twentieth century focus at length on relating the biblical account of events to what archaeologists have discovered.[27] Some commentaries written nearer the end of the century, however, virtually ignore the information gleaned from secular history of the period. First and Second Kings are theological treatises presented through "narrative," not history in the modern sense, these commentators emphasize. These interpreters focus almost exclusively on "the text itself," the canon; if the scripture does not mention something, it is really not relevant to what matters to the inspired writer and hence to the believer, they seem to suggest.[28] There is value in both approaches. Jews and Christians claimed to hear God speak through these books long before the archaeologists began to dig among the ruins of Israel or Iraq. Nevertheless, these books do not claim to be just "narrative." They profess to describe how God was at work in history. So committed to history are the authors that they carefully report historical events that do not fit into their favorite theological pattern of reward and punishment. For example, they report honestly that wicked king Manasseh had a long and relatively secure reign and that good kings Joash and Josiah met violent ends. Moreover, the authors assume that the readers of these books know something of Assyria and Babylon. Some knowledge of ancient history does help to clarify and give a sense of reality to the canon's narratives.

Elisha Does Marvels and Instigates a Revolution in Israel (2 Kings 1—9)

We call these the books of Kings, but their heroes are not monarchs; they are the prophets of the Lord. 1 Kings repeatedly tells its readers how God spoke through prophets Nathan, Ahijah, Micaiah, and especially Elijah. Roughly one-third of 2 Kings is devoted to stories of Elijah's successor, Elisha.

Prototype of the prophets, no other Old Testament spokesperson for God could ever quite equal Elijah. Someday he would come again, lesser prophets sang, to herald the long-awaited kingdom of God (Mal. 4:5). Only Elijah could appear with Moses at Jesus' transfiguration (Mark 9:4). Like Enoch, Elijah never died, we are told, but was transported to heaven in a whirlwind. Millions still sing in the African-American spiritual of that "sweet chariot" which came to carry him home (2 Kings 2:11).

Our writers, however, use many ways to emphasize that Elisha was a worthy successor to his "father" in the prophetic calling. Elijah had placed his mantle upon Elisha (1 Kings 19:19). Now, as Elijah's earthly life is about to end, Elisha can walk with Elijah. When Elijah departs, Elisha tears away his own clothes to don Elijah's mantle. Like a firstborn son, he claims from his spiritual father a double inheritance, not of gold but of the prophet's spirit.

Once the Spirit of God fell on judges and on Saul and David. Now prophets, rather than kings, are the charismatic ones.

Indeed, the stories that cluster about Elisha make him seem almost equal to his master. Like Moses and Joshua, Elijah had parted the waters (2 Kings 2:8). With Elijah's mantle, Elisha does so too (2:14). Through Elijah, God had multiplied a widow's meal and oil (1 Kings 17:12–14). Elisha duplicates the miracle for another widow (2 Kings 4:1–7). Elijah had brought a little boy back from the dead (1 Kings 17:17–24). Elisha does the same thing (2 Kings 4:11–37).

Later generations seem to have loved to tell tales of marvels attributed to Elisha. Through the power of God, they said, he could purify water, make an iron ax float, heal diseases, befuddle a whole army, and predict the end of a famine. The modern reader may be well advised to focus on the theological implications of these legends rather than to debate their historical accuracy. King Jehoshaphat of Judah is said to have sought the prophet's help as he prepared for battle with Moab. Guided by Elisha, Israel won the victory (3:1–27). Like Elijah, in his appearance Elisha may have seemed a strange figure from the wilderness days of Moses. Behind his back one might have dismissed the band of followers of Elisha as "mad" (9:11). But woe to any whom Elisha heard make fun of the prophet of the Lord (2:23–25)!

It fell to Elisha to complete two commissions said to have been given by God to Elijah. He instigated a revolution in Syria (8:13–15). More important for the biblical narrative, it was Elisha, working through one of his band of prophet disciples, who secretly anointed Jehu (9:6–7). Thus Elisha incited Jehu's rebellion, which wiped out the evil dynasty of Omri, Ahab, and Queen Jezebel. The last act recorded of that wicked queen is that she put on her eye shadow and fixed her hair; then she was thrown from a tower to her death (9:30–37). There dogs devoured her body. Through Elisha, Elijah's prophecy had come true (1 Kings 21:23).

In Spite of Efforts at Reform,
Judah Becomes a Vassal of Assyria,
and Israel Falls (2 Kings 10—17)

Formerly an officer in the Israelite cavalry, the new king Jehu undertook to call Israel back to the Lord by means of the sword. He had murdered all seventy of Ahab's male progeny (10:7). Now, with black humor, he invited all the priests of Baal to a "sacrifice." In the temple of Baal, eighty of his soldiers "sacrificed" those priests. The memory of this slaughter still horrified the prophet Hosea a century later (Hos. 1:4). The writers of 2 Kings, however, believed that his end justified his means. They tell us that God rewarded Jehu, promising to preserve his dynasty for four generations (10:30). Soon Israel did turn to other gods, but the threat from Jezebel's Baal of Tyre was ended.

Meanwhile a priest, Jehoiada, led a less violent reform in Judah. Jezebel's niece, Athaliah, had become the Jezebel of the Southern Kingdom. When Jehu, in his excess of zeal, assassinated her husband, she murdered all the princes—probably children of other wives in the royal harem—and claimed the throne for herself. The priest Jehoiada, however, managed to hide one little prince, Jehoash (or Joash). With a popular uprising and a military coup, Athaliah was assassinated and the child was placed on the throne (11:1–21). With the Lord's priest acting as the power behind the throne, the Temple was repaired—and, one suspects, so was Judah's religion. But alas, Joash was assassinated, after a long reign (12:20).

Only one ancient portrait of any of these kings has survived. It is of Jehu. It shows him bowing to the ground as he offers tribute to the king of Assyria.[29] Syria reduced Jehu's son King Jehoahaz to military impotence (13:7). Jehu's great-grandson Jeroboam II, however, gave Israel its last moments of secular glory, reconquering most of what had been Solomon's empire. The writers of 2 Kings faithfully recorded all these ups and downs, usually in a stereotypical formula. Their real concern, however, was with the faithfulness to the Lord of these kings. Not one king of the Northern Kingdom, Israel, meets with their approval. The reason is that they "did not depart from all the sins of Jeroboam son of Nebat, which he caused Israel to sin" (13:11). The great sin among these was that the kings preserved the bull-calf shrines at Dan and Bethel, which Jeroboam I had erected. Second Kings's writers saw this as a violation both of Deuteronomy's prohibition of idolatry and its insistence on one central shrine, now established at Jerusalem.

Meanwhile, in what we call Iraq, offstage, as it were, from the biblical drama but soon of crucial importance to its history, the empire of Assyria was rising to power. Assyrian emperor Assur-Nasir-Pal II boasted that as he conquered his enemies, "the heads of their warriors I cut off. . . . Some I impaled upon the pillar on stakes . . . many . . . I flayed, and spread their skins upon the walls; and I cut off the limbs of the officers."[30] It was to his son that Jehu was forced to pay tribute. Judah survived by buying off Assyria with huge gifts (16:5–9). But Israel could not survive. Chapter 15 describes brief reigns, terminated by assassinations. A few kings endured by paying tribute to Assyria. Tiglath-pileser III, called Pul, gave his account: "As for Menahem, terror overwhelmed him, like a bird, alone he fled and submitted to me. To his place I brought him back and . . . silver, colored woolen garments, linen garments . . . I received as tribute" (cf. 15:19).[31] The Assyrians began deporting Israelites as slaves (15:29). In the end, Pul laid siege to Samaria. For three years, the Israelites held out heroically. Starved at last into submission, they surrendered. In the year 721 B.C., the Assyrians carried them into slavery, never to return (17:6).

Now our book, which has raced through whole dynasties, suddenly slows to thoughtful analysis. Second Kings does not attribute Israel's fall to the power of the Assyrian army or to the political incompetence of Israel's kings. The explanation it gives is the point of the book: "This occurred because the people of Israel had sinned against the Lord their God" (17:7). "Yet the Lord warned Israel and Judah by every prophet . . . saying, 'Turn from your evil ways' " (17:13). By breaking every law in Deuteronomy and ignoring the warnings of the prophets, Israelites had brought tragedy on themselves.

King Hezekiah Brings Reform,
and Judah Survives (2 Kings 18—20)

Jerusalem survived. Historians point out that its relatively isolated position must have made it more secure. Be that as it may, 2 Kings says that Jerusalem endured because the Lord delivered it in answer to prayer.

In contrast to the corrupt kings of Israel in its last, decadent days, Hezekiah is presented as a model Deuteronomic king. "He did what was right in the sight of the Lord just as his ancestor David had done" (18:3). We are told that he even destroyed the "high places," the outlying shrines to the Lord, thus centralizing worship in the Temple.

True, Hezekiah bought off the Assyrians for a while by paying them heavy tribute. But the next king of Assyria, Sennacherib, invaded again. In a carving on his wall in Nineveh, that emperor depicted himself receiving tribute while his armies laid siege to Judah's second largest city, Lachish. Israelite bodies are impaled on high poles while soldiers in armor prepare to rush up their siege ramp or batter down Lachish's walls.[32] Sennacherib sent his "Rab-shakeh" to Jerusalem to spread the propaganda that even Judah's God now had delivered the city to Assyria.

At this point, the second great prophet of 2 Kings appears. Isaiah, whose work is preserved in one of the best-loved books of prophecy, serves as an adviser to good King Hezekiah. Dramatically, the narrative tells how Hezekiah spread the Assyrian ultimatum before the Lord in the Temple (19:14). Isaiah responded by assuring the king that God had heard his prayer and the city would be delivered. "That very night the angel of the Lord set out and struck down one hundred eighty-five thousand in the camp of the Assyrians; when morning dawned, they were all dead bodies" (19:35). There is a hint in the work of the Greek historian Heroditus that the instrument the angel used was the bubonic plague. Sennacherib's account boasts of his victories throughout Judah and says that he caged King Hezekiah in Jerusalem "like a bird," but evidently he did indeed fail to penetrate the holy city. Judah could never forget what seemed to them miraculous deliverance by the Lord.

The very next chapter, however, reminds the reader that God was not bound always to protect the city and the Temple. Now we begin to read that chilling word: "Babylon" (20:12). Hezekiah welcomes a diplomatic delegation from that faraway empire, only just beginning to recover its ancient power. Isaiah warns what the reader already knows: one day Babylon will enslave Judah.

Despite Josiah's Reforms, Judah Falls at Last to Babylon (2 Kings 21—25)

The story of the last days of the kingdom of Judah is dominated by the account of two kings. The evil Manasseh and the righteous Josiah are set in contrast.

No doubt feeling that Judah's only hope lay in knuckling under to Assyria in every way, Manasseh seems to have adopted Assyrian culture, including Assyrian religion. Idolatry, astrology, and even the sacrifice of his son as a burnt offering to a pagan god—everything Deuteronomy condemns, Manasseh did. We read that he "shed very much innocent blood" (21:16). No doubt these executions killed many leaders of the party of the prophets and others loyal to the Lord. Thus he managed to keep his throne for fifty-five years. But the authors of 2 Kings tell us that Manasseh's evil reign was the last straw. After that, God's mind was made up: God would "give them into the hand of their enemies" (21:14).

Two years after Manasseh's death, his son was assassinated, and after a period of anarchy, his eight-year-old grandson Josiah was placed on the throne. 2 Kings glories in the reforms instituted in Josiah's reign. He repaired and no doubt purified the Temple. The high priest produced a book of the law he had "found"; it was taken for authentication to Huldah the prophetess. (Incidentally, nothing is made of the fact that this authority is a woman. That there were women who could speak for God seems regarded as a matter of course.) That book was almost certainly Deuteronomy or major parts of it. Josiah then undertook to make the law of God the law of the land and to be precisely the kind of king for which Deuteronomy called.

His reforms came too late. Tragically, Josiah was killed in battle by the Egyptians. Caught between Egypt and Babylon, Josiah's inept successors vacillated, attempting to give allegiance first to one and then the other. Three months after he took office, Josiah's son Jehoahaz was deposed by the Egyptians. The next king switched alliances back and forth cleverly enough to last eleven years; his son Jehoiachin survived only three months. In 598 B.C., he was carried off to Babylon with the nobles and others who seemed likely to be most useful there. The Babylonians set upon the Jerusalem throne another son of Josiah, whom they called Zedekiah. A few years later, he attempted to rebel, and finally, in 587 or 586 B.C., the Babylonians utterly destroyed Jerusalem. They leveled its walls and its Temple, and carried thousands of its people into slavery. What had been meant to be the kingdom of God had apparently come to an end.

Some years later, a clerk in the royal warehouse in Nineveh, the capital of

Babylon, recording his dispensing of supplies, made this notation: So much food "for Ya'u kinu [Jehoiachin], king of the land of Yahudu [Judah]" and more for his five sons.[33] 2 Kings ends with a note that the captive king was, indeed, after years as a prisoner, finally treated as a palace guest. Perhaps that report hints that the story of the kingdom of God may not have come to an end after all.

3

THE WRITINGS

Hebrew Bibles have their books in a different order from that of the Christians' Old Testament.

Both begin with the *Torah,* the Law (or Instruction), Genesis through Deuteronomy. At an early date, Jews recognized these books as their authoritative guide. Then in Hebrew Bibles come the *Nebi'im,* the Prophets. These books Jews divide into "the Former Prophets" (Joshua through 2 Kings) and "the Latter Prophets" (Isaiah through Malachi).

Finally, in the Hebrew order, come the *Kethubim,* "the Writings"—in Greek, the *Hagiographa,* or Sacred Writings. These include all the other books, none of which quite fits into any other category. Jews placed them last because most of them were among the last to be written and also because several of them, such as the Song of Solomon, were among the last to be accepted as part of the canon, the list of books recognized as making up the authoritative scripture.

This *Guide,* intended primarily for Christian readers, follows the traditional Christian order for the books of the Old Testament. For Jews, Ruth is one of the Writings. Christians place Ruth after Judges because the events it describes occurred during the time of the judges. Recognizing that it is a late book and different from those of the other prophets, Jews placed Daniel among the Writings. Following the traditional Christian order, this *Guide* discusses Daniel as one of the Major (longer) Prophets.

The Writings form a miscellaneous collection of widely differing books. Some, such as the Psalms, are among the best-loved in all the Bible. Others, such as the Song of Solomon, seem relatively less important. All, however, have a place in the canons of both Jews and Christians.

To these works we turn now.

1 CHRONICLES

An Ideal King Plans for the Temple and for Worship by the People of God

"David said, . . . 'The house that is to be built for the Lord must be exceedingly magnificent, . . . I will therefore make preparation for it' " (22:5).

1 **The Genealogy of the People of God**	10 **David, an Ideal King, Reigns in Glory**	22 **David Prepares for the Building of the Temple**	29
The genealogy of all nations, 1	Saul dies for his sins, 10	David secures materials for the Temple and commissions Solomon to build it, 22	
The tribe of Judah, 2	All Israel hails David as king and commander in chief, 11—12	David instructs the Levites and other families of worship leaders in their duties, 23—26	
The descendants of David, 3	David attempts unsuccessfully to bring the ark to Jerusalem, 13	A long list of leaders who serve David, 27	
Others of the tribe of Judah, 4:1–23	He defeats the Philistines, 14	David makes a farewell address focused on the Temple, 28—29	
Other tribes, 4:24–5:26	Now, with the help of the Levites, he does bring the ark to Jerusalem, 15—16		
The Levites, 6	Nathan promises that God will build David's house, 17		
Other tribes, 7	David wins victories, 18—20		
The tribe of Benjamin, 8	An angel guides David in purchasing the site of the Temple, 21		
The families in Jerusalem, especially the worship leaders, 9			

Sources and Date: Probably a Levite, ca. 350 B.C., who copied, revised, and supplemented 2 Samuel
Subject: David's reign as the ideal king and, especially, how he prepared for the building of the Temple and the leadership of the worship by the people of God.
One Relationship to the New Testament: The idealization of David helps build the expectation of the coming messiah

1 CHRONICLES

For modern readers, the books of Chronicles present a puzzle: Why should the Bible include two often identical accounts of the history of the Hebrew kingdom? First and Second Chronicles recount the same story the reader has just read in 2 Samuel and 1 and 2 Kings. In fact, much of 1 and 2 Chronicles is copied word for word from those earlier books.

From time to time "the Chronicler," as the commentaries call the unknown author, does add new information. Those additions, however, provide puzzles of their own. Written six hundred years after David's death, the Chronicler's portrait of that king seems bigger than life. In 1 Chronicles, David's army has grown to an incredible 1,570,000 swordsmen (1 Chron. 21:5; contrast 2 Sam. 24:9). With no mention of any civil war, 1 Chronicles seems to say that from the moment of Saul's death, all Israel, north and south, hailed David as king (1 Chron. 11:1; contrast 2 Sam. 3:1). David is pictured as paying six hundred shekels of gold for the site of the Temple (1 Chron. 21:25), not the mere fifty of silver of the earlier account (2 Sam. 24:24). And in First Chronicles, David hardly sins at all.

Some commentators have a simple explanation for these and other apparent discrepancies between the two accounts of David's history. Robert H. Pfeiffer writes that the Chronicler had "no real concern with the actual facts" and "draws the details . . . from the storehouse of his vivid imagination."[1] Other commentators have been kinder in their evaluation of the Chronicler as a historian.[2] They note that many of details he added may well be factual.

All agree, however, that the Chronicler was a great theologian. "He is the last example of Israel's genius for retelling her sacred story in a way which applies its lessons creatively to the demands of a developing community," writes H.G.M. Williamson.[3] The great artists of the Italian Renaissance painted biblical sites as looking like Italian cities and clothed the crowds in costumes of the painters' own times. We do not criticize them as bad historians; we admire them for using this way of making the Bible's message relevant to their era. In the same fashion, the Chronicler painted a portrait of David and told the story of Judah's history in ways to make God's message most meaningful for his readers' situation.

To that situation and the message the Chronicler saw for it we turn now.

The Background and Purpose of 1 Chronicles

"Here we are, slaves to this day—slaves in the land that you gave to our ancestors" (Neh. 9:36). So Ezra cried to the Lord. A remnant of the Jews had returned from their exile in Babylon. Where once Solomon's magnificent Temple had stood, they had built a much less imposing house of worship.

Gone was the palace of David and Solomon—and their empire with it. Judah was now completely under Persian rule. In such a discouraging time as that, the Chronicler composed this version of Judah's history.

Some scholars date this work as late as 250 B.C., in the time when Judah was under the dominion of Egypt.[4] Jewish tradition attributes these books to Ezra in the late fifth century. Most tend to date the Chronicles to some period between these times, around 350 B.C.[5] In any case, Jerusalem's independence and its days of glory seemed gone forever. In this situation, the Chronicler wrote for many reasons. Four are highlighted here:

1. The Chronicler wanted to bring the sacred history of the books of Samuel and Kings up to date. First and Second Chronicles were originally one book, and while some scholars differ, most believe that the books of Ezra and Nehemiah also were compiled by the same author or editor. Thus what we have as four books constitute a unified history, which begins with Adam (1 Chron. 1:1) and goes through Nehemiah's rebuilding of Jerusalem and Ezra's restoration of the law.

2. The Chronicler wanted to present Judah as a worshiping community. Once prophets advised, even denounced, kings. They could call for a just social order. Once Deuteronomy could serve as a kind of constitution for a righteous government. But "slaves" of Persia had no chance to build a just society. What they could do was sing. What they could do was worship. They no longer had great armies, but they did have Levites, who helped lead worship. The Levites are mentioned twice in 1 and 2 Kings and twice in 1 and 2 Samuel but twenty-nine times in 1 and 2 Chronicles. Through the pages of the books of Chronicles, Ezra, and Nehemiah, priests and Levites lead parades, bands play, choirs sing, and congregations join in beautiful prayers and ceremonies. Perhaps the kingdom of God was never meant to be an earthly kingdom. They were to be a worshiping community; in a sense, a "church."

3. The Chronicler wanted to emphasize the connection between sin and disaster. The Lord was not to blame for Judah's defeat; Judah was. The Deuteronomic history had repeatedly presented the idea that sin leads to judgment. The Chronicler, going even further, seems to affirm that if there are catastrophes, the victims must have brought it on themselves by some sin.

4. But paradoxically, the Chronicler also wrote to give his readers hope. Because the Lord had not been defeated, the Lord could save them yet. He traces their ancestry to show that the Jews are the people whom God chose from the beginning. The glories of David's reign are recounted not simply out of nostalgia; the promised son of David may yet come, bringing that long-awaited kingdom of God. One of the ideas

the Chronicler adds from time to time to his sources is that sinners such as Rehoboam, Jehoshaphat, and even Manasseh could repent and find grace. So, too, the Chronicler believes, may Judah (2 Chron. 6:37–38).

Roughly half of 1 and 2 Chronicles comes from 2 Samuel and the books of Kings. The reader should review the comments on those books in this *Guide*. In what follows, we focus on those things that the Chronicler thought needed to be added or perhaps corrected in those earlier histories.

The Genealogy of the People of God (1 Chron. 1—9)

"Eber, Peleg, Reu"—not many sermons have been preached on that text (1 Chron. 1:25). Most modern readers and, indeed, many scholarly commentators move rather quickly over the first nine chapters of 1 Chronicles. They are almost entirely a list of names.

Those names, however, give us some insight into the writer's purpose. The Chronicler traces the history of the Jews all the way back to Adam. He can assume that his readers know the details from Genesis. But the genealogies place this little group of refugees from Babylon in the cosmic scheme of the Lord's worldwide plan.

Quickly, the lists narrow. Chapter 1 gives the genealogy of all nations. With chapter 2, the list focuses on the readers' own ancestors, the tribe of Judah. The next chapter narrows to the family of the Chronicler's hero, David. Most of the other tribes are dealt with quickly. The tribe of Benjamin, because it stayed loyal to the dynasty of David, gets all of chapter 8. But one other group does indeed merit a full genealogy: the Levites (1 Chronicles 6). Finally, the families who returned from exile to Jerusalem, and especially the priests, Levites, Temple servants, gatekeepers of the Temple, and Temple singers, are listed at length in chapter 9.

If the prophets are the real heroes of the books of Samuel and Kings, the Levites and their associates in the Temple services are the heroes of 1 and 2 Chronicles.

David, an Ideal King, Reigns in Glory (1 Chron. 10—21)

The rest of 1 Chronicles is a glorification of David. It is he who is the real builder of the Temple and the authority for the place assigned to the Levites. In 1 Chronicles, David is presented as the ideal and all-powerful ruler, devoid of the faults recorded in 2 Samuel. To him all the people give undivided loyalty. As such, he is the prototype of the coming messiah.

Though Saul is king for twenty-two chapters of 1 Samuel, he merits only fourteen verses in 1 Chronicles 10. Nothing is said of Saul's being "the Lord's anointed." But the Chronicler does add something not found in 1 Samuel.

Eager to show the connection between sin and trouble, the Chronicler devotes two of those fourteen verses to telling us his understanding of the reason for Saul's tragic death: "Saul died for his unfaithfulness" (10:13).

Now, as will be the case with the messiah, "all Israel gathered together to David" (11:1). First Chronicles gives no hint of the long civil war described in 1 Samuel. There is no tribal rivalry. The mighty warriors and "all the rest of Israel were of a single mind to make David king" (12:38). William Stinespring suggests that the banquet described after David's enthronement is a kind of symbol of the banquet expected when the messiah comes.[6]

First Chronicles reverses the order of the earlier history. In 2 Samuel, David built his palace first, then brought the ark to Jerusalem. In 1 Chronicles, attention to the ark comes first. Moreover, there is an implied explanation for why the first effort to transport that sacred covenant box failed. On the second try, David decreed that "no one but the Levites were to carry the ark" (1 Chron. 15:2). Under the supervision of these official worship leaders, a glorious procession succeeded in bearing the ark into the holy city. Incidentally, David was fully dressed for the occasion (15:27; contrast 2 Sam. 6:20). Most of chapter 16 is a beautiful psalm, which, our writer says, was sung by the choir as part of the ceremony. The Temple singers play so large a part in these books that it is widely proposed that the Chronicler himself may have been a Levite singer in the Second Temple.

Chapters 17 and 18 are copied from 2 Samuel. They contain the important dialogue between David and Nathan in which David expresses his desire to build a house for God and is told that God will build David's house instead (see the comments on 2 Samuel 7 in this *Guide*). Though he quotes these chapters, the Chronicler carefully omits the story of David's adultery with Bathsheba and his murder of Uriah. The Chronicler also leaves out any hint of the rape of Tamar, Absalom's rebellion, Sheba's rebellion, David's slaughter of Saul's sons, or other stories in 2 Samuel that would not fit the idealization of David's reign that he wishes to present.

From 2 Samuel, one unhappy narrative is recorded, the unfortunate census (1 Chronicles 21; cf. 2 Samuel 24). The Chronicler, however, makes two interesting changes. In the earlier history we are told that "the anger of *the Lord* was kindled against Israel, and he incited David against them, saying, 'Go, count the people of Israel and Judah' " (2 Sam. 24:1; italics added). But as the Chronicler tells the story, "*Satan* stood up against Israel, and incited David to count the people of Israel" (1 Chron. 21:1; italics added). The concept of Satan seems not to have developed in Israel until relatively late in Old Testament history. Perhaps the change reflects the influence of Persian thought, in which a supernatural evil being played a prominent role.

The other change that the Chronicler makes is the use of the story as a transition to the subject of greatest interest, how David prepared for the building of the Temple. In 2 Samuel, an angel is related to the plague that follows the census. In 1 Chronicles, that angel of the Lord—not just the human named Gad—guides David to buy the site for the Temple (1 Chron. 21:18; cf. 2 Sam. 24:18).

David Prepares for the Building of the Temple (1 Chron. 22—29)

For the Chronicler, the building of the Temple was the greatest accomplishment of Israel's greatest king. True, the Chronicler knew that the Temple was not actually completed during David's lifetime, and our writer has an explanation for that fact (1 Chron. 22:8). But in 1 Chronicles, it is really David, not Solomon, who gets the credit for the Temple. David is said to have raised for its construction an incredible 3,750 tons of gold and 33,500 tons of silver (22:14). David also provides much of the other materials and the labor force (22:14–15). He guides and encourages Solomon in the work, echoing God's words to Joshua at the death of Moses (22:13; 28:20; cf. Josh. 1:6–7, 9, 18). David is the Temple's architect (1 Chron. 28:11–12). And it is David who organizes the Levites and the various groups associated with them for their various worship tasks (23:1–3; 25:1; etc.).

Of special delight to the Chronicler is the list of those involved in the Temple services. The writer traces their ancestry and describes their duties. The Chronicler glories in the music that the Temple choir and the Temple orchestra provided (25:6–7). (Consistent tradition tells us that David indeed was a musician, and while many psalms obviously were written after David's death, that whole book of temple hymns became known as the Psalms of David.) Four chapters (23—26) are filled with lists of various kinds of worship leaders. Among the musicians are some also named in the headings of some of the psalms: the choirs of Korah (9:19; cf. Pss. 47, 48, etc.) and Asaph (1 Chron. 25:1: cf. Pss. 73, 76, etc.). Surely all this detail is given not simply as a matter of history but as authorization and guidance for the worship in the Temple of the Chronicler's day.

The climax and conclusion of 1 Chronicles is the farewell address attributed to David (28—29). Nothing is said of David's instructions about executing Joab and Shimei (1 Kings 2:5–9). Instead, David makes an eloquent speech to all the leaders of Israel. He reviews God's promises to his dynasty, gives the plans for the Temple to Solomon, encourages Solomon in the work, gathers yet more money for the Temple, and leads the assembly in worship.

"Blessed are you, O Lord. . . . Riches and honor come from you, and you rule over all. . . . We are as aliens and transients before you, as were all our ancestors. . . . All this abundance that we have provided for building you a house . . . comes from your hand. . . . I know, my God, that you search the heart, and take pleasure in uprightness. . . . Keep forever such purposes and thoughts in the hearts of your people. . . ."
. . . And all the assembly blessed the Lord. (1 Chron. 29:10–20)

That lovely prayer forms a fitting conclusion to this first part of the Chronicler's work.

2 CHRONICLES

Hebrew Bibles seem to have the work of the Chronicler backward. Four books—1 and 2 Chronicles, Ezra, and Nehemiah—form one continuous story. The events described in Chronicles occurred before those in Ezra and Nehemiah. Hebrew Bibles, however, put 1 and 2 Chronicles after Ezra and Nehemiah. Second Chronicles is the last book in the Jewish scripture.

Probably this is because the books of Chronicles were among the last books to be accepted into the canon. Ezra and Nehemiah obviously belonged; they alone told how the remnant returned from captivity and rebuilt Jerusalem. But the books of Chronicles seemed unnecessary duplication. The books of Samuel and Kings had already recounted that part of the sacred history.

Compare 2 Chronicles 10 with 1 Kings 12 and you will see the problem. They are almost the same, word for word. And so it is with many other passages. The story 2 Chronicles tells is essentially the same story already told in the books of Kings.

A close reading, however, shows that there are notable differences. The Chronicler, as scholars call the author of the books of Chronicles, retells these stories from the books of Kings in such a way as to emphasize certain ideas. Had the rabbis not decided at last to include these books, something of value would be missing from our Bibles. This chapter focuses simply on illustrating the special theological concerns expressed in 2 Chronicles.

The reader who wishes a quick review of the history that 2 Chronicles reports should read the sections on 1 and 2 Kings in this *Guide*. For the background and purpose of the books of Chronicles, read the brief discussion of that subject in the section on 1 Chronicles. Because the outline of the narrative in 2 Chronicles is essentially that of 1 and 2 Kings (pp. 101, 110), this *Guide* does not give another outline, as has been the pattern in the previous chapters. Instead, using the four special concerns of the Chronicler that were highlighted in the previous section (pp. 120–21), we simply point out some of the ways in which the writer expressed these emphases.

The Jews Are to Be a Holy Race, the Chosen People of God

Perhaps the best-loved and most-quoted verse in 2 Chronicles is a saying that it adds to those reported in 1 Kings. The writer has described at length the dedication of the temple under Solomon's leadership and has quoted from 1 Kings Solomon's long and beautiful prayer. Now, in turn, 2 Chronicles adds, God speaks: "If my people who are called by my name humble themselves, pray, seek my face, and turn from their wicked ways, then I will hear from heaven, and will forgive their sin and heal their land" (7:14).

The Lord calls Israel *my* people; they are called by God's name. When these words were written, the Jews were a poor and oppressed group of refugees, only a few generations removed from slavery in Babylon. But they were, of all the world, 2 Chronicles says, the people of cosmic destiny.

First Chronicles introduced that concept by tracing Judah's ancestry all the way back to Adam. Though that genealogy begins by tracing the ancestry of all the nations of the world, all the foreign lines are quickly dropped. The focus centers on Israel and then, particularly, on the one surviving group, the tribe of Judah.

The narrowing interest is clear from the very structure of 2 Chronicles. Its most obvious difference from the books of Kings is that as little as possible is said about the ten northern tribes, the nation called Israel. The great stories of the prophets Elijah and Elisha, which are so important in the books of Kings, do not appear in Chronicles. Only Judah was faithful to the dynasty of David and to the Temple at Jerusalem; therefore, only the story of Judah, of the Jews, really matters to the Chronicler.

It would not be fair to accuse the Chronicler of racism. Like 1 Kings, 2 Chronicles recalls how Jeroboam set up calf shrines in his Northern Kingdom. But 2 Chronicles adds to that earlier history that the Levites then left their homes and moved to Jerusalem. Lay people, too, "who had set their hearts to seek the Lord God of Israel came after them from all the tribes of Israel to Jerusalem to sacrifice to the Lord" (11:16; cf. 15:9). These northerners from many different tribes were welcomed. Chronicles's discrimination is religious rather than racial. But those two ways of drawing a line between peoples are not always clearly separate. Here are some examples of how 2 Chronicles exalts Judah and warns against association with other peoples.

> In the days of Abijam (or Abijah), 1 Kings 15:6 says only that there was war between north and south. Second Chronicles reports with apparent joy a story that Abijah, the second Judean king after the split, won a great military victory over those apostate Israelites of the north (13:17–20).
>
> The earlier history praises King Asa as a reformer (1 Kings 15:11), but the Chronicler reports that he is condemned for having made an alliance with a foreign nation (2 Chron. 16:7–10).
>
> Jehoshaphat's merchant ships sink because he made an alliance with sinful Israel (20:35–37).
>
> Ahaziah is assassinated because he visited with the king of the north (22:7–8).
>
> A "man of God" roundly rebukes King Amaziah because he hired mercenaries from Israel to serve in his army (25:6–11).
>
> King Ahaz lived to regret his solicitation of help from Assyria (28:16–21).

With apparent approval, the Chronicler also reports in the two books that bear their names the strict segregationist policies of Ezra and Nehemiah. They show how determined the leaders of postexilic Judaism were to maintain Jewish purity (Ezra 10:1–5; Neh. 13:1–3, 23–31). Judah was to be "holy"; the word means "separate." 2 Chronicles was written in part to say that the lessons of history show that any compromise with their pagan neighbors would bring catastrophe to those whom the Lord had claimed as uniquely "my people."

The Jews Are to Be a Worshiping Community, Led by Priests and Levites

"If my people who are called by my name humble themselves, pray, and seek my face," God said to Solomon, then all will be well (7:14). The little group of Jews had survived exile only to be dominated by Persia and then Greece. Only in some longed-for "day of the Lord" could they hope for military power. But what they could do now was to pray, to worship, and to do so in ways pleasing to the one true God. To this end, 2 Chronicles tells us, God gave them a Temple in which to worship and priests and Levites to lead joyful ceremonies as prescribed by the Lord. 2 Chronicles makes this point in many ways.

The book begins with nine chapters devoted to Solomon. Of these, seven are on Solomon's relationship to the Temple. First and Second Chronicles were originally one book. Its focus on the Temple begins with 1 Chronicles 21, continues through the rest of that book, and really dominates through 2 Chronicles 8. Thus some fifteen of Chronicles's sixty chapters—roughly one-fourth of the book—are in praise of the Temple. Less is said about the structure and furnishings of the Temple than in 1 Kings. The little Temple in the days of the Chronicler could never equal Solomon's. But more is said about the ceremonies. Solomon's magnificent prayer is quoted from 1 Kings. The Levitical singers and the Temple orchestra lead the praise (5:11–14). The liturgy was so effective, we are told, that fire from heaven came down to consume the sacrifice (7:1–3).

After the schism, the priests and Levites of the north flock to Jerusalem (11:13). Abijah warns Jeroboam that Judah will defeat Israel because "we have priests ministering to the Lord who are descendants of Aaron, and Levites for their service" (13:10). Sure enough, when "the priests blew the trumpets," a great victory was won (13:14–16).

A similar story is told in the account of Jehoshaphat's victory over the Moabites. In 2 Kings, the army succeeds after hearing the prophet Elisha (2 Kings 3:11–20). In 2 Chronicles, however, the prophet is not mentioned. Instead, Jehoshaphat's army is led to victory by the Levitical choir (2 Chron. 20:18–22).

In 2 Chronicles, it is the priests and Levites (23:4–11), not the hired foreign guards (2 Kings 11:4–16), who achieve the coup that rescues the child-prince Joash from murder by Queen Athaliah. It is priests and Levites who continue to provide his protection (2 Chron. 23:18–21).

The Chronicler glories in Hezekiah's religious reforms, devoting three chapters to them. Second Chronicles, adding to the story in 2 Kings 18, tells how the Temple orchestra, the choir, and especially the Levites guided this revival of true religion (29:26–30) and how worship under their leadership was carefully organized (2 Chron. 31).

Good king Josiah's passover gets three verses in 2 Kings (23:21–23) but nineteen in 2 Chronicles (35:1–19). The place of priests, Levites, and other official leaders of worship is stressed again.

Indeed, what was originally probably the last paragraph of 2 Chronicles shows its ties to Leviticus, a book also full of guidance for worship. That book had so stressed the Sabbath that it commanded that, just as people were to rest one day in seven, so the land was to be given rest one year in seven (Lev. 25:1–7; 26:27–39). That law had not been kept. But now, our writer tells us, the Babylonian captivity lasted seventy years, from the destruction of the First Temple to the building of the Second. Why? So that the land might make up for its Sabbaths, so often missed in the past (2 Chron. 36:21).

In short, in every way one can think of, this writer calls on Judah to be a worshiping fellowship. The Jews have never again built an empire like that of David and Solomon, but the writer's hopes have been fulfilled. In part due to 2 Chronicles, through the centuries the Jews have indeed remained a distinct community, praying and singing their ancient, holy songs.

Jews Must Remember That Sin Brings Punishment

"If my people who are called by my name . . . turn from their wicked ways"—God's blessings promised through Solomon were conditioned on right living. Even more than is the case with the Deuteronomic history (Joshua through 2 Kings), 2 Chronicles stresses the connection between "wicked ways" and disaster. Here are some examples.

On the whole, Asa is regarded in the book as a good king. But when he imprisoned a prophet who denounced his alliance with the king of Aram, he was severely diseased in his feet. He was never cured, we are told, because he turned to physicians for healing rather than to the Lord (16:1–13). Elijah, hero of 1 Kings, appears only once in 2 Chronicles. He sends a letter warning King Jehoram that his sin will bring disease. Sure enough, it does (21:11–20).

Indeed, where 1 or 2 Kings reports some catastrophe, 2 Chronicles frequently adds that some sin was its cause. Why did Jehoshaphat's fleet sink (1 Kings 22:44, 48–49)? Jehoshaphat had made an alliance with apostate Israel (2 Chron. 20:35–37). Why was Joash assassinated (2 Kings 12:20)? He had ordered a political enemy to be executed (2 Chron. 24:20–26). Why was

Amaziah defeated by Israel (2 Kings 14:12–14)? He had imported idols from Seir (2 Chron. 25:14, 27). Why did Uzziah get leprosy (2 Kings 15:5)? He had usurped the prerogatives of the priests, himself offering incense in the Temple (2 Chron. 26:16–19). Why did good King Josiah die in battle (2 Kings 23:29)? "He did not listen to the words of Neco from the mouth of God" (2 Chron. 35:22).

Conversely, evil King Manasseh seems in 2 Kings to have had a long and prosperous reign in spite of his terrible sins (2 Kings 21:1–2). The Chronicler, therefore, tells us that Manasseh was indeed punished. He was kidnapped with hooks and manacles and carried to Assyria until he repented (2 Chron. 33:10–13).

More examples could be given. It may be that some thinkers came to believe that the Chronicler and others had made the link between sin and trouble too automatic. The books of Job and Ecclesiastes were to challenge the view that trouble is always the result of sin.

In the end, Chronicles explains Judah's tragic story with a summary of its philosophy of history:

> All the leading priests and the people also were exceedingly unfaithful . . . and they polluted the house of the Lord. . . . The Lord, the God of their ancestors, sent persistently to them by his messengers, because he had compassion on his people and on his dwelling place; but they kept mocking the messengers of God, despising his words, and scoffing at his prophets, until the wrath of the Lord against his people became so great that there was no remedy. (2 Chron. 36:14–16)

And so Jerusalem fell.

When God's People Truly Repent, There Is Hope of Forgiveness and Salvation

"If my people who are called by my name humble themselves, pray, seek my face, and turn from their wicked ways, then I will hear from heaven, and will forgive their sin and heal their land" (7:14). So, the Chronicler reports, the Lord had promised Solomon. Though it is full of solemn warnings, 2 Chronicles is also a book of hope.

Rehoboam was an evil king. His sins brought the invasion by Shishak of Egypt. But when confronted with that judgment, as interpreted by the prophet Shemaiah, "the officers of Israel and the king humbled themselves and said, 'The Lord is in the right' " (12:6). And God spared Rehoboam.

King Jehoshaphat is condemned in 2 Chronicles for allying himself with Israel. But when he "bowed down with his face to the ground . . . before the Lord, worshiping the Lord" (20:18), and summoned his people to faith, the choir led the way to victory.

Even King Manasseh, the worst of all Judah's kings, repented. Our writer tells us that Manasseh was kidnapped and taken to Babylon. There, "while he was in distress he entreated the favor of the Lord his God and humbled himself greatly before the God of his ancestors. He prayed to him." And even with evil Manasseh, "God received his entreaty, heard his plea, and restored him again to Jerusalem and to his kingdom. Then Manasseh knew that the Lord indeed was God" (33:12–13).[7] Surely the Chronicler told this story of forgiveness as good news to those first discouraged readers.

After all, had not Solomon's prayer been for restoration? "If they sin against you . . . so that they are carried away captive to a land far or near; then if they come to their senses . . . and repent . . . with all their heart . . . then hear from heaven . . . and forgive your people" (6:36–39).

Indeed, as the writer knows, that is exactly what had happened. The appendix (36:22–23) describes how the forgiven Jews were indeed restored to their homeland. But that appendix properly belongs to the next book, Ezra. With that book, the Chronicler's narrative continues.

EZRA AND NEHEMIAH

I am Cyrus, king of the world . . . king of the four rims (of the earth). . . . All the kings of the entire world . . . kissed my feet. . . . I returned to (these) sacred cities on the other side of the Tigris, the sanctuaries of which have been in ruins for a long time. . . . I (also) gathered all their (former) inhabitants and returned (to them) their habitations. Furthermore, I resettled upon the command of Marduk, the great lord, all the gods of Sumer and Akkad whom Nabonidus had brought into Babylon   May all the gods whom I have resettled in their sacred cites ask daily Bel and Nebo for a long life for me.[8]

So Cyrus the Great, emperor of Persia, conqueror of Babylon, boasted. But the author of Ezra and Nehemiah knew the truth. It was not Marduk of Babylon who gave Cyrus the victory; nor was it Bel who moved him to let the displaced persons whom Babylon had enslaved go home. Jeremiah had prophesied it; so had Isaiah. All that pagan Cyrus did was for just one purpose: that there might be fulfilled the word of the one true God, the Lord, the God of Israel.

And so, repeating the ending of 2 Chronicles, the book of Ezra begins with a decree of Cyrus (Ezra 1:1–4). The Jews' forced exile was over. At last, in the year 538 B.C., they could go home.

In the old Hebrew Bibles, Ezra and Nehemiah were one book, and they are treated as one book in this *Guide*. Quite possibly the same author who edited 1 and 2 Chronicles now completes the story. First we are told how, led by Governor Zerubbabel and encouraged by the prophets Haggai and Zechariah, the little group rebuilt the Temple. Then we are told how Ezra, priest and scribe, returned to help make them a community of covenant and law. And, third, we learn how Nehemiah led them in rebuilding the fortress

EZRA AND NEHEMIAH
The Story of the Material and Religious Rebuilding of Jerusalem

"Ezra . . . set his heart to study the law of the Lord, and to do it, and to teach the statutes and ordinances in Israel" (Ezra 7:10).

"So we [the people led by Nehemiah] rebuilt the wall, . . . for the people had a mind to work" (Neh. 4:6).

Ezra		Nehemiah	
1	**7** **10**	**1**	**8** **13**
The First Exiles Return from Babylon and Rebuild the Jerusalem Temple	**Later, Ezra Brings More Exiles Back and Begins Reforms**	**Nehemiah Supervises the Rebuilding of the Wall**	**Climax: Ezra Reads the Law, the Covenant Is Renewed, the People Celebrate**
Freed by Cyrus, a remnant returns, 1—2	Ezra secures permission to return, 7	Nehemiah returns to Jerusalem and plans to rebuild it, 1—2	Ezra leads great ceremonies and programs of covenant renewal, 8—10
They begin to rebuild the Temple, 3	He brings a group, including worship leaders, back from Persia, 8	In spite of opposition, the people begin to build the wall, 3—4	A census is taken, and families are selected to live within the walled city, 11:1—12:26
Opponents harass and delay their building, 4—5	Ezra now begins extensive religious reforms, 9—10	Nehemiah institutes economic reforms, 5	Joyful worship celebrates the completion of the wall, 12:27—13:3
But at last, they finish building the Temple, 6		They complete the walls, 6	Appendix: Measures to preserve purity of worship and people, 13:4—31
		(A census list), 7	

Subject: Taking up where 2 Chronicles leaves off, Ezra–Nehemiah tells how a remnant returned and rebuilt Jerusalem.

Editor and Sources: Originally one book, Ezra–Nehemiah includes firsthand accounts by those two authors, letters, court decrees, and census reports, edited perhaps around 350 B.C. by someone like the author of the Chronicles.

Themes: The importance of the holy race, the holy city, worship in the holy place led by holy leaders, and God's holy law, to be carefully preserved

wall of Jerusalem. The climax of the book is a joyful celebration. God has rescued the holy people!

Ezra

The First Exiles Return from Babylon
and Rebuild the Jerusalem Temple (Ezra 1—6)

It is described as a new exodus. Like the pharaoh of old, Cyrus authorized God's people to leave their slavery so that they might worship the Lord. As the ancient Egyptians had supplied the Israelites, so their Babylonian neighbors assisted the Jews. As under Moses they had provided sacred vessels for the tabernacle, so now they journeyed across the desert with gold and silver basins and bowls for the Temple they would build. And as the book of Numbers recorded the names of the families in that first exodus, so, proudly, the descendants of those later pilgrim fathers and mothers preserved a record of their genealogies (2:1–67).

Even the genealogy gives a foretaste of what will be the emphasis of the book. Lay families are listed, but the special notice is of the priests (2:36–39), the Levites (2:40–42), and the Temple servants (2:43–58). And as in 1 and 2 Chronicles, the sacred choir is especially important (2:65). The first act of these refugees when they return is to make gifts toward someday rebuilding the house of God. Their next is to begin by building the altar (3:1–3). And having just crossed the wilderness, as did Israel of old, they celebrate with the Feast of Tabernacles (or Feast of Booths), memorial to the tent-dwelling wilderness wanderers of Moses' exodus. Our authors tell us little about their economic and political arrangements. They are concerned to emphasize one thing: the Jews were to be a *worshiping* community.

That goal was not to be easily accomplished.

At every step, the returned Jews were harassed and hindered by the "people of the land" (the Samaritans). Two hundred years before, when the Assyrians had deported the ten northern tribes, they had begun importing people from other races (2 Kings 17:24–41). A superstitious mixture, when some of them had been killed by lions they had sent for a priest in hopes of placating "the god of the land." At the same time, however, they had continued in idolatry. Israelites who had avoided being taken into captivity intermarried with them. These halfway Israelites now offered to join in the building of the new Temple. But on one thing the Jewish leader Zerubbabel and the later leaders Ezra and Nehemiah were in agreement: there must be no compromise with paganism or with pagans. The poor little group of Jews, though just returned from slavery, flatly refused the offer of help from their wealthier neighbors.

That rejection brought disastrous results. With the destruction of Jerusalem, these Samaritans had become the dominant people in the area, working closely with the Persian government. Bribing the right officials, the Samaritans soon brought such government pressure on the Jews that they had to quit building (4:4–5).

One of the confusing things about the book of Ezra is that at this point (4:6–23) it reports a similar plot by the Jews' adversaries, which occurred nearly a century later. On that later occasion, "the people of the land" (the Samaritan faction) attempted to stop the rebuilding of the fortress wall around Jerusalem. The editor of Ezra is so interested in historical accuracy that we are given transcripts of the actual correspondence involved, just as the book opened with the actual decree by Cyrus. But this compiler is obviously not as concerned about putting things in chronological order as in making a theological point. That point is that at every stage of rebuilding, the enemies of the Jews attempted to stop them, but nothing could long frustrate the intention of the Jews' God.

Due to Samaritan opposition, however, eighteen years after the exiles had returned, they still had not rebuilt the Temple. Now two prophets, Haggai and Zechariah, began campaigning for the work to begin again (5:1; 6:14). "Is it a time for you yourselves to live in your paneled houses, while this house lies in ruins?" Haggai demanded (Hag. 1:4). Centuries later, the Jews still so honored the words of Haggai and Zechariah that they preserved them as books of their scripture. Once again, the compilers of the book of Ezra have given us transcripts of correspondence. This time research had discovered a decree of Cyrus that had authorized the construction of the Temple (Ezra 6:1–12). With government sanction, in 520 B.C. the work began again (6:13–15).

The prophet Zechariah promised that even Gentiles would want to join in building this house of worship (Zech. 6:15). But to some Jews with less prophetic eyes, their lonely labor seemed to be producing only a disappointing little shrine. We are told that when its foundations had been laid, some who could remember Solomon's magnificent edifice broke down and cried (Ezra 3:12). But unpretentious as it was, in about the year 516 B.C., approximately seventy years after the Babylonians had destroyed the First Temple, the new Temple was completed.

In Ezra and Nehemiah, every great act begins and ends with prayer and worship. Ezra tells us that, led by priests and Levites, the returned refugees sacrificed one hundred bulls, two hundred rams, four hundred lambs, and twelve goats (6:17). And a few days later, they celebrated the Passover. "With joy they celebrated the festival of unleavened bread seven days; for the Lord had made them joyful" (6:22).

Later, Ezra Brings More Exiles Back and Begins Reforms (Ezra 7—10)

With the simple phrase "after this" (7:1), our writers skip some eighty years. Emperors and governors came and went, but they are not the concern of this book. Ezra and Nehemiah are a history of the reconstruction of God's people, and the next act of that restoration is the spiritual rebuilding led by Ezra himself.

Exactly how long "after this" Ezra's reforms took place is a subject of scholarly debate. Our writers carefully note that Ezra's ministry began "in the seventh year of King Artaxerxes" of Persia (7:7). The trouble is that there were two kings by that name. Traditionally, Ezra is dated as arriving from Babylon in about 458 B.C. Ezra's great reading of the law and leadership in the ceremonies of covenant renewal (Neh. 8—10) are described after we are told about the rebuilding of Jerusalem's fortress wall in 444 B.C. (Neh. 7). Unable to believe that Ezra would have waited thirteen years before he began his reform program, many scholars have dated Ezra's return as 398 B.C., during the reign of Artaxerxes II.[9] Others solve the problem by proposing that a copyist made an error—easily done with Hebrew numbers—and that Ezra came in the thirty-seventh, not the seventh, year of Artaxerxes I (428 B.C.).[10] The last two proposals place the work of Nehemiah before that of Ezra. We are told about Ezra's work first, it is said, because to our writers, the religious reforms he led were even more important than the political and economic achievements brought about by Nehemiah's work of reconstruction.

Ezra's work was so influential that some have called him "the father of modern Judaism." Always interested in genealogy, our writers first introduce him by tracing his priestly ancestry all the way back to the first Israelite priest, Moses' brother Aaron (Ezra 7:1–5). More important, they then tell us that "he was a scribe skilled in the law of Moses" (7:6). Writers from before the exile rarely speak of "scribes." But to the editors of 1 and 2 Chronicles, Ezra, and Nehemiah, a scribe was an important person. In those days, of course, there were no printing presses or word processors. Many people were illiterate. The ability to copy the scriptures clearly and quickly was highly valued. Scribes also became interpreters and teachers of the law. The apocryphal book 2 Esdras reports that all copies of the Hebrew scriptures had been destroyed by the Babylonian conquerors. Guided by God, Ezra quoted them all, 2 Esdras claims, while his assistants took dictation.[11] Most readers today regard that story as a dubious legend. Behind it, however, may well be some historical memory. It is quite possible that the sacred books of the Jews were assembled under the guidance of Ezra. Edited by Ezra, perhaps, they began to take something of the form of our Old Testament. Armed with the book of the law, Ezra came to the Jerusalem Jews with a mission, "for Ezra had set his heart to study the law of the Lord, and to do it, and to teach the statutes and ordinances in Israel" (7:10). With Ezra, Judaism became a religion of the law and the Jews the people of the book.

Ezra's commission from the emperor of Persia, of which our editors have given us a copy (7:21–26), suggests that Ezra had achieved a high rank. Perhaps today he might be called "secretary for Jewish affairs for the empire." The emperor gives him a double charge. With initial financing from the government, he is to raise additional money for the support of the Temple. The Temple clergy are freed from having to pay taxes. And Ezra is to "appoint magistrates and judges . . . who know the laws of your God; and you shall teach those who do not know them" (7:25). Evidently, Artaxerxes believed that better law and order might help that part of his domain. As always in these books, Ezra's project is begun with prayer (7:27–28).

Typically, Ezra prays to "the God of our ancestors" (7:27). And typically, his prayer is followed by a list of names (8:1–14). Americans who like to boast that their ancestors came over on the Mayflower will understand the pride with which the descendants of these people preserved the list. "My ancestors came back to Jerusalem with Ezra," they could boast. And again typically, special attention is given to making sure that there are enough Levites. The leader of these clergy whom Ezra recruits is a man who can trace his ancestry all the way back to Levi and to Jacob himself (8:18). And still in the pattern of 1 and 2 Chronicles and typical of the book of Ezra, we are told that as they cross the border, they fast and pray (8:21). Words and phrases in the narrative echo those used of Moses' exodus from Egypt. Arriving safely with their gift for the Temple, they offer sacrifices for purification from sin (8:35).

Now Ezra, the new Moses, takes charge.

Whatever else Judaism is, it is a religion of two things. It is a religion of the Mosaic law. And it is a religion of a holy people. That people is to be separate and pure. Therefore one point of all those repeated lists of ancestors, which form so large a part of Ezra and Nehemiah, becomes clear: the holy race must not be mixed with pagan peoples. It was Solomon's foreign wives, Ahab's marriage to pagan Jezebel, and especially Israel's all-too-ready assimilation with the Canaanites among whom they settled that had brought Israel's downfall. That must never happen again. Therefore Ezra—after a long prayer of confession of his people's sin (9:5–15)—leads the people in a great act of repentance. Under his guidance, they agree to divorce all their foreign wives and to put away all their children who were born to those wives (10:3). A committee is chosen to enforce the agreement. Now yet another list is given, a census of those who, to their shame, had married foreign women but who now had "sent them away with their children" (10:44). Not one word is said of provision being made for those wives or those half-breed babies. No matter if some other people were hurt; the holy people must be kept holy.

While one understands Ezra's goal, many who base their ethic on Jesus' love for all races—even Samaritans (Luke 10:29–37)—regard Ezra's work at this point as falling short of a full understanding of God's will. In the Old Testament itself, such books as Ruth and Jonah may have been written in part to call the Jews to a less narrow outlook. Ezra's brand of Judaism seems legalistic, sexist, and racist. Both the teachings of Jesus in the New Testament and the book of Ruth in the Old Testament present a very different ethic. In Ezra's defense, however, one might argue that without his strictness, the Jewish religion would not have survived and the greatest Jew, Jesus, could not have been born.

Nehemiah

As noted above, scholars debate which came first chronologically, Ezra or Nehemiah. Our editors, however, are clear about the order of theological importance. First, under Sheshbazzar, the Temple was rebuilt (Ezra 1—6). Then, under Ezra, the community was purified (Ezra 7—10). But now another act, third but still important, was accomplished, the building of a wall around Jerusalem. The leader in that project was Nehemiah.

Nehemiah Supervises the Rebuilding of the Wall (Neh. 1—7)

Concerned to report everything accurately, our editors give us an extract from Nehemiah's own first-person account of his achievement.

Long before, when the captivity began, Jeremiah had urged the exiles to work for the welfare of whatever nation they found themselves in. To this day, millions of Jews have followed his command. And so we read of Jews such as Ezra, Nehemiah, and Daniel whose good work wins for them high positions even though they are of a captured people. Nehemiah tells us, "I was cupbearer to the king" (Neh. 1:11). Though it may sound to a modern reader like a menial job, this was actually a position of honor and trust. The cupbearer guarded the king's food against political rivals who might plot to poison him, and he stood beside the king at every meal. And so when Hanani, Nehemiah's brother, brings news that Jerusalem still lies in ruins, the emperor himself sees and is concerned by the grief of his trusted aide.

As always, our writers tell us that Nehemiah makes no move in this matter until he has fasted and prayed (1:4–11). His spending three months in prayer is understandable. The prohibition against rebuilding Jerusalem had been decreed by the emperor himself (Ezra 4:17–22). Artaxerxes had reason to fear any effort toward independence in his empire. He had moved decisively to put down the reconstruction of always-rebellious Jerusalem. But strengthened by his prayers to God, Nehemiah makes his petition to the king. And his request is granted. Armed with a royal decree, he heads for Jerusalem.

The story of how, under Nehemiah, the Jews rebuilt in spite of opposition is skillfully told. Apparently, Sanballat has been governor of the area and sees Nehemiah's actions as a threat to his authority. Even though Nehemiah gives the officials the king's letter, at every step of the way Sanballat and his allies harass the project. During his first three days in Jerusalem, Nehemiah plans in secret. One night, he makes a quiet tour of inspection (2:11–16). Now ready, he publicly announces his design. In spite of Sanballat's ridicule, the people volunteer enthusiastically for the work.

Once again, we have a list of names (3:1–32). Generations later, a Jew could point to some section of that fortress wall and boast, "My family built that part!" Women labored in the building alongside men (3:12). Sarcastic Tobiah scoffed, "That stone wall they are building—any fox going up on it would break it down!" (4:3). Nehemiah answered him with a curse (4:4–5).

Perhaps the most quoted verse in the book of Nehemiah summarizes his success to this point: "So we rebuilt the wall, and all the wall was joined together to half its height; for the people had a mind to work" (4:6).

Enraged, Sanballat and Tobiah now were ready to resort to force. Nehemiah simply armed his workers and carried on.

Chapter 5 seems an interruption in the story, and some scholars suggest that it recalls a later incident. It describes how Governor Nehemiah worked for economic justice among the poverty-stricken people.

Realizing that their efforts to stop the construction were failing, Sanballat and his allies now asked for a conference (Neh. 6). "I am doing a great work and I cannot come down," Nehemiah replied. In the end, even the enemies of the Jews came to realize why the work could not be stopped: "They perceived that this work had been accomplished with the help of our God" (6:16).

"So the wall was finished . . . in fifty-two days" (6:15).

Hanani, Nehemiah's brother who had first alerted him to Jerusalem's need, was appointed governor. Defense preparations were made. And the book repeats a long list of ancestors, the original returnees (7:5–73; cf. Ezra 2:1–70). As is usual in the Chronicles, Ezra, and Nehemiah, special attention is given the leaders of worship: the priests, Levites, gatekeepers, singers, and Temple servants (7:73). Jerusalem is to be a holy city.

Climax: Ezra Reads the Law,
the Covenant Is Renewed,
the People Celebrate (Neh. 8—13)

We arrive now at the events to which 1 and 2 Chronicles, Ezra, and Nehemiah have been pointing. The first of these is that Ezra reads to the people the book of the law of God.

Some scholars suggest that, chronologically, this act must have occurred soon after Ezra's return. The events in Nehemiah 8 may have originally followed those in Ezra 8. The reading of the law now recounted may have produced the reforms described in Ezra 9. Whatever the actual order of events, our editors have been building their story to a climax, and that climax begins with the proclamation of God's law. All morning long, Ezra read from the book. Women as well as men listened to its instruction. "Amen, Amen," they shouted (8:6). Assistants explained the law, perhaps by translating it from the ancient Hebrew into the Aramaic that had become the language familiar to most Jews. If some wept because of their sins, pointed out in the book, the Levites reassured them. And so they heard what now may be called "the scripture" with "great rejoicing."

Some eighty years before, the first Jews to escape from slavery in Babylon had recalled the deliverance from Egypt by celebrating the Feast of Tabernacles. Now, no longer homeless, the heirs of that new exodus celebrate that feast again (8:13–18). And every day of the celebration, Ezra reads from the book, the Torah, the Law or Instruction (8:18).

Now, chronologically, came the previously described expulsion of those foreign wives and children (9:2; cf. Ezra 9—10). We are given a long prayer-sermon. It summarizes the whole story of the Hebrew scripture, from Abraham to this great day. Majestically, it pictures the power and the patience of the Lord. Humbly, it confesses Israel's sin. It pleads for divine help. And it becomes a ceremony of covenant renewal (Neh. 9:38). Like the names of the signers of the Declaration of Independence, the names of those who signed the covenant document for the whole people are preserved in honor (10:1–27). Women and men, led by the clergy, voice the covenant oath. One more list of names is given, a census of pure-blooded Jews. One family in ten from among them will be allowed to live within the walled city (11:1–36). As always, our writers give special attention to the priests, the Levites, and the choir.

And so, on a great day, they celebrated the completion of the wall (12:27–43). Nehemiah gathered the leaders on the broad top of that wall. He divided them into two groups. Half paraded in one direction, led by the band. The other half marched in the opposite direction, led by the choir. Thus they circled the city, antiphonally sounding forth the praises of God. "God had made them rejoice with great joy; the women and children also rejoiced. The joy of Jerusalem was heard far away" (12:43). Probably an earlier edition of the book of Nehemiah ended on that note of joy. And there ended the remarkable historical work of 1 and 2 Chronicles, Ezra, and Nehemiah.

An appendix, however, does record some other reforms, established especially during Nehemiah's second term as governor. Permanent provision for the priests, Levites, and singers was established (12:44–47; 13:4–14). Nehemiah sought rigidly to enforce the Sabbath laws. And when he found Jews who had married Gentiles, he boasts, "I contended with them and cursed them and beat some of them and pulled out their hair" (13:25).

The walls of strict adherence to law and of racial segregation proved far more effective than even the fortress wall Nehemiah had built. Robert Frost was right: "Something there is that doesn't love a wall." But by building walls around the Jews, Ezra and Nehemiah had not only helped mold and define Judaism; they had helped preserve it down to the present day. And it is likely that Christians owe to Ezra, as much as to any one other person, and to his disciples the collecting and editing of that part of the Bible we have been studying, the Jewish scriptures, the Old Testament.

ESTHER

Visitors to some modern Jewish synagogues may be startled if they happen to attend when the book of Esther is being read. The worshipers may stamp their feet, hiss, and boo when they hear the name of the villain, Haman. They may applaud for Esther. Some in the assembly may be wearing masks and funny costumes. At least one rabbi has been known to conduct the service while wearing a gorilla outfit! And in the entire reading of the book of Esther, such words as "God" and "Lord" never occur; for Esther is read at the festival of Purim, the merriest and most secular of Jewish holidays. Gifts are exchanged. Cookies are baked. And some of those cookies are identified as Haman's ears or Haman's nose, to be bitten off by playful children. A medieval commentator proposed that the proper celebration of Purim involved drinking until one could no longer distinguish between "Haman be cursed!" and "Mordecai be blessed!" Jews enjoy Esther.

Esther is undoubtedly one of the most delightful stories in the Bible. But with no direct mention of God and with its climax being the vengeful slaughter of seventy-five thousand Persians—at the recommendation of its lovely heroine—some have questioned what place this book should have in the canon of holy scripture. Before looking at that question, we will review its suspenseful narrative. Because it is told so clearly, there is no need for this *Guide* to include an outline.

Esther Becomes Queen
of Persia (Esth. 1—2)

Cyrus the Great of Persia (modern Iran) conquered Babylon (modern Iraq) in 538 B.C. and allowed the Jews to go home. Many, however, preferred to live in the relative prosperity they had achieved abroad rather than to return to the ruins of Jerusalem. In the reign of Ahasuerus (Xerxes I, 485–464 B.C.), Mordecai and his young cousin Esther, whom he adopted as his daughter, were among these.

The whole narrative centers on banquets. It begins with the king's feast, six months long. Queen Vashti refuses to leave her own banquet, and therefore the king deposes her. When Esther becomes queen, her coronation is celebrated with a banquet. When she schemes to win the king's favor, she begins by inviting him to two banquets. And when at last the Jews are delivered, they are instructed to celebrate this rescue with a feast every year. So the story begins with a banquet.

After six months of eating and drinking, the king decides to entertain his guests by displaying the beauties of his queen. Vashti, however, is having a dinner party of her own, and perhaps she is not eager to display herself to drunken men. Angered by disobedience in a wife, Ahasuerus banishes her. His advisers—all men, of course—urge this divorce lest other wives begin to disobey their husbands.

The search for a new queen begins. There are two beauty contests, of a sort, in the Bible: Abishag was selected to try to bring some life back to the dying David (1 Kings 1), and here, Esther lives up to her name, which in Persian means "star." She wins the competition to be number one in the king's harem. She cannot begin, however, until she has been prepared for twelve months in the royal spa. Months with cosmetics, massage, and perfumes guarantee that she will be fit, beautiful to see, and even lovely to smell (2:12). Appropriately, a banquet celebrates her coronation.

Two hints, however, are given of danger to come. Unknown to the king, she is a Jewess (2:10, 20). And we are carefully told that while each member of the harem might take her turn spending a night with the king, she is otherwise forbidden to enter the royal court unless specifically invited by name (2:14). But one hint of possible victory is given without comment: Mordecai foils a plot to assassinate the king, though at the time this service goes unrewarded (2:21–23).

Haman Plots to Destroy All Jews, but Esther and Mordecai Form a Counterplot (Esth. 3—5)

Now the villain enters. Esther's adoptive father, being a Jew, refuses to bow down to the proud villain, Haman, prime minister of the empire. Haman is so angered that he resolves that to execute only Mordecai would not be vengeance enough; all the Jews must die. He persuades the king to decree a "pogrom," a mass slaughter of Jews. He has the sacred dice, the *pur,* cast to determine the best day for the slaughter. Providentially, the day of doom is scheduled for some months later.

Learning of the plot, Mordecai engages in ceremonial mourning. Probably the most quoted text in the book of Esther is part of Mordecai's appeal to Esther to save her people. From start to finish, this book implies that everything happens providentially. Perhaps it is providence that has placed Esther in the court. "Who knows?" Mordecai challenges Esther. "Perhaps you have come to royal dignity for just such a time as this" (4:14).

Prepared by a three-day fast, Esther acts on that challenge. The first chapter has given us a hint as to the path to the emperor's heart: she resolves to invite him to a banquet. To do so, however, she must defy the ban on harem girls approaching the king without being sent for. Vashti disobeyed the king and had been banished; Esther could be executed. Nevertheless, she will risk all to save the Jews. And as the reader is relieved to learn, the king welcomes her—and her invitation to a banquet.

Esther and Mordecai Turn the Tables on Haman and Save the Jews (Esth. 6:1–9:19)

With Esther's heroic act, everything begins to change. At last, the king learns how Mordecai had earlier saved his life. Vain Haman, thinking he is describing how he himself should be honored, tells the king what should be done for a hero. But it is Mordecai who is to be escorted through the city in glory, and Haman has to walk ahead of him, leading his enemy's horse. Esther invites Haman and the king to one banquet and, to make doubly sure, another. Then she makes her plea for the Jews, and the king agrees. When the terrified Haman falls prostrate on Esther's couch, the king thinks he is trying to rape her. Haman is hanged on the same seventy-five-foot gallows he had erected for Mordecai.

There is still one complication. In the story, no decree issued by the emperor can ever be countermanded, even by the emperor himself. But he does issue a supplemental decree: the Jews may defend themselves. On the day the *pur* had selected for the slaughter of the Jews, the Jews kill five hundred Persians. But Esther is not yet satisfied. The beautiful queen makes two more requests: all ten of Haman's sons are to be hanged, and the Jews throughout the country are to be given another day to kill Persians. So the next day, the Jews massacre seventy-five thousand more.

The Festival of Purim Commemorates This Deliverance (Esth. 9:20–10:3)

A story with so happy an ending deserved retelling. And so the point of the whole book now is announced: every year, around the first of March, the Jews are to celebrate this deliverance with the festival of Purim (it is named for the sacred dice). The celebration should be one of "feasting and gladness, days for sending gifts of food to one another and presents to the poor" (9:22).

Mordecai now is given Haman's old job as prime minister. One almost feels that a modern writer would have ended the story, "And they all lived happily ever after."

The Place of the Book of Esther

What is one to make of this dramatic tale?

There are three things one probably should *not* make of it. First, it is not to be used as a guide to Persian history. To twist it that way leads to all kinds of problems. We know the name of Ahasuerus's queen: it was Amestris, not Vashti and not Esther. The Persian kings did love banquets, but a six-month-long feast seems a bit much even for them. Haman's retribution for his sins seems too neat to believe, with Mordecai getting the rewards Haman expected, Haman having to lead Mordecai's horse, Haman finally being hanged on the gallows he had prepared for Mordecai, and Mordecai inheriting Haman's high office. The prohibition of a queen coming to a king unsummoned and the law that no law can be rescinded seem odd indeed. To make a proclamation warning about the pogrom months in advance seems stupid. But most especially, historians find incredible that a Persian king allowed Jews to slaughter seventy-five thousand Persians. It is true that the writer of this story knows a great deal about life in the Persian court. No doubt Persians did persecute Jews, and yet, heroically, the Jews survived. Esther's truth as history lies not in the story itself but in the horrible fact that, over and over throughout history, pogroms against Jews have been carried out; yet in the end, Jews have triumphed. Esther may be classified as a historical novel. Those Jews who simply enjoy it and have a merry time with it at Purim understand it better than those who try to discover proofs of its historicity. But its theme of Jewish survival against all odds proved true in Egypt, Babylon, Persia, Rome, medieval Europe, and, in modern times, Hitler's "Christian" Germany. In that sense, this book is historically true indeed.

Second, Esther is not a guide to biblical ethics. However ready the Persian Jews may have been to "take revenge on their enemies" (8:13), the Sermon on the Mount does not recommend "slaughtering, and destroying them" (9:5). Even though the protagonist is a woman, not all feminists approve the book. "If you ask me," told me one feminist biblical scholar, "Vashti is the heroine. She took a stand against sexual exploitation." Still, Esther's courage, if not her cruelty, has inspired many women—and men. It is especially important to note, as Brevard Childs has pointed out, that in celebrating their deliverance, this book does not call on Jews of subsequent generations to kill their enemies.[12] Instead, they are to celebrate by "sending gifts of food to one another and presents to the poor" (9:22). A Jewish women's organization devoted to deeds of love and mercy has named itself "Hadassah," the Hebrew name of our heroine.

And third, Esther is not a high point of biblical theology. In this book, the king of Persia is mentioned one hundred ninety times, but God is not named once. Yet here again, one must note the author's faith in a providence that causes everything to work out for the best in the end. Surely the writer thought of that providence as the plan of God.

And so the book of Esther remains part of the canon. As late as the third century A.D., both Christians and Jews were debating whether it belongs there. Martin Luther had his doubts. "I am so hostile to the book and to Esther that I wish they did not exist at all; for they Judaize too much and have much heathen perverseness."[13]

Yet Esther was included in the canon, and precisely because of that, its context has filled it with rich meaning. Left by itself, it might indeed seem only a delightful tale to be read at a jolly party. But in the context of scripture, it does have meaning. The providence that brought deliverance becomes so clearly the plan of God that a reader scarcely notices the absence of God's name. The deliverance of the people is not simply that of a foreign ethnic group; these are the people of God. In its scriptural context, one can read Esther as the story of a mighty act of salvation by the Lord. That God, in spite of all human obstacles, plans a future for the chosen people.

That these things were simply implied, however, by no means satisfied an unknown writer a few decades later. That author added to the story prayers by Mordecai and Esther, prophetic dreams, and overt theological perspective (for a brief description of those additions, see the chapter on the Apocrypha in this *Guide*).

JOB

Martin Luther wrote that Job is "magnificent and sublime as no other book of Scripture."[14] Thomas Carlyle went further: "[Job is] one of the grandest things ever written with the pen. . . . There is nothing written, I think, in the Bible or out of it of equal literary merit."[15]

Job is also very puzzling.

Down through the centuries, Job has inspired artists of many kinds. William Blake gave his interpretation of the book through a series of pictures. In his *Messiah,* George Frideric Handel set to music one of the best-loved passages of Job: "I know that my Redeemer liveth" (19:26, KJV). People from all over the country come to Pikeville, Kentucky, each summer to see a majestic outdoor drama, "The Book of Job", staged nightly and in elaborate costume, every word chanted from the King James Version of Job. Archibald MacLeish won a Pulitzer Prize with his modern play *J.B.,* based on Job.

But Blake's pictures seem to suggest that the point of the story is that Job was converted from legalistic Pharisaism to humble love, a moving but questionable understanding of the book. The excerpt sung in Handel's *Messiah* is one scholars are not sure how to translate, much less interpret. And MacLeish found the ending of the biblical book of Job so unsatisfactory that he added another which suited him better. Biblical scholars have been almost equally diverse in their interpretations of this puzzling poem.

Background and Structure

There is general agreement about the structure of the book. It begins and ends with a prose story, probably an ancient one, about a man who maintained his integrity and his faith in God in spite of undeserved suffering. In the end, God restored all that he had lost. A poet has rewritten this ancient tale, but into it a long poem has been inserted. In the poem, each of Job's three "comforters" undertakes to explain to him the reason for his suffering. It is, they say, because of his sins, but if he will simply repent, God will forgive him and restore his health and his fortune. Job replies after each of these speeches, protesting his innocence. Each friend speaks again, Job

JOB
The Poetic Story of an Innocent Sufferer Who at Last Meets God

"Your maxims are proverbs of ashes . . . but I will defend my ways to [God's] face" (13:12–15).

(Prose)	(Poetry)				(Prose)
1	3 A Poetic Discussion: How Are Mortals to Speak of a God of Justice in a World Where People Suffer?		32	38	42
Prologue	**Job and His Friends Debate, 3—31**	**Elihu Adds His Ideas, 32—37**	**God Speaks, 38—41**		**Epilogue**
God tests Job by taking his wealth and family, 1	Job laments that he was ever born, 3	In four speeches, Elihu condemns both Job and his friends and emphasizes the majesty of God and the helpful discipline that suffering brings	God's first speech: God's wisdom designed the universe, 33:1–40:2		Job repents, 42:1–6
God tests Job again with bodily afflictions, but Job is still faithful, 2	Each friend speaks in turn, proposing that Job's troubles are due to his sins; in turn, Job replies to each, 4—14		Job accepts in silence, 40:3–5		God approves Job but rebukes the friends, 42:7–9
	The cycle of speeches is repeated two more times; Job longs to present his case to God, 15—27		God's second speech: God's freedom and power are shown in God's creation of monsters, 40:3–41:34		God restores everything to Job, 42:10–17
	A poem on God as the source of true wisdom, 28				
	Job makes his final defense and plea, 29—31				

Date: Unknown; probably during the exile (?)

Setting: The land of "Uz" (Edom?), apparently in the patriarchal period

Subject: An ancient story of a wise man who was faithful in spite of undeserved suffering, retold by a poet. Three friends argue that suffering is caused by sin, but God's words depict a deity whose wisdom and justice transcend any simple formula.

Best-loved Passage: "I know that my Redeemer lives, and . . . I shall see God" (19:26).

replies, and each gets a third turn. Job has pleaded for a chance to present his case before God, and in the end, God speaks. Job "repents," not so much admitting that he has violated moral laws as changing his mind about God and his right to make demands on the Almighty. In the prose epilogue, God restores Job's health, wealth, and family.

Alfred Tennyson said that Job is "the greatest poem of ancient or modern times."[16] To some modern readers, however, who are used to watching television dramas that solve all mysteries in sixty minutes with time out for commercials, Job seems tediously long and needlessly repetitious. It helps to remember that thirty-nine of Job's forty-two chapters are poetry and that the poetry is in the Hebrew fashion. For a more complete discussion of the style of Hebrew poetry, read the chapter on the Psalms in this *Guide*. But here note that the ancient Hebrews loved repetition. They did not rhyme sounds, as we do; they rhymed ideas. They loved to read the same thing, or almost the same thing, said again but in different words. Thus Job in a sense says only one thing in the twenty-six verses of chapter 3: I am so miserable that I wish I had never been born! But he says it in an amazing variety of ways. Over and over, Job's three friends repeat their counsel that all will be well if Job will repent of his sins, and yet they do this using different figures of speech. There is contrast and movement in the book, of course, not just repetition, but to enjoy Job it helps to learn to enjoy the Hebrew style of poetry.

Job is unique. It is not a psalm; a history of the Hebrew people, like 2 Kings; or law, like Leviticus. It is the closest thing to Greek drama in the Bible, but it is also quite different from that genre. But while it is different from Proverbs, it is, like Proverbs, classified as "wisdom literature" (for a more complete discussion of the characteristics of wisdom literature, turn to the section on Proverbs in this *Guide*). Job shares with other wisdom literature at least these characteristics:

1. It *praises wisdom,* which it says is based in God (cf. Job 28 and Prov. 1:7). Indeed, the problem with which Job deals is at least in part how may one speak wisely of God in the midst of suffering. The words "wise" and "wisdom" occur some thirty-one times in Job.
2. Like other wisdom literature, Job seeks to present *timeless, universal truth.* Job lives not in Israel but in Uz, which perhaps is meant to be Edom. Neither he nor his friends are identified as Jews. Job seems to be pictured as living in the dim past of the patriarchal age, but scholars cannot date the book; it belongs to every age.
3. In Job, as in other wisdom literature, *God is known through universal experience,* what theologians call "general revelation," not through God's special revelation to God's chosen people. Thus, in the poems, God is usually called "Shadday," "El," or "Eloah," not "Yahweh," God's unique covenant name, usually translated "the Lord." God does not say

to Job, "I am the Lord who brought you up out of slavery in Egypt." Rather, God speaks as the Creator whose works can be seen by all peoples. Thus Job represents all humankind.

One other background reminder is important for understanding Job. The book assumes that the reader is familiar with the theology that presents God as judge, in this life rewarding the good and punishing the evildoers. This is the theology of Deuteronomy; and the books of Judges, Samuel, and Kings were written to show how this theology of rewards and punishments proved true in the course of Hebrew history. With 1 and 2 Chronicles and Proverbs, one can see this concept of God's justice taken two steps further. It is applied not simply to nations over centuries but to individuals within their lifetimes. And now Job's friends are ready to argue not only that sin leads to suffering but that sin is the only cause of suffering. Job suffers, therefore he must have sinned.

The book of Job is clearly an attack on that theology. It wrestles with the problem of evil, of how one can believe in a wise and just God in a world where, the writer is sure, people suffer even though they are innocent. But as we shall now see, it offers no simple solutions to such problems, and it moves beyond them to even deeper concerns.

The Prologue (Job 1—2)

The prose prologue of Job is probably the retelling of an old story about an ancient wise man, probably the one mentioned in Ezek. 14:14. It is told in five scenes, alternating between heaven and earth.

The first scene pictures Job on earth, a man "blameless and upright" (1:1). Job is not so proud as to claim that he has always been perfect, but it is essential to the story to accept this initial evaluation of his character. He is truly good, meriting the blessings of God. And sure enough, he has all the joys that Deuteronomy promises the righteous, including wealth, health, and family.

The second scene, in the heavenly court, sets the basic problem of the book. Ironically, it is Satan who voices it, "Does Job fear God for nothing?" (1:9). Satan, often mentioned in the New Testament, is hardly ever named in the Old Testament. Here, however, Satan does appear. But Satan, at this stage, is not thought of as an opponent battling God but as a kind of prosecuting attorney in the heavenly court. What Satan is proposing is this: Isn't Job good simply because it pays to be good? Could a man learn to love God simply for God's self? God accepts the challenge. It is essential for the reader to remember that we know from the beginning what Job's friends cannot know: Job's suffering is not caused by his sin.

The third scene, on earth again, describes in stylized repetition how all Job's blessings are removed. But Job simply responds, "The Lord gave, and the Lord has taken away; blessed be the name of the Lord" (1:21). It is on this passage that Job's reputation for patience is based (James 5:11).

The fourth scene, back in heaven, depicts God as agreeing to take the challenge one step further. Not only are Job's external blessings removed, but his own body is to be afflicted.

And so, with the fifth scene, we find Job a ruined man, covered with sores, scratching himself with a piece of pottery, yet still faithful. "Shall we receive the good at the hand of God, and not receive the bad?" (2:10), he responds to his nagging wife.

And now the three friends come. There is no question but that they sincerely want to help. However verbose and tactless they may be later, for one whole week they simply sit with him in sympathetic silence.

Job and His Friends Debate (Job 3—31)

In agony, for one whole chapter (Job 3), Job laments that he was ever born. Job is no longer patient. And with his anguished complaint, the poetic discussion has begun.

The first friend, Eliphaz, begins gently, almost apologizing for speaking. He seeks simply to reassure Job. Job himself knows that God blesses good people. Therefore, "is not . . . the integrity of your ways your hope?" (4:6). Because Job is such a good man, God is not going to let him be hurt much. Eliphaz is a mystic. He describes the ghostly experience in which this truth was borne in on him (4:13–17): no mortal is righteous before God (4:17). But if Job will only turn to the gracious God, all will soon be well. For "how happy is the one whom God reproves. . . . For he wounds, but he binds up; he strikes, but his hands heal" (5:17–18). Everything is going to be all right.

Job replies by defending his grief. His afflictions are not light; they are "heavier than the sand of the sea" (6:3). Let Eliphaz teach him what sin he needs to repent (6:24). Job has a right to complain. Ahead of him lies only death, the gloomy grave of Sheol (7:9–10). And there, when, too late, God seeks him, Job will no longer exist (7:21).

Now Bildad takes his turn. He is startled by Job's words. "How long will you say these things? . . . Does God pervert justice?" (8:2–3). He does not attack Job, but he does suggest that Job's children must have sinned, since they have been killed. Job himself, however, need only pray, and if he is pure, he will be rewarded. A traditionalist, Bildad knows that God is just because that truth has been handed down for centuries. "For inquire now of bygone generations, and consider what their ancestors have found" (8:8). The wise men of the past assure us that if one is virtuous, all will be well.

Job has heard all that too (9:1). Yet he protests his innocence. But what chance has he against Almighty God? No matter what tradition says, Job now feels driven to the opposite extreme: he accuses God of being cruel (9:22–23). "There is no umpire between us," Job complains (9:33). Job can only protest God's injustice until he dies (10:21).

The third friend, Zophar, is horrified. This is no way to talk about God! To the dogmatist Zophar, the whole matter is now clear: Job deserves even worse than he is getting (11:6). Yet still he holds out hope to Job. "If you direct your heart rightly, . . . you will be secure. . . . And your life will be brighter than the noonday" (11:13–17).

Job replies with sarcasm: "No doubt you are the people, and wisdom will die with you," you know so much (12:2). But Job protests that he knows all those traditional platitudes they have been saying. And with his reply at the end of the first cycle, Job really turns his attention away from his comforters. "Your maxims are proverbs of ashes" (13:12). Their old, neat theological formulae simply don't apply. Instead, taking his life in his hands, Job appeals for a chance to plead his case not before these friends but before God. "He will kill me; I have no hope; but I will defend my ways to his face" (13:15). "Let me speak," he begs God, "and you reply to me" (13:22). From now on, Job's great concern, repeatedly voiced, is to meet God and present his case to the Almighty.

One thing would make a difference: if only there were a life after death, that would change everything. Old Testament religion is a religion focused on this present life in this world. Though there are hints in other places, perhaps only in Dan. 12:2, itself a late book, is there a clear promise of resurrection. But here Job at least raises the question: "If mortals die, will they live again?" (Job 14:14). Then everything might be straightened out. "But the mountain falls and crumbles away," he sighs (14:18). "So you destroy the hope of mortals. . . . Their children come to honor, and [the dead] do not know it. . . . They . . . mourn only for themselves" (14:19–22).

Even so, at the high point of the second cycle of speeches—for many, the high point of the whole book—Job seems to find hope for a future life. "Have pity on me, have pity on me, O you my friends," he pleads with his would-be comforters, now really his accusers (19:21). But turning from them, he has, at least for a moment, hope for help from a higher source. It seems that only death awaits him. Would that the justice of his claim to innocence could be engraved in a rock with an iron pen, so that at some future time, after his death, he might be vindicated (19:24)! And somehow, at least for the moment, he believes that he will be present at that future vindication. Earlier he had longed for an "umpire," a mediator between himself and God. Now he cries:

> For I know that my Redeemer lives,
>   and that at the last he will stand upon the earth;
> and after my skin has been thus destroyed,
>   then in my flesh I shall see God,
> whom I shall see on my side,
>   and my eyes shall behold, and not another. (19:25–27)

Tragically, the Hebrew here is so difficult that it is widely held that some ancient scribe made a mistake in copying. Scholars translate the passage in different ways to make sense of it. A few verses later, Job seems to have reverted to his despair about a future life (21:23–26). Therefore there is some doubt as to whether Job here really means that there is a life after death. But after some seventeen pages of discussion, J. Gerald Janzen concludes that Job here really does break through to a hope that somehow beyond death, resurrected, he will see God "on my side and whom my eyes shall behold, and not estranged" (Janzen's translation of 19:27).[17] Whatever the writer may have meant, within the canon of the Christian's Bible, this passage becomes a moving expression of faith in the life to come, through Christ the Mediator.

The third cycle of speeches and replies seems confused. No third speech is attributed to Zophar. Many suggest that 24:13–25 is his speech and that his name was dropped inadvertently by an ancient copyist. Here Job seems almost to be saying what his friends have been maintaining. Perhaps the confusion is a sign that the dialogue has run its unsuccessful course.

Near the end of this series, our writer gives us a beautiful poem on wisdom. Some suggest that it once existed outside this book. In any event, it points to the ultimate failure of human wisdom. "Surely there is a mine for silver. . . . But where shall wisdom be found? . . . It is hidden from the eyes of all living. . . . God [alone] understands the way to it, and he knows its place. . . . 'Truly, the fear of the Lord, that is wisdom' " (28:1–28; cf. Prov. 1:7). The "wisdom" of Job's friends has turned out not to be wisdom at all.

Job's final statement (29—31) includes one of the clearest presentations of ethical responsibility found in the whole of the Old Testament. Summing up his case before God, Job recalls his concern for others. He has been devoted to helping the poor, the fatherless, the blind. He has been pure in his conduct with women. He has been fair with the people who worked for him. He has sympathized with the afflicted and never rejoiced in the ruin of those who hated him. It is the climax of Job's defense. Liberation theologian Gustavo Gutierrez proposes that one can see in Job's speeches a gradual turning away from himself. More and more, he identifies with all of suffering humanity. And this, Gutierrez proposes, makes Job ready for his encounter with God.[18] At the very least, one can say that although Job has at times denounced God as unjust, with no reward given for Job's social concern, he believes completely in the importance of that ethic of social justice preached by prophets such as Amos and Isaiah.

And so Job's long speeches come to an end with one more plea for encounter with God. "Oh, that I had one to hear me! (Here is my signature! let the Almighty answer me!)" (31:35).

"The words of Job are ended" (31:40).

Elihu Adds His Ideas (Job 32—37)

Just as we seem ready for God to appear, instead we have four speeches, spanning five chapters (32—37), from yet another friend, Elihu. Many scholars have proposed that these chapters are an addition by a later author, who believed he could solve the problems with which the book has thus far dealt unsuccessfully. Supporting this view is the fact that Elihu is not mentioned in the prologue or the epilogue. These chapters could be skipped without the reader being aware that anything was missing. They seem an unnecessary interruption.

Nevertheless, the prevailing opinion now seems to be that they belong to the book. They heighten the suspense, review the problem, and perhaps do give some new emphases.

"I am full of words," young Elihu announces (32:18). He is so full that he spends one whole chapter just telling us that he is going to speak. A few commentators have suggested that there is a touch of the comic in Elihu, a relief of tension for the reader before the mighty climax of the book. Elihu rebukes both sides in the debate. He seems to emphasize the forgiving grace of God (33:23–30). But Elihu still maintains that, "according to their deeds" God repays sinners (34:11).

His final speech (36—37) is a poem on the majesty of the Creator. Throughout it there are references to clouds and storms and lightning. So the poet has prepared us; for now, "the Lord answered Job out of the whirlwind" (38:1). Beyond the storm, the Creator speaks.

God Speaks (Job 38—41)

For thirty-seven chapters we have been waiting for an answer. Instead, God hurls at Job some forty questions. Instead of clear solutions to his problems, God gives Job descriptions of mythical beasts modeled on the crocodile and the hippopotamus. Job is a puzzling book.

"Who is this that darkens counsel by words without knowledge?" God demands. "Gird up your loins like a man" (stand up and get ready for this meeting you have demanded). "I will question you, and you shall declare to me" (38:2–3).

With that, God bombards this mortal with question after question, contrasting the wisdom and power of the Creator with that of a mere human:

"Where were you when I laid the foundation of the earth?" (38:4).
"Have you commanded the morning since your days began?" (38:12).
"Have you entered the storehouses of the snow?" (38:22).
"Who has cut a channel for the torrents of rain?" (38:25).
"Can you lift up your voice to the clouds?" (38:34).

On and on go these rhetorical questions. Job, who has spoken at such length throughout the book, is now reduced to silence (40:3–5).

But God speaks again (40:6–41:34). God challenges Job to dress himself in all the royal splendor he can claim. Job has challenged God and God's justice.

Then let Job himself "tread down the wicked where they stand," and God will acknowledge Job's right to criticize (40:10–14).

And to cap the oration, God describes two of God's creations, mythical creatures: Behemoth, a kind of super-hippopotamus; and Leviathan, the crocodile-like dragon that, in Babylonian legend, God conquered at creation. Who can limit such a God?

Now Job replies (42:1–6), in apparent contrition, "I know that you can do all things, and that no purpose of yours can be thwarted." Job quotes God's challenging demand, "Who is this?" and confesses:

> Therefore I have uttered what I did not understand,
>> things too wonderful for me,
>> which I did not know. . . .
> I had heard of you by the hearing of the ear,
>> but now my eye sees you;
> therefore I despise myself,
>> and repent in dust and ashes.

All admire the beauty of this poetry. All agree that it is a marvelous picture of the power and wisdom of the Creator. But not all agree on exactly what either God or Job means.

The traditional view, still maintained by most commentators, is that God's speech is to remind Job that God is high above any mortal, that God's ways are a mystery beyond a mortal's understanding, and that no human has a right to make demands on the Almighty. Job's response is one of contrition. It is not that Job now confesses to sins he has so consistently and truthfully denied committing. But overwhelmed by an actual encounter with the majesty of the Creator, he confesses his creatureliness, his finiteness, and that he, a mortal, had been presumptuous to challenge Almighty God.

H. H. Rowley summarizes it in these words, "While the Divine speeches rebuke him for things he said under his trial, their burden is that he cannot have the knowledge on which judgment should rest, and that he is wiser to bow humbly before God than to judge him."[19]

Gutierrez proposes that there is also another meaning in God's speeches. The problem with which the book deals is that the suffering of the innocent seems to undermine the faith that there is order and purpose in God's universe. God's first speech, therefore, is to present God as the celestial architect, the planner, to demonstrate that God does have the wisdom to design, even if in Job's case the plan is not apparent. God's second speech is to show the delightful freedom of God. God can make two outlandish creatures and even play with them (41:5). Such a God is not bound by the neat maxims of Job's friends. God is too free and powerful to be bound by any theologian's narrow concept of justice. Hence there is room in God's plan for grace.[20]

In sharp contrast to the traditional understanding of Job, Janzen emphasizes the challenge God gives this man. Traditionally, the questions posed to Job have been interpreted as intended to overwhelm this mortal with a sense of his inferiority to Almighty God. In effect God asks, "Can you do what I do?" The implied answer is, "No, of course not!" But Janzen quotes Psalm 8. The psalmist, too, has marveled at the creation of the universe. Nevertheless, he sees the glory of human beings. "You have given them dominion over the works of your hands; you have put all things under their feet," including all beasts (Ps. 8:6–8). There is an ambiguity in God's questions. Perhaps humans can meet the challenge and answer, "Yes!" Retranslating the verse about Job's "repentance," Janzen sees it as expressing not contrition but a change of mind about the status of human nature. Human beings are challenged to see themselves as creatures, but creatures in the image of God.[21]

It is probably true that Janzen has gone too far. No human can do the things God describes. God's speech seems designed to overwhelm Job with a sense of the contrast between the Almighty and the mortal. Yet Janzen is right that there is a kind of glory for Job in God's speech. To this mortal in all his misery, God, the majestic Creator, comes. God plays with Leviathan, but God speaks with human beings.

Thus, beyond the content of what God says, there is a kind of answer in the experience of the presence of God. Liberation theologian Gutierrez writes of two streams of thought in Job. There is the prophetic, the emphasis on social justice, exemplified in Job's closing speech. But beyond that there is the mystic, the overwhelming experience of the actual presence of the Divine in the midst of suffering humanity.[22] Job had heard of God, but now he has met God. That personal encounter does not answer all Job's questions, but it makes all the difference.

The Epilogue (Job 42:7–17)

Job has challenged God to meet with him, and God has responded. Job has, in some sense, repented, but he has not been crushed. In the epilogue, God appears not as the God of retributive justice but as the Lord of grace. All that God had taken from Job, God now restores.

William Blake's illustrations of Job draw our attention to one moving bit of the closing scene. God condemns Job's friends but instructs them, "Go to my servant Job, . . . and . . . Job shall pray for you, for I will accept his prayer not to deal with you according to your folly. . . . And the Lord accepted Job's prayer" (42:8–9). There is grace both in God and in Job. Indeed, Christian tradition has often seen this innocent sufferer as a type of Jesus Christ. In Christ, Christians believe, we have the Redeemer and the resurrection for which Job longed.

PSALMS

Praise the Lord!
How good it is to sing praises to our God;
   for he is gracious, and a song of praise is fitting. (Ps. 147:1)

The ancient Hebrews cannot compare with the Greeks or the Romans in the statuary they left us. Their sacred law forbade graven images (Ex. 20:4). They left us almost no paintings. Their architecture, now destroyed, must have been impressive, but they had to import its designers and decorators (2 Chron. 2).

But the Hebrews did excel in one form of artistic expression: they sang. More than three hundred times the Bible uses such words as "sing," "song," "hymns," and "music." The Israelites sang in the Temple when they worshiped God. They sang—and danced—to celebrate military victories. They sang in times of deep distress. When they were captives in Babylon, they still, through their tears, sang the "songs of Zion . . . in a foreign land" (Ps. 137:3–4). Ezra and Nehemiah tell us how the returned Jews celebrated the rebuilding of their Temple and their holy city: they sang (Ezra 3:11; Neh. 12:27). And when, out of Israel, the Christian church was born, it was born as a singing fellowship.

The hymnbook for their songs to God was the book of Psalms.

At the Last Supper, Jesus and the disciples sang, probably Psalms 115—118 (Matt. 26:30). Paul and Silas sang in the Philippian jail (Acts 16:25). Paul urged his readers to sing psalms (Eph. 5:19; Col. 3:16). And the New Testament itself depends more on the Psalms than on any other book of the Old Testament.

Christians in medieval cathedrals heard great choirs singing and chanting psalms. In the Reformation, Protestant martyrs went to their deaths singing psalms. Roman Catholic martyr Thomas More died with a psalm on his lips. John Calvin forbade the singing in church of anything other than the Psalms. Psalm singing became so much a part of the Reformed tradition that it was nearly the middle of the twentieth century before the Associate Reformed Presbyterian Church in America officially endorsed singing in its worship any songs other than the Psalms. Today, in millions of congregations every Sunday, selections from this part of the canon are read—often responsively—chanted, or sung. The scripture-reference index of the typical hymnal will show that the book of Psalms is its most frequently cited source. And individual Christians and Jews still read and pray these poems every day.

Hebrew Music and Poetry

The Psalms are songs. The names of some of the popular melodies to which they were sung remain. One of the tragedies of history is that the ancients did

PSALMS
Outline

In the outline that follows, certain Psalms have been listed in more than one category. Although no system of classification is perfect, anyone who studies the Psalms in groups such as those suggested here will find this classification helpful.

Hymns of Praise
In General—100, 113, 117, 145, 150
Praise to the Lord of Creation—8, 19:1–6, 29, 104
Praise to the Lord of History
The History of Salvation (the mighty acts of God)—68 (?), 78, 105, 106, 111, 114, 149 (compare Exodus 15:1–18)
The Kingship of God (the so-called enthronement Psalms)—47, 93, 96, 97, 98, 99
The Kingship of God's Anointed (the royal or Messianic Psalms; not hymns, but should be studied with the six preceding Psalms)—2, 18, 20, 21, 45, 61, 63, 72, 89, 101, 110, 132, 144
Praise to the Lord of Creation and History—33, 65, 103, 115, 135, 136, 146, 147, 148
Praise to the Lord of Zion
In General—46, 48, 76, 87
Pilgrim Songs—84, 122, 134
Admission to Zion—15, 24

Prayers in Time of Trouble
Laments of the Community—12, 44, 58, 60, 74, 77, 79, 80, 83, 90, 94, 106, 123, 137
Laments of the Individual
In General—3, 5, 6, 13, 22, 25, 28, 31, 39, 42–43, 52, 54, 55, 56, 57, 61, 63, 64, 71, 86, 88, 120, 141, 142
Protestations of Innocence—7, 17, 26, 27, 59 (compare 44)
Imprecations Upon Enemies—35, 59, 69, 70, 109, 137, 140 (compare the following laments of the community: 12, 58, 83)
Penitential Prayers—6, 32, 38, 51, 102, 130, 143 (compare 25)

Affirmations of Faith—4, 11, 16, 23, 27, 46, 62, 63, 90, 91, 121, 125, 131

Songs of Thanksgiving
Thanksgivings of the Community—67, 75, 107, 118, 124
Thanksgivings of the Individual—18, 30, 32, 34, 41, 66, 92, 116, 138 (compare Isaiah 38:1–20 and Jonah 2:2–9)

Wisdom Poetry—1, 19:7–14, 32, 37, 41, 49, 73, 111, 112, 119, 127, 128, 133, 139

Liturgies
Liturgies of Instruction—15, 24
Hymn and Priestly Blessing—134
Royal Liturgies—2, 20, 110, 132
Prophetic Liturgies
In General—12, 75, 85, 126
Hymn and Oracle Blended—81, 95
Freer Imitation of Prophetic Style—14 (53), 50, 82

Mixed Poems
Adaptation of Earlier Materials—36, 40, 89, 90, 107, 108, 144
Freer Compositions—9–10, 78 (compare Deuteronomy 32:1–43), 94, 119, 123, 129, 139

Source: Reprinted, by permission of Westminster John Knox Press, from Arnold B. Rhodes, "The Book of Psalms," in *The Layman's Bible Commentary* (Richmond: John Knox Press, 1960) 9:26–27.

not have our method of writing music. Thus we will never know how such tunes as "Lilies" (Ps. 80) or "Do Not Destroy" (Ps. 75) or "The Deer of the Dawn" (Ps. 22) sounded. The Bible's lists of musical instruments give us hints of how the music sounded. Psalm 150 tells its hearers:

> Praise him with trumpet sound;
>> praise him with lute and harp!
> Praise him with tambourine and dance;
>> praise him with strings and pipe! (150:3–5)

The very word "psalm" comes from the name of a stringed instrument called the "psaltry." Most often mentioned in the Bible are percussion instruments. The popularity of such rhythm instruments suggests dance music, and rightly so. Dancing was very much a part of Jewish celebration, including religious celebration.

We do not now have the melodies, but we still have the beautiful lyrics of the Psalms. At least three characteristics are typical of this Hebrew poetry.

The first characteristic is that Hebrew poets did not rhyme sounds; they rhymed ideas. That is, they delighted in poetry with pairs of lines with matched meanings. Such couplets lent themselves to antiphonal singing. We are told that the women who played, danced, and sang to a popular song of David's day "sang to one another," apparently back and forth (1 Sam. 18:6–7). Traditionally, such couplets of Hebrew poetry have been analyzed as being of three kinds:

1. Sometimes these are pairs, with both lines expressing almost exactly the same idea.

> Enter his gates with thanksgiving,
>> and his courts with praise. (100:4)

2. Sometimes the second line presents the opposite truth to that in the first.

> For the Lord watches over the way of the righteous,
>> but the way of the wicked will perish. (1:6)

3. Sometimes the second line adds a new but related thought.

> I cry aloud to the Lord,
>> and he answers me from his holy hill. (3:4)

Patrick D. Miller, Jr., warns that not all verses in the Psalms fit neatly into one of these three categories.[23] There are many kinds of parallelism. Miller suggests especially that a second line or group of lines may particularize, define, or expand what has gone before. In this couplet, the second line makes the meaning of the first more specific:

> The earth is the Lord's and all that is in it,
> the world, and those who live in it. (24:1)

He gives this example of how additional lines may intensify and elaborate the first:

> The kings of the earth set themselves,
> and the rulers take counsel together,
> against the Lord and his anointed. (2:2)

A second characteristic of Hebrew poetry is figurative language. Often the figures of speech in the Psalms are bold and imaginative. God is compared to a cup (Ps. 16:5), a sheep farmer (23:1), a rock (28:1), a king (47:8), a judge (67:4), a conquering general (68:17), and a loving father (103:13). God's people are compared to sheep that God protects (100:3), trees that stand firm (1:3), and grass that God simply sweeps away (90:5). And enemies are likened to venomous snakes (58:4), howling dogs (59:6), and God's washbasin (60:8), whom God will break with a rod of iron (2:9) or at whom God hurls the divine shoe (60:8).

A third characteristic of Hebrew poetry is that it has rhythm. Often there is what most scholars regard as meter. Miller cautions that the subject of Hebrew meter is much debated among scholars, and the original Hebrew meter is lost in translation. But as broadly defined, the rhythm of many psalms comes through clearly in any language. Sometimes modern translations may sacrifice something of beauty to make the precise meaning of the words clearer. Many people, therefore, prefer the King James Version, where rhythm pulses through every stanza.

The Origin and Structure of the Book of Psalms

The book of Psalms is a collection of collections. The modern reader can still see something of the way in which its collectors organized these songs. Psalm 1 is an introduction to the instruction that the book now gives, and it may be that Psalm 2 is placed next as a tribute both to the Lord and to the king, who was patron of the Temple musicians. The book ends with a group of five "Hallelujah" psalms, a fitting close to a book whose Hebrew name, "Tehillim," means "praises." It is divided into five books, probably so that these "five books of David" could parallel the "five books of Moses." The first four books end with a doxology (41:13; 72:18–19; 89:52; 106:48), and Psalm 150 serves as a doxology for the whole. Among the shorter collections within these five books, one may note the five "Hallelujah" psalms at the end, the psalms of Asaph (73—83), and the "Songs of Ascents" (120—134). Perhaps book 1 of the Psalms was the earliest collection, with other books added as these psalms were assembled. But for the most part, it is impossible to guess why these poems were placed in the order in which we now have them. The Greek version of the Old Testament, called the Septuagint and often indicated by the number LXX, has 151 psalms.

The book is thought of popularly as the work of King David. Seventy-two psalms do have a heading that is usually translated "a Psalm of David." That heading, however, *le David,* could as accurately be translated "to" or "for" David, implying that the psalm is dedicated to the memory of that famous musician rather than that it actually was written by that ancient king. Indeed, it is clear that some psalms with that heading could not have been written by David, because they assume the existence of the Temple, which was not built until after David's death (for example, 5:7; 68:29; etc.) Some songs are related to the Jerusalem choir (84; 88; etc.). Psalm 90 is attributed to Moses. Obviously, Psalm 137 was composed by someone carried into slavery in Babylon. The headings of some psalms profess to place them in particular situations (for example, Pss. 7 and 18), but all agree that these notations were added quite late and cannot be demonstrated to be based on actual historical memory. Therefore scholars have virtually given up the attempt to determine the date or the author of most psalms. They come from generally anonymous poets and from many different centuries.

How the Psalms Were Used

What can be done, with some claim to success, is to classify the Psalms in relation to how they must have been used.

Quite evidently, many were used in services of worship in the Temple. The book of Psalms has been called "the Hymnbook of the Second Temple," and many of the Psalms were sung in Israel's First Temple, built by Solomon. How the choir or the congregation sang antiphonally in some service of worship can be seen most clearly by looking at Psalm 136. As the leader sang or chanted the stories of creation and redemption, the congregation or the choir joined in the response.

> O give thanks to the Lord, for he is good,
> > *for his steadfast love endures forever.*
> O give thanks to the God of gods.
> > *for his steadfast love endures forever.*
> O give thanks to the Lord of lords,
> > *for his steadfast love endures forever.* (Ps. 136:1–3; italics added.)

(See the outline on page 153 for a list of other psalms that were liturgies.)
Together pilgrims sang the "Songs of Ascent."

> > I was glad when they said to me,
> > > "Let us go to the house of the Lord!" (Ps. 122:1)

And knowing that they were to be the kingdom of God, the assembly sang of God as king.

> Clap your hands, all you peoples;
>   shout to God with loud songs of joy.
> For the Lord, the Most High, is awesome,
>   a great king over all the earth. (Ps. 47:1–2)

Not all the Psalms, however, were necessarily intended for the whole congregation. Some thanked God for grace given to an individual, and in some an individual pleaded for forgiveness or healing. It was in the midst of illness that some individual singer wrote Psalm 6.

> O Lord, do not rebuke me in your anger,
>   or discipline me in your wrath.
> Be gracious to me, O Lord, for I am languishing;
>   O Lord, heal me, for my bones are shaking with terror.
>   . . . .
> Turn, O Lord, save my life;
>   deliver me for the sake of your steadfast love. (6:1–4)

And as in several other, similar psalms, the psalmist included a cry of faith:

> The Lord has heard my supplication;
>   the Lord accepts my prayer. (6:9)

Often an individual lament also includes promises to God. And even though written by individuals in particular situations, these psalms often use transcendent language that has universal appeal and can be used by the whole community.

Broadly, the Psalms are often classified as community psalms or individual psalms and as songs of praise and thanksgiving or songs of lament and distress. Each of these classifications, however, can be thought of as having many subcategories. One of the clearest and most complete analyses of the psalms in this way is that of Arnold B. Rhodes (see p. 153).[24] One-hundred-fifty psalms are too many for comment in this section, but we herein note examples in several, though not all, of the major categories that Rhodes identifies.

Hymns of Praise

"Hallelujah"—next to "Amen," this is the Hebrew word most familiar to readers of the Bible in English. The word means "praise the Lord," and many psalms begin and end with that phrase (for example, 113; 117; 146—150). Many psalms retold "the history of salvation," praising God for mighty acts in saving Israel (78; 105; 106; etc.). The law guided Israel's response in daily life to God's mighty acts. The Psalms expressed that response in worship.

Among the best-loved songs of praise is Psalm 100. The singer begins by calling on the whole world to praise God: "Make a joyful noise to the Lord, all the earth." The word used here for the loud noise is the same applied to the roar of wild beasts. This is not quiet, meditative praise. The worshipers are invited into the Temple with joyful song:

> Worship the Lord with gladness;
>> come into his presence with singing.

The typical psalm of praise includes reasons for worship. In Psalm 100, both the Lord's creation and God's shepherd-like ownership and care are noted:

> Know that the Lord is God.
>> It is he that made us, and we are his;
>> we are his people, and the sheep of his pasture.

And so, again, the congregation is called to enter the great courtyard of the Temple thankfully:

> Enter his gates with thanksgiving,
>> and his courts with praise.
>> Give thanks to him, bless [praise] his name.

And now the reasons for such joyful song are given in more detail. The favorite chorus about God's "steadfast love" is included, as in Psalm 138 (above).

> For the Lord is good;
>> his steadfast love endures forever,
>> and his faithfulness to all generations.

Many psalms praise God as king. Similarly, many praise Israel's earthly king. "You are the most handsome of men," cries Ps. 45:2, a song for a royal wedding; and the beauty of the king's bride is also celebrated (45:10–17). Psalm 72 prays for the king, that he will fulfill the goals of social justice proclaimed by the prophets:

> May he judge your people with righteousness
>> and your poor with justice. (72:2)

The Old Testament passage most often quoted in the New Testament is Psalm 110. Perhaps it was first sung at the coronation of a king. It begins by placing the king in triumph side by side with God.

> The Lord [God] says to my lord [the king],
>> "Sit at my right hand
>> until I make your enemies your footstool."

Such a king will not need to draft an army. His people will volunteer.

> Your people will offer themselves willingly
>> on the day you lead your forces.

This king, however, is not just a king. Though he is of the tribe of Judah, not Levi, he is a priest, just as the ancient priest-king of Jerusalem, Melchizedek, was a priest (though not in the usual pattern).

> The Lord has sworn and will not change his mind,
> "You are a priest forever
> according to the order of Melchizedek."

The New Testament, however, does not quote the last stanza, in which this conquering king fills the nations with corpses (110:6). The Second Psalm can even call the king God's "son." A remarkable thing about these "Royal Psalms" or "Messianic Psalms"—or as Rhodes calls them, psalms of "the Kingship of the Lord's Anointed"—is that the Jews kept singing them long after there were no more kings on a throne in Jerusalem. Some day, they said, God will yet send us such a king. The reason the New Testament writers so often quoted Psalm 110 is clear: they saw that promised king in David's greatest son, Jesus.

Prayers in Time of Trouble

The largest group of psalms, however, is not the songs of praise and thanksgiving; it is the laments. In a nation that has experienced so much prejudice and persecution, it should not surprise us that the congregation often gathered to plead with God for help. Sometimes the directness of their prayer startles us. Psalm 44 begins by reminding God of all the Lord's marvelous deeds of deliverance in the past (44:1–8). But now they complain, "You have rejected us and abased us" (44:9). "You have sold your people for a trifle" (44:12). And they do not hesitate to accuse God of being unjust:

> All this has come upon us,
> yet we have not forgotten you,
> or been false to your covenant. (44:17)

And in an agony that might seem blasphemous if it were in another book, these mourners cry to God to wake up, for apparently the Lord has gone to sleep on the job; or else God is hiding, or perhaps God's memory has gone bad:

> Rouse yourself! Why do you sleep, O Lord?
> Awake, do not cast us off forever!
> Why do you hide your face?
> Why do you forget our affliction and oppression? (44:23–24; cf. Ps. 35:23)

But there is still hope in God for one great reason:

> Rise up, come to our help.
> Redeem us *for the sake of your steadfast love.* (44:26; italics added.)

Some laments are prayers for the whole nation in trouble. Some are quite personal and individual. Among the best loved of the latter type is Psalm 51.

Tradition says that it was David's prayer of repentance after his sin with Bathsheba. If so, the last two verses, which seem to have been written after Babylon destroyed Jerusalem, must be a later addition. "Have mercy on me, O God," the psalmist pleads in the opening lines, and for fourteen verses he confesses his sin and pleads for forgiveness. Then the writer vows to spread the good news of that forgiveness. Several penitential psalms voice promises to make sacrifices in response to God's mercy. This psalm, however, promises a special kind of sacrifice:

> The sacrifice acceptable to God is a broken spirit;
>> a broken and contrite heart,
> O God, you will not despise. (51:17)

It has been said that every human emotion is reflected in the Psalms except one: forgiveness. True, many psalmists plead for God to forgive them. But in none is there an expression of forgiveness for one's enemies; rather, psalms beg God to "consume them" (59:13).

> Add guilt to their guilt;
>> may they have no acquittal from you.
> Let them be blotted out of the book of the living. (69:27–28)

The psalmist may even beg God to curse an enemy's family:

> May the creditor seize all that he has. . . .
> May there be no one to do him a kindness,
>> nor anyone to pity his orphaned children. (109:11–12)

At least one may admire the frankness and sincerity with which these poets addressed their God.

Affirmations of Faith and Songs of Thanksgiving

"The Lord is my shepherd." Almost anyone at all familiar with the scripture knows the best-loved "affirmation of faith," the Twenty-third Psalm. Most hymnals contain a metrical paraphrase translation for modern congregations to sing these ancient verses.

Martin Luther taught his followers to sing their affirmation of faith: "A Mighty Fortress Is Our God." It is a metrical paraphrase of Psalm 46.

Pilgrims climbing the mountains toward the holy city sang of their faith in Ps. 121:1–2:

> I lift up my eyes to the hills—
>> from where will my help come?
> My help comes from the Lord,
>> who made heaven and earth.

Other psalmists accused God of going to sleep. This one, by contrast, sings:

> He who keeps you will not slumber.
> He who keeps Israel
>   will neither slumber nor sleep. (121:3–4)

And thus many psalms are songs of thanksgiving for the care the Lord has given. Psalm 107 celebrates how God has delivered people lost in the desert (vv. 4–9), people from prison (vv. 10–16), the sick (vv. 17–22), and sailors from storms at sea (vv. 23–32). Psalm 124 is one of several thanking God for deliverance, apparently from some army that had invaded Israel. Psalm 30 is a prayer of thanksgiving from an individual who had been restored to health after nearly dying: "You have turned my mourning into dancing" (30:11). And the author of Psalm 32 is happy because of receiving not only healing but forgiveness.

Wisdom Poetry

Most psalms are prayers to God or exhortations to others to join in prayer. They were not written for instruction but for worship, though believers have been instructed by them in the kind of worship that is proper for God. But some psalms were written to instruct the hearer, to teach the reader how to live. The longest chapter in the Bible is Psalm 119, a prayer in praise of God's Torah (the Law or Instruction). Psalm 37 exhorts the reader to the virtue of patience. "Happy are those who consider the poor," says Ps. 41:1. And most typical of the moral instruction characteristic of the "wisdom literature" is the First Psalm. It contrasts graphically two ways of life, the way of the wise person who lives by the Torah and the way of the wicked who do not.

But this particular kind of writing, the wisdom literature, so loved by the ancient Hebrews, is the subject of the next two sections.

PROVERBS

> Early to bed and early to rise
> Makes a man healthy, wealthy, and wise.

Like millions of Americans, Hebrew sages would have appreciated America's best-loved wise man, Benjamin Franklin. Like him, they delighted in proverbs, little couplets into which they packed a lifetime of wise observation. In fact, it was almost certainly from the book of Proverbs that Franklin got both the pattern and much of the content of those sayings which he made part of America's folk wisdom. It is sometimes said that today the book of Proverbs has gone out of fashion among both theologians and ordinary church members. Historians tell us, however, that two hundred years ago it was among the most popular books in all of scripture. Perhaps the time has come for a renewed emphasis on its "old-fashioned," practical wisdom. A collection of short sayings and poems, Proverbs does not follow an outline. See p. 165 for a list of its headings.

The Nature of Wisdom Literature

Three books of the Old Testament in Protestant Bibles are classified as "wisdom literature": Job, Proverbs, and Ecclesiastes. Several psalms also are wisdom writings, such as Psalms 32, 34, 37, 49, 112, and 128. Roman Catholic Bibles include two Apocryphal books that are very much in the wisdom pattern: Ecclesiasticus and the Wisdom of Solomon. Wisdom books are by no means all alike, but here are some characteristics of wisdom literature that, to a greater or lesser degree, these works share.

First, Wisdom literature focuses on everyday experience in this world. Sometimes there is no particular moral or religious content to a proverb, only shrewd observation.

> Some pretend to be rich, yet have nothing;
> others pretend to be poor, yet have great wealth. (Prov. 13:7)

The Pentateuch bases its commands on the mighty acts of God, especially God's rescue of the covenant people from Egypt. Proverbs, by contrast, bases its advice on practical common sense. Why should one be generous? Proverbs does not usually urge the reader to be generous because of divine commands, but because one can see that it pays. The sage has observed that

> a generous person will be enriched,
> and one who gives water will get water. (11:25)

Second, wisdom literature deals with the order found in the universe God has created. Job is in agony because he cannot discern that order, but in the end, the Creator points Job to the marvelous planning by which God "laid the foundation of the earth" and "determined its measurements" (Job 38:3–5). Trusting in God's general revelation in creation, the sage can find lessons in ordinary nature:

> Go to the ant, you lazybones;
> consider its ways, and be wise. (Prov. 6:6)

Third, though Ecclesiastes is more skeptical, Proverbs finds that universal order in an observable pattern of consequences. Certain actions are followed by desired results; the opposite actions seem always to lead to trouble:

> A soft answer turns away wrath,
> but a harsh word stirs up anger. (15:1)

> Pride goes before destruction,
> and a haughty spirit before a fall. (16:18)

Anyone who tills the land will have plenty of bread,
but one who follows worthless pursuits will have plenty of poverty. (28:19)

Deuteronomy had promised that God would reward the nation if it obeyed God's laws and would punish it if it sinned. Proverbs goes further, claiming that the pattern of reward and punishment can be seen in the consequences of individual actions in individual daily lives.

Fourth, in the wisdom literature, the goal is to be "wise." Wisdom is to live in accordance with the pattern of life that the sage can teach. Proverbs announces its purpose in its opening verses. The "child" is to study its parent-like advice

for learning about wisdom and instruction,
for understanding words of insight;
for gaining instruction in wise dealing.

Proverbs is written

to teach shrewdness to the simple,
knowledge and prudence to the young. (1:2–4)

The words "wise" and "wisdom" occur more than one hundred times in Proverbs, often contrasted with words such as "fool" or "foolishness." There are two ways of life, that of the wise and that of the fools:

The wise will inherit honor,
but stubborn fools, disgrace (3:35).

Finally, it is characteristic of wisdom literature that it is presented in easily remembered and often witty ways. (For some characteristics of Hebrew poetry see the discussion of "Hebrew Music and Poetry" in the section on the Psalms. All the kinds of couplets described there can be found in Proverbs.) The sages delighted in figurative language, including comic figures:

Like a gold ring in a pig's snout
is a beautiful woman without good sense. (11:22)

Proverbs uses hyperbole, comic exaggeration. Few people are really too lazy even to eat, but the sage can write:

The lazy person buries a hand in the dish,
and is too tired to bring it back to the mouth. (26:15)

The sages also delighted in poems based on numbers:

Three things are too wonderful for me;
four I do not understand:
the way of an eagle in the sky,
the way of a snake on a rock,
the way of a ship on the high seas,
and the way of a man with a girl. (30:18–19)

The foolishness of laziness and the mystery of young love could have been expressed in more prosaic and technical terms, but who would have remembered that? But said as Proverbs puts them, these sayings are quoted thousands of years later.

The Theology of Proverbs

In Man We Trust—so Walter Brueggemann titled a book on the wisdom literature.[25] The point of that rather startling title was to emphasize the "humanism" of books such as Proverbs. In the wisdom literature, human beings are presented as responsible. We make choices and experience consequences, and we do so in the ordinary course of daily life in this world. By paying attention to the sages, the "simple" can become "wise." Proverbs says little about worship, sacrifices, forgiveness, or dependence on divine help. If we are fools, we cannot blame God or the devil; we are on our own.

But this is not at all to say that Proverbs is irreligious. Early in the book, Proverbs announces its theme:

> The fear of the Lord is the beginning of knowledge;
> fools despise wisdom and instruction. (Prov. 1:7)

Or as Prov. 9:10 puts it:

> The fear of the Lord is the beginning of wisdom,
> and the knowledge of the Holy One is insight.

The order of the universe is divine order. Reverence for the Creator is the foundation of true wisdom. True, Deuteronomy bases its ethic on gratitude for redemption from Egypt and on authoritative divine commands, while Proverbs bases its ethic on a kind of pragmatism. But in such works as Psalm 1 and Psalm 119, wisdom and *torah* ("law" or "instruction") are almost synonyms. As Proverbs puts it, "Those who keep the law are wise children" (28:7). The sages discovered that God's law and practical wisdom came out at the same place.

The Source and Structure of Proverbs

"The proverbs of Solomon son of David, king of Israel"—so Proverbs begins. Tradition has made Solomon the author of the entire book. Contributing to that tradition is the report in 1 Kings of the unrivaled wisdom of Solomon:

> God gave Solomon very great wisdom, discernment, and breadth of under-standing as vast as the sand on the seashore, so that Solomon's wisdom surpassed the wisdom of all the people of the east, and all the wisdom of Egypt. He was wiser than anyone else, wiser than Ethan the Ezrahite, and Heman, Calcol, and Darda, children of Mahol; his fame spread throughout all the surrounding nations. He composed three thousand proverbs, and his songs numbered a thousand and five. He would speak of trees, from the cedar that is

in the Lebanon to the hyssop that grows in the wall; he would speak of animals, and birds, and reptiles, and fish. People came from all the nations to hear the wisdom of Solomon; they came from all the kings of the earth who had heard of his wisdom. (1 Kings 4:29–34)

A close reading of Proverbs, however, indicates that the book is a collection of sayings from many authors, composed over perhaps ten centuries. The opening title should be thought of as a dedication to the memory of that first great Israelite collector of proverbs rather than as meaning that King Solomon actually composed them all himself.

As a matter of fact, some of the Proverbs seem to be older than Solomon. It is widely held that Prov. 22:17–23:14 is based on an Egyptian document, *The Wisdom of Amenemope*.[26] Compare, for example, these sayings:

Amenemope	*Proverbs*
See for yourself these thirty sayings.	*Have I not written for you thirty sayings? (22:20)*
Associate not with the hot-head, Nor become intimate with him in conversation.	*Make no friends with those given to anger, and do not associate with hotheads. (22:24)*
Covet not the property of an inferior person, Nor hunger for his bread . . . it is an obstruction in the throat.	*Do not eat the bread of the stingy; do not desire their delicacies; for like a hair in the throat, so are they. (23:6–7)*

Indeed, proverbs are common to all cultures in all ages, including our own, and because the book of Proverbs is based on belief in God as the universal Creator, it should be no surprise that the Hebrews borrowed practical wisdom wherever they found it.

Proverbs itself says that it is a collection of collections from various sources. It is impossible to give a helpful outline of the book of Proverbs. Its sayings have not been put together by subject matter or date. But here are the different collections within the book, as indicated by their headings:

The Proverbs of Solomon (1:1–9:18)
The Proverbs of Solomon (10:1–22:16)
The Words of the Wise (22:17–24:22)
Sayings of the Wise (24:23–34)
Proverbs of Solomon That the Officials of King Hezekiah Copied (25:1–29:27)
The Words of Agur (30:1–33)
The Words of King Lemuel, Taught by His Mother (31:1–31)

(Not all the proverbs under each of these headings need necessarily be thought of as originally belonging to the same collection.)

In the structure of the book, there is one major division that is clear and important. The first nine chapters contain long poems in praise of wisdom, while the rest of the book contains, for the most part, couplets or brief poems (we will return to each of these parts later).

Who were these "wise" people who composed these proverbs? The writer of 1 Kings knew of the Eastern sages Ethan, Heman, Calcol, and Darda. Ezekiel recalled Noah, Daniel, and Job. We are told of David's court adviser Ahithophel that the counsel he gave "was as if one consulted the oracle of God" (2 Sam. 16:23). Though Jeremiah believed that all of them had, in his day, gone wrong, he seems to list four kinds of people through whom God was expected to speak: scribes, prophets, priests, and "the wise" (Jer. 8:8–10). Some scholars, therefore, have proposed that there was an identifiable class of professional teachers of wisdom. These included men such as Ahithophel and women such as the wise woman of Tekoa (2 Sam. 14:1–21), the wise woman to whom General Joab turned (20:14–22), and the mother of King Lemuel (Prov. 31:1). While there were certainly wise advisers to kings (members of the king's "cabinet," as it were), the idea that there was a distinct professional class of the "wise" has been seriously challenged.[27] The word "wise" is used as much of skilled artisans as it is of court advisers. Apparently, one could gain a reputation for wisdom regardless of one's profession.

The best one can say, therefore, is that the book of Proverbs is a collection of miscellaneous sayings gathered over a thousand years from kings, advisers to kings, and anonymous sages and from the folk wisdom of Israel and even of its neighbors.

The Subject Matter of the Short Proverbs (Prov. 10—31)

Space in this *Guide* does not allow for listing many of the subjects that are repeatedly discussed in Proverbs. Basically, Proverbs is concerned with right human relationships and with practical guidance for a satisfying life. Here are just a few ideas emphasized in the short sayings of Proverbs 10—31, with an illustrative proverb for each.

Hard Work versus Laziness

> The appetite of the lazy craves, and gets nothing,
> > while the appetite of the diligent is richly supplied.
> > (13:4; cf. 14:23; 20:4; 24:30–34; etc.)

Good Wives versus Shrews

> It is better to live in a corner of the housetop
> > than in a house shared with a contentious wife.
> > (21:9; cf. 21:19; 27:15–16; etc.)

The book closes, however, with a beautiful tribute to a good wife (31:10–31; cf. 19:14).

Drinking and Overeating

> The drunkard and the glutton will come to poverty,
>   and drowsiness will clothe them with rags.
>   (23:21; cf. 23:1–3, 29–35)

Concern for People in Need

> The righteous know the rights of the poor;
>   the wicked have no such understanding.
>   (29:7; cf. 11:24; 14:31; 19:17; 22:9, 22–23; 29:14)

Talk and the Value of Not Talking Too Much

> Even fools who keep silent are considered wise;
>   when they close their lips, they are deemed intelligent.
>   (17:28; cf. 10:19; 15:1, 4; 17:7; 21:23; 29:20)

Parents and Children

> Do not withhold discipline from your children;
>   if you beat them with a rod, they will not die.
>   (23:13; cf. 10:1; 15:20; 22:6; 23:14–15; 29:15)

Honesty

> Bread gained by deceit is sweet,
>   but afterward the mouth will be full of gravel.
>   (20:17; cf. 11:1; 16:11; 19:5; 20:23)

Quietness and Contentment

> Better is a dinner of vegetables where love is
>   than a fatted ox and hatred with it.
>   (15:17; 17:1, 22; 25:16; 30:7–9)

The Longer Poems: "Dame Wisdom" versus "Dame Folly" (Prov. 1—9)

There are many more subjects discussed in Proverbs. One that is mentioned over and over, concern for which underlies the entire book, is wisdom. Not only do many of the short sayings contrast the wise person and the fool or urge the pursuit of wisdom, but the first nine chapters also contain beautiful poetry contrasting wisdom and folly. These chapters deserve special attention.

The poems that make up the first nine chapters of Proverbs are usually thought to come from the postexilic period, perhaps as late 300 B.C. They may reflect the influence of Greek thought. They are in the form of instruction from a parent to a child:

> Hear, my child, your father's instruction,
>> and do not reject your mother's teaching;
>> for they are a fair garland for your head,
>> and pendants for your neck. (1:8–9)

Over and over, the one who achieves wisdom is promised blessedness:

> Happy are those who find wisdom,
>> and those who get understanding. (3:13)

And now wisdom is personified as a beautiful lady, set over against the prostitute Folly.

> For her income is better than silver,
>> and her revenue better than gold.
> She is more precious than jewels,
>> and nothing you desire can compare with her. (3:14–15)

Vividly, the poet describes folly as a whore, enticing the young person (7:1–27). But over against that evil "woman" there is a remarkable picture of Dame Wisdom, almost equated with God. She speaks:

> By me kings reign. . . .
> Riches and honor are with me. . . .
> My fruit is better than gold, even fine gold. . . .
> The Lord created me at the beginning of his work. . . .
> When he established the heavens, I was there . . .
>> then I was beside him, like a master worker;
> and I was daily his delight . . .
>> and delighting in the human race. (8:15–31)

Greek philosophers of this period were writing of the *logos,* the divine reason, by which all things were created and by which humankind should be guided. Whether the writer of Proverbs 8 was influenced by this concept is debated. It seems clear to many scholars, however, that later Jewish thinkers interpreted Proverbs in the light of Greek thought. They equated the personified wisdom of Proverbs with the Greek philosophers' *logos,* or "word." In the Apocrypha, Ecclesiasticus 24 surely reflects both Proverbs and the Greek concept (see the brief comments on Ecclesiasticus in the chapter on the Apocrypha in this *Guide).*

What makes this important to Christians is that the first chapter of John seems to use the concept of personified wisdom found in Proverbs, using the Greek philosophers' word *logos* to give one answer to the question "Who is Jesus?"[28] The early church made the startling claim that what Proverbs had told humankind to seek had now, instead, found them. Proverbs's "wisdom," the philosophers' *logos,* had become incarnate in Jesus Christ.

ECCLESIASTES
The Teachings of a Disillusioned Philosopher

"Vanity of vanities, says the Teacher, vanity of vanities! All is vanity" (1:2).

1:1 **The Teacher Experiments and Finds All Life Futile**	4:3 **Some Resulting Ethical Observations**	8:1 **Wisdom's One Sure Precept: Enjoy Life When You Can**	11:5 **Enjoy Life Before You Get Old** 12:14
Introduction of the theme: everything is meaningless, 1:1–11	Therefore cultivate the virtues of quiet acceptance, cooperation, and humility, 4:4–5:7	Wisdom does have value, 8:1–15	Make the most of life while you are young, 11:5–10
The teacher has tried all kinds of life; none satisfies, 1:12–2:26	And avoid greedy striving for possessions, 5:8–6:12	But death comes even to the wise, 8:16–9:6	For the miseries of old age are coming, 12:1–8
God sets the time schedule for everything, 3:1–9	(A collection of miscellaneous proverbs), 7:1–29	So be content with what joys happen to come your way, 9:7–18	Appendices: the value of these teachings, 12:9–12
We, however, can never understand it, 3:10–15		(Another collection of miscellaneous proverbs), 10:1–11:4	A pious conclusion, 12:13–14
But only accept it until our time to die, 3:16–4:3			

Author: Traditionally Solomon, but more likely an anonymous teacher who was highly regarded by his students

Date: Perhaps around 250 B.C.

Theme: Life is short, futile, and meaningless, so fear God and make the best of what opportunities for happiness may happen to come your way.

One other related note: when Jesus taught, he did not usually speak in oracles like those of the prophets or in laws like those of Moses. Frequently, he spoke in the pattern of Proverbs:

> Those who are well have no need of a physician,
> but those who are sick. (Mark 2:17)

> The sabbath was made for humankind,
> and not humankind for the sabbath. (Mark 2:27)

Thus Proverbs helped prepare the church for its understanding of Jesus Christ.

ECCLESIASTES

Deuteronomy promised that if the nation was righteous, it would prosper; but the book warned of catastrophe if Israel forsook God's law. The Deuteronomic historians who wrote the books of Judges, Samuel, and Kings demonstrated how this proved true in the rise and fall of Israel. The writers of 1 and 2 Chronicles affirmed even more confidently the pattern of reward and punishment. And Proverbs boldly applied this lesson to individuals in their everyday lives. The First Psalm said it all in a beautiful poem. Of the righteous it promised, "In all that they do, they prosper. . . . But the way of the wicked will perish" (Ps. 1:3–6).

Two books of the Old Testament flatly deny that this pattern is always the case. Job is a dramatic poem filled with the anguished cries of a person who, though innocent, is in agony. And Ecclesiastes, in a far more detached, abstract, philosophical fashion, over and over affirms that there simply is no pattern of reward and punishment or any other discernable order in life as its author has seen it. To the teacher who wrote this book, life is a puzzle. The book is puzzling too.

Ecclesiastes and Proverbs:
A Contrast

To see the startling contrast between Proverbs and Ecclesiastes, look at some quotations from each book, placed side by side. It is true that these quotations are taken out of context, but review their context and the message is still much the same. Many similar quotations could be added.

Proverbs	*Ecclesiastes*
Those who till their land will have plenty of food. (12:11)	What do mortals get from all the toil and strain with which they toil under the sun? . . . Their work is a vexation. . . . This also is vanity. (2:22–23)

Proverbs	Ecclesiastes
I, wisdom, . . . have strength. . . . Riches and honor are with me, enduring wealth and prosperity. (8:12–18)	The race is not to the swift, nor the battle to the strong, nor bread to the wise, nor riches to the intelligent, nor favor to the skillful; but time and chance happen to them all. (9:11)
My child, do not forget my teaching, . . . for length of days and years of life and abundant welfare they will give you. (3:1–2)	The same fate [death] comes to all, to the righteous and the wicked. (9:2)
The wage of the righteous leads to life. (10:16)	Do not be too righteous, and do not act too wise. (7:16)
Happy are those who find wisdom, . . . nothing you desire can compare with her. (3:13–15)	No one can find out what is happening under the sun. . . . Even though those who are wise claim to know, they cannot find it out. (8:17)
The beginning of wisdom is this: Get wisdom, and whatever else you get, get insight. (4:7)	In much wisdom is much vexation, and those who increase knowledge increase sorrow. (1:18)

Repeatedly, Proverbs urges that one can learn to be wise. Wisdom leads to hard work, sobriety, concern for people in need, honesty, and many other virtues. Proverbs seems to promise that those who practice these virtues will receive not only spiritual rewards but quite tangible ones: wealth, long life, and honor. But Ecclesiastes tells us that the writer can observe no such order in the universe. Often the righteous suffer; often the unrighteous prosper; and in the end, the same fate, death, comes equally to both.

The Authorship, Date, and Structure of Ecclesiastes

The author identifies himself as "the son of David, king in Jerusalem," and thus as Solomon, the traditional source of all the wisdom literature. A close reading of the book, however, suggests that the opening ascription should be thought of more as a dedication than as a factual claim to authorship. Two reasons are given for this idea. First, the language of Ecclesiastes is quite different from that of the period of Solomon. It is the Hebrew of centuries later. And second, as noted above, the thought expressed in Ecclesiastes is so different from classical Hebrew thought that it seems clearly to be that of a later age. Most scholars therefore place the book in the third century B.C.

The second verse of the book identifies the author as, in Hebrew, Koheleth. The Greek translation of the Old Testament, the Septuagint, rendered that title by the Greek word *ecclesiastes,* and this became the title of the book in English-language Bibles. Exactly what that word means has puzzled scholars. It is related to the word for "assembly," and thus the King James translation and the Revised Standard Version have called the author "the Preacher." The Good News Bible calls him "the Philosopher." Because, however, we are told that the author taught (Eccl. 12:9), the New Revised Standard Version takes it that the assembly addressed was a classroom and translates "Koheleth" as "Teacher." That is probably the way students addressed this author.

Like the book of Proverbs, Ecclesiastes cannot be neatly outlined. Obviously, there is a brief introduction (1:1–11) setting the theme, "Vanity of vanities! All is vanity" (1:2). That saying recurs throughout the book and serves as a summary at the end (12:8). At the end there is also a postscript— perhaps two or three postscripts (12:9–14). But in between there are collections of the Teacher's sayings, brought together in such a way that it is not possible to say with confidence what the organizing principle was in the mind of the Teacher or his editor. Addison G. Wright finds structural clues dividing the book at 6:9, the first half being "Qoheleth's [Koheleth's] Investigation of Life" and the second, "Qoheleth's Conclusions." "In the first part Qoheleth is concerned with the vanity and emptiness of various human endeavors, and in the second with humankind's inability to understand the work of God."[29] Actually, one can find both ideas repeated in each half. R.B.Y. Scott suggests that, "broadly speaking, the first six chapters set forth [the Teacher's] philosophy and the last six chapters his ethical conclusions and counsel."[30] But again, there is philosophy in the second half and ethics in the first. Scott fully recognizes that "the Words of Qoheleth do not form a clearly structured book." He finds twenty-seven sections in Ecclesiastes. Another scholar analyzes the book into twenty-three blocks of material, and another into thirty-seven. Others regard Ecclesiastes as being almost as loosely organized a collection as Proverbs 10—31.

The reader should be warned, therefore, that the outline on p. 170 of this *Guide* is by no means complete. Many verses do not fit into the pattern presented there. But it may be a useful way of summarizing some of the basic ideas of this confusing book.

Here are some of those ideas.

The Teacher Experiments and Finds Life Futile (Eccl. 1:1–4:3)

> Vanity of vanities, says the Teacher,
> vanity of vanities! All is vanity. (1:2)

So the book states—and repeatedly restates—its basic idea. The word translated as "vanity" occurs more than thirty times throughout this little volume. Scott says that a more literal translation would be "A breath of breaths! A breath of breaths! Everything is a breath!"[31] The New Revised Standard Version similarly translates Eccl. 1:14, "All is vanity and a chasing after wind." Less literally, but helpfully, the Good News Bible renders Eccl. 1:2–3, "It is useless, useless, said the Philosopher. Life is useless, all useless. You spend your life working, laboring, and what do you have to show for it?" Using the vocabulary of a modern existentialist, the New International Version begins Ecclesiastes:

> "Meaningless! Meaningless!" says the Teacher.
> "Utterly meaningless!
> "Everything is meaningless."

The Teacher is a kind of fatalist:

> What has been is what will be,
> and what has been done is what will be done;
> there is nothing new under the sun. (1:9)

The fate that is decreed for all is death (2:14; 3:19; 9:2–3). The Teacher has arrived at this pessimistic view of life by personal observation and experimentation. Indeed, 82 of his 222 verbs are in the first person. "I applied my mind to know wisdom," he tells us (1:17). And he did this by trying various lifestyles for himself. "I said to myself, 'Come now, I will make a test of pleasure; enjoy yourself'" (2:1). He tried wine, great building projects, accumulating slaves and property, and amassing wealth. It was all in vain (2:1–13). Even the wisdom he acquired seemed useless, for he saw that in the end the same fate, death, awaits the wise just as it does the foolish (2:12–17). Soon he would leave to others all that he had amassed. Why, then, should one bother to do all that labor (2:18–23)?

The conclusion to which his observations and experiments led him is this: "There is nothing better for mortals than to eat and drink, and find enjoyment in their toil" (2:24).

God does indeed have a plan, "a time for every matter under heaven" (3:1–8). We, however, "cannot find out what God has done from the beginning to the end" (3:11). The only future we can be sure of is one in which "the fate of humans and the fate of animals is the same; as one dies, so dies the other" (3:19).

Some Resulting Ethical Observations (Eccl. 4:4–7:29)

One might expect such gloomy discoveries to have led the Teacher to despair. Indeed, it did at one point cross his mind, he tells us, that the dead are more fortunate than the living (4:2). But our author is still a life-affirming teacher, and so he deduces from his observations a kind of Stoic ethic. He urges contentment with one's lot:

> Better is a handful with quiet
> than two handfuls with toil. (4:6)

Cooperation is better than competition: "Two are better than one. . . . For if they fall, one will lift up the other. . . . If two lie together, they keep warm. . . . A threefold cord is not quickly broken" (4:9–12). Reverence God (5:1–6). Don't be greedy for wealth (5:10–12). Instead, people should "accept their lot and find enjoyment in their toil—this is the gift of God" (5:19). Be thankful if you can enjoy what you have, for some have plenty and yet cannot enjoy it (6:1–12). As for wisdom, the Teacher has found it in only one man in a thousand, and in no women at all (7:28).

Wisdom's One Sure Precept:
Enjoy Life When You Can (Eccl. 8:1–11:14)

"Who is like the wise man?" the Teacher cries (8:1). Certainly, cruelty and oppression are to be avoided, for in the end, the wicked person dies. But sometimes the righteous "are treated according to the conduct of the wicked" (8:14). Only one thing seems clear:

> So I commend enjoyment, for there is nothing better for people under the sun than to eat, and drink, and enjoy themselves, for this will go with them in their toil through the days of life that God gives them under the sun. (8:15)

The Teacher had begun with a search for wisdom (1:17). But he concludes:

> No one can find out what is happening under the sun. However much they may toil in seeking, they will not find it out; even though those who are wise claim to know, they cannot find it out. (8:17)

Over and over he returns to the realization that "the same fate [death] comes to all, to the righteous and the wicked" (9:2). So you should "go, eat your bread with enjoyment" (9:7). And "whatever your hand finds to do, do with your might; for there is no work or thought or knowledge or wisdom in Sheol [death], to which you are going" (9:10).

Enjoy Life before You Get Old
(Eccl. 11:15–12:14)

Probably the two passages in Ecclesiastes most often read today are the poem about how there is a time for everything (3:1–8) and the closing poetic warning about old age. The student is urged, "Remember your creator in the days of your youth, before the days of trouble come" (12:1). In figurative language, the Teacher describes the blindness and deafness of old age, the lack of sleep, the lameness, the feebleness, the toothlessness, and at last the death that will inevitably come. So, he says to the young student,

"Rejoice . . . while you are young. . . . Follow the inclination of your heart and the desire of your eyes" while you still can (11:9).

The message closes as it began: "Vanity of vanities, says the Teacher; all is vanity" (12:8).

An appendix, perhaps added by devoted students who collected the Teacher's words, commends these wise sayings to the reader. The student is warned not to try to go beyond or add to these proverbs, because "of making many books there is no end, and much study is a weariness of the flesh" (12:12). And a pious note is added that seems not quite in character with some of the rest of the book:

> Fear God, and keep his commandments, for that is the whole duty of everyone. For God will bring every deed into judgment, including every secret thing, whether good or evil. (12:13–14)

Ecclesiastes and the Canon

The rabbinic school of Shammai had a solution to the problem of what to do with this puzzling book: bar it from the canon! Martin Luther tended to agree. But the school of Hillel prevailed, and there it is.

Thus far, our treatment of the book has emphasized the negative. There are, however, passages in Ecclesiastes that sound the more positive message of Proverbs. Many scholars regard these more pious passages in the book as insertions by a later scribe, shocked by the Teacher's arguments that the wise and righteous do not always receive rewards. Perhaps the final verses are such an addition. Another verse that some regard as a "gloss" by a devout editor is "God will judge the righteous and the wicked, for he has appointed a time for every matter, and for every work" (3:17). Most out of keeping with some of the rest of the book is this passage:

> Though sinners do evil a hundred times and prolong their lives, yet I know that it will be well with those who fear God, because they stand in fear before him, but it will not be well with the wicked, neither will they prolong their days like a shadow, because they do not stand in fear before God. (8:12–13)[32]

Sometimes it may be that the Teacher states such positive proverbs in order to examine and refute them. Others argue that they represent the real views of the writer. Whatever is the case, two things are true: they are now part of the book as incorporated into the canon; but the major emphasis of the Teacher seems to be on the uselessness, meaninglessness, and incomprehensibility of life.

Ecclesiastes is not the favorite book of most readers of the Bible, but certain values should be noted.

For one thing, like it or not, much of what the Teacher says is true. The righteous do not always get rich, and often the unrighteous do. Anyone who repeats the Teacher's experiments will discover that virtue is not always rewarded and that the wise and the foolish do die. Standing alone, Proverbs overstates its case. Ecclesiastes has written the corrections on Proverbs. Similarly, the New Testament centers on the story of a virtuous man who suffered a shameful death while still young. Both Proverbs and Ecclesiastes, both Deuteronomy and the gospel, have a place in the canon.

Again, there is a positive ethical message in the Teacher's wisdom. He does not despair over the incomprehensibility of life. Instead, he counsels the virtues of quiet acceptance, contentment with one's lot, refraining from greedy striving, and cooperation with others.

But it is probably by reading Ecclesiastes in the light of Easter that most Christians have found value in it. The earliest extant Christian commentary on the book was written in the middle of the second century A.D. by Gregory Thaumaturgus. He proposed that the purpose of the book was to show that all earthly life is vain and thus to point us to the contemplation of heaven. The Teacher reminds us that things of this world are transient. The gospel agrees, but it gives Christians hope. The Teacher saw death as the end of both foolishness and wisdom. The New Testament promises what the Teacher could not know, that beyond that death is resurrection.

SONG OF SOLOMON

The Hebrews had their own way of expressing the superlative. They called the Lord "God of gods." The king was "King of kings." And so, when they wanted to say that the Song of Solomon was the greatest, the most beautiful song ever written, they gave it this title: "The Song of Songs."

Early in the second century A.D., Rabbi Aqiba went even further. "The whole world is not worth the day on which the Song of Songs was given to Israel, for all the Scriptures are holy, but the Song of Songs is the Holy of Holies."[33] Down through the centuries, Jews have read the Song of Songs as part of the liturgy of the Passover. Perhaps this is because it celebrates the springtime (2:10–12). Perhaps it is also because the song was understood as representing how the loving Lord chose Israel as the divine "bride."

The good rabbi, however, was upset. Young people were singing lyrics from the Song of Solomon not simply in the synagogue but in the tavern. They were understanding the book not as something too sacred for common use but, rather like modern music on MTV, as a celebration of sex and love. In a sense, centuries later, scholars are still debating which was right, the rabbi or the tavern singers, and they are certainly debating just what these lovely poems do mean.

No charted outline seems to quite fit this collection of verses, but see pp. 178–80 for one scholar's analysis.

Interpretations of the
Song of Solomon

"Know, my brother, that you will find great differences in interpretation of the Song of Songs. In truth they differ because the Song of Songs resembles locks to which the keys have been lost." Thus the great Jewish savant Saadia began his commentary on the Song of Songs. In proportion to its size, no book of the Bible has received so much attention and certainly none has had so many divergent interpretations imposed upon its every word.[34]

So Marvin H. Pope begins his commentary on the Song of Solomon. True to his introduction, Pope writes more than seven hundred pages to explain these eight short chapters. Though the Song of Songs is one of the shorter books of the Bible, Pope's commentary is the longest single volume in all the Old Testament in the *Anchor Bible*.

There is agreement among most modern scholars that the work is not by Solomon, though the always-conservative *Harper Study Bible* still assumes that the Solomon tradition is valid.[35] Belief in Solomon as the author is based on the ascription at the beginning of the book; on references to Solomon in 1:5, 3:7–11, and 8:11; and on Solomon's reputation as a composer (1 Kings 4:32; cf. Pss. 72; 127). The ascription, however, can be as accurately translated "to Solomon," a dedication, as "by Solomon." The references to Solomon seem to be about him and do not claim to be by him. A number of scholars have speculated that the author of at least some of the poems must have been a woman.[36]

To date, Pope and others still find indications that some of the poetry is as old as the tenth century B.C. Noting words that seem to have Persian or even Greek origins, however, most scholars believe that the book as we have it comes from perhaps as late as the third century B.C. Hence the book is usually said to be by an unknown author who lived long after Solomon, though it may include folk poems or liturgies that are much older. More important differences of opinion remain.

Building on the prophets' poetic imagery, such as Hos. 2:14–16 and Isa. 50:1, Jewish rabbis interpreted the book as an allegory of the Lord and God's beloved "bride," Israel. Christian interpreters "baptized" this allegory, understanding the book as describing the love of Christ and the church (cf. Eph. 5:25–32). As recently as 1980, Baker Book House, holding to this approach, republished its series from the 1890s, *The Preacher's Complete Homiletic Commentary*. The commentary on Song of Solomon explained 1:2, for example—"Let him kiss me with the kisses of his mouth!"—as meaning, "spiritually, the believer's longing for the sensible presence of Christ as the manifestation of His love. Probably the cry of the Ancient Church for the coming of the Lord's Anointed."[37]

A delightful interpretation became popular in the nineteenth century. The book was understood as a kind of opera with three characters and a chorus. According to this interpretation, the villain is Solomon and the heroine a rustic maiden whom the lecherous old king attempts to add to his harem. The "daughters of Jerusalem" are Solomon's wives and concubines, singing in the background. And the book tells the story of how the heroine remains true to her country swain, who wins out in the end. At least one oratorio has been written around this idea, with prose passages inserted to explain the plot. Unfortunately, there is no way one can really derive that story from these poems.

In *The Interpreter's Bible,* Theophile J. Meek defends a more recent approach.[38] The book, he says, is based on an ancient Hebrew New Year's liturgy, which in turn derived from a pagan fertility cult. Originally, it celebrated the marriage of two pagan deities. He finds phrases in the Song of Solomon that seem to be quoted from such hymns, and he argues that this origin helps explain how a book of love poems came to be incorporated into a sacred volume. In a different cultic interpretation, Pope builds on what he regards as the climactic verse, "love is strong as death" (8:6), and proposes that the book is related to Oriental funeral celebrations. In some Eastern countries, the burial of the dead was accompanied by feasting, drinking, and love making, thus affirming life even in the face of death. *The Interpreter's One-Volume Commentary,* however, rejects any notion of a pagan cultic origin for the book. "For one thing, it seems difficult to explain how such a liturgy could have found entrance into the circles of normative Yahwism [worship of the Lord] or why anyone would have thought it worthwhile to expurgate and preserve it."[39]

The most popular interpretation of the Song of Solomon today is that it is exactly what it seems: a collection of sensuous love songs. God is never mentioned in the entire book. These poems celebrate human, sexual love.

Brevard Childs proposes that the ascription to Solomon places these love poems in the category of wisdom literature. The Song of Songs did not, of course, originate in the same circles that produced Proverbs. Such books as Proverbs, however, did celebrate the work of God in creation. Daily life, according to the wisdom literature, is a gift of God. Hence, so natural a function as sexual union is part of God's good creation. Believing that nature is a gift of the Creator, the sages would not separate the "secular" from the "sacred." Thus love poems, even sensuous love poems, were not out of place in the scripture.[40]

One Understanding of the Content of the Songs

It seems to be impossible to outline this book or to trace with certainty a clear sequence in its poetry. This has not prevented many commentators from attempting to do so. Commentators have grouped these lyrics under three

headings, five, six, twenty, twenty-two, twenty-seven, and—no doubt—
other arrangements. The repetition of phrases and ideas does suggest some
unity in the book, but there really is no clear pattern relating one poem to
another. One of the most interesting attempts to trace some order and
development of themes through these poems, however, is that of Phyllis
Trible in *God and the Rhetoric of Sexuality*. Without commitment to the idea
that this is precisely what was in the mind of the ancient author, we here
summarize briefly Trible's helpful feminist exegesis of the book.[41]

Trible takes as a starting point Adam's love song at the creation of Eve:

> This at last is bone of my bones
> and flesh of my flesh;
> this one shall be called Woman,
> for out of Man this one was taken. (Gen. 2:23)

But with the fall of humankind, the Bible moves from that idyllic love poem
in a garden to tell what Trible calls "A Love Story Gone Awry." The Song of
Solomon, however, she titles "Love's Lyrics Redeemed." In this song, through
true love, another garden appears. Indeed, the woman calls herself a
"garden," in which she invites the man to "eat" (4:16).

To Trible, the Song of Songs is a "symphony of love" unfolding in five
major movements. The end of each of the first four is marked by a verse in
which the woman sings, "I adjure you, O daughters of Jerusalem . . . " (2:7;
3:5; 5:8; 8:4). Not incidentally, in each it is the woman or the chorus of
women who introduces the section, and the woman is the principal speaker
throughout the book.

The first movement (1:2–2:7) begins with the woman telling us of her
desire: "Let him kiss me with the kisses of his mouth!" It ends, as Trible
translates it, with the desire fulfilled, her lover's hands now embracing her.

While the first movement began with the desire for the kisses of the man's
mouth, the second begins with joy at a sound from his lips:

> The voice of my beloved!
> Look, he comes,
> leaping upon the mountains.
> . . . .
> My beloved is like a gazelle. (2:8–9)

It ends when, having sought him in the night, she brings him at last to her
bedroom (3:4–5).

The third movement begins with a question (3:6), marveling at the man as
another Solomon on his wedding day (3:8–11). Later, however—in what is
often interpreted as a dream sequence—her nocturnal search for her lover is
unsuccessful, and indeed, she is abused by city watchmen (5:7). And so this
time her closing appeal to the chorus is for help in finding her lover (5:8).

The fourth movement, therefore, begins with the response of these "daughters of Jerusalem"; they ask who this lover is (5:9). Their question gives her a chance to sing his praises:

> My beloved is all radiant and ruddy,
>> distinguished among ten thousand.
> His head is the finest gold;
>> his locks are wavy,
>> black as a raven. (5:10–11)

This movement ends with a long song by the woman, in which she sings:

> I am my beloved's,
>> and his desire is for me. (7:10)

She even wishes that they were brother and sister so that their public displays of affection would attract less attention (8:1–4; cf. 4:9–10). Again, the movement ends not with a wish but with fulfillment:

> His left hand is under my head
>> and his right hand embraces me! (8:3; Trible's translation)

It is probably the "daughters of Jerusalem" who sing the question that introduces the last movement (8:5–14). In her final song, the woman no longer sings about her lover, as in the other poems. This time she sings to him.

> Make haste, my beloved,
>> and be like a gazelle
> or a young stag
>> upon the mountains of spices! (8:14)

Twice, Trible notes, the woman sings, "My beloved is mine and I am his" (2:16; cf. 6:3). In such love, free from dominance by either sex, characterized by mutuality and equality, Eden's garden is restored.

A Final Note:
God's Passion for Humanity

The old idea that the Song of Songs is an allegory of the love of God for God's people or of Christ for the church has, properly, been largely abandoned. These poems celebrate the human love of man and woman. Nevertheless, as noted above, it is true that the prophets repeatedly compared the covenant relationship between God and Israel to that of husband and wife. Paul compared the love of Christ for the church to married love, and John spoke of the new Jerusalem as like a "bride adorned for her husband" (Rev. 21:2). Medieval thinkers saw in the human love expressed in this book a reflection of that divine love. Perhaps they were not entirely wrong.

Paradoxically, some of the most sensuous love stories among currently popular novels are those of a Roman Catholic priest, Andrew Greeley. He writes of lovers fired with a passion that is indeed "strong as death" (8:6). One of his novels is based on the Song of Songs.[42] As passionate as the lovers Greeley describes are, repeatedly this clergyman-storyteller reminds us of this: the most intense lover's passion is but a shadow of the passion with which God loves us.

4

THE LATTER PROPHETS

Jews call the books of Joshua through 2 Kings "the Former Prophets." Though these are books of history, Jews recognize that they were written by people who were "prophets" in the literal sense of that term: they spoke forth for God. But four scrolls were called "the Latter Prophets": Isaiah, Jeremiah (including Lamentations), Ezekiel, and the "Book of the Twelve" (or the "minor prophets"). Before we look at these "latter prophets," here is some background information.

The ancient Hebrews did not invent or monopolize prophecy; the pagans had prophets too. The archaeologists document what the Bible tells us, that the religions of Israel's neighbors claimed to have men and women who could speak messages from their gods and whose advice was sought by their kings. Balaam is said to have been employed to put a curse on Moses and the Israelites (Num. 22—24). Jezebel brought prophets of Baal to Israel. In 1 Kings 18:20–29, we have a vivid account of that group, singing, dancing, even cutting themselves in their ecstasy as they sought to persuade Baal to send fire from heaven and overcome Elijah's God.

In retrospect, Moses is called a prophet (Deut. 34:10), though 1 Sam. 9:9 suggests that the title may not have been used of him in his lifetime. "Seers" such as Samuel might for a fee help a farmer find stray livestock (1 Sam. 9:8). Sometimes they formed bands called "sons of the prophets" (2 Kings 2:3, 5, 7, RSV). They are described as caught up in "prophetic frenzy," apparently aided in achieving this ecstasy by "harp, tambourine, flute, and lyre." Joining with them, Saul was so inspired that he was "turned into a different person" (1 Sam. 10:5–6). On another occasion, Saul stripped off his clothes, fell into a prophetic frenzy, and lay naked all day before Samuel, "prophesying" (1 Sam. 19:24). Centuries later, Elisha still wanted a minstrel to help get him into the

the spirit for prophesying (2 Kings 3:15). It is no accident, therefore, that many of the oracles found in the books of the prophets are in the form of poetry, apparently chanted or sung by their authors. Indeed, Muslims still regard the beauty of the poetry of the Koran as one proof that Muhammad was a prophet inspired by God.

Elijah could be identified by his odd appearance and primitive dress (2 Kings 1:8). Perhaps he—and the prophet John the Baptist centuries later —renounced more fashionable clothes to remind people of the old days when Israel wandered in the wilderness. Prophets loved to dramatize their messages in what seemed strange ways (Isa. 20:2; Jer. 27:2; Ezek. 12:1–5). It was natural, therefore, that many people ridiculed such prophets, and some regarded them as mad (2 Kings 9:11). Others, however, became their disciples.

Some prophets became advisers to kings. David consulted Nathan and accepted Nathan's word, even when that prophet condemned David's actions (2 Sam. 7:1–17; 12:1–15), and the prophetess Huldah helped give authority to Josiah's reforms (2 Kings 22:14–20). But by the time of Ahab, many such prophets seem to have become hired "yes men," employed to say what the king wanted to hear (1 Kings 22). The prophet Micaiah apparently was imprisoned for speaking God's truth to the king. Perhaps Amos denied being a prophet because he did not want to be associated with the royal sycophants (Amos 7:14).

But prophets who were not on the king's payroll still often engaged in political activity. Ahijah instigated the revolution that split Israel (1 Kings 11:29–40), and Elisha spurred Jehu to revolt against the dynasty of Omri (2 Kings 9). We shall see that many of the prophets whose words formed books of the Bible denounced the injustice and the faithlessness to the Lord of the rulers of their day.

Actually, there seem to have been more false prophets than true prophets in Israel. Deuteronomy proposed one guideline for recognizing which prophets really spoke for God: their words would come true (Deut. 18:22). This criterion, however, though often useful, may have been too simple. Not all the words of the great canonical prophets were literally fulfilled. The Northern Kingdom (Israel) was never restored, for example, in spite of the hope that Jeremiah expressed (Jer. 3:18), and the Temple built after the exile was not equal to the one of which Ezekiel dreamed (Ezek. 40—42). Christians have seen such promises of the prophets as fulfilled in far better ways than even the prophets dreamed, in the coming of Jesus Christ (2 Cor. 1:20).

The prophets did predict the future, and often their predictions did come exactly true. But the prophets whose words form books of the Bible are not remembered primarily as magic fortune-tellers; they were spokespersons for the Lord. They knew the nature of God. Because God is that kind of God, they were sure that God would do certain kinds of things. Amos knew that because the Lord demanded justice, God would punish Israel for its lack of concern for the poor. Jeremiah knew that God would never completely abandon the chosen people. The prophets were the great preachers of their day, calling Israel to repentance and to hope. Thus, far beyond the immediate concerns of their own times, they speak to every age their messages from the Lord.

Elijah is said to have been the representative prophet at Jesus' transfiguration (Mark 9:4). But we have a record of his deeds, not his words. In the eighth century B.C., however, someone recorded some oracles that Amos spoke in Israel. Isaiah tells us that God told him to "bind up the testimony, seal the teaching," putting his words into writing (Isa. 8:16). Baruch recorded prophecies of Jeremiah (Jer. 36:4). And thus the books called "the Latter Prophets" began to come into being. To these we turn now.

ISAIAH

Of all the books of prophecy in the Old Testament, the one the New Testament writers loved best was Isaiah. It was the one they quoted most often. Through it, they interpreted both Christmas and the cross. Both Christians and Jews, as they assembled the books that would be their Bible, the canon, placed first among the prophets the one we examine now: Isaiah.

The Unity and Authorship of the Book

The book seems to have been a growing document. Isaiah, the son of Amoz, whose name appears repeatedly in the first half (Isa. 1—39), prophesied from 742 until 701 B.C. He tells us that he was called to his task "in the year that King Uzziah died" (742 B.C.). His prophecies deal directly with events of the second half of the eighth century B.C., including the invasion of Judah by the combined forces of Syria and the Northern Kingdom and the later invasion by Assyria. In each crisis, we are told, he counseled the king to stand firm, trusting not in military might but in the Lord, and Jerusalem was delivered. A repeated theme of these chapters, however, is that judgment is coming upon Jerusalem for its sins.

The second half of the book (Isa. 40—66), by contrast, deals with an entirely different situation. In these chapters, Jerusalem is in ruins (44:26); Babylon, not Assyria, is the oppressor of Judah; and with Cyrus's imminent conquest of Babylon (538 B.C.) now predicted, the author urges the Jews to prepare to return and rebuild their city. The theme is comfort, pardon, and restoration, not judgment. Isaiah is never mentioned. The style and vocabulary are quite different from those of most of chapters 1—39. Isaiah 9 and 11 glory in the prospect of a coming great king, the messiah. Poems in Isaiah 40—66 sing instead of the coming of a suffering servant. Most commentaries,

ISAIAH 1—39
Warnings of Judgment and Hopes for Peace, Justice, and the Messiah

"The Lord enters into judgment with the elders and princes of His people. It is you who have devoured the vineyard; the spoil of the poor is in your houses" (3:14).

"In returning and rest you shall be saved; in quietness and in trust shall be your strength" (30:15).

1 Oracles of Isaiah, the Son of Amoz, about Israel and Judah	13 Oracles against Various Nations	24 Three Groups of Oracles	37 Assyria Is Thwarted, but Babylon Threatens
Introduction: A plea for justice, 1	Prophecies against:	An apocalypse of cosmic judgment, 24—27	Three chapters, largely repeated from 2 Kings, that tell how God by a miracle saved the city when Assyria invaded, but how Isaiah warned of the Babylonian captivity, 37—39
Prophecies about Judah and Jerusalem, 2—4	Babylon, 13—14	Oracles against various sins, 28—32	
The Song of the Vineyard, 5	Moab, 15—16	Postexilic prophecies of restoration, 33—35	
The prophet's call, 6	Damascus, 17		
Prophecies using a child as a symbol:	Egypt, 18—20		
Immanuel, sign of hope, 7	Babylon, Damascus, Arabia, 21		
Maher-shalal-hash-baz and warning to the enemy, 8	(Isaiah condemns Judah's defense preparations), 22		
The Prince of Peace, 9	Prophecy against Tyre, 23		
A remnant shall survive in spite of Assyria, 10			
The son of David's line, 11			
A joyful day is coming, 12			

Author and Date: Many of the oracles of Isaiah 1—39 are from Isaiah the son of Amoz, who prophesied between 742 and 701 B.C., though these chapters also include some prophecies from a later time (most of Isaiah 40—66 comes from an anonymous poet—or poets—from the time of the exile and later).

Setting: Isaiah, the son of Amoz, lived in Jerusalem at the time of the fall of the Northern Kingdom and the invasion of Judah by enemies, including Assyria.

Theme: Isaiah preached judgment upon Judah for social injustice and trust in arms, but he promised that a remnant would survive if they would trust in "the Holy One of Israel."

One Relationship to the New Testament: Isaiah 1—39 includes promises of a coming son of David. New Testament writers believed these were fulfilled in Jesus (see the outline of chapters 40—66 for the "servant" concept).

therefore, discuss Isaiah 1—39 and Isaiah 40—66 as two separate books, calling them "First Isaiah" and "Second Isaiah." Indeed, many divide the book again: noting that several passages in Isaiah 56—66 seem to presuppose that the Jews have returned from exile, they label these chapters "Third Isaiah."

In fact, only a few commentators still regard the whole book as the work of one writer.[1] Some recent scholarship, however, has argued that in spite of multiple authorship, the book now comes to us as a united whole and should be considered that way.[2] There are passages in First Isaiah that appear to be from a time later than that of Isaiah, the son of Amoz: Isaiah 35, for example, though in the first half of the book, really seems to fit the style and themes of Second Isaiah. The story of Isaiah's warning of the Babylonian captivity to come (Isa. 39), seems to be placed where it is to bind the two parts of the book together. The theme of the holiness of God recurs throughout the entire book. Both halves of the book are focused on God's holy city, Jerusalem. The son of Amoz promised that "a remnant shall return," and the second half of the book witnesses that the fulfillment of that promise is at hand. The message of the first half of the book is judgment; the second half completes God's message by announcing forgiveness. Scholars committed to the canonical approach point out that, whatever the date and origin of each passage may be, the book now comes to us as a connected whole. Jews and Christians have found that its message transcends the original situations in which the various parts were delivered. To emphasize that unity, this *Guide* treats the whole book in this one section; but it notes how passages come alive when some are placed in the crises of the eighth century B.C., and others are seen as expressing the heroic faith of an unnamed poet in the Babylonian exile two hundred years later.

Isaiah 1—39 (First Isaiah)

Oracles of Isaiah, the Son of Amoz, about
Israel and Judah (Isa. 1—12)

"The vision of Isaiah son of Amoz, which he saw concerning Judah and Jerusalem in the days of Uzziah, Jotham, Ahaz, and Hezekiah, kings of Judah" (1:1)—so the first section of the book begins. Some passages in the first twelve chapters are written in the first person, and several describe things the prophet did; hence this section is sometimes called "Memoirs of Isaiah the Son of Amoz."

Chapter 1 is a shocking introduction, perhaps composed of several sayings of the prophet. It begins by picturing the Lord as announcing that God's people are more stupid than donkeys! No wonder their country lies desolate, devastated by invaders. God will not listen to their prayers, Isaiah warns, and all the sacrifices ordained by Moses are a waste of time. Through Isaiah, God announces:

> Bringing offerings is futile;
>   incense is an abomination to me. . . .
> Your new moons and your appointed festivals
>   my soul hates; . . .
> even though you make many prayers,
>   I will not listen. (1:13–15)

Isaiah is not really opposed to prayer and worship; his own call to ministry occurred in the Temple (6:1–8). But prayer and sacrifice, he knows, are no substitute for social justice. Here, he says, is what God really wants:

> Cease to do evil,
>   learn to do good;
> seek justice,
>   rescue the oppressed,
> defend the orphan,
>   plead for the widow. (1:16–17)

Never one to mince language, he calls the holy city a whore (1:21). He denounces the government not only for dishonesty in high places but for its lack of concern for people in need:

> Your princes are rebels
>   and companions of thieves.
> Everyone loves a bribe
>   and runs after gifts.
> They do not defend the orphan,
>   and the widow's cause does not come before them. (1:23)

Judgment, he warns, is coming. And yet Isaiah grieves over Jerusalem and pleads with the once-faithful city to repent. And at least for some in the city, Isaiah offers hope:

> Zion shall be redeemed by justice,
>   and those in her who repent, by righteousness. (1:27)

For the rest, there is only destruction.

At this point is inserted one of the best-loved poems in all of scripture (2:1–4). Curiously, most of the same song is found almost word for word in Micah 4:1–3. Did one copy it from the other? Did both quote a currently popular song? Or as many scholars suggest, was an editor from a later time inspired to insert it appropriately here? One can only say that it comes here as a vision of gospel hope after the bitter denunciation of the city. The "mountain of the Lord" (the Temple Mount) will be raised above all other mountains, and all the nations will come to Jerusalem to worship:

> They shall beat their swords into plowshares,
> and their spears into pruning hooks;
> nation shall not lift up sword against nation,
> neither shall they learn war any more. (2:4)

Today, words from Isaiah's song of hope for peace are inscribed on the wall of the United Nations building in New York.

The next chapters, however, are oracles of judgment on Jerusalem for its sins. Princes are guilty, the Lord says, of "crushing my people" and "grinding the face of the poor" (3:15). The prophet vividly describes the wealthy women of Jerusalem, with their

> finery of the anklets, the headbands, and the crescents; the pendants, the bracelets, and the scarfs; the headdresses, the armlets, the sashes, the perfume boxes, and the amulets; the signet rings and nose rings; the festal robes, the mantles, the cloaks, and the handbags; the garments of gauze, the linen garments, the turbans, and the veils. (3:18–23)

These ladies were stylish enough. But unconcerned now for the poor, their day of terrible poverty is coming. Yet again, the prophecy of judgment is followed by one of hope, at least for the little group that will survive (4:2–6).

Of the prophecies of judgment, one of the most beautiful is the "Song of the Vineyard," chapter 5. Perhaps the prophet sang it at a harvest festival after the maidens had danced in celebration. He offers a "love-song" for "my beloved," and the crowd, one imagines, is delighted. Appropriate to the festival, it is a song about a vineyard. But the carefully tended vineyard produces what could be translated as "stinking fruit." And so the farmer gives up on the vineyard, abandons it. The hearers would have sympathized with the farmer. "What more was there to do?" (5:4). But suddenly the singer explains his song. It is an allegory:

> For the vineyard of the Lord of hosts
> is the house of Israel. (5:7)

In approving the destruction of the vineyard, Isaiah's hearers have condemned themselves. The wealthy have grabbed even the property of the poor.

> Ah, you who join house to house,
> who add field to field,
> . . . .
> Surely many houses shall be desolate,
> large and beautiful houses without inhabitant. (5:8–9)

And rich, luxurious, alcohol-plagued Jerusalem will go into exile (5:11–13; cf. 5:22–23).

Chapter 6 tells of the prophet's call. Some have said that it serves as a kind of model for complete worship in any day. It begins with a vision of the glory of God, before whom a heavenly choir sings, "Holy, holy, holy" (6:1–4). Next comes confession of sin (6:5), followed by forgiveness and cleansing (6:6–7). Now comes the challenge to service, to which the prophet responds, "Here am I; send me!" (6:8). And this worshiper is sent forth now with a commission from God (6:9–13). In the case of Isaiah, it is a commission to warn of judgment to come if Judah does not repent.

Yet the themes of judgment and hope continue to alternate. Chapters 7 through 12 contain oracles from at least thirty years apart, and some scholars believe that some of these poems were written long after the death of the son of Amoz. Perhaps one theme that caused the editor who collected them to group them together is the repeated figure of a "child."

Around 734 or 733 B.C., as mighty Assyria (part of modern Iraq) menaced them, Israel—the Northern Kingdom—and Syria sought to force Judah to join them in a defensive military alliance. They invaded Judah, probably intending to place a Syrian on the throne in Jerusalem instead of King Ahaz, to guarantee Judah's military cooperation (2 Kings 16:1–20). "The heart of Ahaz and the heart of his people shook as the trees of the forest shake before the wind" (Isa. 7:2). Isaiah had already given one of his sons a curious name, Shear-jashub, "a remnant shall return," symbol of his conviction that terrible times were coming but some faithful people would survive. Taking that child with him, Isaiah confronted the terrified monarch and promised him a sign of deliverance. "Look, the young woman [probably Isaiah's wife] is with child and shall bear a son, and shall name him Immanuel ['God is with us']" (7:14). Before that child would be old enough even to know right from wrong, the feared invaders would be gone. Nevertheless, hard times would follow, indicated by the plain fare the child—and presumably, others—would eat (7:15). The immediate meaning of Immanuel's birth, however, has not exhausted its significance in the Christian canon. Though the Hebrew word *alma* is here properly translated "young woman," the Septuagint, the Greek translation used by New Testament writers, translated it using the Greek word for "virgin." Matthew, therefore, was able to see in the promise of "God is with us" a foreshadowing of the birth of Jesus (Matt. 1:23).

Perhaps Matthew's messianic interpretation of the child was aided by the continued theme of "child" in the next chapters. In chapter 8, the prophet goes to a prophetess, presumably his wife, and she is to bear a son. This boy is to have the name Maher-shalal-hash-baz, "The Spoil Speeds, the Prey Hastens," that curious name being another sign of the deliverance of Judah and the destruction of its twin enemies, Israel and Syria. King Ahaz does not seem to have followed Isaiah's advice, and the chapter ends with more warnings of doom. Three children with symbolic names have now become living signs. With the help of his disciples, Isaiah adds another sign: he has his "testimony" written down. Thus it was preserved to become part of our Bible (8:16–18; cf. 30:8). As far as we know, Isaiah engaged in little public activity after this until the reign of Hezekiah, a more responsive king, some thirty years later.

At this point, however, our editor inserts another song about a child, a song beloved by Christians at the Advent season:

> For a child has been born for us,
>   a son given to us;
> authority rests upon his shoulders;
>   and he is named
> Wonderful Counselor, Mighty God,
>   Everlasting Father, Prince of Peace. (9:6)

Perhaps this was sung at the birth of a prince in the royal palace—Hezekiah, for example. Perhaps birth here is used as a symbol for coronation, as a new king begins his reign. Some commentators place this song after the exile. Whatever its origin, Jews continued to sing it long after there was no king in Jerusalem. Someday, they dreamed, that king would come. Christians affirm that this hope of the child, the Prince of Peace, was fulfilled in Jesus.

The next chapter returns to one of Isaiah's repeated themes, expressed in the name of one of his children: the salvation of the remnant. This group, he promises, will survive in spite of Assyria, and they will trust no more in foreign alliances or military might but in the Lord (10:20–27).

And again, the messiah is promised. From the stock of Jesse—that is, David's family—will be born a spirit-filled ruler (11:1). His reign will bring justice to the poor and universal peace. In his glorious messianic age, even enmities in nature will be overcome:

> The wolf shall live with the lamb,
>   the leopard shall lie down with the kid,
> the calf and the lion and the fatling together. (11:6)

And then comes the climax and conclusion of the oracles with the sign of a child: "A little child shall lead them" (11:6).

The section closes with a song of anticipated thanksgiving (12:1–6).

Oracles against Various Nations (Isa. 13—23)

The next section of Isaiah has not elicited quite the same love from Christian readers as have the first chapters of the book. The editor has collected a series of taunt songs and oracles of doom and judgment from the Lord on Judah's neighbors. Of Babylon we read:

> Their infants will be dashed to pieces
>   before their eyes. (13:16)

Of Judah's near neighbor to the southeast the poet sings:

> Therefore let Moab wail,
> let everyone wail for Moab. (16:7)

Damascus, capital of Syria, still today an enemy of Israel, fares no better: "Her towns will be deserted forever" (17:2).

Isaiah was so sure that Egypt would be stripped in defeat and was so strongly opposed to Judah's forming a military alliance with that giant to the southwest that we are told he walked naked and barefoot for three years to attract attention to his protest (20:1–6). Arabia and Tyre also receive prophecies of judgment. (The current tensions in the Middle East are nothing new.)

Unattractive as the tone of these poems may be and remote as they seem to modern readers, thousands of miles and thousands of years later, these oracles, too, have a place in the canon. For one thing, one may note the growing understanding of the universal reign of God. "I will punish the world for its evil," cries Isaiah's God (13:11). The power of the One whom Isaiah worships is by no means confined to Israel. For another thing, remember that Isaiah was quite as severe in his judgment on his own people as he was on his neighbors. And these nations are condemned for sins that have characterized many nations in our own age. Babylon had been an oppressor (14:4). Moab had been proud, even insolent (16:6). Egypt's conquests had terrorized the world (18:2). Note, too, that Isaiah was concerned that his own nation not imitate these neighbors by playing their game of power politics. The prophet found no joy in Hezekiah's defense preparations against these neighbors (22:8–11). Judah must trust not in its fortress walls but in its Lord. Instead of hope through Israel's armies, here and there one finds hints or even direct promises of the coming of a God-given messiah (16:4–5).

Three Groups of Oracles (Isa. 24—36)

The editor has placed next a four-chapter collection of oracles of cosmic judgment. Most scholars regard these as coming from a time much later than that of our eighth-century prophet. They are appropriate here, however, because they carry to new heights the prophecies of judgment on the nations that are found in chapters 13—20. Commentators call chapters 24—27 "Isaiah's Little Apocalypse," that is, his symbolic description of the final events, the end of the world:

> Now the Lord is about to lay waste the earth and make it desolate,
> and he will twist its surface and scatter its inhabitants. (24:1)

The preceding songs voiced doom, much of which lay within history. Many of those prophecies in time literally came true. But the disasters now described transcend anything earthly:

> On that day the Lord will punish
> the host of heaven in heaven,
> and on earth the kings of the earth. . . .
> Then the moon will be abashed,
> and the sun ashamed. (24:21–23)

But the end of these catastrophic events will be the final deliverance of all humankind. They will celebrate with a banquet:

> On this mountain the Lord of hosts will make for all peoples
> a feast of rich food. (25:6)

And in one of the few places in the Old Testament where there is promise of a future life, the poet sings of God, "He will swallow up death forever" (25:7). The author of the great New Testament apocalypse, Revelation, was twice to echo Isaiah's lovely picture of God's final compassion for humanity: "Then the Lord God will wipe away the tears from all faces (25:8; cf. Rev. 7:17; 21:4).

Chapters 28 through 32 contain many prophecies that again relate directly to Isaiah's own day. He condemns "the proud garland of the drunkards of Ephraim [the Northern Kingdom]" (28:1), contrasting their fading power with the "garland of glory" of the Lord (28:5). But Isaiah is equally ready to condemn in his own country the "scoffers who rule this people in Jerusalem" (28:14). Once more he protests their trust in an alliance with Egypt and in military preparedness:

> Alas for those who go down to Egypt for help
> and who rely on horses,
> who trust in chariots because they are many
> and in horsemen because they are very strong,
> but do not look to the Holy One of Israel. (31:1)

To Isaiah, trust in armaments and trust in the Lord were contrasting faiths. No cavalry and no war chariots could save Judah from Syria or Assyria. Instead,

> thus said the Lord God, the Holy One of Israel:
> In returning and rest you shall be saved;
> in quietness and in trust shall be your strength. (30:15)

The story of how God miraculously delivered Jerusalem from the Assyrian army is told to show how Isaiah's prophecy came quite literally true (Isa. 37—38).

First, however, there is a series of poems so like those of Second Isaiah (Isa. 40—55) that they help show that the book in its present form is to be thought of as a unified whole. The destroyer, Babylon, will be destroyed (33:1). Now everything is in chaos (33:7–9). But the Lord is about to perform mighty acts (33:10–12), especially in behalf of the righteous (33:15). Therefore Judah is told, "Do not fear!" (35:4); for as in the days of Moses, "waters shall break forth in the wilderness" (35:6). "A highway shall be there" (35:8), and on it, at last, "the ransomed of the Lord shall return" from their captivity in Babylon (35:10).

Assyria Is Thwarted, but Babylon Threatens (Isa. 37—39)

The transition from the first part of the book (chapters 1—39) to the second part, in which the Babylonian captivity is presupposed, is accomplished by a retelling of two stories from 2 Kings 18—20. The Northern Kingdom had been destroyed by Assyria. Now Assyrian King Sennacherib sent his propaganda agent, the Rabshakeh, to issue his ultimatum and persuade terrified Jerusalem to surrender. King Hezekiah sent to Isaiah for advice. True to the principles he had preached, Isaiah urged that the king trust God and never surrender (37:6). Hezekiah's prayers (37:15–20) would be answered (37:21–35). And indeed, we are told, perhaps by bubonic plague, God destroyed the Assyrian army in a single night (37:36–38).

But to point us to the second half of the book, set in the time of the Babylonian captivity, the first half ends with an account of how a diplomatic delegation from Babylon, a newly rising power, was welcomed in Jerusalem (Isa. 39). Perhaps they had come seeking a military alliance against Assyria. Hezekiah proudly showed them all his royal treasures. With prophetic insight, Isaiah warned of what would come tragically true a little over a century later: all that treasure and, indeed, even the king's own descendants would be carried away into shameful slavery by the country in whom Hezekiah now placed his trust.

And so, as we know from 2 Kings, a little over a century after his death, Isaiah's prophecy of judgment was fulfilled. In 587 B.C. Judah was deported into slavery in Babylon. It is there that the second half of the book of Isaiah begins.

Isaiah 40—55 (Second Isaiah)

> Comfort, comfort, my people,
> > says your God.
> Speak to the heart of Jerusalem! (40:1–2; author's translation)

In this way, God commissions the heavenly host. Moses had commanded that all slaves should be released after forty-nine years. Now the angelic messengers are to proclaim to Judah, enslaved in Babylon, "that she has served her term" (40:2). Her year of jubilee, of liberation, is at hand.

Isaiah 40—55 is filled with this good news of redemption. It had been the task of Amos to warn that what awaited Israel was not salvation but judgment. Isaiah, the son of Amoz, had often given the same warning. But now an unnamed poet sings no longer of judgment but of salvation. Jerusalem's

ISAIAH 40—66
Promises of Restoration and Redemption and Calls to Righteous Living

"Go out from Babylon, flee from Chaldea" (48:20).

"I will give you [my servant] as a light to the nations, that my salvation may reach to the end of the earth" (49:6).

40	49	56
"Second Isaiah"—Prophecies of the End of the Exile and a Summons to Return Home	**A Call to Return Home and to the Servant Mission**	**"Third Isaiah"—Postexilic Prophecies**
The Creator-Redeemer Is Coming to Liberate Judah from Babylon	The twin calls: to return home and to the servant mission, 49	God promises blessings to *all* who keep the Sabbath, 56:1–8
Get ready! The Creator-Redeemer is coming, 40	God has not abandoned the suffering servant, 50:1–11	But both leaders and people are sinning, 56:9–57:21
The nations will stand trial, but Israel will be set free, 41	Instead, God will comfort and redeem Zion, 51:1–52:12	The fast that brings blessings is to help those in need, 58:1–14
The servant, though blind, will be a light to those nations, 42	The servant will redeem humankind, 52:13–53:12	So repent, for God is going to bring a glorious day, 59:1–60:22
So "fear not!", 43:1–44:8	Zion will be restored, 54	A call to mission to those in need, 61:1–13
Not Babylon's idols but God will redeem Israel, through Cyrus, 44:9–46:13	So joyfully return to God and to the covenant mission, 55	God will vindicate Zion and punish its enemies, 62:1–63:6
Babylon will be destroyed, so leave it, 47—48		A prayer to the God of grace and God's severe answer, 63:7–65:16
		New heaven, new earth coming, 65:17–25
		Miscellaneous closing oracles, 66:1–24

Time and Setting: While much of Isaiah 1—39 was addressed to people in the eighth century B.C., Isaiah 40—55 was addressed primarily to the exiles in Babylon shortly before their release in 528 B.C. Many of the oracles in Isaiah 56—66 are addressed to the Jews after their return to Jerusalem, and some may even be from a later century.

Theme: This second half of Isaiah focuses on how the one holy God will restore the captives to their homeland, the mission of the servant of the Lord, and the renewal of living according to the covenant when they have returned.

Special Significance for the New Testament: Though there is debate as to whom the prophet understood by the suffering "servant," the New Testament writers saw these prophecies as fulfilled in Jesus.

"penalty is paid" (40:2). Indeed, she has made the double retribution demanded by God's law (40:2; cf. Ex. 22:7). The rest of the story can now be told; the book of Isaiah is to be completed. Across a highway engineered by God, the Lord's people, about to be marvelously liberated from Babylon, are to march triumphantly home. Now, at last, Isaiah's "remnant will return."

True, Jerusalem is in ruins (44:26). Its people are "prisoners" (49:9). They have been "robbed and plundered" (42:22). The Jews' land is "devastated" (49:19). The people, who had thought themselves "married" to God by a covenant, feel that now the Lord has "divorced" them (50:1). Bel and Nebo, gods of Babylon, seem all-powerful. No wonder the prophet's hearers find his good news so incredible that he calls them "deaf" to the message (42:19; cf. 42:23). But the prophet proclaims a God who "fulfills the prediction of his messengers" (44:26; Isaiah, the son of Amoz, and Jeremiah, for example). This is a God

> who says of Jerusalem, "It shall be inhabited,"
> and of the cities of Judah, "They shall be rebuilt,
> and I will raise up their ruins." (44:26)

Even that little group of very conservative scholars who, on the basis of Isa. 1:1, attribute the entire book to Isaiah, the son of Amoz, agree that the words of Isaiah 40—55 are meant for the period shortly before 538 B.C. In that year, Cyrus of Persia (now Iran) conquered Babylon (now Iraq) and let the captive Jews go free (Ezra 1:1–4). Foreseeing that deliverance coming, this prophet could sing, "Go out from Babylon, flee from Chaldea . . . The Lord has redeemed his servant Jacob' " (48:20).

Who this anonymous prophet was, we will never know. We do know that he or she was inspired to write some of the grandest poetry in all of scripture. This poet was one who had suffered. And this theologian presents what many regard as the highest theology in all the Old Testament.

The Creator-Redeemer Is Coming to Liberate Judah from Babylon (Isa. 40—48)

Wars in the Middle East have made pictures of the Arabian Desert all too familiar to modern viewers of television news. Across that barren, rugged, dry country, the poet sings, God's angels are to build a highway on which the Jews may return (40:3–5). The Lord "will feed his flock like a shepherd" and "carry them in his bosom" back home again (40:11). (The great commentary on many verses from these chapters is in the music of Handel's *Messiah*.)

The prophets liked to write oracles in the style of a courtroom drama—or more precisely, the pleading of a case at the ancient city gate. So now this poet pictures the Creator as challenging the nations and their gods to debate:

"Who has measured the waters in the hollow of his hand?" (40:12). "To whom then will you compare me?" (40:25). Surely no heathen idol can equal the Lord. And so, humiliated as Israel has been,

> Do not fear, you worm Jacob
> . . . .
> I will help you, says the Lord;
>   your Redeemer is the Holy One of Israel. (41:14)

With Isa. 42:1–4, we have the first of four "servant songs," the others being in 49:1–6; 50:4–11; and 52:13–53:12. Many scholars propose that when these were originally composed, they were independent of the contexts in which they are now found. Therefore they should be interpreted as a unit in themselves. A small library could be filled with books seeking to determine who this "servant" was in the mind of the poet.[3] More recently, commentators have reminded us that these oracles come to us now in the context of the book's other prophecies, that we may never be able to read the mind of the prophet concerning exactly who the prophet expected would fulfill the prophecy, and that we may more profitably focus attention of the mission of the servant than on the servant's identity.[4]

The first reference to the servant is clear enough: "But you, Israel, my servant . . . " (41:8). These oppressed Jews are assured that they are chosen to serve God and that therefore God has not cast them off. Therefore, "do not be afraid" (41:10). The point of the first servant song, however, is not the servant's identity but his mission. The servant has been chosen by God and empowered by God's Spirit for a purpose: to "bring forth justice to the nations" (42:1). He will accomplish this international revolution nonviolently (42:3). And he will not stop until the whole world is won (42:4). Other prophets could describe God raining down horrible judgment on other nations, and Isaiah, the son of Amoz, could picture a day when all nations would bring their tribute to Jerusalem and its God. But that Israel had a mission to bring the world to righteousness must have seemed a startlingly new idea. Israel has been blind to this mission (42:19), but now it is called to this task (42:18–25; cf. Gen. 12:3c).

Summoned by such a God to such a destiny, they need not fear. Four times the cry of Isa. 41:10 is now echoed: "Do not fear, for I have redeemed you" (43:1). "Do not fear, for I am with you" (43:5). "Do not fear, O Jacob my servant" (44:2). "Do not fear, or be afraid" (44:8).

They need not fear because the God who promises to bring them home is the one, holy God, the Creator, the Sovereign of all history. By contrast, the gods of the heathen are nothing. Relatively few passages in the Bible are intended to be funny, but Isa. 44:9–20 is an exception. The prophet's purpose is serious, but he makes all manner of fun of idolaters. What a fool is the man who burns part of a log to cook his dinner and then carves an idol to worship out of the rest of it!

And so the prophet arrives at the announcement of the specific means that the Lord of history will use to deliver God's servant, Israel. With prophetic foresight, he declares that Cyrus will set the Jews free (44:28). Cyrus himself does not realize it, but his whole program of world conquest has been ordained by the God of the Jews for just one purpose: to set free the Lord's chosen people (45:4, 13).

> He shall build my city
> and set my exiles free. (45:13)

And the riches of the world will flow to Jerusalem (45:14).

Over and over, the prophet affirms absolute monotheism and makes fun of idolatry (45:14–46:13):

> Turn to me and be saved,
> all the ends of the earth!
> For I am God, and there is no other. (45:22)

Other prophets had rebuked Israel whenever it worshiped other gods, but whether they believed pagan deities had some kind of existence is debated. This prophet knows that only one true Lord exists.

Trusting in false gods, Babylon is bound to fall (Isa. 47). So this section ends with a joyful summons. The new exodus is about to begin. Therefore

> go out from Babylon, flee from Chaldea,
> declare this with a shout of joy, proclaim it,
> send it forth to end of the earth;
> say, "The Lord has redeemed his servant Jacob!" (48:20)

A Call to Return Home and to the Servant Mission (Isa. 49—55)

Up to this point, it is possible to interpret the servant as being Israel, though called to a mission not previously recognized by the Jews. With chapter 49, that simple identification runs into problems. Now the servant is not Israel but, instead, has a mission to Israel, "to raise up the tribes of Jacob" (49:6). The chapter begins in the first person, so one could think of the servant here as being the prophet himself. But the servant is called to a mission beyond that of even so extraordinary a person as this poet:

> I will give you as a light to the nations,
> that my salvation may reach to the end of the earth. (49:6)

The prophet is indeed called to summon the prisoners to return home (49:9). But the servant's mission transcends both the prophet's and Israel's calling.

The third servant song (50:4–11) introduces a new element: the servant suffers. But it is the fourth of these songs (52:13–53:12) that proclaims the purpose of the servant's suffering. In Jewish worship, a lamb could be killed as a kind of substitute for the sinful worshiper. Now the poet sings of the coming servant as being "like a lamb that is led to the slaughter" (53:7):

> But he was wounded for our transgressions,
>   crushed for our iniquities;
> upon him was the punishment that made us whole,
>   and by his bruises we are healed.
> All we like sheep have gone astray;
>   we have all turned to our own way,
> and the Lord has laid on him
>   the iniquity of us all. (53:5–6)

Through his suffering and death, the servant brings salvation to the whole world. And paradoxically, though the servant dies and is buried (53:9), at the end of the song the servant seems to be alive again, as though risen from the dead (53:11–12).

The mission of the servant is quite different from that of the messiah promised by psalmists and other prophets. That conquering ruler would break the nations "with a rod of iron" (Ps. 2:9), "filling them with corpses" (Ps. 110:6). The servant, by contrast, is to proclaim liberation and to be a light to Israel. Thus the servant must fulfill the role of a prophet. The servant must also be a light to the whole world. That is rather more than an ordinary prophet ever attempted, though Israel may be called on to fulfill that mission. The servant has a priestly function, bringing forgiveness of sins by being himself the lamb of God. Surely God has used Israel's suffering as a means of enlightening and blessing to the rest of us, who have so often persecuted that people. And yet the function of the servant seems to go beyond what either the prophet or the chosen people could achieve.

Poetry often has meanings on several levels. Perhaps it is fruitless now to try to read the ancient prophet's mind—to determine precisely whom he hoped for as the one who might be God's servant and achieve this cosmic redemption. It may be that he did not have one precise answer to that question. Within the Christian canon, however, there is an answer. Christians see in the call to mission a summons to the church. But Christians find a deeper meaning still. The New Testament tells of a devout man who, having read Isaiah 53, inquired, "About whom, may I ask you, does the prophet say this, about himself or about someone else?" And Philip "proclaimed to him the good news about Jesus" (Acts 8:34–35).

Second Isaiah ends with good news. "Sing," the prophet cries (54:1). "Do not fear," he repeats (54:4). Like a faithful husband, God will give Jerusalem many sons. And so the prophet calls to the people to come and buy without price the food that really matters (55:1–2). In Israel's new exodus back to Jerusalem, even the mountains "shall burst into song" (55:12). More than mere return to the old city is promised. In an ecstasy of eschatological vision, the prophet promises these exiles that nature itself will be transformed, "for an everlasting sign that shall not be cut off" (55:13).

Isaiah 56—66 (Third Isaiah)

The canonical book of Isaiah comes to us as an example of how the word of God lives and grows. The vision of the new exodus and, in effect, the new Eden does not end the book as we now have it. Eleven more chapters carry the message down to some thirty or more years later.

Several passages show that the oracles of Isaiah 56—66 were written to people of a time somewhat later than that of Isaiah 40—55. Though Jerusalem's walls have not yet been rebuilt (60:10), many Jews have now been gathered back to Jerusalem (56:8). And the Temple has been rebuilt (66:1, 6). This means that these oracles were not completed before 516 B.C. Most scholars, therefore, regard these chapters as the work of yet a third "Isaiah." They are so similar in style and vocabulary to Second Isaiah, however, that some still regard them as the work of the same author. Some explain the similarities as the work of disciples seeking to imitate the great poet of the exile.[5]

Some Themes of Third Isaiah

According to these chapters, Israel's problem, now that the chosen people have returned, is not captivity by Babylon; it is their own sin. Chapter 56 is a plea to keep the Sabbath. But it offers a new promise. Foreigners and even eunuchs, previously barred from God's people by the law of Deut. 23:1, are now welcomed to the fellowship if they keep God's covenant (56:3–4). Some Jews are condemned because they have drifted back into the worship of pagan gods (57:9). The subject of sabbaths, proper worship, and fasting leads to an expression of social concern:

Is not this the fast that I choose:
   to loose the bonds of injustice,
   to undo the thongs of the yoke,
to let the oppressed go free,
   and to break every yoke?
Is it not to share your bread with the hungry,
   and bring the homeless poor into your house? (58:6–7)

The poetic promises of the prophet of the exile have been by no means literally fulfilled. The little remnant of returned exiles is discouraged. "We wait for light, and lo! there is darkness," this writer admits (59:9). But he reassures his disillusioned hearers:

> Arise, shine; for your light has come,
> > and the glory of the Lord has risen upon you.
> . . . .
> Nations shall come to your light,
> > and kings to the brightness of your dawn. (60:1–3)

According to Luke, Jesus defined his own mission by a servant-like passage from Third Isaiah:

> The spirit of the Lord God is upon me,
> > because the Lord has anointed me;
> he has sent me to bring good news to the oppressed,
> > to bind up the brokenhearted,
> to proclaim liberty to the captives,
> > and release to the prisoners;
> to proclaim the year of the Lord's favor (61:1–2; cf. Luke 4:16–21).

Liberation theologians and others concerned for the oppressed have loved these words.

Other warnings of judgment and glimpses of hope are scattered through-out these chapters in no clear order. One eschatological passage is so joyful that it is echoed at the climactic conclusion of the New Testament:

> For I am about to create new heavens
> > and a new earth;
> the former things shall not be remembered
> > or come to mind.
> But be glad and rejoice forever
> > in what I am creating;
> for I am about to create Jerusalem as a joy. (65:17–18; cf. Rev. 21:1–2)

And so this great book ends with the promise that God is like a heavenly mother, caring still for her children (66:12–13).

JEREMIAH

We are told more about the life, thought, and inner struggles of Jeremiah than of any other prophet—probably any other person—in the Old Testament.

We know that at various times he was cursed by the crowds (15:10), beaten and arrested (37:15), nearly lynched (26:8), and tortured (20:2). We know that former friends from his hometown and even family members hated him so much that they plotted to assassinate him (11:21; 12:6). We know that he responded by eloquently cursing them all (12:3; 24:9; etc.). "Let me see thy vengeance upon them" (11:20, RSV), he begged the Lord. "Destroy them with double destruction!" (17:18). As to his own relationship with God, in language that seems blasphemous, he accused the Lord of lying to him (20:7). The God who had once been like a "fountain of living water" (2:13)

JEREMIAH
"The Weeping Prophet"

"Now I have put my words in your mouth. See, today I appoint you over nations and over kingdoms, to pluck up and to pull down, to destroy and to overthrow, to build and to plant" (1:9–10).

1	11	26	46	52
Jeremiah's Account of His Oracles and Experiences	**Jeremiah in Conflict and Suffering**	**Baruch's Account of the Prophet**	**Oracles against the Nations**	
Early Oracles, Mostly of Judgment				
The prophet's call, 1	He endorses Josiah's covenant, 11	Baruch tells how, after the Temple sermon, Jeremiah was arrested, 26	Oracles against	
Israel is faithless, 2—5	And weeps when it is ignored, 12—15	Jeremiah wears a yoke as a warning, 27—28	Egypt, 46	
Therefore judgment is coming for the nation, 6	He continues to warn, 16—17	Jeremiah's "Little Book of Comfort", 30—33	Philistia, 47	
The Temple sermon pleads for repentance, 7	Using clay pots to illustrate the message, 18—19	He gives his final warning, 34	Moab, 48	
But the people continue in sin, 8	He is arrested and tortured, 20	Jehoiakim is warned but cuts up the scroll, 35—36	Ammon, Edom, Damascus, 49	
Jeremiah weeps over Jerusalem and continues to plead, 9—10	Evil leaders versus the messiah, 21—23	The fall of Jerusalem and the fate of Jeremiah, 37—45	Babylon, 50—51	
	Now the king of Babylon is to triumph, 24—25		(A historical appendix: The fall of Jerusalem), 52	

Situation: Jeremiah prophesied from 627 to 587 B.C., in the last days of Jerusalem as it fell to Babylon.

Message: He warned of the judgment coming, pleaded for repentance, and counseled surrender to Babylon. But when all earthly hope was lost, he promised that God would some day restore God's people.

One Special Significance for the New Testament: This book contains the promise of "the new covenant"; Jesus is said to have inaugurated that covenant at the Last Supper (31:31–34; cf. 1 Cor. 11:25).

had so failed him, he complained, that God had become no better than "a deceitful brook" (15:18). No wonder he hated his mission as a prophet and longed to quit (9:2). He became so utterly depressed that he not only cursed his own birthday but also cursed the man who had announced his birth to his proud father instead of killing him in the womb (20:14–18).

But this "weeping prophet" has also been called the most Christ-like figure in all the Old Testament.

The Background and Composition of the Book

Armies march across the pages of the book of Jeremiah, and kings also are among its characters. Young Jeremiah was called to be a prophet in the year 627 B.C., that moment in history when young King Josiah was soon to take the first steps toward making the law of Moses the law of the land. Jeremiah lived to see Josiah tragically killed in battle by the Egyptians; Assyria reassert its control of Jerusalem; and then, in 605 B.C., Babylon crush the Assyrian oppressors in the battle of Carchemish. He cursed as Jerusalem's petty tyrants tried unsuccessfully to play the dangerous game of power politics, vacillating between being a satellite of Babylon and then a satellite of Egypt, in the vain hope of achieving some degree of independence. He wept as he saw his prophecies of doom begin to be fulfilled—as when, in 597 B.C., the armies of Babylon entered Jerusalem and carried off the king, the queen mother, and many of Jerusalem's other leaders. Then, from a prison cell, he heard the daily news reports. In 587 B.C., the army of Babylon laid siege to the holy city, starved it, and finally destroyed it. The reader must picture these horrible historical tragedies occurring in the background in order fully to understand the words of doom—and in the end, of hope—of this tortured prophet.

Yet one thing that makes the book at times difficult to understand is that whoever collected these oracles did not put them in chronological order. Jeremiah does begin with the prophet's call and end with the fall of Jerusalem. But Jeremiah 7, for example, gives us the prophet's report of his famous "Temple sermon," while Jeremiah 26 tells that story again. Chapter 21 is a denunciation of Zedekiah, but chapter 22 contains warnings to two of his predecessors. Clearly, the book is not organized chronologically, and it is not entirely clear just why chapters come in the order in which we have them. The outline of Jeremiah in this *Guide* is admittedly oversimplified and conjectural, though it may be useful as one way of getting an overview of the book.

It is generally agreed that the first half of the book (chaps. 1—25) is in some sense autobiographical, while the last half (chaps. 26—52) rests more directly on the report of Jeremiah's secretary, Baruch. Commentators debate the extent to which the book contains additions and revisions by later editors.[6]

Jeremiah's Account of His Oracles
and Experiences (Jer. 1—25)

Early Oracles,
Mostly of Judgment (Jer. 1—10)

According to Jeremiah 1, in the year 627 B.C., perhaps as good King Josiah was making early moves toward religious reforms (2 Chron. 34:3), a teenager in the little town of Anathoth received a call from God. From the beginning, Jeremiah was not happy about this summons. "Ah, Lord God! Truly I do not know how to speak, for I am only a boy," he protested (1:6). But God would not let him go. "Now I have put my words in your mouth," the Lord replied (1:9). Those words were to become to this driven soul, he tells us, like fire in his mouth, setting on fire the people who heard them (5:14).

The boy was called to an enormous mission.

> See, today I appoint you over nations and over kingdoms,
>   to pluck up and to pull down,
>   to destroy and to overthrow,
>   to build and to plant. (1:10)

In the end, he did speak God's word of hope that would enable God's people "to build and to plant." But for most of his career, Jeremiah was forced to announce the judgment that would destroy.

He reports an early experience that symbolized his mission. With a play on words, he tells how he saw an almond tree (1:11). In Hebrew, that name sounds almost like "a watch tree." And he saw what God was "watching": a boiling pot, pouring out its scalding contents from "the north" (1:13). Did he at that time identify this danger? Was it the Scythians, the Assyrians, or Babylon? In the form in which we now have the report, we are not told, and throughout his ministry there were many threats from the north. Babylon was the final invader. From the beginning, Jeremiah found meaning in these dangers: they were warnings of God's judgment for the people's sins (1:16).

A century before, Hosea had proposed a shocking simile: Israel was like a wife who had turned into a whore. Now Jeremiah develops that figure in chapters 2—5. In the wilderness, God and Israel had been on a kind of honeymoon (2:2). But now Israel has become faithless to its "husband," the Lord (3:1). Like a lawyer pleading a case, God argues through the prophet how unjustified Israel's spiritual adultery is (2:5–9). He pleads for them to return (4:1–4), but the people seem deaf to his warning of judgment (6:10).

As far as is recorded, it was in 609 B.C., perhaps at the time of the coronation of King Jehoiakim, that Jeremiah was arrested for the first time. We can understand why. The popular theology of the time, preached by false prophets, was "No evil will come upon us" (5:12). Had not God promised David that his dynasty would always be on the throne, and had not Isaiah shown that God would defend the Temple? Now, standing on the steps of that very Temple, Jeremiah blasted that hope: "Do not trust in these deceptive words: 'This is the Temple of the Lord, the Temple of the Lord, the Temple of the Lord' " (7:4). Like Amos and Isaiah, Jeremiah shouted that the Lord demanded much more than formal worship. At this stage, Jeremiah had not given up all hope:

> *If* you truly amend your ways and your doings, *if* you truly act justly one with another, *if* you do not oppress the alien, the orphan, and the widow, or shed innocent blood in this place, and *if* you do not go after other gods to your own hurt, *then* I will dwell with you in this place. (7:5–7; italics added)

Jeremiah preached that the covenant was conditional. If Jerusalem showed concern for justice for people of other races, fatherless children, and single women, then the Temple would be a dwelling place for God. But faith that "we are safe" (7:10) based simply on the fact that the Temple was in Jerusalem provided only a false sense of security.

The Jerusalem mob nearly lynched Jeremiah. Baruch's account of the same sermon (Jer. 26) tells us that only by the intervention of friends in high places, one of whom had been prime minister under good King Josiah, did Jeremiah escape with his life (Jer. 26:24; cf. 2 Kings 22:12). And so the book continues its sad report of Jeremiah's plea for repentance to a still-sinful people (chap. 8).

It is here that our editor gives us the first of Jeremiah's laments. Scholars often speak of some of these as his "confessions" (11:18–12:6; 15:10–21; 17:14–18; 18:18–23; 20:7–12, 14–18). "For the hurt of my poor people I am hurt," he cries (8:21). There seems to be no medicine to cure their suffering. "Is there no balm in Gilead?" (8:22). And in moving poetry, the weeping prophet sobs:

> O that my head were a spring of water,
>   and my eyes a fountain of tears,
> so that I might weep day and night
>   for the slain of my poor people! (9:1)

He can only continue to plead (Jer. 10).

Jeremiah in Conflict and Suffering (Jer. 11—25)

In Jer. 11:1–8, our editor summarizes a sermon that Jeremiah may have preached earlier. Second Kings 22—23 has told how Josiah attempted to make the law of God, probably Deuteronomy, the law of the land, renewing Judah's covenant relationship with the Lord. "Hear the words of this covenant," Jeremiah cried (11:2). Apparently, Jeremiah even supported Josiah's closing of such outlying shrines as the one in his hometown of Anathoth. Perhaps that is part of the reason his neighbors and even his family members began to plot to assassinate him (11:21–23).

The prophets loved to use what today might be called "visual aids." Jeremiah displayed a loincloth that had rotted after being buried for months. This, he said in effect, is what Judah now seems to God (13:1–11). Jeremiah announced that he would no longer pray for them (14:11). He refused to marry, his perpetual bachelorhood being a warning that Jerusalem's families were destined for death (16:1–4). Twice he used a clay pot to illustrate his message. The first of these oracles was one that still contained an element of hope. He watched a potter molding a vessel from clay. Something spoiled it, however, and so the potter mashed down the soft material and reworked it into something useful and beautiful after all. "Then the word of the Lord came to me: Can I not do with you, O house of Israel, just as this potter has done?" (18:5). Whole nations are only clay in God's hand, Jeremiah explained. If Judah would yield, the Lord might yet make something of it.

It was too late. The next chapter tells us how the prophet led a strange parade. Elders and senior priests followed him. He was carrying an earthenware jug. Holding it in his hands, he delivered his sermon of warning. Then he smashed the flask in the sight of all the crowd. Now he announced the meaning of this object lesson: "Thus says the Lord of hosts: So will I break this people and this city, as one breaks a potter's vessel, so that it can never be mended" (19:11). The nation, including its king, was doomed.

That sermon was too dramatic to be ignored. Pashhur the priest beat Jeremiah and put him in the stocks (20:3). Far from ceasing his warnings of doom, however, Jeremiah not only announced that his torturer would die in captivity in Babylon but that Pashhur's family would do so also. But the inwardly torn prophet took no joy in this thought; rather, he accused God, who had let the Lord's prophet experience only disappointment, rejection, and danger, of lying to him (20:7). And he cursed the day he was born (20:14).

Jeremiah's whole life seemed to him to be one of conflict. The book's editor has brought together several stories of Jeremiah's verbal battles with Jerusalem's leaders. Near the last, grim days of Jerusalem, King Zedekiah sent Pashhur to the prophet to ask him to make a forecast. All of the nation's defense preparations are a waste, Jeremiah still insisted. Even God would fight on the side of Babylon against Jerusalem (21:5). Here the editor inserted a poem that pleads for a king to "execute justice . . . and deliver from the hand of the oppressor anyone who has been robbed" (21:12). Another sermon begs the king to "act with justice" for "the orphan, and the widow" (22:3). Jehoiakim, who in the midst of the crisis of Judah's last days used forced labor to build himself a fine new palace, is contrasted with his father Josiah: "He judged the cause of the poor and needy" (22:16). King Jehoiachin (called Coniah) is equally denounced (22:24). Religious leaders are said to be just as bad (23:9–40).

Indeed, Jeremiah compares the whole people in those last days before the fall to a basket full of rotten figs. There is, however, one note of hope. He compares those people who, in the first deportation, have been taken captive to Babylon to good figs. To these, God says through the prophet, "I will bring them back to this land. I will build them up, and not tear them down; I will plant them, and . . . give them a heart to know that I am the Lord" (24:6–7). After "seventy years," they will return (25:11).

Baruch's Account of the Prophet (Jer. 26—45)

Much of the second half of the book appears to be a collection of biographical notes on Jeremiah, written by his secretary, Baruch. Baruch's account of the Temple sermon tells of the near-lynching that followed it (26:7–19). He tells how Jeremiah, by wearing a yoke, like an ox, dramatized his protest against Zedekiah's efforts to form an alliance against Babylon. Jeremiah was sure that Judah should submit to the inevitable "yoke" of Babylon. False prophet Hananiah broke Jeremiah's yoke and, in the name of the Lord, promised deliverance within two years. But he was wrong. Chapter 29 contains a letter that Jeremiah sent to the first group of exiles to Babylon. They were to seek the welfare of that place, even though they were exiles there. Jews have remembered these words down through the ages, seeking to be good citizens in whatever country they have lived.

Now, however, the book of Jeremiah takes what might seem an utterly unexpected turn. Chapters 30 through 33 are often called Jeremiah's "Little Book of Consolation." The weeping prophet has spent a lifetime voicing prophecies of doom. At last, the long-delayed fulfillment of his worst fears is at hand. Babylon is at the very gates of Jerusalem. Yet paradoxically, the book of Jeremiah is now filled with songs of hope. Of all of these, by far the best loved and most influential is his prose poem, apparently voiced from a prison cell, about the "new covenant." At the beginning of his ministry, he had based hope on Josiah's renewal of the old covenant (11:1–8). But there was nothing in the law itself that could prevent the people's faithlessness. Only a change of heart could achieve that goal. And so the prophet reports this vision:[7]

> The days are surely coming, says the Lord, when I will make a new covenant with the house of Israel and the house of Judah. It will not be like the covenant that I made with their ancestors when I took them by the hand to bring them out of the land of Egypt—a covenant that they broke, though I was their husband, says the Lord. But this is the covenant that I will make with the house of Israel after those days, says the Lord: I will put my law within them, and I will write it on their hearts; and I will be their God, and they shall be my people. No longer shall they teach one another, or say to each other, "Know the Lord," for they shall all know me, from the least of them to the greatest, says the Lord; for I will forgive their iniquity, and remember their sin no more. (31:31–34)

In the New Testament, the writer of Hebrews twice quotes from this passage (Heb. 8:8–12; 10:16–17). More importantly, Paul tells us that on the night in which he was betrayed, Jesus instituted the Lord's Supper, announcing that this is it: "This cup is the new covenant in my blood" (1 Cor. 11:25). Indeed, the two parts of the Christian Bible get their names from this concept: the Old Testament (or Covenant) and the New Testament (or Covenant).

To dramatize the certainty of his hope, Jeremiah entered into one of the strangest real estate deals in history. Though the Babylonian army may already have been camped on that property, Jeremiah, in prison, agreed to buy the family farm from his cousin. For now, he was sure, God was promising that someday, "houses and fields and vineyards shall again be bought in this land" (Jer. 32:15).

Perhaps because it explains how Baruch came to record Jeremiah's words, the book now tells the story found in chapters 35 and 36. King Jehoiakim had barred Jeremiah from the Temple. The prophet therefore sent Baruch to read his message there. The king confiscated the scroll and, as it was read, cut it up with his penknife and threw it in the fire. But Jeremiah simply dictated the words again, and more were added (36:32). Thus this part of the Bible began to be written.

This section of the book ends with unrelieved tragedy. We have an account of the long siege of Jerusalem, much of it identical to the report in 2 Kings. Because he had so consistently counseled surrender to Babylon, Jeremiah had been denounced and imprisoned as a traitor. When at last Jerusalem fell, the Babylonians, perhaps thinking of Jeremiah as a kind of ally, did not deport him. Chaos reigned, however, within the little group left behind. Jeremiah's protector was assassinated, and the prophet himself, against his will, was taken with a group of refugees to Egypt. There, apparently, the suffering but faithful prophet of the Lord died.

Oracles against
the Nations (Jer. 46—52)

In the very beginning, at his call, Jeremiah had been appointed "over nations and over kingdoms, to pluck up and to pull down" (1:10). The last major section of the book is a collection of oracles ascribed to Jeremiah, promising the judgment of the Lord on seven nations, Judah's neighbors. First, Egypt, Philistia, Moab, Ammon, Edom, and Damascus are warned. With vivid poetry, their fate is described. God's power and God's justice are not confined to Judah.

But the longest set of these prophecies of doom is against Judah's oppressor, Babylon:

> Though you rejoice, though you exult,
>   O plunderers of my heritage,

though you frisk about like a heifer on the grass,
    and neigh like stallions,
your mother shall be utterly shamed,
    and she who bore you shall be disgraced.
Lo, she shall be the last of the nations,
    a wilderness, dry land, and a desert. (50:11–12)

In fact, Babylon was to be conquered fifty years later and today is little more
than an Iraqi village.

The book ends with another brief account of the fall of Jerusalem, largely
a repetition of 2 Kings 24:18–25:30. The Temple was indeed destroyed. King
Zedekiah was captured. His sons were killed before his eyes, and then, so
that their deaths would be last thing he would ever see, his eyes were put out.
Jeremiah's tearful warnings had come true.

LAMENTATIONS

On our television screens, all of us have seen this picture of sheer horror. We
have watched it in Somalia and Biafra and Iraq. Here are men who look like
skeletons. There are boys and girls with bloated bellies, glazed eyes gazing
from faces wrinkled with premature age. And most heart-rending of all, we
have seen starving babies nursing at the shrunken breasts of emaciated
women. We have even seen human beings reduced to the level of animals,
fighting with each other to be the first to grab some food.

Now, imagine yourself a sensitive poet. You are not just watching this
horror as you sit in your comfortable living room; you are right in the middle
of it. For eighteen months the enemy has blockaded your mountain city,
cutting it off from all food. Finally, your government leaders have attempted
to escape, only to be murdered. The enemy has broken through the last
defenses, pillaged, raped, and burned, and it has razed your city to the
ground. Most who have not been killed have been carried away into slavery.
Even your neighbors the Edomites have turned into scavengers, stealing
what they could as the city burned. You have experienced hunger and thirst
so dehumanizing that it has reduced mothers to eating their own children.
Now your tears and rage take form in five poems.

An experience like that produced the book of Lamentations.

Background, Structure, and Use
of the Book

In the year 597 B.C., Babylon invaded Judah, kidnapped its king, and carried
off its Temple treasures and the cream of its leaders. These conquerors
placed on the throne in Jerusalem Zedekiah, demanding that he do their
bidding. Nine years later, however, ignoring the warnings of Jeremiah,
Zedekiah attempted to throw off this foreign yoke. With the most powerful

LAMENTATIONS
Poems of Grief amid the Ruins of Jerusalem

"Is it nothing to you, all you who pass by? Look and see if there is any sorrow like my sorrow, which was brought upon me, which the Lord inflicted on the day of his fierce anger" (1:12).

1 Jerusalem Has Become a Lonely Widow	2 God's Judgment Has Brought This Catastrophe	3 One Survivor's Misery and Hope	4 Memories and the Holocaust	5 A Desperate Appeal to God
The city is like a bereaved woman, 1:1–7	God is angry with Jerusalem, 2:1–8	I have suffered horrible affliction, 3:1–18	How different was the glory of Jerusalem from the shame, terror, and violence of its fall, 4:1–20	Remember our misery, O Lord, 5:1–18
because of her sins, 1:8–11	The result is devastation, 2:9–17	Now remember me, Lord, with love, 3:19–24	Edom, you will be punished, too, 4:21–22	Why do you not restore us?, 5:19–22
She appeals for pity, 1:12–19	So pray to the Lord for mercy, 2:18–22	The reply: Wait! God has compassion, 3:25–39		
and prays to God for vengeance, 1:21–22		So return to the Lord, 3:40–54		
		The response: God, you have heard my plea, 3:55–66		

Author: Traditionally Jeremiah, but actually an unknown survivor—or survivors—of the destruction of Jerusalem by Babylon
Date: Soon after the fall of Jerusalem in 587 B.C.
Situation: Jerusalem is in ruins, many of its people have been killed, others have been exiled to Babylon, and the memory of the horror of the siege still brings agony.
Theme: The tragic suffering their defeat has brought, with here and there a few glimpses of hope through prayer.

armies in the world, the Babylonians laid siege to Jerusalem. For eighteen months the Jews held out, even though they were starving. At last Babylon overran the city, captured and blinded its king, and razed the city, even destroying its Temple. Most Jews who survived the starvation, disease, and mass slaughter were carried off into slavery. A few, like the author or authors of Lamentations, escaped to weep in the rubble.

No one knows who wrote the five poems that make up our book of Lamentations. The tradition that ascribes it to Jeremiah is based on the report in 2 Chron. 35:25 that the prophet wrote some poems of lamentation. Those, however, were at the death of King Josiah many years earlier. The style of Lamentations is so different from that of the book of Jeremiah that few scholars ascribe the former book to him. We do not even know whether Lamentations is the work of one poet or several. What is clear is that it comes out of the grief of one or more of the survivors of the war's destruction of the holy city.

Hebrew Bibles properly place Lamentations not among the Prophets but among the Writings, along with such books as Ecclesiastes and Song of Solomon.

The verses throb with grief, despair, guilt, and even vindictiveness. Yet paradoxically, they are written according to a carefully controlled, stylized formula. The first four poems are acrostics, each stanza beginning with the next letter of the Hebrew alphabet. Jews seem to have been fond of this pattern of poetry. Except for the third poem, each has twenty-two stanzas of three lines each, one for each letter of the alphabet, and the third poem simply triples the others, with sixty-six stanzas. Three poems begin with the Hebrew word that is translated "how," the standard opening of a Hebrew dirge, and the rhythm is that of a funeral procession.

Such formal composition makes these poems especially useful in worship. In many synagogues, they are read at annual observances of the date of the destruction of the Temple. Christians have seen in their picture of innocent suffering a symbol of the passion of Christ, and lectionaries have often prescribed readings from Lamentations during Holy Week.

The Five Poems

Chapter 1 develops the figure of Jerusalem as a widow, bereaved of her husband. Once a princess, now a slave, "she weeps bitterly in the night" (1:2). "Jerusalem sinned grievously," the poet confesses (1:8). But that does not make her suffering less. And so now the "widow" pleads for sympathy:

> Is it nothing to you, all you who pass by?
> Look and see
> if there is any sorrow like my sorrow,
> which was brought upon me,

> which the Lord inflicted
> on the day of his fierce anger. (1:12)

The poem ends with a prayer for vengeance on Jerusalem's enemies (1:21–22).

The second poem (chap. 2) focuses not on Jerusalem but on God:

> How the Lord in his anger
> has humiliated daughter Zion! (2:1)

It is God who has destroyed, cut down, burned, and killed. Indeed, "the Lord has become like an enemy" (2:5). That is why the devastation has been so complete. And so this psalm ends with a plea for mercy in the midst of the almost unimaginable horror of cannibalism:

> Look, O Lord, and consider!
> To whom have you done this?
> Should women eat their offspring,
> the children they have borne?
> Should priest and prophet be killed
> in the sanctuary of the Lord? (2:20)

The third poem (chap. 3) is in the pattern of the individual laments found in a number of psalms. Written partly in the first person, the focus is on one sufferer. For eighteen verses, the poet describes personal affliction. Through starvation and disease in the aftermath of the war, God "has made my flesh and my skin waste away" (3:4). And so the poet appeals to the Lord:

> "The Lord is my portion," says my soul,
> "therefore I will hope in him." (3:24)

Perhaps, in the liturgy, one is to think of the next verses as the reply of a priest:

> It is good that one should wait quietly
> for the salvation of the Lord. (3:26)

The singer is urged to "return to the Lord" (3:40), lifting heart and hands to God. In the end, the poet can write with such faith that it is as if the prayer has already been answered.

> You came near when I called on you;
> you said, "Do not fear!" (3:57)

And as before, there is the cry for vengeance.

The fourth poem (chap. 4) focuses on memory. The poet recalls the past glories of Jerusalem and then compares them with the shocking devastation and humiliation of the present. Again, there is confession that Jerusalem, by its sin, brought its troubles on itself (4:13). The closing prayer for vengeance is directed against Judah's neighbor Edom, which apparently had joined in raiding the hapless city (4:21–22; cf. Obad. 1:1, 12–14).

The final poem (chap. 5) is an almost hopeless prayer. The poet describes to God the terrible conditions in which the survivors find themselves. God, the writer knows, reigns forever (5:19). But even though the poet appeals for mercy, the book ends without strong assurance that help will come:

> Restore us to yourself, O Lord,
> that we may be restored;
> renew our days as of old—
> unless you have utterly rejected us,
> and are angry with us beyond measure. (5:21–22)

Few works in all literature picture more vividly the hatreds and horrors that war brings. Yet here and there, even in the midst of such hopeless suffering, brief flashes of Israel's indomitable faith shine through.

EZEKIEL

We know how some skeptical Israelites regarded the prophets of the Lord: they thought they were crazy (2 Kings 9:11). Some prophets dressed in rough fashion; separated themselves from ordinary society; and in moments of ecstatic inspiration, engaged in what must have seemed strange behavior (1 Sam. 19:24). But of them all, Ezekiel seems strangest to us.

Once, he lay for more than a year beside a model of Jerusalem. On other occasions, he nearly starved himself, knocked a hole in the wall of his house, carried all his possessions in a bag on his back, cut off all his hair and publicly burned part of it, and perhaps actually ate a scroll. He refused to mourn when his beloved wife died, and for a period of many months, he seems to have been struck dumb. Some of his visions are among the strangest in the scripture.

There was, however, a method in this prophet's "madness." He was not really mad. Rather, in dramatic, symbolic ways, he was relaying to his fellow exiles in Babylon messages inspired by God. Centuries later, Christians still study his words and actions for God's warnings of judgment and promises of hope.

The Background and Nature
of this Book

In the year 597 B.C., Jerusalem surrendered to Nebuchadnezzar, who set his own puppet king on the throne and carried off to Babylon the leaders and most capable Jews he could find. Among them was a twenty-five-year-old priest, Ezekiel. On July 31, 593 B.C., that priest became also a prophet.[8]

The effect of the exile was traumatic. The Lord, it seemed, had failed,

EZEKIEL
Prophecy in a Time of Captivity

"Son of man, I have made you a watchman for the house of Israel" (3:17, RSV).

1	25	33	40	48
Prophecies of Judgment		**Prophecies of Hope**		
Prophecies of the Judgment Coming on God's People	**Prophecies against Other Nations**	**Promises to Israel**	**A Vision of an Ideal Temple and City**	
Ezekiel sees God's glory, 1	Against Ammon, Edom, Philistia, 25	Ezekiel's call to be a watchman is repeated, 33	A restored temple, 40—42	
He is called to be a "watchman," 2—3	Against Tyre, 26—28	Now God promises restoration, 34—36	Restored worship, 43—46	
He gives dramatic warnings, 4—9	Against Egypt, 29—32	God's Spirit brings Israel's bones back to life, 37	Restored city and land, 47—48	
But he sees God's glory leave the polluted Temple, 10—11		The final apocalyptic battle of Gog and Magog, 38—39		
He continues to warn until Jerusalem falls, 12—24				

Date: From about 593 B.C. (after the first deportation to Babylon) through and beyond the destruction of Jerusalem in 587 B.C.

Location: Ezekiel is among the first group of exiles deported to Babylon.

Theme: Chapters 1—32 are oracles of coming judgment, but the second half of the book, after the fall of Jerusalem, is a series of visions of hope for a restored Jerusalem.

Some Especially Significant Ideas: Ezekiel emphasizes pure worship in a pure temple, helps the exiles interpret their captivity, gives them hope for restoration, and marks a new stage in the development of apocalyptic thought.

defeated by the gods of Babylon. All the glorious promises about David's dynasty had apparently proved false. Nothing lay ahead but slavery. "How could we sing the Lord's song in a foreign land?" one psalmist mourned (Ps. 137:4). At first, it is true, there still seemed to be some hope. Jerusalem and its Temple still stood. But Ezekiel knew that polluted place of worship and its city would not long endure. And so the first half of the book is a series of warnings by this prophetic "watchman." Jerusalem would be destroyed. This was not, he explained, because the Lord had been defeated; it was because of the abominations that the "holy" city had practiced.

In 587 B.C., Ezekiel's oracles of doom came true: Babylon leveled the city and even the Temple of the Lord. "How then can we live?" Ezekiel's hearers were to demand, in utter despair (33:10). But now, when all human hope was lost, Ezekiel announced visions of hope. Israel's "dry bones" would come to life again. God's enemies would be conquered. And someday God's glory would return to an ideal temple in a truly holy city.

Evidently, the Babylonians gave Ezekiel the opportunity to serve as a religious leader among the people they had deported. We are told that he reported his visions as the elders of Judah sat before him (8:1; 14:1; 20:1), apparently in his own house. There, in the community of deported Jews of Tel-abib, Ezekiel proclaimed his oracles to his fellow exiles.[9]

Prophecies of Judgment (Ezek. 1—32)

Prophecies of the Judgment Coming
on God's People (Ezek. 1—24)

The story of Ezekiel's call begins with a description of one of the strangest visions recorded in the Bible (Erich von Daniken proposed that Ezekiel must have seen a spaceship!).[10] It has been celebrated in an African-American spiritual. Riding in a storm cloud comes a curious chariot, drawn by exotic beasts. Its wheels point in all four directions at once. Seated on a throne in the chariot is "something that seemed like a human form" (1:26), but Ezekiel can see little of this figure except fire and, above it, a rainbow, symbol of the covenant (Gen. 9:13). Even though the vision is presented so mysteriously, Ezekiel does not claim that he is describing what God looks like. Rather, "this was the appearance of the likeness of the glory of the Lord" (1:28). An artist would have a difficult time painting a clear picture of this chariot, but one part of Ezekiel's meaning is clear: God's glory is not confined to one place. The chariot of the Lord can go in any direction and to any place God wills.

Now the call comes to Ezekiel. "Son of man," this transcendent God calls this very mortal prophet (2:1; 3:10, 17, RSV). "I have made you a sentinel for the house of Israel" (3:17). If this watchman fails to warn as disaster approaches, the responsibility is his. But if he warns, the fault lies with those who fail to heed the warning. Ezekiel did warn.

Many prophets liked to use "visual aids." Ezekiel's were the most dramatic. He built a little model of Jerusalem, surrounded it with tiny army tents, and then lay beside it every day for months, to symbolize that the Babylonian army would lay siege to the city (4:1–8). He began eating only the sparse and ceremonially unclean fare that was all that the people would have during that siege (4:9–17). He cut off all his hair, burned a third of it, chopped up a third, and scattered a third to the winds to symbolize the coming destruction of the people of Jerusalem (5:1–17). "End," "disaster," "doom"— these warning words reverberate through chapter 7.

What seemed to have distressed this priest the most were the "abominations" that were going on in what was supposed to be the Temple of the Lord (he uses that word, "abominations," some forty-three times). He describes a vision in which he sees pagan symbols on the walls of the Temple (8:10), women engaged in laments to a pagan god (8:14), and men worshiping the sun (8:16).

And now the symbolism of the heavenly chariot begins to become clear. Ezekiel sees that mobile throne of the glory of God once again. This time, however, it rises up from the Temple (10:4) and settles on a mountain overlooking the city (11:23), leaving the polluted place of worship behind. God, Ezekiel tells the people exiled to a strange land, is not confined to Jerusalem, and God's glory is not limited to the Temple.

Once again, this sentinel dramatizes his warning of coming danger. He knocks a hole in the wall of his house, as the wall of Jersualem would be breached, and he parades around the town with his belongings in a sack on his back, like a man going into exile. Even King Zedekiah will be reduced to this, Ezekiel prophesies (12:1–16). Ezekiel is not, of course, the only person to claim to be speaking in the name of the Lord. He denounces both prophets and prophetesses who still try to reassure Jerusalem (13:1–23). Ezekiel develops at length a figure first used by Hosea: Israel is like a girl whom the Lord loved and married but who has now proved unfaithful to her husband. Yet the chapter that makes this sad comparison also promises that someday the covenant will be renewed (16:59–63).

Ezekiel is sometimes called a pioneer of the concept of individualism. Hearing him denounce their sins, his despairing hearers attempted to place the blame on their ancestors. They quoted a familiar proverb, "The parents have eaten sour grapes, and the children's teeth are set on edge" (18:2). Indeed, Israelite tradition did have a far larger sense of the community, the group, than do most modern Americans. Ezekiel, however, saw the proverb as expressing a dangerous effort to evade responsibility. "It is only the person who sins that shall die" (18:4). God's concern is not for the past but for how a person today treats the poor, how honest that person is, and how free the individual is from idolatry (18:5–9; cf. 22:6–12). Later books, such as the wisdom literature of the Old Testament and the books of the New Testament, were to develop further the emphasis on the individual. This is not to say, however, that Ezekiel was unaware of corporate responsibility. Chapter 20 is a review of the history of Israel, emphasizing how the grace of God has been met by the community's repeated apostasy.

For Ezekiel, the day of tragedy was January 15, 588 B.C. First came the sad news that his prophecies were being fulfilled: Babylon had laid siege to Jerusalem. And then his wife, "the delight of [his] eyes," died. Against all custom, he refused to mourn for his wife outwardly, heartbroken though he was. Rather, he said, mourning should be for the people's sins and for the Temple, the delight of Israel's eyes (24:21).

Perhaps a psychiatrist might explain it: with that double grief, the prophet for a year and a half was struck dumb (24:27).

Prophecies against Other Nations (Ezek. 25—32)

In other lands as well as Israel, prophets were often called on to predict victories in war and to place divine curses on enemy nations. Perhaps in part out of this tradition, several books of prophecy contain oracles against Israel's neighbors (see, for example, Amos 1:1–2:3; Isa. 13—22; and Jer. 46—51). So the two halves of the book of Ezekiel are at this point linked together by a group of such oracles. Perhaps their coming at this point also serves to heighten the tension as we await news from the siege that has begun.

These oracles are carefully organized. Seven nations are judged, and seven oracles are pronounced against the last one, Egypt. All of these nations are said to be doomed. They were all neighbors of Israel. Some were supposed to be allies against Babylon, but none had helped when the crisis came. They had gloated over Jerusalem and had even looted what was left of the city after it fell to Babylon. Ezekiel especially damns Egypt, upon which Judah had so mistakenly relied as it resisted Babylon.

Such passages are not greatly beloved by most modern readers. They smack of the nationalism against which such books as Ruth and Jonah protest. Another prophet could foresee the day when God "will bring to [the Lord's] holy mountain and make . . . joyful" even "the foreigners who join themselves to the Lord" (Isa. 56:6–7).

Ezekiel's angry denunciation of Israel's neighbors, however, was surely deserved. Poor Jerusalem had been shamefully betrayed; it should elicit our sympathy, not our censure. Moreover, such passages remind us that the God of Israel is the Judge of all nations, including our own.

Prophecies of Hope (Ezek. 33—48)

Promises to Israel (Ezek. 33—39)

The book of Ezekiel falls into two parts. Chapters 1 through 32, as we have seen, are the sentinel's grim warning of danger: God's judgment is at hand.

Except for the interruption of the seven chapters of judgment on the seven nations, the first part ends with the horrible news that the siege has begun. Ezekiel is struck dumb.

Paradoxically, however, now that all human hope is lost, the last chapters of the book are oracles of hope. To mark the transition to his new mission, the call of the prophet is repeated. Once again, as at the beginning of the book, he is told that he is to be a "sentinel" for God (Ezek. 33:7). The dreaded news arrives: "The city has fallen" (33:21). But now the prophet can speak again, and this time his visions are of a glorious future.[11]

Israel's shepherds have been failures, but now God will be their shepherd (34:11). That good shepherd will bring them home. And God says, "I will set up over them one shepherd, my servant David" (34:23). The messiah will be God's servant, caring for the restored people. Israel's enemies will be judged (chap. 35), but Israel will be blessed, cleansed from the polluting sins of the past (chap. 36). God announces, "A new heart I will give you, and a new spirit I will put within you" (36:26). And now we are told of perhaps the most familiar and yet most bizarre vision in this book of strange oracles and symbols. It is celebrated in an African-American spiritual. In a vision, Ezekiel is transported to a battlefield strewn with dead bones. There he is told to prophesy to the bones. As he watches, bone by bone, these join together to form corpses. But as he speaks again, the wind, spirit, or breath—these are the same word in Hebrew—comes into them, and they rise up, a mighty army. Now the meaning of the vision is made clear: "Mortal, these bones are the whole house of Israel" (37:11). They may be exiled, hopeless, and "dead," but God is going to bring them back to life again.

This eerie vision is a fit prelude for Ezekiel's description of the end time, of the last days, of eschatology. It has many of the characteristics of "apocalyptic" literature.[12] The classic example of that kind of writing is the book of Revelation in the New Testament. In fact, Revelation gets many of its symbols from Ezekiel. From Ezekiel 38—48, that New Testament Apocalypse picks up such figures as Gog and Magog (Ezek. 38:2; Rev. 20:8), the final battle (Ezek. 38—39; Rev. 20:7–10), carrion birds (Ezek. 39:17; Rev. 19:17–18), the shaking of nature (Ezek. 38:19–20; Rev. 8:5–10), the sacred river (Ezek. 47:1; Rev. 22:1); and the new Jerusalem (Ezek. 48:30–35; Rev. 21:2).

Ezekiel's description of the last days begins with a two-chapter description of a great final battle (38:1–39:29). Gog, chief prince of Meshech in the land of Magog, with many allies invades Israel. In cosmic conflict, Israel defeats all its enemies through the power of God. Numerous efforts have been made to identify Gog. Perhaps the model for Ezekiel's vision was the Lydian king Gyges, described later in Plato's *Republic* as having a magic ring that enabled him to commit crimes undetected. Down through history, it has been proposed that Gog meant the Ethiopians, the Goths, the Muslims, and Hitler. Because of a vague similarity of sound between *rosh*, "prince," and "Russia," fanciful fundamentalists at one time attempted to equate Gog with "godless communism." There is no genuine linguistic basis for that identification. Whatever may have been in Ezekiel's mind, Revelation is doubtless correct in using the term simply to symbolize the forces of evil Satan mustered against the people of God.[13]

If the symbol is obscure, Ezekiel's basic meaning is clear: in the end, God and God's people will triumph. The forces of evil will be destroyed. And at the end of the story, we read that God promises:

> Then they shall know that I am the Lord their God because I sent them into exile among the nations, and then gathered them into their own land. I will leave none of them behind; and I will never again hide my face from them, when I pour out my spirit upon the house of Israel, says the Lord God. (39:28–29)

A Vision of an Ideal Temple and City (Ezek. 40—48)

Nine chapters, nearly twenty percent of the book, are devoted to a vision of a new and perfect temple in a new and perfect city and land.

Some prophets, believing that ceremonies in the Temple had become a substitute for practicing justice toward the needy, protested so vigorously that they seemed almost to reject the whole system of prayers and sacrifices (see, for example, Amos 5:21–24 and Isa. 1:10–17). Not so Ezekiel. He was a priest. He loved the Temple and he grieved, first over its corruption and then over its destruction. More than most of the other prophets, his ideas reflect those of the book of Leviticus. When he wants to describe the ideal future and the end of the age, he does so in terms of an ideal temple. Its measurements are carefully described, perhaps not so much because they constituted an architect's specifications as because they symbolize perfection.

The beauty of the structure of the book is again manifest. It began with a vision of the chariot of the glory of God. In chapter 11, Ezekiel saw that glory rise up and leave the old, polluted Temple, long before the Babylonians destroyed it. But now he sees that chariot once again. This time it comes from the east—from Babylon, the land of exile?—and fills the new temple with glory (43:1–5). That temple's walls will exclude all that is profane and unworthy. At last, a truly purified priesthood will minister there (44:15–31). Ideal princes will rule (45:7–9). And as the river of life flowed through the Garden of Eden, so now from the threshold of the Temple will flow a sacred stream (47:1). In the end, the full twelve tribes of Israel will be restored, and each will be assigned its territory in which to live forever (47:13–48:29).

The Temple that was indeed built again in Jerusalem, soon after Ezekiel's death, was far less magnificent than the one of which he dreamed. In the vision of John, which depends so heavily on Ezekiel, there is no temple in the new Jerusalem, for none is needed (Rev. 21:9–22). Christians look forward to the heavenly city beyond history. In the meantime, though Ezekiel's temple was never built, they affirm with Paul that prophecies of a glorious future in a way have been fulfilled beyond even the prophet's vision. "For in [Christ] every one of God's promises is a 'Yes' " (2 Cor. 1:20).

DANIEL

Of all the books of the Old Testament, Daniel seems to many modern readers the strangest. In it, great beasts rise from the waters: bears and leopards and lions. A goat sprouts horns that are kings. Angels bring mysterious messages. "Weeks of years" are outlined, with hints that one might, by interpreting its curious numbers, predict the time of the end. At that end, the book promises, there will be a resurrection of the dead.

Hardly had the book been written when Jewish writers were reinterpreting its visions. The New Testament gave its own interpretations. Down through the centuries, in every age, some Christian readers have professed to find in it predictions that they were living in those last days.

Its apocalyptic prophecies puzzle us. Most Jews and Christians, however, have been inspired by its stories. Daniel in the lions' den and the faithful Jews in the fiery furnace are models of courage. And when freed of fanciful misinterpretations, Daniel has brought a message of steadfastness and hope to millions who pray, "Thy kingdom come"; for this is a book about the kingdom of God.

The Setting, Nature, and Place of
the Book of Daniel

Every child who has grown up in Sunday school knows the story of Daniel in the lions' den. What makes that story even more inspiring is to set it in the context in which it was written.

Antiochus IV of Syria proudly called himself "Epiphanes," that is, "God Manifest." It was he who, in 175 B.C., inherited rule over an empire that included Judea. Of all the peoples under his control, the group that must have seemed to him most backward were the Jews. Some Jews, it is true, readily adopted the then-modern Greek culture. They wore Greek dress, attended the Greek theater, played in the gymnasium that Antiochus built beneath the Temple, and lived a pagan lifestyle. But many resisted. Antiochus quickly recognized what held them back: it was their religion. The apocryphal books 1 and 2 Maccabees tell how he resolved to stamp out Judaism. He poured hog's blood over the altar in the Temple and erected a shrine there to Olympian Zeus. He forced Jews to eat pork, and if a baby was circumcised, he executed both mother and child.

It was in that crisis, most biblical historians agree, that an unknown writer penned the book of Daniel.[14] He wrote stories of how, four centuries earlier,

DANIEL

Stories of Heroic Faithfulness and Visions of Earthly Kingdoms versus the Coming Kingdom of God

"And in the days of those kings the God of heaven will set up a kingdom that shall never be destroyed" (2:44).

Stories about Daniel and Prophecies about Kingdoms

Daniel heroically holds to Mosaic food laws, 1

He interprets a dream contrasting kingdoms of this world and the kingdom of God, 2

His three friends face a fiery furnace rather than worship an idol, 3

Daniel interprets a dream contrasting an earthly king with the Kingdom of God, 4

Daniel interprets the handwriting on the wall: the earthly kingdom will fall, 5

He faces the lions' den rather than pray to the greatest earthly king, 6

Apocalyptic Visions of Daniel

Four beastly kingdoms are contrasted with the kingdom of the saints, 7

Four beastly kingdoms are contrasted with the kingdom of the Prince of princes, 8

Daniel confesses Israel's sins and prays for deliverance; Gabriel outlines seventy weeks of years before deliverance will come, 9

A heavenly messenger foretells the rise and fall of human empires, 10—11

But in the end, there will be a resurrection of the dead, with glory for the righteous, 12

Date: Daniel is said to have lived in the sixth century B.C., during the Babylonian captivity, but the book was written around 166 B.C., during oppression by the Syrians.

Purpose: To encourage a persecuted people to remain faithful, giving them an example from the past and hope for the future

Theme: The kingdom of God, which, in the end, will triumph over all worldly kingdoms

the legendary wise man Daniel had faced the same kind of pressures that his readers now faced. Daniel and his friends had been instructed to eat pork, worship an idol, and give ultimate allegiance to an earthly king. But they had refused to submit. In the end, even the proud tyrants had been forced to acknowledge that only God is king. After telling those stories, the writer, using what became a favorite Jewish literary device, the apocalypse, traced the history of the rise and fall of earthly kingdoms right down to Antiochus Epiphanes. He promised that Antiochus, like the other kings, would fall. But the Lord, the God of Israel, would be king forever!

It is characteristic of apocalypses that they are written as though by a great person of the past, describing what for that prophet would have been future events, using highly symbolic language. They foretell that tribulation will come but that in the end, often after a cosmic battle, God and the people of God will triumph. Isaiah 24—27 and Ezekiel 38—39 have some of the characteristics of this form. Though this style seems foreign—some would even say dishonest—to us, there is no doubt that Jewish readers delighted in apocalypses. Revelation is the classic book of this kind.[15]

Daniel is so different from other books of the Old Testament that there has been confusion about where to put it. It was probably the last to be written of the Old Testament books, and Hebrew Bibles place it last, including it among the Writings, such as the wisdom literature. Christians, however, have placed it as the fourth of the Major Prophets, following Isaiah, Jeremiah, and Ezekiel.[16]

Stories about Daniel and Prophecies about Kingdoms

The book of Daniel can be divided in half. The first half contains stories about Daniel. He and his friends, exiled to Babylon, repeatedly risk their lives rather than conform to that country's paganism. Each time they are delivered, and over and over, a pagan king is forced to confess that the only true king is the God of Israel. These stories should not be read as curious bits of ancient history, since there is no historical evidence that the emperors of Babylon and Persia ever actually affirmed faith in the Lord. Rather, they should be read for the purpose for which they were written, to inspire heroic resistance to temptation in the days of Antiochus Epiphanes and, by implication, for all subsequent readers. Their truth lies not in their record of the past but in their promise of the future: the final triumph of the kingdom of God.

In the first story (chap. 1) we are introduced to Daniel. Still a boy, he has been exiled to Babylon. Recognized as promising youths, he and his friends are selected for training in the palace for high positions. But there the food and the wine are not kosher, "clean," according to the Mosaic law (at the time the book was written, Antiochus Epiphanes was attempting to force Jews to eat pork and other unclean foods). Daniel and his young friends, however, risk their opportunity for advancement rather than violate God's law. And in the end, they outdo those who conform to the pagan lifestyle.

The next chapter tells how Daniel, like Joseph centuries before, interprets a dream for the king. That dream and its interpretation give the basic theme of the book. Nebuchadnezzar dreams of a great idol made of various metals, but its feet are feet of clay. Though the statue appears so strong, when the foundation is struck by a stone "cut out, not by human hands," the huge image crashes into pieces (2:34). The image, wise Daniel explains, represents four successive empires. But in the end, these earthly kingdoms will perish. The stone that overcomes them represents the kingdom of God (2:44). It will stand forever. Even King Nebuchadnezzar now cries, "Truly, your God is God of gods and Lord of kings" (2:47).

The pressures mount in each story. Beloved through the centuries, chapter 3 tells how Daniel's three friends refused to worship an idol set up by Nebuchadnezzar (at the time the book was written, Antiochus Epiphanes had set up a shrine to Zeus in the Temple in Jerusalem). Condemned to die, Daniel's friends affirmed their faith that God would rescue them. "But if not," they courageously announced, they still would not submit. Daniel's friends were thrown into a fiery furnace. Miraculously, they walked unhurt through the flames, accompanied by one who looked like a god. And so the story ends with a return to the book's theme, the kingdom of God. King Nebuchadnezzar is moved to confess that

> [God's] kingdom is an everlasting kingdom,
>   and his sovereignty is from generation to generation. (4:3)

Continuing the theme, the next chapter tells how the wise man Daniel once again interprets a dream. It is a prophecy that the world's greatest king will be reduced to the level of a beast. The dream comes true. When he is at last restored, this earthly emperor sings of God, "His kingdom endures from generation to generation" (4:34).

Dramatically, chapter 5 tells how, at a drunken orgy, King Belshazzar drank from a goblet stolen from the Temple at Jerusalem. God's hand wrote a mysterious inscription on the palace wall. Only Daniel could interpret it: "You have been weighed on the scales and found wanting . . . your kingdom is divided and given to the Medes and Persians" (5:27–28). That very night, Babylon fell.

The last, climactic story is perhaps the best loved. Daniel is now prime minister. His political rivals conspire to persuade the king to forbid prayer to any but the emperor. Daniel, however, prays only to the Lord. Regretfully, the king has Daniel thrown into a den of lions. Yet the next morning, Daniel is unhurt. In the end, the lions eat Daniel's enemies, and the king sings of the Lord:

> His kingdom shall never be destroyed,
> and his dominion has no end. (6:26)

Story after story affirms the ultimate triumph of the kingdom of God. And in every story the appeal is the same: be like Daniel; be loyal to the only true king.

Apocalyptic Visions of Daniel

The second half of the book (chaps. 7—12) can be thought of as a further development of the vision of successive kingdoms that was described in the second chapter.

Now it is Daniel who has a dream. This time the four empires are symbolized by four beasts (7:17). But Daniel sees before the heavenly throne "one like a son of man" (7:13, RSV), a human being, in contrast to those animals:

> To him was given dominion and glory and kingship,
> that all peoples, nations, and languages
> should serve him.
> His dominion is an everlasting dominion
> that shall not pass away,
> and his kingship is one
> that shall never be destroyed. (7:14)

His kingdom is the reign of "the holy ones of the Most High" (7:18).

In the next chapter, four beasts again symbolize four successive kingdoms. This time three are identified: Media, Persia, and Greece (8:20). The fourth beast is unnamed, but we are told that it will persecute the saints. Apparently Antiochus Epiphanes is intended. The vision is so frightening that it makes Daniel sick, but in the end, he is assured, the persecutor will be "broken, and not by human hands" (8:25).

Daniel prays a long prayer, confessing Israel's sins and begging for deliverance (9:1–19). He is told, however, that he must wait for that deliverance for "seventy weeks" (9:24), reflecting Jeremiah's prophecy of restoration from captivity after seventy years. Daniel's seventy weeks stand for seventy weeks of years, 490 years. Seven is a sacred number, symbolic of perfection. Therefore computations that bring one to the year 107 B.C. miss the point. The writer seems to expect the deliverance in his own day, with the overthrow of Antiochus Epiphanes. In fact, in 164 B.C. Jews did succeed in driving out the Syrians and cleansing the Temple.

Chapters 10 and 11 give a detailed review of the history of the biblical world from the third year of Cyrus (535 B.C.) through the conquests by Alexander the Great (10:1–20) and down to the time of the writer. The figurative language about symbolic beasts is set aside. Specific events are reported. The last evil ruler to be described is evidently Antiochus:

Forces sent by him shall occupy and profane the Temple and fortress. They shall abolish the regular burnt offering and set up the abomination that makes desolate. He shall seduce with intrigue those who violate the covenant; but the people who are loyal to their God shall stand firm and take action. (11:31–32)

And so, at last, the readers are assured, "He shall come to his end, with no one to help him" (11:45).

The last chapter gives the great promise of the book. Though there will be a time of terrible trouble still to come, in the end God's people will be delivered. There are few places in the Old Testament where a future life is clearly promised. Daniel's vision, however, is climaxed with this unambiguous picture of the resurrection:

Many of those who sleep in the dust of the earth shall awake, some to everlasting life, and some to shame and everlasting contempt. Those who are wise shall shine like the brightness of the sky. (12:2–3)

Beyond history and all earthly kingdoms, this book promises, the faithful will share eternally in the kingdom of God.

Subsequent Interpretations of Daniel

The apocryphal books 1 and 2 Maccabees tell how the Jews heroically threw off the yoke of Syria. Antiochus Epiphanes, however, died a natural death some years later, and the end of the world did not come at that time. Though we can be reasonably sure whom the writer of Daniel had in mind by the various symbols he used, his symbolic language left open other possibilities. Therefore Jews and Christians ever since have engaged in reinterpretations of Daniel's visions. The apocryphal book 2 Esdras develops ideas from Daniel, and *1 Enoch,* a popular Jewish work written perhaps a century after Daniel, proposed new understandings of the "son of man." Many Jews and Christians concluded that the fourth empire of Daniel's prophecy must be Rome, and this interpretation was popular for centuries. In the New Testament, the book of Revelation relates the apocalyptic vision to the church, persecuted by that evil empire.

The most important reinterpretation of Daniel is that which the Gospels ascribe to Jesus. Matthew tells us that Jesus rejected Satan's offer of "all the kingdoms of the world" (Matt. 4:8). He summarizes Jesus' message as the announcement that now God's kingdom has come near (Matt. 4:17). But in the Sermon on the Mount (Matt. 5—7), Jesus radically reinterprets the nature of that kingdom. Repeatedly, Jesus identifies himself as the "Son of man" (cf. Dan. 7:13, RSV). But when that heavenly human being comes again at the resurrection, Jesus said, his standard of judgment will be how we have treated "the least of these who are members of [his] family" (Matt. 25:40).

HOSEA

Few prophets have exceeded Hosea in producing startling figures of speech. At one time or another, he compared God to a mother bear, a wild lion, a moth, and dry rot (5:12; 13:7–8). And repeatedly, he compared God's people to a prostitute. Over and over, he announced that the God of justice was about to bring catastrophe on Samaria. Shortly before it was destroyed, he announced bluntly that Israel was dead. He also pictured God as a heavenly lover, a forgiving father, and a rejected husband.

That last figure of speech grew out of his own tragic experience. Shocking though it seems, it was echoed by prophet after prophet, down through the centuries.

A Note about the "Minor" Prophets

From the time of Augustine (ca. A.D. 400), Christians have spoken of the last twelve books of the Old Testament as the "Minor Prophets." Isaiah, Jeremiah, and Ezekiel—and, some would say, Daniel—are called the "Major Prophets." The designation "minor" refers to length, not value. The books from Hosea through Malachi are all relatively short; the Major Prophets are long. The ancient Jews published the scriptures in scrolls. Isaiah, Jeremiah, and Ezekiel each took up one scroll, and one scroll was devoted to the twelve shorter prophets. By around 200 B.C., these twelve had been grouped together so frequently that no one had to ask the poet which prophets he meant when he wrote:

> May the bones of the Twelve Prophets
>   send forth new life from where they lie,
> for they comforted the people of Jacob
>   and delivered them with confident hope. (Sir. 49:10)

Though his prophecy ends probably a bit later than that of his older contemporary Amos, Jews and Christians have agreed in always placing first among these twelve the book to which we now turn, Hosea.

Hosea's Domestic Tragedy: A Symbol of Israel's Broken "Marriage" to God (Hos. 1—3)

The first verse of Hosea presents no problems. It dates the prophet as living in the last, sad days of the Northern Kingdom, roughly 750–721 B.C.

The next verse, however, is so shocking that many commentators try to gloss it over. The Lord, Hosea's biographer tells us, told the prophet to go and marry a prostitute! Believing that God could never tell a man to contract so sinful a marriage, the older commentaries used to propose that the writer meant that the Lord had told Hosea to marry a girl who, only later, turned out to be an adulteress. But most now agree that the book means exactly what it

HOSEA
God's Faithful Love for Israel, God's Unfaithful "Bride"

"For I desire steadfast love and not sacrifice, the knowledge of God rather than burnt offerings" (6:6).

1 **Hosea's Domestic Tragedy: A Symbol of Israel's Broken "Marriage" to God**	4 **Israel's Unfaithfulness to God**	14 **A Closing Appeal**
Hosea marries a whore and gives their children symbolic names, 1	Their spiritual unfaithfulness, 4—6	Return to God, 14:1-3
An appeal to the unfaithful wife, 2	Their political unfaithfulness, 7—10	God will forgive, 14:4-9
He brings her back, redeems her, 3	God's continuing faithful love for God's people, 11—13	

Date: Around 740 B.C.

Place: Israel, the Northern Kingdom

Theme: As Hosea still sought to win back his faithless wife, so God still seeks to win back faithless Israel.

Special Significance: Throughout the rest of the Bible, New Testament as well as Old, God's covenant love for God's people is compared to the love of husband and wife.

says. There was a reason for it. Hosea's life was to be a kind of acted parable. God, says this startling metaphor, had "married" Israel even though Israel was spiritually a whore.

Indeed, it is implied that Hosea's wife, Gomer, was not just an ordinary woman of ill repute; she was probably a temple prostitute, available to men who sought by means of sexual intercourse with her to win the favor of the pagan god Baal. Baal was supposed to be the god of fertility. As a couple mated in his temple, Baal mated with his Ashera, and this, it was claimed, magically brought fertility to one's crops.

Dramatically, Hosea was saying that God had formed a covenant, like a marriage, with Israel even though Israel was unworthy. And, he went on to say, as Gomer now proved an unfaithful bride, so Israel was being an unfaithful "wife" to the Lord, leaving its covenanted God for Baal.

Not only his marriage but his children became living testimonies to Hosea's condemnation of Israel. Each child was made to live with a name that must have been a burden. The first he called Jezreel. If the poor child was asked why he bore that name, he could reply that it was because God had warned, through his father, "For in a little while I will punish the house of [King] Jehu for the blood of Jezreel, and I will put an end to the kingdom of the house of Israel" (1:4). A century before, King Jehu had, at Jezreel, mass-slaughtered worshipers of Baal (2 Kings 10:18–27). That bloody "sacrifice" remained a horror in the memory of Israel. Perhaps, in the United States, naming a child Benedict Arnold or Watergate might attract similar attention.

Hosea named his daughter Lo-ruhamah, "not pitied." Asked why she bore so wretched a name, she could reply that it was because her father said that God "would no longer have pity on the house of Israel" (1:6). Worst of all, the third child was named Lo-ammi, "not my people," because, Hosea announced, Israel was no longer the Lord's people, for the Lord was no longer their God (1:8–9).

By the second chapter, Gomer has returned to her life as a whore. In moving poetry, the prophet begs her children to plead with her to return. "Plead with your mother, plead . . . that she put away her whoring from her face" (2:2). While almost certainly the whole story of domestic tragedy is that of Hosea's own experience, he sees it also as an allegory. The prophet is pleading with the "children of Israel" to bring their mother, the nation, back to its true "husband," the Lord.

The final chapter of this love story (Hos. 3) tells us that God called Hosea again. This time he is not simply to marry but also to love "a woman who has a lover and is an adulteress, just as the Lord loves the people of Israel, though they turn to other gods" (3:1). It is not directly stated that it is the same woman, but the allegory demands it. Now Gomer has fallen so low that she has, apparently, sold herself into slavery. But her loving husband pays a price, brings her home, and, loving her still, seeks to protect and discipline her to make her once again his own. So God, Hosea is saying, still loves Israel, in spite of its infidelity. That loving God still seeks Israel, and someday, Hosea still hopes, "the Israelites shall return and seek the Lord their God" (3:5).

Israel's Unfaithfulness to God (Hos. 4—14)

Though Hosea does not again refer to his own tragic marriage, the rest of the book develops the ideas contained in the metaphor he drew from that sad love story. Shockingly, the sexual symbolism continues, so that it is not always clear whether, as he denounces adultery, Hosea is speaking of Israel's spiritual "adultery" with Baal, its political corruption, or the actual sexual immorality that had become so common in his day. All three are repeatedly deplored. Most of the prophecies are warnings of judgment to come, but here and there are oracles of hope. Just why the collector of these poems published them in precisely the order in which we have them is not clear. (The brief outline in this *Guide* is oversimplified to help the reader get a quick overview of the book.) Broadly speaking, however, the oracles seem to be somewhat in chronological order, covering a period of perhaps twenty-five years.

The first oracles of this section seem to come from the relatively stable reign of Jeroboam II. They focus, therefore, more on the spiritual and moral corruption of Israel than on the political corruption that so concerned Hosea later in his life. Both kinds of sin, however, are denounced from time to time throughout the entire book.

The first three chapters presented God's charges against Israel figuratively, through Gomer's adultery. In the next chapter, God spells out the meaning of the figure, sometimes in quite specific terms:

> There is no faithfulness or loyalty,
> > and no knowledge of God in the land.
> Swearing, lying, and murder,
> > and stealing and adultery break out;
> > bloodshed follows bloodshed. (4:1–2)

Priests and prophets have led the people astray (4:4–5). And idol worship is common (4:12–13). This spiritual adultery leads to physical adultery:

> Therefore your daughters play the whore,
> > and your daughters-in-law commit adultery. (4:13)

But God's wrath falls even more on the men who commit adultery with them (4:14).

Now, as Hosea had warned, Israel began to fall apart. In the ten years following the death of Jeroboam II, five different men in succession ruled in

Samaria, capital of the Northern Kingdom. Four of them got the throne by assassinating their predecessors. At the same time, Assyrian power began to threaten all its neighbors. In 733 B.C., the emperor Tiglath-Pileser moved in and simply annexed to his own domain much of the Northern Kingdom, leaving Israel only Samaria and some of the country around it.

"Blow the horn. . . . Sound the alarm!" cried Hosea (5:8). "Ephraim [Israel] shall become a desolation" (5:9). A misguided attempt by Israel to form an alliance with Syria and force the Southern Kingdom, Judah, to join had backfired (5:10). But even making peace with Assyria would not cure what ailed Israel.

Yet still the prophet pleads: "Come, let us return to the Lord" (6:1). And God, frustrated by Israel's fickleness, cries, "What shall I do with you, O Ephraim?" (6:4). True, Israel still worships, but that kind of worship is not what God most wants. In a verse that summarizes much of the message of the book, the Lord cries:

> I desire steadfast love and not sacrifice,
> the knowledge of God rather than burnt offerings. (6:6)

Hosea pictures God as denouncing as "silly" the foreign policy of Israel's kings. "They call upon Egypt, they go to Assyria" (7:11), vacillating between the two in alliances against the other. "Destruction to them, for they have rebelled against me!" (7:13). The king was supposed to be "the Lord's anointed," but the succession of assassins on the throne in Samaria did not represent the kingdom of God. "They made kings, but not through me," God says of Israel (8:4). Hosea denounces their bargaining with one nation and then another (8:10). But the problem underlying their political corruption, Hosea knows, is religious.

As the Assyrian menace grows, he sounds the alarm again:

> Set the trumpet to your lips!
> One like a vulture is over the house of the Lord,
> because they have broken my covenant,
> and transgressed my law. (8:1)

Hosea deliberately disrupts a harvest festival with a song not of joy but of doom:

> Do not rejoice, O Israel!
> Do not exult as other nations do;
> for you have played the whore,
> departing from your God. (9:1)

Before them lies only captivity (9:3).

As the storm clouds of war gathered, Israel believed in the lie of military preparedness. But:

because you have trusted in your power
and in the multitude of your warriors,
therefore the tumult of war shall rise against your people,
and all your fortresses shall be destroyed. (10:13–14)

Yet in the midst of all this warning of doom, Hosea voices one of the most beautiful poems on God's steadfast love found in all the scripture. God is a heavenly parent who, in the days of the exodus, cared for Israel as a child:

When Israel was a child, I loved him,
and out of Egypt I called my son.
The more I called them,
the more they went from me;
they kept sacrificing to the Baals,
and offering incense to idols.
Yet it was I who taught Ephraim to walk,
I took them up in my arms. (11:1–3)

In an agony of grief, this loving parent cries:

How can I give you up, Ephraim?
How can I hand you over, O Israel? (11:8)

And so, at least for a moment, God seems ready to cancel the threatened punishment:

My compassion grows warm and tender.
I will not execute my fierce anger;
I will not again destroy Ephraim. (11:8–9)

It was too late. Chapter 13 is a kind of funeral dirge over the city of Samaria, by this time so close to death.

In the year 721 B.C., Samaria, after a three-year siege, starved for food and famished for water, finally surrendered to Assyria. Its people were carried off captive, never to return.

A Closing Appeal (Hos. 14)

"Return, O Israel, to the Lord your God" (14:1). To the end, Hosea voiced God's appeal. Somehow, even at that end, he could still picture God as saying:

I will heal their disloyalty;
I will love them freely. (14:4)

Amos, Hosea's contemporary, preached almost nothing but the just punishment about to come from the God of wrath. Paradoxically, Hosea added to that message new insights into God's steadfast love. God did not learn about suffering love from Hosea; Hosea learned it from God. But with literary license, the dramatist Paul Green, in his moving play *Green Pastures,* reverses the order. He pictures the God of wrath as hearing of steadfast love through Hosea. At this point in the play, over the battlements of heaven, the angels can see Christ carrying his cross. There, foreshadowed by Hosea's poetry, justice and mercy are united.

JOEL

Twenty billion locusts! The *Reader's Digest* described a 1988 plague of these grasshopper-like pests thus: "20 billion locusts covered nearly 150 square miles and gnawed through thousands of tons of vegetation every day."[17] Observers of invasions by these incredible insects describe how they work their way through windows, doors, and even cracks in the walls of houses, how they devour all crops and strip the branches from trees, and how nothing humans can do can stop them.

One poet saw such devastation wrought by these horrid creatures that it evoked images of the judgment day. That is how God inspired Joel to give us the little book that bears his name.

No one is sure when Joel lived. Plagues of locusts are too common in the Middle East for that catastrophe to date the book for us. There are hints, however, that it was written late in the Old Testament period. There is no mention of a king, and the almost apocalyptic style also suggests a time after the exile. The Temple has been rebuilt (1:14), and if the reference to walls (2:9) means that Jerusalem's walls have been rebuilt, the book comes from after 444 B.C. Joel quotes many earlier prophets, but he was an original poet. We know nothing at all of his personal life.

A Plague of Locusts Is Seen as a Sign of God's Judgment (Joel 1:1–2:27)

"Cutting . . . swarming . . . hopping . . . destroying"—after a very brief introduction, Joel describes the cloud of insects (1:4). Drunkards, he calls, mourn; for this invading army will leave no more grapes for wine (1:5). "Be dismayed, you farmers" (1:11), "put on sackcloth and lament, you priests" (1:13); for the crops are ruined, the fruit is destroyed, and even the trees are dried up.

And so Joel proposes action. In a day when Israel had its own government and some control over its economy, an Amos or an Isaiah might have proposed renewed emphasis on justice for the poor. Typical of the emphasis of writers after the exile, Joel focuses instead on prayer. He calls for a national day of formal mourning:

> Sanctify a fast,
>   call a solemn assembly.
> Gather the elders

JOEL

A Plague of Locusts as a Call to Repentance

"Sanctify a fast, call a solemn assembly. Gather the elders . . . and cry out ot the Lord" (1:14).

1		2:28		3:21

A Plague of Locusts Is Seen as a Sign of God's Judgment

The plague, 1:1–2:11

A plea: "Return to me . . . with fasting," 2:12–17

A promise: "You shall eat in plenty and be satisfied," 2:18–27

The Day of the Lord Is at Hand

Signs among the people: "I will pour out my spirit on all flesh," 2:28–29

Signs in nature: "The sun shall be turned to darkness," 2:30–32

What these signs point to—judgment upon the nations: "Multitudes, multitudes, in the valley of decision," 3:1–15

But Judah will be blessed, 3:16–21

Date: Unknown, perhaps as late as 350 B.C.; occasioned by a plague of locusts

Purpose: Using that plague as a warning of coming cosmic judgment, the prophet pleads with the people to repent.

Special Significance: Acts 2:17–18 depicts Peter as seeing in Pentecost the fulfillment of the prophecy of Joel 2:28: "Then afterward I will pour out my spirit on all flesh."

> and all the inhabitants of the land
> to the house of the Lord your God,
> and cry out to the Lord. (1:14)

The reason for this action is this: the horror of the plague is a warning that "the day of the Lord is near" (1:15), the judgment day. The prophet himself leads a prayer (1:19).

Poetically, Joel compares the invasion by the locusts to an invasion by an army. He calls on the military sentinels to warn as if Babylon's forces were coming again. "Blow the trumpet," he cries, and again, "Blow the trumpet" (2:1, 15). The locusts are like cavalry. But there is still hope:

> Yet even now, says the Lord,
> return to me with all your heart,
> with fasting, with weeping, and with mourning. (2:12)

And though he calls for formal, liturgical worship, Joel knows that those symbols are not in themselves the important thing:

> Rend your hearts and not your clothing.
> Return to the Lord, your God,
> for he is gracious and merciful,
> slow to anger, and abounding in steadfast love. (2:13)

One reads so often of prophets being ignored or even persecuted that it comes as a surprise to learn that the people seem to have heeded this prophet's appeal. The Lord "had pity on his people" (2:18). Thus the first half of the book ends with promises of blessings to come (2:18–27). "Do not fear," the prophet now twice reassures them (2:21, 22). To starving but praying people he can now relay God's promise: "You shall eat in plenty and be satisfied" (2:26).

The Day of the Lord Is at Hand (Joel 2:28–3:21)

Joel, however, sees the plague of locusts as but a foretaste of the coming "great and terrible day of the Lord" (2:31). The second half of the book is an almost apocalyptic picture of that coming cosmic judgment day.

In the Old Testament, one reads of individual judges and prophets on whom the Spirit of the Lord came. But God says that in the coming day

> I will pour out my spirit on all flesh;
> your sons and your daughters shall prophesy,
> your old men shall dream dreams. (2:28)

Writing with special attention to the place of women in scripture, Beth Glazier-McDonald calls our attention to the fact that in Joel's vision, barriers of age and sex are to be swept away. All kinds of people prophesy.[18]

Catastrophic signs will appear in nature (2:30–32). But in this frightening time, "everyone who calls on the name of the Lord shall be saved" (2:32).

By contrast, those nations that have so long abused Israel will be punished. Singled out for special warning are those that have sold Jews as slaves (3:1–3). The Gentile world is summoned as if to battle (3:9). But they cannot resist the decision, the verdict, of the great Judge:

> Multitudes, multitudes,
>   in the valley of decision!
> For the day of the Lord is near
>   in the valley of decision. (3:14)

The decision, the verdict, will be terrible for them.

But the book ends with a promise of salvation for God's people. If nature has been the scene of cosmic destruction,

> in that day
> the mountains shall drip sweet wine,
>   the hills shall flow with milk. (3:18)

And at long last,

> Judah shall be inhabited forever,
>   and Jerusalem to all generations. (3:20)

Joel and the New Testament

In the light of other parts of the Old Testament and the teachings of Jesus in the New Testament, it would be a mistake to suppose that every natural disaster, such as a plague of locusts, is the result of sins by the people on whom it comes. At the same time, we know enough about ecology to recognize that some sins do indeed sometimes lead to devastation in nature. It is true also that every natural disaster can serve as a reminder of the uncertainty of life in this world and thus be used as a call to dependence on God.

The New Testament book of Revelation borrows the figure of locusts from Joel (Rev. 9:3–11). The most direct use of Joel is in the sermon attributed to Peter on the day of Pentecost. As the Holy Spirit was poured out on the infant church, Peter quoted Joel's promise of the pouring out of the Spirit on all kinds of people (Acts 2:16–21; cf. Joel 2:28). And Joel's promise that "everyone who calls on the name of the Lord will be saved" (Acts 2:21; cf. Joel 2:32) Peter sees fulfilled through faith in Christ.

AMOS

Two things especially make this "minor" prophet a book of major importance: (1) no other Old Testament prophet more resoundingly voiced God's demand for justice for the oppressed; and (2) oracles attributed to Amos were

AMOS

A Warning That God Demands Justice for People in Need

"I hate . . . your festivals. . . . But let justice roll down like waters, and righteousness like an everflowing stream" (5:21–24).

1 **God's Judgment on Israel's Neighbors**	3 **God's Judgment on Israel**	7 **Five Visions of Judgment to Come**	9:9 **An Appendix**	9:15
On Damascus (Syria), 1:3–5	Israel's privileges imply responsibility, 3	1. A plague of locusts, 7:1–3	An addition to give some note of hope even in this book	
Gaza (the Philistines), 1:6–8	Rich women, wrong worship: a warning, 4	2. Judgment by fire, 7:4–6		
Tyre (Lebanon), 1:9–10	A lament over coming judgment and an appeal for justice, 5	3. A plumb line measures crooked Israel, 7:7–9		
Edom, 1:11–12	An attack on indifference, 6	(Amos is interrupted by an angry priest), 7:10–17		
Ammon, 1:13–15		4. The fruit of the "end," 8:1–14		
Moab, 2:1–3		5. The final destruction to come, 9:1–8		
Israel itself, 2:4–16				

Author: Amos, a shepherd and farmer from Judea
Audience: Israel, the Northern Kingdom, at Bethel, a royal shrine
Date: Ca. 750 B.C., roughly thirty years before Israel fell
Purpose: To warn Israel of coming judgment because of their neglect of the poor, the fatherless, the widows
Special Significance: Amos is the first prophet whose words became a book of the Bible.

the first words of a prophet to make up a written book of the Bible. Amos was by no means the first of Israel's prophets; Nathan, Elijah, Elisha, and many others had preceded him. But something new happened with regard to Amos's prophecies: somebody wrote them down. Indeed, they are among the first written words of all our scripture. The recording of Amos's stormy warnings against injustice was a first step in the birth of the Bible we study today.

The Background of the Book

Amos insisted he was a "layman." He was not a professional prophet in the king's court or a priest in the royal chapel. He was "among the shepherds of Tekoa" (1:1). The word used here implies not so much one who tends a flock as a man in the sheep business. He also had a farm (7:14) and was probably a prosperous man. His hometown, Tekoa, was in Judah, the Southern Kingdom. It was to the Northern Kingdom, Israel, however, that he felt sent to deliver his oracles.

The first verse tells us that he prophesied "in the days" of evil King Jeroboam II of Israel (786–746 B.C.). Those days were prosperous. Jeroboam had reconquered much of the old empire of Solomon (2 Kings 14:23–27). Archaeologists have found traces of his royal palace, with paneled walls inlaid with ivory carvings in the style popular in pagan Egypt (3:15). Business was so good that merchants could hardly wait for the Sabbath to end so they could get back to multiplying profits—at the expense of the poor (8:5). Amos could denounce the wives of rich Israelites, drinking as they idled in luxury (4:1–3). These prosperous Israelites were religious too. They loved to worship the Lord in their traditional shrines (4:4–5). God, they knew, had long ago selected them to be the chosen people, rescuing them from Egypt. In that faith they felt secure (6:1). What could bring a farmer from the Southern Kingdom, Judah, north to Israel to denounce them in the name of their God?

Yet sometime around 750 B.C., this angry prophet, Amos, stood at the gate of the royal shrine at Bethel and announced that God was about to annihilate these chosen people. Their worship, he shouted, was repulsive to God. Their sense of security was ill-founded. Their prosperity was based on the exploitation of the poor. Their politics was corrupt. Soon, not only their ill-gotten gain but they themselves would be carried off into slavery.

A generation later, in 721 B.C., all of Amos's worst warnings came true. Starved into submission, Samaria surrendered, and its people were carried into captivity, never to return.

God's Judgment on
Israel's Neighbors (Amos 1—2)

We are told that when the prophet Elijah was in despair, God spoke to him with "a sound of sheer silence" (1 Kings 19:12). Not so with Amos. "The Lord roars from Zion," he begins; and when Amos's God roars, the tops of the mountains wither (1:2).

Luring the crowd into hearing his message, he began by saying things they were probably pleased to hear. He first announces the judgment of God on their enemies. Seven times he chants the same formula:

> Thus says the Lord:
> For three transgressions of Damascus
>   and for four, I will not revoke the punishment. (1:3)

Damascus, Tyre, Edom—one by one, each of Israel's seven neighbors is condemned. Amos does not denounce these pagans for breaking a covenant with the Lord, for failing to keep God's law, or even for worshiping other gods. These foreigners were not part of the Lord's covenant people. But he does denounce each nation for some act of wanton cruelty that even the heathen should know is wrong. Damascus has as cruelly destroyed the people of Gilead as if it had run farm machinery over them. Gaza and Tyre have raided and carried off their neighbors as slaves. Edom, in its military atrocities, has even ripped up pregnant women. So the list goes. And seven times the frightening word of God is revealed, "I will send a fire on" each.

Last in the list of Israel's neighbors is Judah, Amos's home state (2:4–5). Sometimes family feuds are the most vicious; perhaps these words won the most applause. It is interesting to note, however, that many scholars believe the oracle condemning Judah was added later, by scribes from Judah itself, who wanted to make clear that Amos's warnings about justice applied to them too.

God's Judgment on Israel (Amos 3—7)

Either way, Amos now has his audience with him. But suddenly, he springs his trap. Using precisely the same formula with which he proclaimed the coming destruction of Israel's hated neighbors, he condemns Israel itself:

> For three transgressions of Israel,
>   and for four, I will not revoke the punishment;
> because they sell the righteous for silver,
>   and the needy for a pair of sandals—
> they who trample the head of the poor into the dust of the earth. (2:6–7)

Human life is cheap. There is no justice in the courts for the poor. The needy may be sold into slavery for a trifling debt. Sexual immorality is rampant too, even involving "sacred" prostitutes in the shrines of the Lord (2:7–8).

God had rescued them from Egypt and had given them their land, Amos reminds them (2:9–12), but they have rejected God's messengers (2:12). Now the judgment is coming, and they will never be able to escape it (2:12–16).

But were they not God's chosen people, the only ones God "knows" Yes!

Amos pictures God as agreeing. "Therefore I will punish you" (3:2), for God called Israel not simply for privilege but for responsibility. As surely as the roar of a lion means it has caught something or the fall of a bird means it is trapped, so surely God's message of doom must now be voiced (3:3–8). Their violence and oppression within will bring destruction also from without (3:9–15).

Never tactful, Amos calls Israel's wealthy, drunken women "cows" (4:1). He chants a biting parody of the morning call to worship at the traditional shrines of Bethel and Gilgal:

> Come to Bethel—and transgress;
>> to Gilgal—and multiply transgression. (4:4)

They love their holy ceremonies, but they go right on leading unholy lives. God has repeatedly warned them, to no avail (4:6–12).

Chapter 5 begins as a kind of funeral dirge, as if Israel were a dead girl:

> Fallen, no more to rise,
>> is maiden Israel. (5:2)

To turn Israel from its falsehood and decadence, Amos issues a true call to worship and to life. God says, "Seek me and live" (5:4). "Seek the Lord and live" (5:6). "Seek good and not evil, that you may live" (5:14). But do not seek God at the royal shrine at Bethel (5:5). It is futile to worship while at the same time rejecting the prophet who "reproves at the city gate," the place of public assembly. Greed, not need, has guided them and their leaders:

> Therefore because you trample on the poor
>> and take from them levies of grain,
> you have built houses of hewn stone,
>> but you shall not live in them;
> you have planted pleasant vineyards,
>> but you shall not drink their wine. (5:11)

This denunciation of their substitution of ceremony for social justice leads to the most quoted passage in the book. Using all the phrases that priests have used to indicate God's acceptance of sacrifices and ceremonies, Amos depicts God as repulsed by the sight, sound, and even smell of their worship:

> I hate, I despise your festivals,
>> and I take no delight in your solemn assemblies.
> Even though you offer me your burnt offerings and grain offerings,
>> I will not accept them;
> and the offerings of well-being of your fatted animals
>> I will not look upon.
> Take away from me the noise of your songs;
>> I will not listen to the melody of your harps.

Instead, here is what God really wants:

> But let justice roll down like waters,
> and righteousness like an everflowing stream. (5:21–24)

Five Visions of Judgment
to Come (Amos 7:1–9:8a)

Prophets often described symbolic visions. Amos now gives us five, all of doom. God delays at least for a time, plagues of locusts (7:1–3) and of fire (7:4–6). Amos sees a plumb line; by it, crooked Israel is measured (7:7–9).

At this point, Amaziah, priest of the royal chapel at Bethel, has had enough. He reminds Amos that he is preaching in the king's own sanctuary, and he orders Amos to go back where he came from. Let him prophesy there! Amos replies first by denying that he is a professional prophet.[19] Then he roundly curses both Amaziah and his family, predicting that the priest's wife would become a prostitute, his children would be killed, and he and all Israel would be carried captive into slavery (7:14–17).

Israelites seem to have delighted in puns and plays on words. Amos's fourth vision is of a basket of summer fruit. That seems pleasant enough; but in Hebrew, the word for "summer fruit" and the word for "end" sound almost alike. It is a vision of the horrible "end" of Israel. That end will come because they "trample on the needy, and bring to ruin the poor of the land" (8:4).

The final vision (9:1–8a) is the most frightening. A kind of earthquake shakes the royal shrine until it smashes down on the heads of the worshipers there. There will be no escape.

An Appendix (9:8b–15)

The ending of Amos involves a puzzle. For eight and a half chapters, the book has been a prophecy of almost unrelieved doom. Then suddenly, in the middle of a verse, it breaks off and begins to reverse itself, offering some hope. God says of Israel:

> I will destroy it from the face of the earth
> —except that I will not utterly
> destroy the house of Jacob (9:8).

The explanation most scholars give is this. In 721 B.C., Samaria, capital and last stronghold of Israel, the Northern Kingdom, did fall, and its people were exiled into slavery in Assyria. Someone, Amos or somebody else who recognized the truth of his prophecies, survived and carried his written words to Judah. There they were treasured. But it was recognized that they were incomplete. As the written word of God came into being, more needed to be added; for God is not a God only of punishment and doom. And so someone—perhaps Amos himself but more likely another inspired prophet—added this promise.[20] Someday, God says,

the mountains shall drip sweet wine,
    and all the hills shall flow with it.
I will restore the fortunes of my people Israel,
    and they shall rebuild the ruined cities and inhabit them. (9:13–14)

OBADIAH

Obadiah is the shortest book of the Old Testament. It is among the least loved and least familiar. But the situation that produced it is all too familiar.

Catastrophe sometimes brings out the best in neighbors; sometimes it brings out the worst. In 1992, riots destroyed sections of Los Angeles. On our television screens we saw pictures of looters raiding their neighbors' shops. Florida looters also raided their neighbors' stores and homes after the terrible storm of 1992. We have seen relatively comfortable tribes raiding the relief trucks intended for their starving neighbors who are struggling to survive war or famine in Somalia and Ethiopia. Quite properly, few things make us angrier than seeing neighbors deliberately capitalizing on the misfortune of neighbors.

The book of Obadiah voices that righteous indignation. When, at last, Jerusalem surrendered to Babylon and its people were carried off into slavery, the Edomites, neighbors and kinspeople of the Jews, gloated, helped betray survivors to the conquerors, and then looted the ruined city. Obadiah promises the judgment of God on Edom, the ultimate triumph of God's people, and at last, the coming kingdom of God.

Since Obadiah is so short, no chapter-by-chapter outline is needed in this *Guide.*

Date, Background, and Source

We know nothing of the author but his name, Obadiah. The book is not dated. Commentators date the book, or parts of it, anywhere from the ninth century B.C. to the fourth. Most agree, however, that in the form in which we have it, the book does include angry memory of Edom's conduct when, in 587 B.C., Jerusalem fell. The deep emotion of the book makes one think it was written soon after the event. That Obad. 1:1–5 seems almost to quote from Jer. 49:9, 14–16 suggests to some that it comes from a later time, when the words of Jeremiah—and perhaps others—had been collected and had become available to the writer. An attractive suggestion is that the book was read by the exiles at a ceremony on the site of the ruins of the Temple, after their return.[21]

According to Gen. 25:19–25, even before they were born, twins Jacob (Israel) and Esau (Edom) were fighting in their mother's womb. A neighbor of Israel, Edom occupied what is now the south of Jordan. Obadiah refers to the way its cities were built high on cliffs, and modern visitors to ancient Petra can see the remains of a city of this kind. Lamentations 4, especially verses 21–22, expresses rage at Edom that is much like Obadiah's.

The Contents of the Book

Verses 1 through 5 announce that judgment is coming on Edom. At times, verses 5–9 speak of this judgment as having already come. This, however, is probably what is called "the prophetic perfect," simply voicing such assurance of a coming event that it is as though it has already happened.

Verses 10 through 14 give the reasons for God's wrath. The Edomites had "stood aside" when Babylon carried off Jerusalem's wealth (v. 11). They "gloated" over their neighbors' disaster, and they "looted" (v. 13). They even handed over survivors to the enemy (v. 14).

In the last half of this one-chapter book (vv. 15–21), the focus is no longer on Edom alone; "for the day of the Lord is near against all the nations" (v. 15). All will be punished according to their deeds. Israel, however, will be delivered (v. 17). As in the days of Joshua, each tribe is assigned a portion of the land; therefore in the great restoration to come, the exiles will be given territory, now greatly expanded (v. 20).

The book ends with the hope that goes all through the Bible and for which Christians pray in the Lord's Prayer: "the kingdom shall be the Lord's" (v. 21).

JONAH

Ah! City of bloodshed,
    utterly deceitful, full of booty—
    no end to the plunder!
. . . .
I am against you,
    says the Lord of hosts.
                —(Nahum 3:1–5)

So the prophet Nahum depicted God's attitude toward Nineveh. He had good reason: mighty Nineveh starved little Israel into submission, then murdered or kidnapped and enslaved its people.

Similarly, the attitude of many Jews toward the Babylonians who enslaved them was best expressed by a psalmist:

Happy shall they be who pay you back
    what you have done to us!
Happy shall they be who take your little ones
    and dash them against the rock! (Ps. 137:8–9)

Determined not to let any pagan religious influence continue in rebuilt Jerusalem, Ezra and Nehemiah even forced any Jews who had married foreigners to divorce their wives and disown their own children (Ezra 10:44; Neh. 13:23–31).

Here and there, however, one finds Old Testament writers who strongly

JONAH

The Story of the Prophet Who Needed to Learn That God Is Concerned for All Peoples

"Then the Lord said, . . . 'Should I not be concerned about Nineveh?'" (4:10–11).

1	2	3	4
Jonah Tries to Run Away from God but Is Swallowed by a Fish	Inside the Fish, He Prays a Psalm for Help	Delivered, He Preaches to Nineveh; It Repents and Is Spared	Jonah Sulks, but God Affirms Compassion Even for Nineveh

Author: Unknown (It is about Jonah, not by him.)

Date: Jonah lived around 750 B.C.; this book about him was written probably after the exile, perhaps around 400 B.C.

Purpose: To call Israel to repentance, reminding them tht God is concerned for all peoples

affirm that God loves all races. The prophet of the exile saw the Jews as called by God to a mission to the whole world:

> I will give you as a light to the nations,
>   that my salvation may reach to the end of the earth. (Is. 49:6)

The book of Ruth twice reminds its readers that David's great-grandmother was of the hated Moabite race. And perhaps the most delightful—though also seriously thought-provoking—protest against racism and nationalism is the little book of Jonah.

Background and Nature of the Book

When the present writer has asked his students if they believe that the Creator of the universe could make a fish such that a man could live inside it for three days, many have piously agreed that, for God, even that would not be impossible. But when he has asked whether that all-powerful Lord could speak God's inspired word through a funny short story, some have found this a much more difficult question. The position taken in this *Guide* is that in the book of Jonah, Almighty God both could and did.

A century ago, there were commentators who attempted to prove that one could live inside a whale for three days. Their efforts were not successful. If one is to take the story as history, it is necessary to assume a miraculous fish—which, of course, the Creator could create. Historians, however, have an even bigger problem with the book's reports that an unnamed king of Nineveh commanded the entire city—including its animals—to wear sackcloth and that all its people repented and turned to the Lord. The story seems to be not a curious bit of history but, like the stories Jesus told, a parable.[22]

In fact, it is a funny parable. But this is not for a moment to deny the very serious message that the book is intended to convey. Indeed, Jews read this book in solemn ceremonies of repentance. They are right, for the purpose of the story is to show us how foolish we are in our sins.

The prophet Jonah lived in the middle of the eighth century B.C. He blessed the wars of conquest of evil King Jeroboam II. He must have been an older contemporary of Amos and Hosea (2 Kings 14:23–29). No one knows how old the stories about Jonah may be. The book itself is not dated either. The use of certain words and phrases suggests that it comes from after the exile. Its internationalism is like that of Ruth and Second Isaiah, postexilic books. If, as seems quite possible, it was written as a protest against the danger of the kind of nationalism reflected in the policies of Ezra and Nehemiah, it can be dated to around 400 B.C. God's people had been "swallowed up" by distant Babylon, but now they had been delivered. That exile brought a broadening perspective, on other peoples and on the mercy of God.

The Story of Jonah

The first chapter depicts for us a man so foolish that he thinks he can run away from God. God calls Jonah to go east to Nineveh to preach. Jonah boards a boat headed due west (no one is quite sure whether its destination, called Tarshish, inidicates Sardinia or Spain, but both are in the opposite direction from Nineveh). A great storm arises. The Hebrew word *gadol,* "great," recurs in various forms throughout the book. Everything seems bigger than life: the fish, the city, the bush, and so forth. The devout sailors pray, but not Jonah. Even when he explains that their only hope is to throw him overboard, they try to avoid it, rowing hard to save his life. Throughout the book, the Gentiles are presented favorably, in contrast to Jonah.

Finally thrown overboard and swallowed by the great fish, Jonah does indeed pray. Chapter 2 is a beautiful psalm, much like psalms of thanksgiving for deliverance in the book of Psalms (compare Jonah 2 to Ps. 30, for example). Its style and vocabulary are different from the rest of the book, and it seems to presuppose that the author is already delivered. It could be omitted and the story would continue without an obvious break. Therefore it is widely proposed that this psalm is by a different author, though appropriately inserted here.

Coughed up on shore, Jonah did begin to preach. Perhaps his message was one he could enjoy preaching to those hated Ninevites: "Forty days more, and Nineveh shall be overthrown" (3:4). (Nineveh is pictured as being such a huge city that it takes Jonah three days to walk from one end of it to the other, though the historians tell us that the ruins of Nineveh could be crossed in much less than one day. One suspects that bit of archaeological information would not matter to the author.) Amazingly, wicked Nineveh repents. The king himself decrees that all its people must pray to God. Not only all its people but all its animals must wear the dress of mourning. Seeing such repentance, God spares even this wicked Gentile city.

With the last chapter, we come to the biggest message of the parable. Jonah, sulking because God has not destroyed the city, voices the writer's theology as if it were a complaint to God. Jonah wanted God to be a God of vengeance. Instead, he charges, "You are a gracious God and merciful, slow to anger, and abounding in steadfast love" (4:2). Exactly! This is the point of the book. A miraculous bush becomes so great in one day that it shelters Jonah from the Middle Eastern sun. But when the next day it withers, silly Jonah feels so sorry for himself that he says he is ready to die. The Lord of "steadfast love" asks if God should not at least feel that pity for 120,000 innocent children, even if they are Ninevites. And, if Jonah does not care about Ninevites, doesn't Jonah think that God should at least value all those cattle (4:11)? With that question the story ends, leaving Jonah and the readers to answer for themselves.

A Note about the Message of the Book

The great fish is mentioned in three verses of Jonah, but the great God is mentioned thirty-nine times. It is unfortunate that many of us focus attention on the fish rather than on its Creator. This book was not written as a strange fish story. It was written to show how ridiculous Israel and we are in our narrowness. It says that God is too big to run away from. This great Lord cares for all creation—animals too. It insists that God's mercy is wide enough to include even people who seem to us not to deserve God's care at all. There is both warning and gospel in that message.

MICAH

Sennacherib of Assyria boasted of his conquests, even of the atrocities his armies committed. A frieze found on the wall of the ruins of his palace at Nineveh depicts how his army laid siege to the Judean town of Lachish. Futilely, Lachish's soldiers try to defend its fortress. Some, already slain by Assyrian arrows, are shown falling over the town's walls. Three naked bodies, apparently captured soldiers, have been impaled on pointed poles, their corpses displayed for the terrified people of Lachish to see. And a long line of men, women, and children who have surrendered are being led off captive into slavery.

One biblical prophet wept over the Assyrian invasions, though he confessed that there was a reason for this tragedy:

> Harness the steeds to the chariots,
>   inhabitants of Lachish;
> it was the beginning of sin
>   to daughter Zion,
> for in you were found
>   the transgressions of Israel. (Micah 1:13)

Long after Sennacherib's carvings crumble, the book of Micah's prophecies of judgment—and of hope—will preserve the memory and the meaning of those sad days.

The Background of the Book

In 731 B.C. Assyria—today part of Iraq—conquered Damascus, capital of Syria. Ten years later, Samaria, capital of Israel, the Northern Kingdom, fell to Assyria's army. They were starved into submission and carried off into captivity. Twenty years later, the Assyrian armies again swept over the Southern Kingdom, Judah. King Hezekiah was forced to pay tribute to the invaders, but Jerusalem was miraculously spared. The small towns of Judah were not so fortunate.

MICAH
A Small-Town Prophet Warns Judah of Coming Judgment

"What does the Lord require of you but to do justice, and to love kindness, and to walk humbly with your God?" (6:8).

1 **Judgment Coming on the Towns of Judah**	2 **The Sins That Are Bringing The Judgment**	4 **Hope for the Future Beyond the Judgment**	6 **God Presents God's Controversy with the People**	7 **Israel Responds**
		The coming kingdom of peace, 4		The nation reacts in sorrow, 1—7
		The coming king to be born in Bethlehem, 5		but then in hope, 8—20

Date: Around 730 B.C. (It probably includes additions from a later time.)
Place: Judah
Theme: Judgment, but also hope, with a special concern for small towns
Special Significances: The promise of the king to be born in Bethlehem, quoted to guide the wise men (5:2; Matt. 2:6); the promise of world peace, now inscribed on a wall of the United Nations building (4:3).

All we are told about Micah's background is that he was from Moresheth, one of Judah's small towns. He was a contemporary of Isaiah, the great prophet of Jerusalem. Isaiah loved that city, though he condemned its sins. But Micah is the prophet of the small towns.

He tells us that he resolved to dramatize his grief in a startling manner:

> For this I will lament and wail;
> I will go barefoot and naked;
> I will make lamentation like the jackals,
> and mourning like the ostriches. (1:8)

Howling his poetry like a wild beast, and "barefoot and naked," Micah was a prophet many people resented, but he must have been hard to ignore.

Judgment Coming on the Towns of Judah (Micah 1)

For Micah, the tragic events of his time were a prelude to the coming of God. And when the Lord comes,

> then the mountains will melt under him
> and the valleys will burst open,
> like wax near the fire. (1:4)

Micah knew a reason for the catastrophes devastating Israel:

> All this is for the transgression of Jacob
> and for the sins of the house of Israel. (1:5)

The centers of the sins that brought God's horrible judgment were the two capital cities: Samaria and Jerusalem (1:5).

For a century and a half, the stone palace and fortress walls of beautiful Samaria had looked down on the surrounding valley. Soon it would be only "a heap in the open country" (1:6), and "all her images [would] be beaten to pieces" (1:7). Jerusalem, too, would be plowed like farmland.

It is over the smaller cities and the towns, however, that this small-town prophet grieves. As he chants of their destruction, he uses a series of Hebrew puns and plays on words that do not come through in English. James Moffatt's translation attempts to reflect this device:

> Weep tears at Teartown (Bochim),
> grovel in the dust at Dustown (Beth-ophrah)
> fare forth stripped, O Fairtown (Saphir)!
> Stirtown (Zaanan) dare not stir. (1:10–11)[23]

Destruction was coming on them all.

The Sins That Are
Bringing That Judgment (Micah 2—3)

Micah knew the reason for that destruction: greed. The rich were getting richer, but they were doing so at the expense of the poor:

> They covet fields, and seize them;
>> houses, and take them away;
> they oppress householder and house,
>> people and their inheritance. (2:2)

Divine law had attempted to prevent the accumulation of wealth in the hands of a few. Property was supposed to stay in the family that had originally owned it. If the property was leased by someone else, it was to be returned to the family every fifty years (Lev. 25). But shrewd capitalists had learned how to get around the law. Social and economic justice was perverted. Other great eighth-century prophets agree (cf. Amos 2:6–7; Isa. 5:8–9).

Shocked, Micah's hearers tried to shut him up (Micah 2:6), only to hear his sarcastic reply:

> If someone were to go about uttering empty falsehoods,
>> saying, "I will preach to you of wine and strong drink,"
> such a one would be the preacher for this people! (2:11)

Far from being quiet, Micah attacked every influential group: rulers who were unconcerned to see that justice was done for the poor (3:1–3), prophets who falsely promised peace (3:5–8), government officials who accepted bribes (3:9–11), and priests and prophets who were simply in it for the money and said whatever would be popular with the people (3:11).

For these sins, he warns, "Jerusalem shall become a heap of ruins" (3:12).

Hope for the Future beyond
the Judgment (Micah 4—5)

The first three chapters of Micah are largely warnings of judgment to come, though here and there are glimpses of hope. The next chapters, however, describe visions of a glorious future. The words of Micah were recorded and treasured. As they were handed down through the generations, other oracles were preserved by being copied onto the same scroll. After the first three chapters, it is not clear which oracles are the work of Micah and which come from later inspired poets.[24] The most obvious such problem arises with the beautiful poem in Micah 4:1–4. It is almost word-for-word the same as Isa. 2:1–4. Did one writer copy from the other, or, as many scholars suggest, was a later song so beloved that it was added to each? On a wall of the United Nations building in New York is inscribed the poet's promise that someday

> they shall beat their swords into plowshares,
>   and their spears into pruning hooks;
> nation shall not lift up sword against nation,
>   neither shall they learn war any more. (4:3)

The other best-loved oracle of these chapters is the promise of the coming king from David's line. True to the emphasis on small towns, this poem foretells that the promised prince will be born in the little town of Bethlehem, where David was born. Matthew tells us that centuries later, when the wise men came to Herod's sinful court in Jerusalem to find the newborn King of the Jews, it was to Micah that Herod's advisers turned:

> But you, O Bethlehem of Ephrathah,
>   who are one of the little clans of Judah,
> from you shall come forth for me
>   one who is to rule in Israel. (5:2; cf. Matt. 2:1–6)

God Presents God's Controversy with the People (Micah 6)

The form critics point out that a favorite pattern of the prophets pictured God arguing a legal case against the people. This pattern opens Micah 6. Calling on the mountains to serve as a kind of jury, the Lord demands to know in what way God has failed Israel. God's grace throughout history is reviewed (6:1–5). Penitent, the hearer asks what could possibly be an adequate response to all the Lord has done for Israel. Many sacrifices? Even human sacrifice? (6:6–7). God's threefold answer is one of the high points of biblical prophecy:

> He has told you, O mortal, what is good;
>   and what does the Lord require of you
> but to do justice, and to love kindness,
>   and to walk humbly with your God? (6:8)

Bernhard Anderson proposes that into this one verse Micah has packed a summary of the messages of the greatest eighth-century prophets.[25] There is Amos's demand for justice (Amos 5:24), Hosea's emphasis on steadfast love (Hos. 2:19), and Isaiah's humble reliance on the Lord (Isa. 30:15).

Israel Responds (Micah 7)

In the final chapter, Israel personified speaks. The first speech is one of confession (7:1–7). Government officials are corrupt (7:3), neighbors can no longer be trusted (7:5), and the family itself is breaking down (7:6). But this is not the end. "I shall rise," Israel affirms (7:8). Jerusalem's walls will be rebuilt (7:11). The returned remnant will be pardoned (7:18). And at the end of the book, probably edited for use in liturgy, the congregation responds:

> He will again have compassion upon us;
> he will tread our iniquities under foot. (7:19)

And addressing God directly, they sing:

> You will show faithfulness to Jacob
> and unswerving loyalty to Abraham. (7:20)

Note one other thing about the people's response: Micah's prophecies of immediate doom did not come true. Jerusalem survived. A century later, an explanation was given in Jeremiah. That prophet was nearly lynched for preaching the same warnings that Micah had preached. Wise officials secured Jeremiah's release. When Micah said these things, they reminded the mob, the people did not execute Micah. Instead, they listened and repented. And so, in that happier day, God delivered them (Jer. 26:16–19). Perhaps, the officials seemed to suggest, if we repent, we might be spared too.

NAHUM

Though the events occurred long ago, television shows still count on an audience when they portray again the last days of Adolf Hitler. Some readers of this *Guide* still have their own memories of his fall. There was dancing in the streets, and there were drunken celebrations. Many Christians joined in special services of thanksgiving. More than any other individual, it was Hitler who had plunged the world into World War II, had brought about the deaths of hundreds of thousands of his enemies, and had ordered the murder of six million Jews. Somehow his suicide in the rubble of bombed-out Berlin seemed fitting, the long-awaited sentence of a just God.

Something like that experience lies behind the book of Nahum. The Assyrians were the Nazis of the ancient world. For more than a century, they had terrorized the Middle East. Everywhere they had raped, tortured, kidnapped, and slaughtered. But now the messengers began to bring good news (1:15). In 614 B.C., Asshur fell; and in 612, the Babylonians conquered Nineveh. At last, the punishment of God had come upon that hated city.

The book of Nahum is a taunt song, gloating over Nineveh and celebrating its fall. Though it is written as if Nineveh were already destroyed, it was probably written shortly before the conquest of that city. The prophet could already visualize its doom. Chapters 2 and 3 are a cry of hatred and vengeance. But the first chapter, like the church services when Hitler surrendered, sets the story of the fall of Nineveh in a theological context which gives it a place in our Bibles.

A Poem on the Power
of a Jealous God (Nahum 1:1–14)

Too short to require an outline in this *Guide,* the book of Nahum is really two poems. The first (1:1–14) includes an acrostic poem, that is, a poem in which each stanza begins with the next letter of the Hebrew alphabet. Whether it was written by Nahum, was an earlier poem that he adapted, or was an addition by a later scribe is debated among scholars.[26] The inclusion of these verses put the celebration of the horrors befalling Nineveh in a theological context and thus gave the book a place in the scripture.

"A jealous and avenging God is the Lord." The poem begins by voicing the two themes of its theology. First, God is "jealous," that is, loving and protective of the chosen people and concerned for their loyalty; therefore God is "avenging," sure to punish those who deserve it. True, God is "slow to anger" (1:3). God had tolerated Nineveh for a long time. But in the end, "the Lord will by no means clear the guilty" (1:3).

The second theological concept stressed in the poem is the power of this God. All of nature is subject to the Lord (1:3–5). No human power can stand before the divine power (1:6). "The Lord is good" (1:7); that goodness is manifested in God's protection of "those who take refuge in him" (1:7). But this includes the theme to be developed more fully in this poem, God's utter destruction of anyone

> who plots evil against the Lord,
> who counsels wickedness. (1:11)

A Poem Celebrating the Destruction
of Nineveh (Nahum 1:14–3:19)

"Look!" A messenger is bringing the news: Nineveh is falling (1:15). With that assurance, Nahum begins his jubilant, vengeful celebration of the enemy's destruction. Liberated, Judah can resume its festivals to the Lord.

Nineveh is in panic. Its soldiers still wear their famous crimson uniforms (2:3). But now, in confusion, "the chariots race madly through the streets" (2:4), and the officers stumble when summoned. They have plundered others; now they are going to be plundered (2:9). The lion had been their symbol. But "what became of the lions' den?" (2:11).

Now the Babylonians have broken into the city and the battle has begun. The poet lets us see the carnage:

> Ah! City of bloodshed,
> utterly deceitful, full of booty—

> The crack of whip and rumble of wheel,
>> galloping horse and bounding chariot!
> Horsemen charging,
>> flashing sword and glittering spear,
> piles of dead,
>> heaps of corpses,
> dead bodies without end—
>> they stumble over the bodies! (3:1–3)

Charles L. Taylor, Jr., comments that Nahum's poetry "for vividness and force is perhaps unmatched in the Bible or even in all literature"![27]
The reason for Nineveh's destruction is not really Babylon's army. It is this:

> I am against you,
>> says the Lord of hosts. (3:5)

Nahum's Place in Scripture

Nahum is so filled with vengeance and hatred that Elizabeth Achtemeier reports that one commentator has called Nahum a false prophet. At what seems the opposite extreme, Achtemeier writes of the opening hymn that "we have here only a little less than a complete presentation of the biblical witness to God's person."[28] Much more modestly, and writing rather of the second part of the book, Taylor says that Nahum "declares only one small part of the truth about God. Yet that fraction is of untold importance, for it reminds him who will heed that there is no withstanding the Lord who maintains justice and answers human need." Nahum, Taylor says, "is one of the world's classic rebukes to militarism."[29]

Babylon conquered Nineveh but, in its turn, it too fell. The 1990s saw another nation bomb Nineveh's successor in Iraq, Baghdad. Seeking a lesson from this poem on God's justice, another commentator recalls Rudyard Kipling's "Recessional," written for his own country:[30]

> Lo all our pomp of yesterday
>> is one with Nineveh and Tyre.

Perhaps Nahum functions in our Bible like Kipling's closing warning "Lest we forget—lest we forget."

HABAKKUK

If God is good and all-powerful, why is there so much evil in the world? Racked by grief and disease, Job wrestled with that question. Jesus on the cross cried to God, "Why?" (Mark 15:34). Millions of others have agonized

HABAKKUK
Questions and Hope in a Time When Judgment Is Near

"The righteous live by their faith" (2:4).

1	2:6	3
Two Questions and Two Answers	**Five Woes or Judgments**	**A Prayer-Psalm of Praise**
Question: How long will God put up with Israel's sins? 1:1–4	On plundering nations, 2:6–8	God is coming in terrifying majesty to save, as in the days of the exodus, 3:1–16
Answer: Not long. God is raising up the Chaldeans (Babylon) to punish them, 1:5–11	On the greedy, 2:9–11	The singer's trust in God, no matter what trouble may come, 3:17–19
	On violent leaders, 2:12–14	
Question: How can a pure God let wicked Babylon swallow up a nation that, bad as it is, is better than Babylon? 1:12–17	On "drunk" oppressors, 2:15–17	
	On idolaters, 2:18–19	
Answer: Though the wicked will perish, "the righteous [shall] live by their faith," 2:1–5	Contrast: the Lord in his temple, 2:20	

Date: Late seventh century B.C., as Babylon is becoming powerful
Theme: Faith, though in a bewildering time of sin and judgment
Special Significance: Habakkuk 2:4 became the theme of Romans (1:17) and thus, in part, of the Protestant Reformation.

over the problem of the apparent triumph of evil. As he saw his world falling apart, an inspired prophet pleaded with the good God, "Why?"

God's strange answer is the basis of the book of Habakkuk.

The Background of the Book

The last days of the kingdom of Judah were terrifyingly close. In 609 B.C., Egyptian troops killed good King Josiah. Three months later, they jailed his son Jehoahaz; put their own puppet, Jehoiakim, on the throne; and forced Jehoiakim to collect huge taxes each year, which they carried off to Egypt. But in 605 B.C., the Babylonians conquered Egypt, and they, in turn, began extorting tribute. Jehoiakim tried futilely to play the game of power politics, switching loyalty from one nation to the other. It was hopeless. Soon after his death in 597 B.C., the Babylonians deported more than three thousand Jews, Jerusalem's best leaders, into slavery. Yet Jeremiah tells us that during the horrors of his reign, King Jehoiakim had no real concern for the poor and no real concern for God. His response to the needs of his people was to build himself a new palace (Jer. 22:13–17).

It was probably in the midst of the reign of that evil king, perhaps about the year 606 B.C., that Habakkuk begged God for an explanation.

Two Questions and
Two Answers (Hab. 1:1–2:5)

"O Lord, how long?" (1:2). So begins Habakkuk's dialogue with God. "Violence . . . wrong-doing . . . destruction . . . strife and contention" are everywhere (1:3). "Justice never prevails" (1:4). Deuteronomy and earlier prophets had promised that God would punish evil and protect the good. Instead, "the wicked surround the righteous" (1:4). Those in power were getting away with their greedy schemes, and God seemed to be doing nothing about it. "Why?" Habakkuk cried to the Lord (1:3).

God gave an answer that "astonished" and "astounded" the prophet (1:5). The rich and corrupt people will be punished soon, "for I am rousing the Chaldeans" (1:6). Egypt, Jehoiakim's patron, may seem all-powerful now, but Babylon is the power of the future. Through it, Judah's sin will receive its just reward.

God's answer seems only to compound the problem. It leads to the prophet's second question. Granted that Judah is sinful, Babylon is far worse. How can God allow that evil empire to conquer God's own people?

> Why do you look on the treacherous,
>> and are silent when the wicked swallow
> those more righteous than they? (1:13)

Like a sentinel watching in the hope of news, Habakkuk waits for some kind of prophetic vision to give him an answer (2:1). And God speaks again.

For a full vision, a clear answer, the prophet must wait, God tells him, though it will come (2:3). In the end, sin will be punished. Proud Babylon is puffed up, but "the arrogant do not endure" (2:5). And in the midst of that warning to the haughty comes the great text of this book: "The righteous live by their faith" (2:4). No neat explanation of the problem of evil in the world is yet given. But the prophet receives the assurance that one who lives in faithful trust will be given a right relationship with God. That life of faithfulness is what really matters.

Five Woes or Judgments (Hab. 2:6–20)

More in the typical pattern of a prophet, Habakkuk now hurls five taunts at the proud and the greedy.

Plundering nations will find that their "creditors," those whom they have robbed, will someday collect what they are owed. The plunderers will be plundered (2:6–8).

Greedy leaders building up their own "houses" (dynasties) will find those houses crumbling upon them (2:9–11).

Those who seek to rule by violence and sin will discover that the true ruler is God. In the end,

> the earth will be filled
> with the knowledge of the glory of the Lord,
> as the waters cover the sea. (2:14)

Conquerors in a drunken orgy of forcing others to "drink" their wrath will be forced to stagger from that same "drink" (2:15–17).

Idolaters will discover there is no life in an idol at all (2:18–19).

> But the Lord is in his holy temple;
> let all the earth keep silence before him! (2:20)

A Prayer-Psalm of Praise (Hab. 3)

Nobody is certain who wrote the psalm that forms the last chapter of Habakkuk. Perhaps it was the prophet himself. Most scholars think it comes from a later time. Probably it was sung to the tune "Shigionoth" (3:1), and it is dedicated "to the choirmaster" (3:19). Evidently, therefore, it was designed for services of worship. But though it may have been composed by a later writer, it is now part of Habakkuk's book, and indeed, it fits there quite appropriately.

Habakkuk had been told to wait for a vision (2:3). Now a vision comes, an epiphany, a manifestation of God in all the divine glory:

> His glory covered the heavens,
> and the earth was full of his praise.
> The brightness was like the sun. (3:3–4)

As God approaches, everywhere there is a kind of earthquake. Why? Is God angry with nature? No! But there is a reason God's power is displayed:

> You came forth to save your people,
> to save your anointed. (3:13)

Overawed by the vision, the prophet waits quietly for the day he has foreseen (3:16). With the faith by means of which he has said that the righteous live, he will trust in God, no matter what happens:

> Though the fig tree does not blossom,
> and no fruit is on the vines;
>
> . . . .
>
> yet I will rejoice in the Lord;
> I will exult in the God of my salvation. (3:17–18)

Later Influence of Habakkuk

No commentary on this little book would be complete without noting how large its influence on Christianity has been. Paul built on it in Galatians, the book that has been called "the Magna Carta of the Christian faith" (see Gal. 3:11). Especially important, Habakkuk became the text for Paul's most influential work, the epistle to the Romans (Rom. 1:17). With Paul, "faith" came to be understood as trust in Jesus Christ for one's salvation. Nearly fifteen centuries later, Martin Luther made Romans's theme of "salvation by faith" a rallying cry of the Reformation. Protestant readers of this *Guide* are heirs of a heritage that, in part, goes back through Luther to Paul and from Paul to the little book of Habakkuk.

ZEPHANIAH

> I will utterly sweep away everything
> from the face of the earth, says the Lord.
> I will sweep away humans and animals;
> I will sweep away the birds of the air
> and the fish of the sea.
> I will make the wicked stumble.
> I will cut off humanity
> from the face of the earth. (Zeph. 1:2–3)

Zephaniah had a name for this cataclysmic destruction. He called it "the day of the Lord."

ZEPHANIAH
A Warning of the Coming "Day of the Lord"

"For the day of the Lord is at hand" (1:7).

1 **The Coming Judgment**	2:4 **Judgment Coming to All Nations**	3:1 **The Sins of Jerusalem**	3:14 **A Postscript**	3:20
Judgment on the whole world, 1:1–3 Judgment on Judah: for false religion, 1:4–6 for political corruption, 1:7–11 for indifference, especially by the wealthy, 1:12–13 The horrors of that judgment day, 1:14–18 An appeal to repent, 2:1–3	The Philistines, 2:4–7 The Ammonites, 2:8–11 The Ethiopians, 2:12 The Assyrians, 2:13–15	Officials, judges, prophets—all have failed to respond, 3:1–7 Yet on that day, there is hope of conversion, 3:8–13	A song of hope, 3:14–20	

Date: About 625 B.C., after Manasseh's evil reign (2 Kings 21), a generation before Jerusalem was destroyed

Place: Jerusalem

Theme: "The day of the Lord," the coming judgment day

Special Significance: The eschatological concept of the day of the Lord, the coming judgment day, is developed in subsequent books, reaching a climax in Revelation.

The Background of the Book

When the story of the fall of Jerusalem was recorded, the historian had an explanation for it: the sins of the days of King Manasseh were the last straw. After that bloody, pagan tyrant, there was really no hope for Judah (2 Kings 21:10–15). In Manasseh's reign of terror, no true prophet was permitted to preach. Two years after his death, a popular rebellion broke out; his son was assassinated; and around the year 640 B.C., his eight-year-old grandson, Josiah, was placed on the throne.

Now, after more than half a century, there was a chance for a prophet of the Lord to speak openly. Zephaniah was that prophet. Apparently, he began his oracles before Josiah's great reforms of 721 B.C. Perhaps his words helped lead Josiah, when he became a man, to make that final effort to bring Judah back to God. But as Zephaniah had warned, it was too late. God had resolved to destroy Jerusalem.

The great theme of Zephaniah's preaching is "the day of the Lord." (The word "day" occurs some nineteen times in the three chapters of this little book.) The background of the idea seems to have been Israel's ancient belief that God would miraculously destroy their enemies when they were engaged in holy war. Someday, the Lord's great victory would come. Amos, however, warned that the day of the Lord would be "darkness, and not light" (Amos 5:18), with the Lord's judgment falling on Israel, just as on other nations. Gradually, prophets expanded the picture of the coming day in more and more completely apocalyptic oracles (Isa. 24—27; Ezek. 38—39; Joel 2:1–2; etc.). The New Testament's great Apocalypse is the book of Revelation.

An important link in the evolution of that picture of cosmic judgment is the prophecy of Zephaniah.

The Coming Judgment (Zeph. 1:1–2:3)

In the verses quoted at the beginning of this section, Zephaniah pictures God's judgment on all creation. The prophet's great concern, however, is the judgment coming upon Judah. Having announced the coming cosmic judgment, he describes the sins for which Jerusalem will be punished. Even their priests had tried to include Baal worship along with their worship of the Lord (Zeph. 1:4). People in Jerusalem were practicing astrology, worshiping stars from the flat roofs of their homes (1:5). Worship of other gods and superstitious practices were common (1:6, 9). Political leaders were corrupt (1:8). And God's judgment would begin, Zephaniah announces, in the places of business. There, complacently amassing wealth, the rich supposed that the Lord really was not going to do anything at all (1:11–13).

And so the day of the Lord will come, Zephaniah warns. God, the invincible warrior, will completely devastate the city. It is to be a day of "wrath . . . distress . . . anguish . . . ruin . . . devastation . . . darkness and gloom"

(1:15). The people's wealth will not help them (1:18). Every kind of horror the prophet can imagine will come, and then God will make "a terrible end . . . of all the inhabitants of the earth" (1:18).

There is a glimmer of hope. Isaiah had spoken of a remnant that would survive. Now Zephaniah calls:

> Seek the Lord, all you humble of the land,
> who do his commands;
> seek righteousness, seek humility;
> perhaps you may be hidden
> on the day of the Lord's wrath. (2:3)

Judgment Coming
to All Nations (Zeph. 2:4–15)

Like many other prophets, Zephaniah announces that the God who will judge Judah will also judge the nations that surround it (2:4–15; cf. Isa. 13—23; Jer. 46—51; Ezek. 25—32; etc.).

The Philistines will be destroyed and their seacoast towns will become pasture for Judah (Zeph. 2:4–7). The Moabites and the Ammonites will be plundered by the Israelite remnant because they ridiculed God's people (2:8–11). (Some scholars suggest that these verses were added after the fall of Jerusalem because of these nations' actions at that time.)

The Ethiopians (probably Egypt is included) will be killed (2:12). And especially, Assyria, the most powerful enemy, so proud, will become a desolation (2:13–15).

The Sins of Jerusalem (Zeph. 3:1–13)

An oracle in the last chapter returns to the sins of Jerusalem. The city has failed to listen to its prophets; it has no trust in God; its public officials, its judges, its prophets, and its priests have all misused their positions (3:2–5). Therefore, judgment is coming.

Yet now this book contains a note of hope. In it, God speaks of "my scattered ones" (3:10). Some scholars suggest, therefore, that all or part of this oracle comes from after the captivity. Perhaps, instead, Zephaniah became more hopeful because Josiah now—in 721 B.C.—had attempted reform. In any event, the poem promises a kind of reversal of the catastrophe said to have occurred at the tower of Babel. Once people were scattered by diversity of languages. Now they will all be given "a pure speech, that all of them may call on the name of the Lord" (3:9). And the righteous remnant, humble and purified at last (cf. 2:3), will be God's flock, protected by the Good Shepherd (3:13).

A Postscript (Zeph. 3:14–20)

Sing aloud, O daughter Zion;
  shout, O Israel!
Rejoice and exult with all your heart,
  O daughter Jerusalem!
The Lord has taken away the judgments against you. (3:14–15)

Did ever a book end with such a contrast to its beginning? Almost certainly, these last verses come from a time after Judah was exiled, for God's promise is "I will bring you home" (3:20).

Apparently, what happened is this. Devout Jews saw their captivity as the fulfillment of the grim warnings of Zephaniah. But they, a remnant, had survived, even in captivity, as the prophet had said a remnant would survive. And so, with faith and hope and a song so much like that of Second Isaiah, they trusted the word of the Lord:

I will make you renowned and praised
  among all the peoples of the earth,
when I restore your fortunes
  before your eyes, says the Lord. (3:20)

HAGGAI

"The time has not yet come" (1:2). Haggai was not the last religious leader to hear the excuse that "this just isn't the right time." His answer to that objection and his encouragement to the returned exiles to go ahead and rebuild the ruined Temple are the subjects of this two-chapter book.

The Background of the Book

The people who complained that this was no time to build a temple had plenty of reasons. It was only eighteen years since the first exiles had returned from Babylon. They had found Jerusalem and its Temple in ruins. They had tried to begin building. But when they had refused to let the semi-pagan Samaritans join with them, the Samaritans had used political pressure to force them to stop building (Ezra 4:1–5). Now, in the year 520 B.C., the little group of former slaves was experiencing an economic depression. Their crops had failed (Hag. 1:10). Inflation was rampant (1:6). It did seem a bad time for a building program.

The book of Ezra tells us that, in spite of their hearers' poverty and discouragement, two prophets, Haggai and Zechariah, began to urge that the work begin. Moved by them, Zerubbabel, governor under Persian rule, and Jeshua, the high priest, "set out to rebuild the house of God" (Ezra 5:1–2). The two prophets continued to help them. The book of Haggai is the

HAGGAI

Encouragement to Rebuild the Temple

"Build the house, so that I may take pleasure in it and be honored, says the Lord" (1:8).

1:1	2:1	2:23

A Call to Begin Building

The people's procrastination, 1:2

Haggai's answer, 1:3–11

The people respond and begin work on the Temple, 1:12–15

A Call to Continue Building

Words of hope and encouragement, 2:1–9

But worship in that Temple demands purity, 2:10–14

Promise of a glorious future under Zerubbabel, 2:15–23

Date: 520 B.C., eighteen years after the return from exile in Babylon

Purpose: To encourage the Jews to rebuild the Temple

Two Significant Ideas: Promise of a glorious future and a reminder that worship and buildings for worship are important

account, written by one of the prophet's disciples, of the help Haggai gave. Haggai's first recorded oracle was on August 29, 520 B.C.[31]

A Call to Begin Building (Hag. 1)

To the complaint that "the time has not yet come," Haggai had an answer: "Is it a time for you yourselves to live in your paneled houses, while this house lies in ruins?" (1:4). The people returned from exile had hurried to build houses for themselves. Surely now it was time to build the house of the Lord.

Haggai freely admitted that times were hard. There had indeed been a drought. But, he reminded the people, it is the Lord who controls the weather (1:11). The very poverty of which they complained existed because they had neglected God's house while building their own (1:9). Therefore "go up to the hills and bring wood and build the house, so that I may take pleasure in it and be honored, says the Lord" (1:7) A house for worship, for honoring God, is pleasing to God.

Within a month, the work began (1:12–15). Haggai relayed the Lord's message to them: "I am with you" (1:13). And the writer notes that it was not just a building that was built; "the spirit of all the remnant of the people" was "stirred up" (1:14). As they worked together, something happened within their souls.

A Call to Continue Building (Hag. 2)

A few weeks later, Haggai spoke again. Babylon had destroyed Solomon's magnificent Temple sixty-seven years before, but there were still a few old people who could remember it. By comparison, what a tiny, drab little shrine they were building now! And so Haggai urged them on. "Take courage . . . take courage . . . take courage" (2:4), he reassured them. "I am with you, says the Lord of hosts" (2:4). The God who had rescued them from Egypt would keep the promises made long ago.

George Frederic Handel's *Messiah* has helped perpetuate a kind of inspired misunderstanding of the promise in Hag. 2:6–7. The newer translations are correct; what those verses really promise is that all the earth will be shaken and then "the *treasure* of all nations shall come" to the new Temple (italics added). But the Latin Vulgate and the King James translation understood the verse to say that the "desire" of all nations shall come. This, in turn, was thought to refer to Christ's coming. A familiar solo from Handel's *Messiah* reflected this idea. John Calvin pointed out that since ultimately Christ is what all nations really desire, that understanding is not wrong; but, he said, what the verse really promises is that riches will flow to the Temple from all over the world.

On December 18, 520 B.C., the prophet spoke again. The work had begun, but prosperity had not returned. Haggai proposed two answers. First, what is unclean pollutes what is clean (we might say that a rotten apple in a barrel does not become good by contact with good apples; instead, the good apples become rotten). Sins have proved contagious, polluting the nation and delaying its recovery. But, second, they should be patient. The next harvest will bring blessing (2:19).

That same day, Haggai voiced his last recorded oracle (2:20–23). It was a reassertion of the promised kingdom of God. Haggai's hope focused on Zerubbabel, the governor appointed by Persia and a descendent of the royal line. He would be like a ring on the hand of God.

Not all the promises of Haggai came literally true within the "little while" that he seemed to predict. The day did come, however, when that Temple, rebuilt by Herod, did outshine Solomon's, and tribute did indeed come to it from Jews all over the ancient world. And if Zerubbabel did not fulfill Haggai's messianic expectations, the prophet's words kept that hope alive. To the Temple that Haggai helped build, Jesus came. Christians believe that in Jesus, Haggai's hopes were fulfilled.

ZECHARIAH

Paradoxically, two things are true about Zechariah. Of all the minor prophets, the book of Zechariah is the hardest to understand. But of all the minor prophets, it may well be the one that the gospel writers used most to help us understand Jesus.

The Background and Nature of the Book

The book of Ezra tells us that when the Jews returned from captivity in Babylon, two prophets led them in rebuilding the Temple (Ezra 5:1–2). For the message of the first, in the year 520 B.C., see the book of Haggai. A few weeks later, as the work continued, Zechariah began to preach. Within a few months, he began describing visions that helped give the poverty-stricken people the hope they needed to keep up their labor.

Even the first part of this book (chaps. 1—8) is full of strange apocalyptic imagery.[32] Four horsemen form a heavenly patrol. A scroll flies through the air. A woman is thrown into a basket and is carried away by angels. But Zechariah does interpret these visions for his hearers. Clearly, they are designed to encourage that little group of former slaves to go ahead in rebuilding the Temple. In Judah's seemingly hopeless situation, the visions give assurance that God has a destiny for the remnant people and their two leaders, Joshua and Zerubbabel.

Chapters 9 through 14, however, are much more difficult. They do not claim to be by Zechariah. They include poetry, in contrast to Zechariah's prose. They are called oracles, not visions. The Temple, Joshua, and Zerubbabel are no longer mentioned. And Greece rather than Persia seems to be the oppressor. Most scholars, therefore, believe that these prophecies

ZECHARIAH

Visions of Hope, Centered around the Rebuilding of the Temple, the Coming King, and the Final Judgment

"Those who are far off shall come and help to build the temple of the Lord" (6:15).
"Lo, your king comes to you . . . humble and riding on a donkey" (9:9).

1:1 Eight Symbolic Visions of Hope	7 A Question and an Answer	9 The Coming of the Messiah	11 Warning of Judgment	12 The Day of the Lord 14:21
1. Four horsemen, God's heavenly guardians, 1:1–17	The question: Should we continue to mourn and fast, as we have since Jerusalem fell? 7:3	In contrast to violent conquerors, Zion's king comes humbly, riding on a donkey, 9	A good shepherd (leader) is contrasted with worthless leaders, 11	God will deliver them through a Davidic king, 12:1–13:1
2. Four horns of evil destroyed, 1:18–20	The answer: No. Feast and rejoice now, 8:19	The coming return of God and God's restored people, 10		Judah purified, 13:2–6
3. A measuring line that cannot measure the glorified, rebuilt Jerusalem, 2:1–5 (A call to the remaining exiles to return), 2:6–13				God's shepherd stricken and the sheep scattered, 13:7–9
4. Joshua the high priest given glorious new robes, 3:1–10				Final victory, 14:1–21
5. Joshua and Zerubbabel, the governor, as anointed lamps, 4:1–14				

ZECHARIAH (Continued)

6. A flying scroll of
warning against sin, 5:1–4

7. A basket (*ephah*) of sin
carried away, 5:5–11

8. The four chariots of
God's heavenly patrol,
6:1–14

Summary: the glorious
future of the Temple, 6:15

Date: 518 B.C. (the last chapters probably come from a later time)

Themes: Encouragement to the returned exiles as the Temple is being rebuilt; chapters 9 through 14 are on the coming of the messiah and the final victory of God.

Some Especially Significant Ideas: Matthew interprets Jesus' triumphal entry into Jerusalem in terms of the king on the donkey in Zechariah 9. Ezra 5:1–2 says that Zechariah and Haggai led the returned exiles in rebuilding the Temple. In this book, one can see new development of apocalyptic literature. New Testament writers frequently quote Zechariah in their stories of Jesus.

come from a later time, from the late fourth perhaps even to the second century B.C. Some commentaries even refer to these chapters as "Second Zechariah." In them, a good shepherd is rejected, apparently even killed. Plagues and cosmic battles roll over the earth. Even Judah attacks the city of Jerusalem. But in the end, the kingdom of God is established forever.

Eight Symbolic Visions of Hope (Zech. 1—6)

"Return to me, says the Lord of hosts, and I will return to you" (1:3). Zechariah began his preaching with a call to repentance. The positive nature of the rest of his prophecies suggests that his hearers responded to his challenge.

Most of the first half of the book is a series of eight symbolic visions:

1. Zechariah sees four horsemen, God's heavenly patrol, guarding the whole earth. And as he sees them, he hears an angel announce, "I have returned to Jerusalem with compassion; my house shall be built in it, says the Lord of hosts" (1:16).
2. Four blacksmiths strike down four horns, four nations that have long harassed Israel (1:18–20).
3. An angel stops a man from measuring the walls of Jerusalem, for the city will someday be rebuilt too big to be confined by any wall except that of the fire of the Lord (2:1–5).

   "Up, up!" the prophet calls. "Up! Escape to Zion" (2:6–7). He summons those former slaves who have not yet returned and promises them that they will dance in triumph over their former masters (2:6–13).
4. Zechariah sees Joshua, high priest of the returned exiles, clad in dirty clothes and harassed by Satan. But Satan is rebuked, Joshua is provided festival dress, and he is promised that if he follows God's law, he will rule in the house the people are building (3:1–10).
5. In the light of a lampstand lit by the spirit of God, Joshua and Zerubbabel, the governor, are seen as two olive trees, anointed to stand by the Lord of the whole earth (4:1–14).
6. A scroll flies over the earth, bringing punishment to sinners (5:1–4).
7. In a great basket, angels carry away personified sin (5:5–11).
8. Finally, Zechariah sees again a heavenly patrol, four horse-drawn chariots, keeping God's watch over all the earth, and the prophet is assured that God's spirit is at rest "in the north country," from which Babylon and others have so long invaded Israel (6:1–8).

As God's chosen priest, Joshua is to be given a glorious crown. He will build the Temple. And the prophet ends his report of these visions with the promise that "those who are far off shall come and help to build the Temple of the Lord; and you shall know that the Lord of hosts has sent me to you" (6:15).

A Question and an Answer (Zech. 7—8)

Even today, there are synagogues in which devout worshipers still wear black leg bands in mourning for Solomon's Temple. In 518 B.C., a delegation came to Jerusalem to ask a related question: Should they continue the annual fasts with which, ever since the destruction of that Temple, they had mourned its end? Zechariah gave a double answer.

First, he reminded them of the reason for that destruction. Israel had not obeyed its great prophets. What they need to do is "render true judgments, show kindness and mercy to one another; do not oppress the widow, the orphan, the alien, or the poor; and do not devise evil in your hearts against one another" (7:9–10). That, not ceremonial fasting, is what matters.

But, second, there is no need for fasting now. The day is coming soon when Jerusalem will be rebuilt and boys and girls will play in its streets in peace. And as to the fasts, they are to be turned into feasts of joy (8:18–19).

The Coming of the Messiah (Zech. 9—10)

As noted above, Zechariah 9—14 is so different from Zechariah 1—8 and seems to suggest so different a situation that it is widely held that it comes from a later prophet or, more likely, later prophets.

The first oracle (chaps. 9—10) begins with a description of destruction coming upon Jerusalem's neighbors. The enemy is now Greece (9:13), and the invader is quite possibly Alexander the Great. (One is tempted to relate the warhorse of 9:10 to Bucephalus, the famous steed that only Alexander could ride.) But in contrast to the bloody invasion by Alexander—or whatever conqueror is intended here—there is the coming of the messiah:

> Rejoice greatly, O daughter Zion!
>   Shout aloud, O daughter Jerusalem!
> Lo, your king comes to you;
>   triumphant and victorious is he,
> humble and riding on a donkey,
>   on a colt, the foal of a donkey.
> He will cut off the chariot from Ephraim
>   and the war horse from Jerusalem;
> and the battle bow shall be cut off,
>   and he shall command peace to the nations;
> his dominion shall be from sea to sea,
>   and from the River to the ends of the earth. (9:9–10)

Jesus deliberately acted out this entry of the Prince of Peace as he rode into Jerusalem on Palm Sunday (Matt. 21:1–5; John 12:12–15).

The Jews were scattered to Egypt in the south and Assyria in the north as, after his death, Alexander's empire was split apart. They were subject to evil "shepherds" (rulers) (10:3). But the prophet promises that they will be restored in a new exodus (10:11) and will someday glory in the name of the Lord (10:12).

Warning of Judgment (Zech. 11)

The shepherd theme links chapter 11 to chapter 10, but its meaning is not clear. Evil shepherds are denounced (11:4–6). Then the prophet writes, "So, on behalf of the sheep merchants, I became the shepherd of the flock doomed to slaughter" (11:7). Taken literally, he seems to say that he served briefly as governor. Most commentators think he means simply that in some fashion that is not clear, he acted out this role in symbols. He was quickly rejected and was paid off with the price of a slave. Those thirty pieces of silver he threw "into the treasury in the house of the Lord," or as some manuscripts read, he threw it "to the potter" (11:13). Dramatically, he broke the staffs he had labeled "Favor" and "Unity," symbolizing the breaking of the covenant. Centuries later, it is not possible to visualize exactly what the prophet did or to identify exactly whom he was attacking. These strange words were preserved, however, and Matthew found meaning in them. He recognized Jesus as the Good Shepherd, rejected by his people. Evil shepherds set his price at thirty pieces of silver. Judas's blood money, thrown back at the priests in the Temple, became the price of what was probably a cemetery, the potter's field (Matt. 26:15; 27:3–10). Whatever the prophet was thinking, this became his meaning for Christians.

The Day of the Lord (Zech. 12—14)

The book ends (chaps. 12—14) with two somewhat different accounts of the day of the Lord.[33] They agree in describing cosmic conflict, God's victory over all the enemies of Jerusalem, and the ultimate triumph of the kingdom of God.

The whole world seems to turn against Jerusalem, apparently even including, at first, its own tribe, Judah. But realizing now that God is protecting the holy city, that tribe turns and, with God's miraculous help, repels the invaders. The dynasty of David rules, "like the angel of the Lord" (12:8). But now there is a strange tragedy. The whole city mourns a martyr. Apparently they have executed him and now, too late, recognize that this was a horrible mistake. "When they look on the one whom they have pierced, they shall mourn for him, as one mourns for an only child" (12:10). The prophet never identifies this beloved one. But after his death, a fountain is opened to cleanse all Jerusalem from its sin (13:1). Again, we may wish that the prophet had been clearer as to whom he had in mind. Perhaps he here seeks to include in his vision of the future the promise of the suffering servant of Isaiah 53. John knew who in the providence of God actually fulfilled the prophecy. The one who had been pierced was Jesus (John 19:37; cf. Rev. 1:7).

The editor inserted a brief poem (13:7–9) that fits with the shepherd theme of chapters 10 and 11. Many apocalypses include an account of a period of trouble, "the tribulations of the messiah," before God's final victory. In this poem, a shepherd is stricken, and his flock, apparently Israel, is scattered. But in the end, Israel will be purified and restored. Once again, the prophet does not identify the stricken shepherd. New Testament writers, however, saw that prophecy as fulfilled in Jesus (Zech. 13:7; cf. Matt. 26:31; Mark 14:27; John 10:13–15).

The last chapter of Zechariah is another description of the day of the Lord. The warrior God will defeat all Jerusalem's enemies. In the end, "living waters shall flow out from Jerusalem . . . and the Lord will become king over all the earth" (Zech. 14:8–9; cf. John 7:38).

MALACHI

Protestants think of Malachi as the last words of the Old Testament.[34]

It seems likely, in fact, that by the time of Jesus, Jews had come to believe that there would never be another prophet until at last the messenger whom Malachi had promised would usher in the messianic age.

For Christians, however, Malachi serves not just as an end but as a transition. Malachi closes with the promise of "Elijah" coming to usher in that messianic age. Picking up where Malachi leaves off, the Gospels affirm that with John the Baptist that promised messenger did come, forerunner of the Messiah and the new age that Jesus inaugurated.

Malachi, then, is the book that ends the Old Testament but also the book that links the Old Testament with the New.

The Background and Nature of the Book

The promises of the prophets simply had not come true. Ezekiel had promised a glorious new temple and city, but the Temple they had built was a commonplace little shrine. Haggai had promised that the treasures of all nations would flow to it, but the Temple and the people were poverty-stricken. Isaiah and others had promised that there would always be a king of David's line on the throne, but the Jews were still subjects of foreigners. In Jerusalem there was not even a throne, much less the promised messiah. No wonder that they complained skeptically to God, "How have you loved us?" (Mal. 1:2). Deuteronomy had warned that sin would bring catastrophe but righteousness would bring prosperity. But as they looked at the people around them, they found that the warning just did not seem to be true. "It is vain to serve God," they sighed. "What do we profit by keeping his command? . . . Evildoers not only prosper, but when they put God to the test they escape" (3:14–15).

This failure of faith was reflected in the Jews' lives and worship. What they sacrificed at the Temple were the culls from their flocks, and many paid no tithes at all. Even the priests lacked reverence for their own ceremonies.

MALACHI
God's Purifying Messenger

"See, I am sending my messenger to prepare the way before me, . . . and he will purify the descendants of Levi" (3:1–3).

1:1 **God Does Love the People**	1:6 **But They Have Not Kept Pure the Levitical Covenant**	2:17 **The Messenger of the Covenant Is Coming to Purify**	3:13 **Contrasting Responses and Their Contrasting Consequences** 4:6
See how God has punished Israel's enemy Edom, 1:1–5	They are offering impure sacrifices, 1:6–14	Skeptics scoff, 2:17	Some reject the promises, 3:13–15
	And priests profane their covenant duties, 2:1–9	Malachi's warning answer: God is coming, 3:1–7	But some revere God, 3:16–18
	The marriage covenant has been profaned, 2:10–16	So respond with Temple tithes and be blessed, 3:8–12	God's morning will bring them contrasting fates, 4:1–3
			So remember the law and await God's messenger, 4:4–6

Date: Probably around 460 or 450 B.C.

Situation: The third or fourth generation after their return from exile, the people are disillusioned and discouraged and question whether God really cares and whether worshiping the Lord really matters.

Purpose: To reassure the people and to persuade them to purity in worship and in life

Special Significance: The New Testament sees John the Baptist as the promised messenger (Mal. 4:5–6; cf. Matt. 11:10).

Families were in trouble. Many men divorced their wives to marry younger pagan or semi-pagan women. Superstition, adultery, perjury, abuse of workers, neglect of widows and orphans, and prejudice against people of other races were common (3:5–7).

Sometime around 460 or 450 B.C., an otherwise unknown prophet entered into a kind of debate with these faithless Jews. One favorite pattern among the prophets was to picture God as a kind of prosecuting attorney presenting a legal case against Israel. The book of Malachi begins by reversing this. The people are making a case against God. But by the end of the book, it is Israel that is on trial.

Malachi means "my messenger." Because we know of no other Jew with that name, scholars are split on the question of whether the title of the book (1:1) actually gives the name of the prophet or is simply picked up from its promise of "my messenger" (3:1). Either way, Christians and Jews agree that this prophet was indeed a "messenger" from God.

God Does Love the People (Mal. 1:1–5)

From start to finish, the Old Testament affirms the love of God. But "how have you loved us?" the little group of discouraged Jews demands. Malachi's response may not be the high point of biblical theology, but it probably did appeal to his hearers. Look how much better off you are than your enemy, he said in effect. Edom, descended from Jacob's twin brother, is on the verge of extinction; but you have survived.

But They Have Not Kept Pure the Levitical Covenant (Mal. 1:6–2:16)

God, through Malachi, brings a countercharge: even the priests have failed to give God the respect due their heavenly Father (1:6); they have despised God's name and polluted the sacred sacrifices. "How?" they protest. You bring God lame, blind, and crippled animals, not the best as the law requires, Malachi charges. God prefers the worship in pagan temples to such impure sacrifices (1:11).

Priests, descended from Levi, had been called to solemn covenant obligations (2:4; cf. Num. 18:21–24; 25:12–13). Instead, bored, they cry, "What a weariness this is" (1:13). Priests were supposed not only to conduct ceremonies but to teach the law, the instruction of Moses (Mal. 2:6; cf. Deut. 33:8–11). Instead, Malachi charges, they have misled the people and corrupted that covenant.

Faithlessness to their covenant with God has led men to faithlessness in another covenant (2:10). The marriage covenant is being violated. Men have been divorcing the wives they married in their youth to marry "the daughter[s] of a foreign god" (2:11). "I hate divorce," God announces (2:16).

The Messenger of the Covenant Is
Coming to Purify (Mal. 2:17–3:13)

"Where is the God of justice?" the skeptical people reply (2:17). Malachi answers that God will soon be manifest indeed. God's messenger is on the way:

> See, I am sending my messenger to prepare the way before me, and the Lord whom you seek will suddenly come to his temple. The messenger of the covenant in whom you delight—indeed, he is coming, says the Lord of hosts. (3:1)

These scoffers, however, may not be so pleased when this occurs:

> But who can endure the day of his coming, and who can stand when he appears? For he is like a refiner's fire . . . and he will purify the descendants of Levi. (3:2–3)

That messenger—the figure of the messenger seems merged with that of God—"will draw near to you for judgment" (3:5). And he will burn up all impurities, including their theft from God.

"How are we robbing [God]?" they demand (3:8). "In your tithes and offerings," which they have not been bringing to the Temple, Malachi answers (3:8). But God promises that if they will repent their stinginess and become generous again, the Lord will "open the windows of heaven" with blessings for them (3:10).

Contrasting Responses and Their
Contrasting Consequences (Mal. 3:14–4:4)

Malachi ("my messenger") elicited two responses. On the one hand, there were scoffers who still said, "It is vain to serve God. What do we profit by keeping his command?" (3:14). But there were others who "revered the Lord" (3:16).

And so Malachi expands his answer to the problem of God's apparent indifference. Perhaps now it may seem that there is no "profit" in obeying the law of God. But God is recording in a "book of remembrance" (3:16) the names of those who have responded with reverence instead of with the trivialized worship that Malachi has attacked. Thus they will be remembered in the end. At that end there will come a judgment day. As the sun rises on that great dawn, some will be burned like stubble (4:1). "But for you who revere my name the sun of righteousness shall rise, with healing in its wings" (4:2).

Many scholars suggest that the last three verses of the book seem tacked on and may be a later addition. Perhaps they were added to give the whole collection of the twelve Minor Prophets a fit conclusion. Others suggest that they belong with the rest of the book and that Malachi itself was put last in part because they are so fitting an end for that collection. Either way, they summarize the Old Testament and lead us into the New.

First, we are reminded to keep the law or teaching of Moses, so essential a part of the Jewish scripture (4:4).

Second, we are promised again that the messenger is coming before the day of the Lord's advent. Here that messenger is identified as Elijah, that prototype of the prophets, who could indeed come again because he had never died (4:5–6; cf. 2 Kings 2:11–12).

Moses and Elijah—personifications of the Law and the Prophets, together symbols of the whole of the Old Testament—are said to have met with Jesus on the mount of the transfiguration (Matt. 17:3). John the Baptist became the new Elijah, messenger of the coming of the Lord (Matt. 11:11–14).

But to tell that story is to get into the New Testament and its completion of the Old Testament message. In the more than four centuries between Malachi and the New Testament, devout Jews continued to write about God. Many of their works are found in the Apocrypha, much of which is included in Roman Catholic Bibles. The next chapter of this *Guide* gives a brief introduction to those books.

5

THE APOCRYPHA

If a Protestant and a Catholic examine each other's Bibles, it is likely that they will quickly make a discovery: the Catholic Bible has more books in it. Roman Catholics regard as part of their authoritative canon twelve books or parts of books not found in most Protestant editions of the scripture. The Eastern Orthodox churches add three more, including a Psalm 151. To make matters more complex, some Protestant Bibles do include the twelve books found in Roman Catholic Bibles, plus three others. These, however, are usually grouped together between the two authoritative Testaments and labeled the "Apocrypha."

Historically, this confusion goes back to the centuries just before the birth of Jesus. Scattered here and there throughout the Roman Empire, Jews, like other people of that time, spoke and read Greek, the empirewide language of commerce. The Jewish scriptures, which Christians call the "Old Testament," were translated into Greek. According to legend, the translators, who miraculously arrived independently at precisely the same translation, were seventy in number; hence their translation was called the "Septuagint." Scholars often abbreviate this title by using the Roman numeral LXX. Except for 2 Esdras, the books of the Apocrypha, though never part of the Hebrew scriptures, were included in the Septuagint. In about the year A.D. 90, rabbis meeting in Jamnia decided that only the Hebrew scriptures, not the Apocrypha, should be regarded as authoritative, part of their "canon" or "rule" of faith and life. Christians, however, used the Septuagint as their Old Testament. Late in the fourth century, Jerome produced the Vulgate, a translation of the Bible into Latin, which became the authoritative scripture for medieval Roman Catholicism. He did include some of the Apocrypha, but he carefully noted that these books were not part of the canon. Subsequent editions of the Vulgate, however, did not include his notes. Throughout the Middle Ages, therefore, the Apocryphal books were regarded as part of the scripture.

In the sixteenth century, the Protestant Reformers undertook to base their doctrines on the Bible alone. They rejected what they regarded as heresies produced simply by church tradition. In debates, Roman Catholic theologians defended the practice of prayer for the dead by reference to 2 Macc. 12:43–45. The Reformers countered by pointing out that 2 Maccabees was a book of the Apocrypha; Protestants would accept as authoritative Old Testament only the canon of the Hebrew scriptures. In A.D. 1546, the Roman Catholic Council of Trent decreed that the Apocrypha was officially part of the canon except for 1 and 2 Esdras and the Prayer of Manasseh, which should not be included. Protestants rejected the authority of any part of the Apocrypha.

The Reformers did grant that the Apocrypha was valuable. Early Protestant editions of the Bible often included it, but its books were collected and printed either between the two Testaments or as an appendix after the New Testament. The Church of England—in this country, the Episcopal Church—included the Apocrypha in such official translations as the King James Version. But that church stated that these books, while useful "for edification," were not authoritative for doctrine. Gradually, therefore, publishers began to drop the Apocrypha from their editions of the scripture.

There are at least four reasons for Protestants to read the Apocrypha: (1) understanding something of the Apocrypha can help further understanding across the divisions between Catholicism and Protestantism; (2) many of these books are delightful; (3) as is noted at the end of this chapter, the Apocrypha provides background for understanding the New Testament; and (4) most important, the Apocryphal books in themselves are useful "for edification." God did not take a break between the Testaments. Reading the Apocrypha can help to make a person a better Christian.

For these reasons, therefore, this *Guide* includes the following all-too-brief introductions to the Apocryphal books. Quotations are from the New Revised Standard Version.

1 ESDRAS

"Esdras" is the Greek form of the name Ezra, and much of the book is simply another edition of the canonical book of Ezra. Though it appears in the Protestant Apocrypha, it is not included in the Roman Catholic canon. It begins by reproducing much of 1 Chronicles 35—36; repeats the book of Ezra; and includes Neh. 7:38–8:12, with its account of Ezra's reforms.

There is one delightful addition (1 Esd. 3—4). In the court of King Darius, three youths competed to give the best answer to the question of what is the strongest thing in the world. The first spoke eloquently of the power of wine, which can "make equal the mind of the king and the orphan" and "turns every thought to feasting and mirth." The second proposed that the king himself is most powerful, since all the world must obey his commands. But the third spoke first of the power of women. For them, men will give up gold and silver. Even the king was a kind of slave to his concubine Apame. But then, more seriously, he proposed, "Great is truth, and strongest of all!" (4:41). He won the prize. It turns out that the third youth is Zerubbabel, and the prize he requested was authority to lead the exiles back and rebuild the Temple (4:42–57; cf. Ezra 5:2).

2 ESDRAS

Second Esdras, though included in the Protestant Apocrypha, is not regarded as canonical by Roman Catholics and is not found in the Septuagint. It probably originated near the close of the first century A.D., and it includes what many regard as later Christian additions. It is an apocalypse in the style of Revelation, describing seven visions of the last days. Like Revelation, it is filled with symbolic places and creatures, including a forest, an eagle, a lion, a woman, and many others; horrible catastrophes are predicted; and it promises that at the end of the world there will be a resurrection of the dead and a final judgment. Martin Luther is said to have found the book so confusing that he threw it into the Elbe.

It is clear, however, that the author is concerned about why evil seems to be all-powerful and why the good are so often persecuted. "The prophet Ezra" is depicted as asking this question, in various ways, of an angel, who grants him visions in reply. At least part of the answer is that he is to wait patiently, for in the end, God's justice will triumph.

Chapter 14, which in some versions is the last chapter, reports that God's law had been burned, presumably in the Babylonian captivity. Ezra is miraculously enabled to dictate the entire scripture, plus seventy hidden books to be published at a later time, to five scribes. While this story is legend, it may reflect a genuine memory that it was Ezra the scribe who edited and supervised the publication of the Pentateuch in something like the form in which we now have it (cf. Neh. 8:1–8).

TOBIT

Tobit is a delightful short story. A pious man, though he is living in exile in Nineveh, he carefully keeps the law of Moses, both moral and ceremonial. Always ready to share his food, he sends out his son Tobias to invite the poor to a good dinner at his home. The son returns with the news that he has discovered the body of a murdered Jew, whose corpse has simply been thrown into the marketplace. Leaving his feast, Tobit goes to give the poor man a proper burial. When he returns, he is ritually unclean. Therefore he does not enter his house but sleeps outdoors that night. Bird droppings hit his eyes, and he is blinded. Soon he is in financial need. He remembers that a man in Media owes him ten talents of silver, and he resolves to send his son Tobias to collect the debt.

Tobit is afraid for the youth to attempt the trip alone, so a man is secured to accompany him on the journey. But the man is the angel Raphael in disguise. As they cross a stream, Tobias catches a fish and, acting on the advice of Raphael, saves some of its viscera. Arriving at Ecbanta, they stop for the night with a kinsman, Raguel. No sooner does Tobias meet Raguel's beautiful daughter than he proposes marriage. Raguel, however, honestly warns Tobias: Sarah has been married seven times already. But each wedding night, a jealous demon has murdered her bridegroom on his wedding bed. Undaunted, Tobias takes Sarah to the bridal chamber. Acting on the guidance of Raphael, he puts the heart and liver of the fish on the ashes of the incense. When the next morning the maid comes to prepare Tobias's body for the grave that Raguel has already dug, they find that the smoke has so choked the demon that it has fled to Upper Egypt. Tobias collects the money, brings home his bride, rubs more of the fish on his father's eyes, and cures the old man of his blindness. In the end, not only his parents but his parents-in-law have splendid funerals.

The story introduces a new understanding of angels. Raphael is the personal guide and guardian of a pious man. But Tobit's real point is the example of strict Jewish piety in a Gentile culture. Tobit observes the ceremonial law, he gives generously to the poor, and he prays devoutly. Much of his wisdom is expressed in his long address to his son before Tobias begins his journey (Tobit 4). There is included something close to the "Golden Rule": "What you hate, do not do to anyone" (4:15).

Martin Luther called Tobit "a truly beautiful, wholesome, and profitable fiction, the work of a gifted poet. . . . A book useful and good for us Christians to read."[1]

JUDITH

The beautiful heroine of this book has been criticized as "a shameless flatterer, a bold-faced liar, and a ruthless assassin."[2] But the story of how she used her feminine wiles to save her people has inspired artists and delighted readers for centuries.

In the story, Holofernes, leading the Assyrian invaders into Israel, lays siege to the town of Bethulia. All hope seems lost when a devout and beautiful widow, after lengthy prayer, volunteers to save the city. She puts on her most attractive clothes and, with her maid carrying a bag of ritually clean food, goes to the enemy camp, demanding to see Holofernes. She promises him that she will give him guidance through prayer until he has arrived at last in Jerusalem. Charmed by her beauty, he invites her to dinner with him, but she carefully eats only the ceremonially clean food she has brought. On the fourth night, however, she accepts his invitation to a banquet, lies before him on lambskins her maid has prepared, but still eats and drinks only from the bag of kosher food and wine she had brought. "Holofernes' heart was ravished with her and his passion was aroused" (Judith 12:16). But when the others have left and she is alone with Holofernes, who is lying drunk on his bed, Judith says another prayer, takes the sword that is hanging on the tent wall above his bed, and cuts off his head. Placing the head in the now-empty food bag, she and her maid go forth, telling the guards that it is for her nightly prayer; return to Bethulia; and announce that the Lord has delivered the people. When, next morning, the Assyrians discover how they have been tricked by just one Israelite woman, they flee in terror, the Israelite army pursues, and the country is saved.

Whatever modern critics might say against Judith, the author intends to present her as a model of Pharisaic piety. She prays diligently, trusts completely in God, and follows the dietary laws of Moses even while in the camp of the enemy. Through such a woman, the author suggests, God can save the chosen people.

ADDITIONS TO THE BOOK OF ESTHER

In the canonical book of Esther, God is not even mentioned. Some years later, an unknown author remedied that omission. In the Apocrypha, the book of Esther begins with a dream in which Mordecai sees two fighting dragons. They symbolize the struggle between the nations of the world and the "righteous nation." When that nation cries out to God, a great river begins to flow and the people are delivered. We are given long prayers by both Mordecai and Esther, prayed when they hear of the decree against the Jews. It is God, not just Esther, who changes the mind of the king. The king issues a decree announcing that the Jews are "children of the living God, most high, most mighty, who has directed the kingdom both for us and for our ancestors in the most excellent order" (Greek version, Addition E, 16:16). And at the end of the book is added a meditation by Mordecai. He now understands the dream with which the story began: it was an allegory foretelling how God would deliver them through Esther. All has been from God.

THE WISDOM OF SOLOMON

Proverbs, Ecclesiastes, and Job were not the last books of "wisdom litera-ture." In fact, it may be that the author of the Wisdom of Solomon was deliberately trying to make sure that Ecclesiastes would not be the last word. Writing in the century before the birth of Jesus but claiming the authority of Solomon, the writer attacked the skepticism that Ecclesiastes seemed to propose.

The first five chapters are addressed to scoffers. In words that sound like those of Ecclesiastes, the writer quotes disillusioned Jews as saying:

> Short and sorrowful is our life,
> and there is no remedy when a life comes to its end. (Wisd. Sol. 2:1)

Therefore they simply live for pleasure:

> Come, therefore, let us enjoy the good things that exist,
> and make use of the creation to the full as in youth. (2:6)

The righteous, these skeptics observe, seem to receive no rewards.
This writer has a new solution to the problem: there is a future life!

> But the souls of the righteous are in the hand of God,
> and no torment will ever touch them.
> In the eyes of the foolish they seemed to have died. (3:1–2)

But in fact, having been tested by God, these souls are now "at peace" and "their hope is full of immortality" (3:3–4). By contrast, the wicked are punished. Except for the promise of resurrection in Daniel, there is almost no assurance of life after death in the canonical Old Testament. The Wisdom of Solomon seems here to reflect the Greek concept of the immortal soul. The development of hope for a future life is an important step between the Old Testament and the New.

The second part of the book (chaps. 6—9) assures the reader that it is wisdom that brings immortality. Building on Proverbs 8, the writer describes personified wisdom as God's agent in creation and the equivalent of the *logos* of Greek philosophy. The prologue to the Gospel according to John was to use this concept to explain the meaning of Christ.

The last part of the book (chaps. 10—19) is a review of Old Testament history from creation through the exodus. It is Wisdom rather than the Lord who is the center of the story. Repeatedly, the writer sets out to show the rational order of the universe, in which the very things that punished the Egyptians were used by Wisdom to bless God's people.

ECCLESIASTICUS, OR THE WISDOM OF JESUS SON OF SIRACH

The longest and perhaps best loved book of the Apocrypha is Ecclesiasticus, also known as Sirach. Like the Wisdom of Solomon, it is a work of wisdom literature, and like Proverbs, it does not have a clear outline. It records the teachings of a sage in Jerusalem, Jesus ben Sira, around 180 B.C., later translated into Greek by his grandson.

While the Wisdom of Solomon is a theological treatise, Ecclesiasticus focuses rather on down-to-earth, everyday, ethical guidance. The author has a high regard for family values:

> Those who respect their father will have long life,
> > and those who honor their mother obey the Lord. (Ecclus. 3:6)

He also urges charity and concern for the needy:

> Be like a father to orphans,
> > and be like a husband to their mother;
> you will then be like a son of the Most High,
> > and he will love you more than does your mother. (4:10)

The author has been accused of being a woman-hater:

> From a woman sin had its beginning,
> > and because of her we will die. (25:24)

> I would rather live with a lion and a dragon
> > than live with an evil woman. (25:16)

But he can also write:

> Do not dismiss a wise and good wife,
> > for her charm is worth more than gold. (7:19)

The author is grateful for doctors:

> Honor physicians for their services,
> > for the Lord created them;
> for their gift of healing comes from the Most High. (38:1–2)

In contrast to the Wisdom of Solomon, Ecclesiasticus denies that we are immortal:

> The king of today will die tomorrow.
> For when one is dead
> > he inherits maggots and vermin and worms. (10:10–11)

Therefore you should enjoy this life while you can:

> Do not deprive yourself of a day's enjoyment;
> > do not let your share of desired good pass by you.
>
> . . . .
>
> Give, and take, and indulge yourself,
> > because in Hades one cannot look for luxury. (14:14–16)

And so he gives instructions about eating, drinking, music, and etiquette at a banquet, and he generally advocates the pleasant life.

Nevertheless, he is sure that the wise man "will glory in the law of the Lord's covenant" (39:8). Like the Wisdom of Solomon and Proverbs 8, Ecclesiasticus includes long poems in praise of wisdom, personified as a woman; and in this book, wisdom seems almost equated with the law (chap. 24). Ecclesiasticus 42:15–43:35 is a long poem in praise of God the Creator, marveling at God's wisdom as shown in nature.

The most quoted passage in the book begins:

> Let us now sing the praise of famous men,
> our ancestors in their generations. (44:1)

Chapters 44 through 50 recall heroes of the past and on down to the writer's own day.

The last chapter (Ecclus. 51) is a prayer of praise and thanksgiving to God.

BARUCH

This short book is ascribed to Baruch, who was secretary to Jeremiah. Its introduction says that it is a letter which he sent back to Jerusalem from his exile in Babylon in the early sixth century B.C. Actually, most scholars date it five, six, or even seven centuries later than the lifetime of Baruch. Though it purports to be the instructions Baruch gave at the time of the Babylonian captivity, its purpose may have been to guide Jews living under the oppression not of Babylon but of Rome.

The first part of the book (Bar. 1:1–3:8) is a long prayer of confession, based in part on the prayer in Daniel 9. The author instructs the readers to make this prayer. It confesses that the troubles of Israel have come about because the people have disobeyed the Lord, not heeding the voice of the prophets. Penitently, it pleads for mercy:

> O Lord Almighty, God of Israel, the soul in anguish and the wearied spirit cry out to you. Hear, O Lord, and have mercy, for we have sinned before you. For you are enthroned forever, and we are perishing forever. (3:1–3)

The second part (3:9–4:4), probably by a different author, is a poem in praise of wisdom. Why is Israel in exile? he asks. Because it forsook wisdom and the God who is the fountain of wisdom. Wisdom is expressed most clearly in the law of God (4:1).

The book ends (4:5–5:9) with poems of hope, perhaps by other authors. "Take courage, my people" (4:5). "Take courage, my children" (4:21). "Take courage, my children" (4:27). "Take courage, O Jerusalem" (4:30):

> For God will lead Israel with joy,
> in the light of his glory,
> with the mercy and righteousness that come from him. (5:9)

THE LETTER OF JEREMIAH

In some Bibles, this piece of literature is printed as a sixth chapter of Baruch. For seventy-three verses, the author argues how foolish it is to worship an idol. Idols are useless. They are helpless. Birds can light on them. They can be burned. After each argument he repeats, more or less in the same words, this conclusion: "From this you will know that they are not gods, so do not fear them" (v. 23).

ADDITIONS TO THE BOOK OF DANIEL

The book of Daniel is much longer in Greek versions of the Old Testament than in Protestant Bibles. In the English versions of the Apocrypha, these additions to Daniel are usually printed as separate books.

The Prayer of Azariah and the Song of the Three Jews

This Psalm is supposed to be what the three young Hebrews prayed when in the fiery furnace (Daniel 3). First, Azariah (or Meshach, one of the three) prays. He confesses Jerusalem's sins and pleads for mercy, begging forgiveness on the basis of God's covenant with the patriarchs, their contrition, and the nature of God. Then we are told how an angel caused a moist wind to blow through the furnace. The last verses are a litany, said to have been sung by all three. It calls upon nature, then all people, then Israel, and then the three young Jews themselves to "bless the Lord."

Susanna and the Elders

The story of Susanna is a delightful tale, perhaps the first detective story ever written. Wise Daniel is the mastermind, the defense attorney. Two elders lust after the beautiful young wife Susanna. They hide in the courtyard of her home where she bathes. When she is alone, they threaten her if she will not submit to them. Virtuous Susanna screams for help. Frustrated, the elders now bring formal charges against her, alleging that they had found her committing adultery with a young man who, they say, had escaped when they tried to seize him. Susanna is condemned to death. But when, on the way to her death, she prays, wise Daniel enters the story. He separates the two elders. "Under what tree did you catch them being intimate with each other?" he demands (v. 54). "Under a mastic tree," the first replies. "Under an evergreen oak," says the second. Caught by this contradiction, it is the two false witnesses who are executed, not the virtuous and beautiful Susanna.

Bel and the Dragon

This addition to the book of Daniel also features Daniel as a detective. Bel is a great idol worshiped by King Astyages. Proof of its power is that it apparently eats the offerings left for it each night. Wise Daniel, however, devises a test. The next morning, the offerings are indeed gone, though the shrine had been sealed. But Daniel had sprinkled ashes on the floor. On those ashes, Daniel and the king can plainly see the tracks of the priests and their families, who had entered by secret doors during the night and carried off the sacrifices.

There was also a dragon that was worshiped by the Babylonians. Daniel, however, made cakes of pitch, fat, and hair and fed them to the dragon. The poor dragon burst open. In the end the king cried, "You are great, O Lord, the God of Daniel, and there is no other besides you!" (v. 41).

Stories such as these were designed for Jews living in a pagan culture who were tempted to share in its idolatry.

THE PRAYER OF MANASSEH

Though nothing of this event is mentioned in 2 Kings 21, we are told in 2 Chron. 33:10–13 that evil King Manasseh was deported to Babylon. There he humbled himself before God and prayed for deliverance, and God allowed him to return to Jerusalem. Perhaps a century before the birth of Jesus, an anonymous author composed a beautiful prayer he thought appropriate for that king—and others. It begins with acknowledgment of the greatness of God, moves to confession, and then begs forgiveness.

1 MACCABEES

This book is an apparently accurate history of the heroic resistance of the Jews to persecution by the Syrians. It tells how, led by Mattathias and his five sons, they were successful at last in liberating Judea and establishing in Jerusalem the Hasmonean dynasty.

Alexander the Great died in 323 B.C., and his empire was divided. By 175 B.C., the Jews were under the jurisdiction of the Syrian ruler Antiochus IV, who called himself Antiochus Epiphanes (God Manifest). He sought to force the Jews to adopt Greek culture. Many agreed (1 Macc. 1:11–15), but some resisted. To stamp out resistance, Antiochus passed laws against circumcision, observing the Sabbath, and maintaining the Temple sacrifices (1:41–53). He made it a crime even to possess a book of the law (1:57). Women who circumcised their babies were executed with their babies hung around their necks (1:60–61). The ultimate in blasphemy, he sacrificed hogs on the Temple altar and made there a shrine to Zeus (1:54).

A priest named Mattathias assassinated a Syrian official who attempted to make a Jew offer a pagan sacrifice (2:25), and he and his sons fled to the mountains. There they formed a guerrilla army. With the death of Mattathias, his son Judas Maccabeus, "Judas the Hammerer," became the leader. Against all odds he won victories. At last, on December 14, 164 B.C., the Jews were able to rededicate the Temple. Jews still commemorate this triumph with the eight-day feast of Hanukkah (4:41–59).

Judas's time of leadership, however, was never peaceful. Judah's neighbors attacked. Even worse, rival Jewish factions allied themselves with a successor of Antiochus. In 160 B.C., Judas was killed in battle, fighting heroically (9:18).

First Maccabees 9:23–12:53 describes the exploits of Judas's brother Jonathan, who succeeded him. Despite opponents within and without, Jonathan was able, by both military and diplomatic means, to keep Judah relatively independent.

When Jonathan was killed, yet another brother, Simon, assumed the lead (chaps. 13—16). Under Simon, in 142 B.C., Judah became sufficiently independent to begin to date events from that time. First Maccabees reports, however, that Simon still had to wage battles, and at last he was murdered by his own son-in-law.

In the end of the book, however, Simon's son John rules. In spite of all obstacles, the Maccabees had liberated the nation. Though the book does not trace history that far, Judah was to remain an independent state for roughly a century, until the Romans gained control.

2 MACCABEES

Second Maccabees tells much the same story but in what the writer must have considered a more exciting and edifying way. In his account, miracles abound, angels speak, and God seems much more directly involved. The good triumph; the evil perish. Evil Antiochus Epiphanes meets an especially horrible death, but not before even he is converted to faith in God (2 Macc. 9).

Clearly, one major purpose of the book is to encourage Jews to remain faithful to the law in spite of the temptation to conform to Gentile culture. Two stories of heroic martyrdoms dramatize this emphasis. In the first, the Syrians try to force old Eleazer to eat pork. Instead, he voluntarily climbs to the torture wheel. Friends, however, offer to substitute ceremonially clean meat secretly, so that he could pretend to eat pork but really not break the law of Moses. Eleazar refuses, lest he set a bad example for young people. "So in this way he died, leaving in his death an example of nobility and a memorial of courage, not only to the young but to the great body of his nation" (6:31).

Equally designed to inspire is the story of seven brothers. When the first brother refuses to eat pork, the king—present and angry—orders that the young man's tongue, hands, and feet be cut off and that he then be cooked in a great pan. One by one, each of the seven brothers is thus tortured and martyred, yet none yields. And as she watches, their mother cheers them on, saying; "The Creator of the world, who shaped the beginning of humankind and devised the origin of all things, will in his mercy give life and breath back to you again, since you now forget yourselves for the sake of his laws" (7:23). This assurance of a resurrection and a life after death is an important development in the period between the Testaments.

THE APOCRYPHA AND THE NEW TESTAMENT

Bruce M. Metzger, in *An Introduction to the Apocrypha*,[3] lists, among other reflections of the Apocrypha in the New Testament, the growing conflict between those who sought to cooperate with Gentile culture, who became the Sadducees, and those who rigidly adhered more and more closely to the law, the Pharisees; the development of the doctrine of a life after death; and the growing importance of the activity of angels and demons.

There are no direct quotations from the Apocrypha in the New Testament, but Metzger finds New Testament passages that seem to show acquaintance with it. Paul's account of the degeneration of humankind (Rom. 1:18–32) is close to verses in the Wisdom of Solomon 13—14. In Rom. 9:20–22, Paul denies that anyone has the right to question God's judgment. Again, the Wisdom of Solomon provides parallels in 12:12 and 15:7. The "armor of God" passage in Eph. 6:13 may reflect Wisd. Sol. 5:17–20. Paul compares the earthly body to a perishable tent (2 Cor. 5:1), much as does Wisd. Sol. 9:15. When Heb. 11:35 speaks of those who endured torture, confident of a future life, surely the seven martyred sons of 2 Maccabees are among those meant. Metzger finds several parallels between verses in James and verses in Ecclesiasticus. Revelation describes the new Jerusalem as a city of gold with walls of jasper, sapphire, emerald, beryl, and other precious stones (Rev. 21:18–21); its author found those materials in Tobit 13:16–17. Jesus' summons to come and take his yoke is similar to that of Ecclus. 51:23, 26–27. These are among many parallels that Metzger has found.

Most Protestants have followed the Reformers' instruction not to take the Apocrypha as an authority for doctrine. It may be that more Protestants need to remember also the suggestion of many Reformers that these books are indeed valuable for "edification."

PART TWO

THE NEW TESTAMENT

6

THE SYNOPTIC GOSPELS

THE HISTORICAL SETTING OF THE GOSPELS

At first glance, it might seem that we should have no problem in knowing about the life and teachings of Jesus. Four different gospels tell us much the same story. The "plot," as contemporary literary critics like to call it, is somewhat different in each of the four narratives, and yet the basic story is the same. The characters and the conflicts are similar. A preacher from Galilee calls disciples, announces the coming kingdom of God, and performs miracles, especially the healing of the lame and the blind. The disciples come to believe that he is the promised Messiah. But Jesus stirs up the opposition of the religious leaders of the time. He deliberately invades their stronghold, Jerusalem, knowing the fate that awaits him. At the instigation of his enemies, the Roman authorities execute him by crucifixion. But on the third day he rises from the dead and commissions the disciples to tell the world the good news about himself.

But when one begins to inquire about details and compare accounts, problems arise. Historically, did Jesus' message center on the kingdom, as the emphasis seems to be in the first three Gospels (the "Synoptics"), or on himself, as the fourth Gospel, John, implies? Did he claim to be the Messiah, the Son of God, or did he expressly forbid people to say that about him? Was he a radical social reformer, a preacher of the end of the world and of all earthly social orders, or one who focused rather on individuals and their daily personal relationships to one another and to a loving God?

In his 1908 classic *The Quest of the Historical Jesus*, Albert Schweitzer reviewed the bewildering variety of interpretations of Jesus published in the nineteenth century. He found each interpreter reading his own history and interests into his picture of the historical Jesus. Schweitzer was sure that Jesus' message was apocalyptic; Jesus believed that the world was about to end and that one should therefore abandon worldly concerns. In 1991, John Dominic Crossan reviewed late twentieth-century images of Jesus proposed by scholars and found almost as much variety of interpretation in the twentieth century as Schweitzer had found in the nineteenth:

> There is Jesus as a political revolutionary by S. G. Grandon (1967), as a magician by Morton Smith (1978), as a Galilean charismatic by Geza Vermes (1981, 1978), as a Galilean rabbi by Bruce Chilton (1994), as a Hillelite or proto-Pharisee by Harvey Falk (1985), as an Essene by Harvey Falk (1985), and as an eschatological prophet by E. P. Sanders (1985).[1]

Crossan notes that these varying interpretations spring in part from the particular aspects of first-century Palestinian history and sociology that impress each writer. Crossan himself believes that the Jesus of history should be understood as a Mediterranean Jewish peasant. A poor man among poor men, Jesus preached a kingdom of equality and sharing to be lived out in the here and now. John the Baptist, but never Jesus, according to Crossan, preached in apocalyptic language that the end was coming soon.

Late in 1993, the Jesus Seminar, composed of scholars from many of the finest universities and chaired in part by Crossan, published its views.[2] These scholars attempted to isolate what we can know with certainty to be Jesus' actual sayings. Of some fifteen hundred recorded sayings of Jesus, these scholars agreed to regard only 18 percent as actually coming from the lips of Jesus of Nazareth. They argued that any saying attributed to Jesus was really the creation of the church if the saying implied that Jesus anticipated the cross, indicated that he spoke of the end of the world in apocalyptic imagery, said things that were especially useful in the later life of the church, reflected too closely some Old Testament source, was reported in the style and vocabulary of the Gospel writer, or implied that either Jesus or his disciples thought of him as the Messiah during his earthly lifetime.

It is so easy to doubt the historical accuracy of some report in the Gospels that one trend has been to avoid altogether looking historically at Jesus' life. Some modern commentaries prefer to focus primarily on "the text itself" in each narrative, analyzing it almost as one might analyze a work of fiction.[3]

Such scholarship does great service by reminding us that the truth of the Gospels lies not in their meeting some modern standards of historical accuracy but in the good news the Gospels give us about the meaning of the Christ event in the lives of believers. It is Jesus as witnessed to by those first writers whom Christians worship and serve. We cannot and need not completely separate the Jesus of history from the Christian understanding of Jesus that writers closest to his earthly life have given us.

Nevertheless, the Gospels seem to be more valuable historically than the work of the Jesus Seminar might suggest. The first three Gospels especially, the Synoptics, quote Jesus so often as speaking of his coming death and of the final judgment that it hardly seems necessary to doubt that he did warn of future events. Vivid reports of his personal responses and emotions, the unflattering picture of the very apostles who preserved the tradition, and sayings that were preserved even though they were hard to understand all suggest genuine memory. The church did not simply invent stories and sayings of Jesus to fit the Old Testament; it reinterpreted the Old Testament to fit the facts about Jesus. Many of Jesus' sayings were in the form of short, witty proverbs or stories easily remembered. People who remembered Jesus in his earthly life were still alive as the stories and sayings of Jesus were being collected. Above all, the Gospels' picture of the teachings, life, death, and resurrection of Jesus is utterly different from what the contemporary popular expectation of the messiah would have invented. Certainly, the early church produced and shaped the Gospels, but first the traditions based on Jesus of Nazareth produced and shaped the early church.

Without attempting, then, to prove that every word of the four Gospels meets the criteria of all modern historians, we need not regard the Gospels as fiction, even inspired fiction. They come to us as stories of a real man who lived in a real place in a real time. Rudolf Bultmann is right that when Mark wrote the earliest Gospel, he created a new form differing fom any previous work of literature. But after comparing the Gospels and Acts with other literary works of their time, Martin Hengel concludes that the closest analogies are to works of the historians, not the mythmakers, of their day:

> We owe our thorough knowledge of the origins of Christianity above all to the fact that Luke and similarly the authors of the other two synoptic gospels, and indeed to some extent even the author of the fourth gospel, were not simply preachers of an abstract message, but at the same time quite deliberate "history" writers. . . . They did have a theological intent which was at the same time a historical one.[4]

The Gospel writers were not, Hengel warns, modern "objective" historians. But whatever else they were, they believed that they were writers of "history." Therefore we must set the Gospels' stories in their historical context if we are fully to understand them.

Some principles of biblical interpretation used in this *Guide* were described in its first chapter. It was proposed there that the new literary criticism has helped us to see more clearly the particular elements in the Gospels' stories that their writers wished to emphasize and how, step by step, each narrative makes its point. But it was also urged that a study of the historical background and sources of any book of the Bible can help us to understand it. Without for a moment suggesting that what follows solves all problems, here are some elements in the historical background of the life of Jesus that do help us understand the Gospels' story.

To understand fully the story of Jesus' life, it is helpful to be aware of two facts of history:

1. Jesus lived and taught amid the tensions of a people only forty years away from suicidal political revolution.

2. At least by the standards of our twentieth-century secularistic society, many of the people among whom Jesus taught seem almost fanatically religious.

How this political and religious situation came about and how recognition of it sheds light on the Gospels' story is the subject of the following sections.

The Political Situation

To understand the story, you must date it, Luke tells us, and it is to be dated by its political setting. "In the fifteenth year of the reign of Emperor Tiberius, when Pontius Pilate was governor of Judea, and Herod was ruler of Galilee, and his brother Philip ruler of the region of Ituraea and Trachonitis, and Lysanias ruler of Abilene, during the high priesthood of Annas and Caiaphas, the word of God came" (Luke 3:1–2). Matthew also dates his story politically: "In the time of King Herod, after Jesus was born in Bethlehem" (Matt. 2:1).

In this respect, of course, the Bible is quite different from most other religious literature. The Bhagavad Gita of the Hindus is a timeless work, the origins of its story lost in antiquity. The Tao Te Ching of the Taoists gives scarcely a hint of the events contemporary with its origin.

By contrast, Roman soldiers march through the pages of the New Testament. Guerrilla bands pillage the hills around Jerusalem. Passive resisters gaze toward heaven, hoping for a cosmic deliverer from Roman oppressors. Traitors have sold out to Israel's new masters. Heroic legalists try to preserve Judaism against the encroachments of "modern" Greco-Roman civilization. And almost every page of the Gospels reflects one or more of these historical factors.

Here are some especially relevant elements of the situation.

Greco-Roman Culture Threatened Judaism

Students are often surprised to discover the high degree of civilization and sophistication that was characteristic of the world of the first century A.D. Schooled in the idea of progress, some students automatically relate the word "ancient" to such words as "primitive" and "backward." Actually, it was the Dark Ages, centuries later, that saw the Mediterranean world reduced to near savagery.

A. C. Bouquet, in *Everyday Life in New Testament Times*, reminds us of several facts about the Greco-Roman world. Almost all stylish women of the time wore lipstick. Dyed hair (especially red or blond) and permanent waves were in fashion, sometimes even for men. One famous glamour girl kept a herd of three thousand asses to provide milk for her daily bath, to give her a lovely complexion all over. One student wrote home, "Don't fidget about my mathematics, for I'm working hard." Another, with his mind on girls instead of books, wrote, "Brunettes for me. I always did like blackberries." Country folks loved to go to fairs, where they would see sideshows featuring marionettes, acrobats, ropewalkers, jugglers, and fortune-tellers. Beach resorts were crowded each summer. Astronomers not only knew that the earth was round but had calculated the distance around it as being twenty-four thousand miles and the distance to the sun as ninety-two million miles.[5]

In itself, none of these manifestations of a "modern," "secular" culture is significant. But they remind us of a crisis brought about by the intrusion of a new way of life that did threaten Judaism's adherence to a pattern of living, almost every detail of which was supposed to be guided by what Jews regarded as the very law of God.

The crisis had come about in this way.

In the year 334 B.C., Alexander the Great, king of the Greek city-state of Macedon, began to conquer the world. Alexander fought not only for his own glory but also for a kind of missionary purpose. As a youth, he had been tutored by the philosopher Aristotle. No philosopher himself, Alexander nevertheless sought to spread the enlightenment of the Greeks to the barbarian world. Both as a conqueror and as a missionary, he was remarkably successful. When, more than three centuries later, Paul set out as a different kind of missionary to conquer the world for Christianity, he could be understood in every country he visited when he spoke Greek. Greek had become the language of people throughout the empire. The New Testament could be written in Greek and read by literate people anywhere.

With Greek language and philosophy went a non-Jewish way of life. After Alexander's death, his empire was divided, and Palestine was soon under the dominion of Syria. To their Syrian overlords, Jews seemed a stubborn people in their continuing refusal to adopt the ways of Greek civilization. Finally, in 168 B.C., Antiochus IV, who called himself "Epiphanes" (God Manifest), undertook to stamp out Judaism once and for all. Because pork was unclean according to Hebrew law, he sacrificed hogs on the altar at Jerusalem. Circumcision, Sabbath observance, and the keeping of Hebrew festivals were forbidden.

First and Second Maccabees, books of the Apocrypha that appear in Roman Catholic Bibles but are omitted in most Protestant and Jewish Bibles, describe the Hebrew resistance. Ninety-year-old Eleazar climbed bravely up to the torture wheel rather than eat pork. Seven brothers were fried alive rather than submit. (Stories of such martyrdoms still inspired Jews in Jesus' day.)

Passive resistance, however, failed. A thousand Jews were slaughtered when they refused to do battle on the Sabbath. A group of brothers called the Maccabees (the Hammers) gathered a guerrilla band in the hills and began more active resistance. They won against the odds, and Judea was set free. Judas Maccabeus became king.[6]

Unfortunately, the Maccabees and the Hasmonean dynasty they established proved stronger militarily than religiously. Hellenization (spread of Greek culture) continued, and the dynasty grew corrupt. When, in 63 B.C., brothers became rivals to the throne, Pompey of Rome moved in to "reestablish order." Judea became a captive satellite state of the expanding Roman Empire.

In Jesus' Day, Rome Ruled Palestine through Cruel Dictatorship

At the time of the birth of Jesus, Herod the Great, who sat on the throne in Jerusalem, claimed the title "King of the Jews." He owed his throne and his title, however, to his Roman masters.

Matthew was much concerned to set Jesus, whom he depicts the Wise Men as calling by Herod's title, "King of the Jews," in relation to this King Herod.

Herod seems to have been a man of considerable ability. He succeeded in murdering the entire family of certain rival claimants to his throne, some forty-five people. He was so effective in currying favor with changing factions in Rome that he had Roman support throughout his thirty-three-year reign. He instituted a remarkable building program, including the construction of a magnificent theater, an amphitheater, and the Hebrews' Third (and last) Temple, the one in which Jesus was to worship. A strong law-and-order man, he reduced crime and brought stability. Many found it to their advantage to support Herod.

Thousands of Herod's more devout subjects, however, hated him. Herod himself was only nominally a Jew, descended from the Idumeans, a race converted to Judaism by conquest. He introduced Roman sports, dress, and temples in Jerusalem. Above all, his oppressive taxes were regarded as robbery to pay off his foreign masters, the Romans.

Terrified by the slightest hint of threat to his throne, he murdered even his wife and two of his own sons on charges of plotting rebellion. Punning on two similar words, the emperor Augustus is said to have quipped, "I would rather be Herod's *hog* than Herod's *son*." Even during his final illness, Herod gave orders for the execution of forty protest demonstrators and another of his own children. His known cruelty is reflected in the story in Matthew's Gospel that Herod ordered all male babies in Bethlehem to be killed because one of them was reported to be a claimant to his own title, "King of the Jews."

Shortly after an eclipse of the sun in the year 4 B.C., riddled with what was probably venereal disease, the old dictator died. According to Matthew 2, it was during the last days of the reign of this king Herod that Jesus Christ, the "King of the Jews," was born.

Jesus Lived in a Land on the Verge of Suicidal Revolt

Palestinian stability died with Herod.

His will decreed that his kingdom should be divided among three of his sons. The Roman emperor soon deposed Archelaus, the ruler of Judea and Samaria (the southern half of Palestine), because of Archelaus's misrule. Guerrilla bands, perhaps inspired by the memory of the Maccabean revolt, began to form.

Probably in A.D. 6, stirred up in part by a major taxation comparable to the one Luke relates to the birth of Jesus, armed rebels seized the Roman arsenal at Sepphoris, a town in Galilee (northern Palestine) only four miles from Jesus' home in Nazareth. In punishment, the Romans crucified two thousand Jews. It is possible that Jesus as a child walked a road lined with crosses on which hung the bodies of these nationalists. It is also possible that Jesus, as a young carpenter, helped rebuild Sepphoris after it was destroyed by the vengeful Romans.

Perhaps some two hundred thousand Jews died in uprisings against and punishments by the Roman authorities during the century leading up to the revolt of A.D. 66–70.

Secular history has not been much kinder to Pontius Pilate than the Bible has. In A.D. 26, he was appointed Roman procurator (governor) in Judea. He alienated his subjects at the very beginning by causing the Roman soldiers to carry the ensigns, symbols of Rome, into Jerusalem as they arrived. These winged figures were regarded by the Jews as being "graven images," prohibited by the Commandments. Valuing "progress" more than Judaism, Pilate again infuriated the people by taking money from the Temple treasury to pay for an aqueduct to bring water to Jerusalem. When Pilate slaughtered a band of pilgrims under the mistaken impression that they were a revolutionary mob, the Roman emperor finally acceded to the demands of a Jewish protest delegation and dismissed Pontius Pilate.

Insecure in his authority, Pilate had earlier yielded, John 19:12 tells us, to the cry of the mob demanding Jesus' crucifixion: "If you release this man, you are no friend of the emperor. Everyone who claims to be a king sets himself against the emperor."

Tourists who visit the Roman forum today still see the Arch of Titus commemorating the final victory of the Romans over the Jews. In A.D. 66, the rebellion in Palestine reached a pitiful, futile climax. Repeated riots brought hundreds of deaths. Finally, in A.D. 70, after a long siege, Jerusalem fell. Carvings on Titus's arch show captives and the seven-branched candlestick of Herod's Temple being paraded in triumph through the streets of Rome. What Mark 13:2 depicts Jesus as prophesying came almost literally to pass. Of the Temple at Jerusalem, scarcely one stone was left on another.

Even then, not all hope of messianic deliverance was exhausted. In A.D. 132, one Simon ben Kosibah was hailed as the "son of the star," the messiah. His pitiful revolt resulted in the stamping out of the Jews' last hope of rescue by violence.

Matthew's story of the star at Jesus' birth may reflect the association of a star with the expectation of the messiah-king (Num. 24:17). Clearly, the inscription placed on the cross over Jesus' head indicates that he was executed as one whom Roman authorities feared as presenting the threat of revolution: "The King of the Jews" (Mark 15:26).

The Religious Situation

The Gospel events took place in a time of tensions that were not only political but also religious.

One cannot fully understand the New Testament without realizing that religion played a far larger part in the lives of most first-century Jews than is the case with most twentieth-century Western people. Perhaps one would need to travel to India today to observe a culture so dominated by religious concern. There were, of course, many who were relatively indifferent to Judaism's tradition. But far more than is the case for most of our contemporaries, religion was of enormous importance for thousands of Jews in New Testament times.

Knowing the following factors in the religious situation of the day is especially helpful in understanding the New Testament.

Judaism Preserved the Old Testament Faith

In part, at least, Jesus must be understood as a devout Jew living among devout Jews. As we shall see, Jesus differed with Judaism so often that during his ministry he was in constant conflict with Jewish leaders. Nevertheless, we must emphasize that Jesus was a Jew. Jesus worshiped in the Jewish synagogue and taught from the Jewish scripture. The first Christians were Jews. The church emerged at first as a sect within Judaism. Not only in such books as Matthew and Hebrews, which emphasize this idea, but throughout the New Testament, Jesus is proclaimed as the fulfillment of the Old Testament expectation.

To understand the New Testament adequately, therefore, one must study the Old Testament. That study lies beyond the scope of this chapter, though not of this book. Here, very briefly, are only a few of many Old Testament ideas presupposed in the New Testament.

First, the God of the Gospels is the *same God* the Hebrews worshiped: one, sovereign, righteous, just, and loving. Jesus *did* announce that, with his coming, God was about to do something new. Jesus did not announce a new God. He did not even profess primarily to be giving new information about the character of that God. He was proclaiming the God of Abraham, of Isaac, of Jacob, and of the prophets.

Second, Israel's God was one *revealed in mighty acts*. Here the biblical God must be distinguished from the gods of both Greek philosophy and the Oriental religions. Thinkers and holy men and women related themselves to these pagan deities through the discovery of universal concepts or through mystic experiences available to all who would rightly open themselves to them. But the God of the Jewish scriptures was revealed primarily through what God did. This is not to deny the importance of the understanding of these historical events in the minds of the inspired prophets and teachers who wrote the books of Jewish scripture. But one must emphasize the distinctive part that actions attributed to God played in Jewish faith.

Thus the Old Testament centers on one story to which many stories contribute. According to that story, God called Abraham to be the ancestor of a chosen people. God miraculously rescued his descendants, a group of bricklaying slaves, from bondage in Egypt. God conquered Palestine for them; established their kingdom; disciplined them with exile when they sinned; and in the days of Cyrus of Persia, restored them to their homeland. Hebrews saw these events of history as miracles, wonders, signs of the activity of God.

It was a new activity, more than a new concept, of this same God that the Gospel writers claimed to be describing.

Third, these acts of God were understood as being for the establishment and preservation of a *unique, chosen, holy people*. They were expressions of God's loving concern for Israel. Even the judgment of God could be understood as part of the guidance and protection of the elect. Sometimes the concept of the chosen people led to an almost fanatical attempt to preserve the race uncontaminated by any foreign influence. As the Jews sought to rebuild the chosen nation after the Babylonian captivity, Ezra forced all Jews who had married Gentiles to divorce them. Sometimes the concept of the chosen people emphasized the unique mission of the Jews to the world. Isaiah 49:6 pictures God as saying to the elect, "I will give you as a light to the nations, that my salvation may reach to the end of the earth." Christians were to come to think of Christ and the church in relation to Isaiah's vision.

Fourth, Judaism was distinctively a *covenant religion*. Archaeologists have unearthed copies of ancient Middle Eastern treaties by which a powerful emperor might take under his rule and protection a small, weak, neighboring nation. Perhaps such covenants formed a model for the Jews' understanding of their relationship with God. In any event, they held that after God's rescue of them from Egypt, God had condescended to enter into a covenant with them. The Lord would be their king and protector. They, as the prophets were to interpret it, were in a sense "married" to the Lord. They had agreed to respond to God's deliverance and continuing preservation of them by being faithful exclusively to this one God. God had saved and would save them. They in turn agreed to respond in attitudes of the heart, in cultic worship, and in ethical living. Their prescribed response to the grace of God was codified in law.

The New Testament was to speak of Christ as having instituted a "new covenant."

Fifth, in this covenant, God demanded *righteousness in social relationships.* Amos, the first of the Hebrew prophets whose words are preserved for us as a book of the Old Testament, had pictured God as ready to judge Israel

> because they sell the righteous for silver,
>   and the needy for a pair of sandals. (Amos 2:6)

I hate, I despise your festivals,
   and I take no delight in your solemn assemblies.
. . . .
But let justice roll down like waters,
   and righteousness like an everflowing stream. (Amos 5:21–24)

Prophets denounced even kings if they failed to show concern for the poor or used their power simply for their own advantage. Perhaps no other religion has ever tied together so closely love of God and active concern for one's fellow human beings.

Jesus was popularly identified by his contemporaries as being another prophet, perhaps in part because of his insistence that the coming of the kingdom of God demanded godly relationships between people.

Finally, the Jews nurtured and expressed this faith through *cultic practices.* Perhaps few first-century Jews would have drawn a sharp distinction between ethical practices such as honesty and charity and "cultic" practices such as circumcision and Sabbath observance. Both were equally part of the law of God. The modern distinction between the two, however, may be helpful for contemporary students. God, the Jews were sure, not only demanded concern for one's neighbor; the Lord commanded participation in certain ceremonies, in worship, and in practices designed to mark the Jew as distinct from the rest of humankind.

Jesus, like any other Jewish boy, was circumcised in infancy, bearing on his body the indelible mark of his being part of the covenant people.

Particularly in the Gospel according to John, we find Jesus participating in the Jewish festivals conducted annually at the Temple in Jerusalem. Most important among these for the New Testament was the Passover. It involved the yearly celebration of God's redemption of God's people from Egypt and the establishment of the covenant. Participants shared a meal that included a sacrificed lamb. The Gospels record Jesus' eating a meal at this Passover season with his disciples the night before his death, and the Passover imagery helped the New Testament writers to interpret the meaning of Jesus' death as a redeeming, covenant sacrifice.

Perhaps most difficult of all to preserve against the encroachments of Greco-Roman culture, Jews observed the Sabbath, keeping free from all work the period from sundown Friday evening until sundown Saturday evening. Controversy with those who most rigidly adhered to the Sabbath law was a factor leading to Jesus' death.

In Jesus' Day, Competing Groups of Jews Represented Differing Views

Thus far, first-century Judaism has been presented as though its people were all of one mind. This was far from the case. Controversies within the Jewish community are repeatedly reflected within the Gospels' stories.

Josephus, the Jewish writer whose histories, written late in the first century, shed a flood of light on New Testament times in Palestine, speaks of four "philosophies" influential among Jews of his day.

The Pharisees are so prominent in the story that the word "Pharisee" occurs in the Gospels more than eighty times. Though only some six thousand out of perhaps a million and a half Palestinian Jews were Pharisees, their influence with the people and their opposition to Jesus made them of great importance to the Gospel writers.

Though nobody knows exactly how the Pharisees originated, it is known that the sect had been in existence for a century and a half by Jesus' day. The name "Pharisees" apparently means "the separated ones," given them presumably because they sought to be different from other people by being more holy. The Pharisees represented devoutly determined resistance to the threat of Greco-Roman culture. Pharisees saw their worldly neighbors compromising their faith and practice at point after point. Ancient puritans, they resolved to compromise nothing. To preserve the law, they fenced it about with tradition, so that by keeping the strictest traditional interpretations of the law they would be certain not to break even the slightest detail.

Their heroes and heroines were those who, according to their tradition, had most courageously resisted even the slightest surrender to pagan pressures. The Apocryphal book of Tobit describes how an old Jew in captivity lost his sight in his concern to keep ceremonial laws such as those governing the burial of the dead. As a reward, his fortune was restored, his son was given a beautiful wife, and his eyes were healed, all by the miraculous intervention of an angel. Another book of the Apocrypha, Judith, describes how, even in the camp of an enemy, this lovely widow refused to eat food that was not kosher, always carrying her own kosher food and wine.

She was able to beguile the invading general with her charms, murder him on his bed, and rescue her people. The Pharisees were sure that God would protect and deliver those who thus obeyed God's law.

In much the same way as they added their traditional interpretations to the law, so these devout people developed doctrines that went beyond the direct words of the Jewish scripture. They argued for belief in the resurrection and a life after death. They believed in angels and demons. They believed in predestination and foreordination by God, who plans all that will come to pass.

One who knows the Pharisees only through the New Testament is likely to get an inaccurate view of these good people. Jesus' attacks on them need not be applied to all the Pharisees. They were looked on as, and probably were in fact, the best Jews of their day. The word "Pharisee" has come to mean "hypocrite," but their original intent was to be uncompromising guardians of God's law.

The Sadducees were the party of compromise. If the Pharisees chose to protect every word of the law by adding traditional interpretations, the Sadducees accepted as authoritative as little as seemed possible for good Jews. Thus they regarded as binding on them not the whole of the Old Testament but only the Torah, the books of the Law, the first five books of the Bible. They rejected belief in angels and demons. And as to a future life, they rejected that belief, apparently successful in finding rewards of a different kind here on earth.

Most dictators learned long ago that it is easier to dominate a religion than to stamp it out. The Romans chose this shrewder strategy. The Jews continued to have their high priest in their Temple, but the high priest had to be appointed in cooperation with the Roman authorities. He could continue in office only as long as he pleased his Roman lords. Often his stay in office was short indeed.

There were rewards for those who served Rome. The Sadducees came to be the priestly class, the leaders in the Sanhedrin (the Jewish supreme court of seventy members), and the wealthiest of the Jews. Sophisticated, in some ways more Greek than Hebrew, affluent in a poverty-stricken land, and cooperating with their conquerors, the Sadducees tended to be despised by many of their fellow Jews.

Matthew 16:1–12 describes Jesus' condemnation of the Pharisees and Sadducees. Matthew 22:23–33 describes the Sadducees' attempt to ridicule Jesus' belief in a future life.

The Essenes are best known to us through the most remarkable discovery of buried treasure in modern times.

In 1947, a teenaged Arab goatherd who was chasing a runaway found himself in a cave on a mountain overlooking the Dead Sea. There he stumbled on an earthen jar. It contained the first of the famous Dead Sea Scrolls, part of the library of a curious Jewish sect not unlike the later Roman Catholic monks.

The Pharisees tried to live everyday lives as middle-class Jews in the world, but in accordance with God's law. The Essenes, however, turned their backs on the sinful world. To the wilderness they went, away from the corruption of the cities. There they set up their own communes, rather like medieval monasteries. Most of these communes were for men only, though a few included families. An applicant for admission went through a year's probation. When admitted, he deeded over all his property to the community, went through a ceremony not unlike baptism, swore to live a strict and righteous life, and began to share in the common meals.

The Essenes regarded themselves as the army of the "sons of light." Whenever the awaited age of the messiah might come, they would stand ready to fight the forces of evil and darkness.

The Essenes are never mentioned in the New Testament. But their sharing, baptized, kingdom fellowship was so much like the early Christian church that some have proposed that many early Christians, even Jesus himself, might have been members of this sect. Most scholars now reject the suggestion that Jesus was ever an Essene, but we shall see that there are real similarities between the Essenes and John the Baptist.

Finally, there were *the Zealots*, a kind of Palestinian Liberation Organization, secretly plotting violent revolution to be carried out when the messiah came to lead them. We have already noted their heroic but futile raids.

Luke 6:15 tells us that one of Jesus' disciples was "Simon, who was called the Zealot." Fear that Jesus, who was being hailed as Messiah, might stimulate a Zealot uprising was a factor in the execution of Jesus by the nervous Romans.

Three Religious Emphases
of First-Century Judaism Particularly
Influenced Jesus' Life and Its Interpretation

Most Jews did not belong to any of these four parties. The common people, "the people of the land," had little time or means, perhaps, for participation in such movements.

Still, there were synagogues for worship and study in every Jewish town, more and more of them with synagogue schools for teaching the youth. Religious zeal seems to have been widespread, at least by twentieth-century standards. And the movements we have examined exemplified attitudes and concerns not confined to their members.

Three of the religious emphases characteristic of the first century have such bearing on the Gospel accounts that we must take special note of them.

Legalism was highly developed. Only six thousand Jews wore the broad tassels of the Pharisees' band. But Josephus tells us that the common people looked up to the Pharisees as examples of what all should be. The Law, the Torah, was the very word of God.

Strict observance of the Sabbath symbolized obedience to all the law. Pharisaic tradition spelled out precisely what Sabbath observance required. For example, when the question arose as to whether, on the Sabbath, one might put a bowl over an annoying gnat in order to rid oneself of it, it was ruled that doing so would be a form of hunting, strictly illegal on the holy day. One must not wear a new robe on the Sabbath, because there might still be a needle left in it; it would be a sin to carry even that much of a burden on Saturday. Some rules suggested evasions. It was a sin to tie a knot in a rope on the Sabbath, but one might tie a knot in a sash, because getting dressed was necessary for decency. Hence, if the rope in a person's well broke on Saturday, it was permitted to mend it with the temporary use of a sash.

When Jesus set human need above such Sabbath rules, some Pharisees began to plot his death.

Expectation of the messiah seems to have been widespread and to have taken a variety of forms.

Though the Pharisees did not attempt armed resistance to Rome, they were no less dedicated to liberation than were the Zealots. It was simply that their methods were different. If all Israel would but keep two Sabbaths perfectly, they promised, the messiah, the promised king, would come with deliverance.

The Dead Sea Scrolls seem to imply that the Essene communes awaited not just one but two messiahs, one kingly and one priestly. The Essenes would be the Lord's army in that coming day.

The Zealots were all too ready to follow any attractive military leader in the hope that he was the one promised to lead them in the slaughter of the Romans.

Perhaps it was because he rejected all of these ideas of messiahship that Jesus strictly forbade his disciples to tell people that he was the messiah. But the belief that Jesus had brought at last the fulfillment of their hopes and dreams undoubtedly drew the crowds who became his first followers.

Closely related to the expectation of the messiah was the intense *expectation of the final days of this world.*

> And the horns of the sun shall be broken and he shall
> be turned into darkness;
> And the moon shall not give her light, and be turned
> wholly into blood.[7]

So prophesied the author of *The Assumption of Moses,* a work popular among first-century Jews, as he wrote of the coming cataclysm. The Dead Sea Scrolls described the last day thus:

> The heavens shall thunder loud . . .
> and the gates of Hell shall be opened.[8]

A typical apocalypse, falsely attributed to Enoch, described the cosmic judgment of Satan and the nations in these terms:

> Ye mighty kings who dwell on the earth, ye shall have to behold Mine Elect One, how he sits on the throne of glory and judges Azazel, and all his associates, and all his hosts in the name of the Lord of Spirits.[9]

"Eschatology," teaching about the last things, the doctrine of the end of the world, produced its own kind of literature, from which the passages just quoted are taken. Called "apocalyptic" literature, this distinctive kind of writing flourished among a people desperate for deliverance. In many of these apocalypses, there was also the promise of a messiah.

It was with ears at least partly trained by this kind of preaching that Jesus' first hearers heard him announce what Mark reports as a summary of his first preaching: "The time is fulfilled, and the kingdom of God has come near; repent, and believe in the good news" (Mark 1:15).

THE WRITING OF THE GOSPELS

In the beginning was the event.

Jesus lived; Jesus taught; Jesus died. At Easter, something so amazing occurred that it caused the disciples to spend the rest of their lives telling the world that Jesus also rose from the dead. The Gospel stories were born in historical events.

The nineteenth-century German scholar Bruno Bauer seriously proposed that Jesus never actually existed. Recognizing apparent difficulties and inconsistencies in the Gospel accounts, he argued that the Gospels were simply religious fiction. The effect of his proposal was to demonstrate its own impossibility. Today, it would be difficult to find even one competent historian who doubts that Jesus really lived. Mark, the first written Gospel, was penned only about thirty-five years after Jesus' death. The other records of Jesus' life are too early, too many, too diverse, and yet in too much basic agreement not to have their source in some nucleus of actual fact. And it is far easier to suppose that the religious movement which spread so rapidly over the Roman Empire was the creation of a powerful personality than that the personality was the fictional creation of the movement.

In being centered so directly on historical events and the person in the midst of them, Christianity is unique among religions. Devout Muslims respect the memory of Muhammed, surely a historical individual of remarkable gifts. Muslims, however, would be the first to affirm that their religion centers on Allah's message, not on the person of Muhammed the messenger. Whether or not Arjuna ever lived is a question that has no bearing on the truth of the Hindus' Bhagavad Gita. Christianity, however, begins with the story of a real man. Rudolf Bultmann, who devoted much of his study to the comparison of the Gospel stories with other literature of a similar form, writes that the Gospels are unique in this focus among the religious literature of the world. This particular kind of literature cannot quite be paralleled even in style and form to any other anywhere.

In the beginning was the event. But for our knowledge of this crucial event or series of events we are dependent on written sources. The only written sources that really help us are those within the New Testament. There are two brief references to Jesus in the writings of the Jewish historian Josephus, but many scholars regard the longer of these as being an insertion by a Christian copyist. The writings of Jewish rabbis who mention Jesus come from a later period and seem to be simply reflections of Jewish–Christian controversy. Roman historians did not hear of Jesus until the Christian movement had spread over the empire.

We can learn some things about Jesus' life from books of the New Testament other than the Gospels, but the details are disappointingly few. It is the Gospels, the first four books of the New Testament, that tell us almost everything we know about the earthly life of Christ.

Fortunately, one Gospel writer gives us a brief account of how and why he wrote:

> Since many have undertaken to set down an orderly account of the events that have been fulfilled among us, just as they were handed on to us by those who from the beginning were eyewitnesses and servants of the word, I too decided, after investigating everything from the very first, to write an orderly account for you, most excellent Theophilus, so that you may know the truth concerning the things about which you have been instructed. (Luke 1:1–4)

To some, this account of the writing of a Gospel must seem disappointing. The Koran, the Muslims believe, was dictated by an angel. The Book of Mormon was handed down from heaven, according to the Church of Jesus Christ of Latter-day Saints. Pious Christian paintings have shown angels dictating to biblical writers. But the claim Luke makes is simply that he did a careful job of research. Many Christians are ready to warn, however, that they trust a claim of research such as Luke's more than any boast of a "miraculous" origin. This section considers what can be deduced about how Luke went about this task.

Taking Luke's account of how his Gospel was written as typical of the others as well, we use it as a basis for considering the origins of the Gospels.

Oral Traditions about Jesus

Even though Mark probably wrote his account of Jesus' life around A.D. 65, only some thirty-five years after Jesus' death, and though we have letters written by Paul from perhaps as early as A.D. 50, there still remains what has been called a "dark tunnel" of twenty years between Jesus' death, around A.D.

30, and our oldest Christian writings. What kind of sources did the Gospel writers use? How did they penetrate that tunnel?

From the Beginning, the First Preachers Told about Jesus' Life

Luke says that his story came in part from those who, from the beginning, were "ministers of the word."

Acts gives us an account of what these first preachers said. Admittedly, Acts was written fifty or more years after the life of Jesus. There is reason to believe, however, that by comparing the summaries of sermons in Acts with passages in which Paul reports what seem to be accounts of the gospel as he first heard it, the content of the first preaching can be reconstructed.

The Greek word used for the content of the first preaching is *kerygma*. It means "proclamation." It was used for the announcement of victory. It implies the joyful proclaiming of good news. A *keryx* was a herald, and the first preachers thought of themselves as heralds reporting a triumph.

In his highly influential book *The Apostolic Preaching and Its Developments*, the late C. H. Dodd pointed to the following summary in Acts as being very probably typical of the earliest sermons:[10]

> You know the message he sent to the people of Israel, preaching peace by Jesus Christ—he is Lord of all. That message spread throughout Judea, beginning in Galilee after the baptism that John announced: how God anointed Jesus of Nazareth with the Holy Spirit and with power; how he went about doing good and healing all who were oppressed by the devil, for God was with him. We are witnesses to all that he did both in Judea and in Jerusalem. They put him to death by hanging him on a tree; but God raised him on the third day and allowed him to appear, not to all the people but to us who were chosen by God as witnesses, and who ate and drank with him after he rose from the dead. He commanded us to preach to the people and to testify that he is the one ordained by God as judge of the living and the dead. All the prophets testify about him that everyone who believes in him receives forgiveness of sins through his name. (Acts 10:36–43)

Other summaries of sermons in Acts and in Paul's letters are similar.

If this was indeed the kind of thing that the first preachers regularly said, then the part of the typical sermon that described the earthly life of Jesus included the following elements:

1. It began with an account of John the Baptizer and his baptism of Jesus. This baptism was associated with an anointing of Jesus by the Holy Spirit.
2. Some account was given of Jesus' deeds. Emphasis was laid on his power, the goodness of his actions, his healing, and his exorcisms of evil spirits, in conflict with the devil.

3. Some account of Jesus' preaching or teaching was also given.
4. Mention was made of chosen witnesses (the disciples).
5. The story moved from Galilee to Judea and Jerusalem.
6. The one event of Jesus' life specifically described here—and in all other summaries of early sermons—was his death. Details of that death began to be noted, even in this brief summary: the role of his enemies and the manner of his execution.
7. Jesus' resurrection was announced, with specific mention of his appearance to his disciples and his commission to them to spread the good news.

The striking thing about these seven points is that they would serve equally well as a short summary of Mark or, indeed, of any one of the four Gospels.

Luke says that he based his Gospel in part on what he had heard the first preachers say. Similarly, early and consistent tradition affirms that Mark based his Gospel on what he had heard in preaching, including the sermons of Jesus' disciple Peter.

What is proposed, then, is that the kerygma, this form of preaching that seems to have been much the same throughout the early church, included an account of the life of Jesus. No doubt, different stories and sayings of Jesus were told by different preachers in different sermons. But the basic, common kerygma provided the framework, the outline, for Gospel writers when they set down their stories of Jesus' life. And the stories and sayings of Jesus, the sermon illustrations used by these "ministers of the word," made up the body of each Gospel.

The Gospels Contain Stories and Sayings
Handed Down by These First Preachers

Scholars called "form critics" have argued cogently that the individual stories gathered together in the framework of each Gospel show signs of having been told and retold separately before they were written down as we now have them.

This view fits well with the fact that the stories do not appear in our Gospels in the same order. For example, the parable of the sower appears early in Mark's Gospel (chap. 4), a bit later in Luke's Gospel (chap. 8), and not until the middle of Matthew's account (chap. 13). Mark tells of the healing of the man with the withered hand near the beginning of his story of Jesus' life (chap. 3), while Luke puts it in chapter 6 and Matthew not until chapter 12. The Lord's Prayer is given as part of the Sermon on the Mount in Matthew 6; in Luke 11, it is part of private instruction given later by Jesus to his disciples. The simplest explanation is that these stories and sayings were not the invention of the writers but part of the oral tradition of the church handed down by the many early preachers. Each writer used a familiar story at the place in his Gospel where it would best illustrate the point he was making.

One form critic has compared the separate stories of Jesus, handed down by word of mouth, to separate pearls that the Gospel writers have strung together, each in different order to present his distinctive insights into the truth.

Form critics have attempted to analyze these stories on the basis of the forms or patterns in which they seem repeatedly to occur. Such critics have not always agreed in their analyses, but three such patterns or forms are noted here.

The most obvious form is that of the *parable*. The traditional definition serves well: "A parable is an earthly story with a heavenly meaning." Jesus told so many parables that, with a touch of hyperbole, Mark 4:34 says that Jesus never spoke in public without using a parable. Familiar examples of parables are Luke 15:3–7 (the lost sheep), Luke 10:29–37 (the Good Samaritan), and Mark 4:3–9 (the sower and the soils). One can readily see how these little stories could be remembered easily and handed down orally.

A second form has been called the *pronouncement story*. It consists of a saying of Jesus embedded in an account of some incident of his life, so that the two would be remembered together. For example, Mark 2:23–28 tells how Jesus' disciples, walking through a grainfield on the Sabbath, plucked and ate bits of wheat. When the Pharisees accused them of desecrating the Sabbath by threshing grain on the holy day, Jesus replied, "The sabbath was made for humankind, and not humankind for the sabbath." Story and saying would be remembered together. Mark 2:15–17 gives another illustration. Jesus' enemies attack him for associating with the outcasts of society. He replies, "Those who are well have no need of a physician, but those who are sick." Incidentally, it should be noted that many of Jesus' sayings are in this style of witty couplets or balanced phrases, which would be easy to remember and pass on orally.

The third form is the *miracle story*. In a typical miracle story, (1) a need is noted; (2) Jesus' help is sought; (3) there is an expression of faith; (4) a memorable miracle is performed; and (5) the story ends with a notation about the response of those who saw the miracle. The response may be one of faith, astonishment, or even anger. Matthew 9:1–8 contains all five of these elements in its account of the healing of a paralytic.

Some scholars have attempted to determine the age of a story by analysis of its form. Not all agree, however, that this attempt has been entirely successful.[11]

There are hints that enable scholars to make guesses concerning which strands of the tradition are earlier or later. For example, it seems evident that Jesus told a story about a lost sheep and a shepherd who goes out to find it. Luke 15:1–7 sets this story in the context of Jesus' replying to Pharisees who attacked him for associating with sinners. The meaning, in this setting, is clearly a defense of Jesus' association with outcasts. In Matt. 18:10–22, the story is immediately followed by instruction concerning special care to be taken to win back delinquent church members. Many have argued that the setting in Luke is the original one. By placing the same story in a different context, Matthew's Gospel has applied it quite helpfully to the later situation of church discipline. Lastly, John 10:11 does not repeat the familiar parable but richly develops its meaning in relation to Christ and all the faithful: "I am the good shepherd. The good shepherd lays down his life for the sheep."

As different situations arose in the life of the church, different sayings and stories were recalled and new meanings were found in them. We have emphasized the place of preaching in the development of the oral tradition. Worship, instruction, and other concerns of the church doubtless also helped preserve the stories of Jesus. The point here is simply that the stories circulated orally, were easy to remember, and are older than the written Gospels in which we now find them.

Gospel Writers Selected and Arranged
This Material for Their Special Purposes

To return to Luke's account of how he wrote his Gospel, Luke tells us that by the time he writes, "many have undertaken to set down an orderly account of the events that have been fulfilled among us" (Luke 1:1). He was familiar, therefore, with many stories of Jesus' life. Some of these he evidently considered of inferior quality. He selected from among the many stories in circulation those that fit his particular purpose and suited his standards of credibility.

It is John's Gospel that spells out this concern for selection most clearly, in words that would apply in many ways to the other Gospels also:

> Now Jesus did many other signs in the presence of his disciples, which are not written in this book. But these are written that you may come to believe that Jesus is the Messiah, the Son of God, and that through believing you may have life in his name. (John 20:30–31)

With considerable hyperbole, John says that Jesus did so many things that the world could not contain the books it would take to record them all (John 21:25). He has carefully selected those stories and sayings that he believes will win the reader to faith in Jesus as the Christ, the Son of God, and lead that reader to new life.

In short, as we have seen, the Gospels must be understood against the background of the kerygma. They grew out of gospel sermons. They are not simply cold, objective biographies. They are evangelistic tracts. Their contents were selected for evangelistic purposes. This is most obvious in John, the latest of the Gospels, but though less explicit, it is also the case with the others, even the earliest, Mark. Lest we miss the point that he is trying to win us to belief, Mark introduces his story as "the beginning of the good news of Jesus Christ, the Son of God" (Mark 1:1). Every Gospel is written to give us not simply the writer's record of what Jesus said and did but also his understanding of who Jesus really was and what he can mean to the reader. Each Gospel is a call to the decision of faith.

This is why there is so much that the Gospels do not bother to tell us about Jesus. What was his childhood like? We have only one story about Jesus between his infancy and age thirty (Luke 2:41–51). What did he look like? What is the real historical order of the events described in such different sequences in our four Gospels? In what sense did Jesus think of himself as Messiah? Such questions are not answered for us, in part at least because they were not the theological concern of our Gospel writers.

Other pious authors soon undertook to fill in the gaps in the Gospel stories. Here are a few stories about Jesus that are relatively unfamiliar to most modern Christians.

Jesus' parents sent the boy Jesus to school. He knew so much more than the teacher and so confused the poor man that the teacher soon begged Mary and Joseph not to send Jesus back again.

The child Jesus made a pigeon of clay. He clapped his hands, and the bird miraculously flew away.

A playmate accidentally bumped into Jesus, knocking down the Son of God. Jesus cursed him for this blasphemy, and the boy dropped dead. After the child's parents complained to Joseph, Jesus graciously resurrected the boy.[12]

These and many other equally incredible stories are preserved for us in apocryphal Gospels, accounts of Jesus' life beloved by many early Christians but eventually rejected by the church as false. Noting them points us to a second criterion of selection used by the Gospel writers. Luke explains that, aware of other accounts of Jesus' life, he wrote his so that his reader would know what was the truth.

Much recent scholarship has so emphasized the theological purpose of the Gospel writers and the structure of each Gospel as a unified story with its own plot and characters that it has neglected the writers' evident concern for reporting the facts. We have seen that they do not report all the facts. And we have seen that they report not just facts but also their interpretations of the meaning of those facts. But the Gospel writers were not, they tell us, producing fiction to support theology. Had they been doing so, they might well have included stories such as those just described. Each Gospel writer, like Luke, wanted his reader to know the truth, as he had learned it from many sources. Luke claims to have talked with "eyewitnesses." Assuming that he was also the author of Acts, we may well believe that he had opportunity to meet eyewitnesses in the journeys he describes there. A perhaps credible tradition says that Mark was reporting what he learned from Peter, who was very much an eyewitness of the events described. At the very least, our Gospels are based on oral and written sources developed within the lifetimes of the first preachers. And though most scholars deny that our Gospels of Matthew and John, in the forms in which we now have them, are actually from the pens of these apostles, the names of these Gospels suggest that in some way, at least, they rest on a tradition that goes back to two of the original Twelve.[13]

Our Gospel writers, then, selected stories told by the early church and strung these "pearls" together, each in his own fashion, on a thread also spun from the first sermons. They wrote connective narratives, stories with characters and plot, to win readers to faith through confronting them with the truth.

The Written Records

When Luke tells us that "many have undertaken to set down an orderly account," he implies that he is familiar not only with oral sources such as we have been describing but also with written accounts of the life of Jesus. While there are differences of opinion, most scholars believe that we can describe two of the written sources Luke used.

Mark Is Our Oldest Gospel
and Was One Source for Matthew and Luke

Several reputable scholars still support the tradition that Matthew was the first of our four Gospels to be written.[14] The great majority, however, believe that Matthew and Luke already knew Mark's Gospel and made use of it when they wrote.

The chief reason for this view is that so much of Mark seems to have been copied by the other Gospel writers, though adapted by them to fit their language, style, and purposes. Of the eighty-eight paragraphs that make up Mark, only three are not found in either Matthew or Luke. Matthew reproduces approximately ninety percent of the subject matter of Mark. More than half of the contents of Mark can also be found in Luke.

Moreover, where either Matthew or Luke varies from Mark in wording or in outline, the other is likely to agree with Mark. Almost never do Matthew and Luke agree with each other but differ from Mark.

Because Mark's Gospel is a primary source for both Matthew and Luke, its origins are of great importance for New Testament study. Our best source of information is the *Ecclesiastical History* of Eusebius, written around A.D. 330 but quoting from earlier accounts. According to Eusebius, here is what happened.

Emperor Nero undertook to stamp out the church in Rome. Among those martyred was Peter, leader among Jesus' twelve disciples and of the Roman congregation. After the death of Peter, according to Eusebius, "Mark, the disciple and interpreter of Peter, himself handed down to us in writing the substance of Peter's preaching."[15]

Similarly, Eusebius quotes the early church leader Papias as having written around A.D. 140:

> The elder used to say this also: Mark became the interpreter of Peter and he wrote down accurately, but not in order, as much as he remembered of the sayings and doings of Christ. For he was not a hearer or a follower of the Lord, but afterwards, as I said, of Peter, who adapted his teachings to the needs of the moment and did not make an ordered exposition of the sayings of the Lord.[16]

Mark appears repeatedly in the New Testament as a young leader in the church from its earliest days, acquainted with Peter, Barnabas, and Paul (Acts 12:12, 25; 15:39; 2 Tim. 4:11). Though it is challenged, there seems to be no compelling reason to doubt the reports of Eusebius, Papias, and Irenaeus that he was the author of our Gospel. If so, we may infer that Mark gave us the stories of Jesus that he had heard directly from the firsthand accounts of Peter. This fits nicely with the fact that, next to Jesus himself, by far the most prominent character in Mark is the apostle Peter. Mark's Gospel, in a sense, may be Peter's own story of Jesus. At the least, it gives us the story as it was told in Rome soon after Peter's martyrdom.[17]

Matthew and Luke Also Had a Written Collection of Jesus' Teachings: "Q"

There are more than two hundred verses in both Matthew and Luke that cannot have been copied from Mark because they do not occur in that Gospel. These verses are so nearly alike in the two Gospels that most scholars believe that they must have come from one common written source. Almost all of them report sayings attributed to Jesus. A reader wishing to confirm the idea that the two Gospels appear to have used the same source may compare such passages as the following:

Matthew	Luke
5:39–44	6:27–31
6:9–18	11:2–4
8:19–22	9:57–60
13:31–33	13:18–21

At times, one writer seems more complete in his report, at times the other. Therefore it seems likely not that one is copying from the other but that each is copying from some now-lost manuscript.

It cannot be absolutely proved that such a document ever existed.[18] There is such widespread agreement, however, concerning such an early collection of Jesus' teachings that it has been commonly given the name "Q" (from the German word *Quelle,* meaning "source"). The document must have been older even than our Gospels of Matthew and Luke, perhaps as old as Mark itself (ca. A.D. 65). If a copy could be found today, millions of dollars could not buy it!

Using These and Other Sources, Our Writers Composed Their Gospels

We are now ready to describe what seems the likely origin of the Gospels as we have them.

Mark was written around A.D. 65, following the death of Peter, by (tradition says) Peter's young disciple and interpreter. Mark may be based, in part, on the stories told by Peter himself in his preaching and teaching.

Matthew was composed between A.D. 80 and 90 by a writer who put together Mark's account of Jesus' deeds with the collection of Jesus' teachings now commonly designated as "Q." To these two sources he added the material peculiar to his Gospel, which scholars designate as "M."

For centuries, this Gospel has borne the name of one of Jesus' twelve apostles. Eusebius reported that as early as A.D. 140, Bishop Papias wrote, "So then Matthew recorded the oracles in the Hebrew tongue, and each interpreted them to the best of his ability."[19]

Two reasons make it highly unlikely, however, that the Gospel as we have it is the work of a Palestinian Jew such as Matthew, an actual apostle and eyewitness of the events described. First, an eyewitness would not have copied so extensively from Mark's admittedly secondhand report. Second, a Palestinian Jew would probably not have quoted from the Greek translation of the Old Testament (called the "Septuagint"). A Palestinian disciple would have quoted from the original Hebrew. Yet where the Greek version of the Old Testament differs from the Hebrew, this writer almost always based what he said on the Septuagint's version. He quoted from the Septuagint so often that it seems clear that he was himself a Greek-speaking Jew, one of the hundreds of thousands of such "Hellenists" living outside Palestine, not one who followed Jesus in Galilee.

How, then, did the name of Matthew get attached to our Gospel? Though it can be only an attractive conjecture, it has been suggested that the apostle Matthew was in fact the author of Q. According to this proposal, Q was the *logia*, or collection of sayings, attributed to Matthew by Papias. The editor who joined Mark's account of Jesus' deeds to Q, Matthew's account of Jesus' teachings, attributed his work to Matthew as the source of most of what in his Gospel was different from Mark's.

If this theory is true, it means that Matthew does contain many firsthand recollections of the teachings of Jesus. It must be said, however, that this is only one theory and, again, is only attractive conjecture.

In much the same way but with somewhat different emphases, Luke produced his Gospel, also probably in the early eighties. He too added to Mark and Q distinctive material, which scholars designate by the letter "L."

As early as A.D. 175, we find references to this Gospel as the work of Luke, the companion of Paul. Though this identification has been disputed, it still seems the simplest explanation. The argument for it runs as follows: Luke 1:1–4 contains a brief preface to the Gospel, addressed to one Theophilus. Acts 1:1 is apparently addressed to the same person and refers to an earlier book, almost certainly the Gospel. The two books, then, are by the same author. Acts, in turn, from 16:10 on, has frequent stories told in the first person ("God had called *us*," "*we* set sail from Troas," etc. [Acts 16:10–11]). The author appears to be claiming to have been a companion of Paul during much of the latter part of Paul's life. Coupled with this is the fact that in Col. 4:14, Paul speaks of his companion "Luke, the beloved physician," and 2 Tim. 4:11 speaks of the faithfulness of someone named Luke. Luke appears in Paul's letters, but only at places where Acts might suggest that the author was present. He is not so prominent that a Gospel would have been attributed to him had he not written it. Therefore, it is argued, the tradition that Luke is the author seems valid.

This view has been strongly attacked by many scholars, who point to apparent differences between the life of Paul as one might reconstruct it from Paul's letters and the account of Paul's life in Acts. However, the view that Paul's companion Luke is the author of both the Gospel and Acts is still widely held.[20]

Ancient and consistent tradition attributes the Gospel according to John to one of the most prominent of Jesus' twelve apostles. The church historian Eusebius quotes an earlier source as reporting, "Last of all, John, perceiving that the external facts had been made plain in the gospel, being urged by friends, and inspired by the Spirit, composed a spiritual gospel."[21]

John, however, is quite different from the other three Gospels. Questions of its date and authorship are very complex. There are strong reasons for questioning the traditional view. Because of the problems involved and because the Fourth Gospel is, in many ways, the climax of the New Testament, this *Guide* delays discussion of John until its last chapter.

The First Three Gospels, the "Synoptics," May Easily Be Compared

In content, origin, and structure, the first three Gospels are much alike. Because, as we shall see, they may be easily compared by being placed in parallel columns, they are often grouped together. Their common title, the "Synoptics," means that they "see together" the life of Christ.

We have seen that they are mutually related in origin. Adopting B. H. Streeter's "four document hypothesis,"[22] one may chart their relationships in this way:

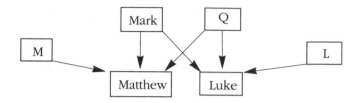

Matthew combined Mark and Q with his particular material, M. Luke combined Mark and Q with his particular material, L. Each arranged the order of this material for his own purposes, but the result is still quite similar. (Most Bibles, in the margins or in footnotes, have cross-references to help the reader compare how the different Gospels tell the same stories.)

Any book called a *harmony* of the Gospels places the Synoptics' accounts side by side for easy comparison. For example, the three Gospels tell the story of how Jesus healed Peter's mother-in-law. Here are the accounts as translated in the Revised Standard Version:

Matthew 8:14–17	*Mark 1:29–34*	*Luke 4:38–41*
And	And *immediately* he left the synagogue,	And he arose and left the synagogue,
when Jesus entered Peter's house,	and entered the house of Simon and Andrew, with James and John.	and entered Simon's house.
he saw his mother-in-law lying sick with a fever;	Now Simon's mother-in-law lay sick with a fever, and *immediately* they told him of her. And he came and took	Now Simon's mother-in-law was ill with a *high* fever, and they besought him for her. And he stood over her and rebuked
he touched her hand,	her by the hand and lifted her up,	the fever,
and the fever left her. . . . That evening they brought to him many who were	and the fever left her. . . . That evening, at sundown, they brought to him all who were sick or	and it left her. . . . Now when the sun was setting, all those who had any that were sick with various diseases brought them to him;
possessed with demons;	possessed with demons. And the whole city was gathered together about the door.	
and he	And he healed many who were sick with various diseases,	and he laid his hands on every one of them and healed them.

cast out the spirits with a word. . . .	and cast out many demons;	And demons also came out of many, crying, "You are the Son of God!" But he rebuked
	and he would not permit the demons to speak, because they knew him.	them, and would not allow them to speak, because they knew he was the Christ.
This was to fulfil what was spoken by the prophet Isaiah, "He took our infirmities and bore our diseases."		

Certain words have been italicized so that typical differences of emphasis may be noted, even in so short a story.

Matthew, writing to Jewish readers to present Jesus as the promised Messiah, quotes from the Jewish scriptures, as he so often does, a passage that he sees Jesus as fulfilling.

Mark, typically depicting Jesus as a man of action, twice uses a favorite word, "immediately." Often, as here, he gives vivid details that to some have suggested that he is reflecting Peter's eyewitness account.

Luke, a physician, seems here (and perhaps elsewhere) to take an interest in details of healing.

John, typically different from the Synoptics, does not tell this story.

The Synoptics, of course, differ in more ways than those here noted. They not only differ in emphasis and in the order in which they tell the stories but also seem at times to be in conflict in their reports of certain facts. Some of these differences are noted in the later sections of this *Guide* on the specific Gospels.

Here, however, our purpose is to call attention to the essential agreement among the Synoptics as a basis for our study of the life and teachings of Jesus.

The Church Selected the Present Four Gospels and the Other New Testament Books as an Authoritative "Canon"

The four Gospels contained in our New Testament were not the only ones written by early Christians. We have seen how pious imagination provided stories of the boyhood of Jesus, with tales of his confounding his teachers and resurrecting dead playmates. Nor are the epistles that are found in our New Testament the only letters revered by early Christians. The *Epistle of Clement* (written around A.D. 96) seems to have been regarded as authoritative by many churches. The book of Acts had its rivals too. The *Acts of John,* for example, described the sufferings and triumphs of that apostle. It reported that one night John had to sleep in a bed so infested with bedbugs that he at last informed the leader of the parasites that he was an apostle and needed exclusive use of the bed. Obediently, the insects filed out, only to return as the apostle left the next morning.

Not only did other books compete for acceptance by the church, but several books now found in the New Testament are not included in early lists. Second Peter, Hebrews, James, and Revelation were among those whose authority was disputed or only slowly accepted.

Gradually, however, the twenty-seven books that form our New Testament were recognized as the New Testament "canon" (from the word for "measuring rod" or "ruler"), the church's rule for faith and practice. The Synod of Carthage (A.D. 397) made official what had already been widely accepted in the church.

The acceptance of these books—and only these books—as the New Testament canon seems to have been based on such beliefs as the following:

1. These books were regarded, rightly or wrongly, as the works of apostles and famous leaders of the early church. Though few now would attribute Hebrews to the apostle Paul, the belief that he wrote it undoubtedly helped establish it in the minds of church members as authoritative. Other books were accepted as they were attributed to other great men of the early church.

2. These books were regarded as inspired by the Holy Spirit. We have noted that they were the work of human authors and that our Gospels were the product of a kind of historical research. This, however, does not mean that the church did not find the Holy Spirit active in the entire process of the writing of its sacred books. God, they were sure, had guided the writers to give the church the good news through these human agents. The inspiration of these books was borne in on church members as they read these little volumes and in them were confronted with the figure of Jesus and the call to the decision of faith. Readers still have this experience today.

3. These books stood closest to the crucial events of the life, death, and resurrection of Jesus. It was, the church believed, in Jesus Christ that God had revealed the Divine Self. No more books could or needed to be added to the canon, they believed, because that revelation was complete in the mighty act of God that these books described. Only at the return of Christ could something really new be added. The canon was complete because it pointed to Christ, who was complete.

It is, therefore, to the Gospels' story of Jesus' life and teachings that we turn next.

THE GOSPEL ACCORDING TO MATTHEW

E. J. Goodspeed writes:

> The Gospel of Matthew is the most successful book ever written. It has had the largest circulation, exerted the greatest influence, and done the most good.[23]

Nobody knows for sure why, but as the books of the New Testament were collected, Matthew was put first. The epistles of Paul were written earlier than any of the Gospels. Mark, not Matthew, was probably the first of the Gospels to be written. Yet Matthew was put first. Perhaps it was placed ahead of Mark because it seemed more complete than Mark; it added more of Jesus' teachings, such as the Sermon on the Mount. Perhaps it was put first because it is so full of quotations from the Old Testament that it was seen as the best bridge between the Old Testament and the New. Perhaps the compilers of the New Testament simply loved it most. Whatever the reason, the canon of the New Testament as we now have it implies that this is the proper place to begin.

Outline and Emphases

Did Matthew think of Jesus as a kind of "new Moses"? So some scholars have argued. The baby Moses was hidden from pharaoh; Jesus was hidden from Herod. Moses came out of Egypt; so did Jesus. Moses wandered in the wilderness; Jesus was tempted in the desert. From Mount Sinai, Moses delivered the law; from another mountain, Jesus delivered the Sermon on the Mount. Tradition attributed the first five books of the Old Testament, the Torah, the books of the law, to Moses. Matthew grouped Jesus' teachings into five major collections or discourses, the new "law" of the Christians. And when, after his resurrection, Jesus gives the Great Commission, in Matthew he does so from a Sinai-like mountain. That commission, as reported by Matthew, is not to preach the gospel to all nations, telling them good news. It is for "teaching them to obey everything that I have commanded you," the new law (Matt. 28:20).

It may be going too far to say that Matthew collected Jesus' teachings into five discourses because there were five books of Moses. Perhaps his organization was simply for convenient, ready reference as his book was used by teachers instructing new converts. If the convert was not now to live by the old Jewish law, how was he to live? As he pleased? By the time Matthew wrote, probably some Christians had misunderstood Paul as saying that. Matthew answers, By no means! "You have heard that it was said to those of ancient times . . . but I say to you. . . . " So Matthew quotes Jesus repeatedly in his first report of Jesus' teachings (Matt. 5). The old law was replaced by Jesus' commands.

Probably from the first century to the twentieth, students have memorized

THE GOSPEL ACCORDING TO MATTHEW
The Gospel of the King of the Jews

"All this took place to fulfill what had been spoken . . . through the prophets" (1:22).
"This is Jesus, the King of the Jews" (27:37).

1 Birth and Infancy: The King Is Born	3 Baptism and Temptation: The King Prepares	5 The Sermon on the Mount: The Kingdom Is Proclaimed	8 Miracle Stories, the Disciples, the Opposition: Conflicting Responses to the King	16 The Great Confession: The King Is Recognized	18 Teachings on the Way to Jerusalem: The Cost of the King's Company	21 The Last Week and Easter: The King Is Crowned	28
Ancestry and angelic announcement, 1	Jesus is baptized, 3 and withstands temptation, 4	Introduction: the Beatitudes, 5:1–16	Responses to Jesus' authoritative deeds, 8—9	Peter makes "the great confession," 16	Stories of the journey to the cross, with teachings about humility and sacrifice, 18—20	Palm Sunday: Jesus enters Jerusalem, 21:1–11	
Birth and plot by King Herod, 2		Relation of the kingdom to traditional laws, 5:17–48	Twelve respond by becoming apostles, 10	God confirms that confession on the mount of transfiguration, 17		Monday: Jesus cleanses the Temple, 21:12–17	
		to traditional ceremonial practices, 6:1–18	Opposition grows, 11—12			Tuesday: Jesus' enemies test him with questions, 21:18–25	
			Parables interpret these responses, 13				

THE GOSPEL ACCORDING TO MATTHEW (Continued)

1	3	5	8	16	18	21	28
Birth and Infancy: The King Is Born	Baptism and Temptation: The King Prepares	The Sermon on the Mount: The Kingdom Is Proclaimed	Miracle Stories, the Disciples, Opposition: Conflicting Responses to the King	The Great Confession: The King Is Recognized	Teachings on the Way to Jerusalem: The Cost of the King's Company	The Last Week and Easter: The King Is Crowned	
		and to traditional worldly concerns, 6:19–24	The pressures mount, 14—15			Wednesday: Judas bargains to betray him, 26:1–16	
		The standard of judgment in the kingdom, 7				Thursday: Last Supper and arrest, 26:17–56	
						Good Friday: Jesus is crucified, 27	
						Easter: Jesus is raised from the dead, 28	

Author: Traditionally Matthew, one of the Twelve, but actually its present form is from a later hand
Date: Probably around A.D. 85
Subject: The life, teachings, death, and resurrection of Jesus as the promised Messiah
Emphasis: Jesus is the Messiah, the king promised in the Jewish scriptures.

the outline of Matthew by counting off the five discourses on the fingers of one hand. (Jewish teachers were fond of numerical helps to the memory.) Between each of the following discourses, Matthew incorporated stories of Jesus' life, taken mostly from Mark:

1. How are citizens of the kingdom to live? The Sermon on the Mount provided clear guidance, set in relationship to Jewish law, tradition, and practice (Matt. 5—7).
2. How are traveling preacher-disciples to conduct themselves on their evangelistic journeys? Jesus' words as he sent out the Twelve supplied the answer (Matt. 10).
3. What were those parables Jesus told? Matthew gathered seven and put them together for ready reference (Matt. 13).
4. How shall Christians conduct themselves toward one another and as they face persecution? Jesus' words about humility and sacrifice, as he journeyed toward Jerusalem and his own martyrdom, provided the answer (Matt. 18—20).
5. How will history end? Matthew collected Jesus' eschatological sayings, predictions of the future and the end of the world, as a final discourse (Matt. 24—25).

Note how Matthew even marks each of these discourses with the phrase "when Jesus had finished saying these things" (Matt. 7:28; 11:1; 13:53; 19:1; 26:1).

Add the stories of Jesus' birth and infancy at the beginning of the book and of his death and resurrection at the end, insert between the discourses miracle stories and stories of Jesus' growing conflicts with his enemies, and the student in the first century or the twentieth finds in Matthew an easily remembered manual for Christian faith and practice.

But it was not simply as a "new Moses" that Matthew interpreted Jesus. Rather, he saw Jesus as the fulfillment of all of the Old Testament. Leaf through the first few chapters of Matthew in any modern translation that sets off Old Testament quotations as though they were poetry and one can see how, time after time, Matthew quotes from the Jewish scriptures. Fifteen times he uses the word "fulfill," often in some phrase such as "All this took place to fulfill what had been spoken by the Lord through the prophet" (1:22). So convinced was Matthew that the whole of the Old Testament was fulfilled in Christ that he could see every detail of Jesus' life as somehow foreshadowed there and could speak of passages in the Old Testament as related to Jesus in ways that would be more acceptable to his Jewish-Christian readers in the first century than to more "scientific" interpreters in the twentieth.

For example, Matthew sees the infant Jesus' return from Egypt as fulfilling the words originally spoken of Israel's deliverance from the land of the pharaoh. "Out of Egypt I have called my son" (Matt. 2:15; cf. Hos. 11:1). Seeing Jesus as, in some sense, a "new Moses," Matthew could interpret the story of the exodus—in ways modern scholars might call "figurative"—as referring also to Jesus. Similarly, the prophecy in Isa. 7:14 of a child to be named "Immanuel" as a sign of deliverance in Isaiah's day could be interpreted as referring to the newly born Emmanuel (Deliverer), Jesus.

It is especially as the prophesied king whose coming ushers in the prophesied kingdom that Matthew presents Jesus. Almost every saying and story of the Gospel can be understood as related to that theme in some sense.

Jesus' ancestry is traced through the kings of Judah. The birth stories set Jesus "who has been born king of the Jews" in contrast to King Herod. John the Baptizer announces that the kingdom is coming and later baptizes Jesus, who then must battle with Satan over the meaning of the heavenly voice that has addressed Jesus with a royal title. Jesus' first preaching is summarized, "Repent, for the kingdom of heaven has come near" (Matt. 4:17). Matthew 5—7 gives the new "law" of the kingdom. Kingly words of authority are followed by deeds of authority (Matt. 8—9), astonishing the crowds. Conflicts arise as the kingdom is proclaimed by Jesus and his disciples. Matthew 13 reports seven parables of the kingdom. At the "great confession," Peter and the disciples hail Jesus with titles reserved for the messianic king. Still speaking of the kingdom, Jesus goes to Jerusalem. As he is crucified, there is placed above his head that same title, "the King of the Jews" (27:37). He dies wearing a crown, but a crown of thorns. Soon, however, the risen Christ in Matthew announces, "All [kingly] authority in heaven and on earth has been given to me. Go, therefore and make disciples of all nations," teaching them to obey the king's commands (28:18).

No literary masterpiece such as the books of the New Testament can be described in a simple outline without threat of serious distortion. Matthew is a complex weaving together of themes and counterthemes. We have already given one outline, focusing on one emphasis of Matthew (see table on pp. 318–19). Others have described the "plot" of Matthew quite legitimately in other ways.[24]

Using the overview that this *Guide* provides of Matthew, however, we turn now to a part-by-part study of the Gospel.

Birth and Infancy:
The King Is Born (Matt. 1—2)

"Where is the child who has been born king of the Jews?" the mysterious Magi inquire (Matt. 2:2). Matthew answers first of all, in effect, "Squarely in the middle of the royal Davidic line of true Judean kings."

The Gentile Luke traces Jesus' ancestry from Adam, father of humankind. But to Matthew, Jesus is the son of King David of Israel and the son of Abraham, the father of the chosen people (Matt. 1:1).

It is through David and Solomon and the other kings that Jesus' ancestry is traced in the Gospel. The whole picture was so perfect to Matthew that he had to describe it with the use of sevens, the perfect, sacred number beloved of Jewish teachers. The whole ancestry from Abraham to Jesus is grouped in three pairs of sevens. It did not matter to Matthew that one must count some ancestor twice or that there are only forty-one names on the list and comparison with 1 Chron. 3:11–12 suggests that some names have been dropped. Matthew was using a Jewish teacher's way of subtly telling his readers that Jesus is the perfect prince of the royal line.

Luke tells the story from Mary's point of view, but Matthew concentrates on Joseph. (We defer discussion of the meaning of the virgin birth until our comments in the section on Luke.)

As we meet Mary and Joseph, they are engaged but not yet married. "Betrothal," or engagement, however, was a formal and very binding affair in Judea, with a public exchange of vows and the giving of a ring. Such betrothals often lasted a full year before the actual wedding. Couples were normally betrothed in their teens, brides in their early teens. There is no biblical basis for the tradition that Joseph was an old man.

Shocked at the discovery that his bride-to-be is pregnant, Joseph is ready to break the engagement. But an angel reassures him. Jesus is to be the fulfiller of prophecy. His name, Jesus, means "Savior"; the title "Emmanuel" means "God with us." Joseph, reassured that a miracle is taking place, goes ahead with the marriage.

Who are the Wise Men who come seeking the true-born "king of the Jews" in the court of the puppet pretender? For Matthew, they seem to represent the foreigners of the Gentile world who at the beginning of the story give a foretaste of the end. Matthew's is the most Jewish of the Gospels, repeatedly, in every way it can, presenting Jesus as the promised Jewish Messiah. Yet it is Matthew who, at the end of the Gospel, specifically speaks of "all nations" as destined to come under the rule of this King. Matthew structured his narrative so that in the beginning, with these worshipers from the East, he hinted at the Gentile mission to come.

The number of Wise Men is not given. Pious legend once set their number at twelve, later at three. Perhaps Matthew thinks of them as magi, Persian priests and astrologers, worshipers of the god of light, who wore round felt hats and long white robes. (The English word "magician" comes from "magi.") Modern astronomers have associated the star with the conjunction of Saturn, said to have been associated in the ancient world with the Jews, and Jupiter, symbol of kingship. This conjunction took place in 7 B.C., appeared, disappeared, and reappeared, as seems to have been the case with the Christmas star (Matt. 2:7–10).

Such speculation, however, may be a modern effort to ask questions about history and science of an account in which the author intends rather to express theological truth. Matthew's only interest is that these Gentiles learn from Micah's prophecy (2:5–6), journey with heavenly guidance to the ancestral home of the great King David, and there bring tribute to the newborn "king of the Jews." Having fulfilled their prophetic task, they disappear into the night.

However, that other king, Herod, remains. So fearful for his throne that he would murder even members of his own family, as we have seen, Herod is pictured as slaughtering every male infant in the village of Bethlehem. Even here, Matthew is sure, Herod is unwittingly fulfilling scripture (2:17–18). But Jesus, like Moses before him, escapes the cruel king, and after crossing the nearby border into Egypt, outside Herod's power, makes his exodus from Egypt some time later. Even then, the family takes up residence not back at Bethlehem but nearly a hundred miles to the north, in Nazareth.

From the beginning, Matthew is saying, there was conflict over King Jesus and the kingdom of God.

Baptism and Temptation:
The King Prepares (Matthew 3—4)

Some fascinating possibilities are opened up by the fact that the traditional location of Jesus' baptism is almost within sight of the cave in which the first Dead Sea Scrolls were found.

As news of the buried treasures of the Qumran commune spread west, a few scholars created a sensation by proposing that Jesus must once have been a member of an Essene community. That suggestion has been largely abandoned. But if John the Baptizer was associated with these holy ascetics, a number of questions may be answered. Why was he there in the wilderness, quoting Isaiah, denouncing the sins of the city, baptizing, and preparing for the coming of the messiah? At least the discovery of the Essene library lets us know that John was not the only Jew in the wilderness or the only one with concerns of this kind. Here are some parallels between John and the Qumran people:

Both had left the city for the rough, Wild West–like wilderness in the region of the Dead Sea.

Both led ascetic lives. John is pictured as wearing skins and eating grasshoppers. The Essenes renounced conventional family life and luxury.

Both renounced the sins of society. John preached against the Pharisees and Sadducees so vehemently that Matthew depicts him as calling them sons of snakes.

Both practiced a purification by water, some kind of ceremony related to forgiveness of sins.

Both looked for the imminent coming of the messiah and his kingdom.

The verse of Isaiah that Matthew uses to introduce his account of John the Baptizer is one repeatedly quoted in the Dead Sea Scriptures: "The voice of one crying out in the wilderness: 'Prepare the way of the Lord' " (Matt. 3:3).

Matthew summarizes John's message in one sentence: "Repent, for the kingdom of heaven has come near" (3:2). Whatever else that coming kingdom meant to John, it was to be a time of cosmic judgment. "Every tree therefore that does not bear good fruit is cut down and thrown into the fire" (3:10).

The crowds flocked to hear this wilderness preacher with the odd clothes and the threatening message. There seems reason to believe that popular Jewish thought of the time had regarded the era of the prophets as over. No more prophets would come until the kingdom dawned at the messianic age. But now, here was a prophet indeed, in the very pattern of the ancient Elijah, announcing the kingdom. A century and more after Jesus, there were traces of a John-the-Baptizer cult, still followers of the desert preacher.

Yet as Matthew describes him, John regarded his mission as only one of preparation. "I baptize . . . with water . . . but one who is more powerful than I is coming after me." He pictured that coming one also in terms of cosmic judgment. "His winnowing fork is in his hand" (3:11–12).

At this point, one must separate John from the Essenes. They had retreated from the world, as monks do to a monastery. John drew the world to him and sought to prepare the masses for what was coming. And while the Essenes dreamed of what would come, Matthew tells us that John recognized the One already come in Jesus.

Eager always to present Jesus in an exalted way, Matthew adds to Mark's account the report of John's proposal that he should be baptized by Jesus, not the other way around. But Jesus identifies himself with John's movement. "Let it be so now" (3:15). John baptizes him.

The significance of the baptism for Jesus, however, comes not in something John does but in something the Spirit of God does. Jesus, Matthew tells us, hears a "voice." There is no indication that the crowd heard the voice. Apparently we are to understand this as an inner experience. "This is my Son, the Beloved, with whom I am well pleased" (3:17).

Footnotes in many Bibles cross-reference the two phrases of this "voice" to two passages of the Old Testament. "This is my son" may be derived from Ps. 2:7. That psalm appears to have been a coronation song for a Hebrew king, given the exalted title "son of God." After the Hebrew monarchy perished, it was regarded as a prophecy of the coming of the great messiah king.

But the phrase "my Son, the Beloved, with whom I am well pleased" has also a completely contrasting origin. It seems to echo Isa. 42:1, the first passage of the songs of the "servant of the Lord." That servant is given as "a light to the nations" (Isa. 42:6). But the salvation that the servant brings comes through vicarious suffering:

> He was despised and rejected by others;
>   a man of suffering and acquainted with infirmity;
> . . . .
> Surely he has borne our infirmities
>   and carried our diseases;
> . . . .
> But he was wounded for our transgressions,
>   crushed for our iniquities;
> upon him was the punishment that made us whole,
>   and by his bruises we are healed. (Isa. 53:3–5)

If the "voice" was recalling these passages, what we are to understand is this: at the time of his baptism, two ideas were borne in on Jesus' soul. Of how he has lived and how he has thought of himself previously, Matthew gives us only one hint: Matt. 13:55 implies that Jesus' neighbors in Nazareth thought of him as living quite an ordinary life. But now Jesus feels a double and apparently conflicting call:

1. He is to be the promised King, the messiah, so exalted that he could be called "Son of God," to whom the psalmist could picture God as promising, "I will make . . . the ends of the earth your possession. You shall break them with a rod of iron" (Ps. 2:8–9).
2. He is to be the Suffering Servant who will be a "light to the nations" by giving his life vicariously for the world.

A careful search of rabbinic literature has yet to discover any Jewish writer of the time who put these two ideas together. The conquering messiah was one thing. The suffering servant was regarded as something else, probably persecuted Israel itself.

Now, however, Jesus feels himself called at the same time to be the Savior of the world and yet to save it by suffering and dying for it.

Mark describes Jesus' reaction as being driven into the wilderness by the Spirit. Matthew tells us that for forty days he did not even eat. Alone in the desert, he had to battle through the meaning of the apparent revelation that had come to him. What could it mean that he was to be King and Servant at the same time?

Television cameras cannot record spiritual struggles. Matthew, in pictorial terms, describes Satan as if he stood visibly before Jesus, addressed him audibly, and took him physically to various places. The meaning behind his graphic language, however, is that of Jesus' wrestling with the implications of the "voice" that had come to him. The temptations are divided into three,

Jewish writers having a love for that number. The first two are prefaced by the phrase translated "if you are the Son of God." The "if," however, might validly be translated "since": "Since you are the promised king . . ." The temptations offer three alternative paths to messiahship.

1. Jesus could be a bread king, an economic messiah. He replies that food is not what really matters (4:3–4).
2. Jesus could be a wonder-working sensation. He could do a public dive off the pinnacle of the Temple and so impress the crowds that his recognition factor and popularity ratings would make him invincible (4:5–7). Significantly, in the Synoptics, the miracles ascribed to Jesus seem always to be intended to help people, never to make a display of his power.
3. He could become the conqueror the Zealots had dreamed of, vanquishing the kingdoms of the world by the devil's methods. The One who taught "Love your enemies" could never choose that (4:8–11).

Each of these routes to messiahship Jesus rejects with a verse of scripture. Somehow he is to be the messiah by being the Servant of God. Already, Matthew is suggesting, there are hints of the coming cross.

The Sermon on the Mount: The Kingdom Is Proclaimed (Matthew 5—7)

"From that time Jesus began to proclaim, 'Repent, for the kingdom of heaven has come near' " (Matt. 4:17). In that one sentence, Matthew summarizes Jesus' whole message.

It can hardly be questioned that the announcement of the kingdom of God was the heart of Jesus' preaching. The first verse of the Sermon on the Mount promises it (cf. Matt. 5:3, 10, 19). Virtually every parable begins, "The kingdom of heaven is like" (see Matt. 13:31, 33, 45, 47). Such verses as Matt. 7:21; 8:11; 11:11; 16:19; 18:1; and 23:13 confirm the kingdom's centrality throughout the Gospel. When Jesus sends out his disciples to preach, it is with the same message that was originally announced by John the Baptist: "The kingdom of heaven has come near" (10:7).

That this summarizes Jesus' proclamation is clear. What is not so clear is what Jesus meant by it. Here are some divergent but widely held views.

The late Albert Schweitzer shocked the world of Christian scholarship with an interpretation commonly called *thoroughgoing eschatology*.[25] According to Schweitzer, when Jesus said that the kingdom had come near, he meant that the end of the world was just about to occur. Many texts seem to support that view. When Jesus sends out his disciples to preach, he tells them, "You will not have gone through all the towns of Israel before the Son of Man comes" (Matt. 10:23). Following the great confession by Peter, Jesus announces, "Truly I tell you, there are some standing here who will not taste death before they see the Son of Man coming in his kingdom" (16:28). His last discourse deals with the end of the world and includes the statement "Truly I tell you, this generation will not pass away until all these things have taken place" (24:34). According to Schweitzer, Jesus grew convinced that if he became the Suffering Servant prophesied in Isaiah, giving his life, God at Jesus' death would send the kingdom. When, on the cross, he realized that the end of the world did not seem to be coming, he cried in disillusionment, "My God, my God, why have you forsaken me?" (27:46). While some Christians have been horrified at the suggestion that Jesus could have proclaimed a mistaken time-table about the kingdom, others have replied that disappointment was part of the suffering that the Savior who was "tempted in all things like as we" had to endure.

The nineteenth-century *liberal view*, against which Schweitzer was reacting, proposed that Jesus thought of the kingdom as beginning first with his followers but gradually growing to include the whole world. The kingdom is compared to seeds that the sower sows (13:3–23), a mustard seed that grows into a tree (13:31), and the yeast that will leaven a whole lump of dough (13:33). Liberals liked to quote from Luke 17:20–21, "The kingdom of God is not coming with things that can be observed. . . . For, in fact, the kingdom of God is among you [or within you]." The kingdom, they said, was simply the response by more and more people to the rule of God in their hearts, an inner, growing fellowship.[26]

British scholar C. H. Dodd proposed a view often called *realized eschatology*.[27] According to Dodd, the kingdom actually did come with Jesus. Jesus, Dodd noted, defends himself to his enemies with these words: "But if it is by the finger of God that I cast out the demons, then the kingdom of God has come to you" (Luke 11:20). "The kingdom of God is among you" (Luke 17:21), wherever Jesus is. The first Christians went out to preach not just a future hope but something that had already begun. The era of death was ended with Christ's resurrection. The new age had begun. The kingdom might look small as a mustard seed now, but in the end its importance would be manifest to all.

More traditionally, many have understood the kingdom to mean *the church*.[28] With Jesus' death and resurrection, the world did not come to an end, but the Christian church as such did begin. While Matthew is the only Gospel that depicts Jesus as using the actual word "church" (and it is only in two places in Matthew), all the Gospels describe Jesus as calling a company of disciples and establishing a fellowship with them at the Last Supper. The rest of the New Testament says relatively little about "the kingdom," but the word "church" is used more than a hundred times. On that church, its members believed, God poured out the Holy Spirit, inaugurating a new age.

Perhaps most Christian thinkers are inclined to synthesize elements from all of these views. That the calendar is divided into B.C. and A.D. bears witness to the fact that a new age did dawn with the coming of Jesus. At the same time, most Christians still look forward to a future coming. Jesus, it must be noted, stated that neither he nor anyone else could predict exactly when the end would take place (Matt. 24:36).

Our records, then, are not entirely clear about any schedule for the coming of the kingdom, implying that the kingdom is somehow both present and future. What is made quite clear, however, is how men and women are to respond to the announcement of the kingdom, how citizens of the kingdom are to live. Two paragraphs after Matthew has summarized Jesus' preaching as "repent, for the kingdom of heaven has come near," he begins three chapters of collected sayings of Jesus about the lifestyle of citizens of that kingdom. Matthew 5, 6, and 7 are commonly called the Sermon on the Mount. They compose probably the best-loved summary of what Jesus had to say.

A look at the cross-references in most Bibles will show that sayings which Matthew has grouped together in these chapters are reported by Luke as having been given at various times during Jesus' career. Luke 6 does report a "sermon on the plain," but it is much shorter than Matthew's three chapters, and such familiar parts of the Sermon on the Mount as the Lord's Prayer are related by Luke to quite different contexts. We have seen that chronological order was not as important to the Gospel writers as theological order or patterns helpful for teaching. Matthew apparently has grouped these sayings together and put them right at the beginning of his account of Jesus' teaching to let his readers know from the start what he regards as the main things Jesus had to say about the new "laws" of the dawning kingdom.

Whether they were put together by Matthew or originally delivered as one address, these sayings do follow each other in a logical order. Matthew 5—7 can be outlined in various ways, such as the following:

1. Introduction: All the joy of the kingdom of heaven is now at hand for those who are willing humbly to accept God's gift (5:1–16).
2. With the coming of the kingdom, the traditional laws will no longer do. They are only halfway measures. Your King now commands complete purity, utterly unselfish love (5:17–48).
3. The traditional ceremonial practices will not help either. God's kingdom is a matter not of the external signs of piety but of the whole heart (6:1–18).
4. The old worldly concerns must be forgotten too. Food and clothes do not matter. You must concentrate on just one thing, God's rule, and leave everything else to God (6:19–34).
5. Conclusion: In the final examination, the judgment, only those whose whole lives are pointed toward serving God in love of their fellow human beings can meet the tests of the kingdom (Matt. 7).

Matthew, the good teacher, begins with three-times-three sayings in the easily remembered "beatitude" form. Because the word translated as "blessed" could well be translated as "happy," some have called these Jesus' rules for happiness. Others, however, have said that they should be read more nearly as exclamations: "Oh, the happiness of the poor in spirit, for theirs is the kingdom of heaven!" A. M. Hunter begins each beatitude with "Congratulations!"

The emphasis in the Beatitudes is on humility and openness to God and to one's fellows. "Poor in spirit" seems to mean "conscious of spiritual need," though some suggest it implies also identification with the poor and needy of the world. William Barclay identifies the happy mourner of verse 4 as one "whose heart is broken for the world's suffering and for his own sin, for out of his sorrow he will find the joy of God!"[29] The meek are those with power, but power under control. Mercy, purity, peacefulness, and a willingness even to undergo persecution are characteristics of citizens of the kingdom (5:7–12). Such people are the kind who can carry out God's mission to the world, who can be the world's "salt" and its "light."

The second half of the chapter focuses on the relationship of the kingdom's "law" to the law of Jewish tradition. The old law is not abolished, but it is transcended. The demands of the kingdom are even more radical than those of the Jewish scriptures (5:17–20).

Twice Jesus gives three specific examples of these radical demands (5:21–48): "You have heard that it was said . . . But I say. . . . " Specific areas of application are to the old laws against murder, adultery, putting away a wife without divorce proceedings, false swearing, exacting more than just retribution, and hating anyone other than one's enemy. In each case, Jesus' point is that the demands of the kingdom go so much further than the old law that they make the old obsolete. Not only murder but anger is now prohibited. Not only adulterous action but lustful thoughts are forbidden. Not simply careless putting away of one's wife but divorce itself is condemned. Not simply false swearing but all swearing is forbidden, unnecessary because of the honesty of the citizens of the kingdom. Not simply justice in retribution but no retribution, coupled with active concern for those who wrong us, is Jesus' command. And the commandment to love can no longer be limited to loving one's neighbor. Even enemies are to be loved. Such commands as these about loving even one's enemies constitute the heart of Jesus' ethical teaching.

Having dealt with the old laws, Jesus now deals with the old ways of showing one's religion. Almsgiving, prayer, and fasting were three pious practices that distinguished the most devout Jews. Jesus seems really to be making fun of those who make a display of such rituals. He laughs at the Pharisee who blows a trumpet to attract a crowd before dropping a coin in a beggar's cup. Such people are hypocrites, actors. What matters is not public practice but one's secret, inner concern (6:1–18).

That concern must be an undivided loyalty to the kingdom. In the crisis of the kingdom's advent, there is no longer any time for concern for material things. No second master can be tolerated. There is no room left for worldly cares and no need for them. Only one thing matters: the kingdom of God and its righteousness (6:19–34).

The coming of that kingdom means the coming of the judgment. But the standards by which we will be judged may be surprising. We will be judged by how judgmental we have been of other people. We will be judged by a Father's mercy; therefore we should treat others as we wish them to treat us. The standards are too narrow for most people. But those who can meet the tests of the kingdom can stand fast, no matter what storms may come (Matt. 7).

The Beatitudes (5:3–12), the Lord's Prayer (6:9–13), and the Golden Rule (7:12) have always been among the best-loved passages of the New Testament. The words about loving one's enemies (5:44) and turning the other cheek (5:39) have inspired not only Christians such as Martin Luther King, Jr., but also non-Christians such as the great nonviolent leader of the Hindus, Mohandas Gandhi.

Miracle Stories, the Disciples, Opposition: Conflicting Responses to the King (Matthew 8—15)

Curiously, what startled the crowd at the Sermon on the Mount the most was not what Jesus said but the way he said it. They "were astounded at his teaching, for he taught them as one having authority, and not as their scribes" (7:28–29). The typical Jewish rabbi claimed no authority for himself. He delighted rather in handing down what his teacher had said that *his* teacher had said. In utter contrast, a repeated refrain of the Sermon on the Mount had been, "You have heard that it *was* said . . . But *I* say. . . ." As we shall see, scholars debate in what sense, if any, Jesus claimed to be the Messiah. But evidently, one could not hear such teachings as those collected in the Sermon on the Mount and doubt that the teacher regarded himself as somehow uniquely related to God's kingdom. The crowd had reason to be "astounded."

Repeatedly, therefore, the Gospel comments on the reactions of people to Jesus. Some interpreters have said that what we know about Jesus consists not so much of historical facts as of the impression he made on people, the effect he had on the lives both of enemies and of followers. By describing the reactions of others, the Gospel writers subtly challenge the reader to decide how he or she also will respond.

Having, for three chapters, described Jesus' words of authority, Matthew now describes his authoritative deeds. Matthew 8 and 9 are largely a collection of miracle stories with comments on the contrasting responses these actions of Jesus began to elicit (the various responses are italicized in the examples that follow).

In direct violation of the law, Jesus touches a leper (8:1–4). Jesus does not contract leprosy. Rather, the leper *becomes clean!*

Jesus heals the servant of a Roman army officer who recognizes authority when he encounters it. This Gentile's response is contrasted with that of many of God's own people (8:5–13). The Roman has shown faith.

Jesus' healing of Peter's mother-in-law leads to a gathering of a crowd of people around Jesus (8:14–17). These people *bring needs.*

No partial response to his authoritative call will do. "Let the dead bury their own dead." "Follow me," Jesus commands (8:18–22). He demands the response of *commitment.*

Though people may hesitate, the winds and the sea obey him, and many men *marvel* (8:23–27).

But the reactions can be negative. After he healed the demoniacs but caused a stampede among the hogs (8:28–34), some people *begged him to leave.*

As Matthew develops the "plot" of his narrative, he builds suspense, tracing how that negative reaction gradually hardens, how the conflict increases. Scribes are *shocked* when Jesus claims authority to forgive sins (9:1–8). Jesus' willingness to fraternize with social and moral outcasts *offends* the Pharisees (9:9–13). Even John's disciples are *puzzled* (9:14–17). Yet in spite of Jesus' deliberate effort to avoid the spread of stories about his healing (9:27–31), "the report . . . spread throughout that district" (9:26). By the end of chapter 9, though the crowds still wonder what to make of such a man, the Pharisees are ready to *attack Jesus as being in league with the prince of demons* (9:32–34).

To summarize, Matthew repeatedly notes one or more of three kinds of response. Most people are simply amazed; they do not know what to think. A few are roused to hatred and begin to attack. But there are also a few who respond in faith and are healed or even, like Matthew himself in Matt. 9:9, answer Jesus' call and become his disciples.

Matthew 10 is devoted to these disciples, important characters in the narratives of all four Gospel writers. They are presented as an odd mixture, these twelve laborers in the kingdom "harvest" (9:37–38).

Peter is always listed first, is mentioned far more often than any of the others, seems to be identified as the leader in such passages as John 21:15–19 and Matt. 16:13–20, and clearly is the spokesman of the earliest church in Acts 2. A rather consistent picture emerges of his character: talkative, impulsive, unstable, capable of cowardice but also of repentance. In view of the tradition that the Gospel stories derive so largely from Peter through Mark, it is especially significant that the portrait we have of him is so honest, so far from flattering.

Andrew, his brother, seems less vocal, though it is noted that it was Andrew who first brought Peter to Jesus. John 1:35–42 identifies Andrew as having been a disciple of John the Baptizer.

James and John were, like Peter and Andrew, fishermen. Mark 1:19–20 speaks of their being associated with their father and with "hired servants," which may imply a relatively prosperous, established fishing business. John is traditionally identified as the "disciple whom Jesus loved," referred to repeatedly in the Fourth Gospel and as the author of that Gospel. Such passages as Mark 5:37; 9:2; and 14:33 imply that these two brothers, along with Peter, constituted the inner circle of the Twelve. Their mother hoped that they would receive the highest places in the kingdom (Matt. 20:20–28). What James actually received was the first martyrdom among the disciples (Acts 12:2).

Of the rest, little is said. Philip has a Greek name and is pictured in John 12:20–22 as instrumental in bringing certain Greeks to Jesus. Bartholomew is usually supposed to be the same as the Nathanael mentioned in John 1:47, "an Israelite in whom is no deceit," praise he so readily accepts that it may be intended to indicate that he is a Pharisee. Thomas is known as the doubter for his failure to believe in the first reports of the resurrection (John 20:24–29). Matthew is identified as a tax collector. Thus he was a social outcast, hated for collaborating with Rome. In complete contrast, Luke 6:15 calls the second Simon a Zealot, one of the militant opponents of the Romans. Of Thaddaeus and the other James we have no information even for conjecture. Last on the list, of course, is the traitor Judas. Later pious tradition told stories of the martyrdom of all but Judas.

Jesus sends the disciples out with the same message that he and John the Baptizer had proclaimed earlier: "The kingdom of heaven has come near" (Matt. 10:7). Matthew 10 now gives instructions to the disciples. They are to move rapidly. They are to expect, but not to fear, persecution. They are to heal as well as preach. Many scholars suggest that these sayings were remembered particularly and perhaps adapted for use by early Christian evangelists after the resurrection.

Chapters 11 and 12 pick up again the story of the varied reactions to Jesus: the questioning of John, the unrepentance of the cities, the faith of those who will accept his invitation. By 12:14, the opposition has reached such intensity, brought to a crisis related to the healing on the Sabbath of a man with a withered hand, that the Pharisees enter into the first plot to kill Jesus.

The longest parable of Matthew 13 is a kind of explanatory analysis of these varied responses. The various kinds of people are compared to various kinds of soil, responding differently to the "seed" of the gospel.

As the conflict grows, more and more frequently, Matthew's narrative implies, Jesus must withdraw from determined opposition. Herod's execution of John the Baptizer causes one withdrawal (14:13). Even his popularity with the people after feeding multitudes twice necessitates withdrawals (14:21–22; 15:38–39). An attack by the Pharisees and scribes over Jesus' failure to keep their traditions precedes another withdrawal (15:21). He is now forced to go to the borders of Galilee and even beyond (Matt. 15:21; 16:13). The last withdrawal takes Jesus all the way to Caesarea Philippi.

The Great Confession: The King Is Recognized (Matt. 16—17)

The great confession at Caesarea Philippi is the turning point in all three Synoptics. For the first time, at least according to Mark's chronology, Jesus' messiahship is openly discussed. Instead of withdrawing from his enemies, Jesus henceforth moves toward the center of his opposition. In Matthew, he now speaks of the founding of the church. For the first time, he clearly announces his intention of dying on a cross. And he now summons his disciples to go with him to Jerusalem and to die. These are developments that merit careful study.

We have seen that Jesus repeatedly was forced to withdraw from bitter opposition. By the time of the event described in Matt. 16:13–28, Jesus had retreated all the way to Caesarea Philippi, perhaps the farthest from Jerusalem he had ever traveled. (The retreat described in 15:21 may have been about the same distance.) There he was out of the reach of Herod Antipas, the Herod who had recently killed John the Baptizer. This distant location is itself significant.

Not only has Jesus withdrawn from enemies; he has retreated from crowds of followers attracted by bread and miracles. Far from claiming to be Messiah, he has repeatedly and sternly forbidden those whom he has healed to tell others about him (see Matt. 8:4; 9:30; Mark 1:25, 34; 3:12, etc.). The message with which he sent out the disciples was that of the nearness of the kingdom, not the coming of the promised Messiah. When John the Baptizer sent messengers to confront Jesus with the question "Are you the one who is to come?" Jesus replied enigmatically: "Go and tell John what you hear and see: the blind receive their sight, the lame walk, the lepers are cleansed, the deaf hear, the dead are raised, and the poor have good news brought to them. And blessed is anyone who takes no offense at me" (Matt. 11:4–6). Demons recognize him, and the crowd wonders. But Jesus refuses any title.

As early as 1901, the German scholar Wilhelm Wrede proposed an explanation for this "messianic secret." The early church, he suggested, had faced a problem. The first preachers were proclaiming that Jesus was the promised Messiah (in Greek, the word is "Christ"). But those who had heard Jesus preach could object that Jesus never made any such claim. Mark, Wrede argued, therefore invented the idea of the "messianic secret." Jesus knew that he was Messiah—Mark claimed—and the demons repeatedly recognized him. But Jesus chose to keep his identity secret. Actually, Wrede believed,

Jesus did not think of himself as the Messiah at all. His message concerned God and the kingdom, not himself.

While New Testament scholars since Wrede have had to deal with this question, by no means all have agreed with Wrede's solution to the mystery. If Jesus did not at least implicitly claim messiahship, why was he crucified? To many, it has seemed more likely that Jesus rejected such titles as "Messiah," "King," and "Son of God" not because he did not in some sense believe them to be properly his but because his understanding of the nature of his messiahship was so completely in contrast to the popular expectation. Jesus saw his role as being not that of a conqueror of Rome but that of the Suffering Servant who would give his life for humankind.[30] Only once did Jesus publicly claim the title "Messiah," but that was at the moment when the claim was sure to bring about his death. In Mark 14:61–62, as Jesus is on trial for his life, he is challenged by the high priest: "Are you the Messiah?" This time he replies, without any equivocation, "I am."

The Synoptic writers hesitate to try to read Jesus' mind or to enter into or speculate about his self-consciousness. Some insight as to what Jesus thought of himself may be found in the story of Peter's great confession.

Now a fugitive in the mountains, with only his closest followers accompanying him, Jesus himself raises the question concerning his identity. "Who do people say that the Son of Man is?" (Matt. 16:13). The answers give us insight into the popular perception of Jesus. People generally regarded him as another in the distinguished line of prophets, another Elijah, Jeremiah, or John the Baptizer.

Then Jesus asks, "But who do you say that I am?" Simon Peter replies, "You are the Messiah, the Son of the living God" (16:15–16).

With that confession, all kinds of new things suddenly begin to happen. In Matthew, Jesus accepts the title, blessing Peter for voicing it. With Peter's confession, Jesus announces the founding of the church. Jesus announces that he is going to Jerusalem to die, and he calls his disciples to accompany him, eventually to lose their own lives for his sake.

The meaning of Jesus' words to Peter have been the subject of bitter Protestant–Catholic controversy. To traditional Roman Catholics, the meaning has seemed simple. Jesus says, "You are Peter" (the Greek word *petros* means "rock"). "On this rock I will build my church" (16:18). To Peter, Christ has given the keys of the kingdom. These keys Peter, in turn, has passed down to his successors, the bishops of Rome, the popes.

Protestants have placed the emphasis on the confession, not on the man. If Peter becomes the foundation of the church, they have argued, it is simply that he is the first to voice this confession of faith in Jesus as the Christ. The power of the keys is given to the other apostles too—in Matt. 18:18, to all the church of believers. Many passages in the New Testament show Peter as a leader in the church, Protestant thinkers have admitted, but none attributes the infallible authority of a pope to Peter, much less to his successors.

The issue is not yet resolved.

In any event, no sooner has Jesus accepted the title "Messiah" and spoken of the church than he announces that he is going to Jerusalem to die. The disciples are shocked and protest vehemently. Instead of withdrawing his announcement, Jesus simply challenges them to come with him and to lose their lives too.

Just one week later, Jesus and three disciples are said to have experienced the only mystic vision of its kind recorded in the Gospels, the transfiguration. The disciples see Jesus with a shining face, talking with the long-dead Moses and Elijah (17:1–8).

Yet once again, Jesus announces his impending death (17:22–23). And now the geographic notations become more pointed (17:22, 24; 19:1; 20:17, 29; 21:1). He is on his way to Jerusalem and the cross.

Teachings on the Way to Jerusalem: The Cost of the King's Company (Matt. 18—20)

Three times Jesus is pictured as announcing that he is going to Jerusalem to die: Matt. 16:21; 17:22–23; and 20:18–19. Over the sayings that Matthew collected to form chapters 18—20 falls the shadow of the cross. All of the sayings are set in the context of the final journey to Jerusalem. While it may not be clear why every one of these sayings is recorded at this point, almost all can be seen as related to the concept of humility and loving sacrifice.

The disciples have recognized who Jesus is. Jesus has accepted the title "Messiah," or "Christ." But now he must help them understand the Servant's concept of salvation through sacrificial suffering.

It is not the ambitious but those who have childlike humility who will be greatest in the kingdom, Jesus explains to these future leaders in Matt. 18:1–6. Undivided loyalty is demanded (18:7–9). All souls, however insignificant or unworthy they may seem, are important in the kingdom. Therefore, citizens of the kingdom are to treat their brothers with the utmost loving patience. God has forgiven us. We must forgive others (18:10–35).

Even the demands of sex may have to be denied in favor of the absolute demands of the kingdom (19:10–12). Childlike humility is the key (19:13–15). The kingdom may demand that one give away everything else simply to follow Christ (19:16–22). The rewards of the kingdom are real, but they are for those who are willing to sacrifice, to be "last" rather than seeking to get ahead (19:23–30).

God alone will decide who is to receive the various rewards of the kingdom (20:1–16). Jesus himself will receive a cross, he reminds his followers (20:17–19). When the mother of James and John, ambitious for her sons, asks that they be given the top places in the kingdom that they feel is surely about to be established, Jesus, the Servant-Messiah, explains, "Whoever wishes to be great among you must be your servant, and whoever wishes to be first among you must be your slave; just as the Son of Man came not to be served but to serve, and to give his life a ransom for many" (20:26–28).

It is not the ambitious disciples but two blind beggars whose eyes are opened (20:34).

With these teachings, the company has arrived at Jerusalem, the city where Jesus will die.

The Last Week and Easter:
The King Is Crowned (Matt. 21—28)

The Gospels' story of Jesus' life is really the story of his death. From one-fourth to nearly one-half of each of the Gospels is devoted to just one week, the last. What has been said of Mark applies equally well to the other three: each Gospel is a passion narrative—a story of Jesus' death—with a long introduction.

As we have seen, Matthew used many literary devices to point us to what is coming. Now, as his story arrives at the account of Jesus' last week, the pace of the narration slows. The time sequence becomes clear as never before in the Gospel. We can trace Jesus' movements geographically and by the days of the week. From the night of his arrest, we can trace events almost hour by hour. The details are so full and vivid that many have suggested that an account of this last week must have been written before any of our present Gospels were set down.

Though scholars who challenge this chronology can be found, the traditional day-by-day sequence, celebrated by Christians in Holy Week ceremonies, seems well enough attested in Mark to be used as a framework for our study here.

Palm Sunday was the day of what has been called Jesus' "triumphal entry" (Matt. 21:1–11). The title is misleading. The little parade into Jerusalem was more in the nature of a nonviolent demonstration in the modern sense than anything military or "triumphant." On the surface, at least, nothing happened except that a group of Galilean pilgrims to the Passover feast shouted slogans while Jesus rode silently among them on a donkey.

However, more was involved. Probably Matthew is literally correct when he writes that "this took place to fulfill what had been spoken through the prophet" (21:4). Zechariah 9:9 had foretold one who would be a king but who would come riding on a donkey. A conquering king might enter a city riding in a war chariot. Zechariah had spoken of a king who would enter humbly, a king of peace. It may be that Jesus was deliberately acting out

Zechariah's prophecy, publicly claiming, without saying a word, to be this kind of king. Some have spoken of this as an "acted parable,"[31] the first of three symbolic actions of Jesus during this last week (the other two were the cleansing of the Temple and the Last Supper).

Two things support the view that Jesus may have been deliberately acting out his claim to this unique kind of messiahship. First, there are indications that the entry was deliberately, perhaps even secretly, arranged in advance, even with a kind of password for securing the donkey (Matt. 21:1–3). Second and more important, while Jesus had previously forbidden any public claim that he was Messiah, on this day he seems to have accepted without protest the crowd's acclamation of him as "Son of David" (the great King).

Monday was the day of the cleansing of the Temple. Matthew makes it appear that this second "acted parable" took place on Palm Sunday, but Mark's Gospel, on which most of Matthew's report seems to be based, makes it clear that the casting out of the money changers took place the following day.

At the time of the Passover, thousands of pilgrims from all over the Mediterranean world swarmed into Jerusalem. Obviously, a Jew who sailed from Ephesus or Corinth could not easily bring with him on the boat a lamb or even a pigeon for sacrifice (see Lev. 12:8). For the convenience of the pilgrims, such animals were sold in the Temple courtyard. Moreover, it was required that the sacrifices be bought with special coins. Those who swapped this Temple currency for the foreign money brought by the worshipers from many lands were allowed to make a sizable profit. The Passover had been commercialized; the Temple had become a market for profiteers.

Jesus was horrified. " 'My house shall be called a house of prayer,' " he quoted, "but you are making it a den of robbers" (Matt. 21:13). For one moment, at least, he turned over tables and drove out these salesmen of "piety for a price."

For Jesus' enemies, this was the last straw. Mark 11:18 tells us that it was in reaction to this episode that the chief priests and scribes began the final plot that, four days later, resulted in Jesus' death.

Tuesday has often been called "the day of conflict." Though they were ready now to kill him, Jesus' enemies were aware that he still had enormous support among a populace never far from riot and revolution. They therefore resolved to discredit him publicly by asking him questions that would have the effect of exposing the ignorance of the country carpenter. Matthew describes four such questions.

First, "By what authority are you doing these things, and who gave you this authority?" the religious authorities (the chief priests) demanded (21:23). Jesus had received no official training as a rabbi. He had not been appointed a priest. Who was he to say what should and should not go on in the Temple and to claim to be a teacher in Israel?

Jesus' answer was to return the challenge with a question of his own: What authority did John the Baptizer have? Unwilling to attack the revered memory of John and aware that to admit that John—and by implication, Jesus—could have authority apart from official channels, the priests retired in confessed confusion.

Matthew here reports three parables that interpret the whole tragedy of the rejection of Christ by the chosen people. Jesus' enemies were all the more frustrated (21:45–46).

Second, the Pharisees took their turn: "Is it lawful to pay taxes to the emperor, or not?" (22:17). The question was designed to place Jesus in a hopeless position either way he answered. If he said no, he could be prosecuted for advocating resistance to the Roman government. If he said yes, he would lose his popularity with the nationalistic crowd. Though on the surface Jesus' answer could be regarded as a clever evasion of a trick question, Christian interpreters see profound meaning in it. Jesus asked his hearers to note Caesar's picture and inscription on a Roman coin. Then he replied, "Give therefore to the emperor the things that are the emperor's, and to God the things that are God's" (22:21). Civic responsibility goes hand in hand with true religion. We read that the frustrated Pharisees "were amazed" and simply "went away."

Third, it was the Sadducees' turn (22:23–33). We have seen that this party rejected belief in a future life. Determined now to succeed where their opponents had failed, they came to Jesus with another trick question. Evidently, they were aware that Jesus had expressed belief in a life beyond death. What, they asked him, would be the future state of a woman who on earth had had seven husbands? Surely, it was implied, when she met all seven again in heaven, it would be a kind of hell.

Jesus gave a double reply. He said that there is no marriage in heaven, but more important, there is a future life. The basis on which he defended this faith was from that part of the Bible which the Sadducees themselves accepted as authority. God in Ex. 3:6 had identified God's self in this way: "I am . . . the God of Abraham, the God of Isaac, and the God of Jacob." "He is God not of the dead, but of the living," Jesus said (22:32). That is to say, God is a God who has a loving concern for living individuals. Such a God will not simply let beloved people die.

Far from destroying his influence with the people, the Sadducees' question had brought Jesus new acclaim as a teacher (22:33).

Finally, the Pharisees made a last attempt. This time, however, the question was a legitimate, if enormously difficult, one: Of all of the many sayings of the Jewish scriptures, which is the greatest law? Jesus' answer this time was straightforward, and its report serves Matthew as a kind of summary of this aspect of Jesus' teaching: " 'You shall love the Lord your God with all your heart, and with all your soul, and with all your mind.' This is the greatest and first commandment. And a second is like it: 'You shall love your neighbor as yourself.' On these two commandments hang all the law and the prophets" (22:37–40).

The questioning ends with a quotation by Jesus from Psalm 110, the passage from the Old Testament quoted more than any other in the New Testament. As understood here and elsewhere, it points to the Messiah as greater even than David himself (Matt. 22:41–46).

Having put his enemies temporarily to flight, Jesus, in complete contrast to his pattern of withdrawal earlier in his ministry, now gives a lengthy and public denunciation of the scribes and Pharisees. The entire twenty-third chapter of Matthew is devoted to an attack in which he brands them as hypocrites, blind fools, whitewashed tombs, snakes, and children of hell. By the end of this day, leaders of all influential factions must have been ready to cooperate in destroying him.

The last of Matthew's five great collections of Jesus' teachings is in some ways the most puzzling. Matthew 24—25 contains Jesus' "Little Apocalypse," his teachings on eschatology, the doctrine of the last things, the end of the world.

We have already noted that there is great difference of opinion concerning how the sayings of Jesus about the end time are to be interpreted. In one sense, it may seem quite simple. "Truly I tell you, this generation will not pass away until all these things have taken place" (24:34). As it stands, such a verse seems to make clear that Jesus expected the end of the world within his lifetime. Cosmic signs and catastrophes seem to be prophesied as preliminaries to the final, cataclysmic event. The faithful are to stand fast, however, in the assurance of imminent deliverance.

More careful study, however, suggests that one must be cautious about accepting too certain a schedule. For one thing, it is to be noted that Jesus' discourse is in reply to two questions. The disciples ask: (1) When will the Temple be destroyed? and (2) When will the end of the world be? (24:1–3). We have seen that Matthew put together sayings of Jesus on similar subjects even though they were spoken at different times. It is possible that some of the sayings of Jesus in Matthew 24 may be thought of as referring to the destruction of the Temple, which occurred in A.D. 70, within the lifetime of many of his hearers, rather than to the end of the world.

There are hints that Jesus expected a future for this world long enough that "this good news of the kingdom will be proclaimed throughout the world, as a testimony to all the nations; and then the end will come" (24:14).

And finally, it may be noted that Jesus flatly states that neither he nor anyone else knows either the day or the hour of the end time (24:36). We are to be always ready, for no one knows when the end will be (24:44; 25:13).

What we have in Matthew 24, then, is a discourse in the standard apocalyptic form, which was beloved by Jews of the first century. That pattern is described in this *Guide* in the section on the book of Revelation. Almost all of the characteristics of such literature described there appear in Matthew 24. In a sense, Jesus is simply depicted in this Gospel as using a standard literary device. What is significant is the meaning he imparts to this pattern, the particular use to which he puts it. That characteristic, uniquely Jesus-like addition is found in the parable with which the discourse ends (25:31–46).

In that parable, one finds the standard imagery of conventional Jewish apocalyptic literature. There is the throne, the judgment, the division of the saved from the lost, and the sentencing of people to heaven or hell. Up until this point, we have been on familiar ground.

But now a new standard of judgment is introduced: "As you did it to one of the least of these who are members of my family, you did it to me" (25:40). The way one treats the poor, the sick, the prisoner, the least worthy, will in the end turn out to be the way one has treated the Judge. No other apocalypse before had proposed quite that.

According to Matthew, that was the last—and some would say the greatest—parable Jesus ever told.

Wednesday has been conventionally referred to as the day of rest in Bethany. Jesus seems to have stayed in this suburb of Jerusalem with friends, walking the two or three miles into the city each morning.

Only two events are recorded. A woman enters the house where Jesus was staying and pours expensive ointment on his head. Jesus now accepts the gesture of worship without protest and interprets it as a prelude to his death (26:6–13).

On the same day, Judas makes his bargain to betray his Lord for thirty pieces of silver (26:3–5, 14–16).

It is not entirely clear either what Judas did or why he did it. Because we read that the next night he led a band of police to the garden of Gethsemane, it seems likely that what he did for Jesus' enemies was to show them Jesus in a remote place. There they could arrest him without fear of the rebellious crowd and have him safely in the hands of Roman authorities by morning.

The only motivation given is money. It seems incredible, however, that one expecting to receive a high place in a kingdom to be established at any moment should exchange an anticipated throne for thirty coins. Some have proposed that Judas was simply impatient. Jesus had been three days in what should have been his capital city. He had done nothing but talk. Judas hoped to force Jesus now to act, to begin the revolution that Judas understood him to have been promising. Others have supposed that Judas had become completely disillusioned. The promised kingdom had not and would not come. He would make the best bargain he could. Thirty pieces of silver was better than nothing.

Maundy Thursday is the name traditionally given to the night of the Last Supper (26:17–35).

The Passover, still faithfully celebrated today in the homes of millions of religious Jews, is a feast in which each family commemorates the rescue of the Hebrew people from Egypt in the days of Moses. Exodus 13:1–16 describes its institution. Each part of the meal was to be significant. The lamb was a sacrifice to God. The herbs were to be bitter, a reminder of the sufferings of slavery. The bread was unleavened, for there had been no time for yeast to make dough rise on the night the Israelites escaped. A son had died, the Exodus story said, in every home where the blood of the lamb was not sprinkled on the doorposts. The rescued people had been led by Moses to Mount Sinai, where they had entered into a covenant with God.

In conventionally Jewish fashion, Jesus ate the Passover with his disciples. But now he made of this traditional ceremony a third "acted parable." As he broke the bread and passed it to his disciples, he announced, "This is my body." The cup, too, was given new meaning. "This is my blood of the covenant, which is poured out for many for the forgiveness of sins" (Matt. 26:26–29). A new covenant was being announced, with a new people. This covenant was to center on a new sacrifice, Jesus' own sacrifice, to be accomplished the next day. Variously called the Lord's Supper, the Communion service, the Eucharist, or the Mass, the reenactment in different forms of this meal has been the heart of Christian liturgy from that time on.

Some years ago, a resolution was proposed in the Knesset, the Israeli Parliament, that the condemnation of Jesus of Nazareth be declared invalid. The one who made the motion did not mean to determine one way or another whether Jesus was guilty of the charges on which he was executed. He simply noted that there appeared to be such irregularities in the judicial procedures that the trial should be declared illegal. The Knesset rejected the proposal on the grounds that it could scarcely reverse an action of a Jewish Sanhedrin of more than nineteen hundred years ago, its court records long ago lost. The resolution did have the merit, however, of noting that the report of the trial, at least as we have it, suggests a kind of legal lynching.

Seized in secret, Jesus is tried at midnight, evidently by enemies concerned to push through a verdict of guilty. No convincing witnesses, however, can be found to accuse Jesus of any major crime. But now the high priest places Jesus on the witness stand. He has heard a rumor, at least, that Jesus claims to be the Messiah. Perhaps there is an opportunity here. "Tell us if you are the Messiah, the Son of God" (26:63). Though Matthew elaborates Jesus' answer, Mark 14:62 quotes Jesus as giving the completely unambiguous reply "I am." That declaration on the part of such a man was enough. It was blasphemy. To the Jews, blasphemy was a capital offense. The trial was no longer needed. The torture could begin.

Outside, the other disciples had run away, and Simon Peter was denying that he had ever heard of Jesus (Matt. 26:69–75).

On *Good Friday,* the Romans crucified Jesus.

Jewish readers have sometimes found what has seemed to be an anti-Semitic bias on the part of certain New Testament writers, including Matthew. Whether that bias is really present or not, anti-Semitism has surely been one of the besetting sins of Christians down through the centuries. So-called Christians have branded Jews as "Christ killers" and have harassed and persecuted them in horrible ways throughout history. Such actions, however, really have not the slightest justification in the Gospels. Whatever their private prejudices may have been, the biblical writers correspond in present-ing the crucifixion as the sin of all humankind, not of any particular race. The African-American spiritual is wisely addressed to all people when it asks rhetorically, "Were you there when they crucified my Lord?" The implied answer is yes, whatever the racial or religious background of the one who answers. This, surely, is the fundamental meaning of the New Testament's teaching about responsibility for Jesus' death.

But even if one deals with the historical facts more narrowly, the responsibility rests equally on Romans, other Gentiles, and Jews. Apparently, Jewish courts were not allowed to carry out sentences requiring capital punishment. Therefore Jesus was taken to the Roman procurator (governor), Pilate. Jesus gave this lackey of the Roman emperor the only response he deserved: "he gave him no answer" (27:14). Seeking to curry favor with the people, Pilate offered to release to the gathering crowd one political prisoner, apparently hoping they would choose the innocent Jesus. Stirred up by their leaders, however, the mob demanded Barabbas, probably a Zealot. Unable to find any crime in Jesus but unwilling to stand against the crowd, Pilate attempted to abdicate responsibility by washing his hands of the whole affair (27:24). It was a futile gesture.

Now, at last, the King was crowned, but with thorns (27:27–31).

Crucifixion was death by slow torture through exposure. Regarded as too cruel for use on Roman citizens, it was a death for criminal slaves. In spite of familiar pictures to the contrary, it seems usually to have been the case that the condemned prisoner carried not the entire cross but only the crosspiece to the place of execution. The upright section of the cross would already have been planted in the ground. It was the custom that the charges on the basis of which a criminal was executed were placed over his head. The inscription over Jesus' head read: "This is Jesus, the King of the Jews" (27:37). Thus the narrative of Jesus' death echoes the title voiced by the Wise Men at Jesus' birth.

The story of the death is told with an economy of words, suggesting rather than spelling out the details of the torture. Brief mention is made of the carrying of the cross, the refusal of a pain-killing drug, the ridicule from the crowd and even from the others being executed, and the continuing thirst.

The climax of suffering is indicated in one horrible cry, often called the "cry of dereliction." It was so firmly rooted in Christian tradition that it was remembered even in its original form in the Aramaic, the language Jesus spoke: " 'Eli, Eli, lema sabachthani?' that is, 'My God, my God, why have you forsaken me?' " (27:46). Some scholars, recognizing that these words are a quotation from Psalm 22, have interpreted them as implying that Jesus was quoting a psalm that ends with assurance of victory. There is no hint, however, in the Synoptics that the "happy ending" of the psalm was in Jesus' mind. Rather, it is a cry of the utmost spiritual torment. Even God seemed to have abandoned Jesus.

One might imagine that the Christian church would have tried to cover up the fact that its founder had died in an agony of defeat. The ancient world still thrilled to Plato's story of the death of Socrates: calm, content, unconcerned in the face of death. Yet far from concealing the story of Jesus' death in misery, the New Testament writers made it the very center of their accounts. The spiritual torment was, for them, even more important than the physical torment. The disappointment, loneliness, and sense of failure that overcame Jesus are made as clear as his bodily suffering. Socrates died in the complacency of self-assured reason; Jesus died in the agony of self-sacrificing love. Even the pagan executioners were moved. "Truly this man was God's Son!" (Matt. 27:54).

On *Easter,* the good news began to be spread: Jesus is risen!

As is noted in the section on Luke's Gospel, our accounts of the events of Easter and the days immediately following it are difficult to put together. No description of the actual resurrection is given. The order and even the location of the appearances of the risen Christ are reported differently in the various accounts. The early records agree completely, however, on one great fact: he rose. For the first Christians, that was the only fact that mattered.

Explanations that offer alternatives to the Christian belief that Jesus really rose have been less than satisfying. Matthew seems to have been familiar with an attempt to brand the story of the resurrection as a hoax perpetrated by the disciples, who stole the body of Jesus in the night (28:11–15). Efforts have been made from time to time to reassert this idea. But people rarely go out and "turn the world upside down" under the inspiration of self-perpetrated hoax. Others have suggested that the disciples were the victims of visions, hallucinations brought on by wishful thinking and expectations encouraged by words of Jesus. There is every indication, however, that the awareness of the resurrection came as a complete surprise to the utterly discouraged followers of Jesus.

Something happened that changed Peter. Once a coward who, before a serving maid, denied even having known Jesus, now he was ready to announce Jesus' messiahship before the very court that had recently condemned Jesus to death. Something happened that turned the scattered, frightened disciples into the nucleus of a dynamic, rapidly spreading church.

Matthew's account of what happened is this: On Sunday morning, two women went to the tomb, found it empty, and were told by an angel that Jesus was risen. The reassembled followers now met in Galilee. There Jesus appeared to them, again, like Moses, on a mountain. Now he spoke with full kingly power. "All authority in heaven and on earth has been given to me. Go therefore and make disciples of all nations, baptizing them in the name of the Father and of the Son and of the Holy Spirit, and teaching them to obey everything that I have commanded you. And remember, I am with you always, to the end of the age" (28:18–20).

The only "proofs" the New Testament was to offer of the resurrection were these: the testimony of these and other witnesses, the life of the spreading church, and the continuing experience of that promised presence.

With this proclamation of Jesus' final words, the "Great Commission," Matthew calls his reader to his or her own decision of response.

THE GOSPEL ACCORDING TO MARK

Four Gospels, the early church felt, were too good to lose. When it collected its sacred books, the church put Matthew first, perhaps because it loved Matthew most. But it did not abandon the other three. Even though ninety percent of Mark was reproduced in Matthew or Luke, they preserved it, and Luke was equally treasured.

Discussion of the Fourth Gospel, John, the climax of the New Testament, is delayed until the last chapter of this *Guide*. We now focus on the distinctive contributions of the second and third Gospels, Mark and Luke.

Much twentieth-century scholarship has attempted to get behind our Gospels to their sources. The goal has been to try to determine what was said about Jesus before our Gospels were written down. More recent scholarship, however, has also been interested in what it has called *redaction criticism* (and other, newer kinds of literary criticism). Redaction criticism is the study of how the Gospel writers put together their material, how they edited and composed their narratives. What their sources were we will never know for sure. What we can work with are their finished products.[32]

In this section and the next, therefore, we look at some of the major themes around which Mark and Luke organized their reports of stories and sayings of Jesus. We do not go through either Gospel in detail or outline these Gospels. Their basic framework is the same as Matthew's. Because most of the content of Mark is reproduced in Matthew, it is not discussed again here. Rather, we look at the special emphases that distinguish the second and third of the Synoptics. What in these narratives makes these stories different from the other Gospels?

Studying Mark was once regarded as rather a waste of time. Early nineteenth-century biblical scholars thought of this Gospel as simply a cut-down version of Matthew.

A century later, Mark was the most studied book in the Bible. Two ideas concerning Mark seemed to make it our most important source of information about Jesus. First, it was regarded as our oldest source, closest to the events it described, probably based on Peter's preaching, and thus, historically, most trustworthy. Second, it was regarded as having the least theological "bias," presenting Jesus "objectively" as the man he really was, not "distorting" the story by reading into it speculation about his divine nature.

The first idea, though challenged today by many reputable scholars, is still widely held.[33] The tradition that the Gospel is the work of Mark, a companion of Peter, who wrote it shortly after Peter's death, is ancient. Detective-like efforts to get behind Mark's writing to oral or written sources have not produced unanimous agreement. Many scholars feel that the story of Jesus' death, the "passion narrative," is so full of vivid and apparently accurate details that it must have been written much earlier than Peter's death (A.D. 64 or 65). Others have suggested that the "Little Apocalypse" (Jesus' teachings about the end of the world) in Mark 13 may have been a written source. Some have noticed a curious duplication of stories in Mark 6:30–7:23 and Mark 8:1–21. There, in the same sequence, are two feedings of multitudes, two crossings of the lake, two disputes with the Pharisees, and two discourses related to food. Perhaps, it is argued, Mark found two accounts of the same events; they had become so different in being told and retold that he did not recognize their basic identity. At best, however, reconstruction of Mark's sources can now be only more-or-less convincing speculation. There are good reasons to believe that the Gospel according to Mark is our oldest written Gospel, that it does come from the church at Rome, and that it may indeed have been written quite soon after Peter's death. That it seems to anticipate the fall of Jerusalem (which occurred in A.D. 70) and that it pauses to explain certain Jewish customs or terms to Gentile readers are facts that fit in nicely with the traditional account of the Gospel's origin. Thus, for our knowledge of the life of Jesus, Mark's Gospel as we have it is our first, basic source of information.

But that Mark is free of theological "bias" has been shown to be completely false. For all of the many human touches in its story of Jesus, Mark lives up to the promise of its opening phrase. Here is "the beginning of the good news of Jesus Christ, the Son of God." Mark, too, is preaching a kind of sermon, giving a theological interpretation concerning who he believes Jesus is: "Christ" and "Son of God." He understands Jesus' death as a "ransom" that will bring the salvation of many (Mark 10:45). He is sure Jesus is the "Son of man" who will come at the end to judge the world. Indeed, one might trace the "plot" of the Gospel as being the gradual recognition and revelation of the "secret" that Jesus is all of these things. Mark begins by telling us that at his baptism, Jesus hears God tell him, "You are my Son, the Beloved" (1:11). At the center of his Gospel, Mark tells how the disciples, on the mount of the transfiguration, hear God say, "This is my Son, the Beloved" (9:7). And at the end of the Gospel, even the Gentile centurion who has crucified Jesus realizes who Jesus is. He cries, "Truly this man was God's Son" (15:39).

Though Greek scholars speak of Mark's relatively rough style, his little booklet is a work of inspired genius. Mark originated a completely new literary form, the Gospel, quite unparalleled in Greco-Roman or Hebrew literature. He filled his seemingly simple account of the events in the life of one man with highly complex theological concepts. Virtually every line of the book bears witness to Mark's faith in Jesus as the Christ (the Anointed One or Messiah) and Son of God. And almost every line at least subtly calls on the readers, themselves facing persecution, to remain faithful, even though they, like their Master, may be on the way toward martyrdom.

Jack Dean Kingsbury classifies the "plot" of Mark's Gospel as a "conflict story":

> At the center of the conflict of Mark's story is Jesus. His struggle is, on the one hand, with Israel (the religious authorities and the crowd) and, on the other hand, with the disciples.[34]

Jesus' struggle with the disciples is to overcome their ignorance of who he is and of his mission. With Israel, it is to win reception of him as God's agent and of the kingdom he ushers in. Though the leaders of Israel crucify him, Jesus is raised from the dead to win in the end—and the disciples, it is implied, at last understand. The response to which the story leads its readers is that they become Jesus' followers too.

Mary Ann Tolbert proposes that after Mark's introduction, two parables help define the two major sections of the book. The parable of the sower (4:1–20) is a summarizing picture of the first half (Mark 1—10), in which Jesus "sows" the "seed" of the gospel of the kingdom everywhere. But the parable of the vineyard (12:1–11), climaxed with the killing of the owner's son, serves as a synopsis of the second half (Mark 11—16).[35]

Within that framework, there are three themes Mark especially develops as he tells this story.

A Call to Faithfulness in the Midst of Persecution

Set Mark's writing in its context, Rome at the time of Nero's horrid persecution of Christians, and its words about the cross come alive with new meaning. The Roman historian Tacitus tells in gruesome detail the situation that Mark's readers faced. It had been rumored that Nero himself had started the fire which, in A.D. 64, had destroyed much of Rome. Tacitus writes:

> To dispel the report Nero made a scapegoat of others, and inflicted the most exquisite tortures upon a class hated for their abominations, whom the populace called Christians. The Christus from whom the name had its origin had been executed during the reign of Tiberius by the procurator Pontius Pilate. The mischievous superstition was thus checked for the moment, but was reviving again, not only in Judea, the original seat of the evil, but even in the capital, where all that is anywhere hideous or loathsome finds its center and flourishes. Accordingly some were first put on trial; they pleaded guilty, and upon the information gathered from them a large number were convicted, not so much on the charge of arson as because of their hatred of humanity. Wanton cruelty marked their execution. Covered with skins of wild beasts they were torn in pieces by dogs, and thus perished; many were crucified, or burned alive, and even set on fire to serve as an illumination by night, after daylight had expired. Nero had offered his own gardens for the spectacle, and exhibited races, mingling with the crowd in the garb of a charioteer, or himself driving. Hence, even for criminals who deserved extreme and exemplary punishment, there arose a feeling of compassion; for it was not, it seemed, for the common weal, but to glut the cruelty of one man, that they were being destroyed.[36]

In all probability, among the many who died in that persecution were Peter and Paul.

It was in that situation that Mark wrote to Christians who were facing the possibility of being crucified, burned alive, or even "set on fire to serve as an illumination." To them he wrote that Jesus had said on the way to his own death, "If any want to become my followers, let them deny themselves and take up their cross and follow me. For those who want to save their life will lose it, and those who lose their life for my sake, and for the sake of the gospel, will save it" (8:34–35).

Thus Mark's story of Jesus' life was written almost as much as a story of Jesus' death, a death in which Jesus' followers were all too likely to share.

Here we recall Martin Kähler's famous saying that the Gospel is "a passion narrative [a story of Jesus' death] with an extended introduction." Nearly half of Mark is devoted to Jesus' journey to Jerusalem and the last week of his life. But even of the rest of the book, Willi Marxsen has written that Mark was composed "backward"—that is, even the first chapters of Mark are written with repeated hints of the cross that is coming at the end.

Norman Perrin proposes that there is a kind of three-way parallelism in Mark.[37] The Gospel begins with John the Baptizer, who came preaching and was "delivered up" to his martyrdom. Jesus came preaching and was "handed over" to be crucified. But also the disciples, Jesus' followers, are sent out to preach, and they are warned explicitly that "they will hand you over to councils; and you will be beaten in synagogues; and you will stand before governors and kings because of me" (13:9).

Mark begins with John the Baptizer, who was to be killed by Herod. As early as the second chapter, Mark pictures Jesus as warning the disciples, with regard to himself, that "the days will come when the bridegroom is taken away from them" (2:20). By the next chapter (3:6), Jesus' enemies are already plotting to kill him. And in the next chapter, a parable warns that Satan will attack all who sow the word (4:15). "Teacher, do you not care that we are perishing?" his frightened disciples say in the storm (4:38). They are saved by his authoritative voice.

After Peter's great confession (Mark 8:27–30), Jesus is pictured as clearly announcing two things: he is going to die, and his disciples will have to die for him. Three times, Jesus specifically foretells his coming death (8:31; 9:31; 10:33). Each such saying is followed by a demand that the disciples sacrifice too. "Those who are ashamed of me and of my words in this adulterous and sinful generation, of them the Son of Man will also be ashamed" (8:38). "Whoever wants to be first must be last of all and servant of all" (9:35). "Whoever wishes to be first among you must be slave of all. For the Son of Man came not to be served but to serve, and to give his life a ransom for many" (10:44–45).

Over and over, Mark tells his readers, who were then facing the very kind of persecution about which he says Jesus warned, that the disciples failed to understand. Indeed, some have said that Mark's narrative is the story of three conflicts: Jesus' conflict with Satan and his demons, Jesus' conflict with the Pharisees, and Jesus' conflict with his disciples.

"Do you still not perceive or understand? Are your hearts hardened?" Jesus demands of them. "Do you not remember? . . . Do you not yet understand?" (8:17–21). When Peter, who has just made the great confession, tries to separate salvation from martyrdom, Jesus calls him Satan (8:32–33). He repeats his announcement of the cross, but "they did not understand what he was saying" (9:32). There are repeated promises to those who sacrifice for Christ. "For those who want to save their life will lose it, and those who lose their life for my sake, and for the sake of the gospel, will save it" (8:35). "Truly I tell you, there is no one who has left house or brothers or sisters or mother or father or children or fields, for my sake and for the sake of the good news, who will not receive a hundredfold now in this age—houses, brothers and sisters, mothers and children, and fields with persecutions—and in the age to come eternal life" (10:29–30).

Yet still the disciples do not understand. Before and after the section concentrating on this instruction of the disciples, Mark sets a story of a blind man who receives his sight (8:22–26; 10:46–52). The disciples, however, remain blind until the resurrection. When Jesus is arrested, Mark tells us—with such candor that his account surely must be historical, not just the invention of a disciple afterward—that the disciples all "deserted him and fled" (14:50).

However historical all this may indeed be, there are several hints that make it clear that Mark was not simply writing about disciples of the year A.D. 30, he was telling his story to later disciples. The warnings and the promises are addressed to "any" (8:34). "Whoever" would be first must be a servant (10:44).

The address to future disciples is most clearly stated in Mark's "Little Apocalypse" (Mark 13). We noted in our discussion of the parallel passage in the section on Matthew how difficult it is to understand this discourse. But one message is clear: Jesus is depicted as predicting to his disciples that they will be persecuted. "When they bring you to trial and hand you over, do not worry beforehand. . . . Brother will betray brother to death, and a father his child, and children will rise against parents and have them put to death; and you will be hated by all because of my name. But the one who endures to the end will be saved" (13:11–13).

And lest any think that these words referred only to those disciples actually present when Jesus spoke them, Mark reports a final note at the end of the discourse: "What I say to *you* I say to *all:* Keep awake" (13:37; italics added).

To early Christians facing the possibility of literal crucifixion, Mark wrote of Jesus' own leadership in facing death. There is symbolism as well as history in his moving notation: "They were on the road, going up to Jerusalem, and Jesus was walking ahead of them" (10:32).

Apocalyptic Battle with the Forces of Satan

As Mark saw it, the struggle that cost Jesus his life and in which Christians were challenged to risk theirs was not simply a this-worldly conflict with human opposition. It was really a battle with Satan and his legion of demons, a cosmic spiritual conflict with a hellish host.

Some ages have found it easier to think in such terms than has our own. The Old Testament speaks of Satan, Belial, and the obscure Leviathan. Mark also speaks of Beelzebul (3:22). Revelation, which develops most fully the idea of cosmic conflict, adds the names "Abaddon" and "Apollyon." By the seventeenth century, when Urbain Grandier was burned after one of history's last great trials for sorcery, he could name Ashtoreth, Essas, Celsus, Acaos, and Cedon, the fallen thrones; and Alexh, Zabulon, Nephtalius, Cham, Nriel, and Achas, the distressed principalities. Indeed, one medieval computation estimated the number of demons at 1,758,064,176, rather more devils than there were people at that time. More conservative sixteenth-century reports, one notes with a certain relief, limited the number to only around 7,500,000. The rise of modern science and the era of the "Age of Reason" in the

seventeenth and eighteenth centuries directed attention toward more natu-
ralistic interpretations of human experience. The latter part of the twentieth
century saw a curious revival of interest in satanism and the occult.

While a modern psychiatrist might explain the phenomenon in different
terms, evidently, in the first century, afflictions popularly diagnosed as
demon possession were all too common. The Jewish historian Josephus tells
us that he personally witnessed the exorcism of one demon; the evil spirit
was drawn out through the patient's nose, with the exorcist using a ring that
was said to be a relic of King Solomon, who had died a thousand years
earlier. Jews boasted that the emperor of Rome had once turned to a rabbi to
exorcise a demon from his royal daughter. Evidently, certain Pharisees were
believed to be skilled in curing demoniacs (Matt. 12:27).[38]

Over and over, Mark depicts Jesus as casting these evil spirits out of the
people whom they have possessed. One indication of a factual basis for
Mark's repeated stories of such cures is his report of Jesus' enemies'
opposition to these exorcisms. At no point do they accuse him of not really
effecting the cures. They never suggest, for example, that the healings are
faked. The healings are so manifestly factual that Jesus' enemies have to try to
explain them away as being the product of satanic rather than divine power
(see Mark 3:22).

Mark is interested in all of Jesus' miracles of healing, but it is especially his
casting out of demons that Mark emphasizes. Matthew begins his account of
Jesus' ministry with the Sermon on the Mount. But Mark begins with the story
of Jesus' victory over an "unclean spirit" (1:21–28). Mark's next story ends
with the comment that Jesus "cast out many demons" (1:34). Two chapters
later, another summary of Jesus' activities emphasizes exorcism (3:11–12).
Jesus' enemies attack him, charging not that he does not really exorcise evil
spirits but that his evident power to do so must come from Beelzebul
(3:20–30). Jesus, however, continues his war with the demons (5:1–13;
7:24–29; 9:14–29).

Just as Jesus' followers are called to follow him in facing suffering and
death, so they are called to join in his struggle against the hosts of Satan.
When the Twelve are appointed, they are specifically given two duties:
preaching and exorcism (3:14–15). When they are sent out on their first
mission, they find that they do indeed have this authority (6:7–13). The story
of a subsequent failure, however, warns of the difficulty the disciples were to
find in this task (9:14–29).

What Mark is telling his readers is not simply that Jesus and the apostles
were able to effect startling cures of a bizarre emotional disturbance. Mark
sees these exorcisms as dramatic hints that Jesus and his followers are
engaged in a cosmic contest. Though Jesus keeps his identity "secret" from
all, the demons know him immediately and scream their protests as he

invades their territory (Mark 1:24). In Jesus, the Spirit of God is waging war with Satan. It is, Mark tells his readers, an apocalyptic struggle.

Right at the beginning, at Jesus' baptism, the Spirit of God had descended on him. "The Spirit immediately drove him out into the wilderness . . . forty days, tempted by Satan" (1:12–13). Jesus himself interprets his exorcisms as a sign that Satan's house is being entered and plundered and that Satan himself is being bound (3:20–30). Jesus' struggle, in which Mark's readers are challenged to participate, is a spiritual fight to the death not simply against human opposition but with an unseen, hellish host. Another New Testament writer was to voice the same idea: "For our struggle is not against enemies of blood and flesh, but against the rulers, against the authorities, against the cosmic powers of this present darkness, against the spiritual forces of evil in the heavenly places" (Eph. 6:12).

Probably it is this eschatological context, this interpretation of Jesus' ministry in terms of the final struggle with Satan, that gives us the key for understanding Mark's enigmatic title for Jesus, the "Son of man." Ask Mark who Jesus is, and repeatedly, this title seems to be his answer. Yet no one is quite sure what "Son of man" means. Thirteen times the title occurs in Mark: 2:10, 28; 8:31, 38; 9:9, 12, 31; 10:33, 45; 13:26; 14:21, 41, 62. Strangely, the phrase appears only on the lips of Jesus. According to Mark, "Son of man" seems to be Jesus' favorite title for himself, but nobody else ever uses it about him. What adds to the mystery is that it is rarely used in the letters of Paul or the other epistles; nor is it frequent in John. Many scholars have suggested that Jesus did use it but that, except for the Synoptics with their report of Jesus' own practice, New Testament writers tended to avoid it because they, too, were not quite sure what it meant.

A popular misunderstanding has set it over against another title frequently used of Jesus, "Son of God." Jesus, later creeds affirmed, had two "natures": divine and human. The title "Son of man" has been used to affirm Jesus' humanity, "Son of God" his divinity. In the New Testament, however, the two titles are never contrasted in this way.

Some interpreters have argued forcefully that the title does particularly relate to Jesus' involvement in human suffering and death. "Then he began to teach them that the Son of Man must undergo great suffering, and be rejected by the elders, the chief priests, and the scribes, and be killed" (Mark 8:31; cf. 9:9, 31; 10:33–34, 45; 14:21, 41). It is proposed that from Ezekiel, itself an eschatological book, Jesus selected a title focusing on his identification with suffering humanity. Some scholars translate the title simply as "the Man."[39]

By contrast, others have noted that Jesus repeatedly uses the title in relationship to the coming eschatological judgment. It is used most strikingly in this way when such use is sure to bring Jesus conviction for blasphemy. "And 'you will see the Son of Man seated at the right hand of Power,' and 'coming with the clouds of heaven' " (14:62; cf. 8:38; 13:26). This is the way "Son of man" is used in the Old Testament apocalyptic book of Daniel:

> As I watched in the night visions,
>> I saw one like a human being [Son of man]
>>> coming with the clouds of heaven.
>> And he came to the Ancient One
>>> and was presented before him.
> To him was given dominion
>> and glory and kingship,
> that all peoples, nations, and languages
>> should serve him.
> His dominion is an everlasting dominion
>> that shall not pass away,
> and his kingship is one
>> that shall never be destroyed. (Dan. 7:13–14)

The book of *Enoch,* a "pseudepigraphal" book, a "false writing" that did not get recognized as worthy of inclusion in the Old Testament, similarly depicts the Son of man as a cosmic judge of nations and of demons.

Noting that Jesus speaks of the Son of man in the third person, some have suggested that Jesus did not claim to be the Son of man but rather looked forward to that figure's coming at the end of the age. To take that view, however, one must throw out those sayings, already noted, in which Jesus speaks of the coming sufferings of the Son of man. There are also sayings in which Jesus seems to claim already to possess the authority of the future judge (Mark 2:27–28).

The understanding of the title that seems to the present writer to fit best with its varied uses is this: Jesus did avoid the title "Christ," which to most Palestinian Jews would have connotations of kingship in revolt against Rome. He did deliberately choose an enigmatic and ambiguous title. But as he used it, it was full of eschatological implications. It suggested an invader of the demons' domain, whom the evil spirits recognized as having come to destroy them (1:24). As Son of man, Jesus invades even death itself (8:31; 9:9; 10:45; etc.). But in winning that victory, he prepares for his coming as the Son of man, the cosmic judge (14:21, for example). It would seem that Mark understood the title and told the story in this way.[40]

This whole theme of Jesus as the leader in the battle of heaven against hell reaches its climax in Mark's "Little Apocalypse" in chapter 13. Here, as we have seen, Mark's readers are warned of persecution. But the events there described go far beyond Christians being human torches for Nero's garden party. "In those days, after that suffering, the sun will be darkened, and the moon will not give its light, and the stars will be falling from heaven, and the powers in the heavens will be shaken. Then they will see 'the Son of Man coming in clouds' with great power and glory" (13:24–26).

Mark's readers face almost certain death. But they have nothing to fear. Jesus is the Son of man. As Son of man he has invaded Satan's domain, even ransomed victory from death itself. That Son of man will come again. And when he does, "he will send out the angels, and gather his elect from the four winds, from the ends of the earth to the ends of heaven" (13:27).

The Memory of the Human Jesus

People were bringing little children to him in order that he might touch them; and the disciples spoke sternly to them. But when Jesus saw this, he was indignant and said to them, "Let the little children come to me; do not stop them; for it is to such as these that the kingdom of God belongs. Truly I tell you, whoever does not receive the kingdom of God as a little child will never enter it." And he took them up in his arms, laid his hands on them, and blessed them. (Mark 10:13–16)

To Mark, Jesus is a martyr leading martyrs to the cross. He is an eschatological conqueror of demons and a cosmic judge. But he is also a human being who takes little children in his arms and blesses them.

Mark's account of Jesus' life was shaped in part by the desperate situation in which his readers found themselves. It is no simple biography of a man but a work with apocalyptic overtones, picturing Jesus as a conquering Judge. But we must now note that Mark's Gospel is also filled with vivid scenes and human touches, which many scholars see as genuine reflections of the life of Jesus of Nazareth as a man on earth. The story of Jesus with children in his arms has no parallel in merely apocalyptic literature. Mark presents a picture of a man.

Repeatedly, the other Gospel writers, as they quote from Mark, seem to think it necessary to add phrases or omit ideas in order to point up for readers the divinity of Jesus. Where Mark reports Peter's great confession as simply "You are the Messiah" (8:29), Matthew has "You are the Messiah, the Son of the living God" (Matt. 16:16). To Mark, Jesus is "the carpenter" (Mark 6:3). Matthew alters this to make Jesus "the carpenter's son" (Matt. 13:55). In Mark, the Spirit drove Jesus into the wilderness (Mark 1:12). Matthew reports rather that the Spirit simply led Jesus (Matt. 4:1). In Mark, Jesus sighs (Mark 7:34; 8:12), feels compassion for hungry people (6:34), is sometimes surprised (6:6), and can become angry (3:5; 8:33; 10:14). He can become so tired that he needs to rest (4:38). All three Synoptics tell the story of the rich young ruler, but it is only Mark whose account still contains the words "Jesus, looking at him, loved him" (10:21; cf. Matt. 19:16–30; Luke 18:18–30).

Some thirty times, Mark uses the word "immediately," usually referring to some action by Jesus or some response to him. Perhaps this is only an idiosyncrasy of Mark's style. Perhaps it reflects the character of Peter, Mark's teacher. But perhaps there is in it memory of Jesus' own personality, his sense of urgency.

Mark does not hesitate to report what seem to be human limitations on Jesus' knowledge. Luke omits the story of the Syrophoenician woman, through whom Jesus seems to have had to learn that the gospel is not limited to Jews (Mark 7:24–30). Mark can report that Jesus needed a second effort to cure the blind man at Bethsaida (8:22–26). And the way in which Matt. 13:58 revises Mark 6:5 shows the trend of later writers: Matthew says that in Jesus' hometown, "he did not do many deeds of power there, because of their unbelief," whereas Mark has written flatly, "And he *could* do no deed of power there" (italics added). Sometimes, Mark seems to suggest, Jesus had to experience even failure.

We have already noted, similarly, the honesty with which the Gospels, perhaps especially Mark, report the far-from-heroic behavior of the disciples, whom later legend was to canonize as "saints."

It is the contention of this *Guide* that Mark does represent a vivid, historical memory of what scholars have called "the Jesus of history." The story has been written to meet the needs of a later period. It has been given profound theological interpretation. But it has not been invented by pious imagination. Mark wrote, as we have seen that Luke claims to have written, on the basis of reports about an actual person and real events, that his readers might know the truth (cf. Luke 1:1–4).[41]

A Note about the Ending of Mark

In the oldest Greek manuscripts, this Gospel ends with Mark 16:8: "So they went out and fled from the tomb, for terror and amazement had seized them; and they said nothing to anyone, for they were afraid."

Recently, most scholars, noting this manuscript evidence, have argued that that is where Mark did actually end his story. He repeatedly gave Jesus' promise that he will return at the eschaton, the end of the world (8:38; 13:26; 14:62). Mark ended his story precisely where his readers were, looking forward hopefully to that coming judgment day.[42]

Other scholars, however, believe that the ending of Mark has been lost. While none of the various endings added in ancient manuscripts are from Mark's original, their existence bears witness to the fact that early Christian copyists sensed that the ending was missing. Long before Mark wrote, the story of Easter was an essential part of the first preaching (see, for example, 1 Cor. 15:1–8). Mark 14:28 and 16:7 seem to suggest that Mark is preparing the reader for an account of a resurrection appearance in Galilee. Language scholars report that hardly any other sentence in any known Greek manuscript ends, as does Mark's Gospel, with the Greek preposition *gar* ("for"). It is evident, therefore, they say, that the manuscript is broken off in mid-sentence. The remarkable thing is not that the end of the scroll has been lost but that copies of so much of it have been preserved for more than nineteen centuries. We can be grateful that we have as much of Mark's Gospel as we do.

THE GOSPEL ACCORDING TO LUKE

Luke is a different gospel. True, as was described in the section on "The Writing of the Gospels," Luke is based on Mark and shares with Matthew the source known as Q. But a number of characteristics of Luke make it unique.

For one thing, Greek scholars have called Luke the literary masterpiece of the New Testament. For another, the plot of the story has its own emphasis. Donald Juel proposes that one might think of its particular approach in this way: Luke begins the story by telling how God makes promises to Elizabeth and Mary and others. Then the narrative focuses on the tension between the fulfillment of those promises and the opposition to their fulfillment by the enemies of the gospel.[43]

Though currently this is much disputed, traditionally commentators have spoken of Luke as the Gospel to the Gentiles and have suggested that Luke may be the only book of the New Testament whose author was not a Jew.

Recently, interpreters have focused on Luke's picture of Christ as the great Liberator, champion of the poor (and, some have claimed, forerunner of the movement for women's liberation).

The emphasis on liberation is made clear in the way in which Luke begins his account of Jesus' ministry. Matthew followed his account of Jesus' baptism with the Sermon on the Mount, Jesus' teaching of a new law. Mark told instead of an exorcism. Luke, however, places first a story of Jesus' announcing that he has come to bring release to captives and good news to the poor.

While it is an expansion of Mark 6:1–6, this dramatic story is found only in Luke 4:16–30. Though it is the first sermon that Luke recorded, verse 23 indicates that Luke did not think of it as chronologically the first sermon that Jesus ever preached. Apparently, Luke put it first because he saw it as expressive of the purpose of Jesus' whole ministry.

Jesus has returned to Nazareth, the town in which he grew up. At the synagogue on the Sabbath, he is given the opportunity to read the scripture and to speak, not an unusual privilege in a synagogue for a Jewish man. What he reads, however, and the interpretation he gives it produce a riot.

The passage read is from the second half of the prophecy of Isaiah and is similar to the "Servant poems" we discussed in the section on Isaiah in this *Guide*. These poems had usually been understood as referring to the mission of the nation of Israel. But Jesus announces, "Today this scripture has been fulfilled in your hearing." Apparently, he is claiming that it is in his own ministry that these words are to come true.

Here, then, is Jesus' understanding of what he had come for, according to Luke:

> The Spirit of the Lord is upon me,
> because he has anointed me

> to bring good news to the poor.
> He has sent me to proclaim release to the
>   captives
>   and recovery of sight to the blind,
>   to let the oppressed go free,
> to proclaim the year of the Lord's favor. (Luke 4:18–19, quoting from Isa. 61:1–2)

Jesus had come for "the poor," "the captives," "the blind," "the oppressed." When he went on to suggest that God's people had failed in this mission, which he now was assuming, the angry mob attempted to lynch him.

By placing the story at the beginning of his account of Jesus' ministry and by telling it in such detail, Luke has signaled to his reader that it is important. It is a kind of brief introductory summary of Luke's version of the whole Gospel. We confine our study here of what is unique in Luke primarily to examining certain themes suggested by these verses.

The Gospel for All Peoples

As traditionally interpreted, Luke's Gospel is written to a Gentile, by a Gentile, and for Gentiles. To him, Jesus is one who has brought a revolution that has broken down the old barriers of race.[44]

Whoever is meant by the "most excellent Theophilus" to whom the Gospel is addressed in Luke 1:3, that person has a Greek, not a Jewish, name. Tradition says that the author was Luke, a man with a Greek name, one who enters the story in Acts as a companion of Paul when in Acts 16:10 (the beginning of the "we" passages) Paul crosses from Asia into Europe. Primarily because of the difficulty of reconciling Acts's account of Paul's life with that which Paul himself gives in Galatians, many have rejected this tradition. But many—though not all—of those who do not ascribe the book to a companion of Paul agree that the Gospel appears to be the work of a Gentile. Over and over, it emphasizes that Jesus came not for one race but for all.

When the child Jesus was brought to the Temple for ceremonies traditional at the birth of Jewish boys, Luke tells us, old Simeon took the baby in his arms and sang that he would be "a light for revelation to the Gentiles" (Luke 2:32; cf. Isa. 42:6–7).

Matthew had traced Jesus' ancestry through Abraham and the Hebrew kings (Matt. 1:1–17). Luke, however, has a different genealogical table, leaving out most of the Hebrew kings but going back to Adam, the father of all races (Luke 3:23–38). Matthew tells us that when Jesus sent out the disciples, he charged them, "Go nowhere among the Gentiles" (Matt. 10:5). Luke tells the same story but carefully omits those limiting words (Luke 9:1–6).

It is Luke alone who tells the story of the Good Samaritan, the man of the wrong race and religion who is held up as a model in preference to certain respectably pious leaders among the traditional people of God (10:29–37).

Other Gospel writers report Jesus' enigmatic saying "Some are last who will be first, and some are first who will be last" (13:30; cf. Matt. 19:30; Mark 10:31). But it is clear from the context in which Luke sets this saying that Luke understands it as having a racial meaning. The Gentiles, formerly last, are now to have a high place in the kingdom of God.

Jesus as the Bringer of Economic "Revolution"

Mary's Magnificat (Luke 1:46–55) has been called "the most revolutionary song ever sung."

Matthew's account of Jesus' birth, as we have seen, prepares us for the coming of the promised Jewish king, a new Moses. Luke's account promises instead a kind of revolution, one especially for the cause of the poor and oppressed. Unique to Luke is a psalm attributed to Mary, Jesus' mother, as she looks forward to the birth of her child. She sings of God that now

> he has shown strength with his arm;
> he has scattered the proud in the thoughts of their hearts.
> He has brought down the powerful from their thrones,
> and lifted up the lowly;
> he has filled the hungry with good things,
> and sent the rich away empty. (Luke 1:51–53)

Luke's story of Jesus' birth goes on to report that the news is announced not, as in Matthew, to rich Magi from the East but to "certain poor shepherds" in Judean fields.

As we have seen, Luke pictures Jesus announcing his mission as being to "bring good news to the poor" and "release to the captives" and "to let the oppressed go free" (4:18). At least three parables develop the theme of concern for those in need. Luke 10:29–37 extols the Good Samaritan as a true "neighbor" because he does not let lines of race or religion prevent him from helping the man in need. Luke 12:13–21 pictures gentle Jesus as bluntly calling a rich man "fool" for trusting in his wealth when judgment is at hand. And in Luke 16:19–31, Jesus depicts a rich man and poor Lazarus as swapping places in the life to come. The rich man had been unconcerned for the poor. Jesus is willing to use standard apocalyptic symbolism and picture this rich but selfish miser as damned for eternity, "in agony in these flames."

Luke's version of the Beatitudes spells out his revolutionary concern unambiguously. Matthew 5:3–12 interprets the Beatitudes spiritually: "Blessed are the poor *in spirit*"; "Blessed are those who hunger and thirst *for righteousness*" (italics added). But Luke 6:20–23 reports these sayings in unadorned economic terms: "Blessed are you who are poor. . . . Blessed are you who are hungry now, for you will be filled. Blessed are you who weep now, for you will laugh." An economic reversal is promised.

And to add emphasis to the promise of a world turned upside down at the coming eschaton (the end), Luke's report adds a series of warnings: "But woe to you who are rich, for you have received your consolation. Woe to you who are full now, for you will be hungry. Woe to you who are laughing now, for you will mourn and weep" (6:24–25). However justified Matthew may have been in interpreting the Beatitudes in terms of the spirit that receives blessedness, many scholars believe that Luke's version may be closer to the actual words of Jesus.

It is Luke also who tells us the story of one man who got Jesus' message. Zacchaeus is depicted as wealthy, dishonest, and one of the hated tax collectors. But when he meets Jesus, his repentance manifests itself both in a new honesty in his business and in a new concern for the poor (19:1–10).[45]

Forerunner of a Kind of "Women's Liberation"

Long before the modern movement for asserting the rights of women, students had noted a third group for whom Luke shows a special concern. We have seen his concern to voice the good news that no one is to be excluded from the kingdom because of race or economic class. But as most commentators have understood him, Luke also depicts Jesus as ignoring the ancient boundaries that lower the status of half the world because of their sex.[46]

Matthew's account of Jesus' birth centers on Joseph. But Luke's is the story of two women. One is Elizabeth, Mary's cousin and the mother of John the Baptist. The other is Mary herself, the mother of Christ. It is to a woman that the angel Gabriel comes. It is a woman who blesses Mary as the mother-to-be of the Lord (1:41–45). A woman, Anna, recognizes in the baby at the Temple the future Savior (2:36–38). It was many women, Luke tells us, who provided the financial support for Jesus' ministry (8:1–3). And in Luke's account of the resurrection, it is a whole group of women who first hear the news that Jesus is risen and are the first to spread the good news (24:9–10).

In all four Gospels, Jesus is pictured as ministering to women. Luke adds to the others the story of Jesus' raising from the dead the son of a widow of Nain (7:11–17).

But what may have been for Luke's readers the most shocking story of this kind is one that he alone reports. Jesus is in the home of Mary and Martha. He actually teaches Mary as if she is intellectually the equal of a man, to the distress of Martha, who would prefer to have her sister join her in the more traditional "woman's work" in the kitchen (10:38–42). In much of the Gentile world, women were regarded as a man's property. To Aristotle, for example, they were but a little above the rank of slaves. Jews had perhaps the highest regard for women of any people in the first century. And yet even among them, there were disputes as to whether women should be taught. "I would rather teach my daughter obscenities than to teach her the law," one sexist rabbi is quoted as saying. But Luke's Gospel is one in which women have a place equal to that of men.[47]

The Matter of Miracles

Among the "oppressed" for whom Luke says Jesus came were the sick and the blind.

Early in the twentieth century, W. K. Hobart proposed that this Gospel's detailed accounts of healings and use of technical medical terms showed that the author really must have been the one whom Paul calls "the beloved physician" (Col. 4:14). Further study called this view into serious question, suggesting that the vocabulary would be equally suitable for a lawyer or for many other educated Greeks. Nevertheless, there is in Luke sufficient emphasis on healing that the following comments on miracles are appropriate at this point.

The Buddhist scriptures contain a lovely story of a miracle alleged to have been performed by Siddhartha Gautama. An evil man attempted to seduce a beautiful young virgin, beginning by praising the beauty of her eyes. "Then take them!" she protested, and she plucked her eyes out. Her sacrifice to preserve her chastity so shamed the lecher that he was converted. And the Buddha, on hearing the story, miraculously restored the virtuous maiden's sight.

Now, it must be said that most twentieth-century Americans, on hearing this tale, dismiss it as pious legend from a superstitious land and age. But the question inevitably arises concerning the miracles reported in the New Testament: Are they to be rejected in the same way? Most ancient religions have claimed miracles that would be disputed today. It has been wisely remarked that in the first century, Christianity could not have been believed without miracles, but that today, it is hard to believe precisely because of those same miracles.

Students of the Bible have given many answers to the problem of miracles, most of which are variations on one or another of the following four.

1. Some flatly reject the miracle stories. The eighteenth-century philosopher David Hume, for example, argued that miracles would be a violation of the laws of nature created by nature's God, a contradiction. More important, one ought not to believe a report of an alleged miracle unless it is more difficult to believe that the report was in error than that the miracle took place. A story from centuries ago, written perhaps by one who does not even claim to have been an eyewitness, told among superstitious people in a pre-scientific era, can hardly be accepted in

modern times, Hume alleged.[48] Following a similar line of reasoning, Thomas Jefferson produced an edition of the New Testament from which all miracles had been excluded.

2. Some accept such stories as spiritually but not literally true. Many devout scholars assume it as a dogma not to be questioned in a scientific age that miracles, at least of a physical kind, simply do not and cannot happen. Yet they recognize that to cut out all the miracle stories would be to leave the Gospels in shreds. The task of the interpreter, therefore, is to find what meaning there may be for modern readers in these ancient tales. The story of the cleansing of a leper, for example, may symbolize for us the sense of cleansing from sin that the believer may experience today. A disciple of Rudolf Bultmann might "de-mythologize" the story of how Jesus gave sight to a blind man by speaking of the new insights the good news brings to those who encounter the figure of Christ in the pages of the Gospel. The stories of Jesus' raising the dead suggest the transition from "inauthentic existence" to "authentic existence" described in existential philosophy.

3. Some accept some or all of the miracles but seek to justify their views critically.[49] A number of these more conservative scholars have accepted Hume's challenge that each report of a miracle must be judged on its own merits. Nevertheless, they also accept many such stories as historically true. The understanding of the universe as a clocklike, cause-and-effect machine, assumed in Hume's day, has now been discarded, these scholars argue, by science itself. Discoveries such as those leading to Werner Heisenberg's uncertainty principle are said to challenge the assumption that every event is predictable. Modern psychosomatic medicine gives us at least partial insights into how healings may, in extraordinary circumstances, take place quite apart from the use of medicines or surgery. While New Testament reports of miracles need be accepted no less critically than those attributed to the Buddha, for example, they need not be rejected on the basis of a presupposition that only mechanically predictable events can happen. Where so remarkable a personality as Jesus was present, one may believe that remarkable, unexpected things did occur.

4. Some, on theological grounds, accept it as a matter of faith that every biblical story reported as history must be believed as factually true. God created the universe, these conservative scholars note. The Creator therefore can alter its usual pattern of operation whenever that seems wise. Jesus, being God incarnate, God come to us as a human being, could and did do the miracles reported in the scripture. To doubt these stories, fundamentalists argue, would be to doubt both the deity of Jesus and the authority of God's word. This would violate Christian theology as they understand it.

Whatever may be the correct view concerning miracles, it is important to note that Jesus did not want faith in his gospel to rest on belief in such wonders and signs. The Synoptics agree that when asked to prove himself by doing miracles, Jesus flatly refused (Matt. 16:1–4; Mark 8:11–13; Luke 11:29). The miracles he did were to help people, not to impress the credulous. Jesus demanded faith on the basis of moral, not physical, authority. Typically, the Christian today does not arrive at faith in Jesus because she or he has first believed the reports that Jesus did miracles. On the contrary, because one has first been grasped by the spiritual power of Jesus, one may, indeed, come to believe that Jesus did physical miracles too.

The Birth of Jesus

Of the many stories in the New Testament, few are more loved or more debated than that of Jesus' birth.

While some see belief that Jesus was born of a virgin as a fundamental of the faith, others regard the story simply as typical primitive religious myth. Millions celebrate it every Christmas in carol and pageant. Yet it must be admitted that, as history, the story abounds in problems.

One problem concerns the date. Luke carefully sets the story in the context of a worldwide taxation "while Quirinius was governor of Syria" (Luke 2:2). Quirinius, however, does not seem to have become governor of Syria until several years after the death of Herod (4 B.C.), in whose lifetime Matthew says Jesus was born. And the first worldwide taxation of which we have any record did not occur until A.D. 7. An uncertain solution that some have proposed to the problem rests on the fact that Quirinius did hold a lesser office in Syria as early as 7 B.C., in which year there was a decree for census and taxation in Egypt. Perhaps, it is proposed, that census also included Palestine.

Much more serious is the problem that relates the story to the traditional pattern of religious legends. Greek and Roman mythology abounded in stories of children born to human mothers after intercourse with mythical gods. Tourists may yet see on the walls of the temple at Luxor a carving in which an Egyptian pharaoh depicted his mother as encountering a god and then bearing him a son, that pharaoh thus being both human and divine. Legends of miracles related to the birth of Siddhartha Gautama are part of Buddhist tradition. Defenders of the historicity of the biblical narratives have replied that the highly moral nature of these accounts, their relative contemporaneousness with the events described, and their setting in real history distance the stories of Jesus' birth significantly from myths such as those of Greek religions.

Another problem is the complete silence of the rest of the New Testament concerning Jesus' birth. Not Mark, not John, not Paul, not any other New

Testament writer ever mentions the virgin birth. Did they not believe it? Did they not know of it? Did they simply not think it important for their purposes?

Finally, there is the problem of the apparent differences between the story as Luke tells it and the story as we have it from Matthew. One has only to ask who Jesus' grandfather was to discover an apparent discrepancy. Luke 3:23 tells us that Jesus' earthly father, Joseph, was the son of Heli, but Matt. 1:16 says that Joseph was the son of Jacob. A traditional answer, that Luke is tracing Jesus' ancestry through Mary, ignores the difficulty that Luke seems clearly to say that he is speaking of Joseph's ancestors. The two lists do not even agree concerning all the ancestors of King David.

Reading the two stories, one seems to find completely different under-standings of how it happened that Jesus of Nazareth was born in David's hometown of Bethlehem. Luke tells us that the Holy Family makes a special trip from their home in Nazareth to Bethlehem because of a census for tax purposes. The child is laid in a manger because there is no room for these travelers in the local inn (Luke 2:1–7). Matthew, however, says nothing of any previous residence in Nazareth. In Matthew, the family welcomes the Wise Men in a "house" (Matt. 2:11), with no hint that it is not their own home. The reason Jesus grew up in Nazareth, according to Matthew, is that the family had to flee Bethlehem to avoid persecution by Herod—a persecution apparently unknown to Luke.

At least a partial understanding of some of the differences between Matthew and Luke comes from a recognition of their different purposes and emphases. For example, Matthew used a genealogical list that would trace Jesus' ancestry through all the kings of Israel and back to Abraham, the father of the Hebrews. This fits his concern to show Jesus as the fulfiller of the hope for the promised King of the Jews. The Gentile Luke, however, was quite content with a genealogical list that included no Jewish king except David but which traced Jesus' ancestry back to Adam and to God, from whom all races have come (Luke 3:23–38). Matthew the Jew was concerned to set Jesus in opposition to the false king of the Jews, Herod. The Gentile Luke, writing to the "most excellent Theophilus," was more concerned to relate Jesus to the Roman Empire. For some Christians, however, problems still remain.

What makes such problems especially important to many is the emphasis placed on the virgin birth of Jesus by traditional theology. As they recite the Apostles' Creed, millions of Christians affirm faith in Jesus as "conceived by the Holy Ghost, born of the Virgin Mary." Originally, it seems, "born of the Virgin Mary" was included in the creed to emphasize Jesus' humanity. He was born of a woman, not handed down from heaven. "Conceived by the Holy Ghost" affirmed Jesus' deity. Fundamentalist theologians, however, have often interpreted doubt concerning the virgin birth to be doubt concerning the deity of Christ.

In contrast, other devout Christian scholars have replied that the story of the virgin birth seems peripheral to New Testament Christianity. Only Matthew and Luke mention it, and having told their stories, they refer to it no more. The rest of the New Testament writers say nothing about it at all.

Some may find a partial reconciliation of conflicting views by thinking of the virgin birth in terms of two miracles. The *biological miracle* that Jesus was born without an earthly father to a virgin mother does not seem to have been important to most New Testament writers. Christian historians may face honestly the difficulties noted above, though the present writer does not find these insurmountable.

The *theological miracle* of the uniqueness of Jesus as both God and man, the doctrine symbolized in the creed by "conceived by the Holy Ghost, born of the Virgin Mary," may indeed be regarded as essential to New Testament Christianity. Every part of the New Testament affirms both the humanity of Jesus and the uniqueness of his relationship to God. That faith, however, rests on grounds quite independent of historical analysis of the stories of Jesus' birth.

Finally, it is important to note the literary form of the birth stories. As Matthew has filled his account with quotations from the Jewish scriptures— music to his readers' ears—so Luke has filled his story with songs, ancient Christmas carols. The angel who appears to Jesus' uncle Zechariah bursts into song (Luke 1:13–17). Mary's Magnificat has been sung through the centuries (1:46–55). When speech is restored to Zechariah, he sings his prophecy (1:67–79). To the shepherds, angels announce Jesus' birth by singing a carol (2:14). And old Simeon's Nunc Dimittis, sung as he held the infant Jesus in his arms, was to become part of the musical liturgy of the church through the ages (2:29–32). (The Revised Standard Version and other translations of the New Testament print these passages in such a way as to show the reader that they are poetry.) Luke has written not a newspaper account but a kind of grand opera or oratorio on the birth of Jesus.

Historical analysis of the birth stories is helpful.[50] But the literary interpreter must also note that one has not fully grasped the good news Luke intended to convey until one has, with joy, sung Christmas carols.

The Resurrection

At least one miracle, the New Testament affirms, is essential. "If Christ has not been raised," Paul writes, "then our proclamation has been in vain and your faith has been in vain" (1 Cor. 15:14). Every Gospel ends with the announcement of the good news of the resurrection. Every other book of the New Testament assumes or affirms it. Every line of the New Testament is written by a Christian committed to belief in the resurrection of Christ.

Again, it must be admitted, there are problems. It has sometimes been said that the Easter stories of the four Gospels agree on almost nothing except the one big fact that on the third day, Jesus rose (but on the truth of that fact, each writer would stake his life).

Who first saw the risen Christ? Matthew 28:9 indicates that two women did so. Luke 24 gives no hint that the women saw Jesus. Rather, in Luke, Jesus appears first to two disciples on the road to Emmaus and then to the Eleven. John 20 makes the first appearance to Mary Magdalene alone, not to the other women, and then describes an appearance to ten, not eleven, disciples. Paul, in 1 Cor. 15:5, seems to specify that the first appearance was to Peter, then to the Twelve.

Where did the resurrection appearances occur? Matthew records the appearance to the disciples as occurring on a mountain in Galilee. Mark 16:7 hints that the lost ending of Mark must have described an appearance there. Luke 24, however, sets all appearances in or near Jerusalem. John has Jesus appear in both places.

Such problems are probably not now completely solvable on the basis of historical research.[51] That such differing accounts had developed by the time the New Testament books were written shows that the accounts of Easter must have been told and retold very early indeed and in every diverse place to which the gospel first spread. Thus the resurrection affirmation itself was no gradually developed legend. It was central to the good news from the very beginning.

What the New Testament writers emphasize is that men and women in various places and ways began to experience the presence of the risen Christ. They give no account of the actual resurrection. They never tell what a television camera would have recorded had there been one outside the tomb on Easter morning. John Dominic Crossan, leader of the Jesus Seminar, discounts completely the literal historicity of resurrection stories such as that of Jesus' appearance at a meal with two disciples at Emmaus (Luke 24:13–32). He affirms, however, his faith that Jesus is alive spiritually and is still repeatedly encountered by believers: "Emmaus never happened. Emmaus always happens."[52]

The repeated mention of the empty tomb does bear witness to the Gospel writers' certainty that there had occurred an actual, material event. John even pictures Jesus as still bearing the marks of the nails in his risen body. The ressurected Christ, however, is not presented simply as an ordinary physical body come back to life but as one miraculously transformed, entering a new kind of existence. The Gospels' emphasis is not on a physical phenomenon; it is on a spiritual triumph and its continuing significance in the lives of people.

The skeptic may argue that the New Testament writers offer no absolute proof of the resurrection. These writers do profess to offer strong evidence. They give the witness of those who encountered the risen Christ. They challenge each reader to learn in his or her own experience. They describe also the experience of the community of believers, the church, in the mighty acts that they report Jesus continued to do in and through them by means of his living Spirit.

But the story of those acts and those witnesses is the subject of the next section of this *Guide*.

7

THE ACTS
OF THE APOSTLES

"In the first book, Theophilus, I wrote about all that Jesus did and taught." So begins Luke in Acts 1:1. In this second book by Luke, the same author, writing to the same reader, picks up precisely where the first volume ended. Now, Luke implies, he will tell what the risen Christ continued to do, by means of his Holy Spirit, in and through the infant church.[1]

THE NATURE AND PURPOSE OF ACTS

Acts as History

For nineteen centuries, readers have found Acts's story fascinating. Suddenly filled with a new sense of power from on high, Acts tells us, the apostles began to shout their message to the world. Heroically, they braved persecution, performed miracles, won converts, and spread the infant church. So Acts tells the story. Serious questions have been raised, however, as to whether Acts is true to the facts.

Nineteenth-century critics were almost unanimous in regarding Acts as worthless, at least as history. The book was regarded as a second-century collection of legends, slanted to cover up the split between Peter and Paul which Galatians was thought to reveal. In Gal. 2:11, Paul writes of Peter, "I opposed him to his face, because he stood self-condemned." Acts had been written, the critics argued, to suppress the scandalous memory of the early rift about the place of Gentile converts in the church and to make the relationships among early leaders appear to have been all sweetness and light. Acts was believed to be full of edifying fiction and distortion that had been produced more than a century after the events it professed to report. The crucial period between the events recounted in the Gospels and the clear

THE ACTS OF THE APOSTLES
The Story of the First Deeds of the Holy Spirit through the Church

"You will receive power when the Holy Spirit has come upon you; and you will be my witnesses in Jerusalem, in all Judea and Samaria, and to the ends of the earth" (1:8).

1 Witness in Jerusalem	8 Witness in Judea and Samaria	13 Witness to the Ends of the Earth	
		Paul's Missionary Journeys	21 Paul's Trials and Journey to Rome
Jesus ascends, and the church waits, 1	Philip, Peter, and others win converts in Samaria, 8	First missionary journey, 13—14	Paul is arrested in Jerusalem, 21:17–23:35
The Spirit comes at Pentecost; the first converts are won, 2	Saul (Paul) is converted, 9:1–31	The Jerusalem Council decides to accept his Gentile converts, 15:1–35	Paul goes on trial in Caesarea, 24—26
First miracle, 3	In Lydda and Joppa, Peter performs miracles, 9:32–42	Paul's second missionary journey, 15:36–19:20	Having appealed to Caesar, Paul sails to Rome, 27:1–28:15
First arrest, 4	A Gentile, Cornelius, is converted, 10:1–11:18	Paul's third missionary journey, 19:21–21:16	Paul lives two years under house arrest in Rome, 28:16–31
First notable sin; first beating, 5	The interracial church at Antioch grows and ministers, 11:19–29		
First "deacons," including Stephen, the first martyr, 6—7	Peter escapes, but James is martyred, 12		

Author: The author of the third Gospel, traditionally Paul's companion Luke
Subject: How, empowered by the Spirit, the church grew and ministered. More than half the book is devoted to the ministry of Luke's hero, Paul.
Themes: the power of the Spirit, the spread of the gospel, the gospel crossing of racial lines, the sharing fellowship of the church, and more
Date: Probably around A.D. 85

picture of the early church found in Paul's letters was described as a kind of twenty-year "dark tunnel." Into it, it was said, Acts failed to shed any dependable light.

Curiously, it was the almost accidental discovery of a boundary marker in Turkey that caused the pendulum of critical evaluation of Acts's accuracy to swing toward the opposite extreme. British archaeologist Sir William M. Ramsay—no kin to the writer of this *Guide*—set out, about the turn of the century, to retrace the journeys of Paul. He began his expedition assuming the prevailing view about Acts, that it was a collection of legends written in the middle or late second century. His discovery of a stone boundary sign showed him that Paul, in fleeing from Iconium to Lystra and Derbe, really would have crossed the border into Lycaonia, as stated in Acts 14:6. What made this minor detail significant was that the boundary of Lycaonia had been there only from A.D. 37 to A.D. 72, during which period Paul's alleged flight had taken place. A writer of a century later, relying simply on legend or imagination, could have neither known nor invented this little detail. Startled by his discovery, Ramsay began to unearth other archaeological evidence that seemed clearly to indicate that the author of Acts possessed accurate, detailed, and probably firsthand information.

By 1922, the pendulum had swung so far that J. W. Hunkin could write the following as propositions to which the great majority of scholars, at least in Great Britain, would agree:

> (i.) That the Acts is a product not of the second century but of the first.
>
> (ii.) That there is a very strong probability that the author of the "we sections" is the author both of Acts and of the third gospel: [The "we sections" are the passages in which the author states that "we" did certain things, apparently claiming to have been present at the time. See Acts 16:9–10; etc.]
>
> (iii.) That he possesses a great deal of accurate information with regard to St. Paul's journeys, some of it being first-hand:
>
> (iv.) That whatever be his sources for the early chapters of the Acts these "Scenes from Early Days" are well chosen and consistent, and give a picture of the march of events which is at any rate, on the whole, correct in outline.[2]

The second half of the twentieth century, however, saw the pendulum of critical thought swing back in the direction of skepticism with regard to the historicity of Acts's stories. Three major lines of argument have convinced many that Acts is of limited value to the historian.

1. Acts, especially in its early chapters, includes stories of miracles. It reports that language barriers crumbled (2:6), the sick were healed (5:16), prisoners were miraculously released (12:6–11), and the dead were raised (9:36–42). Especially if he or she begins with the assumption that all miracle stories must be false, the critic is likely to be skeptical about the historicity of Acts.

2. Repeatedly, Acts seems to be in conflict with the genuine letters of Paul. For example, it is said that "speaking with tongues" in Acts 2 is quite different from what Paul describes in 1 Corinthians 12—14; Galatians 1—2 gives a picture of Paul's actions after his conversion that is quite different from the picture in Acts 9; and the true story of the Jerusalem Council in Galatians 2 apparently conflicts with that in Acts 15.

3. Finally, recent scholarship has emphasized that the author of Acts wrote as a theologian, not as a historian. There are dozens of events that any modern historian would have reported but about which Acts is completely silent. When, near the end of Acts, Paul at last arrives at Rome, the church has already been founded there. But the author gives us no hint as to how this occurred. Whatever happened to the apostle John and to most of the other disciples? Acts quickly lets them drop from the story. From other sources, we know that there was soon a flourishing church in North Africa. Acts gives us detailed accounts of the founding of some insignificant congregations in Turkey but tells us nothing of so prominent a church as that in Alexandria, Egypt. Rather, the author has picked stories or, it is alleged, even invented stories that would illustrate the particular theological themes that he wanted to develop.[3]

In spite of these objections, however, many scholars have continued to argue—effectively, in the view of the present writer—that Acts may be regarded as a valuable source of historical information about the infant church. The arguments to the contrary, however, are so strong that we need here to review the case given in defense of the general historicity of Acts's account.

1. Consistent, repeated, and very early tradition attributes the book to Luke, a companion of Paul. This is the more noteworthy because Luke was not otherwise especially distinguished in church history (see the section on "The Writing of the Gospels" in chapter 6 of this *Guide*). Apocryphal books created by the imagination of later Christians were usually attributed to much more prominent early leaders.

2. The use of the first person at the beginning of Luke, again in Acts 1:1, and repeatedly from Acts 16 on (in the "we passages") can be explained most simply by supposing that the author of the whole two-volume work, known to Theophilus, is claiming to have been present at the times indicated. Every test of vocabulary and style seems to indicate that the "travel diary" in Acts is by the author who wrote the rest of the book.

3. The differences between Acts and certain of Paul's writings, especially Galatians, are real, and they certainly suggest that Acts is not infallible

as history. Some of these differences may be explained partially, however, in ways to be noted in the discussion of Galatians in this *Guide* (Paul, too, is straining to make some theological points). As a matter of fact, the detailed agreements between Acts and the letters of Paul are more striking than the differences. They are especially remarkable because the writer of Acts shows no sign of having before him copies of the letters themselves. Agreement on so many details, incidental in both Acts and the epistles, seems inexplicable in a work of later pious imagination. The writer clearly had access to a great deal of accurate information.[4]

4. We have already noted that archaeologists such as Ramsay found Luke accurate on many details that would have been difficult for a second-century writer to know.[5]

5. Finally, there are indications that Luke had access to and made use of both written and oral sources. This, of course, is what the author claims in Luke 1:1–4. Some of these sources show traces of going back to the earliest days of the church.[6]

It is possible that some Christian scholars, in their pious effort to be scrupulously honest and not to base their theology on a theory of biblical infallibility, have actually leaned over backward to be skeptical about the historical accuracy of their sacred book. The Jewish scholar Joseph Klausner, by contrast, writes of Acts:

> But even in the first part of the book, that is to say, in the first twelve chapters, there is so much information containing details and names, that it would have been difficult to obtain them by hearsay and to remember them so exactly unless the author had had a written source before him. Thus it is necessary to assume that also in the first chapters the author made use of written sources along with oral.[7]

Acts as Theology

If Luke's accuracy as a storyteller and historian continues to be debated, his originality as a theologian is currently more and more admired. Whatever one's view concerning the historicity of Luke's stories, any careful reader will find that Acts is not meant to be a modern newspaper report or a research paper "objectively" describing the early church. Luke wants to persuade Theophilus. He has chosen to tell some stories and to ignore others because he has certain ideas he wishes to emphasize. He introduces these themes in the very beginning of Acts.

The disciples, Luke begins by telling us, were confused. Jesus had risen. And yet the world still went on. "Lord, is this the time when you will restore the kingdom to Israel?" they asked (Acts 1:6). Is the kingdom at last really at hand? Is the final judgment now about to come?

> He replied, "It is not for you to know the times or periods that the Father has set by his own authority. But you will receive power when the Holy Spirit has come upon you; and you will be my witnesses in Jerusalem, in all Judea and Samaria, and to the ends of the earth. (1:7–8)

Into these verses, deliberately emphasized by their placement at the beginning, the author has packed much of the message that he plans to develop. Here are three major theological emphases of Acts that these verses introduce.

Acts Is a Book about the Powerful Acts of the Holy Spirit

More than half a century after Good Friday and Easter, the end of the world still had not come. Jesus, Mark had reported, had promised that there were some who heard him teach who would live to see the kingdom of God come with power (Mark 9:1). Matthew 16:28 even quoted the saying as being that they would see the Son of man himself coming. Now decades had passed and that end had not come. In his Gospel, Luke did not quote Mark 9:1.

Who *had* come, Luke was sure, was the Holy Spirit. "Is this the time when you will restore the kingdom?" "It is not for you to know" about God's schedule, the risen Christ replies in Acts 1:7. "But you will receive power when the Holy Spirit has come upon you." Acts 1 is the story of that promise. Acts 2 is the story of Pentecost, the fulfillment of the promise. The rest of Acts is the story of that Spirit's power.

In his Gospel, Luke had written of "the Holy Spirit" (translated "the Holy Ghost" in the King James Version) about as often as had the other two Synoptic writers put together. Now, in the twenty-eight chapters of Acts, he uses that phrase or its equivalent nearly fifty times.

Acts 2 describes in highly dramatic fashion the first outpouring of that Spirit. In the power of that ecstasy, the disciples speak in tongues, begin their mission of witnessing, and win their first converts.

In subsequent chapters, the power of the Spirit is directly related to the disciples' bold witness when on trial (4:8; 5:32), the writing of scripture (4:25; 28:25), the authority of the apostles (5:3), the character of those to be selected for church office (6:3), the restoration of sight to the blind Saul (9:17), comfort (9:31), Jesus' own power (10:38), conversion (10:44), the character of the saintly Barnabas (11:24), the appointment of the first officially designated missionaries (13:2), Paul's authority (13:9), joy (13:52), common Christian experience across lines of race (15:8), divine guidance for the church (15:28) and for individuals (16:6), prophecy (19:6; 20:23; 21:11), and the work of elders (20:28). In short, Luke implies that all of the good things the apostles do or have are through the power of the Holy Spirit.

Acts Is a Book about the Acts of the Church

More than fifty years after Easter, the kingdom of God had not come—not, at least, in the way in which it had been expected. What had come, however, was the Spirit-filled community, the church.

Jesus himself is never recorded as using the word "church" except in Matt. 16:18 and 18:17. Many regard these two verses as employing a term that was not used until after Jesus' earthly life. But not only is the word "church" used repeatedly in Acts but the idea of the ongoing Christian community is basic to the whole book.

Hans Conzelmann proposes that Luke saw all history as divided into three periods.[8] The first was the age of the Law and the Prophets, ending with John the Baptist (Luke 16:16). The second, "the midpoint," was the period of Jesus' life described in Luke's Gospel. The third is the era of the Spirit and of the church, which begins with Acts. It will continue until the return of Christ. The eschatological hope has not been abandoned. Luke still expects Jesus to return at the end of the age (Acts 1:11). But the community is not to "stand looking up toward heaven," concentrating on the future (1:11). It has a job to do and a fellowship in which to participate here and now. Someday the kingdom will come, but now there is the church.

In Acts 1, the risen Christ gives the church its commission. Later in that chapter, the church replaces Judas, thus beginning to organize for its task. In Acts 2, it begins its witness, adding three thousand converts to its number. An ideal, sharing community is described in Acts 2:42–47. Acts 3—4 describes the community heroically and prayerfully facing persecution. Again, Acts 4:32–37 describes a church in which the kingdom ideals of the Sermon on the Mount are being realized (for a similar summary picturing the ideal church, see Acts 5:12–16). The church again expands its organization (6:1–6), for the purpose of even better sharing. Through the whole book, Luke continues the story of how this community dealt with problems and spread its gospel and its fellowship.

In his Gospel, Luke had depicted Jesus as having to break down barriers between races and classes (see the section on Luke's Gospel in chapter 6 of this *Guide*). Now he pictures the church as the community in which that ideal fellowship has been realized. "All who believed were together and had all things in common; they would sell their possessions and goods and distribute the proceeds to all, as any had need" (2:44–45). Gentiles, too, are welcomed into that loving company. The story of the admission to the church of the Roman centurion Cornelius (Acts 10) is so important to Luke that he tells it all over again in the next chapter (11:4–17). From Acts 13 on, the book is the story of the spread of the church into Gentile lands and among Gentile peoples.

Acts Is the Missionary Story of the Apostles Witnessing to the "Word" through All the World

We have noted that Christ's Great Commission, as recorded in Acts 1:8, calls on the church to be "witnesses in Jerusalem, in all Judea and Samaria, and to the ends of the earth." The whole book of Acts can be thought of as outlined around that theme verse.

The witness in Jerusalem is described in Acts 1:12–6:7. That section ends with the editorial summary "The word of God continued to spread; the number of the disciples increased greatly in Jerusalem" (6:7).

The witness beyond Jerusalem is introduced in Acts 6:8 with the story of Stephen. His address seems designed to protest restriction to a sacred temple, land, or race. And with his death, we are told, the church members "were all scattered throughout the region of Judea and Samaria" (8:1). Thus Acts 6—12 can be thought of as telling how the second part of the Great Commission began to be fulfilled. A summary in Acts 9:31 reports, "Meanwhile the church throughout Judea, Galilee, and Samaria had peace and was built up." A similar summary in Acts 12:24 ends the section.

The witness to the world has already been hinted at by the story of the conversion of the Gentile Cornelius (10:1–11:18) and the founding of the church at Antioch (11:19–30). But from Acts 13 on, the book concentrates almost exclusively on the worldwide witness of the church. The missionary activity of Luke's great hero, Paul, becomes the center of the whole story. Acts ends with Paul's arrival at Rome, the capital of the world.

A characteristic summary that Acts uses at the end of the first section is "the word of God continued to spread" (6:7; cf. 12:24; 19:20). Catching the significance of this phrase, the title of a popular study book calls Acts the story of *The Word in Action*.[9] Acts is the story of witnesses, but it is also the story of the spreading power of the "word" to which their witness was borne.

Luke the theologian writes as a witness to that word.

The Purpose of Acts

Is Acts history or theology? It is certainly theology. Luke undoubtedly selects and to some extent shapes his stories to illustrate the gospel he is preaching to a church more than fifty years after some of the events he describes.

Yet we have seen that Acts contains accuracies most easily explained on the theory that Luke did have access to much historically valuable information. The present writer attaches more value to Acts as a work of history than do most who currently write on this subject.

Perhaps a figure to suggest how Luke has blended fact and faith may be provided by an ancient legend, itself probably pure fiction. Tradition says that Luke was an artist. At least two medieval churches contain paintings of the Virgin Mary that are piously believed to have been painted by Luke. Luke really was a kind of artist—with words.

Luke has painted for us a word portrait of the infant church. No good portrait is limited to the exactness of a photograph. An artist attempts to bring out the character of the subject, expanding a line here, deepening a shadow there. But the artist does not thereby seek to produce fiction. He or she attempts rather to present the truth more profoundly than a photographer could. In this sense, at least, we may believe that the author, more than fifty years after some of the events he was seeking to describe (but not without information), wrote so that his readers might know the truth.[10]

SCENES FROM THE EARLIEST DAYS

For nineteen hundred years, Christians have been inspired by the word pictures of the earliest days of the church that have been "painted" in Acts 1—12. Just what these controversial vignettes present is now summarized here.

The Ascension

Two centuries after Jesus' resurrection, pious pilgrims began to visit Jerusalem to see an empty tomb. Where was Jesus' body? Ascended into heaven, Acts 1 replies. But when Christians began to recite, as part of the Apostles' Creed, "He ascended into heaven," they meant more than just a spatial relocation of Jesus' flesh and bones.

Every part of the New Testament affirms that Christ is risen from the dead. Repeatedly, he is also spoken of as in heaven and at "the right hand of God" (Rom. 8:34; Col. 3:1; 1 Peter 3:22; cf. Eph. 1:20; Heb. 1:3). That Jesus now has the status symbolized by these words is basic to the New Testament faith.

Except for the disputed ending of Mark (16:19), however, it is only Luke who describes Jesus' ascension—going "up" bodily into heaven—as an event seen by his disciples.

The story in Acts 1 is written in terms of a first-century cosmology in which heaven was thought of as "above" a flat earth. Subsequent recognition that the earth is round and that "up" is a relative term has not altered the significance of what the theologian Luke intends. His story implies at least three things:

1. Jesus was not raised from the dead simply to die again. Modern efforts (such as *The Passover Plot*)[11] proposing theories of a temporary resuscitation of Jesus' body miss the point of the biblical claim. Jesus, the church was sure, had permanently triumphed over death, had entered a new kind of life.

2. Jesus' ascension into heaven is a sign of his heavenly status, his conquest of all that opposed him in this world of human sin and limitation. Jesus is now "beside" God, exalted, in a position of equality with the Almighty.

3. The ascension of Jesus' body into heaven is a necessary preliminary for the coming of the Spirit. That Spirit, free from all physical, spatial limitations, becomes at Pentecost the moving force behind the witness of the apostles all over the world.

The Election of Matthias

After the death of Judas, there seemed to be the need for a new apostle to lead in that witness. As far as we know from the New Testament, however, Matthias, the one selected, never did much leading.

Late legend said that the cannibals were about to eat him. He had gone as a missionary to the Ethiopians. Just in time, however, this thirteenth apostle was rescued—by Andrew. An apocryphal Gospel that taught a heresy usually called Gnosticism was falsely attributed to Matthias. The New Testament, however, never mentions his name again after his selection in Acts 1.

The choosing of an additional apostle, however, is significant. Luke is saying that, from the first, the church regarded organization for its task as important. As there had been twelve tribes of Israel, the ancient people of God, and twelve apostles in the days of Jesus' earthly life, so the new community must have its Twelve. But first, Luke tells us, the church had to wait for the Spirit to come before it could begin its witness.

Pentecost

Suddenly, Luke says, that witness began, born in spiritual ecstasy.

Almost every book of the New Testament speaks of the Holy Spirit. Belief in this powerful presence was clearly part of the Christian faith from the beginnings of the Christian witness. Only Acts 2, however, describes the coming of that Spirit as an identifiable event on a particular day, the Jewish feast day of Pentecost. With miraculous manifestations of fire and the sound of wind, Luke tells us, the confused disciples were suddenly transformed. Once they had timidly waited. Now, so moved that some onlookers thought that they were drunk, the disciples began to shout out the gospel to the world.

The Gentile Luke pictures Pentecost itself as already pointing to the fulfillment of Jesus' command to be witnesses "to the end of the earth." The setting is Jerusalem at the feast of Pentecost (so called because it came fifty days after Passover). From all over the world, Jewish pilgrims, speaking every language, had come "home" to their holy city for the ceremonies. As the Spirit-baptized disciples began to "speak with tongues," some of these pilgrims heard only what sounded to them like the babbling of drunkards.

But miraculously, others heard in these same voices the disciples' praise of God, transcending all barriers of language and nation.

Scholars have proposed various explanations of this puzzling story:

1. More conservative scholars have said that here, at the beginning of the Christian mission, a miracle occurred and the disciples were temporarily enabled to speak foreign languages that they had never been taught.[12]
2. C. S. Mann suggests the possibility that the disciples spoke classical Hebrew, the language of the Old Testament, rather than the locally popular Aramaic dialect, and thus, to their surprise, the Jews from abroad understood.[13]
3. More liberal students have suggested that the "speaking with tongues" of the early church was always a pouring forth of unintelligible sound (such as is described in 1 Cor. 14:2), which "nobody understands." Luke, writing at a later time and unfamiliar with the practice, reported an ideal crossing of language barriers that did not then literally take place. Rather, his story reflects how, by his day, the gospel had begun to cross barriers of race, nation, and tongue.
4. Still others have suggested that the miracle was more in the hearts and ears of the hearers than in the tongues of the speakers. To some, the utterances did sound like drunken nonsense (Acts 2:13). But those more open to the Spirit were able to understand, each in his or her own way, the praise of God (Acts 2:11).

Whatever is the true explanation of the historical facts, Luke hints at theological meanings in the phenomena he depicts. Jewish tradition said that when the law was given to the Jews, seventy tongues of fire appeared on Mount Sinai—one for each of the other nations of the world. Now these tongues of fire reappear. The separation of nations and languages at the tower of Babel has now been reversed. The Jewish scriptures had pictured isolated instances of the Spirit's coming upon individuals (Judg. 14:6; 1 Sam. 10:10; etc.). But Luke sees in the worldwide church the fulfillment of Joel's prophecy that the Spirit will be poured out upon "all flesh" (Acts 2:17). Jesus' own promise had come true (Acts 1:5–8).

The "speaking in tongues" brought a mixed reaction from the crowd, Luke tells us. But Peter's sermon, presumably in common Aramaic, is said to have won three thousand converts (2:41).

The Preaching

In the twentieth century, the sermons summarized in the book of Acts have gained new recognition as expressions of the kerygma, the gospel proclaimed by the early church. In his now classic *The Apostolic Preaching and*

Its Developments, British scholar C. H. Dodd compared these sermons with passages in which Paul seems to be quoting tradition that he himself had been taught (Rom. 1:1–5; 10:8–9; 1 Cor. 1:23; 2:1–2; 15:1–7; Gal. 3:1; 1 Thess. 1:9). Running through both, Dodd found what appeared to be almost the same pattern. Dodd summarizes the sermons in Acts in the following propositions:

> First, the age of fulfillment has dawned. . . .
> Secondly, this has taken place through the ministry, death, and resurrection of Jesus, . . . with proof from the Scriptures that all took place through "the determinate counsel and foreknowledge of God. . . . "
> Thirdly, by virtue of the resurrection, Jesus has been exalted at the right hand of God, as Messianic head of the new Israel. . . .
> Fourthly, the Holy Spirit in the Church is the sign of Christ's present power and glory. . . .
> Fifthly, the Messianic Age will shortly reach its consummation in the return of Christ. . . .
> Finally, the *kerygma* always closes with an appeal for repentance, the offer of forgiveness and of the Holy Spirit, and the promise of "salvation."[14]

Several lines of investigation suggest that these sermons, thus summarized, do reflect the ideas characteristic of the earliest preachers:

1. As Dodd has shown, there is a distinct similarity between these sermons and the ideas that Paul seems to have learned from his predecessors.
2. A word study of the use of the Greek verb *kerussein* ("to preach") throughout the New Testament shows that its objects are nearly always the kinds of things described in Acts's sermons.
3. The language and style of the sermons, though that of Luke's good Greek, are said to bear uncharacteristic echoes of Aramaic, a Palestinian dialect foreign to our Greek author. Some have argued that he must have used an Aramaic source for some of these sermons.
4. The eschatology (doctrine of the end) and Christology (doctrine concerning who Jesus is) implied in these passages are not those of Luke's emphases. They seem more characteristic of an earlier time.

This is not to say, of course, that Luke has given us stenographic reproductions of the actual sermons. He says quite explicitly that he is attempting only a summary (Acts 2:40). But for the reasons stated above, we can believe that Acts does give us insight into the kind of things that the early preachers really did say about Jesus.[15]

If, then, we ask what was the earliest Christology, what was the earliest understanding of who Jesus was, the answer we get from these earliest sermons is perhaps surprising. It does not appear that the first Christians could have recited the Nicene Creed, with its phrases about Jesus that have been borrowed from Aristotelian metaphysics (such as that Jesus was "of one substance" with God the Father). But at the same time, there is no hint that, as some scholars once argued, Jesus was first thought of as a man and only gradually came to be revered as God. Rather, the sermons say such things about Jesus as the following.[16]

First, Jesus was described in terms of the *cosmic Judge of popular Jewish eschatological expectation.* Peter is depicted as quoting Joel's account of the final catastrophic events, now said to be at hand:

> I will show portents in the heaven above
> and signs on the earth below,
> . . . .
> The sun shall be turned to darkness
> and the moon to blood,
> before the coming of the Lord's great and glorious day.
> (Acts 2:19–20; cf. Joel 2:30–31)

The day spoken of in a book of the Pseudepigrapha, or "false writings," the *Assumption of Moses,* would arrive when

> the horns of the sun shall be broken and he shall be turned into darkness;
> And the moon shall not give her light, and be turned wholly into blood.[17]

In that eschaton, that end, Peter announces, Jesus "is the one ordained by God as judge of the living and the dead" (Acts 10:42).

This kind of understanding of Jesus is not a characteristic emphasis of the Greek Luke. Vivid descriptions of cosmic judgment were popular, however, among some first-century Jews. Later, the book of Revelation was to develop this aspect of the primitive kerygma.

Second, Jesus was seen as the *fulfillment of the Jewish scriptures.* "David says concerning him . . . " (2:25); "God fulfilled what he had foretold through all the prophets, that his Messiah would suffer" (3:18); "All the prophets testify about him . . . " (10:43)—over and over the sermons in Acts affirmed that all of the Old Testament had pointed to Jesus. We have seen how Matthew developed this idea in his Gospel. Hebrews explores this idea even more fully.

Third, Jesus was described also as *a man who had lived on earth.* "Jesus of Nazareth, a man attested to you by God with deeds of power, wonders, and signs that God did through him among you," is the subject of Peter's sermon in Acts 2:22. In Acts 10, Peter preaches of "how he went about doing good and healing all who were oppressed by the devil, for God was with him" (v. 38). One fact about Jesus' life that is mentioned in all of the sermons is his death. We have seen that an outline of the sermon in Acts 10 would serve almost equally well as an outline of Mark, so firmly was this story built into the primitive kerygma (see the section on "The Writing of the Gospels" in chapter 6 of this *Guide*).

Fourth, central to the sermons was the announcement of *Jesus' resurrection* (2:24, 32; 3:15; 10:40; etc.). It is the resurrection that is particularly to be associated with the two great titles for Jesus that Peter is depicted as proclaiming at Pentecost: "Lord" and "Messiah" (2:36). That the title "Lord" was used of Jesus even as early as the days of the Aramaic-speaking church seems clear from Paul's quotation of the formula *Marana tha* in its original Aramaic (1 Cor. 16:22). Probably it is to be understood as meaning originally that Jesus was the messianic king who had been promised in Psalm 110, the passage from the Old Testament most often quoted in the New Testament. The frequency of the use of the title and of the quotation of that psalm throughout the New Testament bears witness to its antiquity. The title "Christ" or "Messiah" also was soon so widely used of Jesus that it came to be almost a second proper name for him. But in the early days, its original connotation of "the Anointed One" surely must have been felt. Hebrew kings were anointed for office. When the dynasty of David was dethroned, the hope still endured of the great anointed king to come. Peter was announcing the fulfillment of that hope.

Is it possible to penetrate back to the very earliest Christian "creed" or confession, which stated what the very first Christians believed about Jesus? Tracing back the earliest formulas in scripture and the liturgies for baptism and worship, one always arrives at an original formula. It is the one implied by the climax of what Luke presents as the first Christian sermon: "Jesus Christ is Lord" (cf. 2:36).

Finally, the first sermons spoke of Jesus as a *living and present power*. It is Jesus who has poured out the Holy Spirit upon the believers (2:33). In his name, miracles are performed and forgiveness is granted (2:38; 3:16; etc.). He is the church's "Leader" and "Savior" (5:31).

Norman Perrin has argued forcefully that for Luke, Jesus is in a sense "the first Christian," the example and model for his followers. That, however, is not the emphasis of these sermons. In these early utterances, Christ is not presented simply as the first of a group. He is uniquely the author of ecstasy, the object of devotion, and one who, in his relationship to the believers, occupies a place and assumes titles heretofore reserved for God. He is not simply the church's example and leader but its Lord.

The Ideal Community

Was this first church a "commune"? Were the first Christians "communists"? We read such summaries as the following: "All who believed were together and had all things in common; they would sell their possessions and goods and distribute the proceeds to all, as any had need" (2:45; cf. 4:32). In his Gospel, Luke had pictured Jesus as preaching a kind of economic revolution on behalf of social justice. Now, he tells us, at least for "one brief, shining moment," Jesus' ideal was realized.

A closer reading, however, makes clear that such a verse as that quoted above is not to be taken as the whole picture. Luke does want to present the first church as an inspiring ideal. He wants to show the church as a sharing, praying, preaching, daring community. But Acts also records quite frankly selfishness, dissension, and dishonesty among the first church members. Ananias and Sapphira, we are told, sold a piece of property, brought half the proceeds to the apostles, and claimed to be giving them the whole price. The sin for which they were condemned was not that of keeping back half the money. Whatever sharing there was, it evidently was strictly voluntary, not required of all church members. It was when they were caught in a lie that Ananias and his wife fell dead (5:1–11).

We are also told of an early dispute between the native Palestinian Jewish Christians and their Greek-speaking brothers over the distribution of food to the poor (6:1–6). Again the church added to its organizational structure, selecting what were later called "deacons"—all of whom had Greek names—to see that the Greek-speaking widows would get their fair share. That dispute may have been the ancestor of subsequent disagreement resulting from the spread of the church beyond Palestine and the Jewish race, as at least one faction of the church aggressively spread the gospel through the Roman Empire.

Though he pauses in this way to caution us not to imagine that the first Christians were really sinless, Luke continues to picture the church in ideal terms, a model for his own generation. These exemplary Christians witness heroically and with marvelous success. They share all they have. And in persecution, they so pray that "the place in which they were gathered together was shaken" (4:31). Equally shaking to the reader is the account of what they prayed for. As Luke tells it, they did not pray to be spared; they prayed to have the courage to go on preaching, even though they faced persecution (4:29).

Persecution

Face persecution they did!

There are so many stories of arrests, trials, and escapes in Acts that Adolf Harnack supposed they must include duplicate reports of the same events. No doubt all were written to inspire a later generation of Christians still facing persecution, as well as to inform them. In any event, the first chapters of Acts abound in accounts of troubles with the authorities.

Acts 4 tells of an arrest and trial of Peter and John. This first time they are let off with a warning. Acts 5 tells of a second arrest, with the apostles being set free by angels. Then, arrested again, they are freed through the intercession of the wise Rabbi Gamaliel. Acts 7 describes the first martyrdom, that of Stephen. Acts 12 reports the execution of James, the first of the Twelve to give his life for his Lord. And Acts 12 records a fourth arrest of Peter, who is again set free by an angel. Meanwhile, we are told, persecution has begun to scatter the first Christians.

It is ironic that, for a few years, Jews seem to have persecuted Christians. Christians have been persecuting Jews for sixteen centuries. Soon, of course, it was the Roman, not the Jewish, authorities who threatened the church.

In our study of the Synoptic Gospels, we noted certain reasons for the antagonism between Jesus and even the best Jews. The reader should also recall that only by tenacious adherence to the law, usually coupled with a love of the holy land and the Temple even by those living far away, did Judaism survive. Jews grew up on the story of the seven brothers who were skinned and fried because they refused to eat pork. Jews grew up daily scanning the skies for a deliverer from the hated Romans. Naturally, they would not look kindly on the spread of a new teaching that seemed to undermine their faith. And authorities whose jobs depended on pleasing the Romans were not going to be happy that the "rebellion" they thought they had crushed now seemed to be rising again. Twenty-eight times in one century, the high priesthood changed hands, usually at the insistence of those who took orders from Rome. Fearful that their turn to lose power was at hand, the establishment moved to crush the new sect.

In the case of Stephen, one of those elected to administer food (Acts 6:1–6) but who seems also to have been a prominent preacher, antagonism finally led to violence. They lynched him.

Stephen

Presumably, Stephen's trial began in orderly fashion. Following custom, he would have been brought in wearing mourning clothes, a sign of the prisoner's penitence for sin. The seventy judges and their leader in the Sanhedrin, the Jewish court, would have been seated in a semicircle. Two notaries would have kept a record, one to record evidence in Stephen's defense, the other the evidence for the prosecution.

For centuries, the long address attributed to Stephen in Acts 7 has puzzled the commentators. "Stephen's reply at first seems absurd and inept," wrote John Calvin. "Many things in this speech have not very much pertinency to the matter which Stephen undertook," admitted Desiderius Erasmus. One modern commentator suggests that Luke himself did not understand it. At the very least, it is so different from anything else in Luke's book of Acts that we may believe that here, surely, Luke made use of some written source that purported to summarize what Stephen at some time had actually said.

Perhaps a key to understanding Stephen lies in his reference to Jesus as the "Son of Man" (7:56). This is almost the only place in the New Testament outside the Gospels in which this enigmatic phrase is used of Jesus, almost the only place where it appears except on the lips of Jesus himself. Apparently, later Christian thinkers went on to titles that made more sense to them than did this one from Jewish apocalyptic literature. The apocalyptic book of Daniel had described the Son of man:

> To him was given dominion
> and glory and kingship,
> that all peoples, nations, and languages
> should serve him. (Dan. 7:14)

Perhaps this Christian with the Greek name, who worked among people from other nations resident in Jerusalem (Acts 6:9) was the first to take seriously the idea that Jesus' kingdom must break out of Judaism, "that *all* peoples, nations, and languages should serve him."

The charges brought against Stephen involved his speaking against both the Temple and the law. Puzzling as his long address in Acts 7 is, three themes emerge: God is above the holy land, the chosen people, and the holy Temple. Repeatedly, God has worked outside these limits of place and race.

Infuriated, Stephen's hearers became no longer a court of law but a kind of lynch mob. Jewish law called for an orderly procession to the place of execution, with opportunity given right up to the last minute for a reversal of the death penalty. But now they "rushed together against him" (7:57). Praying, like Jesus, for the forgiveness of those who killed him, Stephen was stoned.

To be stoned, a criminal was thrown into a pit or a cell in which the witnesses against him could stand above him and drop big rocks on him. If the missiles of the witnesses themselves failed to kill him, then the whole crowd might join in crushing him with their stones. Guarding the coats of Stephen's executioners was young Saul of Tarsus (7:58).

The Spread of the Church

In the persecution that followed, in which Saul/Paul later confessed he had indeed been a leader (Gal. 1:13), the church at last began to spread into Judea and Samaria and beyond.

Later, writers repeatedly affirmed that the Christian world mission was really at the command of the risen Christ (Acts 1:8; cf. Matt. 28:19; etc.). But Acts is probably right that the first Christians remained largely in Jerusalem until they were driven out.

It is probably no accident, however, that the radiating forth of the gospel begins in relation to Stephen. We have seen it hinted that his was the vision of a kingdom of the Son of man that would include "all peoples, nations, and languages"—even Samaritans.

"You are a Samaritan and have a demon," Jesus' enemies had snarled, according to John 8:48. "Samaritan" was the worst name they could think to call him. Desperate as they had been for funds and friends, the little group of Jews who had set out to rebuild the Temple after the Babylonian captivity had rejected the offer of help from Samaritans, half-breed Israelites (Ezra 4:1–3). These Samaritans, in turn, had set up their own temple on Mount Gerazim (John 4:20). Stephen, however, had little regard for temples (Acts 7:48). We are told that after Stephen's death, "Philip went down to the city of Samaria and proclaimed the Messiah to them" (8:5). Even these hated Samaritans received the Holy Spirit (8:17).

Chapters 8 through 11 continue to describe how the gospel radiated from Jerusalem, as foreshadowed in Acts 1:8. An Ethiopian eunuch, possibly a Jew by birth but prevented from full participation in Judaism by the law of Deut. 23:1, was baptized.

The crucial departure from Judaism, however, is dramatized for us in the story of the baptism of Cornelius, a Roman. So important to Luke is the account of this Gentile's conversion and acceptance into the church that he devotes nearly two chapters to the story, in effect telling it twice (10.1–11.18). Peter is pictured as the leader in the matter, and he acts as the result of special revelation.

Critics have questioned the story in the light of Peter's subsequent refusal to eat with Gentiles (Gal. 2:12). Paul tells us on the basis of firsthand observation, however, that Peter did frequently eat with Gentiles, in violation of Jewish law. Luke has highlighted this particular instance as a dramatic way of telling his readers that the gospel did break out of all racial restrictions.

The critics are surely right, however, that the great leader in taking the gospel to the Gentiles and in working out the theology of that world mission was not Peter. It was that Saul of Tarsus who guarded the coats of Stephen's executioners and who helped lead the persecution that drove the Christians from Jerusalem. To Luke, Saul/Paul is so important that Acts 13—28, more than half of the book, is devoted to the life of this one man. To his story we must now turn.

PAUL

He was "a man rather small in size, bald-headed, bow legged, with meeting eyebrows, a large, red, and somewhat hooked nose," says the *Acts of Paul and Thecla,* a book of pious fiction popular in the second century. "Strongly built, he was full of friendliness, for at times he looked like a man, at times like an angel" (author's trans.).

As a description of Paul's physical appearance, the passage is too late to be of much value, though it is so unflattering as to suggest that it may owe something to memory, not just hero-worship. But the last clause is one Luke himself might have liked. At times Paul "looked like a man, at times like an angel."

He never succeeded in becoming a perfect saint, and indeed, Paul would have been the first to admit it (Phil. 3:14). He did become, next to Jesus, the dominant figure of the New Testament. Of its twenty-seven books, thirteen bear Paul's name. Some of these, as we shall see, probably should be thought of rather as dedicated to his memory than as actually from his pen, yet even so, his influence on them is clear. Two more books, Luke and Acts, are traditionally attributed to a disciple of Paul. Thus well over half of the New Testament is related to this one apostle. Paul has, in fact, been called "the second founder" of the Christian faith.

Clearly, he was Luke's hero. Acts 9 is the story of Paul's conversion. From Acts 13 on, the other apostles almost fade out of the story. Nearly the first half of Acts consists of scenes from the early church. But the rest of Acts is devoted entirely to stories of Paul.

Early Life and Conversion

Paul was born, Luke tells us, a Jewish citizen of Tarsus, a prominent city in what is now Turkey. He bore the name of history's most famous man of his tribe, King Saul. But as a Roman citizen, he also had a Roman name, Paul. Tarsus contained one of the great universities of the ancient world, and Luke pictures Paul as able to quote Stoic philosophers when presenting the gospel to Greek thinkers (Acts 17:28). Yet it was as a strict Pharisee in Jerusalem, taught by Rabbi Gamaliel, that Paul was trained, according to Acts 22:3. Some have interpreted Acts 7:58 and 26:10 as implying that Luke thought of Paul, though still young, as having already risen to be a member of the Jerusalem Sanhedrin, a kind of Jewish supreme court. More modestly, Paul simply wrote, "I advanced in Judaism beyond many among my people of the same age, for I was far more zealous for the traditions of my ancestors" (Gal. 1:14). Paul did admit that he had been "a Hebrew born of Hebrews" and "blameless" in his rigidly righteous adherence to the Jewish law (Phil. 3:5–6).

As such, Luke tells us, this young man fairly snorted with murderous rage as the Christian movement grew (Acts 9:1). Extremely "zealous," to use his own phrase, he once persecuted "the church of God and was trying to destroy it" (Gal. 1:13–14; cf. Phil. 3:6).

His conversion amazed his new brothers and sisters in Christ, both Luke and Paul tell us (Acts 9:26; Gal. 1:23–24). It has puzzled scholars ever since.

The story is so important to Luke that he tells it three times (Acts 9:1–30; 22:1–21; 26:1–23). Some details vary in the retelling. In Acts 9:7, Paul's companions hear a voice but see no one; in Acts 22:9, his companions see the great light but hear no voice. Perhaps mystic experiences do not lend themselves to the kind of factual reporting one expects on television's evening news. But the basic outline is the same. Paul was sent from Jerusalem to Damascus to lead in suppression of the church there (Gal. 1:17 implies that Paul had already become a resident of Damascus). On the road to that Syrian city, he was struck blind by a vision. In Gal. 1:15–16, Paul simply says that

God "was pleased to reveal his Son to me." Three days later, the persecutor of the faithful had become a baptized, seeing Christian.

Determined to understand the story in modern terms, some have proposed that Paul was subject to some kind of epileptic seizures or trances. Acts does picture him as having repeated "visions" (Acts 9:3; 16:9; 22:17; 23:11), and in 2 Cor. 12:1, Paul confirms this picture. Was epilepsy or perhaps recurring (hysterical?) bad eyesight (related to the Damascus road blindness) the "thorn in the flesh" complained of in 2 Cor. 12:7 (cf. Gal. 4:15; 6:11)? It must be noted that only a man of considerable mental and physical vigor could have done all that both Acts and Paul's letters indicate he did.

Other psychologically oriented students have noted that the "voice" is reported as saying to Paul at his conversion, "It hurts you to kick against the goads" (26:14). Does Luke mean to imply that Paul's conversion climaxed a long spiritual struggle, comparable to that which Paul described later in Romans 7?

Actually, neither the historian nor the psychiatrist can fully explain such experiences. Paul's letters bear witness to his conversion but give us no details (see, for example, 1 Cor. 9:1; 15:8; Gal. 1:15–16). What is certain is that he who once persecuted the church became its most influential writer, its most celebrated missionary, and the hero of the second half of Acts.

His temper was never fully converted. He still could call his enemies "dogs" (Phil. 3:2). Translators discreetly gloss over it, but what he really says about his opponents who continue to advocate circumcision is that he wishes they would go castrate themselves (Gal. 5:12). Even Luke could picture Paul as cursing the high priest and calling him an ugly name (Acts 23:3). "At times he looked like a man."

But to use one of Paul's favorite phrases, he was a man "in Christ."

The First Missionary Journey

One of the unsolved mysteries of biblical study is that while Acts pictures Paul as preaching in Jerusalem soon after his conversion, Paul himself, in Galatians, swears that instead he went to Arabia and did not go to Jerusalem for three years (Gal. 1:17–21). If, in the years described in these verses, Paul was already a missionary, what is usually called Paul's "first missionary journey" was really his second. Acts 9:30 does speak of a journey to Tarsus (cf. Gal. 1:21).

Nevertheless, what began at Antioch in Cilicia was a "first." Antioch, a seaport, was the third largest city in the Roman Empire. There, in that multiracial metropolis, an interracial church had already been established (Acts 11:20). Barnabas had secured Paul to help in the leadership of this unusual congregation. And there, Luke tells us, for the first time as far as we know, two men were formally commissioned to be missionaries (13:1–3).

Jesus' Great Commission, sending his disciples "to the ends of the earth," was at last beginning to be carried out fully.

Because Paul is depicted as setting out on journeys from Antioch three times, it is customary to speak of Paul's "three missionary journeys." These are found in Acts 13—14; 15:36–18:22; and 18:23–21:16. The route of each of these travels as recorded by Luke is readily traceable in any Bible atlas.

Paul's companion Barnabas was from Cyprus (4:36); it was to Cyprus that they went first. (Much later tradition said that Barnabas finally was martyred in Cyprus.) Though they crossed the island preaching, Acts saves its account of their message until its story of Paul's arrival on the mainland. In Cyprus, he is depicted as making a favorable impression on the proconsul (13:6–12). At least one inscription has been found indicating that a few years later, Cyprus was indeed governed by a proconsul and that his name was Paulus. There is, however, no record anywhere else of Sergius Paulus having actually become a Christian, though it is known that the church in Cyprus was quite strong two centuries later.

It is Paul's experience at Antioch in Pisidia—not to be confused with the Antioch in Cilicia, from which Paul's journey began—that Luke describes in detail (13:13–52). Apparently, Luke means us to understand that this is typical of Paul's message and method everywhere and of the response that Paul received.

In Paul's day as in ours, there were Jews in every city. Josephus quotes the geographer Strabo as having written, "This people has already made its way into every city, and it is not easy to find any place in the habitable world which has not received this nation and in which it has not made its power felt."[18] To the synagogue Paul and Barnabas go. In accordance with custom, they are given the opportunity to speak. The sermon is typical not so much of Paul as of the early kerygma common to all. Acts 13:38–39, however, with its promise of a freedom the law of Moses could not give, may be Luke's hint of a distinctive Pauline emphasis, one we will see developed at length in Paul's letters.

Equally typical is the response. Some become Christians; others run Paul and Barnabas out of town (13:48–50).

Curiously, it is Gentiles who are converted in this Jewish synagogue. The explanation is this: For one brief period in its history, Judaism was itself a missionary religion (Matt. 23:15). Disillusioned, even repelled, by pagan religions, many non-Jews had been attracted to the worship of the biblical God. Some had actually become Jews, undergoing circumcision as a sign that they were "proselytes." Others, known as "God-fearers," worshiped at the synagogue without being circumcised or restricting their diet to kosher food. It was among these Gentile converts and near-converts to Judaism, Luke tells us, that Paul had his greatest success. The synagogue split. The Gentile group, with some Jews, became the nucleus of a church. But the leaders of the more conservative Jewish establishment brought political pressure to bear on Barnabas and Paul and forced them to leave town.

The Jewish–Gentile pattern was repeated in Iconium (Acts 14:1–7). But at Lystra, Luke describes Paul's first recorded head-on encounter with real paganism.

> Toues Macrinus also called Abascantus, and Batasis son of Bretasis having made in accordance with a vow at their own expense [a statue of] Hermes Most Great along with a sun-dial dedicated it to Zeus the sun-god.[19]

So reads an inscription dug up near the little Turkish village where the great city of Lystra used to be. Another inscription read, "Kakkan and Maramoas and Iman Licinius priests of Zeus."[20] Clearly, the two gods for whom Paul and Barnabas were mistaken were worshiped in Lystra. In fact, the good people of that province believed that Zeus and Hermes might arrive incognito at any time. They had been taught as children the story of how the two gods, disguised as mortals, had been hospitably received by a Lystra couple, Philemon and Baucis, who had been rewarded. Now Paul and Barnabas, having healed a lame man, were mistaken for these gods themselves. The speech attributed to Paul in Acts 14:15–17 is our oldest account of a Christian address to a pagan audience.

Again forced by a Jewish faction to flee for their lives, Paul and Barnabas retraced their steps and eventually returned to Antioch in Cilicia, the city from which their journey had begun.

Their report is significant. They had been opposed in Cyprus, evicted from Antioch in Pisidia, nearly stoned in Iconium, and actually stoned almost to death in Lystra. But what they are said to have reported is that God had "opened a door of faith" (14:27).

The Jerusalem Council

The church, Luke tells us, was shaken by its own success. Were all those Gentiles really to be let into the church and, if so, on what basis? Luke's story of the council has also shaken modern critics.

The issue was both racial and religious. The Jews were God's chosen people, not the Gentiles. If Gentiles were to be admitted, surely they must first become good Jews. The first Christians were law-abiding, orthodox, circumcised Jews, worshiping in the Temple. There is no indication that the Christian leaders in Jerusalem overtly sought to exclude all Gentiles. But they did see the process of becoming part of God's people as including the ceremony of circumcision. This had been the sign of the covenant, Gen. 21:4 affirmed, since the days of Abraham and Isaac.

Acts 15 describes a kind of formal apostolic council to deal with the issue raised by the flood of Gentile converts. Apostles, elders, and others gather in solemn assembly. Peter makes a speech. James, Jesus' brother, whom later tradition called the first bishop of Jerusalem, presides. A formal, written decree is adopted and circulated to the churches. It represents a victory for Paul, but there are certain compromises in that a few dietary restrictions are to be imposed on the new converts (15:28–29).

Critics have objected that nowhere in his epistles does Paul mention such a decree, though he is repeatedly involved in the issue. The author of Galatians, it is argued, would never have accepted the "compromise" on food. (Defenders of the account in Acts have replied that pork chops are never served at conference dinners involving Christians and Jews today, though Christians do not thereby feel they are involved in "compromise.") The account in Galatians 2 of the same or a somewhat similar meeting represents a much less formal gathering with no written decree. Luke, it is charged, has idealized and enlarged the story to emphasize the importance of the decision for his Gentile readers.

Either way, Luke has dramatically presented an issue that certainly arose. And he is clearly right that the church did come—not without dissension—to accept Gentiles apart from the Jewish Law.

The Second Missionary Journey

"Saint" Barnabas and "Saint" Paul did not always get along. Their partnership ended with a spat over "Saint" Mark (Acts 15:36–40). A nephew of Barnabas, John/Mark—presumably the Mark to whom the Gospel is traditionally ascribed—had accompanied them at the beginning of the first missionary journey but had turned back (no reason is given for his retreat, but the stonings and threats of stonings they faced might have discouraged some later Christians). Paul refused to go again with Mark, and he and Barnabas went their separate ways. (2 Timothy 4:11 implies a later reconciliation.) Paul now set out with a companion named Silas.

Paul's original goal was to revisit the churches founded on his first trip in what is now Turkey (Acts 15:36). In response to what Luke is sure was divine guidance, however, Paul made a momentous decision: he crossed over into Europe (16:6–12). It is at the time of this decision, incidentally, that Luke seems to be claiming that he himself first entered the story (16:10).

Readers whose ancestors came from Europe may be disappointed to find that Paul's reception in Macedonia (northern Greece) was as stormy as it had been in Asia Minor. Again it was a "God-fearer," a Gentile who worshiped with the Jewish community, who was his first convert. Thus a traveling saleswoman, Lydia, was the first known Christian convert on European soil (16:14). Her home became headquarters for the church to which Paul was later to write the Philippian letter.

Soon, however, Paul was arrested at the instigation, Luke tells us, of the owners of a slave girl who was a fortune-teller. They were incensed because Paul, by exorcising her, had destroyed their livelihood. Delivered by an earthquake, a frightened jailer, and his own claim to the privileges of Roman citizenship, Paul was able to go on south through Greece.

A repeated theme is the prominent place of women in the churches established by Paul. Priscilla was to be a leader in the work (18:26; cf. 1 Cor. 16:19; Rom. 16:3). Lydia has been mentioned. "Leading women" are specifically noted among converts at Thessalonica (Acts 17:4). Women were again important at Beroea (17:12). At each of these places, also, it was the Gentiles from the fringes of the synagogues who formed the nucleus of the infant church. In his Gospel, Luke had pictured Christ as having come to break down barriers of race and sex. Now, he is saying, that process was underway.

By the time Paul arrives at Thessalonica for the usual pattern of preaching and the buildup to a riot, his fame has preceded him. "These people who have been turning the world upside down have come here also," his enemies exclaim, "saying that there is another king named Jesus" (17:6–7). The revolution Jesus had announced had already upset the world.

Paul's brief stay at Athens does not fit into the preach-and-riot pattern—or any other. Luke uses it to present, with all his dramatic skill, the encounter of the Christian gospel and Greek philosophy. At the intellectual capital of the world, Paul is invited to present his new ideas to a group of Epicurean and Stoic philosophers. Unlike his hearers in a Jewish synagogue, these men have no knowledge of the Jewish scriptures. The announcement about Jesus is the same, but the long introduction from the Old Testament, characteristic of almost all other sermons in Acts, is missing here in Acts 17:22–31. In its place are an attack on superstitious, pagan religion, likely to please his Epicurean hearers, and actual quotations from Stoic philosophers concerning the kinship of humankind as children of an omnipresent God, an idea calculated to please Paul's Stoic hearers. Though some modern critics have questioned whether Paul would really have made such use of pagan thought forms, others have replied that Paul confessed himself ready to adapt and adjust to his audience in many ways (1 Cor. 9:19–23). A century later, Justin Martyr was ready to argue that Socrates had been a Christian before Christ. Paul was not ready to go that far in relating his message to Greek philosophy, but Acts 17 bears witness to an early trend of Christian thought that was to lead in that direction.

Paul's longest stay on this journey was eighteen months at Corinth. To the church there he subsequently wrote letters that became part of the New Testament. The usual pattern again emerges, with the synagogue split and the Gentiles related to the synagogue forming the nucleus of the church. A minor detail is crucial for New Testament chronology. The proconsul called in as the inevitable riot is brewing is one Gallio. He is known to have been a half-brother of the Stoic philosopher-statesman Seneca. He occupied the position of proconsul only briefly, around the year A.D. 51. Apparently, the legal charge brought before him against Paul was that Paul was trying to win people to a new religion. Jews were granted religious freedom in the Roman Empire, but proselytizing was illegal. Gallio, however, chose to regard the whole matter as simply a squabble among Jewish sects.

Acts 18:22 pictures Paul as reporting in again at Jerusalem and Antioch at the end of the second journey.

The Third Missionary Journey

Naked to the waist, Artemis bared her multiple breasts in her images to show that she was goddess of sex and fertility. Her first stone idol, legend said, had fallen from heaven (19:35). Rich King Croesus had contributed columns fifty-five feet high to surround her temple of marble and gold. Hundreds of prostitutes there were the priestesses with whom intercourse constituted the worship of the goddess.

It was at Ephesus, the center of this worship of Artemis, that Paul spent more than two years, the major stay of his last missionary journey.

Acts 19 attributes so many miracles to Paul that the sick are pictured as being cured even by contact with his handkerchiefs. Exorcisms are especially mentioned.

Such stories have caused many to dismiss this chapter as "legendary." Two things, however, should be noted in its defense. Writing at this time from Ephesus back to Christians at Corinth, Paul himself, in an undisputedly authentic passage, could speak of things that he and his readers had witnessed which they both regarded as "signs and wonders and mighty works" (2 Cor. 12:12). How one explains these may be debated. But that such things occurred appears to be presented as an irrefutable claim.

And we know that exorcism was practiced in the ancient world, by pagans and Jews as well as Christians. Jewish law did not forbid it. The only question was whether it was in the name of the true God or of evil powers. An early medieval text seems to indicate that Jewish exorcists sometimes used certain names, unaware that they included those traditionally attributed to the "three Magi" of Matthew 2.

The inevitable riot occurred apparently in the thirty-thousand-spectator stadium, later to be unearthed by archaeologist J. T. Wood in the nineteenth century. "Great is Artemis of the Ephesians!" chanted the hysterical mob, egged on by merchants of temple souvenirs who had begun to see Paul as a threat to their business. As so often, Luke depicts the civil authorities as refusing to find Paul guilty of any crime.

Though Luke mentions Paul's returning to visit the churches he had founded in Greece, the emphasis is now placed on his solemn return journey to Jerusalem. It is reminiscent of Jesus' last trip to that same city. Repeatedly, Paul is warned that as he goes there, he is going to his death (Acts 20:22–23; 21:11).

The Arrest and Trial of Paul

Of the twenty-eight chapters of Acts, the last eight center on Paul's arrest at Jerusalem and the court proceedings that followed. Such emphasis on legal affairs seems so out of proportion that Harnack proposed that Acts was written as a brief for Paul's trial in Rome and that the "most excellent Theophilus" was Paul's judge. More likely, Luke in this form was presenting a model defense of Christian faith at a time when many later Christians were being threatened by many later judges.

Paul was arrested, Luke tells us, in yet another riot, this one growing out of the false charge that he had brought a Gentile into that part of the Temple restricted to Jews (21:28). Arrested, he was smuggled to Caesarea just in time to escape a lynch mob.

Antonius Felix, Paul's first judge, appears in a bad light both in Acts and in secular history. In A.D. 53, the emperor Claudius had appointed him procurator of Judea, the same position Pilate had once held. Born into slavery, Felix and his brother Pallas had been set free, and Pallas had become a favorite of the emperor until he fell into disgrace in the year A.D. 55. Josephus says that Felix did suppress robbers and murderers, but slaughtered even his friends when it suited his purpose. It seems likely that he was involved in the murder of the high priest Jonathan. He married three times, one wife being Drusilla, sister of one of the infamous Herods. Tacitus writes of Felix that "with all manner of cruelty and lust, he exercised the functions of a prince with the disposition of a slave."[21] He was eventually called to Rome to stand trial for misgovernment, and he was banished. He still had not received the bribe he had hoped to collect from Paul (24:26).

About the year A.D. 60, Festus was chosen by Nero to succeed Felix. He emerges in Acts and elsewhere as a more just and vigorous administrator. Had he lived, perhaps he might have been able to delay or prevent the suicidal revolution that brought about the destruction of Jerusalem within a decade. But Festus died only two years after coming to Palestine.

Beginning in 509 B.C., Roman law, the *Lex Valeria,* had made it obligatory that citizens of Rome who appealed to the Roman rulers be given the privilege of trial before the high court. Though originally the law had applied only to Rome and its suburbs, six centuries later it evidently had been broadened to include citizens of Rome everywhere. Most inhabitants of the Roman Empire, of course, were subjects but not citizens. Having waited in prison for two years because of Felix's hope for a bribe and resisting Festus's proposal to return him to authorities at Jerusalem, who almost certainly would condemn him, Paul exercised his special right as a citizen.

"I appeal to the emperor!" he cried.

"You have appealed to the emperor; to the emperor you will go" (25:11–12).

Yet Luke gives us one more dramatic court scene. King Herod and the princess Bernice would have worn robes of royal purple, with golden circlet crowns on their heads. Festus, as a Roman governor, would have worn a scarlet robe. The captains of the five cohorts of the Roman legion stationed at Caesarea would have stood behind him, and a phalanx of legionnaires must have formed the ceremonial guard. The occasion was the first state visit by the neighboring king to the new Roman governor. Bernice was not the current Herod's wife but his sister. Their relationship was the subject of public scandal. In this dramatic scene, Luke presents for one last time Paul's testimony. Once more, Paul is found guiltless. But his appeal to Caesar must stand. Paul will go to Caesar (26:32).

Acts 27 gives what is perhaps the most vivid and detailed account of a historic sea voyage in all of ancient literature. The largest boats of the time were only about 140 by 36 feet. Two hundred and seventy-six people and the cargo must have been packed in. When he describes the shipwreck, Luke depicts the prisoner Paul as actually assuming command.

The Ending of Acts

William H. Willimon points out that it is appropriate that Acts is an open-ended story. The story of the church is still going on! Nevertheless, the ending of Acts has puzzled commentators for decades. The story breaks off with Paul enduring two years of house arrest at Rome, still preaching (28:30–31). Inevitably, the reader asks, "What happened then? Why does Luke not tell us more?"

Some have suggested that Luke stopped there because it was at that point in time that Acts was written.

Others have proposed that Luke intended to write a third volume or even that he did write one, which is now lost.

Most, however, believing the book to have been written in A.D. 85 or later, have assumed that Luke stopped here because the movement of the gospel from Jerusalem to Rome provided for this Gentile the climax of history. Nine chapters earlier, he had alerted his readers that Rome was Paul's goal (19:21). Now, providentially but not at all in the way Paul had intended, Paul's goal is accomplished. He is preaching in the capital of the world.

Tradition says that Paul was not crucified, as a Jew or a slave might have been. He was given the "privilege" of a Roman citizen convicted of a crime. He was beheaded.

But his letters continued and multiplied his ministry. To them we now turn.

8

THE EARLIER LETTERS
OF PAUL

INTRODUCING THE LETTERS OF PAUL

[Paul was] the second founder of Christianity.
—Wilhelm Wrede

There has really never been a more monstrous imposition perpetrated than the imposition of the limitations of Paul's soul upon the soul of Jesus.
—George Bernard Shaw

[Paul was] the first Christian, the inventor of Christianity! Before him there were only a few Jewish sectaries.
—Friedrich Nietzsche

Christian theology is a series of footnotes to St. Faul.
—Sydney Ahlstrom[1]

Our beloved brother Paul wrote to you . . . letters. There are some things in them hard to understand.
—2 Peter 3:15–16

More than half of the books of the New Testament are either by Paul or traditionally attributed to him. Obviously, to understand the Christians' book, one must understand Paul's letters. But Paul has been understood—or misunderstood—in a bewildering variety of ways, as the quotations above indicate. One modern commentator suggests that nobody ever understood Paul, from the first century on—until that commentator wrote his book!

Here are a few of the varying efforts to get at some key idea by which to unlock Paul's meaning.

Some Contrasting Interpretations
of Paul in History

Paul "was a Greek, child of a Greek mother and a Greek father. He went up to Jerusalem . . . and . . . was seized with a passion to marry a daughter of the priest. For this reason he became a proselyte and was circumcised. Then, when he failed to get the girl, he flew into a rage and wrote against circumcision and against Sabbath and Law."[2] So a group of third-century Christian opponents of Paul's doctrines attempted to "explain" him, by smearing his reputation, in a book they falsely attributed to James. Ebionite heretics, conservative Jewish Christians still holding to the Mosaic law, continued for years to attack Paul as a subverter of the "true Christianity" of Jesus the Jew.

In complete contrast, the second-century heretic Marcion taught that Paul was the only true apostle precisely because Paul had attacked Judaism. A kind of anti-Semite, Marcion argued that the Jewish Creator-God described in the Old Testament was a false deity of law, even vengeance; but "our Christ was commissioned by the good God to liberate all mankind."[3] Marcion rejected Matthew's Gospel as too Jewish a book. But he regarded Paul's letters—after he had censored out of them what he disliked—as truly authoritative.

"Paul is the most heretical of heretics,"[4] wrote Martin Luther, identifying with him as he faced being excommunicated as a heretic himself. Battling with a sense of guilt that has fascinated modern psychiatry, Luther had attempted to find salvation through the most zealous legalism of medieval Christianity. He had watched his fellow monks. "They wore hair shirts; they fasted; they prayed; they tormented and wore out their bodies. . . . And yet the more they labored, the greater their terrors became."[5] He himself had tried to outdo them. It was in his study of Paul's letters to the Galatians and the Romans that Luther found release. Justification, getting right with God, came not by such ascetic practices or by any other good works. Salvation, Paul seemed to be saying, was God's free, unearned gift, received by faith alone (Rom. 1:17). Luther interpreted Paul's struggle against Pharisaic legalism as he understood it. To Luther, the key to Paul's gospel could be expressed in these words: "The truth of the Gospel is this, that our righteousness comes by faith alone, without the works of the Law." On this "heresy" of Paul's protest against Orthodox Jewish legalism, Luther took his stand against the orthodoxy of his day.

With Paul, Christianity left Judaism and took on aspects derived from Greek culture—so certain nineteenth-century thinkers decided. With the aid of Greek philosophical concepts, he universalized and rationalized what might otherwise have become simply a Jewish cult; or according to the so-called History of Religions school, Paul aided the process by which Jesus' teachings of love were fitted out in the trappings of the Greek mystery religions. In such religions as Mithraism and the Isis cult, one might be initiated into a kind of religious fraternity under a "lord," a mediator-savior who linked man and God. Such a "lord" might die and rise again. The candidate might be "born again" by being sprinkled with the blood of a sacrificed bull or even gain union with his "lord" by drinking blood. Scholars influenced by this approach drew comparisons between such practices and Paul's ideas concerning baptism, the Lord's Supper, and the role of the "Lord" Jesus.

To Albert Schweitzer, Paul and such Greek religions "have in common their religious terminology, but, in respect of ideas, nothing."[6] Rather, "it is only the acceptance of the fact that the Apostle's doctrine is integrally, simply and exclusively eschatological"[7] that enables us to understand it. Jesus had proclaimed that the kingdom was at hand. Paul believed that Jesus, the eschatological Messiah, was soon to return to bring in that kingdom. In the meantime, the believer might have the new life of one who is "in Christ." This mystic union, this "'being-in-Christ' is the prime enigma of the Pauline teaching; once grasped it gives the clue to the whole."[8]

No great believer in eschatology, Adolf Harnack argued that Paul transformed the simple religion *of* Jesus into a religion *about* Jesus. Jesus had taught the Fatherhood of God and the brotherhood of all humanity. But with Paul, "the formation of a correct theory of and about Christ threatens to assume the position of chief importance, and to pervert the majesty and simplicity of the Gospel. . . . Paul became the author of the speculative idea that not only was God in Christ, but that Christ himself was possessed of a peculiar nature of a heavenly kind."[9] The center of Christianity became not love but orthodox belief about Jesus as "Son of God."

Existential philosophy was the key by which the twentieth-century thinker Rudolf Bultmann sought to unlock Paul's meaning. Paul does not offer us metaphysical speculations about the nature of God, Bultmann affirms. Rather, he presents God always in relation to humanity and humanity in relation to God. Paul's theology, according to Bultmann, is really "anthropology."[10] When Paul talks about God, he is to be understood today as really talking about the possibilities of human beings. The "salvation" Paul proclaims can be interpreted in the light of the "authentic existence" that Bultmann's one-time colleague, existentialist philosopher Martin Heidegger, described.

Finally, among many contemporary thinkers, one may note that to the "post-Bultmannian" Ernst Käsemann, Bultmann's approach seems too individualistic. History, apocalyptic, and Christology are as important to Paul as anthropology, and they cannot be reduced to statements about an individual Christian. Like Schweitzer, Käsemann sees apocalyptic as "the mother of Christian theology." And Paul writes not first of all about the individual Christian but about Jesus Christ. For Paul, Käsemann says, Christ is the center of a historical process, "salvation history," as well as Savior of individual men and women.[11]

Perhaps 2 Peter 3:15–16 was right about Paul's letters. "There are some things in them hard to understand." This section has presented—in admittedly very brief and oversimplified form—eight interpretations. There are many, many others. Study Paul for yourself and arrive at your own understanding of these letters.

But first, it is important to note that the word "epistle" means simply "letter." These books of the Bible are in the form of everyday correspondence.

The Form of the Letters

Early in the third century A.D., a student named Thonis wrote home. Apparently, he wanted his father to come and bring him money for his school fees.

> To my lord and father Arion from Thonis greeting. Before all else I make supplication for you every day, praying also before the ancestral gods of my present abode that I may find you and all our folk thriving. Look you, this is my fifth letter to you, and you have not written to me except only once, not even a word about your welfare, nor come to see me; though you promised me saying "I am coming," you have not come to find out whether the teacher is looking after me or not. He himself is inquiring about you almost every day, saying, "Is he not coming yet?" And I just say "Yes." Endeavour then to come to me quickly in order that he may teach me as he is eager to do. . . . I send my salutations to all our folk, each by name, together with those who love us. Salutations also to my teachers. Goodbye, my lord and father, and may you prosper, as I pray, for many years along with my brothers whom may the evil eye harm not. [Postscript] Remember our pigeons. [Addressed] To Arion my father from . . .[12]

Whether Thonis's father ever came with the money to pay the teacher to continue Thonis's education, we will never know. The point in reproducing the letter here is this: the form of that very ordinary letter from a student to his father is the form of nearly every one of the New Testament epistles of Paul.

Thonis's request for his father's help could be outlined like this:

1. The name of the sender and the receiver
2. A salutation
3. A prayer to the writer's god for the one to whom the letter is sent
4. The message
5. Personal greetings to others
6. A concluding blessing
7. A postscript about something the writer had forgotten to say earlier

If the reader looks at 1 Thessalonians, usually regarded as the earliest of Paul's letters, he or she will find that it follows very much the same outline:

1. First Thessalonians 1:1 gives the names of the senders and tells us to whom the letter is written.
2. There follows, in the same verse, a salutation: "Grace to you and peace." ("Grace" is a word especially loved by Christians; "peace" is still a traditional Jewish greeting.)
3. Verses 2–3 contain the prayer for the recipients, though this prayer, of course, is in the name of Christ, not of Thonis's ancestral gods.
4. The message now follows.
5. First Thessalonians 5:26 conveys greetings to friends.
6. Paul started to conclude with 1 Thess. 4:1, thought of more he needed to say, and finally concluded with a blessing in 5:28.
7. There is no real postscript on this letter, but note that 2 Thessalonians has one in 3:17–18.

That postscript in Paul's own hand implies that the rest of the letter was dictated to a secretary. Galatians 6:11 adds to the impression that this was Paul's habit. No doubt either Silvanus (Silas) or Timothy, both of whom are mentioned in the first verse of both 1 and 2 Thessalonians, often served as Paul's secretary.

Paul wrote letters, therefore, in quite the ordinary form, and he wrote in quite ordinary language. Many years ago, scholars noted that the Greek of the New Testament was different from that of the classical Greek writers. Some even proposed that the sacred books were written in a special "language of the Holy Spirit." Quite the opposite, we now know from hundreds of letters that have been found (such as that of Thonis) that Paul's language was the popular Greek of his day, the *koine,* or common dialect.

There is no hint that Paul thought of himself as writing sacred scripture. To him, the Old Testament was the inspired book. Because he was writing to the whole church at Thessalonica, he did urge that the letter be read publicly (1 Thess. 5:27). Christians for centuries have been sure that though Paul was not aware of it, he was miraculously inspired by the Holy Spirit as he wrote. But Paul writes simply as a pastor, quite unconscious that, centuries later, his words would be regarded as in some sense part of the "Word of God."

Finally, concerning Paul's letters, Wilhelm Wrede's comment about Galatians applies to some extent to almost all of Paul's writings. Wrede called Galatians "a fighting epistle." Paul wrote to particular situations in particular churches. He wrote to meet challenges. He usually wrote in the midst of controversies, if not to defend himself personally then at least to defend the gospel to which he had dedicated his life. For example, in 1 Thess. 2:1–12,

Paul was defending himself against many kinds of slander. He wrote with high emotion, and his letters are not really grasped if the emotions behind them are not felt. Often his letters follow no more carefully planned outline than do the letters of most readers of this book. Paul may break off a sentence in the middle in his excitement; may call his enemies ugly names; may flatter, apologize, preach, coax, or even quote poetry. He was a real man, writing to real people, often in some real crisis.

To understand a letter of Paul, therefore, it is highly important to look for clues as to what situation or occasion caused him to write it. Paradoxically, readers often tend most clearly to find Paul speaking eternal truths when they are most conscious that he was speaking a particular message to a historical situation.

The letters to the church at Thessalonica illustrate all of these ideas.

1 THESSALONIANS

Timothy brought Paul good news and bad news and a set of questions. Moved by what he had heard, Paul began to dictate a letter. It was a memorable moment in the history of literature. "Paul, Silvanus, and Timothy, To the church of the Thessalonians. . . ." With those words, according to the most widely accepted chronology, the writing of the New Testament began.

The Occasion of 1 Thessalonians

We have noted that every letter of Paul has grown out of a particular situation, often a crisis. To understand a letter, the student must look for hints as to the events that caused the author to write it. Reading through 1 Thessalonians, one comes upon a clear indication of the immediate occasion for this epistle:

> But Timothy has just now come to us from you, and has brought us the good news of your faith and love. He has told us also that you always remember us kindly and long to see us—just as we long to see you. (1 Thess. 3:6)

The verses leading up to this announcement give further background for understanding the letter. Forced out of Philippi, Paul had preached in Thessalonica, in spite of great opposition, he reminds his readers (1 Thess. 2:2). He had had particular success with the Gentiles but violent opposition from some Jews (2:14–16). All this had happened quite recently (2:17). He had been prevented by "Satan" from returning to them (2:17–18). Therefore, having gone as far down the road as Athens, he had sent Timothy back to check on the progress of the new church. Now, presumably a bit farther down the road at Corinth, he has heard Timothy's report and hastens to write them this letter.

1 THESSALONIANS
Their Exiled Pastor Writes to a Very Young Church

"Finally, brothers and sisters, we ask and urge you . . . that, as you learned from us how you ought to live . . . (as, in fact, you are doing), . . . you should do so more and more" (4:1).

1:1 **Thanksgiving and Rejoicing because of Good News from the Church**	2:1 **Paul's Continued Concern for Their Church in the Midst of Opposition**	4:1 **An Exhortation to Keep Up the Good Work, Living in a Way Pleasing to God**	4:13 **Answers to Two Questions They Have Asked**	5:12 **Final Exhortation and Closing Greetings**
Paul's prayer of thanks, 1:1–3	A reminder of how he ministered among them, in spite of opposition, 2:1–12	Live moral lives, 4:1–8	What about those who have died before Christ's return? 4:13–18	
The good news he has heard which has made him thankful, 1:4–10	Their good response, even though he had been driven out, 2:13–16	Live lives of love and industriousness, 4:9–12	When will that return be? 5:1–11	
	His continuing concern, though separated from them, 2:17–3:5			
	The good news Timothy has brought, 3:6–13			

Author: Paul
Recipients: The church at Thessalonica, which Paul had founded but had been forced to leave quickly
Date: A.D. 50–51
Occasion: Timothy had brought Paul a report and some questions from the church.
Purpose: To rejoice with them in their faithfulness, to encourage them in spite of difficulties and attacks on Paul, and to answer their questions

All of this fits perfectly with the account that Acts gives us of Paul's second missionary journey. Even commentators who brand Acts's stories as "legendary" do not hesitate to use Acts 17 to reconstruct the occasion of the writing of this letter. A quick review of that chapter will remind the reader that after a brush with the law at Philippi, Paul did indeed found the church at Thessalonica. He was assisted by Silas (the "Silvanus" mentioned in 1 Thess. 1:1) and Timothy (also mentioned in the letter). He did have his best success with Gentiles—and, by the way, with women—as is noted in Acts 17:4. But certain Jews stirred up such opposition that Paul escaped only by being smuggled out at night, just ahead of a lynch mob (Acts 17:5–10). Opponents from Thessalonica had even driven Paul out of the next town, Beroea (Acts 17:13). Paul had indeed gone on alone through Athens, instructing Silas and Timothy to join him later with a report. Soon he settled down a little farther west in Greece for an eighteen-month stay in Corinth. The account in Acts harmonizes so perfectly with what seems implied in 1 Thessalonians that Acts's additional details must be thought of as shedding trustworthy light on the letter.

We can even date the letter. The archaeologists have discovered an inscription which shows that Gallio was proconsul of Achaia only briefly, so that Paul's stay at Corinth during Gallio's period of office (Acts 18:12) must have been in about A.D. 51 or 52. If, as is implied, the letter was written soon after Paul's arrival in Corinth, then 1 Thessalonians gives us a picture of Christianity only some twenty years after the earthly life of Jesus.

The Purpose of 1 Thessalonians

First Thessalonians, then, is written as a substitute for a visit that is probably too dangerous for Paul to make and in response to the report of the visit that Timothy did make. Paul writes out of joy to congratulate the church at Thessalonica for all of the good things that he has heard about them. He writes to defend himself against false charges that his opponents are still spreading about him. He writes to assure the newly established church of his continuing concern. He writes, as in all of his letters, to exhort them to Christian living. And he writes to answer certain questions that, it appears, have been brought to him from the church by Timothy, perhaps in a letter of their own.

About Outlines of the Epistles Proposed

Except perhaps for Romans, all of Paul's letters are informal. None fits neatly into a systematic outline. All do fit into the general framework of letters that we noted earlier in this chapter. Any outline is helpful only as it simplifies a letter, but to simplify is in some sense to distort. Though there are dangers, an outline is included in a table this *Guide* for each epistle, except for the short, one-chapter letters. These outlines are intended to show how each letter may be seen as unified by certain principal themes. For one useful way of outlining 1 Thessalonians, see p. 399.

Some Comments on the Content
of 1 Thessalonians

The first chapter of the letter is all joy. Acts implies that Paul had been able to teach the Thessalonians only for three weeks. He has been worried about the church, so soon left without its leader. But now Paul has heard good reports through Timothy. These simply confirm other good reports that, he tells them with pardonable exaggeration, have spread everywhere. As a matter of fact, the main street of Thessalonica was the Via Egnatia, the great highway linking Rome with Asia. News of what happened there would spread, which is doubtless one reason Paul was concerned that there be a strong church in that city. Macedonia was the country of Alexander the Great, who, as a missionary for Greek culture, had conquered the world. Thessalonica was named for his sister, as Philippi was named for his father. The news of the church at Thessalonica could have an impact in many places (1:8). Paul no doubt had been worried about the infant church that he had had to leave so suddenly. But these Christians had proved examples of the faith, just as Paul, Timothy, and Silas had tried to be examples to them.

Some commentators suggest that 1 Thess. 1:9–10 echoes a kind of early creed, one learned by Paul and taught to these Christians before a word of the New Testament was written. If so, perhaps one might summarize the faith heroically spread by these first Gentile converts somewhat like this:

> We turn to God from idols,
> to serve a living and true God,
> and to wait for his Son from heaven,
> whom he raised from the dead—
> Jesus, who rescues us from the wrath to come.

Their loyalty to such beliefs has not been easy. Paul's enemies, having run him off, have continued to attack him by slander. Reading between the lines in 1 Thessalonians 2, one can find that the Thessalonians had heard such attacks on their former teacher as the following:

"He is sexually immoral." 1 Thessalonians 2:3 speaks of what the translators discreetly call "impure motives." Acts 17:4 specifically mentions the prominent place of women in the church Paul founded. Perhaps this gave a chance to the scandalmongers. At the beginning of this chapter, it was noted that centuries later this kind of lie was still being spread about Paul.

"He is tricky, a liar" (cf. 2:3).

"He is in it for money and what he can get out of it" (cf. 2:5–6). Paul was not the last traveling evangelist to face that charge. There were, in the ancient world, many traveling preachers of various religions who professed to work miracles (Acts 13:6; 19:13). Many deserved their bad reputations. In Paul's absence, the charges against him may have sounded reasonable.

In reply, Paul reminds the Thessalonians of the life he and his associates had lived among them when he was their pastor. He had earned his own living, working with his hands (1 Thess. 2:9–12). Acts 18:3 tells us that Paul paid his own way by working as a tentmaker. He assures them of his continued concern. He negatively implies that the activity of his enemies is really that of "Satan" (1 Thess. 2:18). He gloats over his assurance that God is cursing those sinners (2:16). ("At times he looked like a man," said a later description of Paul, as we have noted; and Paul can be quite human in his attitudes toward those who oppose what he regards as God's work. See p. 383.) To remind them of his continued concern, he reviews his sending Timothy to them and his receiving Timothy's report (2:17–3:10). The first half of the letter ends with a prayer for God's continued blessing on them.

Some editions of the New Testament leave a blank space between chapters 3 and 4 to show that the letter now moves to a different subject. It is typical of Paul's letters that the second half deals with more practical matters. Thus 1 Thess. 4:1–12 gives ethical instruction to new Christians, to whom the Christian ways may still have seemed strange. For example, New Testament standards concerning sex were quite different from those popular in the ancient pagan world, just as they are quite different from those which surveys indicate guide the practice of most Americans today. Paul flatly prohibits adultery and seeks to confine sexual intercourse to marriage (4:1–8).

His exhortation to love is typically loving. He assures them that they do not need to be reminded to love one another (4:9). He then proceeds to remind them to love one another, more and more!

The two questions that form the subject of the next two paragraphs in the letter reflect the eschatological expectation that was still strong in the church of A.D. 50–51. Jesus had come preaching that the kingdom was at hand. We have seen that many interpreters of Paul emphasize that his letters can be understood only in the light of his eschatology. The little "creed" quoted above (1:9–10) pictures the church as waiting for the "Son from heaven, . . . Jesus, who rescues us from the wrath that is coming." In the light of this expectation, the Thessalonians, new in the faith, have become concerned about some of their number who have died. Have they missed out on the great day?

Paul's answer is to assure them that both the living and the dead will share equally in the coming of the Lord (4:13–18). In fact, the dead will be the first to join him in his return. "Therefore encourage one another with these words." This passage is the best loved in 1 Thessalonians, having been read at the funerals of many Christians.

In recent years, this passage has also been the subject of curious distortion. Bumper stickers have proclaimed: "In case of the Rapture, this car will be driverless." "The rapture," often pictured in sensational detail by certain preachers, is supposedly described in 1 Thess. 4:17, understood to mean that at some time, Christ will gather "up" all believers off the earth, leaving unbelievers to assorted trials. Actually, however, Paul is simply affirming the good news that the dead in Christ will have a full share in the great day. The paragraph says nothing about unbelievers, on or off the earth. The very next paragraph, rather, seems to be a warning against trying to establish some kind of timetable or schedule of events of this sort. Paul's concern is not to map out details about the future but to comfort the bereaved.

Therefore, to the second question—which was apparently "When will the end be?"—Paul replies that nobody knows or needs to speculate about that. The Thessalonians need not try to guess about God's timetable. They are already "children of light and children of the day." They know that they are destined to obtain salvation (5:1–10). Nothing else about the end need concern the Christian.

Rather, Paul says in his closing exhortation, they are to do now the work given them. Note how 1 Thess. 5:15 sounds almost like a quotation from the Sermon on the Mount. And they are to respect their leaders, to be patient, to be loving.

Before his benediction, Paul returns briefly to one theme that has been touched on previously in the letter: the importance of doing one's daily work. He had reminded them earlier how he himself had worked for a living even when he was their pastor (2:9). He had hinted that this was part of his example to them. Again, in 4:11, he had urged them to work with their hands. Now a third time he is concerned to "admonish the idlers" (5:14).

Evidently, however, these hints were too gentle. Within a few weeks, most scholars believe, Paul was writing again on this subject, this time harshly. "Anyone unwilling to work should not eat" (2 Thess. 3:10).

But that is a theme of the next letter.

2 THESSALONIANS

So excited were these new Christians about the end of the world, which they understood to be at hand, that they had actually quit their jobs. Why save money for an old age that will never come? Horrified by their idleness, apparently reported to him soon after his first letter was delivered to the church at Thessalonica, Paul wrote the second letter.

So, at least, tradition has understood 2 Thessalonians. We must note that this interpretation has been challenged.

2 THESSALONIANS
On Working until the End

"As to the coming of our Lord, . . . we beg you . . . not to be . . . shaken in mind" (2:1–2).

1:1 Thanksgiving and Encouragement for Their Faithfulness in the Midst of Trials	2:1 A Correction: Only after Further Trials Will the End Come	2:13 Paul's Prayer That They Will Stand Firm and a Request That They Pray for Him Too	3:6 A Strong Closing Appeal That Everyone Work for a Living until the End	3:18
Thanksgiving, 1:1–4	The end is not yet, 2:1–2	His prayer, 2:13–17		
Encouragement, 1:5–12	The "man of lawlessness" must come before the end, 2:3–12	His request, 3:1–5		

Author: Paul (some question this)
Recipients: The young church at Thessalonica
Date: A.D. 50–51 (some put it much later)
Occasion: Paul has received further news from Thessalonica telling of persecution from without and misunderstandings within that church.
Purpose: To encourage their faithfulness and work and to correct misunderstandings about the end of the world

Problems concerning the Authorship
and Date of 2 Thessalonians

At least four difficulties have been noted concerning the usual interpretation of this book:

1. Parts of 2 Thessalonians are so similar to 1 Thessalonians that some have regarded it as a paraphrase of the first letter, with additions by a later author.
2. The tone of 2 Thessalonians is much more severe than that of the warmly affectionate first letter.
3. The Christology (the doctrine of who Christ is) is said to be more advanced in 2 Thessalonians.
4. Most important, it is said that the eschatology in the second letter is quite different from that of the first. In 1 Thessalonians, Paul says that there is no way to predict when the end will be. It will come entirely without warning, "like a thief in the night" (5:2). But 2 Thessalonians describes various things that must happen before the end can come (2 Thess. 2:1–12).

Some scholars, therefore, have proposed that 2 Thessalonians comes from a later time and is by a later author.[13] Others have suggested that the two letters fit together better if 2 Thessalonians is thought of as having been written first.

Most, however, hold to the traditional view, believing that the alleged differences either have been exaggerated or can be explained on the basis of the growing problem in the Thessalonian church.[14] That situation, as usually understood, is now described.

The Occasion of 2 Thessalonians

The kingdom of heaven must indeed be at hand. Paul had preached it; now his letter had reaffirmed it. So, at least, the Thessalonians understood it. Indeed, there is a hint that, in a "dirty tricks" campaign, Paul's enemies had circulated yet another letter, forged by them, designed to whip up even more unfounded enthusiasm. Some members of the church at Thessalonica had actually quit their jobs to wait for the imminent return of the Lord. New in the faith, the infant church was confused.

Paul received a report of this situation, perhaps from whoever had carried his first letter to Thessalonica. Therefore, within a few weeks after the first letter, he wrote a second one.

The Purpose of 2 Thessalonians

As in 1 Thessalonians, Paul writes to encourage the new church in a time of confusion and opposition. But especially, he seeks to stop the members of the congregation from supposing that the end of the world is necessarily to arrive within the next few days. Various trials must be endured first, he tells them. Therefore, the members of the church should go back to work and to godly living in the world.

Some Comments on the Content of 2 Thessalonians

Because 2 Thessalonians is one of the briefest of Paul's letters, only brief comment is given here.

The most puzzling passage is the one concerning "the lawless one" (2:1–12). Most scholars believe that Paul's words would have made more sense to his Thessalonian readers if he had referred to someone or something threatening or expected to threaten in his own day. But none of the various explanations suggested seems to fit perfectly. Here are three possibilities:

The Roman emperor (or some soon-to-come emperor), with the forces of the empire. A few years earlier, Caligula had attempted to set up his image in the Temple at Jerusalem. Perhaps Paul is thinking of another Caligula who will take "his seat in the temple of God, declaring himself to be God" (2:4), as Caligula did.

The Jewish high priest, with Paul's Jewish opponents. The reference to the Temple hints at this.

Some completely supernatural force of evil. First John 2:18 speaks of the expectation of a coming "antichrist" and indicates, in fact, that several "antichrists" have already come. The standard Jewish eschatological expectation, brought over into Christian apocalyptic literature, pictured the "woes of the Messiah," a time of great trouble just before the end (see the section on "Revelation" in chapter 12 of this *Guide* for the characteristics of apocalyptic literature). Perhaps we can say no more than that Paul is reflecting this convention.[15]

It is equally unclear what Paul means by "what is now restraining" the lawless one (2 Thess. 2:6). Perhaps Paul refers to the restraints placed by Roman law on Paul's opponents. Perhaps Paul means his own activity. The whole passage obviously refers to some idea that Paul had already taught the Thessalonians and therefore did not need to explain again here (2:5).

Disappointed in predictions of dates made repeatedly in history, most Christians have come to recognize that the Bible over and over refuses to announce any clear timetable for the end of the world. Rather, the Christian is expected to live and work each day with that earnestness of purpose which might come with the conviction that any day could be the last before the judgment. Indeed, God's judgments do not always wait until the end of the world.

Fortunately, the main point is clear enough. Paul is saying that the Thessalonians are not to suppose that the world and all its troubles necessarily are at an end. They must be prepared to carry on through difficulties ahead.

The most quoted verse, one that was made law in the first permanent English settlement in America, Jamestown, is 2 Thess. 3:10: "Anyone unwilling to work should not eat"—or as Bruce Metzger has paraphrased it, "No loaf for the loafer!"

1 CORINTHIANS

Corinth was a major intersection in the transportation system of the ancient world. All north-south land traffic in Greece had to pass through Corinth, since it commanded the narrow isthmus that linked the two halves of the Greek peninsula. More important, seagoing vessels docked at its harbor, and their cargoes, or even the boats themselves, were pulled on rollers across the short stretch of land to the port on the other shore, a procedure quicker and cheaper than sailing around half of the country to get there. (A short canal now cuts through the tiny isthmus.)

A sailors' town, famous for its sacred prostitute-priestesses of Aphrodite, Corinth attracted a polyglot population.

Into this town, around A.D. 51, had come the itinerant tentmaker-turned-preacher, Paul. Archaeologists have unearthed portions of a synagogue that may have been the one in which he began to preach. Paul became a partner, both in tentmaking and in teaching, with two refugees from Rome, Aquila and Priscilla (Prisca) (Acts 18:2–3; 1 Cor. 16:19). Though he was later to confess that he had begun his work at Corinth with "fear and in much trembling" (1 Cor. 2:3), the three, together with Silas and Timothy, were so successful that Paul stayed more than a year and a half. Apparently, even leaders of the synagogue, Crispus and Sosthenes, were converted (Acts 18:8, 17; 1 Cor.1:1, 14). After Paul left, a convert named Apollos had carried on as pastor of the new church (1 Cor. 1:12; 3:5; cf. Acts 19:1). (Incidentally, Acts 18:1–18 and the Corinthian letters fit so well together, including the mention in both Acts and the letters of precisely these same people, that even those otherwise inclined to dismiss much of Acts as "legendary" admit that this part of Acts reflects accurate historical memory and do not hesitate to use it to interpret these epistles.)[16]

How many letters Paul wrote back to the church he had founded in Corinth we will never know. At least one appears to have been lost (1 Cor. 5:9). Gunther Bornkamm claims to have found fragments of at least six letters in what we call 2 Corinthians.[17] Together, what has been preserved for us forms the largest body of correspondence in our Bible. A number of passages are among the best-loved in the New Testament.

1 CORINTHIANS
Response to a Divided, "Spiritual-minded" Church

"Now concerning the matters about which you wrote . . ." (7:1) *". . . the greatest . . . is love"* (13:13).

1:1	7:1	16:1	16:24
Comments on Some Reports Paul Has Received about the Church at Corinth	**Replies to Questions Asked in a Letter They Have Sent**	**Brief Miscellaneous Concluding Notes**	
They are splitting up; Paul pleads for unity around the cross, 1—4	What about marriage for the Christian? It isn't sin, but Paul doesn't recommend it, 7:1–40	A solicitation for funds for the Jerusalem poor, 16:1–4	
A case of incest has been reported; Paul pleads for strict sexual morality, 5:1–13	May a Christian eat meat that has been sacrificed to a pagan god? Yes, but not if it gives the wrong impression to someone else, 8—10	Personal comments and greetings, 16:5–24	
Some are involved in a lawsuit; Paul pleads for settling issues among themselves, 6:1–8	What is the place of the women? It is subordination "in the Lord," 11:1-16		
Some claim to be above rules about the body; Paul renews his plea for morality, 6:9–20	Response to reported disorder in worship and an account of the Lord's Supper, 11:17–34		
	What is the relative importance of spiritual gifts? Different Christians have different gifts, but all should seek love, 12—14		
	What about the resurrection? It is the central truth, 15:1–58		

Author: Paul

Recipients: The church at Corinth, which Paul had founded

Date: A.D. 55–56

Occasion: Paul has received a report of dissension in the church and a letter full of questions.

Purpose: To plead for unity, to comment on reports he has received about them, and to answer their questions

First Corinthians contains several such passages:

First Corinthians 11:23–26 is still read regularly in millions of celebrations
of the Lord's Supper.
Parts of 1 Corinthians 15 are likely to be read at the funeral of any Christian
reader of this *Guide.*
The prose poem on love in 1 Corinthians 13 is the best-loved chapter in all
the writings of Paul.

But it is also true that 1 Corinthians has been used as a battleground for
sexists (1 Cor. 7; 11:2–16); for believers in church union (chaps. 1—3); for
Roman Catholics versus Protestants (11:24); for "tongues-speakers" (chaps.
12—14); and even for vegetarians (chap. 8).

Manifestly, the letter both merits and needs study.

The Occasion of 1 Corinthians

"I will stay in Ephesus until Pentecost," Paul writes in 1 Cor. 16:8, so we can
be pretty sure where he was as he wrote this letter. Obviously, he had already
been to Corinth at least once. So we may assume that 1 Corinthians was
written sometime during his more than two-year stay in Ephesus on his third
missionary journey, probably around A.D. 55 or 56 (Acts 19:10).

It was news from Corinth that prompted Paul to write. He had received
a disturbing report of dissension in the church, brought him by "Chloe's
people" (1 Cor. 1:11), perhaps slaves or business associates of some woman
of the church at either Corinth or Ephesus. Paul had also received from the
church at Corinth a letter full of questions, which he now attempted to
answer (7:1). And perhaps others had brought additional word from the
church that Paul had founded some three years earlier (16:17).

The news had not been all good. Somehow, the church was being split
into factions, each adopting the name of one leader: Paul, Apollos, Cephas
(Peter), or even Christ (1:12). Paul was horrified. He now wrote to plead for
unity.

Precisely what these different groups believed is not clear. Some relate
them to the "Judaizers," the conservative faction advocating circumcision
and obedience to all the Old Testament law, which was centered, perhaps,
back in Jerusalem. Apparently, it is with them that the letter to the Galatians
does battle. In the Corinthians' letters, however, there is no mention of the
ceremony of circumcision, the focus of the controversy with the Judaizers in
Galatians. Indeed, more of Paul's opponents at Corinth seem to have been
the opposite of legalists, advocating rather a very "liberated" kind of lifestyle. A curious variety of ideas is attacked by Paul, either directly or by
implication:

A claim to superior wisdom (1:18–31; 2:6–7; 8:1; etc.)

A tendency to condone sexual immorality (chap. 7)

A claim to be above restrictions against practices related to idol worship (chaps. 8 and 10)

Attacks on Paul's authority (chap. 9)

Drunken disturbances at the Lord's Supper (11:17–34)

A schismatic boasting about special gifts of the Spirit, such as "speaking with tongues" (chaps. 12—14)

Misunderstandings about the resurrection (chap. 15).

It may be that all these diverse errors can be grouped together around one idea, the claim of one or more of the factions at Corinth to have special, superior, spiritual wisdom. Perhaps some member of one group might have defended his position in this way:

> We "Apollos" Christians are not beginners in the faith any longer, as were those whom Paul first baptized. We are now filled with the Spirit. Our spiritual gifts, such as speaking in tongues, show our superiority. We now have a knowledge of higher, more spiritual things. We know that Christians are not under the law. Our motto is "All things are lawful" [1 Cor. 6:12; 10:23]. Hang-ups about food offered to idols and the old taboos about sex and drinking concern material things. We spiritual Christians know that material things don't matter one way or the other. We have already, in the Spirit, begun to live the resurrection life. As for Paul and those other factions, they are just beginners.

Different parties may have made similar claims. But because there were apparently several rival cliques, it is not necessary to suppose that all of Paul's opponents in Corinth fell into all of the errors he attacks. His opponents may have represented a wide spectrum, from very conservative Judaizers to libertine Hellenists, even semi-pagans close to the later "Gnostics," who in the next century boasted that they had a superior *gnosis,* or knowledge.[18]

The Purpose of 1 Corinthians

Paul writes to respond to the reports from "Chloe's people" and to answer the letter sent him by the young church at Corinth. His replies deal with a great variety of both theological and practical questions. His first great concern, however, is to reunite the church around the kerygma he had preached, the basic gospel centered on the death and resurrection of Jesus. Secondarily, Paul earnestly urges that these new Christians live in this world, as long as it lasts, the kind of lives appropriate for Christians.

Some Comments on the Content of 1 Corinthians

"I appeal to you, brothers and sisters, by the name of our Lord Jesus Christ, that all of you be in agreement and that there be no divisions among you, but that you be united in the same mind and the same purpose" (1:10). So begins the body of the letter, and with it, the major theme is introduced.

To modern readers used to the fact that the Christian church in the United States alone is split into more than three hundred groups, each with a different name, a different denomination, Paul's concern seems strange. To him, however, only one name matters, "the name of our Lord Jesus Christ," and schism is sin. It is not the use of different names that is in itself the sin. He condemns all the groups, including the faction that boasts simply, "I belong to Christ" (1:12). It is the factions' separation from one another and the claims on which their schism is based that upset the apostle.

If one counts the times the words "wise," "wisdom," and "foolishness" occur in 1 Cor. 1:17–2:13, it becomes evident that at least one faction has been claiming superior *knowledge*. Counting the occurrences of such related words as "power" and "weakness" discloses a secondary theme, *power,* in which that party or some other was greatly interested.

Paul bluntly reminds the Corinthians that few in that church had any real claim either to wisdom or to power. Most of these first Christians were relatively poor and uneducated people, many even slaves. Even Paul himself had made no claim to power or wisdom (2:1–5). Power and wisdom for the Christian could come from only one source, the cross. By all worldly standards that cross represented defeat and absurdity. Nothing could seem more foolish to a Jewish Zealot, dreaming of butchering the Romans, than the story of the promised Messiah dying on a Roman cross. Greeks schooled in the rational philosophies of Plato and Aristotle were likely to dismiss accounts of God's self-sacrificing love for humankind as absurd. Now, within the church, factions claiming new spiritual gifts of higher insight or miraculous abilities were repeating the blindness of their non-Christian neighbors. Paul had claimed to "know" nothing "except Jesus Christ, and him crucified" (2:2). It was around that original, basic kerygma (gospel) that the Corinthian church must reunite.

Not only did some members of the church at Corinth claim to have such spiritual knowledge that they were "above" Paul's theology; they also claimed to be above Paul's morality. "All things are lawful for me" (6:12) is placed in quotation marks in many modern translations (cf. 10:23) on the assumption that these "liberated" Christians were repeating this as a kind of slogan. They were so "liberated" that they had even tolerated the continued church membership of a man living in adultery with his own stepmother (5:1). They were willing for members to sue each other in courts of law (6:1–8). And they permitted church members to patronize the fabled prostitute-priestesses of Corinth (6:9–20).

"Do you not know that your body is a temple of the Holy Spirit?" Paul demands (6:19). Repeatedly using the word "body," Paul tries to bring these advocates of a purely "spiritual" morality back down to earth (6:9–20). To a morality of physical license for "Spirit-filled" people, 1 Corinthians says a flat no.

Paul's views on marriage and on women, presented in 1 Corinthians 7 and in 11:2–16, have caused some advocates of women's liberation to brand the apostle a kind of "male chauvinist pig." He recommends that a man should not even touch a woman, much less marry one! Marriage is permitted, but here the only basis mentioned is its being better than to "burn" with desire or to engage in fornication. No woman, he says here, should ever go to church without a veil. And "the husband is the head of his wife" (11:3). (It must be admitted about Paul that "at times he looked like a man.")

However, Christian advocates of women's liberation (and others) have defended Paul's views here on several grounds. It is noted that the old bachelor does allow marriage, even if not on the highest grounds. Indeed, he even commands a concern for *mutual* sexual satisfaction (7:3). (Perhaps his very "spiritual" opponents especially needed this earthy advice.) He speaks of the woman as ruling over the man's body in the same verse in which he speaks of the man ruling over the woman's (7:4). If he puts severe dress standards on women at Corinth, it is in part because Corinth is a special case, a city with an international reputation for prostitutes. He forbids a man's divorcing a faithful wife. And he bases his recommendation against marriage on his expectation of the imminent end of the world (7:29). Subsequently, as we shall see, a more carefully worked out eschatology was to make that approach somewhat obsolete. Paul admits that he is not in these matters always giving commands from the Lord (7:25).

Temples supplied the butcher shops of the ancient world. First Corinthians 8—10 deals with a question that must have confronted every first-century Christian household: Should a Christian eat meat that has first been offered to an idol? Suppose a church member is having lunch with a pagan and the entrée is from the altar of Aphrodite? Should he or she refuse and offend the host, or eat and appear to condone idolatry? The issue in its first-century form is now irrelevant in countries where sacrifices to idols are completely out of fashion, but the principles on which Paul's answer rests are applicable to many ethical questions of the present day. Here Paul sides with the "spiritually enlightened" party, agreeing that, in itself, there is no harm in eating meat offered to idols. But with the more conservative faction, he argues that the effect which one's action may have on another person is all-important. "Eat whatever is sold in the meat market without raising any question on the ground of conscience" (10:25). But if a person's example may cause someone to think that he or she is condoning idol worship, one should be a vegetarian (8:9–13). One need not be concerned about meat. The Christian must be concerned about other people.

Reports of disorder in the church services at Corinth led Paul to write some of the most familiar—and some of the most controversial—parts of this letter. He seems concerned, at least here, to "keep women in their place" in worship (11:2–16). Of much more permanent influence is the following account, the oldest that we have, of the Lord's Supper, which has been read in almost every service of Holy Communion through subsequent centuries (11:23–26). The words with which he introduces it—"received" and "handed on" —are terms to show that he is passing down a tradition which he himself was taught when he first became a Christian, perhaps only about three years after the event he describes. Thus the passage gives clear witness to the antiquity of the ceremony. The idea of the "new covenant," which Paul says Jesus announced at the Last Supper, is so basic to the faith that the two parts of the Christian Bible are named the Old Covenant (or Testament) and the New Covenant. How literally one is to take Jesus' words "This is my body," whether the bread in the Mass is "substantially" Christ's flesh, has been a point of major controversy between Catholics and Protestants.

Evidently, worship at Corinth was rather different from the formal ceremonies of most twentieth-century churches. "Each of you goes ahead with your own supper, and one goes hungry and another becomes drunk" (11:21). Determined that "all things should be done decently and in order" (14:40), Paul urges the men to take turns in speaking, rather than several speaking at once, and the women to do their questioning only at home (14:26–40).

Among the elements that apparently produced a kind of chaos in Corinthian worship was the practice of some of the "spiritually gifted" people to "speak in tongues." The spread of the "charismatic movement" in recent years has caused 1 Corinthians 12—14 to be one of the most discussed parts of the Bible. Are certain Christians given a "second blessing," a "baptism with (or in) the Holy Spirit," which ordinary Christians lack? Apparently, there were those in the church at Corinth who thought that their gifts of tongues showed that they were superior, Spirit-filled Christians.

Paul answers in at least three ways. First (1 Cor. 12), he proposes that the church is like a body. In an extended metaphor, he asserts that each Christian (each part of that body) has his or her own gift from the one Spirit. Each part of the church and each gift is necessary for the welfare of the whole "body," the whole church. None can look down on another. For a church member with one gift to think of himself or herself as superior to another with a quite different gift would be as stupid as for a foot to feel superior to a hand.

Second, some gifts are better than others. "Strive for the greater gifts" (12:31). But the highest is neither tongues nor knowledge, the two boasts of the "spiritual" people. The highest, which all should seek, is love. First Corinthians 13, the chapter in which that gift of Christian love is described, is the best-loved passage in all of the writings of Paul. At the end of this section, 1 Corinthians 13 is printed in such a way as to suggest its poetic structure.

Note how, even here, the last stanza reflects Paul's eschatological orientation: in the end, only love matters.

Third (1 Cor. 14), in public worship, one should try to "prophesy," to say things that will make sense and will edify other people. Paul does not forbid speaking in tongues. He professes to do it himself, privately. But "in church I would rather speak five words with my mind, in order to instruct others also, than ten thousand words in a tongue" (14:19).

First Corinthians 13 is best loved, but for the historian of Christian doctrine, 1 Corinthians 15 is the most revealing. Perhaps the "spiritual" party in the church were claiming to be living so completely in the Spirit that for them, no future bodily resurrection was necessary. In any event, somehow the resurrection had been brought into question. Paul again begins his answer with the words "delivered" and "received," apparently reminding them of a kind of creed he had been taught at his own conversion. Here, then, presented in the form of the Apostles' and Nicene Creeds, is the gospel of the very first Christians:

> Christ died for our sins
>   in accordance with the scriptures, . . .
> he was buried, . . .
> he was raised on the third day
>   in accordance with the scriptures, . . .
> he appeared to Cephas,
>   then to the twelve. (1 Cor. 15:3–5)

Paul offers neither description nor proof of the resurrection, but he does cite witnesses, including many who were still alive as he wrote (15:6). His own encounter with the risen Christ is for him the final "proof." The fact of the resurrection is essential to the Christian faith. Without it, nothing else in the gospel matters (15:14). With it, there is hope for all people.

The resurrection is no present and purely "spiritual" experience, as apparently some of his "Spirit-filled" opponents had claimed. It is a "bodily" resurrection (15:38). And it is something to be hoped for beyond the ecstasy of the "spiritual" faction at Corinth. But that hope does add a new quality to life now, for the Christian lives in the confidence that because Christ rose, the dead will rise too. In an ecstasy of his own, Paul breaks into song (15:54–55). And he closes the chapter with a shout of "thanks be to God, who gives us the victory" (15:57).

Practical preacher that he was, Paul adds a few words about taking up the offering. Several references in Paul's letters speak of his solicitation of funds for the poor of Jerusalem (Rom. 15:25, for example).

The letter ends with personal greetings, including those from Aquila and Priscilla (Prisca), with whom he had worked in Corinth (16:19). Finally (still at times looking like a man, in spite of the angelic thirteenth chapter), Paul roundly damns those who have no "love for the Lord" (16:22).

Paul's Prose Poem on Love

If I speak in the tongues of mortals and of angels,
    but do not have love,
I am a noisy gong or a clanging cymbal.
And if I have prophetic powers, and understand all mysteries and all knowledge,
And if I have all faith, so as to remove mountains,
    but do not have love,
I am nothing.
If I give away all my possessions,
And if I hand over my body so that I may boast,
    but do not have love,
I gain nothing.
Love is patient; love is kind;
Love is not envious or boastful or arrogant or rude.
It does not insist on its own way;
It is not irritable or resentful;
It does not rejoice in wrongdoing,
But rejoices in the truth.
It bears all things,
    believes all things,
        hopes all things,
            endures all things.
Love never ends.
But as for prophecies,
      they will come to an end;
As for tongues,
      they will cease;
As for knowledge,
      it will come to an end.
For we know only in part, and we prophesy only in part;
But when the complete comes,
      the partial will come to an end.
When I was a child,
    I spoke like a child,
      I thought like a child,
        I reasoned like a child;
When I became an adult,
    I put an end to childish ways.
For now we see in a mirror, dimly,
    but then we will see face to face.
Now I know only in part;
    then I will know fully, even as I have been fully known.

And now faith,
> hope,
>> and love abide,
These three;
And the greatest of these is Love. (1 Corinthians 13)

2 CORINTHIANS

A dramatic story of defeats and triumph—thus many scholars reconstruct 2 Corinthians as they read between its lines.

One must hasten to say that not all scholars agree on the reconstruction. Gunther Bornkamm chops up 2 Corinthians into perhaps six different fragments from the pen of Paul, plus one (6:14–7:1) by another author, included here by mistake.[19] W. G. Kümmel is equally sure that 2 Corinthians is just one complete, unified letter, needing no reconstruction.[20]

A large number of scholars, however, find hints that suggest a view between these extremes. Second Corinthians 2:3–4 speaks of a painful letter, written "out of much distress and anguish of heart." Can that be 1 Corinthians? There is nothing very painful in 1 Corinthians, and there are no signs that Paul was in anguish as he wrote it. Of course, the "painful" letter may have been lost. But perhaps—many scholars would say probably—at least part of that letter has been preserved as our 2 Corinthians 10—13. The first nine chapters of 2 Corinthians, according to this view, contain another letter—or perhaps parts of more than one letter—written after the severe letter of chapters 10 through 13.

Surely, the mood and content of the last four chapters are different from those of the first nine. If, with many scholars, we swap their order,[21] the following story emerges.

The Occasion of 2 Corinthians 10—14

First Corinthians seemed to have been a failure. Factions still divided the immature church. And now outsiders had come, stirring up more trouble. Precisely what doctrines these intruders taught is not clear, but Paul speaks of them as preaching "another Jesus" (2 Cor. 11:4–5). One thing is clear enough: in every way they could, they attempted to undermine the authority of the apostle Paul.

Here are some of the charges these outsiders seem to have made against him:

His letters sound big, but in person he is a weakling, nothing. What a poor preacher Paul is (10:10)! (Perhaps they contrasted Paul with Apollos, famed for his eloquence [Acts 18:24].)

Paul is dirt poor (11:7–11). But look, we are raising lots of money.

2 CORINTHIANS
Paul's Ministry—and Their Partnership in It

"Our consolation is abundant through Christ" (1:5).
"Are they ministers of Christ? . . . I am a better one" (11:23).

1:1
A Joyful Letter in Response to Titus's Report: Paul and the Corinthians Are Reconciled, Partners Again in Ministry

A review of how Paul had been distressed over the apparent rejection of him, and his joy at the news of reconciliation Titus had brought, 1—2

Paul's ministry, in which confidence is renewed and in which the Corinthians are partners again, 3:1—4:12

The encouragement in that ministry that comes from the eschatological hope, 4:13—5:21

A plea for continued partnership in ministry, in spite of difficulties, 6:1—7:4 (6:14—7:1 is a parenthesis on some who are excluded from that partnership.)

Picking up from chapter 2, Paul's joy in the good news of reconciliation Titus has brought, 7:2–16

A plea for financial partnership in ministry to the poor of the Jerusalem church, 8—9

Author: Paul
Recipients: The church he had founded in Corinth
Date: About A.D. 53–54
Occasion: Chapters 1—9 grow out of a report from Titus that the Corinthian church is ready again to work with Paul in ministry. All is well again. Chapters 10—13 reflect serious attacks on Paul that have spread in Corinth.
Purpose: 1—9: To rejoice and to encourage the church in mutual ministry with Paul 10—13: Desperately to seek to reestablish Paul's authority before he visits them

10:1
A Severe Letter Defending Paul's Ministerial Authority as an Apostle against Attacks Being Spread in Corinth

Paul's apology for defending ("boasting of") his authority, 10:1–11:21a

The signs that Paul really has apostolic authority:
his credentials as a good Jew, 11:21b–22
his sacrifices for Christ, 11:23–33
his religious experiences, 12:1–10
his miracles and mighty works, 12:11–13

A plea that they repent and accept his authority before his coming visit, 12:14–13:13

13:14

Paul was "crafty." He put on an act of being poor and humble to get control over you (12:16).

But look at us! We are at the same time true Jews (11:22)—not like that half-Gentile Paul—and really true apostles (11:5), preaching the genuine gospel of Jesus (11:4). What proof has Paul that he speaks for God (13:3)?

Horrified, Paul had made a quick trip from Ephesus across the bay to Corinth. He had publicly warned these rivals that he would "not spare them" if they did not stop (13:1–3).

They had not stopped. Paul had been publicly humiliated (12:21). He recalls that earlier he had been so "utterly, unbearably crushed" that he had thought he would die (1:8).

Torn between resolve to visit them a third time (13:1) and fear of another debacle (1:23; 2:1), Paul wrote this letter "out of much distress and anguish of heart and with many tears" (2:4).

The Purpose of 2 Corinthians 10—13

Though Paul later protested that he wrote "not to cause you pain, but to let you know the abundant love that I have for you" (2:4; cf. 11:11), obviously he was also writing in a desperate effort to defend his own authority, in order to defend the gospel he had preached at Corinth. He writes to "undermine the claim" of those who boast that they are "superlative apostles" and who are preaching "another Jesus than the one" Paul had preached. But though he writes about himself, he does so for the sake of the church he has founded (12:19–21; 13:9). Finally, he writes in the hope that a letter will cause them to repent, so that he will not need to have another stern confrontation with them when he comes in person (13:10).

Some Comments on 2 Corinthians 10—13

Paul's defense centers on an incomparable autobiography:

> Five times have I received from the Jews the forty lashes minus one. Three times I was beaten with rods. Once I received a stoning. Three times I was shipwrecked; for a night and a day I was adrift at sea; on frequent journeys, in danger from rivers, danger from bandits, danger from my own people, danger from Gentiles, danger in the city, danger in the wilderness, danger at sea, danger from false brothers and sisters; in toil and hardship, through many a sleepless night, hungry and thirsty, often without food, cold and naked. And, besides other things, I am under daily pressure because of my anxiety for all the churches. (2 Cor. 11:24–28)

Paul also reveals a good many other things about himself in these chapters. He shows a fine flair for sarcasm as he calls his rivals "super-apostles" (11:5; 12:11) and as he pleads for "forgiveness" for the "sin" of not having gotten the Corinthians to support him financially (11:7; 12:13). He shows, too, his pastoral love for the people in his churches. He does write to assert his authority. "And why? Because I do not love you? God knows I do!" (11:11). Paul can even compare himself to a jealous lover who is desperately trying to prevent his girl from being seduced (11:2). He also reveals himself to be a mystic, given to ecstatic experiences he could not attempt to put into words (12:1–10). Finally, he speaks of a thorn "given me in the flesh," presumably some kind of illness, which even his own prayers could not cure (12:7–8). Some have argued that the sickness might have been some kind of epilepsy related to his frequent visions. Others have proposed that Paul, who went blind at the time of his conversion, continued to suffer from bad eyesight. No one really knows.

Against his every instinct as a Christian, Paul is forced to "boast," feeling like a "fool" as he does so. Counting the times such words as "boast" and "foolishness" occur between 2 Cor. 10:7 and 12:13 helps one realize how embarrassed Paul felt in having to try to match credentials with his critics. These chapters have been compared to Plato's *Apology,* in which Socrates, on trial, with an appealing mixture of humility and pride, also reluctantly defends his life.

In summary, Paul's defense rests on such arguments as the following: It was he who had first brought the Corinthians the gospel (10:14). His refusal to take money from them showed the purity of his motives (11:7–11). His credentials as a good Jew were equal to those of any of his critics (11:22). He had undergone for the gospel all the dangers and difficulties listed above (11:23–33). He had even been granted mystic experiences of the highest kind (12:1–10). And finally, the Corinthians themselves could remember seeing in him "the signs of a true apostle . . . signs and wonders and mighty works" (12:12).

But his only boast, really, is not himself but Jesus Christ. "Let the one who boasts, boast in the Lord" (10:17). The letter ends with an appeal that, before he comes, they should examine themselves (13:5) and mend their ways (13:11), lest his next visit be as wretched as his last (12:20–21).

The Occasion of 2 Corinthians 1—9

"Consolation"—ten times in the first paragraph Paul uses that word in one form or another. Paul had been "utterly, unbearably crushed," as though he "had received the sentence of death" (1:8–9). But now he has been delivered from a "deadly . . . peril" (1:10). The crisis has passed.

Clearly, the mood of 2 Corinthians 1—9 is different from that of chapters 10—13, the chapters we have just been studying. The two parts fit together beautifully if we assume that when Paul's letters were collected, perhaps forty or fifty years later, two letters that now make up our "2 Corinthians" were put together in reverse order.

By following this assumption, we can reconstruct Paul's activities between the letters. He had sent Titus to Corinth, perhaps carrying the letter that we have as chapters 10—13. He was so anxious for a reply that he could not wait for Titus's return but went as far as Troas to meet him. Even though he had great success there in his preaching, Paul was so disturbed that when he did not find Titus at Troas, he pushed on to Macedonia (2:12–13). There, at last, he found Titus and received the good news. Titus reported that the Corinthian Christians longed to see Paul and had been grieved by his letter, and that he had every reason to be proud of his church again (7:5–16). "I rejoice," Paul writes, "because I [again] have complete confidence in you" (7:16). The letter ends, "Thanks be to God for his indescribable gift!" (9:15).

The Purpose of 2 Corinthians 1—9

Many themes are woven together in this very personal and emotional letter, but the most frequently recurring one is Paul's expression of restored comfort, joy, and pride, both in his own apostleship and in the share the Corinthians have with him in ministry. He writes to encourage them to continue to share in the ministers' work.

His newly restored joy in the midst of affliction and the contrast between the glorious ministry and the limitations of human ministers leads Paul to write to encourage the Corinthians with the thought of the hoped-for eschaton, the heavenly things to come at the end of earthly life (4:13–5:21).

Chapters 8 and 9, in contrast, are pointed toward one very practical purpose: raising money. That money is not for Paul, however, but for the gift Paul plans to take back to the poor in Jerusalem.

Some Comments on 2 Corinthians 1—9

"Anyone whom you forgive, I also forgive," Paul now writes happily (2:10). All was forgiven. The conflict was over. In chapters 1 and 2 he reviews the agony of the past, climaxed by his failure to find Titus, from whom he had hoped to get some reassuring news.

"But thanks be to God" (2:14)! Paul breaks off the story, aware that his readers already know its happy ending. Paul does not pick up the narrative again until 2 Cor. 7:5. Rather, his cry of thanksgiving over the renewal of their acceptance of and partnership in his ministry moves Paul into a discussion of what it means to be a Christian minister. Here Paul seems to use the word in a very different way from that which is familiar to modern church members. As Paul uses it, "minister" does not refer simply to himself or to any religious professional. It is applied also to ordinary members of the church at Corinth (3:6). Not only professional clergy but also lay people are "ministers of a new covenant."

Paul uses at least three figures to describe the work of "ministers":

1. "You are a letter of Christ," he writes to these Christians (3:3). They are "written not with ink but with the Spirit." Paul's "letters"—Spirit-filled lives—are contrasted with Moses' letters inscribed in dead stone. These lay ministers are Paul's message, and Christ's message, to Corinth.
2. These ministers are only clay pots ("earthen vessels"). But in them, people may find the treasure of the gospel of Christ (4:7). "Ministers" may wear out their earthly bodies in service to others. Christ gave his life. But they are sustained by the hope of heavenly bodies to come (4:16–5:10). Read at many funerals, Paul's description of the resurrected body makes these verses especially valuable.
3. It is to spread this good news and the reconciliation that accompanies it that Christians are called to be "ambassadors" of heaven on this earth (5:20). Christ gave his life to reconcile us to God. Christians spread the good news of this reconciliation.

To this last task Paul now summons his readers (6:1–13).

Anyone reading 6:11–13 and skipping directly to 7:2 will see how perfectly these two fit together and why most scholars regard 6:14–7:1 as misplaced. Paul's letters were not collected until the end of the century. The wonder is that so many of Paul's writings have been preserved, not that one fragment should be out of place. Perhaps this passage is part of the letter referred to in 1 Cor. 5:9–11. It fits nicely the description of the letter given there. Finally, Paul picks up again the story broken off in 2 Cor. 2:14, the account of the good news Titus had brought Paul from Corinth (2 Cor. 7:5–16). The story ends with Paul rejoicing in the restoration of his "perfect confidence" in the church.

Paul flatters the church members at Corinth by assuring them that they are so generous that there is no need for him to write about the offering he is collecting for the poor of Jerusalem (9:1). Nevertheless, he writes them two whole chapters on precisely that subject (chaps. 8—9).

Noting the abrupt shift from the heights of theology in chapters 1—7 to the mundane subject of money in chapters 8—9, some scholars have proposed that these two chapters must be part of yet another letter. But the cause of the poor was dear to Paul's heart, and it does not appear to have seemed out of place to Paul to move from the sublime to this down-to-earth subject (cf. Rom. 15:25–27; 1 Cor. 16:1–4; Gal. 2:10). Paul had refused to take any money from the church at Corinth for his own personal support (2 Cor. 11:7–10), but he was willing to use every argument he could think of, psychological as well as theological, to raise money for the poor.

He begins with the example set for the Corinthians by their neighbors to the north, the Macedonians (8:1–7). The Corinthians already excel in faith, in utterance, in knowledge, he praises them. Of course they will not want to let the Macedonian churches get ahead of them in giving!

He is only asking them, he insists, to do their fair share (8:13–14).

The funds will be carefully guarded and audited, not by Paul alone but by Titus and another "brother," unnamed but apparently known and trusted by the Corinthians (8:16–24).

They have a reputation for generosity, Paul says. He just knows that they will want to live up to it (9:1–5).

They will be rewarded by God to the extent that they give—or fail to give (9:6–14).

Perhaps in some of these arguments "he looked like a man." But his pleas are all set in the framework of his deeper, theological argument. Early in chapter 8 he had written, "For you know the generous act of our Lord Jesus Christ, that though he was rich, yet for your sake he became poor, so that by his poverty you might become rich" (8:9). It is really in response to Jesus Christ that Paul expects the Corinthians to give. And in the same vein, he ends with a shout concerning the real motivation he proposes for giving: "Thanks be to God for his indescribable gift!" (9:15)

GALATIANS

Building especially on two letters, Galatians and Romans, Augustine penned the best-known Christian works written in the thousand years following the New Testament.

The Protestant Reformation was born out of Martin Luther's militant interpretation of these two epistles.

Twentieth-century pastors still preach these letters, and scholars still debate the implications of every major idea in them.

Together, Galatians and Romans have proved to be the most influential and perhaps the most controversial pair of letters ever written.

Most scholars date the letters as coming from approximately the same time (somewhere between A.D. 52 and 57), interpret them as dealing with many of the same basic themes, and think of them together as representing the most mature and distinctive thought of the New Testament's most prolific writer. Exactly how close they are in date and subject may be debated, but Galatians and Romans obviously have much in common.

Introducing Galatians

"I confess I have sinned."
"Then God will punish you."
"No, He will not do that."
"Why not? Does not the Law say so?"

GALATIANS
Living by Faith

"For in Christ Jesus neither circumcision or uncircumcision counts for anything; the only thing that counts is faith working through love" (5:6).

1:1 **A Personal Defense by Paul of His Authority as an Apostle**	3:1 **A Defense of His Gospel of Freedom from the Law**	5:1 6:18 **A Plea to Continue to Live by Faith the Free, Spirit-filled Life of Love**
Salutation, 1:1–5	The Galatians' own experience proves it. They, too, have begun to live by the Spirit through faith, not law, 3:1–5	Since Christ has set us free, let us live free from the law, not slip back into legalism, 5:1–12
Paul's distress at the attacks on his gospel, 1:6–10	The Jewish scriptures themselves also teach that we live by faith, not law, 3:6–4:31	The free, Spirit-filled life is the life guided by love, 5:13–6:10
A brief autobiography to show that Paul does have authority, 1:11–2:14		An emotional postscript written in Paul's own hand, 6:11–18
The relation of that gospel to life: "the life I now live . . . I live by faith," 2:15–21		

Author: Paul

Recipients: Christians in some churches founded by Paul, in what is now Turkey

Date: A.D. 55 (A.D. 49?)

Occasion: "Judaizers" have attacked Paul and urged these new Christians to live by the Jewish law, of which circumcision is an important symbol.

Purpose: Paul writes to defend his teaching that we are to live by the Spirit, by faith, not law.

"I have nothing to do with the Law."

"How so?"

"I have another law, the law of liberty."

"What do you mean—'liberty'?"

"The liberty of Christ, for Christ has made me free from the Law that held me down. That law is now in prison itself, held captive by grace and liberty."[22]

So Theodore Graebner translated part of Luther's commentary on Galatians. Most commentators today, Roman Catholic and Protestant, would agree that here Luther was correctly dramatizing a major theme of the epistle.

Commentators do not agree, however, concerning to whom Paul was writing this message of freedom from the law. As early as John Calvin, scholars identified the term "Galatians" as referring to inhabitants of the region that is now northern Turkey. Paul traveled through this area on both his second and third missionary journeys (Acts 16:6; 18:23). The term "Galatians" had been applied to its inhabitants ever since it had been invaded by "Gauls" centuries earlier.

Others believe the letter was written to churches in the south of what is now Turkey. They argue that Luke says nothing of Paul's preaching in the north but describes in detail his founding and revisiting several churches in the south (Antioch, Iconium, Lystra, Derbe, etc. [Acts 13—14; 15:36–16:5]). These cities were within the Roman province called Galatia, and, it is argued, Paul usually used such Roman legal names. Barnabas had helped found these churches and is mentioned in Gal. 2:13.

In itself, it makes little difference in the understanding of the meaning of the letter as to whether the "North Galatian theory" or the "South Galatian theory" is correct. However, if the letter was written to the southern churches, founded on the first journey, then a much earlier date than is usually assigned is possible for Galatians. It may have been the first of the canonical letters of Paul, the earliest book in the New Testament. And if this is the case, the problem of Galatians' seeming conflict with Acts concerning the Jerusalem Council is solved. Comments on this highly uncertain hypothesis are reserved, however, for the section "Some Comments on Galatians."

The Occasion of Galatians

Martin Luther, in his classic *Commentary on St. Paul's Epistle to the Galatians,* described the situation that Paul faced in these words:

> These Jewish-Christian fanatics who pushed themselves into the Galatian churches after Paul's departure, boasted that they were the descendants of Abraham, true ministers of Christ, having been trained by the apostles themselves, that they were able to perform miracles.
>
> In every way they sought to undermine the authority of St. Paul. They said to the Galatians: "You have no right to think highly of Paul. He was the last to turn

to Christ. But we have seen Christ. We heard Him preach. Paul came later and is beneath us. Is it possible for us to be in error—we who have received the Holy Ghost? Paul stands alone. He has not seen Christ, nor has he had much contact with the other apostles. Indeed, he persecuted the Church of Christ for a long time."[23]

These troublemakers were attacking not just Paul but the gospel he had preached. The churches in Galatia were "quickly deserting" the understanding of Christianity that Paul had taught (Gal. 1:6). To their initial faith in Christ, they began to add an emphasis on law and ceremony, especially circumcision.

No one is quite sure who the intruders were. Traditionally, commentators have called them "Judaizers" and have thought of them as very conservative Jewish Christians, perhaps having their headquarters in Jerusalem. These Jews apparently argued that for a man to be a good Christian, he should go through the ceremony of circumcision and live by the Jewish law. Some recent interpreters have noted that the Galatians seem also to have been tempted to return to the worship of "elemental spirits" and to an emphasis on the observance of "special days, and months, and seasons, and years" (4:9–10). Perhaps, it has been argued, Paul's opponents were Gentiles who sought some kind of syncretism, a merger of Christianity, Jewish legalism, and some elements of paganism. More recently, scholars have answered that there are hints of such an emphasis on spirits and special days in certain Jewish sects. It is not necessary, perhaps, to suppose that Paul's enemies had their roots outside Palestine.

Whatever else these teachers may have advocated, they preached a kind of Jewish legalism that Paul believed could not be combined with the Christian faith. Angered by their attacks on his apostleship but even more by their subversion of the gospel he had preached, Paul wrote this highly emotional letter.

The Purpose of Galatians

Luther misunderstood Galatians; so, at least, it can be argued. Galatians is not about "*justification* by faith," as Luther and his followers through the centuries have believed. It is about *sanctification* by faith. It is not about how one gets sins forgiven. It is about how one is to live when that initial forgiveness has been received.

Now, Luther was right that Galatians does affirm that we are justified—forgiven, made right with God—by God's grace, received by faith. Yet Paul's emphasis in Galatians is on the subsequent, continuing life of freedom. The Galatians had, they knew, already received the Spirit by faith, not law (3:2). Now they were to continue to live not by law but by the Spirit. "If we live by the Spirit, let us also be guided by the Spirit," Paul pleads (5:25). To revert to legalism, symbolized by circumcision, would be to revert to slavery. Paul writes to encourage the Galatians to live the Spirit-filled lives of persons set free from the law.

Some Comments on Galatians

Nicaea the slave was now free! The inscription gives no hint concerning where the money came from by which her freedom was purchased. In a religious formality, the price had been given to the god Apollo, though then it had gone to her master Sosibis. The inscription that the archaeologists found at Delphi reads, in part, as follows: "Apollo the Pythian *bought* from Sosibis of Amphissa, *for freedom,* a female slave, whose name is Nicaea . . . *with a price* of three minae of silver and a half mina. . . . The *price* he has received."[24] Henceforth Nicaea was a slave to her god, "bought" by the god for a price. But with respect to all human slavery, she could live free.

It is something like this that Paul argues in Galatians, often called "the Magna Carta of Christian liberty." Christ "redeemed" us (4:5), bought us back, "for freedom" (5:1). "You are no longer a slave" (4:7) to anything human, Paul says. Christians are known to have been bought and paid for by their God. Therefore the Galatians must live as free men and women, lives energized by the Spirit, guided not by law but by love (5:14).

Galatians, as Wilhelm Wrede said, is a "fighting letter." How concerned Paul is to defend the Galatians' freedom is shown by two peculiarities of the letter's structure. In every other letter, Paul begins with a prayer of thanksgiving; but in this letter he omits all that, plunging right into his angry defense. And at the end, he adds in his own hand a long postscript in unusually large letters (6:11–18). Perhaps the letters were big because Paul had poor eyesight. But perhaps he wrote large to shout his message in ink: "For neither circumcision nor uncircumcision is anything; but a new creation is everything!" (6:15).

The focus of the conflict was circumcision. To be perfect, thereby spiritual rather than carnal, it had been argued, what better symbol could be imagined than the actual cutting away of a piece of flesh—and the flesh sacrificed from the part of the body associated with lust. Paul, his opponents apparently charged, had not demanded that step toward perfection simply in order to make things easy for his converts, to please men (1:10).

Paul begins to defend his gospel by defending his own apostleship. In this defense, Paul gives us a kind of two-chapter autobiography, his testimony to his Christian experience and authority as an apostle. In this autobiography, Paul is concerned to affirm two points. First, his authority is independent, "sent neither by human commission nor from human authorities, but through Jesus Christ" (1:1). He had not simply been a pupil of the Twelve at Jerusalem (1:16–24). He had such authority that he had even stood up against Peter ("opposed him to his face" [2:11]), "Cephas," who was later to be called "the first pope."

But Paul is also concerned to show that his gospel of freedom from the law, though not derived from the leaders of the Jerusalem church, had the full approval of the Jerusalem apostles. He had "laid before them" what he had been teaching, ready to change if wrong (2:2). Yet Jesus' own brother James, as well as Peter and John, the great apostles, had shaken his hand and told him to carry on (2:9).

Galatians's story of this meeting is often said to be a more accurate account of the Jerusalem Council of Acts 15. Luke, it is said, expanded into a large ecclesiastical assembly, climaxed by formal decrees, what was really a small, private, and informal discussion. John Calvin and many twentieth-century scholars have held, however, that Galatians is describing an earlier meeting, which took place during Paul's second visit to Jerusalem following his conversion (Acts 11:29–30). Galatians implies that the meeting it describes was during the second visit Paul made to Jerusalem as a Christian.

If Galatians is describing a meeting that took place prior to Paul's missionary journeys, then it may be that this letter was written as early as A.D. 49, even before 1 and 2 Thessalonians. Against this view, it is argued that Gal. 4:13 implies that Paul had been to the Galatian churches twice. That verse, however, can be understood in other ways. The North Galatian theory would prohibit an early date for Galatians, but that theory also is uncertain. Those who tend, as does the present writer, to set a relatively high value on the historicity of Acts are likely to hold to the view that Galatians is an early letter and that it describes a meeting several years prior to the Jerusalem Council of Acts 15. The issue can probably never be settled to the satisfaction of all.

What is clear is that in the first two chapters of Galatians, Paul presents the case for both his independence of and his endorsement by the mother church at Jerusalem. He also introduces the theme of the letter. We already know, he says, "that a person is justified not by the works of the law but through faith in Jesus Christ" (Gal. 2:16). Now we must not slip back into legalism, "build up again the very things that I once tore down" (2:18). The Galatians, in their legalism, have gone to the opposite extreme from the "Spirit-filled" people of 1 Corinthians. The Corinthians simply lived as they pleased. In this letter, Paul must urge the Galatian legalists to forget their hang-ups and to live the truly Spirit-filled life. He can describe it in these words: "It is no longer I who live, but it is Christ who lives in me. And the life I now live in the flesh I live by faith in the Son of God" (2:20).

Belief in a life received by faith from the Spirit, not according to the rules and regulations of the Jewish Torah, is defended in a two-chapter argument (Gal. 3—4). The Galatians' initial experience of receiving salvation by faith, not by obedience to circumcision or any other law, shows that the Jewish law is no longer relevant for Christians (3:1–5). And in a long, involved, and at times dubious exposition, Paul sets out to prove that the Jewish scriptures themselves have taught the priority of faith over law. In Gal. 3:11, he defends his position with a quotation from Habakkuk: "Their spirit is not right in them, but the righteous live by their faith" (Hab. 2:4; cf. Rom. 1:17); and Paul argues that Abraham had lived by faith long before the law was given (Gal. 3:6).

Paul now uses a bit of Roman law to illustrate how the promises to Abraham have spread outside Judaism. As interpreted by G. M. Taylor,[25] the pattern is as follows. Roman inheritance laws were originally enacted to protect Roman citizens. Eventually, however, if a Roman wished to leave part of his estate to some non-Romans, he could do this: Technically, he left all to one Roman heir. That heir, however, knowing that he was actually supposed to act for others as the executor of the estate, would, by another legal convention, "adopt" the others to whom the estate would go. He could then divide the inheritance with them. Christ, as Abraham's true heir, now "adopts" us, Paul says, and we also become heirs of the promises of Abraham (3:15–18).

Changing the figure, Paul says that the Old Testament law was a temporary necessity until the eschatological deliverance brought by Christ. It was a "disciplinarian" (3:24; cf. 4:2), a kind of stern baby-sitter. Entertainments of the time poked fun at such sour-faced guardians, who shouted, "No!" to freedom-loving children as they protected them. A child under such restraint was little better than a slave. But now, Paul says, the Galatians have been set free and are not slaves but are bought for freedom and adopted as grown-up sons and daughters, heirs of the promises.

Galatians 3:28 summarizes what must have been among the most shocking implications of Paul's argument. In the familiar liturgy of the day, a man might pray, "I thank thee, Lord, King of the universe, that I have not been born a Gentile, a slave, or a woman." Paul announces that precisely these three barriers have been blasted away by the coming of Christ: "There is no longer Jew or Greek, there is no longer slave or free, there is no longer male and female; for all of you are one in Christ Jesus." In civil rights struggles and in the battle for women's liberation in the twentieth century, this verse was to become a rallying cry.

Paul concludes the theological argument by using a dubious device popular among first-century biblical scholars: allegory. Paul compares those who live by the law to the children of Abraham's slave, Hagar, and those who live by faith and the Spirit to Abraham's free sons (4:21–31).

The final two chapters of Galatians are an appeal to live out the implications of this theology. You are free, Paul says. Therefore—at least, as Augustine interpreted him—Paul says, "Love God—and do as you please!" In the twentieth century, Joseph Flctcher was to argue, in part on the basis of Galatians, that the Christian is bound by no laws, not even the Ten Commandments.[26] The Christian is simply to do whatever love demands in a given situation. Even adultery may be the right thing for a Christian, Fletcher suggests, if in some situation it is required by love. The Judaizers must have been scandalized.

But there does remain the law of love (5:14). There does remain the guidance of the Holy Spirit (5:25). The one who loves God may do as he or she pleases. But that one will wish freely to choose to do as God's Holy Spirit guides, Paul is saying. And that guidance will lead Christians to "bear one another's burdens, and in this way you will fulfil the law of Christ" (6:2). Thus the Christian will live not by license but by the liberty of unconstrained love.

Martin Luther summarized Galatians's paradox of Christian freedom and servanthood in these famous words: "A Christian man is the most free lord of all, and subject to none; a Christian man is the most dutiful servant of all, and subject to everyone."[27]

ROMANS

To Martin Luther, at least, Romans represented the high point of the whole Bible:

> This epistle is in truth the principal part of the New Testament and the very purest Gospel. It fully deserves that every Christian should know it by heart, word for word, and should feed upon it every day, as daily bread for his soul. It cannot be read too often nor too deeply pondered, and the more it is studied the more precious and sweet to the taste does it become.[28]

Augustine, John Calvin, Karl Barth, and many other giants of Christian theology have also built their thought on Romans. It is generally recognized as the fullest, clearest, most systematic statement of Paul's most distinctive doctrines, especially his belief in "justification by faith."

It may seem odd, however, to speak of Romans as "the very purest Gospel." Matthew, Mark, Luke, and John are the books the church has called the "Gospels." Romans gives us hardly any information at all about the earthly life of Jesus. This is one reason why critics of Paul, including Adolf Harnack, have charged that a book such as Romans actually "ruins" the gospel. It substitutes religion about Jesus, they argue, for the religion of Jesus.

In answer, Paul would probably reply that concern about the Jesus of the past is valid, of course. The next generation of Christian writers would explore that subject well. But Paul was interested in the present, in the risen Christ now, and in the new age the risen Christ was now bringing. Paul's concern in Romans is "existential." He writes about his understanding of what Christ means to the believer now and in the future. That meaning is, for Paul, "gospel" (good news).

The Occasion of Romans

Surprisingly, Paul seems to have written his longest letter to a church he had never visited. Though Roman Catholic tradition speaks of Peter as founding the church at Rome, the New Testament gives no hint as to the Roman

ROMANS
The Good News of the Righteousness of God

"For in it [the gospel] the righteousness of God is revealed through faith for faith; ...
'The one who is righteous will live by faith'" (1:17).

1:1 Introduction	1:18 The Righteousness of God Revealed in Judgment	3:21 The Righteousness of God Revealed in God's Free Justification of Those Who Have Faith	5:1 The Righteousness of God in the Experience of the Individual	9:1 The Righteousness of God in History: God's Dealings with the Jews	12:1 The Believer's Response to God's Righteousness: Righteous Living in the World	15:14 Concluding Doxology, Personal Comments, and Postscripts 16:27
Salutation, 1:1–7	On pagans, 1:18–2:16	The good news that righteousness announced, 3:21–31	The experience of tension between law and grace, 5:1–7:24	Paul's concern over the apparent rejection of the Jews, 9:1–33	The response of love, 12–13	
Paul's desire to visit them, 1:8–15	On Jews, 2:17–3:8	That righteousness illustrated in Abraham, 4:1–25	The experience and hope of victory, 7:25–8:39	The responsibility of Christians to spread the gospel to them and others, 10:1–21	Concern especially for weaker brothers, 14:1–15:13	
The theme of the letter stated: the gospel of the righteousness of God, 1:16–17	On all people, 3:9–20			Paul's continuing hope for the Jews, 11:1–36		

Author: Paul
Recipients: The church at Rome
Date: A.D. 56
Occasion: Paul hopes to visit the church soon.
Purpose: To prepare for his visit by explaining to them his understanding of the gospel as good news about the righteousness of God

church's origin. Hero though Paul was to Luke, Acts accurately admits that the church was established in Rome before Paul got there (Acts 28:14–15).

He had not been there yet, but Paul did want to visit Rome. Acts 19:21 quotes Paul on his way to his last tragic visit to Jerusalem as exclaiming, "After I have gone there, I must also see Rome." Paul begins his letter by swearing before God how eager he is to visit that church: "I am longing to see you" (Rom. 1:9–11). "I desire, as I have for many years, to come to you," he repeats as he closes his epistle (15:23).

"At present," he writes, "I am going to Jerusalem in a ministry to the saints" (15:25). He had collected for poor Christians in Jerusalem the money he had been seeking as he wrote to Corinth (15:26; cf. 1 Cor. 16:1–4). His ambition is to go to Jerusalem with this gift, then to travel to Rome, and at last to take the gospel all the way to Spain (Rom. 15:28). Probably he writes from Corinth during his three-month stay in Greece on his last missionary journey, around A.D. 57 (Acts 20:1–3). Paul writes to prepare the church for his visit and to explain to them his particular approach to the Christian faith.

Because Paul has had little contact with the Roman church, this epistle, unlike his other letters, is not written to deal with some special problem in a particular congregation. Some things, however, can be inferred about this church at Rome:

1. It was a church of great importance, at least symbolically, because it was located in the capital of the world. Johannes Munck has called attention to Paul's belief that a mission among the Gentiles would make the Jews "jealous," causing them to want to become Christians too (Rom. 11:11).[29] No greater symbol of the spread of God's promises to the nations could be given than the spread of Christianity at the heart of the empire.

2. "Peril," "distress," "persecution," "sword"—there are strong hints in such words in Rom. 8:31–39 that the church had already experienced some persecution. The Roman historian Suetonius tells us that around A.D. 52, "since the Jews were continually making disturbances at the instigation of Chrestus, he [Claudius] expelled them from Rome"[30] (cf. Acts 18:2). Perhaps "Chrestus" is a misspelling of "Christus"—an error common among non-Christians a century later—since Chrestus was a familiar name and sounds almost like the title given Jesus. If so, then the disturbances may have been caused by dissension in the Jewish community in Rome over the first Christian preachers. In any event, those Christians who were Jews had experienced Claudius's persecution by the time Paul wrote Romans.

3. The church at Rome was a mixed congregation, containing both Jews and Gentiles. Scholars differ as to which group predominated. Most think of the church at Rome as largely Gentile. This view seems to be

supported by Rom. 1:5–6; 1:14; 11:13; and 15:16. But other verses seem addressed much more to Jews. Paul speaks to his readers about "Abraham, our ancestor according to the flesh" (4:1), and "our ancestor Isaac" (9:10). "I am speaking to those who know the law [the Jewish law]," he writes in 7:1. "You call yourself a Jew," he challenges his imaginary reader (2:17). Three whole chapters (Rom. 9—11) trace God's relationship to the Jews. And indeed, almost the whole book is to describe God's righteousness as set in relationship to the Jewish law. It seems to the present writer, therefore, that the letter can be more easily understood if it is thought of as being addressed to a largely Jewish congregation, though one in which uncircumcised Gentiles were participating more and more.

Paul is writing, therefore, to Jewish Christians and to Gentile converts who have been taught the Jewish law. He is writing to a church that is growing, however, in the midst of Gentiles, in the very capital of the Gentiles, persecuted by Gentiles, and yet itself gradually coming to be dominated by members who are themselves uncircumcised Gentiles. It is to the theological tensions growing out of the relationship of the Jewish Christians to Gentile Christians, of those schooled in the Jewish law to those who had previously scarcely heard of the Jewish law, that Paul, apostle to the Gentiles, writes this letter.

The Purpose of Romans

Paul writes to prepare the Roman Christians for his coming by describing for them his own understanding of the good news, the gospel. That seems clear enough. The whole letter is a systematically outlined, carefully reasoned exposition of that gospel—in contrast to his highly personal, belligerent, and sometimes disjointed defense in Galatians.

What was that gospel? At first, the answer seems clear. The whole message is summarized at the beginning in just two verses:

> For I am not ashamed of the gospel; it is the power of God for salvation to everyone who has faith, to the Jew first and also to the Greek. For in it the righteousness of God is revealed through faith for faith; as is written, "The one who is righteous will live by faith." (Rom. 1:16–17; cf. Hab. 2:4)

Paul writes to present good news about "the righteousness of God" that is revealed "through faith." But readers of Romans are divided as to what these words mean.

The classical Reformation understanding is that Paul writes to describe a "righteousness," a getting right with God, that the believer receives through faith, not by any legalistic good deeds. God's kind of righteousness for humankind is set over against all human righteousness, which one might claim on the basis of one's own goodness by obedience to the law (10:3). The book is written, according to this view, to answer the question, "How can I get right with God?"

Luther, for example, defines "the righteousness of God" in these words: "how a person becomes righteous before God, namely, alone by faith." It is the believer's "justification." Similarly, Calvin comments, "I take the righteousness of God to mean, that which is approved before his tribunal." The extreme of this approach is that of Rudolf Bultmann, who can speak of the book as a presentation of Christian "anthropology," a book about humankind.[31]

While the believer's justification by faith is surely a great theme of the letter, the present writer finds that the book as a whole makes more sense when the basis of that message is understood as being first good news not about humankind but about God. The believer's hope of salvation rests on the goodness, the righteousness, the love of God. Paul writes to celebrate the goodness of God in God's dealings with humankind.

The German scholar Gunther Bornkamm seeks to combine these two views:

> Astonishing as it may seem, in Romans 1:17 Paul speaks, *in one and the same sentence,* of the righteousness of God and that of the believer: nor are these two things, but one, God's righteousness. . . . God attributes his righteousness to man who is a sinner and not righteous in himself. God is righteous and proves his righteousness by justifying [forgiving, pardoning, declaring acquitted] the person who has faith (Rom. 3:26).[32]

Romans is good news about God. It does answer the question "How can I be saved?" But is it also written to answer such questions as these: Does the faithlessness of some Jews nullify the faithfulness of God (3:3)? Is God unjust to inflict wrath on us (3:5)? Is God the God of Jews only? Is God not the God of Gentiles also (3:29)? Is God's law sin, since we are justified apart from it (7:7, 13)? Is there injustice on God's part (9:14)? Has God rejected God's own chosen people (11:1)?

However, the righteousness, the goodness, that Paul ascribes to God is not a static attribute such as the goodness of the god described by such Greek philosophers as Aristotle. Aristotle wrote of "the Unmoved Mover." For Paul, by contrast, God's righteousness is in God's activity—Christ's death and resurrection—on behalf of humankind. God is "for us" (8:31). The good news about God's active, loving concern for sinful humanity is now revealed, made clear, in the eschatological event of the coming of Christ.

This good news is revealed, Paul says, "through faith for faith" (1:17). The ancient scholar Jerome thought of that phrase as meaning "from the Old Testament faith into the New Testament faith." Calvin took it to imply the believer's growing, deepening trust. But Karl Barth is probably closer to

Paul's theology when he understands it as "where the faithfulness of God encounters the fidelity of men."[33]

"Faith," as Paul uses the term, is never an end in itself. Paul never praises faith as such; it is always faith in something or, more accurately, in Someone. Nor is faith simply belief that certain statements are true. Faith, to Paul, is trust. It is commitment. It is a personal relationship to the God whose faithfulness to us is revealed in Christ.

That kind of faith leads both to forgiveness and to a special kind of life, now and in the eschaton (the end), Paul is sure. The just shall live by their faithfulness—God's faithfulness to the believer and the believer's faithfulness to God.

To describe the righteousness of God and the forgiveness, the "justification," the righteousness God freely gives to those who have such faith, as well as the kind of life that results from it—this is the purpose of Romans.

Some Comments on Romans

In Romans, Paul presents his most original contributions to Christian theology, what he can call "my gospel" (2:16; 16:25). It is surprising, therefore, that he begins with what many scholars believe is a quotation from a very early Christian creed. Romans 1:3–4 summarizes a faith common to all the church, probably in a liturgical formula that Paul could expect some of his readers to know by heart. "His" gospel, he believed, was implied in the earliest kerygma preached everywhere.

Paul could, at times, be blunt. With these strangers, however, he moves tactfully from this common faith, that Christ the Lord has come, to the apocalyptic implications that Paul sees in that eschatological event. We have already examined the key verses in which he announces his understanding of the revelation of God's righteousness (1:16–17). The rest of the letter develops this theme so systematically that some commentators have speculated that Romans is an expansion of a lecture Paul may have given many times.

First, he deals with the negative side of God's righteousness, what Karl Barth calls the "no" of God. God's righteous judgment on sin is already being revealed in this messianic age. That judgment on sin turns out to be sin itself. It reaches its climax in a double perversion, the opposite of God's good creation: (1) in idolatry, humankind worships its own creations, not its Creator (1:23); (2) in homosexual practice, Paul sees a symbol of the reversal of the Creator's intention in human relationships (1:26–27).

If one asks, "What about people who don't know any better?" Paul replies that all should know better. Nature's Creator is revealed in creation (1:19), and moral standards are recognized even in untrained consciences (2:12–15). Yet neither Jew nor Gentile lives up to the good each knows.

Paul climaxes this section by pulling together passages from many parts of the Old Testament to show that every human being deserves condemnation by the righteous judgment of God. "There is no one who is righteous, not even one" (3:10–18). Even those who have tried hard to obey God's law are lost. In fact, what the law has done for them is to make them more aware of their sin (3:20).

One can cite ancient Jewish rabbis who would agree with almost everything Paul has said up to this point. They had read these same verses concerning how all humankind deserves condemnation, but their prescription for this malady was usually repentance, fasting, prayer, and a new resolve to obey the Commandments.

Paul's is the announcement of the new age. But now, he says emphatically, an apocalyptic event has occurred. The righteous God has revealed his saving grace apart from the law (3:21–26). The Jewish commentator H. J. Schoeps says that some rabbis of the time taught that the law would end with the messiah.[34] For Paul, that messianic age had begun. Humankind now lives in the new era, not of law but of faith.

The eschatological element is so strong in Romans that Paul Achtemeier outlines the whole book around the concept of God as the Lord in history. The traditional Jewish apocalyptic had divided history into two eras, the present and the age to come. But Paul sees a new age begun with the coming of Christ, though we still await the final era. Thus Achtemeier outlines Romans around three ages: "God's Lordship and the Problems of the Past: Grace and Wrath" (1:1–4:22); "God's Lordship and the Problem of the Present: Grace and Law" (4:23–8:39); "God's Lordship and the Problem of the Future: Israel and God's Gracious Plan" (9:1–11:36); with the final (ethical) section of Romans returning to the present for a discussion of "God's Lordship and the Problems of Daily Living: Grace and the Structures of Life" (12:1–16:27).[35]

Paul replies in chapter 4 to Jewish Christians, children of Abraham shocked by the announcement that the law is no longer needed, that Abraham himself had never heard of the law. Abraham received God's righteousness by faith long before God's law was given.

In Christ, Paul has said, God in heaven has declared sinful people righteous, forgiven. In chapters 5 through 8, Paul turns to the consequences of God's action in the lives of individuals here on earth. When, in Rom. 1:16, Paul spoke of the gospel as the "power" of God for salvation, the Greek word he used for "power" was the word from which our words "dynamite" and "dynamics" are derived. Paul now describes the "dynamics" of God's salvation. For the person of faith, there are joyful consequences of God's action: "peace," "character," "hope," "love" (5:1–11). Reconciled to God through Christ's death, the Christian also is saved by his life, a life the believer is now enabled to begin to share, at least in hope.

But there is a continuing, "dynamic" conflict, a cosmic struggle within and for the souls of men and women. Scan Rom. 5:12–6:23 and make two lists. Over and over, one will find such words as the following set in opposition to each other:

sin	free gift
death	life
law	grace
Adam (one man)	Christ (one man)

Paul attempts to illustrate in a series of figures how, in this conflict, the believer is freed from the righteousness of the law and enabled to live by the righteousness of God:

1. We were all children of Adam, the fallen sinner, he says. But now, through Christ, humankind has a kind of second start (5:12–21).
2. We have "died" with Christ to the law. Schoeps quotes an ancient rabbi as saying, "As soon as a man is dead, he is free from the obligation of the commands."[36] In baptism, the believer has "died" with Christ and begins a new life of resurrection freedom (6:5–14). The law has not died, but we have died in relation to it.
3. We were "slaves" of sin. But Christ has freed us to be "slaves" of God (6:15–23).
4. We were once "married" to the law. But now our former "husband" is dead, and we are free (7:1–6).

In all of these figures, Paul argues not only for the reality of Christian freedom but also for the importance of living daily the righteous lives of those set free by the righteousness of God. The basis of the appeal, however, is no longer legal obligation but new opportunity, new power for living.

The description of the dynamic, personal struggle of these conflicting forces within the soul builds to a climax in Romans 7. In 7:7, Paul switches to the first person, using *I* to dramatize the personal intensity of the warfare. He gives his own spiritual autobiography, but only as typical of all believers. At the climax of the tension, Paul cries, "Wretched man that I am! Who will rescue me from this body of death?" (7:24). Some commentators have argued that here Paul is simply recalling, from his Christian perspective, his life before his conversion as it now appears to him. Yet he is writing to people who are already Christians, and this language seems too dramatic to be simply a theological analysis of a memory. Luther and Calvin are right that this dynamic tension still exists in the souls of "born-again" Christians, the best of whom, in Luther's phrase, is "at the same time justified and yet a sinner." Like a prisoner whose partner on a chain gang has died, the tormented sinner drags a corpse, a "body of death," his old nature, with him.

But the believer also knows deliverance. "Thanks be to God!" (7:25).

Romans 8 is Paul's almost-lyrical celebration of Christ's victory for the believer in the struggle described in the preceding chapters. Now Paul uses yet another figure, the courtroom. The believer is pardoned, "set free," and "lives" in spite of deserving the death penalty. The Holy Spirit takes over in the soul of the one who has faith. "We are children of God," the Christian can exult, not prisoners condemned by the heavenly Judge (8:16). All history has longed for this eschatological era, which Christians have and will share with Christ (8:18–25).

True, these Roman Christians still face persecution. But "in all these things we are more than conquerors through him who loved us" (8:37). Romans 8 is the believer's shout of triumph.

What about those Jews who have not believed? Paul is so concerned for them that he could wish himself damned if that would convert his fellow Jews (9:3). Romans 9—11 expresses his agonizing meditations on what was, to this Christian Jew, a distressing question. Paul's reasoning about it sometimes seems tortured, and his answers do not always seem consistent. But here are answers he proposes:

1. However it may seem, God is working out God's righteous plan in history, the plan of election. Romans 9:1–29 presents one of Paul's most controversial doctrines, the idea of God's "election" or "predestina-tion" of men and women, not because of their merit but purely by God's grace.
2. If some Jews are lost, it is not because God is unrighteous but because they are, Paul argues. It is their own fault (9:30–33).
3. Christians must take the responsibility. Christians must be missionaries, must spread the good news of salvation to all people (10:1–21).
4. As a matter of fact, some Jews are Christians (11:5).
5. Whatever the situation, Christians must never look down on Jews. Rather, Gentile Christians' highest hope is that through Christ, they have been allowed to be grafted onto the tree that is Israel. The Christian has become, in a sense, an adopted Jew (11:17–24).
6. In the end, the eschaton, the third age in Achtemeier's outline, "all Israel will be saved" (11:26).
7. For now, the whole matter is a mystery beyond even Paul's understand-ing (11:33–36).

Chapters 12 through 15, the last major section of Romans, form our best statement of Christian ethics according to Paul. Even so, these chapters do not give a complete statement of ethical principles but rather deal with specific issues relevant to the Roman church. Several points are worth particular notice.

First, it is essential to understand the motivation of Christian living according to Paul. It is not that the Christian is to be a loving person in order to earn God's favor. To say that would be to get everything exactly backward. Rather, the Christian ethic is an ethic of response, a "therefore" ethic. Because all that has been said in the first eleven chapters of Romans is true, Paul begins chapter 12 with *therefore:* "I appeal to you therefore, . . . by the mercies of God." In gratitude to God for God's righteous action of giving justification to us sinners, Paul says, we are to give ourselves to God.

That response is to be shown in humble service to others within the body, the church (12:1–8). Paul also writes of Christian love in action toward those persecuting the church. His words sound very much like those of Jesus in the Sermon on the Mount (12:14; cf. Matt. 5:43–44). Christians are to carry out faithfully their civic responsibilities, even in Nero's Rome (Rom. 13:1–7). The guide and summary of Christian living can be put in one word: love (12:9–13; 13:8–10). In this eschatological hour, there is no longer time for drunkenness and quarreling, opposites of living out that love (13:11–14).

A long discussion concerns the particular problem of care for Christians who are "weaker" in the faith. The subject of those timid converts who refuse to eat meat lest they seem to participate in sacrifices to pagan gods is discussed again (14:1–15:6; cf. 1 Cor. 8—10). Paul counsels tolerance and concern: "We who are strong ought to put up with the failings of the weak" (Rom. 15:1).

The letter concludes with some personal comments. Chapter 16 consists largely of personal greetings to friends.

Some ancient manuscripts omit all or most of chapter 16. It is suggested by many scholars that Paul would probably not have known as many people in the church at Rome as are listed in chapter 16, since he had never been there. Perhaps, it is proposed, this list belonged originally with another letter of Paul's; or perhaps Paul sent another copy of this letter to some church such as the one at Ephesus, in which he did know many people, attaching these greetings to that copy. Romans may originally have been a sermon or a kind of circular letter to which the salutation and conclusion were added when it was sent as a letter. There is no way to be sure.

At any rate, the list is interesting. Priscilla (Prisca) and Aquila, whose home had indeed been at Rome, are mentioned first (16:3; cf. Acts 18:2; 1 Cor. 16:19). Several members of Paul's otherwise almost unknown family are included (Rom. 16:7, 11, 21; cf. Acts 23:16). Even the secretary adds a greeting (16:22).

Romans is a profound theological treatise. But its closing list of common names reminds the student today that Paul expected ordinary church members to read it, to understand it, and to live by it.

9

THE PRISON EPISTLES

"I am an ambassador in chains" (Eph. 6:20).

Paul did make the journey to Rome he had so long and so eagerly anticipated, but he made it as a prisoner of the Romans. Acts gives us an account of Paul's arrest in Jerusalem, his defenses in various courts, and his appeal to Caesar. His dangerous voyage to Rome is described in vivid detail. We are told that he was welcomed in Rome by Christians but received a very mixed response from the leaders of Rome's large Jewish community. Acts ends with Paul a prisoner under a kind of "house arrest," living in a private home under guard. Here believers and inquirers might visit, and here, presumably, he could still write letters (Acts 28:30–31).

Ancient Christian tradition says that in Rome, under Nero, Paul was martyred. The most likely date is around A.D. 64. Because he was a Roman citizen, he was not crucified. Crucifixion was the proper execution for an outsider, especially a slave. According to tradition, Paul was killed more "humanely": they beheaded him.

From as early as the middle of the second century until the twentieth, at least four letters—Philippians, Colossians, Philemon, and Ephesians—were thought of as written by Paul during this time of Roman imprisonment. They have been regarded as, in a sense, Paul's last will and testament. "Remember my chains," Col. 4:18 had exhorted the reader. And picturing Paul "a prisoner of Christ Jesus" (Philemon v. 9), awaiting his martyrdom in Rome, readers have fulfilled the hope expressed in Phil. 1:14, "having been made confident in the Lord by my imprisonment."

Recently, however, many scholars have found reasons to believe that Paul may have written one or more of these letters during an earlier imprisonment, perhaps at Ephesus or while awaiting trial at Caesarea (Acts 23:33;

24:27).[1] Indeed, serious question has been raised as to whether it was Paul who wrote Colossians, and a large number of scholars now doubt that Paul wrote Ephesians.[2]

The case for dating these letters during some earlier imprisonment—for example, at Ephesus—rests on such grounds as the following:

1. It is eight hundred miles from Rome to Philippi. Some estimate that in the first century, that journey might have taken as long as seven weeks. Yet Paul appears to have had repeated communication with the Philippian church. Similarly, Rome is a long way from Colossae. Is it not much more likely that the runaway slave Onesimus would have sought refuge in Ephesus, a port only a hundred miles from his home?

2. Paul expresses high hope for visiting "soon" both in Philippi and in Colossae (Phil. 2:23–24; Philemon v. 22). Paul could have had much better reason for such hope during some short imprisonment in relatively nearby Ephesus.

3. Paul has with him Timothy, Mark, Aristarchus, Demas, Tychicus, and Luke (Eph. 6:21; Phil. 1:1; Col. 4:7–14; Philemon v. 24). Of these, Acts mentions only Luke as being with Paul at Rome.

4. In Philippians, Paul is faced with Jewish opposition, a situation suggesting to some commentators that the letter belongs to the same period as Galatians.

5. Finally, the references to the "imperial guard" (Phil. 1:13) and "those of the emperor's household" (4:22) were once thought to make clear that the letter was written in Rome. It has now been discovered, however, that these terms were used for certain Roman garrisons and civil servants throughout the empire.

Nevertheless, probably most scholars still think of these four letters as written—or purporting to be written—by Paul from Rome.[3] Placing them during the Caesarean imprisonment helps little with the problem of geography. As for relating them to an imprisonment in Ephesus, the big problem is that we have no clear record that Paul ever was in prison there. The problems of travel time are not unsolvable, given the length of Paul's imprisonment in Rome and the fact that "all roads led to Rome," the center and focal point of the ancient world.

Fortunately, whichever way one decides, the meaning of the letters is not greatly changed. Without strong conviction about the matter one way or the other, the present writer is inclined to believe that they were written from Rome for four reasons:

1. The tradition that they came from Rome is ancient and consistent.
2. We know that Paul was a longtime prisoner in Rome.

3. Paul seems to be facing seriously and with a certain resignation the prospect of death.
4. The thought expressed in some of these letters, if all of them are by Paul, seems to reflect a later stage in his theological development.

PHILIPPIANS

"If there were a competition to decide which is the most beautiful of Paul's letters, the odds would be strongly on Philippians," writes A. M. Hunter.[4] "In no other letter does he share his inner spiritual life so freely with his readers," adds Kenneth Grayston. Philippians is so personal, so cordial, and so affectionate that Grayston gives it a subtitle, "The Apostle and His Friends."[5]

Christ's prisoner here writes such a courageous letter of good cheer that its theme might well be summarized as "joy in a jail."

The Occasion of Philippians

In which city Paul is confined can be debated, but it is clear that he is in prison (Phil. 1:7, 13, 14, 17). Yet the letter is not a complaint but a thank-you note. "I have received from Epaphroditus the gifts you sent," Paul writes (4:18). "It was kind of you to share my distress" (4:14). Long before, Paul had founded the church in Philippi (Acts 16). He had been in jail there too. Since then, that church had supported him repeatedly, and now again, they had come to his aid (Phil. 4:15–18).

A friend from the church, Epaphroditus, had brought the gift, probably money. While with Paul, he had fallen ill and had nearly died. Paul sends the letter with Epaphroditus, rejoicing with the Philippians that they will see that he is well again (2:25–30).

As Paul writes, he does not know whether he will be released or executed (1:20). Yet he reassures his friends that even while he is in prison, the gospel is being spread. And he cheerfully predicts that he will be set free to visit them "soon."

Two facts, however, do distress Paul. First, some kind of false teaching is being spread. "Some proclaim Christ from envy and rivalry" (1:15). "Beware of the dogs," he warns the Philippians (3:2). Perhaps these verses refer to two different groups of false teachers, the first simply capitalizing on Paul's imprisonment to grab places of leadership in the church. More likely, the partisan preachers mentioned in Philippians 1 are the same teachers attacked more fully in the second half of the letter. Second, there is some kind of dissension in the church at Philippi. Two women of the church have had a quarrel (4:2). Others evidently have taken sides. Concern about a threatened church split moves Paul to a plea for unity.

PHILIPPIANS
Joy and Love in a Jail

"I rejoice . . . greatly that . . . you have . . . concern for me" (4:10).

1:1 Paul's Own Situation: Joy in Spite of Prison and Dissension	1:27 A Plea: Increase My Joy by Christ-like Humility and Cooperation	2:19 Good News about Two Friends	3:1 A Warning against Certain False Teachers	4:1 Miscellaneous Concluding Notes	4:23
A prayer rejoicing in their partnership, 1:1–11	The plea for unity, 1:27–2:4	Timothy will visit them, 2:19–24	Paul's own authority and example, 3:1–16	A plea to two female leaders to end their quarrel, 4:1–3	
Joy at the spread of the gospel, in spite of prison and partisanship, 1:12–18	The example: Christ's sacrifice, 2:5–11	Epaphroditus has recovered and is returning to them, 2:25–30	Follow Paul, not false teachers, 3:17–21	A concluding benediction, 4:4–7	
Joy in Paul's hope for the future, 1:19–26	Now they must be humble and sacrificial too, 2:12–18			A thank-you note and some personal greetings, 4:8–23	

Author: Paul
Recipients: The church which Paul had founded at Philippi
Date: A.D. 64 (A.D. 57?)
Occasion: Paul, in prison, has received a gift and news from the church at Philippi.
Purpose: To thank them and to encourage them to mutual cooperation and self-sacrifice

The Purpose of Philippians

Paul writes this letter for several purposes:

1. He writes to thank the church for their gift. "It was kind of you to share my distress" (4:14).
2. He writes to reassure and encourage his friends at Philippi, even though he is in prison and facing possible execution. "I want you to know, beloved, that what has happened to me has actually helped to spread the gospel" (1:12). "Rejoice in the Lord always; again I will say, Rejoice" (4:4).
3. He wants to reassure them about their friend Epaphroditus, "that you may rejoice at seeing him again" (2:28).
4. He writes to plead with the church for Christ-like humility and love in the quarrel that threatens the congregation. "Make my joy complete: be of the same mind, having the same love, being in full accord and of one mind" (2:2).
5. He writes to warn against some kind of false teaching that has reached or that he fears may soon reach Philippi. "Beware of the dogs, beware of the evil workers, beware of those who mutilate the flesh" (3:2).

Some Comments on Philippians

"Rejoice . . . again I will say, Rejoice" (4:4). Though it is written by a man facing death, Philippians is perhaps the most joyful letter in the New Testament. If he or she looks for the words "joy" and "rejoice," the reader will find them in almost every paragraph. In jail, Paul is praying, but he is "praying with joy" (1:4). Even when Christ is preached out of partisanship, Paul can still exult that "Christ is proclaimed in every way . . . and in that I rejoice. Yes, and I will continue to rejoice" (1:18). Paul expects to visit Philippi if and when he is released, "for your progress and joy" (1:25). "Make my joy complete," he pleads with those who are disputing, by being "of the same mind" (2:2). (The reader may trace the theme on through 2:28–29; 3:1; 4:1, 4, 10.)

Paul is joyous in the face of difficulties. Some, Paul feels, are preaching Christ in the wrong way and from the wrong motives (1:15–18). Too little is said in chapter 1 about these preachers for us to know who they were or even if they were the same people whom he denounces as "dogs" in Phil. 3:2. It is clear that their false preaching disturbs Paul almost as much as his own imprisonment.

He is in prison—probably has been for some time—and is facing possible death. This seems to fit Paul's experience in Rome better than any imprisonment we know of earlier in his life. He has reached the point in life in which he would really welcome death, again a hint that this letter is written toward the end. He is confident that he will "be with Christ" if he does die. Yet he cheerfully reassures the Philippians that he probably will be released and visit them again soon (1:19–26).

Paul is courageously sacrificing himself in Christ's service. He uses his report on his own situation and attitude to launch his plea for the Philippians to forget their personal differences and, surrendering their own pride, join in "striving side by side with one mind for the faith" (1:27–30). Paul's real example of self-sacrifice, however, is not himself but his Lord.

Many scholars have recognized that Phil. 2:6–11 is an early Christian hymn. In this best-loved passage in Philippians, Paul is quoting a song probably familiar to those on both sides of the Philippian discord. The song voices a plea for harmony based on Christ,

> who, though he was in the form of God,
>> did not regard equality with God
>> as something to be exploited,
> but emptied himself,
>> taking the form of a slave,
>> being born in the human likeness.
>
> And being found in human form,
>> he humbled himself
>> and became obedient to the point of death—
> even death on a cross.
>
> Therefore God also highly exalted him
>> and gave him the name
>> that is above every name,
> so that at the name of Jesus
>> every knee should bend,
>> in heaven and on earth and under the earth,
> and every tongue should confess
>> that Jesus Christ is Lord,
>> to the glory of God the Father.

Printing it thus, as three stanzas, emphasizes the three stages of the drama of salvation that the hymn celebrated: Christ's preincarnate life in heaven, his servanthood and death on earth, and his exaltation now in heaven. Theologians have found profound meaning in the concept of Christ's "emptying" himself (*kenosis*) of his divine prerogatives of omniscience and omnipotence for his human, earthly service. The pattern of the "servant" is clearly that of Isaiah 53 (the reader may compare Phil. 2:7 with Isa. 53:12; Phil. 2:8 with Isa. 53:7, 12; and Phil. 2:9 with Isa. 53:12a). You disputing Philippians, Paul is pleading, follow Christ by laying aside the rights each side claims, as Christ laid aside his rights in order to serve us. The song ends with all creation uniting in that oldest of Christian creeds, "Jesus Christ is Lord."

"Beware of the dogs!" (Phil. 3:2). That Paul abruptly called these heretics by such an ugly name has so startled many scholars that they have suggested that the passage it introduces cannot originally have been part of this lovely letter. Perhaps Philippians 3—4 was once not the second half of this epistle but a separate note, or perhaps Phil. 3:2–20 is a fragment of another letter, inserted here by mistake. Some scholars profess to find parts of three different letters in Philippians.[6]

In support of this position, it is noted that Polycarp, in his own epistle to the Philippians a century later, reminded them that Paul had written them *letters,* implying that he knew of more than one. Yet themes from the first half of the letter recur in the second. Those who divide Philippians do not agree on precisely where the different parts end. We know that within one letter, Paul could move from one kind of emotion to another. While the possibility that Philippians was composed of parts of more than one epistle is widely recognized, it is probably true that most scholars still treat it as a unity.[7]

Who are these "dogs" who arouse such shocking wrath? The particular ways in which Paul defends his gospel and attacks theirs give us some clues. Apparently, they advocated circumcision (3:2–3). They boasted of their credentials as model keepers of the Jewish law (3:4–6). They claimed a special maturity, quite possibly that they had achieved perfection (3:12–16). And yet they tolerated such sensuous living that Paul could laugh at them, deriding them that "their god is the belly" (3:19). Walter Schmithals has argued that these heretics must have championed an early form of what was later called "Gnosticism."[8] Of this odd blend of Judaism, Christianity, and Greek paganism more will be said in relation to Colossians.

Paul's reply is to stress that true circumcision is spiritual, not physical (3:3). His own credentials as a Jew are as good as anyone's (3:4–6). But in language echoing that of Galatians and Romans, Paul rejoices now as a Christian in a "righteousness" given from God through faith, not the Old Testament law (3:7–11). Humbly, Paul makes no claim to the perfection of which the "Gnostics" boasted. Using a figure from a track meet, Paul writes modestly and simply, "I press on toward the goal" (3:14). His salvation will come not from his own achievements but from Christ (3:20–21).

Tactfully, Paul praises the women who are quarreling at Philippi. Here there is no hint of commanding these women to "keep silence in the churches" (contrast 1 Cor. 14:34). Rather, these two are his equal partners who "have struggled beside me" (4:3).

Tactfully, too, Paul accepts the Philippians' gift with thanks, at the same time carefully asserting his independence. Paul wants to take no chances of being accused of being in the ministry simply for the money (4:10–20).

With personal greetings, he ends this quite personal letter.

PHILEMON

Reading between the lines, one finds that the little letter to Philemon suggests one of the most appealing stories in the New Testament.

Onesimus the slave, having stolen from his master Philemon, had escaped to the city. (Whether it was in Rome or in Ephesus that he was hiding does not change the story.) Somehow, he had come in contact with the apostle Paul. Perhaps he had heard Philemon speak of the preacher who had won him to Christ. Where Paul, who had never been to Philemon's home in Colossae (Col. 2:1), had come to know Onesimus's master is never said. Paul could remind Philemon, the master, however, of "your owing me even your own self" (Philemon v. 19). Surely, this must mean that it was through Paul that Philemon had become a Christian.

Now, through Paul, Onesimus had been converted too. He is "my child," Paul writes, "whose father I have become during my imprisonment" (v. 10). Paul has resolved to send the runaway thief back to his master.

The best Onesimus could hope for would seem to be a return to slavery. The law would fully support Philemon's punishing this fugitive by beating him and branding an *F* on his forehead; and it was within Philemon's rights under Roman law to crucify this thief and runaway.

Cautiously, tactfully, Paul pleads for his "child." Paul speaks of his own imprisonment. To that touch of pathos he adds the light touch of a pun. The name Onesimus means "useful." "Formerly he was useless to you, but now he is indeed useful both to you and to me" (v. 11). But the basic appeal is to love. In sending Onesimus, "I am sending . . . my own heart" (v. 12).

It need not seem strange that Paul does not denounce the institution of slavery. Sixty million slaves were such an accepted part of the social system of the Roman Empire that it does not seem to have occurred to the tiny infant church to attempt to overthrow the whole institution. But Paul could lay down the principles that would some day bring about slavery's end (Gal. 3:28; Col. 3:11). He pleads with Philemon to take back Onesimus, "no longer as a slave but more than a slave, a beloved brother" (Philemon v. 16). Both are now men "in Christ."

He pleads also on the basis of personal affection. Paul even offers his own "IOU" for anything Onesimus may have stolen (vv. 18–19). "Refresh my heart in Christ," he ends his appeal (v. 20).

Competent scholars have proposed that Philemon and Onesimus may have lived not in Colossae but in nearby Laodicea, and that Philemon may be the letter to the Laodiceans mentioned in Col. 4:16. In view of the mention of Onesimus in Col. 4:9 as "one of you," most have rejected this idea.

Of much more interest is the question "How did the story end?" The answer is that nobody knows.

If, however, one looks for a hint of a happy ending beyond the letter itself, there is at least one possibility. Some fifty years later, Ignatius wrote a letter to the church at Ephesus. Early in the letter, he wrote praise of their great bishop. He even made exactly the same pun as had Paul, for that bishop's name was Onesimus.

And if one wants to carry even further such romantic speculation, this may be added: At some time, perhaps in the nineties, a disciple of Paul collected Paul's letters, beginning to gather those we have now. All the letters he collected were epistles dealing with great theological and ethical issues and addressed to whole churches—except for one single, private letter, the little epistle to Philemon. Is E. J. Goodspeed's conjecture purely wishful thinking, that this one private letter was included because the collector was the former slave Onesimus, now bishop of Ephesus?[9] But perhaps such speculation goes beyond the proper scope of this *Guide*.

COLOSSIANS

Most people have understood Genesis 3 to be saying that it was Satan in the form of a snake who tempted Adam and Eve to eat the fruit of the tree of knowledge. Eating that fruit is regarded as the original sin. Some of the Gnostics, however, said that the one who persuaded Adam was not Satan; it was Christ! The evil Creator-God of Judaism, they said, gave Adam a material body to hold him down to Eve. But Christ sought, by the tree of "knowledge" (*gnosis* in Greek), to lift Adam's soul up through the heavens toward the true, spiritual God.

Most scholars believe that the epistle to the Colossians was written to attack a "philosophy" (Col. 2:8) that was an early form of such Gnosticism. That attack included what is widely considered to be the highest statement of the nature of Christ that Paul ever wrote—if, indeed, Paul wrote it.

The scholars are not nearly so well agreed, however, that Paul really was the author of Colossians.[10]

At least four arguments are used by those who believe the letter is from a later hand:

1. Though brief, Colossians contains many words and phrases found rarely or never in the other letters of Paul. Several are found nowhere else in the New Testament.
2. We know from attacks written against it that Gnosticism existed in the second century. It is by no means certain, however, that the odd mixture of Greek, Hebrew, Christian, and Eastern thought that is attacked in Colossians existed as early as Paul's day.
3. Colossians contains ideas, especially those concerning Christology (the doctrine of the nature of Christ), that are quite different from any found in the known letters of Paul.
4. There are telltale suggestions of copying from earlier letters of Paul. For example, the list of names in Colossians 4 is suspiciously like that in Philemon.

COLOSSIANS
The Genuine Wisdom Incarnate in Christ versus "Gnostic" Speculation

"See to it that no one takes you captive through philosophy . . . not according to Christ.
For in him the whole fullness of deity dwells bodily" (2:8–9).

1:1	1:15	2:16	3:12	4:7	4:18
Paul's Prayers	**The Superiority of Christ and His Salvation to the "Knowledge" False Speculation Offers**	**A Practical Consequence: Rejection of the Ethics of the False Teachers**	**Instead, a Plea for Morality of the Truly "Wise"**	**Concluding Personal Notes and Greetings**	
A prayer of thanksgiving for their church, 1:1–8	The superiority of Christ, 1:15–20	Legalistic rules, rituals, and ascetic practices are useless, 2:16–23	Its spirit, especially love, 3:12–17		
He is praying that they may have the true, saving kind of knowledge that is in the gospel of Christ, 1:9–14	What Christ has done for them, 1:21–23	The opposite, giving in to lust, anger, etc., must also be avoided, 3:1–11	Its concrete applications in human relationships in this world, to		
	Paul's concern to spread true knowledge, 1:24–2:7		wives, 3:18		
	The true spiritual power that is in Christ, 2:8–15		husbands, 3:19		
			children, 3:20		
			fathers, 3:21		
			slaves, 3:22–25		
			masters, 4:1		
			all, 4:2–6		

Author: Paul (Some scholars believe it is by a later disciple of Paul.)
Recipients: The church at Colossae, which Paul has never visited
Date: A.D. 64 (Some put it about A.D. 57; others as late as the nineties.)
Occasion: In prison, Paul has received news of the spread of false, Gnostic-like, speculative preaching.
Purpose: To present the superiority of Christ and of the Christian life to such teaching

Those who believe that Paul wrote Colossians reply as follows:[11]

1. There are many unusual words and phrases in Colossians, but these may be explained in part, at least, by the fact that Paul uses the vocabulary of the Gnostics as he seeks to show how Christ is superior to what Gnosticism offers.
2. Similarly, Paul is stimulated to use new ideas, directly related to Gnosticism, in dealing with the heresy at Colossae. It would be foolish to suppose that Paul never had a new idea after he wrote Romans.
3. The similarities to Paul's other letters need not imply copying. They may instead suggest that Colossians is by the same author. Especially, Colossians is so similar to and fits so well with Philemon that it is surely by the same author, generally admitted to be Paul. It must even have been written at the same time.
4. Gnosticism or something very similar to it may well have existed in the first century. It is true that our copies of Gnostic writings come largely from the third century or even later. But there are hints of Gnostic-like ideas in what is attacked in such certainly Pauline books as 1 Corinthians and Galatians. The Dead Sea Scrolls include ideas that, though not a part of Gnosticism, are not unlike some of the ideas that the Gnostics later developed. And writings by or about the Gnostics claim first-century roots for their doctrines.
5. Ancient and consistent tradition ascribes the letter to Paul, as does the epistle itself.

Two things are probably true: (1) most commentaries and introductions still ascribe the book to the apostle, but (2) the number of those who believe that it is the work of a later disciple of Paul is growing.

For the reasons listed above, this *Guide* sides cautiously with the tradition of Pauline authorship.

The Occasion of Colossians

"I am in prison," Paul writes, presumably in Rome.

"We have heard of your faith," he begins in Col. 1:4, though the Colossians "have not seen me face to face" (2:1). Apparently, Paul has received a report brought by the founder of the congregation, Epaphras (1:7; 4:12).

The report has contained good news and bad news. Paul has been told of the Colossians' faith and love. But he also has been warned that there is spreading among them something that he calls "philosophy and empty deceit" (2:8). Knowing about this heresy helps us understand the letter.

According to the second-century theologian Irenaeus, there were many types of heresies with somewhat similar views ("Gnosticism" is a name later given to several of them). The oldest, however, he traces to Simon the

Magician, who, according to Acts 8:9–24, tried to buy the gift of the Spirit from Peter. Irenaeus reports several legends about Simon.

His traveling companion was a former prostitute named Helen, who was said to be a reincarnation of Helen of Troy. Simon, however, "said she was the first conception of his mind, the Mother of all, through whom in the beginning he had the idea of making angels and archangels. This Thought, leaping forth from him . . . descended to the lower regions and generated angels and powers, by whom the world was made." When Helen was ensnared in a material body, Simon the savior came to earth to rescue her and "to offer man salvation through his 'knowledge.' "[12] Because we are saved by grace, not works, Simon taught, it does not matter how we live. Knowledge of heavenly makers is the only thing that counts.

For reasons that are suggested below in the comments on Colossians, most scholars believe that it was some similar heresy that threatened the church at Colossae. Warned about its spread, Paul wrote this letter.[13]

The epistle is sent by Tychicus and Onesimus, the runaway slave (Col. 4:7–9; cf. Philemon).

The Purpose of Colossians

Paul writes, he says, so "that no one may deceive you with plausible arguments" (2:4). He wants his readers instead to "be filled with the knowledge of God's will in all spiritual wisdom and understanding" (1:9). The words sound like the claims of the Gnostics.

The knowledge Paul offers, however, will not be based on Gnostic speculations about angels and "elemental spirits of the universe" (2:20). It will be based on Christ, the image of God himself.

And it will have very practical ethical results. Each Colossian is to be guided to lead a life "worthy of the Lord" (1:10). This life, Paul insists, must be demonstrated in down-to-earth human relationships.

In summary, Paul is writing to set the cosmic Christ over against the cosmic speculations of the Gnostics and to set loving duties toward other people over against Gnostic taboos, rituals, or license.

Some Comments on Colossians

Paul and the Intellectuals—so the late A. T. Robertson titled a commentary on Colossians.[14] Clearly, the great theme of the letter is the relationship of Christ to certain intellectual and religious speculations about the cosmos.

Paul is not, of course, opposed to knowledge. Rather, Paul believes that Christ is the key which opens the door to the real knowledge of the highest kind. "Be filled with . . . spiritual wisdom and understanding," Paul prays, increasing "in the knowledge of God" (1:9–10). Christ has revealed "the mystery that has been hidden throughout the ages and generations but has now been revealed to his saints" (1:26). We are, he says, "teaching everyone in all wisdom" (1:28). He strives that they "may have all the riches of assured understanding and have the knowledge of God's mystery, that is, Christ himself, in whom are hidden all the treasures of wisdom and knowledge" (2:2–3).

Christian wisdom, however, is set in contrast to false "philosophy and empty deceit" (2:8) and "human commands and teachings" (2:22). Rather, those who are in Christ are "renewed in knowledge" (3:10). Movingly, Paul asks the Colossians to pray that in spite of his being in chains, he may still make clear "the mystery" revealed in Christ (4:2–4; cf. 4:18).

When Paul describes this mystery which is revealed in Christ, he does so in such lofty terms that some scholars have doubted that it could be Paul using this kind of language within only thirty-five years of Jesus' death. The writer takes the highest terms of Gnostic speculation and sets Christ above them all.

For example, the Gnostics developed elaborate theories concerning angels and cosmic realms that separated God from the earth. Early speculation imagined seven such gradations, one for each day of the week; later, thirty were described, one for each day of the month, with one female for the extra half-day. And finally, the followers of Basilides spoke of the "principalities, angels and powers of the three-hundred-sixty-five . . . heavens," one for every day of the year.

Colossians, however, pictures Christ as involved in the very creation of all "thrones or dominions or rulers or powers" (1:16). If any of these are opposed to Christ, he has "disarmed the rulers and authorities" by his death and resurrection (2:15)

The Gnostics spoke of the divine "fullness" (*pleroma*). Having been used in various ways of the highest powers about which the Gnostics speculated, the word is now applied by Paul to Christ himself. "For in him all the fullness of God was pleased to dwell" (1:19; cf. 2:9). What fills God also fills Christ.

But Colossians pictures Christ not simply as the fulfillment of the Gnostics' speculations but as, in certain very significant ways, their contradiction and reversal. On one point the varieties of Gnosticism agreed: God is spirit or mind; matter, this material world, eons away from God, is evil. The true God was so far removed from the material earth as to be unknowable, and the creator of this world was by no means the highest god. Therefore, they believed that salvation could be attained by rising above this material world through spiritual knowledge of heavenly mysteries. (Recall the brief account of how Simon the Magician is said to have presented these ideas.)

In language that must have shocked the Gnostics, Paul says that in Christ, the whole *pleroma* dwelt "bodily" (2:9). He is the head of the "body" (the church) (1:18). In him, all things are held together not simply by his "thought" (as in the case of Simon the Magician) but by his "blood" (1:20) and "his fleshly body" (1:22), an odd phrase designed to emphasize the flatly material nature of the incarnate Christ. This material world was created "in him" (1:16).

Salvation, the letter announces, comes not through "philosophy" but through the actual death and resurrection of Christ here on earth (2:11–15). The early Gnostic Basilides proposed that Jesus, as pure mind, could not have been crucified. Instead, he magically took the form of Simon of Cyrene, who had helped Jesus bear the cross. According to Basilides, Jesus stood by and laughed while Simon was crucified. After all, one can't nail pure mind to a cross. Paul affirms the literal, physical death and resurrection of Jesus, to which the believer is united by baptism.

The second half of the letter relates this down-to-earth theology to a practical, down-to-earth ethic.

The Gnostics, believing God to be far removed from material things, divided in their ethics. Some became ascetics, abstaining as far as possible from material things. They developed regulations about "food and drink" (2:16). With regard to material things, the best rules seemed to them to be "Do not handle, Do not taste, Do not touch" (2:21). By contrast, like Simon the Magician with his Helen, some announced that moral rules were only conventions. It did not matter to the spiritual god what you did with your body. "Worship of angels" (2:18) might be more important than whether or not one was sexually chaste.

Paul pleads for a different kind of spirituality. Those who truly set their "minds on things that are above" (3:2) have "died" to "anger, wrath, malice, slander, and abusive language" (3:5–8). They have put on love (3:12–17).

That love will manifest itself not in speculation or in taboos about food but in the day-to-day relationships between people. The traditional barriers have all been transcended. "In that renewal there is no longer Greek and Jew, circumcised and uncircumcised, barbarian, Scythian, slave and free; but Christ is all and in all" (3:11).

The writer goes through specific applications of this principle in the mundane areas of family life: to wives, husbands, children, fathers, slaves, and masters (3:18–4:1). Even conduct toward outsiders and such trivial, earthy matters as daily speech must reflect Christian love (4:5–6). A modern Christian saying is "Bread for myself is a material matter. Bread for my brother is a spiritual matter." Paul would have approved of that kind of spirituality.

A long list of personal greetings ending the letter reflects the warmth of Paul's own love for people.

EPHESIANS

"Paul, an apostle of Christ Jesus by the will of God, to the saints who are . . . faithful in Christ Jesus" (Eph. 1:1).

Many regard Ephesians as one of the high points of the New Testament.

EPHESIANS
God's Plan to Unite All in Christ's Church

"He has made known to us the mystery of his will . . . in Christ . . . to gather up all things in him" (1:9–10).

1:1	2:1	3:1	4:1	6:24
A Lyrical Celebration of God's Plan to Unite All Peoples in Christ's Church	**The Working Out of God's Plan in the Actual Experience of the Gentile Readers, Now Equally Included in the Church**	**Paul's Prayerful Concern That They Share His Vision of God's Plan and Be Strengthened by It**	**Four Resulting Charges to Gentile Converts**	
Praise to God for choosing to include us in God's plan, 1:1–10	They have been saved by God's grace, 2:1–10	Paul's concern to share his insight into this plan of God, 3:1–13	Promote the church's unity, 4:1–16	
Early (Jewish) Christians and later (Gentile) converts share in the Spirit, 1:11–14	Now they are united with Jewish Christians in the church 2:11–22	Paul's prayer for his readers: understanding and strength, 3:14–21	Break with pagan ways, 4:17–5:20	
A prayer that they will understand this plan of God, 1:15–23			Manifest Christian unity through Christian family life, 5:21–6:9	
			Be good soldiers in God's army, the church, 6:10–20	
			Concluding personal note and benediction, 6:21–24	

Author: Paul? (Most modern critical scholars believe it is by a later disciple of Paul.)

Recipients: Gentile converts (in Ephesus? Ephesus is not named in the earliest manuscripts.)

Date: A.D. 64? (Most put it a few years later, after Paul's death.)

Occasion: Paul is in prison (actually or in the memory of a later writer).

Purpose: To celebrate the unity of the church and to guide new converts in understanding that church and living as good church members

But the very first verse plunges the reader into two problems: (1) Was the letter really written by Paul? and (2) Was it really written to the Ephesians?

The oldest Greek manuscripts of Ephesians have no name for the destination of this letter. Only later did scribes fill in the blank with the words "in Ephesus." In the second century, Marcion wrote of the letter as being to the Laodiceans (we know from Col. 4:16 that Paul did write an important letter to Laodicea; the letter is now lost, unless Ephesians is it).

To add to the mystery, the letter seems to assume that Paul and its readers are not personally acquainted. "I have heard of your faith," the author writes (1:15). He assumes that they "have heard" of his ideas (3:2; cf. 4:21). Yet Paul had spent more than two years as pastor of the church in Ephesus (Acts 19:10). The letter contains no references to individuals or to particular problems in the Ephesian church—or in any other congregation, for that matter. In most of his letters, Paul is engaged in a struggle over some problem affecting people whom he knows and loves. This epistle, however, sounds more like a circular letter or a relatively impersonal essay designed to be read in many congregations. Perhaps, then, Ephesians was originally sent to many churches and got its name because it was at Ephesus that some early collector of epistles first found a copy.

More controversial is the question of authorship. The letter contains the name of Paul as its author (1:1; cf. 4:1), and from early in the second century until the nineteenth, it was regarded as Paul's work. It must be said, however, that today most—though by no means all—scholars believe it to be the work of a later disciple of the apostle.[15] The following reasons are given:

1. The style and vocabulary are different from those of the letters that all scholars agree are by Paul. Indeed, one enterprising critic fed Ephesians into a computer and received a printout to the effect that Paul would never have used those words and phrases. In fact, some eighty-two words found in Ephesians are not found elsewhere in Paul's letters, and thirty-eight are found nowhere else in the New Testament. The sentences are longer and more involved than are most of Paul's. Most of the first three chapters are filled with prayers or liturgies, perhaps largely poetry. One commentator writes of Ephesians as "Paul set to music."

2. Ideas in Ephesians sometimes seem to conflict with those Paul expresses elsewhere. For example, in 1 Corinthians 7, Paul grudgingly admits that "it is better to marry than to be aflame with passion" (7:9). But Eph. 5:21–33 movingly praises marriage as the earthly relationship most comparable to that of Christ and his church. Could Paul have changed that much? Again, "You have been saved," the author writes in Eph. 2:8; but Paul elsewhere speaks of salvation as a continuing process or a future hope. In other letters, Paul speaks of Christ as the

coming eschatological Messiah whose imminent advent is eagerly awaited (1 Cor. 7:26, 31; 1 Thess. 1:10; 4:16–17). But in Ephesians, the apocalyptic revelation is the church, not some coming catastrophic judgment.

3. Ephesians seems to reflect an attitude both toward Paul and toward the other apostles which suggests that they are venerated as figures from the past. The apostles are themselves now called the "foundation" of the church (2:20). (For Paul in 1 Cor. 3:11, the only possible foundation is Christ himself.) Paul's own great insight into divine mysteries is praised in Eph. 3:2–5 (Paul wrote of such boasting as "foolishness" in 2 Cor. 10—11). Such attitudes seem more appropriate for a later generation looking admiringly back on Paul and the apostles.

4. Much of Ephesians is so nearly word-for-word like Colossians that many suspect copying (for example, compare Eph. 6:21–22 with Col. 4:7–8).

5. Finally, Ephesians seems to presuppose the emergence of a largely Gentile church, in which the conflicts of Paul's day concerning Jewish law are forgotten (2:11–13; contrast Galatians and Romans).

Nevertheless, at least one relatively recent major commentary, the Anchor Bible volume on Ephesians, by Markus Barth, has argued strongly that Paul may have been the author.[16] Differences in style and in thought may simply reflect the fact that Paul, when he wrote Ephesians, was fourteen years older and was writing for a different purpose from what he was pursuing when he wrote 1 Thessalonians. The similarities to Colossians are explained by assuming that both letters were written at the same time, to be carried to different churches by Tychicus. Many ideas in Ephesians are so typical of Paul that it is difficult to believe that one who was only an imitator could have written the letter. Finally, it is universally agreed that Ephesians is a profound statement of the faith. If not Paul, conservative critics ask, then who could have produced this original masterpiece?

The present writer finds the case against Paul as the author so strong that he cannot with assurance interpret the letter as by the apostle. Ralph P. Martin makes the attractive suggestion that the letter was written by

> a well-known disciple and companion of Paul who published this letter under the apostle's aegis either during the apostle's final imprisonment or (more probably) after his death. He did so by gathering a compendium of Paul's teaching on the theme "Christ-in-his-Church," and added to this body of teaching a number of liturgical elements.[17]

Perhaps, in the case of Ephesians, the author, even if he was later than Paul, was so close in thought to the apostle that no great difference in interpretation is required, whichever way one decides about who the author was. Francis W. Beare, in his commentary in the *Interpreter's Bible,* denies that Ephesians is by Paul. Nevertheless, Beare writes:

> Certainly no other writer of the early centuries shows anything remotely comparable to this man's grasp of the fundamental Pauline ideas, or a like ability to bring out their universal implications. There is a kinship of thought here that is not to be explained on less intimate grounds than those of close personal discipleship. . . . Ephesians stands in extraordinarily close relationship to the Pauline epistles.[18]

Perhaps, then, we may think of the letter as a genuine reflection of the mind of Paul, even if doubts remain that all its words actually came from his pen. With this understanding, we will refer to the author as Paul.

The Occasion of Ephesians

Paul, "a prisoner for Christ Jesus," is pictured as writing as "an ambassador in chains" (3:1; 6:20; cf. 4:1). The letter is apparently sent by Tychicus, as was Colossians. The setting of the letter, therefore, as traditionally understood, is Paul's imprisonment in Rome—the same time as the writing of Colossians and Philemon, about A.D. 63–64 (cf. Col. 4:7–8). The Christians addressed are evidently Gentiles (Eph. 2:11; 3:1). If the letter was written to the church at Ephesus, it must have been for the newer, Gentile members who had not known Paul when he was pastor in that city.

While the use of such words as "fullness" (1:23) and "mystery" (3:3) hint at some form of Gnostic heresy, there is not enough evidence of this kind to indicate that the letter is the result of any particular conflict in a particular congregation or at a particular time. E. J. Goodspeed proposed that an early publisher of Paul's letters composed Ephesians as an introduction to his collection around A.D. 90. What appear to be quotations from Ephesians occur in other works as early as A.D. 115. There is a kind of timeless quality about Ephesians that perhaps is responsible in part for its popularity in many different eras, including our own. The proposal that it was originally a circular letter sent to several churches seems reasonable.

The Purpose of Ephesians

Ephesians is a celebration. It is written to express the author's joyful, prayerful realization that in Christ, God is achieving the climax of God's purpose in history, the uniting of all peoples in Christ's church. The letter is also written to promote that unity. And it is written to encourage Gentile converts to live as loving members of that church in a pagan world.

This purpose is clear, no matter who the author was or when the letter was written. If the letter is the work of a later hand, it may have had the additional purpose of reaffirming the authority of Paul and his gospel against the spread of early Gnostic heresies discrediting his memory.

Some Comments on Ephesians

John Calvin said that Ephesians was his favorite epistle. "It is the crown of St. Paul's writings," Markus Barth quotes J. A. Robinson as writing. And Barth himself adds that in Ephesians, "Paul writes more openly and sublimely than in any one of his previous letters."[19]

The understanding of the plan of history that Paul had begun to work out in Romans 9—11 is now developed fully. Instead of the early church's expectation of the immediate end of history with the coming of Christ, Ephesians presents the uniting of all things in Christ as the now-manifest plan God has been working out all along.

Surely, this theme of God's plan and purpose—the King James translation called it "predestination"—is a repeated one, especially in the first chapter. God "chose us in Christ before the foundation of the world" (1:4) and (pre-) "destined" us (1:5, 11) simply according to the purpose of his will (1:5, 9, 11). All is part of God's "plan" (1:10).

For those disturbed by the logical problem involved in reconciling Paul's doctrine of "predestination" or "election" with the equally emphasized fact of individual responsibility, there may be some comfort in noting two things. First, much of chapter 1 seems to be poetry, or almost poetry. Poets often can express paradoxical truths that defy the logic of prose. Second, the author readily admits that he is describing a "mystery," something that theological reasoning cannot explain (1:9; 3:1–4, 9).

That mystery involves the emerging unity of all peoples in the church. Christ "has broken down the dividing wall, that is, the hostility" separating Jews and Gentiles (2:14). Perhaps the only inscription still in existence that Jesus of Nazareth actually read is one that archaeologists have found which marked the limits in the Temple at Jerusalem beyond which no Gentile might pass: "No foreigner may enter within the balustrade and enclosure around the Sanctuary. Whoever is caught will render himself liable to the death penalty which will inevitably follow."[20] There were barriers not simply of stone but of hostility. The Roman historian Tacitus, typical of the anti-Semitic prejudice of his time, wrote, "The Jews regard as profane all that we hold sacred; on the other hand, they permit all that we abhor. . . . The ways of the Jews are preposterous and mean."[21] In reaction, Jewish rabbis sometimes hated back. At least one is quoted as saying, "To the best of the Gentiles, death; to the best of snakes, a broken back."[22]

But now, Paul says, in Christ, Jew and Gentile are united. "All things" (1:10, 22), including all races, Jews and Greeks, have become "one new humanity" (2:15) in one "body" (1:23; 2:16), sharing one "access in one Spirit" to one "Father" (2:18; 3:14) as fellow "citizens" and "members of the household of God" (2:19), and are now built together as one structure, God's new "temple" (2:20–22). Gentiles and Jews are now "fellow heirs, members of the same body" (3:6), maintaining "the unity of the Spirit in the bond of peace" around "one hope . . . one Lord, one faith, one baptism" (4:3–5), under "one God" (4:6). Through the unity of the faith, all church members form one "body" (2:16), in which, under Christ as the head, they are "members one of another" (4:25). The best earthly figure for such union is that of the perfect family, beautifully described in Eph. 5:21–6:9.

Ephesians abounds in poetic metaphors for the church. Ephesians 2:10 says that we are what God "has made us." The word in Greek is *poema*. The Jerusalem Bible translates that verse, "We are God's work of art." The writer's own artistic figures for the church include the following: "the body of Christ" (4:12; 5:23), "the bride of Christ" (5:21–23), "the commonwealth of Israel" (2:12–19), and "a holy temple" (2:21–22). Each figure expresses a different facet of the meaning the writer sees in the emerging church. He glories in this new manifestation of God's ancient plan.

Typical of letters of Paul, Ephesians falls into two halves. The first half glories in the good news of reconciliation. The second half urges the readers to live out this new unity in their relationships with others. "I therefore . . . beg you to lead a life worthy of the calling to which you have been called" (4:1), this second half begins.

All church members are to use their gifts in service to each other. All are to do the work of "ministry" (4:1–16). These Gentile converts are to renounce their old pagan ways (4:17–5:20). They are to live out in their families the kind of love that Christ showers on his "bride," the church (5:21–6:9).

Finally, the letter closes with an elaborate metaphor in which Christians are urged to "take the shield of faith" to fight against the forces of evil about them (6:10–17). And as part of that fight, they are to pray, including prayer for Paul, "an ambassador in chains" (6:18–20).

These may have been the last words Paul ever wrote.

10

THE PASTORAL EPISTLES

Ephesians celebrates joyfully, sometimes lyrically, the emergence of a great new apocalyptic fact, the church. The pastoral epistles lay down day-to-day guidelines for the faith and order of that developing organization.

Rules are not as exciting as celebrations. Often regarded as late (perhaps early second-century), not really by Paul, and moralistic, the pastorals (1 and 2 Timothy and Titus) are far from the best-loved books of the New Testament. Yet at least three things make them a valuable, if sometimes neglected, part of the canon.

First, they give us insight into the life of the church in a period later than most New Testament books and let us know what it was like to be a church member or leader in the days between the sudden bursting of the gospel upon the world at the time of the apostles and the establishment of the formal pattern of church organization, which soon developed.

A little past the middle of the second century, Justin Martyr described a typical Sunday worship service:

> And on the day called Sunday there is a meeting in one place of those who live in cities or the country, and the memoirs of the apostles or the writings of the prophets are read as long as time permits. When the reader has finished, the president in a discourse urges and invites [us] to the imitation of these noble things. Then we all stand up together and offer prayers.[1]

For anyone who would like in imagination to worship with such a congregation, to see with them their leader, and to hear both the leader's words and those of the prayers and songs of the congregation, these pastoral letters, though written before the time of Justin, give a helpful picture. In them, we hear echoes of the liturgy, hymns, creeds, and discipline of the postapostolic congregations.

Second, many of the guidelines laid down in these letters are still regarded as applying to the church today. Scarcely a minister, elder, deacon, vestry member, or steward is installed in a modern congregation without the reading of a passage such as 1 Timothy 3 or Titus 1.

Third, the pastorals represent one of the earliest efforts to do what Christian thinkers have sought to do in every age: to apply to new situations the teachings of the apostles.

These proposals, however, presuppose a highly debatable view of the authorship and date of these little books. These problems must now be examined in detail.

THE PROBLEM OF THE PASTORALS

Authorship and Date

First and Second Timothy and Titus have been grouped together at least since the Muratorian Canon in the latter part of the second century. That document spoke of them as revered for their help "in the arrangement of ecclesiastical discipline." In 1726, Paul Anton used of them the name "the Pastoral Epistles," recognizing that each is in the form of a letter of guidance from an older pastor, Paul, to a younger pastor. These three booklets are generally agreed to be on the same subjects and by the same author.

But was the author Paul?

There are certainly scholars who do believe that they are the work of that apostle.[2] Arguments for this view include the following:

1. The letters themselves say clearly that they are by Paul (see the first word in each).
2. The Muratorian Canon attributes them to Paul, and other early documents quote from them as Paul's.
3. They are filled with personal references for which it is hard to imagine any purpose if they were created at a later date. For example, Paul requests that the cloak he had left at Troas be brought to him, and he warns against one "Alexander the coppersmith," unknown to us from any second-century literature (2 Tim. 4:12–15). Why would anyone in the second century invent these details?
4. Certain ideas seem typical of Paul. For example, in 2 Tim. 1:9 we read that God "saved us . . . not according to our works but according to his own purpose and grace." These words could have come right out of Romans.

Some Christians, of course, feel required by their theology to hold that these letters are by Paul simply because they say they are. The majority who decide such matters on purely historical grounds, however, do not believe that these three letters, at least as we have them now, are by the apostle.[3] They give the following reasons:

1. The style and vocabulary are quite different from those of other letters ascribed to the apostle. Approximately one-third of the words in these books occur nowhere else in all of the other letters attributed to Paul, and some one hundred seventy words are found nowhere else in the New Testament.

2. They are not included among Paul's writings in such early lists as that of Marcion; nor are they in the Chester Beatty Papyri.

3. Certain ideas and the ways in which certain words are used in the pastorals seem to reflect a stage in the life of the church later than the life of Paul. For example, "faith" to Paul means a dynamic, personal relationship, commitment, trust; and it is faith in a person, Jesus Christ. But in the pastorals, we read about *the* faith, referring rather to a set body of teachings, a creed, to be held against all false teachings: 1 Tim. 4:1 warns "that in later times some will renounce the faith"; 1 Tim. 4:6 speaks of the "words of the faith and of the sound teaching"; 2 Tim. 3:8 speaks of heretics as "worthless as regards to the faith" (author's translation); and the first verse of Titus couples "the faith" with "knowledge of the truth." And a new emphasis on creed is indicated by much more than the use of the article before "faith." The pastor writes of "sound teaching" or "sound doctrine" or "sound speech" (1 Tim. 1:10; 2 Tim. 4:3; Titus 1:9; 2:1, 8); "sound words" (1 Tim. 6:3; 2 Tim. 4:3 RSV); and being "sound in the faith" (Titus 1:13; 2:2). "Sound" here seems to mean "correct" or "orthodox." Moreover, the pastorals repeatedly give some "standard of sound teaching" (creed) to be followed with care (2 Tim. 1:13). "The word stands firm" would be a valid translation of a phrase the pastor repeatedly uses in relation to some creedal formula (1 Tim. 1:15; 3:1; 4:9; 2 Tim. 2:11; Titus 3:8). This emphasis on formal creeds to be remembered and preserved seems to reflect life in the church a generation removed from Paul.

4. The pastorals presuppose a church organization with a more elaborate, set structure than seems to have existed in Paul's day. There are bishops or elders (1 Tim. 3:1–7; 5:17–22; Titus 1:5–16); deacons (1 Tim. 3:8–13); and widows who are officially "enrolled" if they meet specified qualifications (1 Tim. 5:3–16). Neither the other letters of Paul nor Acts reflects such a well-defined structure.

5. While the differences should not be exaggerated, the ethical stance of the pastorals seems somewhat different from that previously found in Paul. The attitude toward the law expressed in 1 Tim. 1:8 is rather different from that in Romans or Galatians. The ethic proposed is not

one lived by the Spirit as one awaits the imminent end of the world. Instead, it is one quite similar to that of the best secular moralists of the time. "Prudent" or one of its cognates occurs nine times in the pastorals, only six times in all the rest of the New Testament.

6. The personal references cannot be fit into the life of Paul as we know it from Acts. In Titus, for example, Paul has spent some time in Crete, and he expects to spend the winter in Nicopolis (Titus 1:5; 3:12). Acts says nothing of either sojourn.

7. That the letters contain the name of Paul and personal references does not prove that he wrote them. We know that devout Christians in the early centuries composed books not found in our New Testament and attributed them to Thomas, John, Paul, Peter, and other apostles. To us, this may seem dishonest; to them, it obviously did not. Rather, it may have seemed a kind of modesty to attribute ideas to one's teacher rather than proudly to claim them for oneself. Perhaps these letters should be thought of as dedicated to the memory of Paul rather than as actually from his pen.

Those who believe that Paul wrote these letters readily admit that they cannot be fit into Paul's life as we know it from Acts. They note hints in early tradition, however, that Paul was released after two years in prison in Rome (Acts 28:30–31). His trial, then, was his "first defense," mentioned in 2 Tim. 4:16. Paul then went to Spain (Rom. 15:24), they argue, and he also then did the traveling implied in the pastorals. The imprisonment mentioned in 2 Tim. 1:8, 16–17; and 2:9 followed a second and final arrest, according to this view. The differences in style, vocabulary, and thought are explained by assuming that Paul is now some ten years older than when he wrote Romans, that he is dealing with a different set of problems, and that he is making use of a different secretary.

Real as the differences are, there are certain areas of agreement. Those who believe that the letters were written during the lifetime of Paul still place them as late as possible within that limit, A.D. 67–68, and recognize that as an old man, Paul is dealing with situations from a time later than that of his other letters. In contrast, many who believe that the letters come from a later time—around A.D. 110, it is frequently suggested—admit that they may well contain valuable tradition from the thought and life of Paul. There is no need to deny the historical accuracy of the situation described in many of the personal references, and indeed, a number of scholars suggest that they may be based on fragments of letters actually written by Paul or may even be later revisions of Pauline letters.

While the present writer believes the evidence against Pauline authorship must be accepted, he would recognize the truth in the comment of William Barclay:

In the Pastoral Epistles we are still hearing the voice of Paul, and often hearing it speak with a unique personal intimacy; but we think that the form of the letters is due to a Christian teacher who summoned the help of Paul when the Church of the day needed the guidance which only he could give.[4]

The Purpose of the Pastorals

"Timothy, guard what has been entrusted to you," the pastor writes, speaking of the orthodox faith expressed in the "sound" teaching or doctrine he is defending. "Avoid the profane chatter and contradictions of what is falsely called knowledge [*gnosis*]" (1 Tim. 6:20). It was to combat that *gnosis* with a disciplined church, witnessing to a disciplined faith, that the pastor wrote.

The heresy attacked seems to be very much like that early Jewish form of Gnosticism which we have already examined in relation to Colossians, and we will not repeat the description of it here (see the section on "Colossians" in the preceding chapter). Those whom the pastorals attack seem to have taught a kind of asceticism with regard to food and drink (1 Tim. 5:23; Titus 1:15) and even discouraged marriage (1 Tim. 4:3).

In contrast, the pastor can accuse these heretics of gross immorality, perhaps because some of them regarded bodily matters such as adultery as of no importance once one had obtained truly spiritual knowledge (2 Tim. 3:6). The enigmatic reference to their denial of a future resurrection probably reflects their view that the body, being mere matter, is valueless (2 Tim. 2:18).

Their heresy involved elements of Judaism (Titus 1:10, 14).

They loved "endless genealogies" (1 Tim. 1:4) and "profane myths" (1 Tim. 4:7; cf. 2 Tim. 4:4).

Above all, they evidently loved to argue (1 Tim. 1:6; 6:4, 20; 2 Tim. 2:16, 23; Titus 3:9).

In all of these tendencies, they sound like the Gnostics.

Against these heretics the pastor proposes a double weapon: (1) there is the church, which must be led by godly and heroic leaders; and (2) there is the faith, which must be preserved with the help of formalized, traditional, heresy-free sayings. As Brevard Childs puts it, "The content of the witness has not changed [in a later generation], but the means by which the message is preserved and transmitted has been altered."[5]

The pastor's model for both sound doctrine and heroic leadership is the apostle Paul. In his name and in his tradition, the pastor writes.

1 TIMOTHY

"I have no one like him." So Paul had written of Timothy, his young companion and assistant. "Like a son with a father he has served with me in the work of the gospel" (Phil. 2:20–22). Repeatedly, Paul groups Timothy with himself as a "brother" and co-author of letters (2 Cor. 1:1; Phil. 1:1; Col. 1:1;

1 TIMOTHY
Instructions to a Young Pastor

"If you put these instructions before the brothers and sisters, you will be a good servant of Christ Jesus, nourished on the words of the faith and of . . . sound teaching" (4:6).

1:1 **Opening Charge: Suppress Heresy, Teach Only What Is Proper**	2:1 **Proper Worship**	3:1 **Proper Church Officers**	3:14 **Proper Doctrine**	5:1 **Proper Conduct Pertaining to Particular Groups**	6:2b **Proper Life versus Worldly Life**	6:21
A warning against improper teaching, 1:1–7	Prayer for and by all men, 2:1–8	The bishop, 3:1–7	A summary of proper doctrine, 3:14–16	Older and younger church members, 5:1–2	Heresy is accompanied by selfishness and greed, 6:2b–10	
A warning against improper ethics, 1:8–11	But with women kept subordinate, 2:9–15	The deacons, 3:8–13	A warning against heretics, 4:1–5	Widows, 5:3–16	By contrast, you must live righteously, 6:11–16	
A reminder of Paul's own experience, 1:12–17			The minister's duty to teach proper doctrine, 4:6–16	Elders, 5:17–22	Be rich, but in good deeds only, 6:17–19	
The charge now delivered to the young pastor, 1:18–20				(Miscellaneous instructions), 5:23–25	A closing charge, 6:20–21	
				Slaves, 6:1–2a		

Author: Paul? (Most say a later disciple of Paul, writing in his honor and memory.)
Recipient: "Timothy" (a young pastor)
Date: A.D. 68? (Most say early second century.)
Occasion: False teaching, accompanied by unrighteous living, threatens the church.
Purpose: To remind the young pastor of the tradition of sound doctrine and righteous living handed down from Paul

1 Thess. 1:1; 2 Thess. 1:1). Acts 16:1 pictures Timothy as joining Paul at Lystra early in Paul's second missionary journey, and he appears to have been closely associated with the apostle from that time on. Whether in fact or in symbol, it is appropriate that Paul's message to the next generation should come in the form of a letter from the old apostle to his younger "brother" and "son."

The Occasion of 1 Timothy

There are fewer references to Paul's situation in 1 Timothy than in the other pastorals. "I urge you, as I did when I was on my way to Macedonia, to remain in Ephesus," Paul begins (1 Tim. 1:3). Paul hopes to rejoin Timothy soon, 3:14 and 4:13 imply. In the meantime, Timothy is pictured as a young pastor at work (4:12; cf. 5:1), to whom Paul gives fatherly advice (1:2).

"Some people have deviated from these and turned to meaningless talk, desiring to be teachers of the law," we are told (1:6). It is the need to respond to the spread of their heresy, "what is falsely called knowledge [*gnosis*]" (6:20), that, whether in Paul's day or a generation later, is the real occasion of the writing of this booklet.

The Purpose of 1 Timothy

"Timothy, guard what has been entrusted to you," cries the writer at the conclusion of the epistle (6:20). The very reason the young pastor has been placed there is to "instruct certain people not to teach any different doctrine, and not to occupy themselves with myths and endless genealogies that promote speculations rather than the divine training that is known by faith" (1:3–4). To this end, the letter repeatedly reminds the reader of brief statements of sound doctrine, in the tradition handed down from Paul, which will stand firm against the false Gnostic teachings. Its purpose is to exhort the young pastor to teach the true faith.

It is known that certain Gnostic sects in the second and third centuries were fond of quoting Paul and claiming his authority for their ideas. It may be that the author of 1 Timothy chose to write in the form of a letter by Paul in order to dramatize his certainty that Paul would have opposed all Gnostic fanaticism.

The letter is concerned, however, to guide not only the teaching but also the practice of the church: "I am writing these instructions to you so that . . . you may know how one ought to behave in the household of God, which is the church" (3:14–15). The writer wants to make sure that only godly people guide the congregation, that worship is properly conducted, and that all members live exemplary lives. Indeed, though the letter is ostensibly addressed only to one reader, the author really wants the whole church to hear the message. To this end, specific instructions are given concerning church officers, women, widows, and even slaves. A strict but not ascetic morality is commanded for all.

Some Comments on 1 Timothy

Those who hold that 1 Timothy is the work not of Paul but of one of his admirers a generation later believe they find signs of this in the first chapter. Paul would not need, they say, to remind Timothy that he is an apostle (1:1) or to review for Timothy the story of his conversion (1:12–17). The chapter is appropriate, however, they say, for beginning a solemn warning against un-Pauline fanaticism to a later generation.

First Timothy 2—3 has been called the oldest extant guidebook on church order. The modern reader wishes that the pastor had described the duties of the bishop and the deacons. Apparently, by the time this letter was written, those duties were already well known. Here only the high moral requirements for those offices are listed. Though "bishop" is used in the singular, it is widely held that the word refers to the same office as does "elder," the two terms apparently being used synonymously in Titus 1:5–7. If so, there were apparently several bishops or elders and several deacons in each congregation. The word for "bishop" could be translated "overseer" or "supervisor," and it soon came to be used of one church official who had oversight for several churches.

The description of the prayers (1 Tim. 2:1–8) sheds light on early Christian worship. Even in times of persecution, Christians prayed for the emperor. There is relatively little evidence of persecution, however, in the pastoral epistles. The expected Christian life seems here to be one of respectable citizenship.

This letter's strict limits on women's participation in the life of the church (2:9–15) contrast sharply with Paul's more permissive attitude, shown in other letters. Paul had hailed Priscilla (Prisca) (Rom. 16:3), Euodia, and Syntyche (Phil. 4:2) as fellow workers, and Phoebe he commended as a "deaconess" (Rom. 16:1). In spite of his restrictions on women at Corinth, he could write that in Christ, all barriers enslaving women had been eliminated (Gal. 3:28). Perhaps the writer of 1 Timothy was driven to his extreme position in part as a reaction to practices of some Gnostics (see the section on "Colossians" in chapter 9 of this *Guide* for the place of Helen in the sect associated with Simon the Magician).

Actually, the writer probably thought of himself as occupying a reasonable and moderate position in the matter of women, as in other ethical questions. He strongly resists sexual license—so strongly as to make all women keep quiet in church. But at the same time, he rejects the fanaticism of those who would prohibit marriage (4:3; cf. 5:14). He recognizes the service of enrolled "widows" (5:10) and would have all women treated as "mothers" and "sisters" (5:2). Writings from the third century show us that the widows continued to be a kind of special order in the church in that era. Eventually, various orders of enrolled "sisters" developed in the Catholic church.

The writer's moral ideal, as has been noted, is one of prudence, a balance between license and asceticism. The godly man must avoid intemperate use of wine (3:3), but Timothy should not be such an ascetic as not to use wine for medicine (5:23). Lustful desires are to be shunned (1:10), but marriage and having children are repeatedly encouraged (2:15; 3:2–3, 11–12; 4:3; 5:14). Food and clothes are good (6:8). But riches present too much temptation, and from the love of money may come all kinds of evils (6:9–10, 17–18).

Indeed, "everything created by God is good, and nothing is to be rejected, provided it is received with thanksgiving" (4:4). (Contrast the Gnostic view that all created things are evil.) The pastor's ideal is that of the chaste Christian family contentedly doing its duties in a respectable way within the Roman world. His is a practical Christianity.

Finally, brief note must also be taken of the "sound doctrine" he urges his reader to guard. The pastor reminds Timothy of the saying that "Christ Jesus came into the world to save sinners" (1:15). "There is one God; there is also one mediator between God and humankind, Christ Jesus, himself human," the pastor affirms against the multitude of Gnostic divine mediators (2:5). First Timothy 3:16 is probably quoted from a hymn familiar at the time this letter was written. First Timothy 6:12–16 may be a fragment of the liturgy used when the young pastor was ordained or when he was baptized.

The young Christian's confession of faith is related to that of Christ before Pilate. And though the eschatological hope that was so central to Paul seems now to have become less prominent, Timothy is still to fight on "until the manifestation of our Lord Jesus Christ" (6:14).

2 TIMOTHY

Addressed from one generation to another—in the form of a letter from the aging church leader Paul to one who was to be a leader of the next generation—the letters to Timothy are written to urge the preservation of the true Christian tradition. Integrity of doctrine in a church led by people of integrity was the theme of 1 Timothy.

These themes of 1 Timothy are repeated in 2 Timothy, but a new emphasis is developed. The tradition being passed from Paul to the ongoing church is not simply one of sound doctrine or correct church order; it is the tradition of Paul's own self-sacrificial example of courage. In a time when many were deserting him and his gospel, Paul had faced loneliness, persecution, and death. The reader must now carry on Paul's legacy of faithful witness.

"I have fought the good fight, I have finished the race, I have kept the faith," Paul the prisoner is presented as writing (2 Tim. 4:7). So you, in your generation, the letter pleads, must with the same courage "guard the good treasure entrusted to you" (1:14).

2 TIMOTHY

Paul's Example of Life and Teaching for the Next Generation

"Hold to the standard . . .you have . . .from me" (1:13).

1:1 **Timothy's Heritage of True Faith**	2:1 **The Charge: Be Faithful to That Heritage**	3:1 **Defenses against Heresies**	4:1 **A Summary Charge to Faithful Ministry**	4:6 **Personal Appeals by Paul**	4:22
His heritage from two generations and from Paul, 1:1–7	Pass on what you have received, in spite of difficulties, 2:1–7	A warning against the heretics to come, 3:1–9		His own testimony in the face of death, 4:6–8	
Paul's example of faithfulness, 1:8–14	Be loyal to the gospel, as Paul has been loyal, 2:8–13	Two sources of sound guidance: Paul's example, 3:10–13		Personal requests and greeting, 4:9–22	
Some others have been heroically faithful; some have not, 1:15–18	By contrast, do not be like the heretics, 2:14–19	the scripture, 3:14–17			
	Instead, be a good vessel of truth, not a disputer, 2:20–26				

Author: "Paul" (Most say a later disciple of Paul writing in his honor.)

Recipient: "Timothy" (a third-generation pastor)

Date: A.D. 68? (Most say later than Paul's life, perhaps early in the second century.)

Occasion: Paul, in fact or in the memory of the writer, is in prison facing death. Heresy threatens the church.

Purpose: To strengthen a later pastor in ministry and in faithfulness to sound doctrine through a reminder of the witness of Paul

The Occasion of 2 Timothy

Whether in actual fact or—more likely—in the memory of the later writer, Paul is writing from prison. I am suffering, "even to the point of being chained like a criminal," he writes (2:9), apparently in Rome (1:17). "I am already being poured out as a libation, and the time of my departure has come" (4:6). In Philippians, Paul expected to be released. In 2 Timothy, he knows he is about to die.

The imprisonment indicated in 2 Timothy does not seem to fit well into the story in Acts. Paul had left a cloak and some books in Troas, though Acts implies that Paul had not been in Troas for years (2 Tim. 4:13; contrast Acts 24:27). Similarly, Paul had left Trophimus ill at Miletus (2 Tim. 4:20). The journey to a Roman prison described in Acts scarcely allows for visits at Troas and Miletus. If the letter was written by Paul, it was probably during a second Roman imprisonment.

Not only is Paul pictured in chains, imprisoned in a shameful way, and facing death, but repeated references are made to the fact that he is lonely, with many forsaking him (1:15–17; 4:10–11, 16).

It is not clear where we are to think of Timothy as living. In 1 Tim. 1:3, he has been left to be pastor at Ephesus. In 2 Tim. 4:12, he is informed that Paul has sent Tychicus to that city. But the situation Timothy faces is still much the same as that described in 1 Timothy. And that situation is one which contains parallels to the difficulties Paul is depicted as facing at the end of his life. Timothy is beginning in his generation to meet something of the loneliness and discouragement that Paul had endured. "Indeed, all who want to live a godly life in Christ Jesus will be persecuted" (3:12). "Distressing times" are at hand (3:1), "when people will not put up with sound doctrine . . . and will turn away" (4:3–4). In his own generation, the first reader of this letter was to face something of what Paul so courageously endured.

The Purpose of 2 Timothy

"Do not be ashamed . . . of the testimony about our Lord or of me his prisoner," the letter is written to urge the young pastor (1:8). The recipient, too, faces the discouragement of seeing members of his flock fall away into a heresy proving more popular among some than does the orthodox faith. "But join with me in suffering for the gospel, relying on the power of God" (1:8). You know the courageous example of Paul, the letter is written to say. Now follow it in your own ministry in your own situation.

To carry on that tradition, the young pastor is to "hold to the standard of sound teaching" handed down from Paul (1:13). He is to "guard the good treasure entrusted" to him (1:14). In the name of the apostle, the writer summarizes his exhortation: "In the presence of God and of Christ Jesus, . . . I solemnly urge you: proclaim the message; be persistent whether the time is favorable or unfavorable; convince, rebuke, and encourage, with utmost patience in teaching" (4:1–2). The picture—in the present or in memory—of Paul's own "testifying" (the word can even be translated "martyrdom") is summoned to inspire and encourage a pastor as he faces the troubles of testifying in his generation.

Some Comments on 2 Timothy

The theme of passing on the faith from generation to generation is introduced at the very beginning of the letter. Timothy is said to be of the third generation of believers (1:5). Timothy's gift of ministry also has been passed down to him in the laying on of Paul's hands at his ordination (1:6; cf. 1 Tim. 4:14).

But in the generation in which the original reader of this letter lives, there is the temptation to find testifying for the gospel a source of embarrassment, even shame. Over against such shame, the reader must be reminded that the gospel really brings power "of love and of self-discipline" (2 Tim. 1:7).

Paul had not given in to shame, that reader is reminded, in spite of his suffering and imprisonment (1:8). Rather, he had been confident that God would continue to protect the gospel, which had been entrusted to him (1:12). Onesiphorus had not been ashamed to visit Paul even in a Roman jail (1:16). And now Timothy, preacher to a new generation, is to hand on that gospel in such a way that he need not be ashamed (2:15).

One reason for shame and discouragement in this third-generation Christian is that so many are deserting the gospel. This, too, the letter reminds its reader, is nothing new. The book includes the names of several people, otherwise unknown to us in the twentieth century but apparently still familiar at the time the letter was first read, who forsook or opposed Paul, names set over against those of heroes who remained faithful. Phygelus and Hermogenes (1:15), Demas (4:10), and Alexander (4:14) are contrasted with Onesiphorus, who had been undaunted by Paul's chains (1:16), and Luke, who alone faithfully remains with Paul (4:11). Others are separated from Paul because of their duties (4:10–20). The note of wistfulness and loneliness in the personal references in 2 Timothy 4 seems so real that it has convinced many that at least these verses are actually from Paul's pen. Even if they are not, there is no reason to doubt that they rest on accurate memory of the suffering that, as we know from other sources, Paul certainly endured. Remember that Paul went through the same kind of thing that you face in your time, the writer is saying, knowing people who "will accumulate for themselves teachers to suit their own desires, and will turn away from listening to the truth and wander away to myths. As for you, always be sober, endure suffering, do the work of an evangelist, carry out your ministry fully" (4:3–5), even as Paul did. "Share in suffering like a good soldier of Christ Jesus" (2:3).

There are hints that the reader may also face quite tangible suffering (Heb.

13:23 tells us that Timothy did go to prison). Twice we are reminded that Paul was in chains (1:16; 2:9). Second Timothy 2:11–13 appears to be an early Christian hymn, perhaps sung at the time a convert gave his testimony at his baptism. But one can well imagine that it had also been sung by martyrs who had gone to their deaths in the persecutions that had already cost many Christians their lives and which would soon bring the deaths of thousands more. They sang:

> If we have died with him, we will also live with him;
> If we endure, we will also reign with him.

Timothy is urged to pass correct tradition along to teachers who will deliver it to future generations (2:2). The concern continues for fixing the tradition, setting it in forms that cannot be twisted to please those "having itching ears" (4:3), ready for Gnostic heresies. At least three times there are passages that seem to reflect early creeds, liturgies, or hymns (1:10; 2:8, 11–13). And Timothy is urged to make use of the Old Testament scriptures (3:15–16; and probably 4:13). Could the writer have guessed that the next generation would begin taking this letter itself as an official, written standard in its battle with heresy?

At this stage, however, the church does not look primarily to a set of writings. Rather, it is the example of a person who has suffered that is to inspire the reader of the letter with a "spirit of power." The example is the courage of Paul. "I have fought the good fight, I have finished the race, I have kept the faith. From now on . . . the crown" (4:7–8). "You then, . . . be strong" (2:1).

TITUS

"My brother Titus," Paul had called him (2 Cor. 2:13). This earnest man (2 Cor. 8:16–17) had been the go-between in the dispute between Paul and the church at Corinth, and it was he who, at last, had been able to bring Paul the good news that all was well again in that church. A Gentile who had been an early convert to Christianity, Titus had accompanied Paul on the visit to Jerusalem in which Paul had discussed with Peter, James, and John the status of Gentile Christians in the church (Gal. 2:1–10).

It was appropriate, therefore, that the third of the pastoral epistles should bear the name of this assistant to the great apostle to the Gentiles.

The Occasion of Titus

According to the letter, Paul has been to Crete (Titus 1:5) and expects to spend the winter in Nicopolis (3:12)—probably the city of that name in northern Greece. The epistle is addressed to Titus, who has been left to be

TITUS
More Guidance for a Young Pastor

"As for you, teach what is consistent with sound doctrine" (2:1).

1:1	2:1	3:1	3:15
Salutation and a Reminder to Select a Good Group of Elders	**Teach Each Group in the Church Its Proper Behavior**	**Remind All to Live Lives Appropriate for Those Who Have Become Christians**	
Greetings from a preacher of the true gospel, 1:1–4	Older people, 2:1–3	A call to moral virtue befitting those truly converted, 3:1–7	
	Younger people, 2:4–6		
A reminder: choose elders sound in life and teaching, not typical Cretans, 1:5–16	(Through example), 2:7–8	No speculative (Gnostic) disputes, 3:8–11	
	Slaves, 2:9–10	Closing personal note, 3:12–15	
	All, 2:11–15		

Author: Paul? (Most scholars believe it to be by a later disciple of Paul, writing in his memory and honor.)

Recipient: "Titus," a young pastor

Date: A.D. 67? (Most critics date it after Paul's life, early in the second century.)

Occasion: "Titus" has been left in charge of a church given to Gnostic disputes and unrighteous living.

Purpose: To remind the young pastor of the importance of sound doctrine, leadership, and life

the missionary pastor in Crete (1:5). Acts gives no hint of Paul's doing mission work in Crete or Nicopolis. Again, therefore, we must assume that if Paul actually wrote this letter, he did it at a time later than that described in Acts.

The situation implied in Titus is really much the same as that of 1 and 2 Timothy. The author addresses Titus as his "loyal child" (1:4) and gives him advice concerning his work as a pastor. As in the other pastorals, the need is for leadership that will teach sound doctrine (1:9; 2:1) and good deeds (2:7). Presumably, the kind of unsound doctrine against which the younger pastor is to contend is that early form of Gnosticism we have already examined.

The Purpose of Titus

As with the other pastorals, the letter is to guide and encourage a pastor of a new generation by sharing the wisdom of the apostle Paul.

Some Comments on Titus

As in 1 Tim. 3:1–13 and 2 Tim. 2:1–2, the author emphasizes the importance of having the right leaders in the church. These are to be people of the highest character, but they also must be able to give instruction in doctrine (Titus 1:9).

These leaders are called "elders" (*presbuteroi*), the term in 1:5 apparently, at this stage in the life of the church, being synonymous with the term "bishop" (1:7). In their commentary, Martin Dibelius and Hans Conzelmann print a long description in which the pagan Onosander prescribes for a Roman general many of the same qualities that the letter to Titus demands for a bishop.[6] There are close parallels between Titus 1 and 1 Timothy 3 concerning the qualifications of church officers:

Titus	*First Timothy*
above reproach (blameless)	above reproach
married only once	married only once
hospitable	hospitable
a lover of goodness	respectable
self-controlled	not a drunkard
children are believers	children who are obedient
prudent	prudent
concerned with preaching	able to teach
just	
pious	
not arrogant	gentle
not irascible	peaceable
not given to wine	not given to wine
not given to brawling	not given to brawling
not fond of dishonest gain	not greedy
children who are obedient	governs own house well
	not newly converted

The belief that the typical Cretan is a liar (1:12–13) can be traced back as far as Epimenides in 490 B.C. Callimachus, in the third century B.C., wrote that "Cretans were always liars," his example being that they even claimed to have on Crete the tomb of Zeus, who, as king of the gods, could scarcely be dead!

The exhortations to moral living by different groups again parallel those found in Colossians, Ephesians, and the other pastoral epistles (2:1–10). Obviously, the writer of the letter had in mind guiding the conduct not simply of Titus but of his whole congregation.

Chapter 3 may contain echoes of an early liturgy for baptism. Some question may be raised as to whether the apostle Paul would ever really have used the words of Titus 3:3 to describe his life before his conversion.

One final note: Titus 2:13 apparently contains one of the few places in which the New Testament unqualifiedly calls Jesus Christ "God." Repeatedly, Jesus is called Son of God or described in other ways that imply his equality with God the Father or his doing work previously regarded as exclusively that of God. But in this verse, we read of "our great God and Savior, Jesus Christ." Christian theology was moving toward the Nicene Creed.

11

FIVE "OPEN LETTERS"

James L. Price suggests that we call the books discussed in this chapter "open letters to Christians."[1]

Since early in the fourth century, the church has given the name "Catholic Epistles," or "General Epistles," to seven letters: James; 1 and 2 Peter, 1, 2, and 3 John; and Jude. That name has meant not that they were addressed to the Roman Catholic Church but that they were not addressed, as were the letters of Paul, to particular congregations named in their opening salutations. Rather, they are for the whole church, the church universal. These letters have in common also the fact that they are the only ones in our New Testament not traditionally attributed to Paul.

Because the letters of John have so much in common with the Fourth Gospel, we will delay discussion of them for now. But we here do discuss Hebrews with four of the "Catholic Epistles." Most scholars believe that Hebrews, too, was not written by Paul; and it, too, contains the name of no particular congregation in its greetings. (As was earlier proposed, the Christian reader always seeks to read any book of the Bible as, in some sense, a letter addressed to himself or herself.)

HEBREWS

Harold W. Attridge describes the paradox of Hebrews: "The document known as the Epistle to the Hebrews is the most elegant and sophisticated, and perhaps the most enigmatic, text of first-century Christianity."[2]

Donald George Miller used to tell his classes that the critics agreed on only one thing concerning Hebrews: nobody really knows anything about it!

HEBREWS
Christ: the Better Priest of the Better Covenant

"Since we have a great priest . . . let us hold fast to the confession of our hope without wavering" (10:21–23).

1:1 **Christ Is Better Than Angels**	3:1 **Christ Is Better Than Moses**	4:14 **Christ Is Better Than the Old Priesthood**	8:1 **Christ's New Covenant Is Better Than the Old**	11:1 **Faith's Heroes of the Old Testament Sought to Go Forward to This Better Covenant We Have in Christ**	12:1 ... 13:25 **Therefore, Let Us Go Forward with Christ in Faith, Love, and Obedience**
The Old Testament exalts not angels but the Son, 1:1–14	Moses was God's servant; Jesus was God's Son, 3:1–6	Being truly human, he can better represent us to God, 4:14–5:11	The old covenant rested only on symbols, 8:1–9:10	Abel, 11:1–7	Go forward in faith, in spite of opposition, 12:1–28
Therefore, be faithful, 2:1–4	Under Moses, the Hebrews never got what was promised, 3:7–4:13	So do not be sluggish, but go forward on God's promises, 5:12–6:20	But Christ has entered the real sanctuary, heaven, 9:11–10:18	The patriarchs, 11:8–22	Go forward in love and obedience, 13:1–25
for in Christ, God has identified not with angels but with us, 2:5–18		Christ is a special kind of high priest, like Melchizedek, 7:1–28	Therefore, do not waver, 10:19–39	Moses, 11:23–31	
				Many more, 11:32–40	

Author: Unknown

Recipients: Christians—"holy partners in a heavenly calling" (former Jews? in Rome?)

Date: Unknown (A.D. 90? A.D. 60?)

Occasion: Some are tempted to "turn away" (3:12) to apostasy (6:6).

Purpose: Having shown the superiority of Christ to everything in the Old Testament (Covenant), to encourage apathetic Christians to move forward in the New Covenant

Consider, for example, the question "Who wrote it?" The list of suggested authors is bewilderingly varied:

The letter itself bears *no name.*

It was finally accepted into the canon in part because it was believed by some to have been written by *Paul.* Most early writers in the Western (Roman) wing of the church doubted this, however, and almost all scholars today regard Hebrews as quite different from Paul's letters in vocabulary, style, and theological approach.

Tertullian, in the second century, had been taught that it was by *Barnabas.*

Other ancient authorities attributed it to *Luke;* still others said it was by *Clement,* an early bishop of Rome.

Martin Luther suggested that it was by *Apollos,* basing his proposal on the similarities between the thought of Hebrews and the thought character-istic of Philo and other teachers from Alexandria (Apollos was from Alexandria [Acts 18:24]).

A modern suggestion has been that it was written by *a woman,* perhaps *Priscilla.* The argument for this is that even though the author was evidently a teacher of skill and authority, the name has been lost. Was this, perhaps, because some church members were embarrassed that a woman had so prominent a place?

The early church father Origen's famous summary is really the best one can say: *God only knows* who wrote Hebrews.

From the letter itself, one can infer only that the author was a master of Greek style, was thoroughly familiar with the Septuagint (the Greek transla-tion of the Old Testament), and was a highly competent Christian theologian in a pattern rather different from that of Paul.

Is Hebrews really a letter?

The writer of Hebrews calls the work not an epistle but a "word of ex-hortation" (13:22), and the opening address found in other biblical letters is missing. Hebrews is a carefully constructed essay, tightly reasoned, building to a planned climax. It is probably the closest thing to a Sunday-morning sermon to be found in our New Testament.

Some scholars, therefore, have argued that Hebrews is not really a letter at all but a sermon. The last chapter, they have proposed, was tacked on later, perhaps to make it seem like one of Paul's letters and thus gain wider acceptance in the church. Chapter 13 fits so well, however, with the rest of the book and such personal knowledge of the readers is shown in other parts (6:9–10; 10:32–34; 12:4) that most scholars reject the view that the chapter is a later addition.[3]

To whom was Hebrews written? This question is more important for interpreting the letter, and yet it is equally disputed.

The traditional view is that the epistle was written to a group of Jews who had become Christians but who were now tempted to drift back into Judaism. To them the writer presents Christ as superior to all that their old religion might offer: angels, Moses, the priesthood, and the old covenant. The traditional title, "Letter to the Hebrews," reflects this understanding of the book.

Most modern interpreters, however, have argued that the letter may be as easily understood as addressed to Gentile Christians. It does not say that it is to Jewish Christians. It never mentions any revival of circumcision or legalism. The conflicts between Judaism and Christianity that were so bitter when Galatians was being written now seem forgotten. The people now addressed are becoming weak-kneed (12:12) and are falling "away from the living God" (3:12). They are becoming indifferent; but they could as well be Gentiles as Jews. The extensive use of Old Testament ideas, it is argued, proves nothing, because the Septuagint was the Bible of Gentile Christians as well as of Jews.

The present writer's own teacher, the late William Manson, made a strong case for a version of the traditional view. The letter, Manson argued, was written to a house-church in Rome composed of Jewish converts to Christianity who still maintained ties with the Jewish community. They were teetering on the dividing line between the original way of life of the first Jewish Christians and the growing fellowship of the world mission to the Gentiles. They were Christians, but they were reluctant to break their ties to Judaism and its older forms of worship.

It is certainly possible that the writer of Hebrews presents the superiority of Christ to the Old Testament religion as a way of encouraging Gentile Christians to persevere in the faith. It does seem simpler, however, to understand the letter in the more straightforward way characteristic of tradition and defended by Manson: that it presents Christ as superior to the Old Testament because it was into Judaism that the readers were tempted to backslide.[4]

The Occasion of Hebrews

Some Christians—whether former Jews or pagans—"holy partners in a heavenly calling" (3:1), are now being tempted to "turn away" (3:12). They are in danger of apostasy (6:6, RSV), of "wavering" (10:23), and are even neglecting to attend worship services (10:25).

These Christians had an admirable record in the past. In "earlier days" they had "endured a hard struggle with sufferings, sometimes being publicly exposed to abuse and persecution" (10:32–33). The persecution had not, apparently, gone as far as the execution of martyrs (12:4), but it had caused the plundering of some Christians' property (10:34). Now both apathy and

new persecution threaten (12:7). The readers now need to be told, "Do not
. . . abandon that confidence of yours" (10:35).

That minority who, like Manson, assign Hebrews to an early date suggest
that the earlier persecution referred to was the one in A.D. 49, in which
Claudius expelled the Jews from Rome because of riots said to have been
instigated by one "Chrestus." The letter itself, then, is written as the more
severe persecution under Nero threatens the church at Rome. Most scholars
relate the letter to later persecutions.

That it was written to Christians in Rome is itself uncertain. Rome is
suggested, however, by the greetings from "those from Italy" (13:24) and by
the fact that Bishop Clement of Rome quoted the letter in an epistle of his
own from around A.D. 96.

The Purpose of Hebrews

The letter is written for a double purpose: (1) theologically, it is to present the
superiority of Jesus Christ to any alternative, such as the things the Old
Testament offered; and (2) practically, it is to encourage the readers to move
forward, not backward, in their faith.

Over and over, one finds the readers urged not to "drift away" (2:1), not to
"turn away" (3:12), not to "become dull in understanding" (5:11), not to
commit apostasy (6:6), and not to "abandon . . . confidence" (10:35).
(Hebrews warns so solemnly against backsliding that, a few years later, the
Shepherd of Hermas was written in part to say that God does sometimes give
lapsed Christians a second chance, though there are strict limits to God's
patience.)[5] Rather, Hebrews encourages its readers to "hold . . . confidence"
(3:14); strive "to enter" (4:11); draw near, "with boldness" (4:16); "go on
toward perfection" (6:1); "be strongly encouraged to seize the hope set
before" them (6:18); "hold fast" (10:23); and "run with perseverance the race
. . . looking to Jesus the pioneer and perfecter" of that faith (12:1–2).

That encouragement lies in the fact that Christ is "much superior to" and
"more excellent than" anything the Old Testament offered (1:4). His priesthood and covenant are "enacted through better promises" (8:6). He offers
entrance into a place of worship "greater and perfect" (9:11). He has opened
a "new and living way" of access to God (10:20).

The letter is an exhortation to carry on, to go forward, encouraged by the
realization of the transcendent value of Christ.

Some Comments on Hebrews

How do we know God? Hebrews begins with an answer: through Christ.
Other, earlier ways are not condemned. But Heb. 1:1–4 affirms that the
revelation in God's Son is superior to all others. As early as verse 3, however,
the author introduces his (or her) particular emphasis. John writes of the

revealed *logos,* or wisdom of God. Paul stresses the *righteousness* of God and our *justification.* But Heb. 1:3 speaks of *purification.* The atmosphere of the letter is not that of the philosophy class or the law court but of the Temple, ceremony, worship. The writer finds new meaning in religious symbols and cultic practices now transformed by Christ.

As seen from this perspective, the human problem is that we are stained with sin and cannot enter into the presence of God.

One solution, in the thought of both Jews and pagans, was the concept of angels. These creatures were regarded as halfway between God and human-kind and thus able to link the two. Angels were said to have assisted at creation and to have given the law. They could go up and down a ladder between God and sinful Jacob. And speculation about these heavenly beings exercised a fascination for the ancient world in some ways analogous to the modern preoccupation with space travel and UFO's. Hebrews argues that God's Son is above God's angels. Yet at the same time, angels can never quite get low enough to make contact with people. This is because they have never been tempted or suffered. God is not really concerned about angels but people (2:16). Christ has identified himself completely with humanity. "Because he himself was tested by what he suffered, he is able to help those who are being tested" (2:18). As mediator, he is higher than the angels and yet more completely down to earth.

"Jesus is worthy of more glory than Moses" (3:3). To the Hebrews, Moses was Abraham Lincoln and George Washington in one, their "Great Emanci-pator" and the founder of their nation. It was through him that God gave the law. It was he who led God's people to the Promised Land; he was a kind of "pioneer" (12:2). Yet the story of Moses is one of frustration, Hebrews says. The religion of Moses never delivered on its promises because it could not overcome the sinfulness of a stubborn people. Of all those who left Egypt with Moses, only two made it into the land of Canaan. Three times the author quotes God's final announcement to those backsliders: "They will not enter my rest" (3:11; 4:3, 5; cf. 3:18). Let us, however, go forward, the writer pleads, into what is promised through our leader, Christ (4:11–13).

In Heb. 4:14 we are introduced to the most distinctive theme of Hebrews, the concept of Christ as the great High Priest. For most Protestants, at least, priests today are somewhat out of fashion. To grasp the writer's message, we need imaginatively to recover the sense of dependence Jews felt regarding the priesthood. The priest was a kind of middleman between God and God's people. He represented God to them; he represented them to God. God was too holy to be approached by ordinary men and women. It was only through the priest that impure humans had access. The high priest might enter the Holy of Holies, the inner part of the tabernacle, only after elaborate ceremony, and then only once a year. But Jesus has entered heaven itself. True, Jesus was not born into the priestly tribe of Levi. But neither was

Melchizedek, called a priest in Gen. 14:17–20 and Ps. 110:4. It was in Melchizedek's pattern of special priesthood that Jesus exercised his priestly mediation between God and people. (The use of the figure of Melchizedek is one parallel that some modern scholars find to ideas in the Dead Sea Scrolls.) But Christ has "no need," like those high priests, "to offer sacrifices day after day, first for his own sins, and then for those of the people; this he did once for all when he offered himself" (7:27).

Hebrews sees the symbols and ceremonies of Leviticus as "types," pictures, in a sense, of the reality of access to God that the Christian was to claim in Christ. The book expresses this reality by making use of an idea well known among such Hellenistic-Jewish teachers as Philo, an idea derived ultimately from Plato. It is surely one of Plato's oddest ideas, but that philosopher proposed that there are really three kinds of beds: there are pictures and shadows of beds; there are what one sleeps on every night; and there is the "ideal form" bed, in the mind and in heaven. What one sleeps on at night is only a temporary manifestation of the ideal, heavenly bed, which is what is really real. This is Plato's perhaps exaggerated way of saying that spiritual, heavenly things are what really matter, what are eternal. Material things, like shadows, pass away.

As Hebrews describes Christ's priesthood and the new covenant, it presents these as the heavenly realities. The law, found in books such as Leviticus, with its ceremonies, "has only a shadow of the good things to come and not the true form of these realities" (10:1). The tabernacle and the altar served only as "a sketch and shadow of the heavenly [sanctuary]" (8:5). But in Christ we have the reality. Jeremiah's dream of a new covenant has come true (8:8–12; cf. Jer. 31:31–34). The risen Christ has actually entered the true sanctuary of God, heaven itself, on our behalf. The whole Bible gets its subtitles from the idea developed in these chapters: the Old Testament (or Covenant) and the New Testament.

"Therefore, my friends, since we have confidence to enter the sanctuary . . . and since we have a great priest . . . let us approach . . . in full assurance of faith" (10:19–22). So the writer summarizes.

The most celebrated chapter in Hebrews is the "roll call of heroes of the faith" (Abel and Abraham and Moses, etc.) in Hebrews 11. The point of the chapter, however, is that all of these were looking forward to something that lay beyond themselves.

That goal, the author announces, is in Christ (12:1–2). Yet Christ himself is seen as the "pioneer" (12:2), the one who leads forward in faith. "Faith" to the writer of Hebrews is courage, the vision to keep going forward into what Christ has promised.

"Let us then go to him outside the camp" of Judaism or of anything less than Christianity, he pleads, on toward heaven, "the city that is to come" (13:13–14).

JAMES

There are many different men named James mentioned in the New Testament. Unfortunately, it seems unlikely that any one of them was the author of our epistle of James.

The brother of John, the first of the Twelve to be martyred, hardly had time to write the book (Acts 12:2).

James the son of Alphaeus (Mark 3:18) was one of the Twelve, but neither the Bible nor tradition indicates that he was a man of distinction.

James the younger (Mark 15:40), perhaps the same as James the son of Mary (Mark 16:1), is perhaps also James the son of Alphaeus. Again we know nothing, though we cannot absolutely exclude the possibility of authorship.

James the father of Jude (Judas) (Luke 6:16; Acts 1:13) could possibly be the same as one of these other Jameses. We know nothing about him, either.

James the brother of Jesus (Mark 6:3; Acts 12:17; 15:13; 21:18; 1 Cor. 15:7; Gal. 1:19; Jude v. 1) is the James to whom tradition finally attributed this letter. It was partly on the basis of the belief that he was the author that the book at last received acceptance into the canon.

Several reasons make it seem unlikely that that tradition is historically accurate:

1. As late as the fourth century, Eusebius listed the book "called the Epistle of James" as "among the disputed books," said it was still "considered spurious," and noted that very few of the church fathers ever made any use of it. If the letter really had been by such a prominent leader in the early church as Jesus' brother, it is highly unlikely that there would still have been debate about its being included in the canon three hundred years later.
2. Language scholars tell us that the letter is written in polished Greek, not the dialect one would expect of the son of a Galilean carpenter.
3. The content of the letter shows no signs of its being by James the brother of Jesus and "bishop of Jerusalem." The author makes no claim to being Jesus' brother; gives few, if any, hints of personal memory of Jesus' earthly life; discusses none of the problems that the rest of the New Testament indicates were so much debated in the early church; and gives no reflection of James' leadership in the Jerusalem congregation (Acts, Galatians, and tradition agree that James really was the leader of that church).
4. The discussion of faith and works in James 2:18–26 seems to reflect a relatively late time, when the letters or at least some of the ideas of Paul, misunderstood, had been circulating throughout the church.
5. It seems likely that James 1:1 reflects 1 Peter 1:1 and that James 4:10

JAMES
The Wisdom That Produces Good Works
"So faith by itself, if it has no works, is dead" (2:17).

1:1 The Wise Person Faces Temptation with Good Deeds	2:1 True Wisdom Results in Loving Actions, Not Just "Faith"	3:1 The Truly Wise Control the Tongue and Show Wisdom by Life, Not Words	4:1 The Truly Wise Also Control the Passions	4:13 Thus the Truly Wise Are Patient 5:20
In trouble, rejoice and seek wisdom from God, 1:1–18 Face your difficulties not with angry words and wickedness, 1:19–20 Instead, face difficulties with good deeds, 1:21–27	Show no partiality, 2:1–7 But obey the law of love, 2:8–13 because not "faith" but good work is what counts, 2:14–26	The difficulty of controlling one's tongue, 3:1–12 The marks of genuine, God-given wisdom, 3:13–18	Be humbly content, not covetous and jealous, 4:1–10 And keep God's law by not judging others, 4:11–12	Submit humbly to God's plans, 4:13–17 Though the selfish prosper now, their judgment will come, 5:1–11 Wait for it with patience, prayer, and concern for each other, 5:12–20

Author: "James" (according to tradition, Jesus' brother, but probably an unknown Christian Jew)
Recipients: Apparently all Christians
Date: A.D. 50–120 (Most critics put it around A.D. 90–100.)
Occasion: Again, we do not know.
Purpose: Practical moral instruction emphasizing life, not just words or "faith"

reflects a knowledge of 1 Peter 5:6, thus putting the letter of James later than 1 Peter.

While the letter is probably not by Jesus' brother James, it is clear that it was gradually accepted into the canon because it was often associated with that early church leader. It is proper, therefore, to interpret the letter in part against the background of that tradition.[6]

Writing in the fourth century, Eusebius tells us that James was the first "bishop of Jerusalem." While that church historian may be reading back into the first century the fixed forms of government developed by his own time, it is clear that James really was an important leader in the Jerusalem church.

Paul tells us that on his first trip to Jerusalem after his conversion, he consulted with only two apostles, Peter and James (Gal. 1:18–19). He names James first among the three "pillars" of the church (the other two being Peter and John) before whom he later laid out his version of the gospel for assurance that he had not "run in vain" (Gal. 2:2, 9). Acts seems to picture James as presiding at the Jerusalem Council (Acts 15:13–21). When Paul arrived at Jerusalem after this third missionary journey, Luke tells us that it was to James that he made his formal report (Acts 21:18).

While both Galatians and Acts say that James was in agreement with Paul and his mission to the Gentiles, there are in both books hints that James was himself associated with the more conservative Jewish faction in the church (see Acts 15:20; 21:20–24). It was when "certain men came from James" to Antioch that Peter stopped eating with Gentiles (Gal. 2:12).

The first-century Jewish historian Josephus—no Christian —tells us a story that fits rather nicely with part of the biblical picture. He says that James was known as "the Just." Seizing a moment of power after the death of Festus (Acts 25:1) and before a new governor arrived, the high priest Ananias had James—and certain others, presumably Christians—executed by stoning. James was so respected for his piety that protests were sent to King Agrippa.[7]

Eusebius reports legends that elaborate the story. "James the Just" was so far removed from the lusts of the world that he ate no meat, never got a shave or a haircut, used no sweet-smelling oil, and—perhaps most obvious of all such signs of this type of piety—never took a bath. He spent so much time praying that his knees became calloused like a camel's! He bore witness to Christ at his trial, was thrown off the wall of the Temple, stoned, and finally clubbed to death. But he died as had his brother, praying, "Father, forgive them, for they know not what they do." According to Eusebius, even Josephus says that the fall of Jerusalem, just a few years later, came about as divine retribution for the murder of so holy a man.[8]

Whatever its actual origin, therefore, the letter eventually came to be included in the canon because it had come to be understood as part of the legacy of this model early Jewish-Christian martyr.

The Occasion of James

The book is addressed "to the twelve tribes in the Dispersion" (1:1). By the time of the New Testament, Hebrew tribal organization had long since vanished. Surely the greeting means "to the Christian church scattered over the world." Writing, then, to so broad a group, the author makes no clear reference to any particular local situation. It is impossible to determine the occasion of the letter.

Some, building on the letter's association with the first "bishop of Jerusalem," have argued that the epistle reflects early Palestinian Jewish-Christian piety. Most, for reasons such as those given above for rejecting the tradition that Jesus' brother was the author, have regarded it as the work of an unknown Hellenistic Jewish-Christian of late in the first century. This seems to the present writer more likely.

The fact is, however, that the book itself gives no clear indication of a special time or place in which it originated or of any unusual situation to which it was addressed.

The Purpose of James

Form critics like to use of certain passages in the Bible the Greek word *paranaesis,* meaning "exhortation" or "moral instruction." Though Paul's letters typically begin with discussion of the kerygma (the good news of the gospel) theology, they usually move on to *paranaesis* (see, for example, Rom. 12—14; Eph. 4—6; Col. 3—4).

James is entirely a book of *paranaesis.* Bruce Metzger counts sixty verbs as imperatives in the 108 verses of the epistle.

Indeed, one may question whether the book really should be called a letter. Though it has a letterlike beginning—even that is of a broad, impersonal kind—the ending is not at all like that of a letter. This writing is more like a sermon.

James, then, is a book of practical, moral instruction, urging every Christian to manifest religion not in words but in deeds of love.

Some Comments on James

Although an outline for the letter is given in this *Guide* (p. 483), perhaps the first thing that must be said about James is that it cannot really be outlined. Martin Luther, who, as we shall see, had other reasons for disliking James, complained that the author "makes a jumble of things."[9]

He does. But there is a reason. James is not attempting to write in the introduction-three-points-and-a-conclusion style of a modern preacher. His model is much more near to that of the ancient Hebrew "wisdom literature."

Proverbs, for example, cannot be outlined either. Many of its passages are simply collections of the wise, even witty, sayings of the kind beloved by the writers and readers of wisdom literature (see, for example, any chapter in Proverbs 10—28).

James shares with Proverbs and other books of Hebrew "wisdom" much more than a tendency to the disconnected style of a collection of wise sayings. The author, like Proverbs, writes in praise of Godly wisdom (3:13, 15, 17; cf. Prov. 8—9; etc.). He exhorts his readers to many of the same virtues: giving to those in need (James 2:14–16; cf. Prov. 11:25); controlling one's tongue (James 3:1–12; cf. Prov. 17:28); and controlling one's temper (James 4:1; cf. Prov. 16:32). And James employs something of Proverbs's tendency to a kind of Jewish humor.

It may seem blasphemous to the more pious readers of this volume to suggest that anything in the Bible is meant to be funny. But there are passages in Proverbs where many centuries and translations have not obscured the humor. Proverbs intends at least a smile when it notes:

> Like a gold ring in a pig's snout
> is a beautiful woman without good sense. (Prov. 11:22)

No one is really quite as lazy as Proverbs's drone, who cannot find the energy even to eat:

> The lazy person buries a hand in the dish,
> and is too tired to bring it back to the mouth. (Prov. 26:15)

It is in this same vein that James writes of some of the sins that he denounces.

James can picture at the church a rich man with gold rings being attentively ushered to a seat, while a poor man is made to stand somewhere or even told to sit on the floor (James 2:1–7).

He can laugh at the hypocrite who piously says to the beggar, "Go in peace; keep warm and eat your fill," but then does nothing to help (2:14–17).

He can compare people who are perhaps dirty and disheveled, see the mess in a mirror, and forget to do anything about it to Christians who read about their sins in the Bible and then forget to clean up their lives (1:22–25).

And he can propose that it is easier to put out a forest fire or to tame all kinds of wild animals than for a Christian to control his or her tongue (3:1–12). (One other biblical teacher was fond of such humorous exaggeration; see Matt. 7:3; 19:24.)

Almost all readers can see wisdom in the wit of these passages. But debate has raged about such sayings of James as that "faith without works is also dead" (James 2:26).

The present writer has sometimes placed the following quotations side by side on the chalkboard and asked his classes to vote on which sounds more like the New Testament:

For by grace you have been saved through faith . . . not the result of works.	A person is justified by works and not by faith alone.

Both are in the New Testament, of course, one being from Eph. 2:8–9, the other being from James 2:24.

Martin Luther took his stand on Paul's preaching of salvation through faith, not works. James's emphasis on works so upset Luther that he denounced it as a "rather straw-like epistle," by "some Jew or other," and proposed to drop it from the canon.

It is difficult to avoid the feeling that James is deliberately attempting to correct a view that must have been associated with Paul. A partial reconciliation of the conflict, however, can be achieved when one recognizes that James and Paul are using the word "faith," in quite different ways. By "faith" Paul means a personal trust in Jesus Christ as Lord and Savior. James is using "faith" to mean intellectual acceptance of certain doctrines as true. Thus James can write that "even the demons believe—and shudder" (2:19). But such demons do not have what Paul means by saving "faith." James is attacking a misunderstanding of Paul's ideas. Paul advocated faith, salvation by faith alone, but it was the kind of faith described as "faith working through love" (Gal. 5:6).

Finally, it should be noted that, for all its emphasis on works in the style of Hebrew wisdom, James is a Christian book. There seems, at first glance, so little that is specifically Christian in James that some have proposed that it really was a bit of pre-Christian Jewish wisdom, slightly edited for church use. The writer, however, describes himself as "a servant of God and of the Lord Jesus Christ" (1:1). His readers, he says, "believe in our glorious Lord Jesus Christ" (2:1). He recalls that God "gave us birth by the word of truth, so that we would become a kind of first fruits of his creatures" (1:18). This sounds more like a formula for Christian baptism than a bit of Old Testament wisdom. "The implanted word that has the power to save your souls" (1:21) surely must be the gospel, not the law. The "excellent name that was invoked over you" is evidently that of Christ (2:7). And James 5:8 places us in the midst of the typical Christian expectation that "the coming of the Lord is near."

Indeed, it could be argued that James is, in certain ways, closer to the teachings of Jesus in style and in content than are many of the other books of the New Testament that say more about Jesus. W. G. Kümmel lists parallels such as the following:

James	1:5, 17	Matt.	7:7–11
	1:22		7:24–27
	4:12		7:1
	1:6	Mark	11:23–24

James is probably not copying from the written Gospels. He knows the same tradition of teachings on which the Gospels rest.

He knows especially the commandment that Jesus says really matters: "If you really fulfil the royal law according to the scripture, 'You shall love your neighbor as yourself' " (James 2:8).

Jesus would say, "Amen!"

1 PETER

In the case of the apostle Peter, it is impossible completely to separate history from the rich legend that quickly became a part of the tradition associated with his memory.

Persecution, says one story, had broken out in Rome. Peter made his escape down the Appian Way. Suddenly, he encountered Jesus, who was walking toward the city.

"Where are you going, Lord?"

"Into the city, to be crucified again."

Shamed by the vision, Peter returned courageously to face prison and death. Arrested and thrown into a dungeon, Peter still witnessed to his captors. At length, won by the holiness of the apostle, two of his guards were converted. How could he baptize them in his cell? Miraculously, a fountain sprang from the floor, and Peter was able to wash clean from sin these newborn Christians. Then he was led out to be crucified—upside down, at his request, because he felt unworthy to die in the same manner as his Lord.

Perhaps the best-loved part of the tradition that comes from the memory of Peter is the first of two letters that bear his name. It, like the legend, centers on courage, holiness, and baptism in the midst of persecution.

Several factors make most scholars cautious about attributing 1 Peter to the pen of the apostle: (1) it is written in polished Greek, though we are told that Peter was an "uneducated" man (Acts 4:13); (2) it is so much like letters of Paul that it appears to come from a time when Paul's epistles were known throughout the church; and (3) most important, it seems to fit perfectly into the situation of worldwide persecution of the nineties and later, in which even to be called a Christian was a crime. We know of no such persecution in Asia Minor, where churches to which the letter is addressed were located, during Peter's lifetime.

As a matter of fact, the letter itself hints of some mediation in its authorship. "Through Silvanus, whom I consider a faithful brother, I have written this short letter to encourage you," we are told near the end (5:12). Is the author perhaps hinting that the spirit but not the actual words are Peter's?[10]

Nevertheless, there are modern critics who still attribute the letter more directly to the apostle. The early church, they note, rejected the so-called

1 PETER

Hope and Holiness in Persecution

"He has given us a new birth into a living hope. . . . You are a . . . royal priesthood, a holy nation" (1:3; 2:9).

1:1 **A Call to Hope and to Holiness**	2:11 **Specific Ethical Instructions for Living as Holy "Priests" in a Pagan World**	3:13 **Priestly Witness to These Pagans in a Time of Persecution**	4:12 **That Time of Persecution Has Now Arrived. Do Your Duty in It with Joy and Hope** 5:14
Salutation, 1:1–2	Among pagan neighbors, 2:11–12	Witness with a clear conscience, 3:13–22	There is joyful meaning in the persecution you face, 4:12–19
Even in persecution, rejoice that you have been born anew to a "living hope," 1:3–9	In relation to the government, 2:13–17	Use what little time is left for holy living, 4:1–11	Let each elder and each younger person do his part, 5:1–5
All history has awaited this day, 1:10–12	For servants, 2:18–25		Face the persecution with humility, patience, and hope, 5:6–11
So leave your old life behind, 1:13–21	For wives, 3:1–6		A closing postscript, 5:12–14
	For husbands, 3:7		
And become part of the church, the new, holy priesthood, 1:22–2:10	For all, 3:8–12		

Author: Peter (at least, according to tradition)
Recipients: Christians in what is now Turkey
Date: A.D. 64 (A.D. 112?)
Occasion: Persecution by the Roman government
Purpose: To encourage new converts and to exhort them to holy living

Apocalypse of Peter and the *Gospel of Peter,* and many rejected 2 Peter, but 1 Peter was early and widely accepted as an authoritative word from the leader of the Twelve. If we do not know of comparable persecution in what is now Turkey during Peter's lifetime, we do know of it in Rome itself, and Peter may have written from the midst of that persecution, warning others of what he sensed would soon spread (persecution was widespread a few years later). And if the Silvanus (Silas) by whom the letter was actually penned was the companion of Paul and his secretary in the letters to the Thessalonians (Acts 15:40; 1 Thess. 1:1; 2 Thess. 1:1), this might explain both the use of polished Greek and the echoes of Pauline phrases and ideas. The presupposition of a relatively undeveloped system of church government (still by "elders"; see 1 Peter 5:1), the hopeful attitude still taken toward the Roman government (2:13–17; cf. Luke 3:13), and the still-strong expectation of "the end of all things" (1 Peter 4:7) are cited as evidence for a date within Peter's lifetime.

Only two things can be said with certainty: (1) the letter does speak directly to the kind of persecution that swept the Roman Empire early in the second century; and (2) 1 Peter was so integral a part of the tradition of the apostle that the early church interpreted it as his authoritative word.

The Occasion of 1 Peter

Pliny the Younger was puzzled. He had been sent to Bithynia, one of the provinces to whose Christians 1 Peter is addressed, to straighten things out. One of his problems was what to do with those stubborn Christians who absolutely refused even token worship of the emperor. Around A.D. 112, seeking official advice, he wrote to the emperor Trajan:

> Meanwhile this is the course I have taken with those who were accused before me as Christians. I asked them whether they were Christians, and if they confessed, I asked them a second and a third time with threats of punishment. If they kept to it, I ordered them for execution; for I held no question that whatever it was they admitted, in any case obstinacy and unbending perversity deserve to be punished. . . .
>
> Before long . . . an unsigned paper was presented, which gave the names of many. As for those who said that they neither were nor had ever been Christians, I . . . let them go, since they recited a prayer to the gods at my direction, made supplication with incense and wine to your statue . . . and moreover cursed Christ—things which (so it is said) those who are really Christians cannot be made to do.

The emperor wrote back his approval:

> You have adopted the proper course. . . . They are not to be sought out; but if they are accused and convicted they must be punished—yet on this condition, that whoso denies himself to be a Christian, and makes the fact plain by his

action, that is, by worshiping our gods, shall obtain pardon . . . however suspicious his past conduct may be.[11]

Several facts about the situation of Christians are clearly indicated by this correspondence:

1. They are experiencing persecution not only in Rome but in other places throughout the empire.
2. Just bearing the name of Christian is itself a crime.
3. Though they are not actually sought out by the government, the Christians may be arrested if their pagan neighbors choose to report them.
4. They then faced a simple choice: they could renounce their faith and easily go free, or they could confess that they were Christians and die.

How similar is the situation to which 1 Peter is written!

1. "Resist him, . . . for you know that your brothers and sisters in all the world are undergoing the same kinds of suffering" (5:9). It is a "fiery ordeal" (4:12) in which Christians actually share in the very sufferings of Christ himself (4:13).
2. They are "reviled for the name of Christ" (4:14). One might be arrested simply "as a Christian" (4:16).
3. Peter—in fact or in tradition—warns concerning pagan neighbors, that they may "malign you as evildoers" (2:12), though he is hopeful that if they maintain friendly conduct among their non-Christian neighbors, they may not need to fear the government (2:13–17; 3:13).
4. But they must be prepared to confess their faith, no matter what danger that may bring (3:15–18). In a time of "fiery ordeal," Peter writes to Christians that "like a roaring lion your adversary the devil prowls around, looking for someone to devour" (5:8).

The Purpose of 1 Peter

"I have written this short letter," the author summarizes at the end, "to encourage you and to testify that this is the true grace of God. Stand fast in it" (5:12). Clearly, the first purpose of the letter is to help its readers see God's plan and purpose in the persecutions they may experience, so that they can face those trials with courage and hope. We have been given "a new birth into a living hope" (1:3). "In this you rejoice, even if now for a little while you have had to suffer various trials" (1:6). "Set all your hope on the grace that Jesus Christ will bring you when he is revealed" (1:13). "Christ . . . suffered for you, leaving you an example" (2:21). "Do not be surprised at the fiery ordeal that is taking place among you to test you, as though something strange were happening to you. But rejoice insofar as you are sharing Christ's sufferings, so that you may also be glad and shout for joy when his glory is revealed" (4:12–13).

Second, the book is written, apparently to new converts (especially former pagans), as an exhortation to moral living. Christians are to be "holy" (different, separate). "You have already spent enough time in doing what the Gentiles like to do, living in licentiousness" (4:3), he pleads. "Do not be conformed to the desires that you formerly had in ignorance. Instead, as he who called you is holy, be holy yourselves in all your conduct" (1:14–15). "You were ransomed from the futile ways inherited from your ancestors" (1:18). Now these readers are to live as part of the church, "a holy nation" (2:9), following Christ "in his steps" (2:21). Over and over, the writer urges his readers to witness to their neighbors by loving conduct.

Finally, though the extent to which one may base interpretations of the letter on this is debated, there are strong hints that the letter is written as a kind of sermon for a baptism, perhaps for use at the Passover-Easter season.[12] Once the church had sent Peter to meet with newly baptized converts in Samaria (Acts 8:14). No apostle could have visited with every new group being baptized, but by means of this circular letter, something of the apostle's authoritative voice can be heard by new converts as they are told that baptism "now saves you" (3:21). Some who deny that the whole letter was itself written for use in the actual ceremony of baptism agree that it may well contain fragments of baptismal hymns or liturgies.

Some Comments on 1 Peter

The word "baptism" occurs only once in 1 Peter. The Anchor Bible translates 1 Peter 3:20–21 in part, "Just this [is the] analogous baptism [that] now saves you. It does not involve putting away the filth of the flesh, but is a pledge of good will to God. [And it saves you] through the resurrection of Jesus Christ."[13] Ideas implied here, however, are repeated themes throughout the whole letter: water, purification, pledge of holy living, salvation, resurrection, and new beginning. It is easy to imagine the use of this letter at an early church baptism.

"Blessed be the God and Father of our Lord Jesus Christ!" the leader cries in his opening praise. His hearers include beginning converts, born "into a living hope" (1:3). Through faith, they have now obtained salvation (1:9). The whole history of the world has looked forward to this moment (1:10–12).

Now, therefore, they are exhorted to live lives of hope and of holiness. They are to prepare their "minds for action" (1:13). The allusion is to the preparation of the old Israel for the Passover journey out of Egypt and across the sea (Exod. 12:11). It may reflect also that, at least according to the baptismal rite described by Hippolytus of Rome early in the third century, those who were about to be baptized removed their outer clothes. (Men and women were separated for the sacrament.) Together they say the "Our Father," as the New English Bible translates it, the Lord's Prayer (1:17). Now they are purified by the blood not of the Passover lamb but of Christ (1:19).

A few commentators suggest that the baptism is to be thought of as actually occurring between verses 21 and 22. The word from the apostle can therefore resume in a different tense: "Now that you have purified your souls" in this act of baptism, "you have been born anew" (1:22–23).

So "rid yourselves" of "all malice, and all guile" (2:1), the sermon continues, leaving such attitudes behind as the baptized did their old clothes in order to put on the new robes symbolizing their new natures (cf. 1 Cor. 10:2; Gal. 3:27). In the liturgy described by Hippolytus, infant Christians were given a ceremonial bowl of milk to drink following baptism (cf. 1 Peter 2:2).

But now they are no longer called "babies." They are summoned, as it were, from the place of baptism to the communion table, to the altar of sacrifice. "Come to him, a living stone, . . . and like living stones, let yourselves be built into a spiritual house, to be a holy priesthood" (2:4–5). Once they were pagans, nobodies. Now they are called "priests." The church is built of these people, "a chosen race, a royal priesthood, a holy nation, God's own people" (2:9).

There is a rich, complex imagery in this passage. On the one hand, surely there is intended a reflection of the experience of Peter himself, who had been so changed that he had received a new name, "the Rock." On such living stones the church itself was to be built (Matt. 16:13–20). Now these new church members are "living stones" too. But on the other hand, there are also echoes of the experience of Israel, that first people of God. When they had passed through the water of the sea, they came to Mount Sinai and there entered into a covenant pledge in which they were told that they were to become "a priestly kingdom and a holy nation" (Exod. 19:6). These Gentile converts, having also passed through the water, have now joined a holy priesthood.

It is necessary, however, to spell out in more detail what holy, priestly living means. These "aliens and exiles" on their journey are no longer quite at home in the wilderness of the pagan world (1 Peter 2:11). The letter moves on to describe specific areas in which they must act out their holiness. In almost all of these areas, the emphasis is on submission, peaceable subordination of their selfish desires to the concerns of others.

"For the Lord's sake," they are to "accept the authority of every human institution . . . the emperor . . . governors," and so on (2:13–17).

Servants are to be obedient to their masters, as Christ, the Suffering Servant, was obedient and never vengeful. First Peter 2:18–25 clearly echoes the suffering servant passage of Isaiah 53. Does it not also reflect the actual memory of Jesus' life and death?

Wives are to show their holiness in their family role and in the inner beauty of their lives (3:1–6).

Husbands equally are to show concern for their wives (3:7).

Turning now to the whole group, the letter summarizes by exhorting them all to love. "Do not repay evil for evil," they are told, in words reminiscent of those of Jesus himself (3:8–12; cf. Matt. 5:38–48).

Such passages of *paranaesis* (ethical instruction), addressed specifically to different members of the household, occur so often in the New Testament as to suggest that they may have been a standard part of the oral tradition at baptism (cf. Eph. 5:21–6:9; Col. 3:18–4:1; Titus 2:2–10).

The function of a holy priest is, of course, to be a link between human beings and God. Built now into the church, these new Christians are to live submissive, loving lives for a purpose: they are to give priestly witness to their neighbors.

They are to be "zealots," it is true, but not "zealots" like the Jews who led pathetic revolts against their Roman persecutors (1 Peter 3:13). Rather, by word and deed they are to manifest Christian love, even to enemies.

This concern for witness to others, even persecutors, leads the author into the most obscure passage in the letter, 1 Peter 3:19–22 (cf. 4:6). In his death, the passage seems to say, Christ entered the world of departed spirits and even there bore witness to the gospel. The pseudepigraphal *1 Enoch* related the spirits who mated with human women and brought the evils of Noah's day (Gen. 6:1–8) to past rulers of this world. If Christ bore witness even to them, the author is saying, his readers ought to witness to those in places of power today, even if in their own deaths. The water of the Flood of Noah's day is compared to the water of baptism that the hearers have so recently experienced.[14]

The former companions of these new converts will be "surprised" that their old friends "no longer join them in the same excesses of dissipation" (1 Peter 4:4). But Christians must hold firm in their new way of life, not reverting to pagan immorality in spite of their neighbors' opposition.

The "sermon" closes with an assurance that the eschaton, the end, is at hand. Therefore these church members are to make every act count for God in the few days that remain (4:7–11).

With 1 Peter 4:12, we encounter one of the unexplained puzzles of the book. The "sermon" had seemed to end with the doxology of 4:11. Now, however, it resumes, and the situation seems to be somewhat different. Up until this point, persecution has been presented as a real possibility but only a possibility. The author has written that "you have had to suffer various trials" (1:6). There is hope that "by doing right you should silence the ignorance of the foolish" (2:15). "Now who will harm you if you are eager to do what is good?" the author reassures his readers (3:13). They must be prepared to suffer "if suffering should be God's will" (3:17). But there is still hope, apparently, that that may not come to pass.

With 1 Peter 4:12, however, the "fiery ordeal" is now coming upon the church. The same experience of suffering is required of sisters and brothers throughout the world (5:9). "Like a roaring lion . . . the devil prowls around" (5:8). There is no longer doubt about it.

Perhaps the first part of the letter was a sermon originally composed by the author earlier. Now he sends it out in writing, adding the last verses in the light of the new, worsened situation.

What can enable these Christians to endure such persecution? There is the sense of the plan of the sovereign God (1:10–12). This is coupled with the apocalyptic conviction that persecution is a necessary part of the expected last stage of history, the tribulations. There is the example of Christ in suffering (2:21–25). There is the hope of resurrection, based on the memory of Christ's resurrection (1:3, 21; 3:21–22). There is the testing and purification that suffering brings (4:1, 12). There is the sense of sharing in the sufferings of Christ himself (4:13). And there is the eschatological hope: "After you have suffered for a little while, the God of all grace, who has called you to his eternal glory in Christ, will himself restore, support, strengthen, and establish you. To him be the power forever and ever. Amen" (5:10–11).

2 PETER

Second Peter is "the least valuable of the New Testament writings," says noted biblical scholar E. F. Scott. It is surely among the least read, studied, and loved.

As far back as we can trace, the church doubted that it was really by the apostle Peter.

It was among the very last books to be accepted into the canon, with its authority seriously questioned down into the fourth century.

Yet in spite of all the doubts about its authorship and its frightening picture of coming judgment, it did finally become part of the canon. Perhaps the church began to see values in it that need to be rediscovered today.

The doubts were ancient and well founded. As late as the fourth century, Eusebius still contrasted 2 Peter with 1 Peter. The latter was everywhere accepted as having been written by the apostle. Second Peter, however, Eusebius classed as "disputed." It was not rejected in the way the so-called *Apocalypse of Peter* was (and the Gospel and the Acts attributed to him). But it was not included in the oldest list of canonical books; it is not found in some ancient versions of the New Testament; and to this day, most scholars believe it to be the work of a much later writer, who modestly and piously attributed his essay to the great leader of the early church.

Here are some of the reasons for doubting that Peter wrote 2 Peter.

1. Most early Christian writers did not quote from it. We find no traces of the book before the middle of the second century.

2 PETER
The Apostolic Tradition and the Coming Judgment Day

"Remember the words spoken in the past by the holy prophets and the commandment of the Lord and Savior spoken through your apostles" (3:2).

"There will be false teachers among you" (2:1)

1:1	2:1	3:1	3:18
Seek the True, Apostolic Knowledge, Which Results in Godly Living	**Beware of the Teachers of Falsehoods**	**Wait Patiently for the Judgment Day, Avoiding the False Teachers' Immorality and Error**	
True knowledge and the progress in godliness that it produces, 1:1–11	A warning: false prophets must be expected, 2:1–3	Though delayed, the great day is surely coming, 3:1–10	
Its basis: the divine authority of the apostolic tradition, 1:12–21	God's judgment on such people in the past, 2:4–10	Therefore wait patiently, living holy lives, 3:11–13	
	The immorality of such false teachers, 2:11–16	and avoiding error, 3:14–18	
	The judgment on them, 2:17–22		

Author: "Peter" (Most scholars would say a later disciple of Peter, writing in his memory and honor.)

Recipients: All Christians

Date: A.D. 64? (probably much later, perhaps A.D. 125)

Occasion: False teachings are spreading, and hope of Christ's return is fading.

Purpose: To remind the readers of the authoritative apostolic teaching and to restore hope in the coming again of Christ

2. It is so different in style, vocabulary, and approach that it is hard to believe that it could be by the same man who wrote 1 Peter.
3. Its content implies a late date. Paul's writings apparently have been collected and are known to the readers. They are even referred to now as "scripture" (2 Peter 3:14–16). Apparently some years have gone by since "our ancestors died" (3:4); the first generation of Christians has passed away. One major concern of the letter is to deal with the problem that so many years have gone by and Jesus still has not come again. The great purpose of the letter is to remind the readers of the tradition that comes down through the years from the apostles.
4. The author almost certainly quotes from Jude, itself a relatively late book, and he probably makes use of other New Testament books.

Yet the church did include 2 Peter—genuinely apostolic or not—in the canon, perhaps because it needed its message.[15]

The Occasion of 2 Peter

"There will be false teachers among you, who will secretly bring in destructive opinions" (2:1), Peter is depicted as warning shortly before his death (1:14). In 2:10, the future tense is dropped. Actually, these teachers are already at work. "Bold and willful, they are not afraid to slander the glorious ones" (2:10). Immoral, "they count it a pleasure to revel in the daytime" (2:13). "They have left the straight road and have gone astray" (2:15).

Precisely what they were teaching is not clear. Some had begun to scoff at the hope of Christ's return (3:3–12). Some had twisted things in Paul's letters (3:16). They had practiced immorality and had attempted to make money by their heretical teaching (2:12, 14). Probably they were among the various Gnostic groups we have previously encountered.

Perhaps as late as well into the second century, an orthodox teacher in the tradition of Peter now attempts to warn against these heretics.

The Purpose of 2 Peter

I have written to you "that you should remember the words spoken in the past by the holy prophets, and the commandment of the Lord and Savior spoken through your apostles" (3:1–2); so the writer summarizes his purpose.

The author wishes to remind his readers that there is an orthodox tradition from Christ and the apostles. Christians must hold to it over against all novel heresies brought in by greedy and immoral heretics. They are especially urged not to lose their faith in the prophecies of the coming again of Christ for judgment and salvation.

Some Comments on 2 Peter

It is perhaps a hundred years after Jesus had promised that "the kingdom of God has come near" (Mark 1:15). For a century, Christians have waited for Christ's return in judgment. "Where is the promise of his coming?" scoffing teachers now demand. "For ever since our ancestors died, all things continue as they were from the beginning of creation" (3:4). In the name of the authoritative tradition that comes from Peter, leader of the apostles, 2 Peter undertakes to refute these heretics and to encourage orthodox believers.

The letter is written as from a Jewish Christian to Gentile Christians. William Barclay notes that the only other place in which Peter's name appears in the form "Simeon" in the Greek is in Acts 15:14, when Simon Peter helps to open the door for Gentiles to be admitted into the church. After the salutation in 2 Peter 1:1, these Gentile Christians are praised as having a faith of equal standing with that of the first Jewish Christians.[16]

There are hints that the letter is intended to appeal to readers who are products of the Greco-Roman culture of their time, influenced by Greek philosophy, especially Stoicism. Readers are instructed to seek knowledge, not "passion," and thereby "become participants of the divine nature" (1:4), an idea more frequent in Stoic than in Christian literature. The resulting virtues are described in a list and are much like those advocated in Stoic ethics. The list begins, however, with "faith," and it ends with "love," so that however adapted it may have been to appeal to Stoic readers, it is distinctly Christian. The earth, we are told, was "formed out of water" (3:5), an idea that would appeal to readers familiar with the thought of Thales, "the first Greek philosopher." And that the world will be destroyed by fire was an idea as familiar to the Stoics as to Jews and Christians (3:7).

While designed to appeal to readers within a pagan culture, the letter reasserts strongly the authority of the Christian tradition handed down from Peter and the apostles. Over against "cleverly devised myths" of the heretics (1:16) are set the facts about Jesus. All facts of which the author reminds his readers—such words as "remind" and "remember" are favorites of his— could be learned from the New Testament writings and need not require belief that the author was actually the eyewitness Peter, in whose name he writes. The transfiguration is seen as a foretaste of Christ's glory on the coming day of judgment (1:17–18; cf. Matt. 17:1–8). The basis of sound Christian doctrine, the author insists, must be such facts of Christ and the teachings of the prophets interpreted not by the whim of any teacher but according to the Holy Spirit and in the apostolic tradition.

Chapter 2 denounces the alternative to this tradition, the teachings of the immoral heretics. Much of this chapter seems to be an expansion of the book of Jude, which also denounces heretics. Here are a few of the many parallels:

There will be false teachers among you, who will secretly bring in destructive opinions. They will even deny the Master . . . bringing swift destruction. . . . Many will follow their licentious ways. (2 Peter 2:1–2)

Certain intruders have stolen in among you, people who long ago were desginated for this condemnation as ungodly, who pervert the grace . . . into licentiousness and deny our only Master. (Jude v. 4)

God did not spare the angels when they sinned, but cast them into . . . deepest darkness. . . . Sodom and Gomorrah . . . he . . . made . . . an example. (2 Peter 2:4–6)

The angels . . . he has kept . . . in deepest darkness. . . . Sodom and Gomorrah . . . serve as an example. (Jude vv. 6–7)

Those . . . indulge their flesh . . . and . . . despise authority. . . . They . . . slander the glorious ones, whereas angels . . . do not bring against them a slanderous judgment. . . . like irrational animals . . . (2 Peter 2:10–12)

These . . . defile the flesh, reject authority, and slander the glorious ones. But . . . the archangel Michael . . . did not dare to bring a condemnation of slander . . . but . . . like irrational animals . . . (Jude vv. 8–10)

The heretics are said not to respect prophets, apostles, angels, or even Christ. Bo Reicke, in the Anchor Bible, speculates that their contempt for authority (2 Peter 2:10) even included political subversion.[17] Second Peter graphically warns of their condemnation at the coming judgment, using symbols derived from Jewish literature popular in that day, including some not found in our Bibles.

To those who have lost faith that the judgment day will ever come, the letter offers several answers: (1) God made the world in the beginning, and God can bring it to an end (3:5–7); (2) God's timetable is not ours: "With the Lord one day is like a thousand years, and a thousand years are like one day" (3:8); and (3) the reason for the delay is the patience of God, God's hope that people will yet repent (3:9). But that day will surely come, unexpectedly, "like a thief" (3:10).

The true believer need not fear, however. The stories of destructive judgment recalled from the past (the Flood and the burning of Sodom) also include the stories of rescue for the righteous (Noah and Lot; 2:5–7).

Therefore, though the letter vividly describes judgment, the readers need not lose hope. As true believers, "in accordance with his promise, we wait for new heavens and a new earth, where righteousness is at home" (3:13).

JUDE

Apparently, it was to Jesus' family that the Jerusalem church looked for leadership for nearly a century after his death.

Joseph never participates in the Gospel story after the account in Luke 2 of Jesus' visit to the Temple at age twelve. Tradition has it that Joseph died while Jesus was still a youth.

Mary, so highly regarded in the Gospels, appears briefly with the disciples of Jesus in the upper room after the resurrection (Acts 1:14), then drops out of the story. Perhaps she died soon after Pentecost.

The brothers of Jesus, however, are placed side by side with the apostles in Acts 1:14. We have seen that James, one of these brothers, became the leader of the Jerusalem church. Two centuries later, Eusebius spoke of him as having been "bishop of Jerusalem." According to Eusebius, after the martyrdom of James, the surviving apostles and disciples, "with those that were related to our Lord according to the flesh," came together to choose James's successor. They selected Simeon, a cousin of Jesus, who was "bishop" until well into the second century.[18]

Two grandsons of another of Jesus' brothers, Jude, were almost martyred under Domitian. Apparently fearing that, as descendants of David, they might be involved in some underground rebellion, the authorities interrogated them. The two were able to convince their questioners, however, by displaying their calloused hands and describing their thirty-nine-acre farm, that they were harmless. The only kingdom to which they laid claim, they assured the judge, was "not of this world." They were dismissed.[19]

The little book of Jude was finally accepted into the canon in part because it came to be regarded as the work of Jude, one of the four brothers of Jesus (Mark 6:3). Actually, Jude (or Judas) was a very common name—there were five men of that name in the New Testament—and the author makes no claim to being a brother of the Lord. He does call himself a brother of James, however (Jude v. 1), and it is argued that modesty prevents his boasting of being related to Christ.

Defenders of the tradition argue that no other person named Jude was prominent enough to have his work treasured by the church. (Judas Iscariot is out of the question, of course, and the other Jude among the Twelve was the son, not the brother, of someone named James [Luke 6:16].) Jude's claim to be "brother of James" clearly identifies him as Jesus' brother also, it is argued.

Most scholars, however, note hints that the book is from a time later than the first generation of Christians. Jude urges his readers to "contend for the faith that was once for all entrusted to the saints" (v. 3), a concern, like that of the pastoral epistles, for the preservation of correct doctrine handed down from the past. His readers are urged to "remember the predictions of the apostles of our Lord" (v. 17), as if these were prophecies of leaders of the past, now (at a later time) being fulfilled.

Moreover, if the book was indeed by a brother of Jesus and of the "bishop of Jerusalem," James, it seems unlikely that it would have been so little used by early Christian writers and that it would have been so slow in winning a place in the canon.

In any event, it gives us no hint of the kind of information about Jesus of Nazareth we might have hoped for from one who had grown up with Jesus as a brother.[20]

The Occasion and Purpose of Jude

The author had intended, he tells us, to write of "the salvation we share," perhaps a sermon summarizing the gospel. But he has now received news that admission has been secretly gained by "ungodly" persons (vv. 3–4), teachers who have perverted the faith. The letter is a ringing denunciation of these heretics in the name of apostolic orthodoxy.

Some Comments on Jude

Second Peter, especially chapter 2, appears to be a revision of Jude (see the preceding section on "2 Peter").

Precisely who the heretics were is not clear. Jude's emphasis on "the only God" (Jude v. 25) suggests the possibility that they taught the Gnostic doctrine that there were two gods, the true God and the evil creator of this world. They are said to "deny our only . . . Lord" (v. 4). This may imply that they regarded Christ, as did some of the Gnostics, as only one link (though the highest) in the chain between humankind and the true God. These heretics apparently both practiced and encouraged immorality, perhaps arguing, as did Simon the Magician, that because we are under grace, not law, licentiousness will be forgiven (v. 4). Clearly, they rejected orthodoxy and authority (vv. 3, 4, 8, 18, for example).

The body of the book is a thunderous warning of the coming damnation of these heretics. Three examples of judgment are cited from the past. God "destroyed those who did not believe" among the Israelites whom he had liberated from Egypt (v. 5). The angels of Genesis 6 who lusted after human women were damned to hell (Jude v. 6). And the cities of Sodom and Gomorrah were burned for their sins (v. 7; cf. Gen. 19). So, Jude warns, these heretics will be destroyed.

The obscure story in Gen. 6:1–4 concerning the "sons of God" who mated with human women and thus precipitated the Flood was elaborated in a noncanonical (pseudepigraphal) Jewish book called 1 Enoch, said to be a prophecy composed by the character mentioned in Gen. 5:21–24. The Old Testament itself does not tell us that these angels were put "in eternal chains in deepest darkness" (Jude v. 6). But 1 Enoch vividly develops the story.

Verses 8 and 9 of Jude also contain an allusion to another book of popular legend. The noncanonical Assumption of Moses told how God had sent the archangel Michael to bury Moses, who died alone (Deut. 34). According to this literature, the devil had tried to claim Moses' body on the grounds that the body was matter and thus the devil's domain and that Moses was a murderer (Exod. 2:12). Recognizing that the devil was an angel, even though a fallen one, Michael had respectfully refrained from abusing him (Jude v. 9). But the heretics, Jude charges, have not hesitated to revile duly constituted authority. "Woe to them!" (v. 11). They are compared to Cain, the first murderer (Gen. 4:8), to Balaam (Num. 22—24), whom Jewish tradition had come to portray as a villain; and to Korah (Num. 16), who led a rebellion against even Moses himself (Jude v. 11).

Again Jude cites, even quotes, *1 Enoch* to support his picture of the coming judgment (vv. 14–15). Many years later, Jerome, who produced the great translation of the Bible into Latin, speculated that the reason that Jude was rejected by many in the early church was because of his use of these noncanonical books.

With its angry denunciations of heretics long dead, whose doctrines we can now only guess at, and with its warnings based on allusions that, however forceful in their own day, are obscure now, Jude is not a favorite book in the twentieth century. But the doxology that forms its two closing verses has been used for centuries in the liturgies of many denominations. It forms a fitting close for this chapter.

> Now to him who is able to keep you from falling, and to make you stand without blemish in the presence of his glory with rejoicing, to the only God our Savior, through Jesus Christ our Lord, be glory, majesty, power, and authority, before all time and now and for ever. Amen.

12

THE JOHANNINE
LITERATURE

Now two days later there was the dedication-festival of the idol-temple [of Artemis at Ephesus]. So while everyone was wearing white, John alone put on black clothing and went up to the temple; and they seized him and tried to kill him. . . . But John . . . went up on a high platform, and said to them, Men of Ephesus . . . You all say that you have Artemis as your goddess; so pray in her name that I and I alone, may die; or if you cannot do this, then I alone will call upon my own God and because of your unbelief I will put you all to death. . . . And while John was saying this, of a sudden the altar of Artemis split into many pieces, and all the offerings laid up in the temple suddenly fell to the floor, and its goodness was broken, and so were more than seven images; and half the temple fell down, so that the priest was killed at one stroke as the roof came down. Then the assembled Ephesians cried out, "There is but one God, the God of John!"[1]

There is a happy ending to this story. Through the faith of one of John's followers, the pagan priest who had been killed was raised from the dead. But, John told him, he still was not really living. Believe in Christ, the apostle urged, "and you shall live for all eternity." "And then and there he believed on the Lord Jesus, and from that time kept company with John."

Actually, that tale is a bit of pious fiction, written probably no earlier than a century after the death of John. It is found in a kind of holy novel about this "son of thunder" called the *Acts of John*. One cannot really learn from it anything about the destruction of the pagan temple at Ephesus, which certainly did not occur during John's lifetime.

What it does tell us is something of the high place that the apostle John had in early Christian tradition. It probably does preserve some memory that the apostle taught in Ephesus and had followers and disciples. It is fact that in John's name tradition was to group five books of our New Testament.

More New Testament books are attributed to John than to any other single writer except Paul. This does not mean that John, the son of Zebedee and one of the twelve apostles, actually penned them all. We have seen that Timothy and Silas assisted Paul in writing some of his letters, that 1 Peter came to us "by Silvanus," and that Hebrews was admitted to the canon in part because it was attributed to Paul, even though he probably had nothing to do with its composition. It is widely held that more than one writer was involved in the production of such varied books as Revelation, the Gospel according to John, and the three epistles of John. In all probability, we are dealing with a school of disciples that grew up around the apostle and with a tradition that grew up around his memory. As a matter of fact, none of the five works claims to be by the apostle. But it was to this great leader that the church later attributed the authority of some of its best-loved—and most puzzling—sacred books.

In this final chapter we turn to them.

REVELATION

If one had to describe certain passages from Revelation in one word, that word might well be "weird."

A great beast rises from the sea. It has ten horns and seven heads, each horn having a crown, and the beast is said to combine the characteristics of a leopard, a bear, and a lion. It is associated with a dragon and with another beast having two horns like a lamb and a voice like a dragon. A great prostitute is seated on many waters and at the same time on a dragon and also on a beast which has seven heads, each of which is seven hills! From above, a Lamb looks down—or is it a warrior on a white horse?—and prepares to conquer. Holy martyrs cry from heaven for vengeance. What is the reader to make of all this?

One solution has been to ignore or even to reject Revelation. After all, its traditional attribution to the apostle John is dubious. The book names its writer as John (Rev. 1:1, 4, 9; 22:8), but there were many men of that name. The writer nowhere calls himself an apostle but rather seems to speak of the twelve apostles with the reverence of a later Christian (21:14). As early as about A.D. 200, Bishop Dionysius of Alexandria noted that Revelation was so completely different from the Gospel according to John in style, vocabulary, and thought that the two could not possibly be by the same author. If Revelation was by the apostle, it is strange that the church was so slow in accepting it into the canon. As late as the fourth century, Eusebius wrote that there was still much dispute about the authority of Revelation. He himself was not at all sure that it was by the apostle.[2] It was one of the last books to be admitted to the canon. Martin Luther loved the Bible, but he held Revelation in low esteem. John Calvin wrote commentaries on almost every book but

REVELATION

The Apocalypse: A Symbolic Vision of Catastrophic Conflicts and the Final Victory of Christ

"Come up here, and I will show you what must take place after this" (4:1).

1:1 **Opening Vision of Christ and Letters to Seven Churches**	4:1 **A Vision of Heaven**	6:1 **The Seven Seals of the Scroll of Destiny**	8:1 **The Seven Trumpets Sounded by Angels**	11:1 **Christians Are Persecuted All over the Earth**	15:1 **Seven Bowls of Troubles Are Poured on Earth**	21:1 **The End: The New Heaven and the New Earth** 22:21
Introduction, 1:1–8	The scene around God's throne, 4	Six seals of troubles opened, 6	Six plagues fall on earth, 8—9	A "beast" battles God's witnesses, 11	Seven catastrophes, climaxed by the fall of "Babylon", 15—16	John's final vision of a transformed, perfected cosmos, 21:1–22:5
A vision of the exalted Christ, 1:9–20	The scroll of destiny being opened by the Lamb (Christ), 5	But God's people are protected, 7	But a scroll of yet further prophecy is given, 10	A "dragon" pursues a "mother" (God's people), 12	The destruction of "Babylon" (Rome), 17—18	Closing blessings and words of assurance, 22:6–21
Letters to seven churches about their particular needs, 2—3				"Beasts" of political and religious power war on God's people, 13	The conquering Christ revealed, 19	
				But the "saints" are saved, 14	The millennium and final victory over Satan accomplished, 20	

Author: "John" (traditionally the apostle, but this is not stated)
Recipients: Seven churches in what is now Turkey
Date: A.D. 96
Occasion: Widespread persecution of Christians by Rome
Purpose: To inspire Christians to endure to the end through a vision of Christ's final victory

Revelation, admitting that he did not understand it. Swiss Reformation leader Huldrych Zwingli announced, "Revelation is not a book of the Bible."

By contrast, many, including some fanatics, have found Revelation a kind of "happy hunting ground" for fanciful interpretations, professing to discover in its symbols predictions of events in their own times which showed that the end of the world was at hand. Tensions mounted all over Europe as the year A.D. 1000 approached. Surely this must be the end of "the millennium," the thousand years mentioned in Rev. 20:4! At the time of the Reformation, radical groups were sure that the prophesied end was at hand. Several denominations were born in the nineteenth century out of computations which indicated to their satisfaction that the predictions of Revelation were then taking place. Shortly before World War I, thousands were persuaded, in part on the basis of Revelation, to accept the slogan "Millions now living will never see death," convinced that Christ would return within their lifetime. The present writer remembers the evangelists of his youth who saw the approaching World War II as clearly foretold in Revelation. The number of the beast, 666 (Rev. 13:18), was "clearly" shown to be a cryptogram for the name of Benito Mussolini and later, as Mussolini became less important than his German disciple, for Adolf Hitler. Russia and Germany were Gog and Magog (20:8). Armageddon, the final battle, was at hand.

As late as 1970, Hal Lindsey's *The Late Great Planet Earth* carried on this tradition, its sales totaling more than a million copies.[3] It identified the ten horns of the beast (13:1) with the (then) ten nations of the European Common Market, which was in the news at that time. Lindsey found the People's Republic of China, which he called "the Yellow Menace," and the pan-Arab union, which the late president Gamal Abdel Nasser of Egypt was, in the sixties, attempting to form, predicted in Revelation's picture of the very last days. The "great harlot" was said by Lindsey to be the Methodist, Presbyterian, Baptist, Episcopalian, Lutheran, and other churches that form the National and World Councils of Churches. It seemed obvious to thousands of Lindsey's followers—and to followers of others of like mind—that those living in 1970 were all members of what the title of another of Lindsey's best-sellers was to call the "Terminal Generation."

How Lindsey's successors will reinterpret Revelation to show it predicting the news events of subsequent decades cannot yet be foreseen. There is a sense, however, in which all these "millenarian" interpreters have been correct. If one consults the writer of Revelation about the time schedule for his predictions, his own answer is quite clear. The very first verse of the book says that it is about things which "must soon take place" (1:1). The book ends with the promise of Christ, "Surely I am coming soon." John's readers were to live, then, as those who might encounter Christ's judgment and deliverance at any moment. His readers then, and by implication, his readers in every age who read him with faith are expected to respond, "Amen. Come, Lord Jesus!" (22:20).

To get at what John actually meant by his strange figures, however, it is essential to remember two things that we noted earlier. In chapter 1 of this *Guide,* certain principles of interpretation were laid down, and we have tried consistently to follow them. One of these was that any book must be interpreted in the light of its historical context. Revelation, like any other New Testament book, was written in a certain historical situation, to readers in that situation; knowing that occasion will help us to understand the letter. Whatever its lessons for subsequent ages, we must try first to see what it must have meant to those seven churches to which it is addressed.

Second, Revelation is a book typical of what is called "apocalyptic literature." One can trace the development of this kind of writing from Amos's warning of the coming "day of the Lord" (Amos 5:18–20) through such longer apocalyptic passages as Isaiah 24—27 and Ezekiel 38—39 to the fully developed apocalypse of the book of Daniel. Many Jewish books outside the canon also used this form. Among the characteristics of apocalyptic literature are these, all of which are found in Revelation:

It professed to be giving secret information about the coming future.

It was in a style full of symbols that only insiders might understand.

It viewed this world from the perspective of heaven, as though the author were watching events on earth from the point of view of some heavenly being.

It divided history into periods.

It predicted the blackest troubles as coming in the period just before the climax of the story.

At the climax, there would be a cosmic battle between the forces of evil and the forces of good, with God's legions triumphing.

It envisioned a great judgment day, the vindication of the righteous, and the conquest of evil.

It hinted or flatly stated that all these cataclysmic events would happen very soon.

Often the apocalypse included the promise of the messiah.

Revelation accepts this general framework and takes its figures from Daniel, Ezekiel, and other apocalyptic works. The reader, however, must look for the Christian meaning that the writer has poured into this ancient mold. It is the church that he sees persecuted, and it is Jesus Christ whom he expects to come and conquer in the end.

The writer tells us that his name is John (Rev. 1:1, 4, 9; 22:8). He makes no claim, however, to being John the apostle. Indeed, he seems to look back on the Twelve with respect (21:14). His vocabulary, thought, and style are so different from those of the Gospel according to John that they can scarcely be by the same author. If Revelation were by the apostle, it would probably not have been so long delayed in receiving acceptance into the canon.

But who the author was is of little importance in a book of this type. Had it been an account of the life of Jesus, it might matter a great deal whether it was by one of the Twelve. But it is an account of mystic visions. Such visions do not derive their authority from the one who receives them but from the One who gives them.

The Occasion of Revelation

Consistent ancient tradition dated Revelation as having been written during the persecution of the church under the emperor Domitian, thus probably A.D. 90–96.

The Roman historian Tacitus tells how, earlier, Nero had blamed Christians for the burning of Rome, which Nero himself may have started:

> Wanton cruelty marked their execution. Covered with skins of wild beasts they were torn in pieces by dogs, and thus perished; many were crucified, or burned alive, and even set on fire to serve as an illumination by night, after daylight had expired. Nero had offered his own gardens for the spectacle. . . . To glut the cruelty of one man . . . they were being destroyed.[4]

Now, thirty years later, it seemed that Nero had come to life again to persecute the church not only in Rome but all over the world. The fourth-century Christian historian Eusebius describes the persecution of the nineties in these words:

> Domitian, indeed, having exercised his cruelty against many, and unjustly slain no small number of noble and illustrious men at Rome, and having, without cause, punished vast numbers of honorable men with exile and the confiscation of their property, at length established himself as the successor of Nero, in his hatred and hostility to God. He was the second that raised a persecution against us. . . . In this persecution, it is handed down by tradition, that the apostle and evangelist John, who was yet living, in consequence of his testimony to the divine word, was condemned to dwell on the island of Patmos. . . . Tertullian also has mentioned Domitian thus: "Domitian . . . was, in fact, a limb of Nero for cruelty."[5]

For entertainment, Domitian used to spend hours sticking sharp points through the bodies of flies! He murdered friends and even relatives. It did seem that Nero had come again, worse than ever.

John writes that "the devil is about to throw some of you into prison" (2:10). He writes of those "who have come out of the great ordeal" (7:14). The "great harlot," "Babylon" (seated on seven hills and hence surely standing for Rome, the city set on seven hills), is "drunk with the blood of the saints and the blood of the witnesses to Jesus" (17:6). He sees "the souls of those who had been beheaded for their testimony to Jesus and for the word of God. They had not worshiped the beast or its image" (20:4). John is obviously writing in a time of terrible persecution.

The reason for this martyrdom is indicated in the verse just quoted. Beastly Rome had now demanded not only obedience, which Christians had always carefully given, but worship of the emperor. The cult of emperor worship had been growing. But it reached its climax with Domitian, who attempted to enforce it throughout the empire. He decreed that all his official proclamations should begin, "Our lord and god orders this to be done." Shrines were set up, some of them in the cities to whose churches Revelation was addressed. The persecution was more active than some later attacks.

Among those arrested, apparently, was the author of Revelation. "I, John, your brother who share with you in Jesus the persecution and the kingdom and the patient endurance, was on the island called Patmos because of the word of God and the testimony of Jesus," he begins (1:9). Tourists are still shown the traditional site of this preacher's island prison.

The Purpose of Revelation

"Be faithful until death, and I will give you the crown of life" (2:10). "To the one who conquers I will give a place with me on my throne" (3:21). Over and over, in the letters to the seven churches, the risen Christ makes some promise of this kind for persecuted Christians (cf. 2:7, 17, 26; 3:5, 12).

John writes to help his readers view the persecution they face from the perspective of heaven. He writes to help them see it from the perspective of the One who can say, "I am the Alpha and the Omega, the beginning and the end" (21:6; cf. 1:8; 22:13). He writes to help them see it from the perspective of followers of the One who was himself martyred but who has now risen to glory.

He wrote in this strange, figurative, apocalyptic style because it was familiar to his readers. But it may be that he used it partly because it was a kind of code, which would have attracted less attention from Roman police. To predict with joy the downfall of Rome would have been treason. To speak of the destruction of a "beast" or "Babylon" might have seemed harmless enough to a confused Roman censor. There is a story of a letter sent to a former missionary from Christians in Communist China, in the days of persecution soon after the revolution there. The letter consisted of a recital of the Marxist teachings against religion. But it ended with one word that slipped by the censors: "Emmanuel," which means "God is with us" (Matt. 1:23). This is the spirit of Revelation. The book is written as a kind of secret, coded word of encouragement to Christians who may soon be going to die for their faith rather than worship the emperor.

Some Comments on Revelation

From the first chapter, the author warns us that we are to take his words not literally but as symbols. He reports a vision of the risen Christ in all his majesty, but this is not a portrait of the actual physical appearance of the human Jesus of Nazareth. Little children would hardly be attracted to this figure with a sword protruding from his mouth (contrast Mark 10:14). It is carefully explained that the seven lampstands are symbols of the seven churches to whom the letter is addressed (1:20), and much of the other symbolism is clear. Christ's eyes are like flames, penetrating everything. The feet are like brass, in contrast to the image of this world's empires, which are described in Daniel as having feet of clay (Dan. 2:33), a foundation sure to collapse. Most important, this cosmic Christ stands among the churches and holds their guardian angels in the hollow of his hand (Rev. 1:12–20).

There follow seven quite straightforward letters to the seven individual churches to which the book is addressed. Though they may be representative of the whole church, these are real churches in real communities, and the letters deal with their real problems. The very popular *Scofield Reference Bible,* many of whose notes have been found helpful by thousands of users since its publication in 1917, proposes that these letters are to be interpreted in three ways. They are, as stated above, letters to these particular churches for their time. They are also of value to all churches in all ages. Christians have discovered this in their own experience. But C. I. Scofield, editor of the reference Bible, also maintained that each of these letters referred to the church in a given period of history. Thyatira, for example, is said to stand for the medieval church, dated from A.D. 500 to A.D. 1500. Sardis, according to Scofield, is the Reformation church. We are now in the Laodicean age, the age of apostasy.[6] There is not one shred of evidence in scripture for this last scheme, which is entirely imposed on the Bible by the imagination of Scofield. This view, however, has been widely circulated as though it were scriptural. Rather, each letter in Revelation 2—3 is to a clearly identifiable church in what is now Turkey, encouraging it in the midst of persecution at the time the letter was written.

In Revelation 4, the writer is summoned to look at the world scene from the perspective of heaven. Again, there is no biblical evidence that the writer here has in mind a "rapture" in which all Christians are caught up into heaven, as Scofield proposed. It is the writer himself who, from his prison, is given a vision of heaven. He sees God seated on the heavenly throne, described in imagery derived in large part from the Jewish scriptures. Precious stones and symbolic animals indicate that all creation praises the Creator, and twenty-four elders, the representatives of the church, sing his praises. The rainbow (4:3) around the throne is the reminder of the covenant (Gen. 9:12–13).

Revelation 5 centers on one other symbolic animal, the Lamb, who is, of course, Jesus Christ (John 1:29). Only he can open the seals of the scroll on which is written the destiny of the world.

As the seals in turn are opened, the writer gazes down from heaven on the catastrophes that now befall the earth. When the first astronauts landed on the moon, the most fascinating pictures that they took were not those of the barren moonscape; they were pictures of earth, seen from that transcendent perspective. So now Revelation describes in vivid imagery a succession of terrible times coming upon the earth. But it does so from the new vantage point of heaven.

These are described, as the outline shows (p. 505), in terms of seven seals, the seventh of which turns into seven trumpets, the last of which introduces seven bowls. Each seems to present troubles worse than its predecessor. It would seem to be a mistake to try to take these literally. John is an artist who, with his series of sevens (a holy number to the Jews), paints a growing picture of spreading chaos.

For example, the four horsemen of the apocalypse (Rev. 6:1–8) seem to stand for conquest, war, famine, and death, a hellish sequence that has recurred in every age. Typically, however, the fifth seal shows the martyrs safe beneath the throne of God (6:9–11). Nature itself begins to fall apart with the sixth seal (6:12–17), but once again, we are assured of the salvation of those whom God has "sealed" (chap. 7). "And God will wipe away every tear from their eyes" (7:17).

Again, it would be to miss the biblical symbolism if one were to take literally the number "one hundred forty-four thousand"—twelve times twelve thousand (7:4). Twelve is the number of completion in Hebrew poetry, and as such, it is used repeatedly in Revelation (12:1; 21:12; 22:2, for example).

Chapters 8 through 10 repeat the same kind of scene, with the seven trumpets heralding troubles even more intense than those of the seals. Yet these horrors at their worst last only "forty-two months" (11:2), only half of "seven" years, the period of perfection on God's timetable.

In chapters 12 through 15, the sequence of seals, trumpets, and bowls seems to be interrupted while we are introduced to strange creatures, which appear to symbolize very real dangers that John's readers were encountering. The creatures harass "a woman clothed with the sun" (12:1), who gives birth to a child. Apparently, she stands for the people of God, the Jews, from whom Christ was born, and the church, pursued through the "wilderness" of this world.

One pursuer is a red dragon, clearly identified as the devil or Satan (12:3, 9). In league with him is "a beast rising out of the sea, having ten horns and seven heads" (13:1), who receives authority on earth from the beast (Satan). Apparently, this is the Roman Empire, because in 17:9–10 we are told clearly that what is represented here is a series of kings. Domitian was, in fact, the seventh emperor ("head") of the Roman Empire to establish any permanent reign. The ten horns are also kings, the reason apparently being that, after the reign of Nero, there were three rulers whose reigns were so brief that they are here regarded as only "horns," not "heads." Note that all have crowns to show that they stand for kings (13:1). "One of its heads seemed to have received a death-blow, but its mortal wound had been healed" (13:3). This apparently refers to the idea of the return of Nero, feared in popular thought, much as after World War II it was rumored that Hitler was not dead and would someday return. In a sense, Domitian, as we have seen, could himself be regarded as a kind of reincarnation of Nero.

Yet a third beastly creature appears in 13:11, making all the earth worship the beast from the sea. This would appear to be a reference to the agency of the emperor-worship cult, now seeking to force every resident of the empire as a patriotic duty to worship Caesar as "lord and god." Marvelous ingenuity has been exercised through the centuries to identify this beast, who has the cryptic number 666 (13:18). The most likely explanation is that the letters of the name Neron, given their value as numbers—Romans did not use arabic digits in those days—add up to 666. If one takes the other form of the name, Nero, the total is 616, a number found in some manuscripts instead of 666.

In spite of these threats, chapter 14 again gives assurance of the superior power of divine protection for God's people.

Seven bowls now shower seven plagues on this world (chaps. 15—16). With the sixth we are prepared for the great final conflict between God and the forces of Satan. "Harmagedon" (16:16) apparently refers to the area of Megiddo, where many of the great battles of Hebrew history were fought. That bloody plain was far more a symbol to the Jews than Gettysburg is to Americans or Waterloo to Europeans. The concept of a final conflict is standard in apocalyptic literature.

As the forces assemble, we meet the "great whore" (17:1), cryptically but clearly identified by the fact that she sits on seven hills (17:9). Rome was known as the city on seven hills. Thus we find arrayed against the church the Roman Empire, the emperor-worship cult, and now the city of Rome itself.

Yet already (chapter 18) an angel sings a taunting song of victory over this "Babylon." Babylon was the imperial city that was the oppressor of God's people in the Old Testament; it is here a symbol for Rome in the New Testament. "Fallen, fallen is Babylon the great!" (18:2).

A final horseman appears in 19:11–16, this one being Jesus Christ himself. Under his leadership, Satan and all his hosts are thrown into hell (19:20). The victory is won!

Perhaps the most debated chapter in the Bible is Revelation 20. Early in church history, some forms of "chiliasm" or "millenarianism," taking this chapter literally, were branded as heresy. Throughout history, however, many devout and scholarly Christians have continued to take it quite literally. They have expected Christ to come to earth; help lead a big physical battle in which Satan is defeated; and then set up an actual kingdom on this material earth, with Jerusalem as its capital city, for a period of exactly one thousand years. "Millennium" means one thousand years, and those who expect the coming of Christ before such a thousand-year period on earth are often called "premillennialists." After the one-thousand-year period, Satan, they say, is to be released briefly. Then the devil will be defeated again, and there will be the final judgment and the new heaven and the new earth.

Since the days of Augustine, most Christians have understood this chapter figuratively. Satan was "bound" with the first coming of Christ, and the "thousand years" of Christ on this earth, according to this view, is the period of the church, his kingdom on earth here and now. In the end, it will be replaced by the transcendent new heaven and new earth.

What was in John's mind may be more near to the following: Hebrew eschatology sometimes pictured the reign of the messiah as on this earth, sometimes as completely transcending this domain of space and time. John has combined these two views. Before anything else, there is a special reward for the martyrs. Their outstanding devotion gives them a thousand years of reign on earth with Christ, before believers who have not had to pay such a price receive their reward. It is to be noted that the thousand years of ruling with Christ is limited to "those who had been beheaded for their testimony to Jesus and for the word of God. They had not worshiped the beast" (20:4). Probably all that is meant here is a beautiful way of saying to those who are suffering most that they will have their special reward. To take Revelation literally here, when its figurative character is so clear elsewhere, is to be inconsistent in one's interpretation.

One must also emphasize that the millennium is not mentioned anywhere else in scripture and therefore should not be made central to one's doctrine, however it is interpreted.

The final scene in Revelation (chaps. 21—22) is an artistic picture of the new heaven and the new earth. The church, the new Jerusalem, is depicted as the bride of Christ, as Israel was the Lord's "bride" in the Old Testament (Jer. 31:32) and as Paul had spoken of the church (Eph. 5:21–33). Twelve, the number of completion and perfection, abounds in the description of the city. All now, at last, is peace and glory.

There is one final note concerning the style of Revelation, which is of great importance for understanding the book: Revelation is full of songs. A glance through it in any modern translation will show many lines printed as poetry. The heavenly court around the throne is pictured as singing, "Holy, holy, holy" (Rev. 4:8). From that point on, we find song after song.

Donald George Miller used to tell his classes of a student who complained, "I don't understand Revelation, but every time I read it, I feel like singing." "That is understanding it!" was the reply.

Thus it is not surprising that the classic commentary on Revelation is not a book but part of an oratorio. George Frideric Handel set to music verses from Revelation to produce his "Hallelujah" chorus:

> Hallelujah! For the Lord God omnipotent reigneth.
> The kingdom of this world is become
> The kingdom of our Lord, and of his Christ,
> And he shall reign for ever and ever.
> King of kings, and Lord of lords,
> Hallelujah! (cf. Rev. 19:6; 11:15; 19:16.)

1 JOHN

According to tradition, James was so far removed from the pleasures of this world that he never took a bath. By contrast, we are told that John did bathe. Once, according to Eusebius, John jumped from the bath and ran shouting into the street. The heretic Cerinthus had entered the bathhouse, and John feared that at any moment the roof might fall in judgment on that teacher of false doctrine.[7]

It is not necessary to take that story as historical fact to recognize the truth it dramatized. First John was written to help its readers distinguish between true and false versions of the Christian faith. It is a warning against Gnostic heresy, of which Cerinthus was one teacher.

The letter is anonymous. Tradition ascribes it to John the apostle and the son of Zebedee. The letter is so similar in thought and language to the Fourth Gospel that it must be either by the same author or at least by someone of the same "Johannine school." There are hints, however, that the epistle, with its strong effort to combat Gnosticism, is in part endeavoring to correct misunderstandings that sprang from the Fourth Gospel's repeated use of Gnostic-like words and concepts.[8]

Regardless of who wrote 1 John, the view of many scholars, summarized by D. Moody Smith, is that the epistles join with the Fourth Gospel to present "the capstone of theological and ethical thought within the New Testament."[9]

The Occasion of 1 John

"Now many antichrists have come," the author writes. "They went out from us, but they did not belong to us" (1 John 2:18–19). Evidently, these "antichrists" who have split off from the church are false teachers. "Many false prophets have gone out into the world." (4:1).

Something of what these false teachers taught can be inferred from what seem to be quotations from them scattered through the letter. Apparently, they claimed to "have fellowship" with God (1:6), to "have no sin" (1:8; cf. 1:10), to "know" God in some special way (2:4), to be "in the light" (2:9), and to "love God" (4:20). Evidently, they claimed perfection, piety, and the

1 JOHN
Love: The Test of True Christianity

"We know that we have passed from death to life because we love one another" (3:14).

1:1 **A Brief Written Summary of the True Christian Message**	2:18 **A Warning against the Teachers of a False Message**	3:1 **The Life of Love for All Abiding in the True Fellowship of the Family of God**	4:1 **How to Tell the Truth from False Doctrine** 5:21
Prologue—the basis of that message: the incarnation in the real man Jesus, 1:1–4	Heretics have split off from the fellowship, 2:18–25	God accepts us as his children, 3:1–3	The doctrinal test: true Christians confess that Jesus Christ has come in the flesh, 4:1–6
Our need for the message: we are all sinners, 1:5–10	A plea that the readers will remain in the fellowship and in true Christianity, 2:26–29	Children of God are characterized by right living, 3:4–10	The test of love: those born into God's family as his children love their brothers, 4:7–21
The good news of the message: Jesus Christ saves us from sin, 2:1–2		The essence of right living is love, 3:11–18	The victory God gives his children through faith, 5:1–5
The proper response to the message: obedience, love, and the rejection of worldliness, 2:3–17		Living as God's children, we pray with confidence in our Father, seek to please God through love, and have God's Spirit in us, 3:19–24	The guarantees of the true faith: the experience of the Spirit, the pledge of baptism, and the fact of Jesus' death, 5:6–12
			Postscript repeating some themes, 5:13–21

Author: Unnamed (according to tradition, John)
Recipients: Christians who may be tempted by these false teachings
Date: ca. A.D. 100?
Occasion: False teachers have caused a split in the church (2:19).
Purpose: To guide the readers to continue in the true faith, which is manifested in love (2:26)

enlightenment of divine knowledge. Yet they showed little concern for their brothers in the Christian fellowship (2:9; 3:14–15; 4:20–21; etc.) and had now abandoned them (2:18–19). The writer regards them, in spite of their boasted "knowledge," as living sinful lives (2:4, 19; 3:8–10, for example).

The Christology (the doctrine concerning who Jesus Christ is) of these false teachers was heretical too. "Who is the liar but the one who denies that Jesus is the Christ?" (2:22), our writer demands bluntly. Probably these teachers professed to believe in "Christ," but they did not want to identify "Christ" with the man "Jesus." According to the ancient scholar Irenaeus, Cerinthus

> represented Jesus as having not been born of a virgin, but as being the son of Joseph and Mary according to the ordinary course of human generation. . . . Moreover, after his baptism, Christ descended upon him in the form of a dove from the Supreme Ruler, and that then he proclaimed the unknown Father, and performed miracles. But at last Christ departed from Jesus, and that then Jesus suffered and rose again, while Christ remained impassible, inasmuch as he was a spiritual being.[10]

Believing that the physical was evil, these "enlightened" and "spiritual-minded" Gnostics denied a genuine incarnation, the belief that in Jesus the Christ had really died for us. Later, the term "Docetists" (from the Greek word *dokein*, "to seem") was applied to heretics who proposed that Christ only *seemed* to be a real man. If it is not the heresy of Cerinthus specifically, it is at least this general kind of error that John is attacking.

The Purpose of First John

"I write these things to you concerning those who would deceive you," the author tells his readers (2:26). His repeatedly expressed concern is to provide tests by which the Christian may distinguish true knowledge (*gnosis*) from its false imitation. "By this we know," he writes over and over, in one form or another (see 2:5; 3:10, 14, 16, 19; 4:2, 13; 5:2; etc.). The Greek word *ginoskein* ("to know") occurs twenty-five times in 1 John, and the similar word *oida* occurs fifteen times. Seventeen times the letter says "we know," and twelve times the readers are assured that "you know."

John's concern, however, in contrast to that of the Gnostics, is not just intellectual. "My little children, I am writing these things to you so that you may not sin" (2:1). He knows that the life of love ranks with sound doctrine among the tests of true Christianity. Over and over, he points his readers to these two tests: a true belief in Jesus and a life of obedience to God through love for one's brothers and sisters.[11]

Some Comments on 1 John

Commentators agree on only one thing about outlining 1 John: the task is impossible. Over and over, the author repeats his major themes, saying the same thing in new ways. The figure of a spiral has often been used to describe the structure of the letter. It goes around and around, yet it rises as it repeats. The outline given in this section (p. 515) may be useful, however, for pointing to some main ideas of the epistle.

It begins with a prologue much like that of the Gospel according to John 1:1–18. The basis of the true Christian message is the genuine incarnation, the material, physical fact of the real human Jesus. "What we have seen with our eyes . . . and touched with our hands . . . we declare to you" (1 John 1:1–3). A later Gnostic work, by contrast, falsely depicted John as saying that sometimes when he touched Christ, his hand could pass through Christ's body as if it were not really there. The author of 1 John will have nothing to do with such Gnostic contempt for the material world. His down-to-earth gospel rests, he begins, on historical fact. William Temple, late archbishop of Canterbury, is said to have called Christianity "the most materialistic religion in the world."

The problem we face, as 1 John presents it, is not matter, and it is not ignorance. It is sin. In 1 John, "light," a favorite word of the Gnostics, is not the "enlightenment" of knowledge of which they boasted. To "walk in the light" is not to know something but to be something, to live in a certain way. Though the Gnostics may have boasted that they had achieved perfection, 1 John 1:5–10 realistically protests that we all walk in darkness because we all sin.

Jesus Christ saves us from sin. The proper response to that salvation is to seek to avoid further sinning (2:1–17). The readers of this letter have no need for some additional, special "knowledge." Knowing the gospel message, they already know the truth (2:21).

Set over against that basic Christian "message" (1:5) is the teaching against which this letter is written (2:18–29). Throughout the letter, tests are given for distinguishing true Christianity from false. "Test the spirits," the readers are urged (4:1).

One test is doctrinal. "By this you know the Spirit of God: every spirit that confesses that Jesus Christ has come in the flesh is from God" (4:2). Gnostics would be horrified at that use of the word "flesh" (cf. 2:23; 4:15; 5:1, 12).

A second test is righteous living. And "by this we may be sure that we know him [have real *gnosis*], if we obey his commandments" (2:3; cf. 3:10, 24; 5:3; etc.).

The most important commandment is the commandment to love. "We know that we have passed from death to life because we love one another" (3:14; cf. 2:10–11; 3:23; 4:7, 16, 20–21). That verse is probably the best summary of the message of this letter. Any claim to Christianity that does not manifest itself in active concern for others is a lie (4:20).

That love has its roots in the very nature of God. "God is light" (1:5), as the Gnostics knew. But "God is love" (4:8, 16). That is a distinctly Christian description of the character of God.

Indeed, the author of this little book, in showing the difference between true Christianity and its Gnostic perversion, has shown the basic difference between Christianity and all other religions. In many ways, Christianity is much like Hinduism, Buddhism, and Islam, but there are at least two points at which Christianity is unique. First, Christianity takes love as its ultimate concern. It announces that God's self is love, and it summarizes its ethical demand in response to that God in one word: love. Second, Christianity proclaims the real, historic person Jesus as the incarnation of that God of love and is centered on him.

Thus 1 John can summarize much of Christianity in one very brief sentence: "We love because he first loved us" (4:19).

2 JOHN

John was a frail old man, says the legend told by Jerome, but he was still loved by his congregation at Ephesus. Eventually, they had to carry him to the church services. Repeatedly, they would ask him to preach, but he would only reply, "Little children, let us love one another."

"Tell us more," they would beg him. Would he not tell them other things about the Lord?

"Little children, let us love one another," he would simply repeat. "That is his commandment; it is enough."

"I ask you, not as though I were writing you a new commandment, but one we have had from the beginning, let us love one another" (2 John v. 5). This is the heart of the little letter called 2 John. The command is not new, indeed, being a repeated theme of 1 John and of the Fourth Gospel (cf. 1 John 3:23; 4:7, 21; John 15:12; etc.).

In fact, the second letter of John seems to be largely a brief summary of the first. Again, there is encouragement for true belief (2 John v. 4; cf. 1 John 2:21–23). There is again a warning against false teachers, "deceivers" who "have gone out into the world, those who do not confess that Jesus Christ has come in the flesh" (2 John v. 7; cf. 1 John 4:2). Apparently, these are the same "Docetic" heretics denounced in 1 John 2:18–27. The writer's hope is that his readers will "abide" in the true faith (2 John v. 9; cf. 1 John 2:27–28; 3:24; 4:15).

It may be pleasant to imagine that the letter is written by "the elder" (2 John v. 1) to his wife. Almost certainly, however, "the elect lady" (v. 1) is a beautiful figure for some particular church beloved by "the elder." The last verse gives greetings from the "children" of the elect lady's "sister," almost certainly meaning the members of one congregation greeting another. The church is becoming a worldwide "family."

Who was this "elder"? Eusebius quotes from Papias's mention of one "John the Presbyter," a second, respected leader of the church at Ephesus, a younger contemporary of the apostle John.[12] Third John is also attributed to "the elder." Perhaps this man was the author of all three epistles and even of the Gospel according to John. The letters themselves, however, do not name their writer, and we cannot with any assurance do so either.

Verses 10 and 11 touch on what became a problem in the church in the second century, hospitality for itinerant evangelists and teachers. For light on that problem, we must turn to 3 John.

3 JOHN

Paul was not the last Christian teacher to go from city to city, needing some place to stay in each town. By the middle of the second century, hospitality for such traveling evangelists had become a problem. Some were apparently a nuisance, overstaying their welcome. And how were true teachers, worthy of free room and board, to be recognized?

In *The Teaching of the Twelve Apostles,* often called the *Didache,* a manual on church order written in that period, we read:

> Everyone "who comes" to you "in the name of the Lord" must be welcomed. Afterward, when you have tested him, you will find out about him, for you have insight into right and wrong. If it is a traveler who arrives, help him all you can. But he must not stay with you more than two days, or if necessary, three. If he wants to settle with you and is an artisan, he must work for his living. If, however, he has no trade, use your judgment in taking steps for him to live with you as a Christian without being idle. If he refuses to do this, he is trading on Christ. You must be on your guard against such people.[13]

Third John deals with a related problem. In this little letter, "the elder" writes to his friend, Gaius, a respected leader in some church, apparently asking him to provide hospitality for a traveling teacher, Demetrius. (Perhaps Demetrius carried this note as a letter of introduction.) Someone else in the church, by contrast, a man named Diotrephes, "who likes to put himself first" (3 John v. 9), has refused to receive such teachers when they come from "the elder." He has even excommunicated those who have entertained these travelers, has refused to accept the elder's authority, and apparently may ignore a letter—1 or 2 John?—sent to the church (v. 9). The elder expects a confrontation with the rebellious Diotrephes soon (v. 10). (We know nothing of Diotrephes except from this letter.)

Because, like 2 John, the letter is written by "the elder," and because its ending is so nearly identical to that of 2 John (vv. 13–15; cf. 2 John vv. 12–13), it seems likely that 2 and 3 John are by the same author. Perhaps 1 or 2 John is the letter mentioned in verse 9, and Demetrius carried it to the congregation along with 3 John, his letter of recommendation to the loyal Gaius.

However, there is a contrast between 2 and 3 John. In 2 John, the elder warns against showing hospitality to false teachers. In 3 John, Diotrephes has had the elder's own representative turned away as a false teacher. Rudolf Bultmann has even raised the question as to whether the author of 3 John may have been regarded as a Gnostic heretic and therefore excluded by the orthodox Diotrephes.[14] We wish we had Diotrephes's response.

First John seems to have been accepted into the canon without dispute. But 2 and 3 John were disputed into the fourth century. Perhaps this was because they were written late, because they were so brief, because 2 John seemed to repeat parts of 1 John, and because 3 John dealt mostly with individuals unknown outside one particular congregation. Perhaps it was because there was uncertainty as to whether they really were—as was later believed—by John the apostle. We turn now to the most important of the Johannine books, the Fourth Gospel, and the complex question of its authorship.

THE GOSPEL ACCORDING TO JOHN

James Sprunt once wrote, "The Gospel according to John has been translated into more languages, read by more people, beloved by more readers, carried by more Christians, and used of God for more good than any other piece of literature in the history of the world."[15]

Probably it has also been the most debated.

Some Contrasts between John and the Synoptics

The biggest cause of debate about John is that it is so different from the Synoptics, the other three Gospels.[16]

True, the story as John tells it is essentially the same as that found in Mark. In both, that story begins with John the Baptist. It tells how Jesus called the disciples, healed, fed the five thousand, even walked on water, taught in such a way as to win the intense love of some and the undying hatred of others, rode at last into Jerusalem on a donkey at the Passover season, met on the last night with his disciples, was arrested, was condemned by both Jewish and Roman authorities, and died on a Roman cross. It describes his triumphant resurrection. And this story of Jesus is interpreted as the story of the Son of God.

Mark and John are so similar, even in wording and details, that some—though not most—scholars believe that the author of John had read Mark before he wrote his Gospel.

There are, however, differences between John and the Synoptics as well as similarities. Charles H. Talbert, in his 1992 commentary *Reading John,* summarizes John's "plot" as the story of

> One who came as a revealing, empowering, presence; who picked/produced a
> new community and provided them and others during his public ministry with

THE GOSPEL ACCORDING TO JOHN
The Spiritual Gospel

"I am the way, and the truth, and the life" (14:6)

1:1 Introduction	2:1 Seven Signs	and Their Meanings	12:1 Last Entry, Last Supper	18:1 The Cross and the Resurrection	21:25
Prologue, 1:1–18		Christ transforms, changing the Temple (2:12–25), giving new birth (3:1–21); transforming "water" (3:22–4:54)	Entry into Jerusalem and coming of the Greeks to Christ, 12	Arrest and trials, 18	
The witness of John the Baptizer and his disciples, 1:19–51	1. Water changed to wine, 2:1–11		Jesus washes his disciples' feet, 13	Crucifixion, 19	
	2. A son healed,	Christ is the Son of God, carrying on his Father's work, 5:10–47	He promises to return but also to send the Spirit, 14	Resurrection, 20	
	3. and a lame man healed on the day of rest, 4:46–5:9		The vine and the branches, 15	Epilogue, 21	
	4. Five thousand fed bread, and	Christ is the bread of life, 6:22–71	The Spirit will guide, 16		
	5. Christ walks on water, 6:1–21		Christ's high-priestly prayer, 17		
	6. Christ heals a blind man, 9:1–41	Christ is the light of the world, 7–10			
	7. Christ raises Lazarus, 11	Christ if the resurrection and the life, 11			

Author: Unnamed (traditionally the apostle John, more likely disciples of John)

Recipients: Unnamed, apparently all seeking greater faith

Date: Probably A.D. 90–100

Occasion: No special occasion is stated. Probably some conflicts between church and synagogue are reflected.

Purpose: "That you may come to believe that Jesus is the Messiah, the Son of God, and . . . have life" (20:31)

warrants for a different kind of worship; who privately predicted what their future would be like, offering promise, parenesis [ethical instruction], and prayer for that time; and who ultimately made provision for their future community life, worship, and ministry before he returned to whence he had come.[17]

This is probably not how one would describe the "plot" of Mark.

Moreover, there are particular differences in the narrative itself. Some can be partially explained, as we shall see, by John's special purposes and method in writing. Some of these differences we may never understand. Here are a few of the contrasts:

1. There is a difference in the location of the events reported. Almost all of Jesus' ministry appears in the other three Gospels to have taken place in Galilee. John concentrates on Jesus' teachings in Jerusalem at the time of the great feasts, as they are celebrated there. (It is not unlikely, by the way, that John is here helpfully giving us new, factual information, since as a devout Jew, Jesus surely must have participated in such festivals. Indeed, the Synoptics hint that he did so frequently but give us no details [see Matt. 23:37].)

2. In John, the form in which Jesus' teachings are reported is quite different. In Matt. 13:34, we are told that "without a parable he told them nothing." Over and over, the Synoptics report stories such as the prodigal son, the Good Samaritan, or the parable of the soils. In John, Jesus does use figures of speech, but there are no parables at all, no stories, at least none comparable to those of the Synoptics. Jesus' sayings are preserved in the Synoptics typically in brief, often rather witty couplets: "Those who are well have no need of a physician, but those who are sick" (Mark 2:17). "The sabbath was made for humankind, and not humankind for the sabbath" (Mark 2:27). In John, Jesus seems often to speak in long monologues or to engage in debates with his enemies.

3. In the three Synoptic Gospels, the heart of Jesus' message is "the kingdom of God has come near" (Mark 1:15). Almost every parable is about the kingdom. The Sermon on the Mount describes its citizens. The disciples are sent out to proclaim it. In John, the phrase "the kingdom of God" appears only twice (John 3:3, 5).

4. The first three Gospels conclude their accounts of Jesus' teachings with the record of a discourse by Jesus on the coming of the Son of man at the end of the world for the last judgment (Matt. 24—25; Mark 13; Luke 21). The last teachings of Jesus reported in John also look forward to a coming, but it is the coming of the Holy Spirit to be continually present with the disciples (John 14:26; 15:26; 16:7; etc.). The more conven-

tional eschatological hope is not abandoned in John, though a few scholars propose that references to it are insertions by later, more "orthodox" editors (see John 5:27–29; 6:39–40, 44, 54; 12:48; 14:3). But the emphasis in John is on what C. H. Dodd has called "realized eschatology." We saw that 2 Peter had to deal with scoffers disillusioned because the promised coming of the glorious end of time still had not occurred, years and years after Jesus' death and resurrection. John's answer, in effect, is to say, Look! What is there that you have hoped for and have not already received in the coming of Christ and the Holy Spirit? We now already have resurrection (John 11:24–25), judgment (12:31), and eternal life (5:24; 17:3). And he depicts Jesus himself as preaching this kind of eschatology.

5. In the Fourth Gospel, Jesus seems to have been recognized as the Son of God right from the beginning of his ministry (John 1:49), at least by his disciples. In the other Gospels, while the devils know who Jesus is (Mark 1:24), others seem only gradually to come to an understanding of his nature. Peter's great confession that Jesus is the Christ produces a crisis and turning point in the story.

6. The greatest contrast of all, however, and the one that is by far the most difficult to explain, is that in John, Jesus appears from the very first quite openly and publicly to proclaim that he is the Christ, the Son of God, and to teach at length concerning his own nature and his relationship to the Father (John 1:51; 4:26; 5:19). Quite openly he announces himself to be the Son of God (5:19–46), who existed before the birth of Abraham (8:58), and announces to everyone such sayings as "I am the bread of life" (6:48), "I am the good shepherd" (10:11), and "I am the light of the world" (8:12). How one explains "the messianic secret" of the Synoptics may be debated, but all explanations seem to agree emphatically that Jesus of Nazareth did not go around publicly preaching about himself in this way. Rather, he is said in the Synoptics to have forbidden people to spread the news that he was the Messiah and to have concentrated his message on the kingdom. In John, however, Jesus publicly and repeatedly demands belief that he is the Son of God and does his miracles in order to win that kind of faith. His words are not about the kingdom but about himself.

"John or the Synoptics—you can believe one or the other, but you can't possibly believe both!" So, on the basis of the contrasts listed above (and a number of others, some of which will be noted subsequently), certain critics have been arguing for a century. There simply is no easy answer to this challenge. Some partial solution to the problems raised by these contrasts can be found, however, by noting the special purposes for which John wrote.

The Purpose of John in Relation
to the Synoptics

Soon after the year A.D. 200, a Christian professor in Alexandria, Clement, noting the contrast between John and the Synoptics, undertook to explain it in this way: "John, last of all, perceiving that what had reference to the body in the gospel of our Savior, was sufficiently detailed, and being encouraged by his familiar friends, and urged by the spirit, he wrote a spiritual gospel."[18] Apparently, the relationship this ancient professor recognized was this: John believed that the other Gospels had adequately recorded the "bodily," observable facts. He now wrote to give the "spiritual" meaning of those facts.

To illustrate: What happened on July 4, 1776, and the days immediately following? A chemist might reply that ink of a certain chemical composition adhered to a piece of paper of a certain material structure. He would be right, of course. A historian would say that the Declaration of Independence was adopted and might debate about the day on which it was signed. He, too, would be correct. But Abraham Lincoln would reply to our question in this way: "Fourscore and seven years ago our fathers brought forth on this continent a new nation, conceived in liberty, and dedicated to the proposition that all men are created equal." It did not matter to Lincoln that on July 4 there was not literally a "conception" or a "birth" or a "dedication." He was not interested, for the purposes of his Gettysburg Address, in whether or not the Declaration was adopted and signed on the same day. He was describing the "spiritual" meaning, the abiding significance, of the great events of the past. He was telling us the truth, the profound truth, of that bit of history as we have come to know it in our lives over the decades.

John, like Lincoln, seeks to tell the abiding "spiritual" significance of the events of the past, to show in the ancient stories meanings that he believes the risen Christ has now made clear through the Spirit.

For example, the other three Gospels had told the story of how Jesus fed the five thousand. John tells it too. But it is John who now, perhaps sixty or seventy years later, hears in that story what Christ is saying through it: "I am the bread of life" (John 6:48).

Again, Luke retold the parable of the lost sheep, setting it in what seems a most natural context, as Jesus' defense to the Pharisees of his associating with outcasts (Luke 15:1–7). Matthew retold the same story, but he included with it sayings that helped make it applicable to the later problem of how to deal with a straying church member (Matt. 18:10–18). John can assume that his readers already know the parable; he does not tell it again. But many years later he hears, with the help of the Spirit, what Christ is eternally saying in that parable: "I am the good shepherd" (John 10:11).

It is important, of course, not to exaggerate the difference in purpose between John and the Synoptics. The Synoptics, too, are theological interpretations of the meaning of Jesus for us. Mark, first to be written and perhaps closest to the memory of the "bodily" facts of Jesus' life, was written to present his Lord as "Jesus Christ, the Son of God" (Mark 1:1). (See the section on "The Gospel according to Mark" in chapter 6 of this *Guide* for a description of some of the theological points that Mark was making as he wrote his Gospel.) And it must be noted that John is also interested in "bodily" facts.

Nevertheless, there is a difference in emphasis. John makes much better sense in relation to the Synoptics when one keeps in mind the difference in purpose. Compare Luke 1:1–4 with John's statement of purpose in John 20:30–31, and both similarity and difference of aim appear.

To John's statement of purpose we must turn now.

The Stated Purpose of the Gospel according to John

Now Jesus did many other signs in the presence of his disciples, which are not written in this book. But these are written that you may come to believe that Jesus is the Messiah, the Son of God, and that through believing you may have life in his name. (John 20:30–31)

So John himself summarizes his purpose. Several words and phrases are of special importance in this statement.

First, John tells us that he has carefully selected what he has told. No doubt he knows many more stories, those of Jesus' ministry in Galilee, for example, which, perhaps because they have been told by others, he does not repeat. Indeed, with considerable hyperbole, we are told in the last verse of the book, "But there are also many other things that Jesus did; if every one of them were written down, I suppose that the world itself could not contain the books that would be written" (21:25). From a great body of material, John has selected only what best suits his particular aim.

Second, what he has chosen to tell us are what he calls "signs." A sign is something that points beyond itself to what it signifies. John 2—11 is often called the "Book of Signs." Of Jesus' many miracles, John has chosen to describe only seven (see the outline on p. 521). But each miracle is interpreted as a sign, its significance being presented in a long meditation related to it. Thus, for example, in John 9, Jesus gives sight to a blind man. This is related to the truth that Jesus is "the light of the world" (John 8:12; 9:5). And in John 11, Jesus raises Lazarus from the dead. The meaning seen in this sign is that Jesus is the "resurrection and the life" (11:25).

These signs are reported so that we may "believe." The word "believe" occurs nearly a hundred times in John, and such related words as "belief" and "unbelief" are frequently repeated. Noting the use of the Greek philosophical concept of the Logos, the "Word" or "Reason," in John 1, some scholars have proposed that John is writing to win Gentiles to faith. Others have noted the long arguments with "the Jews" in such passages as John 5, 6, and 9 and have proposed that John wrote to persuade his fellow Jews to join in becoming Christians. The upper room discourses, however, seem obviously to be meditations designed for developing the faith of those who are already Christians. Repeatedly in John, one reads of some person who has a little faith but needs to have his belief deepened. John writes primarily to deepen and strengthen the faith of Christians. The climax of the book is when "doubting Thomas" comes to full faith as he meets the risen Christ and cries his confession, "My Lord and my God!" (20:28).

"Jesus is the Christ, the Son of God." John writes to help the reader understand who Jesus is. John presents the most highly developed Christology (doctrine of the nature of Christ) in all the New Testament. His most distinctive contribution of this kind is a series of sayings, usually with accompanying meditations, using an emphatic form of the Greek almost as if the words "I am" were in capitals. These "I am" sayings are:

"I am the bread of life" (6:48).
"I am the light of the world" (8:12).
"I am the gate for the sheep" (10:7).
"I am the good shepherd" (10:11).
"I am the resurrection and the life" (11:25).
"I am the way, and the truth, and the life" (14:6).
"I am the vine" (15:5).
"Before Abraham was, I am" (8:58).

Thus, repeatedly, the book explains the meaning of Jesus by using what are, in a sense, the most familiar and simple and universally understandable symbols: light, bread, a vine, and so forth. Into these, John pours profound meaning.

Finally, John says that he writes so that his readers may have "life." This word occurs more than forty times in John. In a sense, John is a very practical book. The author is not greatly interested in speculation about the future, and his primary concern is not a report of interesting events of the past. He wants to help the reader to a new kind of life right now. "This is eternal life," he writes of a present reality, not something to come after death, "that they may know you, the only true God, and Jesus Christ whom you have sent" (17:3).

Secondary purposes may be noted, most being clearly related to special situations that the church faced near the end of the first century. The writer wants to describe Christ in relation to the continuing movement begun by John the Baptist, the growing Gnostic heresy, and the bitter controversies developing between church and synagogue. These are discussed below. But noting these more particular concerns of the writer leads us to the questions of authorship and date of the Gospel.

The Authorship of John

The Fourth Gospel is given to us as an anonymous work. It is true that all editors now print as its heading "The Gospel according to John," but this is the editor's title, not part of the text itself. As to the identity of the writer, the Bible itself simply leaves us to guess.

People have been guessing for centuries. Curiously, one early group of very orthodox Christians believed that John was too "spiritual" and branded it the work of the heretic Cerinthus. But the overwhelming majority of early Christian writers, from at least as early as the Muratorian Canon of about A.D. 170, have ascribed it to someone named "John," and that John has usually been understood to be the son of Zebedee and one of the twelve apostles. That John was an important early Christian leader is attested by the Synoptics, Acts, and later legend, and Paul refers to him as one of the "pillars" of the Jerusalem church (Gal. 2:9).

While the Gospel does not name its author, it does indicate its source as being "the disciple whom Jesus loved." Several times this unnamed person is mentioned (John 13:23; 19:26; 20:2; 21:7). At the end of the book, this disciple appears once more (21:20), and now we are told, "This is the disciple who is testifying to these things and has written them, and we know that his testimony is true" (21:24). Somewhat similarly, the story of Jesus' death is interrupted with the comment "He who saw this has testified so that you also may believe. His testimony is true, and he knows that he tells the truth" (19:35).

Who is this disciple who leans on Jesus' breast as the Twelve recline around the table at the Last Supper, to whom the dying Jesus commits the care of his mother, and who is said to be the source of the Gospel? Several have proposed that he is simply an ideal figure, standing for all who believe.[19] Ideal figures do not write Gospels, however. Floyd Filson, in the Layman's Bible Commentary volume on John, argues that it is Lazarus.[20] Four times, Filson notes, it is stated specifically that Jesus loved Lazarus (11:3, 5, 11, 36). Then, in chapter 13, we begin to read simply of "the disciple whom Jesus loved." Few scholars, however, have followed Filson in this identification. To most, it seems incredible that Jesus' "beloved disciple" could be one who is never mentioned in the New Testament outside of this Gospel and around whom no church tradition ever gathered.

It has been generally argued that this especially beloved disciple must be one of the most prominent of the Twelve. Peter, Andrew, and several others are referred to by name in the Fourth Gospel. John, however, so frequently mentioned elsewhere in the New Testament, is never named in this book. It is proposed, therefore, that John refers to himself this way, modestly concealing his own name.

Supporters of the traditional view that John the apostle wrote this Gospel have offered such arguments as the following: The earliest Christian writers who discuss these matters affirm it. The book has always borne John's name in its title. The writer must, it is said, have been a Palestinian Jew, as was John. This is shown by the fact that he knows Jewish law and customs and opinions (1:21; 4:25; 7:40–41; 12:34; 18:31; etc.); the language of Palestine (19:17); details of Palestinian geography (1:28, 2:1; 3:23; 11:54; etc.); and the ceremonies of the Jewish feasts (7:2, 37; 10:22; etc.). There is such vividness of detail that even some who doubt that the book comes to us in its present form from an apostle believe that it must go back for its ultimate source to someone who was an eyewitness at many of the events described.

Some twentieth-century discoveries have been used to support the traditional view. At one time it was argued that the Fourth Gospel might have been written as late as A.D. 175, obviously beyond the lifetime even of a man famed in part for his longevity (21:22). The discovery in Egypt of a papyrus containing part of John and written no later than A.D. 125 or 130 has forced acceptance of an earlier date. Most scholars now place John between A.D. 90 and 100. Similarly, the discovery of the Dead Sea Scrolls has indicated that certain ideas such as the warfare of light with darkness, characteristic of John, were current in first-century Palestine and need not have been derived from later Gentile thought. Finally, some linguists find hints of oral or written sources in John that were originally in Aramaic, the language of John's native Palestine, not of the later mission to the Gentiles.[21]

It must be repeated, however, that the Gospel comes to us an anonymous book. Only very conservative scholars today are likely to ascribe it actually to the pen of the apostle. There are several reasons.

Most important, the differences between John and the Synoptics, noted above, are so great that it is difficult to believe that the Fourth Gospel, in the form in which we now have it, is the work of one who actually remembered Jesus of Nazareth from long personal experience. If we assume that the historical facts are roughly as Mark presents them, it seems unlikely that one who was present then could, for example, picture Jesus as publicly debating his own divine nature with his enemies early in his ministry. Such debates belong to a later stage in Christian history.

Actually, a careful reading of the ascription to the beloved disciple suggests that the work has more than one author. "We know that his testimony is true" (21:24). Who is "we"? The most natural understanding of the verse is that "we" refers to the writers of the volume in the form in which we now have it. They are claiming, however, that its ultimate source is the testimony, including the written testimony, of the beloved disciple.

The phrase "the disciple whom Jesus loved" is scarcely a modest way for one to describe oneself. It would be highly appropriate, however, for students of John to describe their revered teacher in this way. Even if it is suggested that, as may indeed be the case, John 21 is an appendix added to the book after his death, we have almost the same phrase in the body of the book in 19:35: "his testimony is true." Taken as they stand, these verses seem to indicate that while the book rests on the authority of the beloved disciple, it comes to us through the work of later writers also.

As a matter of fact, there are hints in ancient tradition that John was not alone in the production of this Gospel. Clement of Alexandria, as we have seen, speaks of John as writing after "being urged by his friends." The Muratorian Canon says that John wrote "aided by the revision of all" his bishops and fellow disciples. To the present writer, as to many others, it seems likely that that "revision" was more extensive than has traditionally been recognized.

Though there was still disagreement, in 1991 Gerard S. Sloyan could summarize the most popular view as being that this Gospel is based on an oral collection of stories and sayings of Jesus independent of the other Gospels, sermons that helped interpret those stories and sayings through the dialogues and monologues, a written Gospel, and perhaps two revisions or editings of that document.[22]

Of written sources, the one most often suggested is a "book of signs" reporting seven miracles of Jesus.[23] In view of the consistent tradition that relates the Gospel to John, it would seem to the present writer likely that excerpts from sermons of that apostle were among these sources. Moreover, it would seem likely that the Gospel was produced in a church of which John had been the leader. He was the "author" in the sense of being the "authority" on which the Gospel rested. But those who actually wrote what we now have probably completed their work after John's death. They applied the apostle's message to issues of their own day. And in so doing, they gave us what most Christian scholars would consider among the most mature, advanced, and profound theological treatises ever written.[24]

We cannot identify these pupils of John, perhaps in Ephesus, who penned what we now have. The second-century Christian scholar Papias speaks of two men in Ephesus named John: the apostle John and the elder ("presbyter") John. Apparently, the elder was a younger contemporary of the apostle. In view of the fact that 2 and 3 John are said to be by "the elder" (see the first verse of each) and are traditionally ascribed to "John," many have suggested that John the elder was also the final writer of the Gospel. This helped attach the name "John" to the book. This, however, is only attractive speculation.

Currently, many scholars prefer the approach of the "new literary criticism," which de-emphasizes questions about sources and authorship. R.

Alan Culpepper, for example, focuses on the narrative itself, showing how the characters are presented and the plot is constructed to carry the reader to the desired goals.[25]

For convenience, and out of respect for a helpful tradition, we refer to the anonymous author as John in the section-by-section comments on the Gospel.

The Prologue and the Witness of John the Baptist (John 1)

O God most glorious . . .
Nature's great King, through endless years the same;
· ·
Vehicle of the universal Word, that flows
Through all, and the light celestial glows
· ·
One Word through all things everlastingly.
One Word—whose voice alas! the wicked spurn.[26]

By the time the Gospel according to John was written, men and women for three centuries had been singing Cleanthes' "Hymn to Zeus," quoted above. In it, they had sung of God's "Word," the Logos.

Bridging the gap between pagan and Christian thought, John begins with another hymn about the Logos, the Word of God. Stoics and Christians knew that there was really only one God and that in the beginning it was through that Word, that manifestation of the Divine Mind, that the world was created. "In the beginning was the Explanation," one could translate John's first words. There was that through which God sought to show how everything makes sense. Both Stoics and Christians knew that humankind had often rejected that expression of divine reason.

Three centuries after John, the great Augustine was to write that before he became a Christian, he had learned from Greek philosophy almost everything in the prologue of John until he came to verse 14: "And the Word became flesh and lived among us." That was the good news unknown to any pagan. In Jesus, the Logos had become flesh, had become completely human.

The rabbi-philosopher Philo had already proposed relationships between biblical religion and Greek philosophy. Indeed, it must be emphasized that John is written not by a Greek philosopher but by a Jewish Christian. For an introduction, he uses the Logos concept. But his roots are in the Jewish scriptures. The concept of the divine wisdom in Proverbs 8 is surely part of the background of John's hymn. John begins by expressing the meaning of Christ in terms derived from the Jewish scriptures, as do the first sermons, but also in terms familiar to former pagans.

These were Gnostic terms too. But the strong word used about the incarnation, that in Jesus, the Word had become *flesh,* clearly separated John from these heretics. John uses so many Gnostic figures and concepts that, as was noted earlier, some Christians later claimed that the book was written by the Gnostic heretic Cerinthus. Yet from time to time John reminds the reader of the genuine humanity of Jesus. It is John who tells us that Jesus wept (11:35). It is John who records Jesus' cry from the cross, "I am thirsty" (19:28). Here, in the prologue, he insists on the fact that in Jesus, the Logos became "flesh."[27]

John begins by setting Jesus in relation to philosophical and Gnostic speculation. But he also relates Jesus to the movement of John the Baptist. In Mark, Jesus' ministry begins when John the Baptizer's ends. But in the Fourth Gospel, for a brief period, at least, the two are working at the same time. Here there may be some reflection of the fact that a John the Baptist cult survived for many years after the prophet's death. Acts 19:1–7 implies the existence of this group in Ephesus, the traditional center of the apostle John's ministry. The Fourth Gospel, therefore, though it follows the convention of beginning its story of Jesus with the ministry of John the Baptizer, says nothing of Jesus' having been baptized by John. That might imply to some followers of John the Baptist that their prophet had been somehow superior to Jesus. Instead, the whole emphasis in this Gospel's account of John is on his witness to the superiority of Jesus. "Here is the Lamb of God," John cries as he sees Christ (1:29). The figure is from the Passover celebration, which will be the season of Jesus' death. Followers of John now transfer their allegiance to Jesus, as the Gospel writer wants the contemporary disciples of John the Baptist to do. And John the Baptist appears once again, briefly—in a passage that some think may originally have been part of the first chapter—to say of Jesus, "He must increase, but I must decrease" (3:30).

The Book of Signs (John 2—11)

John 2—11 contains the story of seven miracles, selected from many and interpreted as "signs." Around each of five of these, the book gives us a meditation in the form of a monologue by Jesus, usually introduced by a dialogue with an individual or—more often—a group. The outline on p. 521 shows how this part of the book can be understood as being built around these signs and their interpretations. As stated above, several scholars have suggested that the "book of signs" originally recounted the miracles independently, the discourses being added later. If this is so, it is not possible now to separate out the original source with certainty.

Surprisingly, John places the story of the cleansing of the Temple at the beginning of Jesus' ministry, right after the sign of changing the water into wine. We have seen that the Synoptics are more interested in the theological points that a story illustrates than in its historical sequence. They do not agree on the order of all events. Nevertheless, it does seem important to place historically the cleansing of the Temple within the last week of Jesus' ministry, because—in Mark, at least—it is this act that so infuriates the authorities in Jerusalem that it brings about the final plot to destroy Jesus. In John, however, the raising of Lazarus from the dead is given as the climax of Jesus' signs and the final blow to the old order which eventuates in the crucifixion.

Apparently, John places the cleansing of the Temple here because his opening theme is the transformation, the new life, that the coming of Christ brings. That transformation is symbolized in the first sign; at a wedding, water is changed to wine (2:1–11). Next, at Passover, the Temple is transformed, with a hint of the coming resurrection in which the church, the body of the risen Christ, will replace the old structure (2:19). The transformed life is demanded of an official of Judaism, Nicodemus: "You must be born from above" (3:7). We are left unsure of whether that representative "ruler of the Jews" has responded, but symbolically, when the new life, "living water," is offered to a woman of the hated Samaritans, she responds gladly (4:15). Soon these once-despised people are proclaiming Jesus Savior of the whole world (4:42). Now new life is displayed as the dying son of a Roman official, a Gentile, is rescued from death (4:46–54). Old barriers between races and sexes and old patterns of worship are broken down. Christianity is seen breaking out of the old Temple, officialdom, race, and cult. The old, lifeless water is being changed into wine.

The second sign is the healing of the son of a loving father, a Roman official (4:46–54). It introduces a long discussion in chapter 5 of the Father–Son relationship existing between God and Jesus.

The immediate occasion of the controversy that produces this discussion is that Jesus heals a man on the Sabbath (5:2–9). This act, his enemies charge, involved forbidden "work" on the Sabbath. Jesus' reply is to say, "My Father is still working, and I also am working" (5:17). Like the healing on the Sabbath described in Mark 3:1–6, this incident so infuriates the authorities that already they begin to plot to kill him.

What infuriates them here, however, is not simply the violation of the Sabbath law but the claim implied in Jesus' answer that he is the Son of God. The rest of the chapter analyzes for the reader what it means that Jesus is the Son of the Father. "Who is the man?" (John 5:12). John never mentions Jesus' being conceived by the Holy Spirit and born of a virgin. Rather, he interprets what Christians mean when they call Jesus "Son of God" in ways such as these: He is the one through whom the Father continues to work (5:17); he has authority from God (5:19); he is especially beloved by God (5:20); through him, God gives life to mortals (5:21); he is the agent of God's judgment (5:22, 27); he is like God in that he has "life" within himself (5:26); and through him, God speaks (5:28).

How do Christians know that this is true? Some answers here are that John the Baptist bore witness to Christ (5:33); Jesus' great deeds show who he is

(5:36); God the Father speaks directly to the heart of the believer about Jesus (5:37–38); and the scripture itself tells us who he is (5:39).

The story of the feeding of the five thousand is one of the relatively few events, other than the crucifixion and the resurrection, that are found in all four Gospels. No doubt it was frequently retold among Christians because it seemed especially appropriate at the Communion service. It is in the light of the Eucharist that John interprets it in chapter 6. The other three Gospels have told the story; it is John who tells its meaning. In it, Jesus is saying, "I am the bread of life" (6:48). Though John has the longest account of the Last Supper, five whole chapters (John 13—17), nowhere in them does he mention the actual institution of the Lord's Supper. His readers already know how the Lord's Supper began. Rather, he gives us a Communion meditation here. "Those who eat my flesh and drink my blood have eternal life" (6:54).

The whole story is set in the context of the Passover (6:4). That ancient festival celebrated how the Jews, having first eaten a meal of special bread, crossed the sea to freedom and entered into a covenant with God. Wandering in the wilderness, they again ate a special bread, the manna that God miraculously sent down to them daily from heaven. The disciples, too, cross a sea (6:16–21), with Jesus walking on the water. Jewish expectation of the eschaton, the end of the world, included the hope of a great messianic banquet with the messiah. All of these ideas are now used to explain the meaning of the Communion service. "Your ancestors ate the manna in the wilderness, and they died. This is the bread that comes down from heaven, so that one may eat of it and not die" (6:49–50).

Chapters 7 through 10 have as their background the Feast of Tabernacles (or Booths). The outline on p. 521 takes the seven signs as the basic structure of the first half of John, but it is equally valid to outline the book around Jewish festivals, now transcended in Christianity. Chapters 2 through 4 are set in the context of the Passover, chapter 5 involves the Sabbath, and chapter 6 returns to the Passover. In the ceremonies related to the Feast of Booths, each day for a week a golden pitcher of water was carried in a procession to the Temple to remind the people how God had provided water for them when, centuries earlier, they had wandered in the desert as they escaped from Egypt. It is against this background that we are to understand Jesus' invitation "Let anyone who is thirsty come to me, and let the one who believes in me drink" (7:37).

Similarly, during this festival, great fires were lit high on the Temple each night, a reminder of the pillar of fire that guided the Israelites through the wilderness (Exod. 13:21). This, too, is used to explain the meaning of Jesus: "I am the light of the world" (John 8:12; 9:5). The sign related to this saying is, appropriately, the restoring of sight to a man born blind (John 9).

Much of this section, like chapters 5 and 6, centers on long disputes between Jesus and "the Jews." Such passages have sometimes been misused as proof texts for anti-Semitic bigotry. This, however, is a gross misunderstanding. Jesus himself was a Jew. The Holy Family were Jews, the twelve apostles were Jews, and all the first Christians were Jews. John uses the term to refer not to a race or an ethnic group but to those who reject Christ. These passages must be read in the light of the controversy between church and synagogue that raged at the time this book was being written. "The Jews had already agreed that anyone who confessed Jesus to be the Messiah would be put out of the synagogue" (9:22). The use of the word "already" implies that the writer knows how, later on, Christians were everywhere put out of the synagogues. Sometime after the fall of Jerusalem in A.D. 70, a council of rabbis convened at Jamnia to take steps to preserve Judaism in the crisis brought on by no longer having a Temple or a homeland. They inserted the following bit of liturgy into synagogue worship:

For the apostates let there be no hope
. . . .
Let the Nazarenes [Christians] and
the Minim [heretics] be destroyed in a moment.
And let them be blotted out of the Book of life and not
be inscribed together with the righteous.[28]

Between the lines of John, one can read the equally bitter reply of the church to the synagogue. To perpetuate today late first-century controversies between the synagogue and the emerging church would be to pervert what is best in both Judaism and Christianity.

Actually, these chapters present three parties: Jesus, boldly defying his enemies (7:26); Jewish leaders, seen not so much as individuals but as symbols of unbelief, seeking to discredit Jesus (7:47–48); and the crowd, confused and vacillating (7:40–44).

Jesus' enemies try to have him arrested (7:32), but the police return empty-handed. "Never has anyone spoken like this" is all that they can say to explain their hesitation (7:46). The Jewish leaders hate Jesus because he is a threat to their high position. Jesus has no official sanction (7:48), they argue; he does not come from their ranks in Jerusalem (7:52). He is a nobody, and they are somebodies, yet he is challenging their hold on the people (7:26).

The people are confused and divided. Some believe in Jesus (8:30). Some think him a devil (8:48). All the way through this section, they are asking questions: "Where is he?" (7:11). "Can it be that . . . this is the Messiah?" (7:26). "What does he mean?" (7:36). "Where is your Father?" (8:19). "Who are you?" (8:25). "Who do you claim to be?" (8:53).

Jesus claims no earthly authority. Over and over, he tries to explain that he has come from God (8:16, 23, 42). It is not the town he comes from (7:27) or the approval of the authorities (7:48) but his life that shows who he is (8:46–47).

All this controversy reaches a climax in chapter 9 with the story of Christ's giving sight to a man born blind. The man stands as a symbol of those in the confused crowd who do come to believe in Jesus. Over and over, the crowd and the authorities question him after he has been healed: "Where is he?" (9:12). "What do you say about him?" (9:17). The simple fellow can only answer, "I do not know whether he is a sinner. One thing I do know, that though I was blind, now I see" (9:25). It is the Pharisees (the unbelievers) who are really blind (9:40–41). They have rejected "the light of the world."

The section ends with a meditation that is this Gospel's developed version of the parable of the lost sheep. The Jews, of course, are the people of God, his "sheep" (Ps. 100:3). But the discourse looks forward to the inclusion now of Gentiles too: "I have other sheep that do not belong to this fold. I must bring them also" (John 10:16). For Jews and Gentiles, the Good Shepherd lays down his life (10:11).

The end of the dispute is set against the background of the Feast of the Dedication, which commemorated the restoration of the Temple in 164 B.C., after the Syrians who defiled it had been expelled. Efforts to kill Jesus are now repeated (10:31, 39). Jesus is forced to retreat beyond the Jordan, and the public disputes cease.

The seventh and the climactic sign is the raising of Lazarus, the sign that Jesus is "the resurrection and the life." The conventionally expressed eschatology of Martha is not contradicted: "I know that he will rise again in the resurrection on the last day" (11:24). But there is added to it the "realized eschatology" of John. Already the resurrection has begun. With Christ, the new life is already here.

But "from that day on they planned to put him to death" (11:53).

The Entry into Jerusalem and the Last Supper (John 12—17)

John 12 is a pivotal chapter, summarizing the themes of the first half of the book and, at the same time, preparing the reader for what is to come. Mary anoints Jesus, a foreshadowing of the anointing of his body for burial (12:1–8). Jesus enters Jerusalem humbly, on a donkey, much as in the Synoptics, but here the crowds proclaim him king (12:12–19; cf. 6:15; 18:33–38; 19:3, 15–22). John builds to the climax of his account of Jesus' public ministry by telling how a group of Greeks, symbols of the coming spread of Christianity to the whole world, come seeking Jesus (12:20–26). Throughout the Gospel, John has referred to Jesus' coming "hour" (2:4; 4:21; 8:20; 7:30; etc.). Now, with the coming of these Gentiles, Jesus can announce at last, "The hour has come" (12:23).

Members of the community that produced the Dead Sea Scrolls wrote of themselves as the children of light, who would war against the children of darkness. This Gospel has so stressed the theme of light versus darkness that James Charlesworth has argued that after that community's dispersion by the

Romans, some of its members must have fled to Ephesus and become Christians in the church in which this Gospel was written.[29] John records as Jesus' last public words: "While you have the light, believe in the light, so that you may become children of light" (12:36; cf. 1:4–5; 8:12; etc.). Finally, John closes the first half of the book and opens the second half with a kind of summary, which includes the words "I have come as a light into the world, so that everyone who believes in me should not remain in the darkness" (12:46).

Five whole chapters (John 13—17), probably the best-loved part of the book, are devoted to the Last Supper, largely to a meditation on the coming of the Holy Spirit and on the continuing relationship of Christ to those who love him.

The scene is introduced by an acted parable. Jesus, said at this point to be fully aware that he has come from God, takes the role ordinarily assigned to the lowest servant: he washes the disciples' feet. His gesture is a symbolic, preparatory acting out of the sacrifice that is to occur on the next day. Later in chapter 13, Judas goes out to betray Jesus, and Jesus announces that his death is at hand.

In chapter 14, Jesus is depicted as promising his return, "that where I am, there you may be also" (14:3). Perhaps the best known of the "I am" sayings is then given: "I am the way, and the truth, and the life" (14:6). But the coming that is especially promised is not simply the return of Jesus at the end but the imminent coming of the Holy Spirit. Though the promised return of Christ has been delayed, John seems to be saying, the experience of the coming of the Spirit is one in which his readers have already shared or can share. Christ will send the "Advocate" (14:16), who is the Spirit (14:17), who is actually Jesus' own presence with them (14:18)—a special gift to those with faith (14:19).

Through this Spirit, chapter 15 adds, Christ and his church will be linked as a vine and its branches. Thus joined, believers will share in his power to do great things, to "bear much fruit" (15:8). The vine (Christ with his church) is to be bound together by love (15:12–17). The commandment to love is not new, but love is given a new standard. "I give you a new commandment, that you love one another. Just as I have loved you, you also should love one another" (13:34). That is new!

That Spirit also will continue, even after Jesus is no longer with them, to teach Christians new things, chapter 16 adds. "I still have many things to say to you, but you cannot bear them now. When the Spirit of truth comes, he will guide you into all the truth" (16:12–13). Indeed, many of the sayings of Christ in John may be thought of as among these new things being said by the risen Christ through his Spirit.

The picture of Jesus' last words with his disciples before his crucifixion is closed with what is sometimes called Christ's "high-priestly prayer" (John 17). He glorifies the God who has given him all power, even power to give eternal life to all. "And this is eternal life," we are told, "that they may know you, the only true God, and Jesus Christ whom you have sent" (17:3). What had been the focus of the eschatological hope for centuries is now present for believers: eternal life itself. Christ's great prayer is for the unity of the church, not just a spiritual unity but a unity so visible that the world will be won by it. He prays "that they may all be one . . . so that the world may believe" (17:21).

That prayer has not yet been answered fully.

The Crucifixion and the Resurrection (John 18—21)

We have already seen that in the Synoptics, the account of Jesus' arrest, trial, and crucifixion is given with far more attention to detail than that of any other part of Jesus' life. There is every reason to believe that it is historically of high accuracy. Not surprisingly, therefore, John's account is quite similar.

One thing that this Gospel adds is a conversation said to have taken place between Jesus and Pilate. (Richard J. Cassidy has shown that one purpose of this Gospel may well have been to encourage its readers as they, too, stood on trial for the name of their Lord.)[30] In his conversation with Pilate, the sense in which Jesus is a "king" is discussed: "My kingdom is not from this world. . . . I came into the world, to testify to the truth" (18:36–37). Moreover, John pictures Jesus as acting throughout with the calm authority of a king. Not only is he entirely innocent, as his judges admit, but he has more power than the Jewish police (18:6) or even the Roman governor (19:11). He talks to Pilate not as a prisoner but as a king (18:33–38). Indeed, Pilate recognizes that Jesus really is a king (19:14). And as a king, Jesus calmly disposes of his affairs from the cross (19:25–27). In John, he dies not with a cry of dereliction ("My God, my God, why have you forsaken me?") but with a triumphant announcement, "It is finished" (19:30). In John, it is in the cross itself, not just the resurrection, that Jesus is "glorified."

And yet John pauses from time to time to emphasize that Jesus really did suffer. John has presented the heavenly Christ in Jesus, the one who has come from heaven and returns to heaven, the one who is "not of this world" and whose kingdom is light against this world's darkness. He does this so much that Rudolf Bultmann proposes that the writer must have been a converted Gnostic, repeatedly using Gnostic ideas to describe the meaning of Christ. The Gnostics, too, believed that the Spirit would reveal new truths and had, in fact, done so for them. There is so much language in John similar to that of the Gnostics that they subsequently liked to quote from this Gospel, even claiming that John had been a kind of Gnostic. In reaction, as noted previously, some very orthodox Christians later proposed that the Gnostic heretic Cerinthus had written the book. (Contrast the legend, described in the opening of this chapter, that John ran from the bathhouse when Cerinthus entered.)

Yet John's account of the crucifixion is in sharp contrast to that found in the *Acts of John,* a kind of holy novel composed by the Gnostics a century later. In the Gnostic account, at the moment of the crucifixion, Christ is said to come to John, who was hiding in a cave on the Mount of Olives, to explain to him that the man dying on the cross was not really the eternal Christ:

> And I saw the Lord himself above the Cross, having no shape but only a kind of voice . . . which said to me . . . This Cross of Light is sometimes called Logos by me for your sakes, sometimes mind, sometimes Jesus, sometimes Christ, sometimes a door. . . . But this is not that wooden Cross which you shall see when you go down from here; nor am I the (man) who is on the Cross. . . . So then I have suffered none of those things which they will say of me.[31]

The Son of God, to the Gnostics, was too "spiritual" to suffer.

By contrast, John depicts for us Jesus Christ scourged, dressed in a royal purple robe, with a crown of thorns on his head, and ridiculed. "Here is the man!" Pilate cries (19:5). And from the cross this very human Christ gives a cry of very human need, "I am thirsty" (19:28). "Then he bowed his head and gave up his spirit" (19:30).

While the other Gospels indicate that Jesus was crucified after eating the Passover meal the night before, John seems to say that Jesus was crucified on the day when the Passover lamb was being slain (19:31). Thus Jesus' earthly ministry ended in fulfillment of the words with which John introduced it: "Here is the Lamb of God who takes away the sin of the world!" (1:29).

We have already seen that our accounts of the resurrection differ in details but agree on essentials. In John, the risen Christ appears to Mary Magdalene at the tomb, then, as in Luke, to the disciples on Sunday evening.

John's special contribution to the resurrection story, however, is his account of "doubting Thomas" (20:24–29). Representative of all who come later than Easter and who have difficulty with faith, Thomas, not in the fellowship at first, now is privileged to see the risen Christ for himself. This Gospel has been filled with titles for Jesus: Logos, Son of God, light, the way, and many others. But Thomas is allowed to voice the confession that is the climax of New Testament Christology. He encounters the risen Christ, the print of the nails still visible on his real body, and Thomas cries, "My Lord and my God!" (20:28).

Most scholars regard John 21 as an appendix added later by the same writer or by others of the Johannine school.[32] It adds the story of an appearance of the risen Christ in Galilee, thus helping to bring the account more into line with Matthew's report. It also describes an encounter between the risen Christ and Peter, possibly giving details of an appearance mentioned by Paul (1 Cor. 15:5) and perhaps included in the lost ending of Mark (Mark 16:7).

There are also words to the "disciple whom Jesus loved" (John 21:20–23).

Apparently, John had lived to be a very old man, and the church had believed that Jesus would return before his death. The paragraph makes clear that this was not literally Jesus' promise.

It is probably with the statement of purpose in John 20:30–31 that the book originally ended. We have seen that John had purposes that, in certain ways, were quite different from those of all other writers in the New Testament. And yet what John says of his own aim would apply in many ways to the aim of every New Testament book.

From start to finish, the New Testament is a call to decision. One has not really been introduced to the New Testament when he or she has simply memorized dates and outlines of its twenty-seven books. The introduction is complete only as the reader meets the Figure who is central in these pages and senses the challenge that Person represents.

Therefore, it is appropriate to close the present volume as John originally closed his, by quoting again his words:

> Now Jesus did many other signs in the presence of his disciples, which are not written in this book. But these are written so that you may come to believe that Jesus is the Messiah, the Son of God, and that through believing you may have life in his name. (John 20:30–31)

NOTES

INTRODUCTION: INTERPRETING THE BIBLE

1. Among helpful studies of the various methods of interpretation discussed in this chapter are John Barton, *Reading the Old Testament: Method in Bible Study* (Philadelphia: Westminster Press, 1984); and Terence J. Keegan, O.P., *Interpreting the Bible: A Popular Introduction to Biblical Hermeneutics* (New York: Paulist Press, 1985).

2. Carol A. Newsom and Sharon H. Ringe, eds., *The Women's Bible Commentary* (Louisville, Ky.: Westminster/John Knox Press, 1992).

3. R. Alan Culpepper, *Anatomy of the Fourth Gospel: A Study in Literary Design* (Philadelphia: Fortress Press, 1983).

4. Charles H. Talbert, *Reading John: A Literary and Theological Commentary on the Fourth Gospel and the Epistles* (New York: Crossroad, 1992).

5. The pioneer work in canonical criticism is Brevard S. Childs, *Introduction to the Old Testament as Scripture* (Philadelphia: Fortress Press, 1979).

6. Harry Emerson Fosdick, *A Guide to Understanding the Bible: The Development of Ideas within the Old and New Testaments* (New York: Harper & Brothers, 1938), 53–54.

1. INTRODUCING THE FIVE "BOOKS OF MOSES": THE PENTATEUCH

1. See, for example, Magnus Magnusson, *Archaeology of the Bible* (New York: Simon & Schuster, 1977), 72–75.

2. For a brief survey of the history of the study of the Pentateuch, see Ronald E.

Clements, *One Hundred Years of Old Testament Interpretation* (Philadelphia: Westminster Press, 1976), 7–30. The analysis of the Pentateuch as based on four sources has been widely accepted since the publication of Julius Wellhausen's *Geschichte Israels I* in 1878.

3. Hermann Gunkel, *The Legends of Genesis: The Biblical Saga and History* (New York: Schocken Books, n.d.).

4. Ibid., 130–31.

5. John Bright, *A History of Israel,* 3d ed. (Philadelphia: Westminster Press, 1981), 95. For a contrasting view, see note 10, below.

6. Brevard S. Childs, *Introduction to the Old Testament as Scripture* (Philadelphia: Fortress Press, 1979).

7. Walter Brueggemann, *Genesis* (Atlanta: John Knox Press, 1982).

Genesis

8. For the full translation of this creation myth, see J. B. Pritchard, ed., *Ancient Near Eastern Texts Relating to the Old Testament* (Princeton, N.J.: Princeton University Press, 1955), 67.

9. Ibid., 93–95.

10. John Bright's affirmation, after extensive study, that the patriarchs were historic individuals has already been quoted; see his *History of Israel,* 95, and the extensive arguments he gives for his belief that they actually lived in the early second millennium B.C. In contrast to the claim that the stories of the patriarchs are rooted in Bronze Age history, see John Van Seters, *Abraham in History and Tradition* (New Haven, Conn.: Yale University Press, 1975), 309. Van Seters summarizes his conclusions: "Arguments based on reconstructing the patriarch's nomadic way of life, the personal names in Genesis, the social customs reflected in the stories, and correlation of the traditions of Genesis with the archaeological data of the Middle Bronze Age have all been found . . . to be quite defective." See also Thomas L. Thompson, *The Historicity of the Patriarchal Narratives—The Quest for the Historical Abraham* (Berlin: Walter de Gruyter, 1974). Thompson urges that we see these stories as Israel's way of expressing its hope for the future rather than as historical recollections of the past.

11. Hermann Gunkel has developed the theory that the stories of the patriarchs often represent the movements of tribes rather than individuals; see Gunkel, *Legends of Genesis,* 19–23ff. The accounts often include etiological stories, that is, legends preserved at various shrines to explain origins. These have been collected to form "sagas." As Gerhard von Rad has emphasized, however, as these were collected, they were given new theological meaning. See Gerhard von Rad, *Genesis: A Commentary,* trans. John H. Marks (Philadelphia: Westminster Press, 1961), 19.

12. A translation of the Egyptian story is found in Pritchard, ed., *Ancient Near Eastern Texts,* 23–25.

Exodus

13. George W. Ramsey (*The Quest for the Historical Israel* [Atlanta: John Knox Press, 1981], 48–49) notes that the 1200s B.C. are the most popular dating for the

exodus and summarizes reasons for this view. He warns, however, that there is great disagreement among scholars about not only the date but even to what extent one may regard the exodus as a historical event (65–98).

14. As quoted in Pritchard, ed., *Ancient Near Eastern Texts,* 119.

15. Terence E. Fretheim, *Exodus* (Louisville, Ky.: Westminster/John Knox Press, 1991), 63.

16. Brevard S. Childs, *Exodus: A Critical, Theological Commentary* (Philadelphia: Westminster Press, 1974), 49. Childs's is the most thorough commentary on Exodus known to this writer.

17. Martin Noth, *The History of Israel,* 2d ed. (New York: Harper & Row, 1958; English translation 1960), 128.

18. For a translation of the actual text of this treaty, see Pritchard, ed., *Ancient Near Eastern Texts,* 203–5. Ramsey (*Historical Israel,* 52–58) lists the arguments for and against the view that the Mosaic covenant is modeled on a treaty of this kind.

Leviticus

19. James L. Mays, *Leviticus, Numbers* (Atlanta: John Knox Press, 1963), 7.

20. For understanding the reasons for the different kinds of sacrifices, G.A.F. Knight, *Leviticus: A Commentary* (Philadelphia: Westminster Press, 1981), is especially helpful.

21. For a discussion of the complex literary origins of Leviticus, see Martin Noth, *Leviticus: A Commentary,* (Philadelphia: Westminster Press, 1962), 12–17.

22. Among the many books containing descriptions of modern Jewish observance of traditional feast days is Jacob Neusner, *The Life of Torah: Readings in the Jewish Religious Experience* (Belmont, Calif.: Wadsworth Publishing Co., 1974).

23. See, for example, such contrasting works as Ronald J. Sider, *Cry Justice: The Bible on Hunger and Poverty* (New York: Paulist Press, 1980), 78–82; and Gustavo Gutierrez, *A Theology of Liberation* (Maryknoll, N.Y.: Orbis Books, 1973), 294–95.

Numbers

24. Foster R. McCurley, *Genesis, Exodus, Leviticus, Numbers* (Philadelphia: Fortress Press, 1979).

25. For a discussion of the complex literary origins of Numbers, see Martin Noth, *Numbers: A Commentary* (Philadelphia: Westminster Press, 1968), 4–11. Noth regards most of the material as coming from the Priestly writers and from a time following the exile, though he recognizes some very old passages embedded in it.

26. See the brief discussion of J, E, D, and P on p. 18 in this *Guide.*

Deuteronomy

27. Patrick D. Miller, *Deuteronomy* (Louisville, Ky.: Westminster/John Knox Press, 1990), 16. He also quotes with approval Wellhausen's statement that Deuteronomy is the "connecting link between old and new, between Israel and Judaism," and Elizabeth Achtemeier that "there is no book of more importance in the Old Testament."

28. Miller argues that a case can be made for each of the following as the editors of Deuteronomy: prophets, Levitical priests, and scribes working with teachers of wisdom (ibid., 5–8). Building in part on the work of Martin Noth, A.D.H. Mayes describes a complex process of editing and re-editing; see his *Deuteronomy*, New Century Bible commentary series (Grand Rapids: Wm. B. Eerdmans, 1979), 29–55.

29. S. Dean McBride, Jr., building on Josephus, explores some of the political implications of Deuteronomy in "Polity of the Covenant People: The Book of Deuteronomy," *Interpretation* 41, 3 (July 1987): 229–44.

30. Patrick D. Miller, lecture on Deuteronomy (Union Theological Seminary, Virginia, Reigner Recording Library).

2. THE FORMER PROPHETS

Joshua

1. As quoted in Jack Finegan, *Light from the Ancient Past* (Princeton, N.J.: Princeton University Press, 1948), 105.

2. See "Scholar's Dispute," letters by Diana Edelman and Anson F. Rainey in *Biblical Archaeology Review* (March 1992): 21, 72–76, for discussion of this issue.

3. John Bright, *A History of Israel*, 3d ed. (Philadelphia: Westminster Press, 1981), 130.

4. See Magnus Magnusson, *Archaeology of the Bible* (New York: Simon & Schuster, 1977), 86–88.

5. Ibid., 92–96.

6. As quoted in Finegan, *Ancient Past*, 100.

7. For a summary of the various views and the arguments for them, see George W. Ramsey, *The Quest for the Historical Israel* (Atlanta: John Knox Press, 1981), 5–98.

8. Walter Brueggemann, *The Land* (Philadelphia: Fortress Press, 1977).

Judges

9. On the question of the extent to which Israel entered Canaan as conquering invaders or as more gradual infiltrators, see the section in this chapter on "Joshua," esp. note 7.

10. For a description of the religion of Baal, see Bernhard W. Anderson, *Understanding the Old Testament*, 4th ed. (Englewood Cliffs, N.J.: Prentice-Hall, 1986), 184–93. The Ras Shamra tablets, discovered at the site of ancient Ugarit in Syria, give us much information about one form of this ancient rival to the religion of Israel.

11. See G. Ernest Wright, *Biblical Archaeology*, rev. ed. (Philadelphia: Westminster Press, 1962), 89–90.

12. A. Graeme Auld, *Joshua, Judges, and Ruth* (Philadelphia: Westminster Press, 1984).

13. John Bright, *The Kingdom of God* (Nashville: Abingdon Press, 1953). See esp. p. 32.

Ruth

14. Phyllis Trible, *God and the Rhetoric of Sexuality* (Philadelphia: Fortress Press, 1978), 166.

15. Ibid., 173.
16. Ibid., 196.

1 Samuel

17. For a detailed account of this period in Israel's history, see Bright, *History of Israel,* 184–228.
18. David F. Payne, *I and II Samuel* (Philadelphia: Westminster Press, 1982), 4.
19. Baruch Halpern, *The First Historians: The Hebrew Bible and History* (San Francisco: Harper & Row, 1988). The histories of the more conservative John Bright and the more skeptical Martin Noth are sometimes contrasted in their treatment of early Israel. But from the time of the monarchy on, Bright and Noth are essentially in agreement that the books of Samuel and Kings contain a great deal of factual material.
20. See Magnusson, *Archaeology of the Bible,* 98–118, for an account of the Philistines.

2 Samuel

21. For a full account of the history of this period, see Bright, *History of Israel,* 184–228. For a commentary more oriented toward the newer emphasis on narrative criticism and with more overt concern for the theological meaning of the story of David, see Walter Brueggemann, *First and Second Samuel* (Louisville, Ky.: Westminster/John Knox Press, 1990).

1 Kings

22. For a full account of the history of this period, see Bright, *History of Israel,* 195–266.
23. These books include Proverbs, Ecclesiastes, and the apocryphal Wisdom of Solomon.
24. See James B. Pritchard, ed., *Ancient Near Eastern Texts Relating to the Old Testament* (Princeton, N.J.: Princeton University Press, 1955), 263–64.
25. Ibid., 320.

2 Kings

26. As found in D. Winton Thomas, ed., *Documents from Old Testament Times* (New York: Harper & Row, 1958), 60.
27. For example, Bernhard W. Anderson, *Understanding the Old Testament* (Englewood Cliffs, N.J.: Prentice-Hall, 1957). Also Norman H. Snaith, *The First and Second Books of Kings* (Nashville: Abingdon Press, 1954). Both commentators, of course, are also interested in the theology of the books of Kings.
28. For example, Richard Nelson, *First and Second Kings* (Atlanta: John Knox Press, 1987); see esp. pp. 2–4. Nelson, of course, is well aware of the history behind the narrative.
29. Shown in Bernhard Anderson, *Understanding the Old Testament,* 4th ed. (Englewood Cliffs, N.J.: Prentice-Hall, 1986), 350–51.
30. As quoted in Finegan, *Ancient Past,* 170–71.
31. Ibid., 173.
32. See Anderson, *Understanding the Old Testament,* 4th ed., 350–51.
33. As found in Thomas, ed., *Documents,* 86.

3. THE WRITINGS

1 Chronicles

1. Robert H. Pfeiffer, *Introduction to the Old Testament* (New York: Harper & Brothers, 1941), 786–87.

2. For example, John Bright, *A History of Israel,* 3d ed. (Philadelphia: Westminster Press, 1981), passim.

3. H.G.M. Williamson, *1 and 2 Chronicles* (Grand Rapids: Wm. B. Eerdmans, 1982), 23.

4. For example, Pfeiffer, *Introduction,* 811–12.

5. William F. Stinespring, in his introduction to 1 Chronicles in *The New Oxford Annotated Bible, New Revised Standard Version,* eds. Bruce M. Metzger and Roland E. Murphy (New York: Oxford University Press, 1991), says that the matter is still disputed but implies that the late fifth or fourth century B.C. is still the most popular date.

6. William F. Stinespring, introduction to 1 Chronicles, *The New Oxford Annotated Bible, Revised Standard Version,* eds. Herbert G. May and Bruce M. Metzger (New York: Oxford University Press, 1962), 511.

2 Chronicles

7. The Apocrypha contains a book called the Prayer of Manasseh, which is supposed to be the prayer that Manasseh prayed.

Ezra and Nehemiah

8. From "The Cyrus Cylinder," as cited in James B. Pritchard, ed., *Ancient Near Eastern Texts Relating to the Old Testament* (Princeton, N.J.: Princeton University Press, 1955), 316.

9. See, for example, Raymond A. Bowman, "The Book of Ezra and the Book of Nehemiah," in *The Interpreter's Bible* (Nashville: Abingdon Press, 1954), 3:561–63.

10. See, for example, Bright, *History of Israel,* 363, 375–86.

11. See 2 Esdras 14. For brief comments on 2 Esdras, see chapter 5, "The Apocrypha," in this *Guide.*

Esther

12. See Brevard S. Childs, *Introduction to the Old Testament as Scripture* (Philadelphia: Fortress Press, 1979), 605. His whole discussion of the place of Esther in the canon is helpful (603–5).

13. As quoted in Pfeiffer, *Introduction,* 747.

Job

14. As quoted by Samuel Terrien, "The Book of Job," in *The Interpreter's Bible* (Nashville: Abingdon Press, 1954), 3:877n.

15. As quoted in Pfeiffer, *Introduction,* 683.

16. Ibid.

17. J. Gerald Janzen, *Job* (Atlanta: John Knox Press, 1985), 144.

18. Gustavo Gutierrez, *On Job: God-Talk and the Suffering of the Innocent* (Maryknoll, N.Y.: Orbis Books, 1991).

19. H. H. Rowley, *The Book of Job* (Grand Rapids: Wm. B. Eerdmans, 1970), 241.

20. Gutierrez, *On Job,* 67–75.

21. Janzen, *Job,* esp. 245 and 251.

22. Gutierrez, *On Job,* 94–97.

Psalms

23. Patrick D. Miller, *Interpreting the Psalms* (Philadelphia: Fortress Press, 1986), 33–35.

24. Arnold B. Rhodes, *Psalms,* vol. 9 of the Layman's Bible Commentary series (Richmond: John Knox Press, 1960), 26–27.

Proverbs

25. Walter Brueggemann, *In Man We Trust* (Atlanta: John Knox Press, 1972).

26. As quoted in D. Winston Thomas, ed., *Documents from Old Testament Times* (New York: Harper & Row, 1958), 180–85.

27. For extended discussion of this subject, see Dianne Bergant, C.S.A., *What Are They Saying about Wisdom Literature?* (New York: Paulist Press, 1984).

28. See also the brief discussions of the *logos* in the section on "The Gospel according to John" in chapter 12 and the sections on the "Wisdom of Solomon" and "Ecclesiasticus" in chapter 5 in this *Guide.*

Ecclesiastes

29. As summarized by Bergant, *Wisdom Literature,* 63.

30. R.B.Y. Scott, *The Way of Wisdom in the Old Testament* (New York: Macmillan, 1971) 174.

31. Ibid., 178.

32. James Moffatt, in his translation, puts the following verses in double brackets to indicate that, in his view, they were not part of the original book: 2:26; 3:17; 5:7; 7:18b–19, 26b; 8:11–13; 11:9d; 12:1a (*A New Translation of the Bible,* 3d ed. [London: Hodder & Stoughton, 1934]).

Song of Solomon

33. As quoted by Marvin H. Pope, *Song of Songs: A New Translation with Introduction and Commentary,* Anchor Bible (Garden City, N.J.: Doubleday & Co., 1977), 19.

34. Ibid., 89.

35. Harold Indsell, ed., *Harper Study Bible* (New York: Harper & Row, 1964), 984.

36. See Renita J. Weems's article "Song of Songs," in *The Women's Bible Commentary,* eds. Carol A. Newsom and Sharon H. Ringe (Louisville, Ky.: Westminster/John Knox Press, 1992), 157.

37. Thomas Robinson, *The Preacher's Complete Homiletic Commentary on the Song of Solomon* (1892–96; reprint, Grand Rapids: Baker Book House, 1980), 7.

38. Theophile J. Meek, "The Song of Songs," in *The Interpreter's Bible* (Nashville: Abingdon Press, 1956), 5:94–96 and passim.

39. Robert C. Denton, "The Song of Solomon," in *The Interpreter's One-Volume Commentary*, ed. Charles Laymon (Nashville: Abingdon Press, 1971), 325.

40. Childs, *Old Testament as Scripture*, 573–79.

41. In what follows I summarize some of what Phyllis Trible says in *God and the Rhetoric of Sexuality* (Philadelphia, Fortress Press, 1978), 144–45.

42. Andrew M. Greeley, *Love Song* (New York: Warner Books, 1988).

4. THE LATTER PROPHETS

Isaiah

1. Even the conservative evangelical authors William Sandford La Sor, David Allan Hubbard, and Frederic William Bush, while affirming that Isaiah is "the dominant personality" in the entire book, attribute many of the oracles to "disciples" of that prophet down through the centuries; see their *Old Testament Survey: The Message, Form, and Background of the Old Testament* (Grand Rapids: Wm. B. Eerdmans, 1982), 376.

2. See, for example, R. E. Clement, "The Unity of the Book of Isaiah," *Interpretation* 37, 3 (April 1982): 117–29. See also Brevard S. Childs, *Introduction to the Old Testament as Scripture* (Philadelphia: Fortress Press, 1979), 328–30; and Edgar W. Conrad, *Reading Isaiah* (Minneapolis: Fortress Press, 1990), 1–33.

3. For one list of the various efforts to identify the servant, see James Muilenburg, "The Book of Isaiah," in *The Interpreter's Bible* (Nashville: Abingdon Press, 1956), 5:406–14.

4. See the discussion of this subject in John A. Sawyer, *Isaiah* (Philadelphia: Westminster Press, 1986), 2:143–49.

5. So, for example, James Luther Mays, *Ezekiel, Second Isaiah*, (Philadelphia: Fortress Press, 1978), 56.

Jeremiah

6. A few scholars want to delete from Jeremiah all promises of hope. This seems to be going too far. Many, however, are cautious about ascribing to the prophet himself many of the prose oracles. Even though some of these may be later additions, some may be accurate reflections of Jeremiah's thought, if not his poetic words. John Bright defends many of these oracles as the work of Jeremiah; see his article "The Date of the Prose Sermons of Jeremiah," *Journal of Biblical Literature* 70 (1951): 15–35. Of course, whether they originated from the prophet Jeremiah or not, the oracles are part of the canonical book of Jeremiah now.

7. John Bright comments about the "new covenant" passage, "As regards its authenticity, one can only say that it ought never to have been questioned" (*Jeremiah*, Anchor Bible 21 [Garden City, N.Y.: Doubleday, 1965], 289). R. E. Clements, however, still argues that few if any of the actual words of the "Little Book of Consolation" are by Jeremiah; the style, he says, is not his. See R. E. Clements, *Jeremiah* (Louisville, Ky.: Westminster/John Knox Press, 1989), 184, 189–90. Clements proposes, however, that the new covenant passage does put in theological language the kind of hope the prophet expressed.

Ezekiel

8. This date is indicated in Ezek. 1:2 as interpreted in *The New Oxford Annotated Bible* (1991 ed.), 1058.

9. Because the oracles in the first half of Ezekiel are directed against the sins of Jerusalem, many commentators have argued that some or all of them must have been delivered there. Perhaps the prophet was able to make a journey back to Jerusalem or was not taken captive as early as the book seems to indicate. On this subject, see Herbert G. May, "The Book of Ezekiel," in *The Interpreter's Bible* (Nashville: Abingdon Press, 1956), 6:41–56.

10. Erich Von Daniken, *Chariots of the Gods? Unsolved Mysteries of the Past* (New York: G. P. Putnam's Sons, 1969), 55–57.

11. The book seems to me to display considerable unity; but see May, "Ezekiel," for an approach ascribing it to many different authors. James Luther Mays (*Ezekiel, Second Isaiah* [Philadelphia: Fortress Press, 1978], 22–24) reports that the recent trend has been to see the book more nearly as a unit.

12. For a brief discussion of apocalyptic literature, see the section on Revelation in chapter 12 of this *Guide;* for other examples, see Zechariah 12—14 and Daniel 7—12.

13. For lists of the various efforts to identify the enemy Ezekiel describes, see Robert H. Pfeiffer, *Introduction to the Old Testament* (New York: Harper & Brothers, 1941), 562; and May, "Ezekiel," 6:273.

Daniel

14. For a more complete review of views concerning the authorship and setting of the book, see Childs, *Old Testament as Scripture,* 611–13. See also D. S. Russell, *Daniel* (Philadelphia: Westminster Press, 1981), 3–6.

15. See the brief discussion of apocalyptic literature in the section on Revelation in chapter 12 of this *Guide;* and cf. Zechariah 12—14.

16. On the relation of this book to other books of prophecy, see Klaus Koch, "Is Daniel Also among the Prophets?" *Interpretation* 39, 3 (April 1985): 117–30.

Joel

17. Joseph A. Harriss, "Return of the Locust," *Reader's Digest* (May 1989): 123.

18. See Beth Glazier-McDonald's commentary on Joel in *The Woman's Bible Commentary,* eds. Carol A. Newsom and Sharon H. Ringe (Louisville, Ky.: Westminster/John Knox Press, 1992), 204.

Amos

19. Like some other scholars, James Luther Mays interprets Amos to mean that he was not *originally* a prophet and would not prophesy now except that God had called him; see Mays's *Amos* (Philadelphia: Westminster Press, 1969), 137–39. Many others believe that this layman was dissociating himself from the hired professional prophets of the court, paid to say what the king wanted, as in 1 Kings 22:5–17; see, for example, James Limburg, *Hosea–Micah* (Atlanta: John Knox Press, 1988), 116–18.

20. See, for example, Limburg, *Hosea–Micah,* 80–81; and Hughell E. W. Fosbroke, "The Book of Amos," in *The Interpreter's Bible* (Nashville: Abingdon Press, 1956), 6:774–75.

Obadiah

21. Peter C. Craigie places the book in the decade after the fall of Jerusalem; see his *Twelve Prophets* (Philadelphia: Westminster Press, 1984), 1:197. Limburg (*Hosea–Micah,* 131) places it soon after the return of the exiles from Babylon, around 538 B.C.

Jonah

22. For a brief summary of various interpretations, including arguments defending the historicity of the book, see La Sor, Hubbard, and Bush, *Old Testament Survey,* 349–53.

Micah

23. James A. Moffatt, *A New Translation of the Bible,* 3d ed. (London: Hodder & Stoughton, 1934).

24. James Luther Mays (*Micah* [Philadelphia: Westminster Press, 1976]) attributes almost nothing of Micah 4—7 to the eighth-century prophet. Craigie (*Twelve Prophets,* vol. 2) finds no convincing reason why most of chapters 4—7 might not come from Micah. References to Babylon, the exile, and return suggest to the present writer that most of those chapters are from a time later than the eighth century.

25. Bernhard W. Anderson, *Understanding the Old Testament,* 4th ed. (Englewood Cliffs, N.J.: Prentice-Hall, 1986), 34.

Nahum

26. Charles L. Taylor, Jr. ("Nahum," in *The Interpreter's Bible* [Nashville: Abingdon Press, 1956], 6:954) places it in "the third or second century B.C." Elizabeth Achtemeier (*Nahum–Malachi* [Atlanta: John Knox Press, 1986], 6) regards it as an earlier poem that Nahum revised for his own use. Either way, it is part of the canonical book now.

27. Taylor, "Nahum," 6:953.

28. Achtemeier, *Nahum–Malachi,* 8.

29. Taylor, "Nahum," 6:954.

30. Craigie, *Twelve Prophets,* 2:71. Craigie and Kipling are both British.

Haggai

31. I am following the dating given by Achtemeier, *Nahum–Malachi,* 94.

Zechariah

32. See comments on apocalyptic literature in this *Guide* in the sections on "Revelation" (chap. 12) and, more briefly, "Zephaniah" and "Daniel" (chap. 4).

33. See comments on the day of the Lord in this *Guide* in the section on Zephaniah (pp. 256–60).

Malachi

34. It is probably true historically that some books of the Old Testament were written after the time of Malachi (ca. 450 B.C.), and we know that oracles of later prophets were attached to books by earlier prophets. In Hebrew Bibles, the Writings, such as Psalms and the wisdom literature, are placed last. Jews and Christians agree, however, in placing Malachi last among the books of prophecy. On the place of the

Apocrypha, see chapter 5 of this *Guide*. Traditionally, most Protestants place Malachi last in their Old Testament canon.

5. THE APOCRYPHA

1. As quoted by Bruce M. Metzger, *An Introduction to the Apocrypha* (New York: Oxford University Press, 1957), 37.

2. Bruce M. Metzger and Roland E. Murphy, eds., *The New Oxford Annotated Bible with the Apocrypha* (New York: Oxford University Press, 1991), 20.

3. Metzger, *Introduction to the Apocrypha*, 151–73.

6. THE SYNOPTIC GOSPELS

The Historical Setting of the Gospels

1. John Dominic Crossan, *The Historical Jesus: The Life of a Mediterranean Jewish Peasant* (San Francisco: HarperCollins 1991), xxvii–xxviii.

2. The findings of the Jesus Seminar are published in Robert W. Funk, Roy W. Hoover, and the Jesus Seminar, *The Five Gospels: The Search for the Authentic Words of Jesus* (New York: Macmillan, 1993).

3. For example, R. Alan Culpepper, *Anatomy of the Fourth Gospel: A Study in Literary Design* (Philadelphia: Fortress Press, 1983); and Jack Dean Kingsbury, *Conflict in Mark: Jesus, Authorities, Disciples* (Minneapolis: Fortress Press, 1989). Culpepper and Kingsbury are well aware of first-century history, but their commentaries focus on the stories as told by John and Mark, respectively, not on using the narratives to reconstruct "what really happened," as a historian might.

4. Martin Hengel, *Acts and the History of Early Christianity* (Philadelphia: Fortress Press, 1979), 41–42.

5. Adapted from A. C. Bouquet, *Everyday Life in New Testament Times* (New York: Charles Scribner's Sons, 1954).

6. See the brief review of 1 and 2 Maccabees in chapter 5, "The Apocrypha," in this *Guide*.

7. *The Assumption of Moses* 10:5; in *The Apocrypha and Pseudepigrapha of the Old Testament*, trans. and ed. R. H. Charles (Oxford: Clarendon Press, 1913), 2:422.

8. From *The Book of Hymns or Psalms of Thanksgiving*, Psalm 3, in *The Dead Sea Scriptures*, trans. Theodor H. Gaster (Garden City, N.Y.: Doubleday, 1957), 136–37.

9. *I Enoch* 55:4; in *The Apocrypha and Pseudepigrapha of the Old Testament*, trans. and ed. R. H. Charles, (Oxford: Clarendon Press, 1913), 2:221.

The Writing of the Gospels

10. C. H. Dodd, *The Apostolic Preaching and Its Developments* (London: Hodder & Stoughton, 1944), 20.

11. For a classic introduction to form criticism, see Rudolf Bultmann, "The Study of the Synoptic Gospels," in Frederick Clifton Grant, ed. and trans., *Form Criticism: A New Method of New Testament Research* (New York: Willett, Clark & Co., 1934), 11–75. For a more complete discussion, see E. Basil Redlich, *Form Criticism: Its Values and Limitations* (New York: Charles Scribner's Sons, 1939); and Edgar V. McKnight,

What Is Form Criticism? (Philadelphia: Fortress Press, 1969). For briefer descriptions of some of the methods, values, and limitations of this approach, see William Manson, *Jesus the Messiah* (London: Hodder & Stoughton, 1943), 20–32 and passim; William Barclay, *Introduction to The First Three Gospels* (Philadelphia: Westminster Press, 1975), 24–28; I. Howard Marshall, ed., *New Testament Interpretation* (Grand Rapids: Wm. B. Eerdmans, 1977), 153–64; and most of the New Testament introductions and general reference works cited in notes below.

12. For a collection of such apocryphal stories, see Hugh J. Schonfield, *Readings in the Apocryphal Gospels* (London: Thomas Nelson & Sons, 1940).

13. For a much more skeptical view of the Gospels as history, see Rudolf Bultmann, *The Historical Jesus and the Kerygma* (Nashville: Abingdon Press, 1964), and his "Study of the Synoptic Gospels." The view the present writer prefers is closer to that of Vincent Taylor, *The Life and Ministry of Jesus* (Nashville: Abingdon Press, 1955), 35–44; and of William Manson, *Jesus the Messiah*. For a scholarly and persuasive defense of a very conservative position, see I. Howard Marshall, *I Believe in the Historical Jesus* (Grand Rapids: Wm. B. Eerdmans, 1977). Another reaffirmation of a more skeptical approach is that of Norman Perrin, *The New Testament: An Introduction* (New York: Harcourt Brace Jovanovich, Inc., 1974), 278–82; who questions any story or saying in the Gospels that can be explained on the basis of the later needs of the church or paralleled in rabbinic Judaism. This seems to the present writer to take too lightly the facts that the church grew out of the coming of Jesus and that Jesus, whatever else he was, was a Jew.

14. For examples of those denying the priority of Mark and the dependence of Matthew on that Gospel, see W. F. Albright and C. S. Mann, *Matthew,* Anchor Bible (Garden City, N.Y.: Doubleday, 1971), esp. xxvii–clxxvii; and William R. Farmer, *The Synoptic Problem* (New York: Macmillan, 1964). The vast majority of scholars, however, at least among Protestants, argue for the priority of Mark. There are so many verbal agreements that one must be copying from another, and it seems incredible that Mark, in abbreviating Matthew, would add details to some stories but leave out the Sermon on the Mount, for example.

15. Eusebius, *Ecclesiastical History* 5.8; in *Documents of the Christian Church,* ed., Henry Bettenson (New York: Oxford University Press, 1947), 40.

16. Ibid. 5.3.39 (p. 39).

17. The traditional view presented here has recently been attacked by many. See, for example, Frederick C. Grant, "Mark," in *The Interpreter's Bible* (Nashville: Abingdon Press, 1951), 7:629, 647; Eduard Schweizer, *Jesus,* trans. David E. Green (Richmond: John Knox Press, 1971); and Lamar Williamson, Jr., *Mark* (Atlanta: John Knox Press, 1983). Among their arguments are these: The Gospel is said to reflect too much the influence of developing oral and perhaps written tradition to rest on the memory of an apostle (Peter). Its theology is too highly developed. And it betrays a lack of knowledge of Galilean geography. In reply, scholars have argued that the tradition ascribing the Gospel to Mark is very ancient and widespread and is inexplicable if not based on fact, since Mark was not especially prominent otherwise in church history. Peter's sermons were themselves a good source for "oral tradition." Peter's prominence in the Gospel indicates that it is by one of his disciples. As a native of Jerusalem, Mark need not have been an expert on Galilean geography. And the Gospel itself shows signs of having been written for Romans at a time of persecution and at a date around the time of Nero's

persecution. Ancient tradition from several sources places Peter in Rome at that time (see also the section on "The Gospel according to Mark" note 2, in this *Guide*). Scholars who are hesitant about giving the traditional name "Mark" to the author are still likely to place the writing of the Gospel in Rome at a time shortly after Peter's death.

18. Among those who reject the Q hypothesis are the German scholar Joachim Jeremias, who believes that oral tradition was strong enough to provide the common source; Farmer, *Synoptic Problem;* and John Drury, *Tradition and Design in Luke's Gospel* (Atlanta: John Knox Press, 1976), who holds that Luke used Matthew. The great majority of scholars, however, still support the view that there was a written document, Q.

19. Eusebius, *Ecclesiastical History* 5.3.39; in Bettenson, ed., *Documents,* 39.

20. For the classic presentation of the arguments for and against this traditional view, see F. J. Foakes Jackson and Kirsopp Lake, eds., *The Beginnings of Christianity* (London: Macmillan, 1922), 2:209–359. Most of what has subsequently been written on the subject on either side is anticipated there.

21. Eusebius, *Ecclesiastical History* 6.14; as quoted in James L. Price, *Interpreting the New Testament,* 2d ed. (New York: Holt, Rinehart & Winston, 1961), 539.

22. B. H. Streeter, *The Four Gospels* (London: Macmillan, 1924). For a contrasting approach, see J.A.T. Robinson, *Redating the New Testament* (Philadelphia: Westminster Press, 1976). Robinson puts the writing of all four Gospels within the decade of the fifties. At this writing, however, Robinson's views have not been followed by many.

The Gospel according to Matthew

23. Edgar J. Goodspeed, *Matthew, Apostle and Evangelist* (Philadelphia: John C. Winston Co., 1949), 20.

24. For example, Culpepper (*Anatomy of the Fourth Gospel,* 85) describes Matthew as exploring "the relationship between old and new in the ministry of Jesus; the connections between his teachings, mighty works, and death; and the significance of the story for a church of Jewish Christians sharing their faith with Gentiles."

25. The classic development of this approach is in Albert Schweitzer, *The Quest of the Historical Jesus* (1906; reprint, New York: Macmillan, 1948).

26. See, for example, Walter Rauschenbusch, *A Theology for the Social Gospel* (New York: Macmillan, 1918), 131–45.

27. C. H. Dodd, "The Life and Teachings of Jesus Christ," in *A Companion to the Bible,* ed. T. W. Manson (New York: Charles Scribner's Sons, 1939), 373–89.

28. Augustine, *The City of God* 20.9.

29. William Barclay, *The Gospel of Matthew,* 2d ed. (Philadelphia: Westminster Press, 1958), 1:90.

30. For an example of this explanation of the "messianic secret," see Dodd, "The Life and Teachings of Jesus Christ," in *Companion to the Bible,* ed. Manson.

31. I have borrowed this phrase from Price, *Interpreting the New Testament.* Earlier, Dodd (in *Companion to the Bible,* ed. Manson) had called them "acts of prophetic symbolism."

The Gospel according to Mark

32. A pioneer work in redaction criticism is Willi Marxsen, *Mark the Evangelist* (Nashville: Abingdon Press, 1969). For a brief critical review of its values and

limitations, see the article by Stephen S. Smalley, "Redaction Criticism," in *New Testament Interpretation,* ed. Marshall, 181–95.

33. See pp. 551–52 and the section "The Writing of the Gospels," note 17. The view here defended is well stated in A.E.J. Rawlinson, *St. Mark,* 7th ed. (London: Methuen, 1949), xxiv–xxx. It is also that of A. M. Hunter, *The Gospel according to Saint Mark* (London: SCM Press, 1948), 13–18; Vincent Taylor, *The Gospel according to Saint Mark* (London: Macmillan, 1952), 26–32; and C.E.B. Cranfield, *The Gospel according to Saint Mark* (Cambridge: Cambridge University Press, 1966), 3–6; and it is defended in various works by William Barclay, E. F. Scott, Bruce Metzger, and C.F.D. Moule. Reginald Fuller rejects the view that Mark is by an actual companion of Peter yet suggests that the Gospel may go back ultimately to Peter's preaching (*A Critical Introduction to the New Testament* [London: Duckworth, 1966], 104–6). Those who, like Fuller, reject the identification of the author with the John Mark mentioned frequently in the New Testament (Acts 12:12; 15:37; 2 Tim. 4:11; 1 Peter 5:13) still usually regard Mark as the earliest Gospel, coming from the church at Rome and from within a few years after Nero's persecution of the church. A minority place it as late as A.D. 71, believing that they see in it signs that Jerusalem has been destroyed and that the writer wishes to distinguish Christians from the ill-fated Zealots.

34. Kingsbury, *Conflict in Mark,* 28.

35. Mary Ann Tolbert, *Sowing the Gospel: Mark's World in Literary-historical Perspective* (Minneapolis: Fortress Press, 1989); see esp. 121–24.

36. Tacitus, *Annals* xv.44; as quoted in Price, *Interpreting the New Testament,* 196.

37. Norman Perrin, *The New Testament: An Introduction* (New York: Harcourt Brace Jovanovich, 1974), 144.

38. On the subject of the devil and demonology, see such books as R. H. Robbins, *The Encyclopedia of Witchcraft and Demonology* (New York: Crown Publishers, 1959); and S. Vernon McCasland and David Cole Wilson, *By the Finger of God* (New York: Macmillan, 1951).

39. So Albright and Mann, *Matthew,* lxxxviii–xciv.

40. On the title "Son of man," see note 39, above; and the article "Son of Man" by S. E. Johnson in *The Interpreter's Dictionary of the Bible* (Nashville: Abingdon Press, 1962), 4:413–20.

41. On "the Jesus of history," see the section in this chapter on "The Writing of the Gospels," note 13.

42. For example, see Norman Perrin, *The Resurrection according to Matthew, Mark, and Luke* (Philadelphia: Fortress Press, 1977). Perrin does not propose, however, that Mark did not believe in the resurrection. Mark's picture of the risen Christ is given in his story of the transfiguration (Mark 9:2–8), according to Perrin. Mark assumed that his readers already knew stories of appearances. Mark wanted, instead, to leave his readers looking forward to the coming great appearance of Christ at the end of the world.

The Gospel according to Luke

43. Donald Juel, "Luke and Acts," in *The Apocrypha and the New Testament,* vol. 2 in Bernhard W. Anderson, ed., *The Books of the Bible* (New York: Charles Scribner's Sons, 1989), 175–76.

44. One form of the concept of Jesus as liberator is that of Christ as the "Black

Messiah," presented by black theologians such as Albert Cleage and James H. Cone; see Cone's *Black Theology of Liberation* (Philadelphia: J. B. Lippincott, 1970), 204.

45. The concept of Christ as liberator in relation to economic and political oppression has been especially developed by Gustavo Gutierrez, *A Theology of Liberation* (Maryknoll, N.Y.: Orbis Books, 1973).

46. See Letty M. Russell, *Human Liberation in a Feminist Perspective* (Philadelphia: Westminster Press, 1974).

47. According to Jane Schaberg, "the Gospel of Luke is an extremely dangerous text, perhaps the most dangerous in the Bible." Schaberg recognizes that Luke devotes more space to women than do the other Gospels, and she rejoices in Mary's Magnificat. But she sees women in Luke as almost always presented as models of submission, faith, and service, never as aggressive or as leaders. See her article, "Luke," in Carol A. Newsom and Sharon H. Ringe, eds., *The Women's Bible Commentary* (Louisville, Ky.: Westminster/John Knox Press, 1992), 275–92. Schaberg is certainly right that there is "androcentrism" even in Luke, which today we should condemn. In Luke's defense, however, one might note at least that Luke does not confine his emphasis on service to women.

48. David Hume, *An Enquiry concerning Human Understanding,* sec. 10; as found, for example, in L. A. Selby-Bigge, ed., *Enquiries concerning the Human Understanding and concerning the Principles of Morals,* 2d ed. (Oxford: Clarendon Press, 1957), 109–31.

49. C. S. Lewis (*Miracles* [New York: Macmillan, 1947]) gives a popular and, to the present writer, persuasive case for the traditional Christian belief in miracles. For a discussion from the point of view of form criticism, affirming the antiquity of the tradition that Jesus did miracles, see Reginald H. Fuller, *Interpreting the Miracles* (Philadelphia: Westminster Press, 1963).

50. The most thorough study of the subject of Jesus' birth, one that examines all of these problems in scholarly fashion, is that of Raymond E. Brown, *The Birth of the Messiah* (Garden City, N.Y.: Doubleday, 1977). Brown makes a helpful defense of belief in the virgin birth (pp. 517–33).

51. For a careful effort to try to harmonize the apparent differences in the accounts of the resurrection, written from a very conservative point of view, see George Eldon Ladd, *I Believe in the Resurrection of Jesus* (London: Hodder & Stoughton, 1975), 79–103. Though helpful, even Ladd's book perhaps does not succeed in solving all the problems. Vincent Taylor (*The Formation of the Gospel Tradition* [London: Macmillan, 1935], 59–62) is helpful in suggesting reasons why the early church retold various stories about the resurrection in many different places and thus soon had varying accounts. Rudolf Bultmann, whose views are quite different from those of Ladd, writes, "In the word of preaching and there alone we meet the risen Lord" (*Kerygma and Myth* [London: SPCK, 1960], 43). More traditionally minded Christians, including the present writer, would hold that Bultmann's view is helpful though incomplete. Bultmann is correct that it is the claim of Christian faith that in "the word of preaching"—one might add teaching and Christian fellowship—the believer does meet the risen Lord. Thus belief in the resurrection rests not simply on historical research but also on inner experience, "existential encounter."

52. John Dominic Crossan, *The Historical Jesus* (San Francisco: HarperCollins, 1991), xiii.

7. THE ACTS OF THE APOSTLES

1. It is usually argued that Luke must have been written after the fall of Jerusalem because certain details in Luke's account of the predicted fall (Luke 21), added to his source in Mark 13, suggest knowledge of the actual event. It is often alleged also that Acts relies on a knowledge of the works of Josephus, which would mean that it could not have been written before sometime in the nineties. The evidence for this, however, is quite uncertain. The present writer would date Acts about A.D. 85.

2. J. W. Hunkin, "British Work on the Acts," in *The Beginnings of Christianity,* eds. F. J. Foakes Jackson and Kirsopp Lake (London: Macmillan, 1922), 433.

3. For example, Gunther Bornkamm indicates early in his biography titled *Paul* (trans. D.M.G. Stalker [New York: Harper & Row, 1971], xxi) that he will not regard Acts as a reliable source. Somewhat inconsistently, however, he finds Acts so helpful that he uses it repeatedly in his book. For example, in dealing with Paul at Corinth in Acts 18, he writes, "The account in Acts furnishes reliable, detailed information about which there is no dispute" (p. 68).

4. Can the following be only coincidences? In Acts, believers are called "disciples," "saints," or "brethren," but though Luke knows the title "Christians," he, like Paul, avoids it. The Twelve, with Peter and John particularly named, are pictured as heading the church, and certain others share in its leadership, such as James, and the other brothers of Jesus, and Barnabas. Assuming that Galatians was written to churches mentioned in Acts 12—14, we find in Galatians coincidences with Acts such as the mention of Barnabas as prominent, miracles having taken place, persecution as a problem, and the reception of Paul as a god. The Thessalonian epistles agree with Acts 17 as to the presence of a large Gentile element in the church there, the hostility of the Jews, the close association of Silas and Timothy, and perhaps certain elements in Paul's teaching. Both Acts and the letters to the Corinthians indicate that at Corinth, Paul worked at a trade. Crispus is named as a prominent convert, and Aquila and Priscilla and Apollos are related to Corinth in both. Paul's escape from Damascus by being smuggled over the wall in a basket appears in both Acts 9:25 and 2 Cor. 11:32–33. Romans agrees with Acts in implying that Paul planned to visit Rome after traveling to Jerusalem first. Minor characters in Acts appear also in Paul's letters: Silvanus (Silas), Sopater, Aristarchus, Tychicus, Trophimus, and Gaius. That Luke's name never occurs in Acts—only references to "we"—is itself significant. Acts's picture of Paul's bringing alms on his last trip to Jerusalem fits with numerous references in the epistles. In the chapters on the letters of Paul, we will see other points at which Acts helps us understand the epistles. If Luke is accurate in so many details that we can check, it may be argued that he is accurate in others that we cannot.

5. For example, Acts is correct concerning the proconsulship of Sergius Paulus (Acts 13:7) in name, date, and title, a fact remarkable in view of the constantly changing political situation in the Roman Empire. Acts is correct about such geographical details, according to Ramsay, as that Pisidian Antioch was the center of what was officially called a "region" and that it technically was not in Pisidia. The proconsulship of Gallio, though only a brief one, has been confirmed. See such books as Sir William M. Ramsay, *St. Paul the Traveller and the Roman Citizen* (London: Hodder & Stoughton, 1895).

6. Assuming that the author of the "we passages" in Acts was the author of the rest of the book, he was personally acquainted with Paul, had visited with Philip, and had been to Jerusalem, where he had been welcomed by Jesus' brother (Acts 21:18). It is widely held that here and there, especially in the speeches in Acts, there are hints of sources in Aramaic, the dialect spoken in Palestine in the first century. Similarities of stories have caused some to propose that Luke had before him two accounts of the same event.

7. Joseph Klausner, *From Jesus to Paul,* trans. William F. Stinespring (New York: Macmillan, 1944), 218. For a good presentation of the view, shared by the present writer, that Luke is both theologian *and* historian, see William Neil, *The Acts of the Apostles* (London: Oliphants, 1973), 14–60.

8. Hans Conzelmann, *An Outline of the Theology of the New Testament* (London: SCM Press, 1969), 149–52.

9. J. A. Ross Mackenzie, *The Word in Action* (Richmond: John Knox Press, 1973).

10. William H. Willimon speaks of Acts as "an imaginative reconstruction" and yet writes, "Luke is writing neither theological romance nor secretly received personal revelation. He is interpreting the stuff of history, actual events. History and proclamation are not exclusive categories. To preach Christ is to preach history 'that you may know the truth' (Luke 1:4)" (*Acts* [Atlanta: John Knox Press, 1988], 7).

11. Hugh J. Schonfield, *The Passover Plot* (New York: B. Geis Associates, 1966).

12. For a survey of various views about "speaking with tongues" and a defense of the view that at Pentecost a unique miracle occurred, see John B. Polhill, *Acts* (Nashville: Broadman Press, 1992), 98–100.

13. C. S. Mann (*The Acts of the Apostles,* Anchor Bible [Garden City, N.Y.: Doubleday, 1967], 271–75) notes this idea and also suggests that perhaps the disciples amazed the crowd simply by their interpretation of passages used in the Pentecost liturgy.

14. C. H. Dodd, *The Apostolic Preaching and Its Developments* (London: Hodder & Stoughton, 1944), 21–23.

15. It is often objected that the speeches in Acts are in the style and vocabulary of Luke. Luke, however, put sayings of Jesus from Mark into his own style and vocabulary without greatly altering them, and many find echoes of Aramaic sources in the sermons in Acts. It is true that Thucydides speaks of composing speeches as he wrote history, but he also says that he tried, as nearly as he could, "to give the general purport of what was actually said." Luke would seem to have done the same. Cf. Neil, *Acts of the Apostles,* 38–45. Neil holds that the speeches are a valid source of knowledge of early Christian thought.

16. The present writer has developed what follows in much more detail in William M. Ramsay, *The Christ of the Earliest Christians* (Richmond: John Knox Press, 1959).

17. *The Assumption of Moses* 10:5; in *The Apocrypha and Pseudepigrapha of the Old Testament,* trans. and ed. R. H. Charles, (Oxford: Clarendon Press, 1913), 422.

18. Josephus, *Antiquities* 14; as quoted in C. K. Barrett, ed., *The New Testament Background: Selected Documents* (New York: Harper & Row, 1961), 137.

19. W. M. Calder, "Lystra," in James Orr, ed., *The International Standard Bible Encyclopaedia* (Grand Rapids: Wm. B. Eerdmans, 1939), 3:1944.

20. Ibid.

21. Tacitus, *Histories* 5.9; as quoted in G.H.C. Magregor, "The Acts of the Apostles," in *The Interpreter's Bible* (Nashville: Abingdon Press, 1954), 9:307.

8. THE EARLIER LETTERS OF PAUL

Introducing the Letters of Paul

1. These and several of the following quotations are selected from various ones found in Wayne A. Meeks, ed., *The Writings of St. Paul* (New York: W. W. Norton, 1972).

2. From a lost Ebionite document, as quoted by Epiphanius (A.D. 315–403); found in Meeks, *Writings of St. Paul,* 177–78.

3. Marcion, *The Antitheses* 18; as quoted in Meeks, *Writings of St. Paul,* 190.

4. Martin Luther's "Lectures on Galatians"; as quoted in Meeks, *Writings of St. Paul,* 242.

5. Ibid., 248.

6. Albert Schweitzer, *Paul and His Interpreters* (1912; reprint, London: Adam & Charles Black, 1948), 238.

7. Ibid., 244.

8. Albert Schweitzer, *The Mysticism of Paul the Apostle;* as quoted in Meeks, *Writings of St. Paul,* 389.

9. Adolf Harnack, *What Is Christianity?* trans. Thomas Bailey Saunders, 3d and rev. ed. (New York: G. Putnam's Sons, 1904), 186–88.

10. "Every assertion about God is simultaneously an assertion about man and vice versa. For this reason and in this sense Paul's theology is, at the same time, anthropology" (Rudolf Bultmann, *Theology of the New Testament,* trans. Kendrick Grobel [London: SCM Press, 1952], 1:191.)

11. Ernst Käsemann, *Perspectives on Paul* (Philadelphia: Fortress Press, 1971), 65, presenting his own view in contrast to that of Rudolf Bultmann in *History and Eschatology.* Cf. also Ernst Käsemann, *New Testament Questions of Today* (London: SCM Press, 1969), 137.

12. As quoted in C. K. Barrett, ed., *The New Testament Background: Selected Documents* (New York: Harper & Row, 1961), 38–39.

2 Thessalonians

13. Among those rejecting the Pauline authorship of 2 Thessalonians are Norman Perrin, *The New Testament: An Introduction* (New York: Harcourt Brace Jovanovich, 1974), 119–20; and Gunther Bornkamm, *Paul,* trans. D.M.G. Stalker (New York: Harper & Row, 1971).

14. Among many defending the traditional view are John W. Bailey, "I and II Thessalonians," in *The Interpreter's Bible* (Nashville: Abingdon Press, 1955), 11:249–51; and Werner Georg Kümmel, *Introduction to the New Testament,* trans. A. J. Mattill, Jr. (Nashville: Abingdon Press, 1966), 264–69.

15. Bailey (*Interpreter's Bible,* 11:326–30) gives a more complete discussion of "the man of lawlessness." For a different approach, based on a different translation, which sees "what is . . . restraining" (2 Thess. 2:6) as "what is oppressing" and notes signs of persecution at the time of the letter, see Gerhard Kroedel, *Deutero-Pauline*

Letters, Proclamation commentary series (Philadelphia: Fortress Press, 1978), 88–96. (Kroedel believes 2 Thessalonians was written after Paul's lifetime.)

1 Corinthians

16. For example, see Bornkamm, *Paul,* 68–77; and Kümmel, *Introduction to the New Testament,* 181–82.

17. Bornkamm, *Paul,* 244–46.

18. The identification of Paul's chief opponents as "spiritual-minded" rather than as the same kind of Judaizing legalists who upset the Galatians' churches seems to be that of Bornkamm, Johannes Munck, and many others. While Hans Conzelmann does not want to call them "Gnostics," he speaks of them as "proto-Gnostics" (*1 Corinthians* [German ed., 1969; Philadelphia: Fortress Press, 1975], 15).

2 Corinthians

19. Bornkamm, *Paul.*

20. Kümmel, *Introduction to the New Testament,* 211–15.

21. Among those who place 2 Cor. 10—13 as a letter earlier than 2 Cor. 1—9 are such scholars as Floyd Filson, T. W. Manson, C. H. Dodd, R. H. Strachan, Edgar J. Goodspeed, William Barclay, C. Milo Connick, E. F. Scott, and, more recently, Charles H. Talbert. C. K. Barrett divides 2 Corinthians at chapter 10 but believes that chapters 1—9 are earlier than 10—14. F. F. Bruce shares Barrett's view; see his *1 and 2 Corinthians,* New Century Bible series (London: Oliphants, 1971), 166–72. See also, more recently, Ernest Best, *Second Corinthians* (Atlanta: John Knox Press, 1987), 1–3.

Galatians

22. Martin Luther, *Commentary on St. Paul's Epistle to the Galatians* 2:19, abridged translation by Theodore Graebner, 4th ed. (Grand Rapids: Zondervan, n.d.), 76.

23. Ibid. 1:1 (p. 9).

24. As quoted in A. Lukyn Williams, *The Epistle of Paul the Apostle to the Galatians* (Cambridge: Cambridge University Press, 1936), 67–68.

25. Greer M. Taylor, "The Function of PISTIS XRISTOU in Galatians," *Journal of Biblical Literature* 85 (1966): 58–76.

26. Joseph Fletcher, *Situation Ethics* (Philadelphia: Westminster Press, 1966), 30, 49, and passim.

27. Martin Luther, "Concerning Christian Liberty," in Harry Emerson Fosdick, ed., *Great Voices of the Reformation* (New York: Random House, 1952), 81.

Romans

28. Martin Luther, "Preface to St. Paul's Epistle to the Romans," in Fosdick, ed., *Great Voices,* 118.

29. Johannes Munck, *Paul and the Salvation of Mankind* (Richmond: John Knox Press, 1959), 42–49.

30. Suetonius, *Vita Claudii* 25.4; as found in *Documents of the Christian Church,* ed. Henry Bettenson (New York: Oxford University Press, 1947), 4.

31. See chapter 8, note 10, above.

32. Bornkamm, *Paul,* 137.

33. Karl Barth, *The Epistle to the Romans,* trans. E. C. Hoskyns, from 6th German edition (London: Oxford University Press, 1933), 42.

34. Hans Joachim Schoeps, *Paul: The Theology of the Apostle in the Light of Jewish Religious History,* as cited in Meeks, ed., *Writings of St. Paul,* 349.

35. Paul Achtemeier, *Romans,* (Atlanta: John Knox Press, 1985).

36. Schoeps, *Paul,* in Meeks, ed., *Writings of St. Paul,* 349.

9. THE PRISON EPISTLES

1. Among those who prefer the Ephesian location for some or all of the prison epistles are Leander Keck, Norman Perrin, and Eduard Lohse.

2. See below, pp. 447–49 and 454–56; and notes 11 and 16, below.

3. For a full discussion and defense of the traditional location, Rome, see Ernest F. Scott, "The Epistle to the Philippians," in *The Interpreter's Bible,* (Nashville: Abingdon Press, 1955), 11:5–8; and Francis W. Beare, "The Epistle to the Colossians," in *The Interpreter's Bible,* 11:134–37. Cf. James L. Price, *Interpreting the New Testament,* 2d ed. (New York: Holt, Rinehart & Winston, 1961), 419–22.

Philippians

4. Archibald M. Hunter, *Philippians,* vol. 22 in the Layman's Bible Commentary series (Richmond: John Knox Press, 1959), 78.

5. Kenneth Grayston, *The Letters of Paul to the Philippians and to the Thessalonians* (Cambridge: Cambridge University Press, 1967), 11.

6. Among those who divide Philippians are Norman Perrin, Francis W. Beare, and E. J. Goodspeed.

7. Philippians is regarded as a unity by Scott, "Epistle to the Philippians," 8–9; cf. various commentaries and introductions by A. M. Hunter, Bruce Metzger, Martin Dibelius, and C. Milo Connick.

8. Walter Schmithals, *Paul and the Gnostics,* trans. John E. Steely (Nashville: Abingdon Press, 1972), 65–122.

Philemon

9. See the case for this made by John Knox, "Philemon," in *The Interpreter's Bible* (Nashville: Abingdon Press, 1955), 11:557–60.

Colossians

10. Among those who deny that Paul wrote Colossians are Joseph Burgess, *The Letter to the Colossians,* Proclamation commentaries series (Philadelphia: Fortress Press, 1978), 61–67. See also Norman Perrin, *The New Testament: An Introduction* (New York: Harcourt Brace Jovanovich, 1974); and Gunther Bornkamm, *Paul,* trans. D.M.G. Stalker (New York: Harper & Row, 1971). Eduard Lohse, in his widely acclaimed *Colossians and Philemon* (Philadelphia: Fortress Press, 1971), agrees. For a full discussion of the issues, see Beare, "Colossians," 133–45. He, too, doubts that Colossians is by Paul.

11. Among those defending Pauline authorship of Colossians are Robert M. Grant, *A Historical Introduction to the New Testament* (New York: Harper & Row, 1963),

190–92; Price, *Interpreting the New Testament,* 431–32; Ralph Martin, *Ephesians, Colossians, and Philemon* (Louisville, Ky.: John Knox Press, 1992), 98–99; and more conservative scholars such as William Barclay, *The Letters to the Philippians, Colossians, and Thessalonians* (Philadelphia: Westminster Press, 1959), 121–22.

12. Irenaeus, *Against Heresies,* as cited in Robert M. Grant, ed., *Gnosticism: An Anthology* (London: William Collins Sons, 1961), 24–25.

13. For a helpful discussion of the kind of "Gnostic" heresy Paul seems to be combating in Colossae and why Paul was so opposed to it, see Martin, *Ephesians, Colossians,* 82–96.

14. A. T. Robertson, *Paul and the Intellectuals* (Garden City, N.Y.: Doubleday, 1928).

Ephesians

15. See, for example, J. Paul Sampley, *Ephesians,* Proclamation commentaries series (Philadelphia: Fortress Press, 1978), 9–12; cf. Bornkamm, *Paul;* Perrin, *New Testament;* and Grant, *Historical Introduction.*

16. Markus Barth, *Ephesians,* Anchor Bible 1 (Garden City, N.Y.: Doubleday, 1974), 36–50. See also A. Van Roon, *The Authenticity of Ephesians* (Leiden: Brill, 1974).

17. Martin, *Ephesians, Colossians,* 4.

18. Francis W. Beare, "Ephesians," in *The Interpreter's Bible* (Nashville: Abingdon Press, 1953), 10:603–4.

19. Barth, *Ephesians,* 1:50.

20. As quoted in Jack Finegan, *Light from the Ancient Past* (Princeton, N.J.: Princeton University Press, 1946), 246.

21. Tacitus, *Histories* 5.4–5; as quoted in Lamar Williamson, Jr., *God's Work of Art* (Richmond: CLC Press, 1971), 34–35.

22. *Mekilta* of Rabbi Ishmael, Exodus 14:7; as quoted in Williamson, *God's Work of Art,* 35.

10. THE PASTORAL EPISTLES

1. Justin Martyr, *First Apology* 67, in Cyril C. Richardson, trans. and ed., *Early Christian Fathers* (New York: Macmillan, 1970), 287.

2. For a defense of Pauline authorship of the pastorals, see J.N.D. Kelly, *A Commentary on the Pastoral Epistles* (New York: Harper & Row, 1963), 1–34; and Donald Guthrie, *New Testament Introduction* (Chicago: Inter-Varsity Press, 1962), 2:198–237.

3. See, for example, the very scholarly commentary by Martin Dibelius and Hans Conzelmann, *The Pastoral Epistles* (Philadelphia: Fortress Press, 1972). Compare the works of more moderate critics such as E. F. Scott, *The Literature of the New Testament* (New York: Columbia University Press, 1932), 191–97; and more recently, Thomas C. Oden, *First and Second Timothy and Titus* (Louisville, Ky.: John Knox Press, 1989), 10–15. William Barclay (*The Letters to Timothy, Titus and Philemon,* rev. ed. [Philadelphia: Westminster Press, 1975], 3–13) adopts the view that these letters as we have them contain fragments of letters actually from the pen of Paul but edited by a later hand.

4. Barclay, *Letters to Timothy, Titus,* 17.

5. Brevard S. Childs, *The New Testament as Canon: An Introduction* (Philadelphia: Fortress Press, 1985), 472. Childs is writing here both of the pastoral epistles and of 2 Peter.

Titus

6. Dibelius and Conzelmann, *Pastoral Epistles,* 158–60.

11. FIVE OPEN LETTERS

1. James L. Price, *Interpreting the New Testament,* 2d ed. (New York: Holt, Rinehart & Winston, 1961), 485.

Hebrews

2. Harold W. Attridge, *The Epistle to the Hebrews,* Hermeneia series (Philadelphia: Fortress Press, 1989), 1.

3. For example, R. H. Fuller ("The Letter to the Hebrews," in *Hebrews, James, 1 and 2 Peter, Jude, Revelation,* Proclamation commentaries series [Philadelphia: Fortress Press, 1977], 21–23) interprets chapter 13 as an addition by the author himself, as he sent off as a letter what had been one of his sermons.

4. For the position here taken, see William Manson, *The Epistle to the Hebrews* (London: Hodder & Stoughton, 1951). For a recent presentation of the more popular view, see Fuller, *Hebrews,* 1–5, 25–27; cf. Werner Georg Kümmel, *Introduction to the New Testament,* trans. A. J. Mattill, Jr. (Nashville: Abingdon Press, 1966), 279–81.

5. "He has opportunity to repent but once" (*Shepherd of Hermas* 2.4.3, in Alexander Roberts and James Donaldson, eds., *The Ante-Nicene Fathers* [Grand Rapids: Wm. B. Eerdmans, 1956], 2:22 [cf. 1.3.5 and 7]).

James

6. Among those rejecting the tradition that the epistle is by Jesus' brother are Kümmel, Price, and Burton Scott Easton; see Easton's discussion of various views on the authorship and sources of the book in "James," in *The Interpreter's Bible* (Nashville: Abingdon Press, 1957), 12:3–15. For a defense of the view that the book is by Jesus' brother, see John Wick Bowman, *James,* Layman's Bible Commentary series 24 (Richmond: John Knox Press, 1962), 93–94.

7. Josephus, *Jewish Antiquities* 20.9.1.

8. Eusebius, *Ecclesiastical History* 2.23, in C. F. Cruse, trans., *The Ecclesiastical History of Eusebius Pamphilus* (London: G. Bell, 1917), 66.

9. Martin Luther, "Preface to the Epistles of Saint James and Saint Jude," as quoted in Kümmel, *Introduction to the New Testament,* 287.

1 Peter

10. For a relatively recent, full discussion deciding against Peter as author, see Ernest Best, *I Peter,* New Century Bible series (London: Oliphants, 1971), 49–63. For an older, classic defense of Peter's authorship, see Edward Gordon Selwyn, *The First Epistle of St. Peter* (London: Macmillan, 1949), 7–38. Selwyn allows Silvanus a large

share in the actual wording of the letter in Greek. Cf. Bo Reicke, *The Epistles of James, Peter, and Jude,* Anchor Bible 37 (Garden City, N.Y.: Doubleday, 1964), 71–72. Reicke believes the content is from Peter.

11. Pliny, *Epistles* 10.97, as quoted in Price, *Interpreting the New Testament,* 479–80.

12. Reicke, *Epistles of James, Peter,* 74–75. For a more complete discussion of this interpretation, see Best, *1 Peter,* 21–27. Best, however, rejects this view but does believe that 1 Peter includes bits of baptismal liturgy.

13. Reicke, *Epistles of James, Peter,* 106.

14. This interpretation is proposed by Reicke, *Epistles of James, Peter,* 106–13.

2 Peter

15. Virtually all of the New Testament introductions and commentary series to which reference has been made previously reject the view that 2 Peter is from the pen of the apostle himself. Petrine authorship is defended, however, by the consistently conservative Donald Guthrie, *New Testament Introduction* (Chicago: Inter-Varsity Press, 1962), 2:143–71.

16. William Barclay, *The Letters of James and Peter,* rev. ed., Daily Study Bible series (Philadelphia: Westminster Press, 1976), 145.

17. Reicke, *Epistles of James, Peter,* 166–67.

Jude

18. Eusebius, *Ecclesiastical History* 3.11, trans. Cruse, 88.

19. Ibid. 3.20 (p. 92).

20. For a more complete discussion of the authorship of Jude, see Kümmel, *Introduction to the New Testament,* 300–301; and Albert E. Barnett, "Jude," in *The Interpreter's Bible* (Nashville: Abingdon Press, 1957), 12:317–19. Both reject the view that it is by a brother of Jesus. Donald Guthrie defends the tradition in *New Testament Introduction,* 2:227–29.

12. THE JOHANNINE LITERATURE

1. *The Acts of John* 38–42, in Edgar Hennecke, *New Testament Apocrypha,* ed. and trans. R. M. Wilson (London: Lutterworth Press, 1965), 2:236–37.

Revelation

2. J. Massyngberde Ford (*Revelation,* Anchor Bible [Garden City, N.Y.: Doubleday, 1975], 28–57) argues that much of Revelation is the work of a disciple of John the Baptist and is thus really pre-Christian. Others have believed that they detected Jewish sources in the book. However, the similarities to Jewish apocalyptic writings may be explained in part on the basis of a general similarity among most works in this form. While the writer probably did use sources, as is indicated by the apparent repetitions and fresh starts from time to time, current emphasis among critics has been on the unity of the book. See Elisabeth Schüssler Fiorenza, "The Revelation to John," in *Hebrews, James, 1 and 2 Peter, Jude, Revelation,* Proclamation commentaries series (Philadelphia: Fortress Press, 1977), 100. Only the most consistently conservative

commentators, such as Donald Guthrie (*New Testament Introduction,* vol. 3 [Chicago: Inter-Varsity Press, 1962]), argue that the apostle is the author.

3. Hal Lindsey, *The Late Great Planet Earth* (Grand Rapids: Zondervan, 1970).

4. See chapter 6, note 36, above.

5. Eusebius, *Ecclesiastical History* 3.17–20, in C. F. Cruse, trans., *The Ecclesiastical History of Eusebius Pamphilus* (London: G. Bell, 1917), 101–3.

6. C. I. Scofield, ed., *The New Scofield Reference Bible* (New York: Oxford University Press, 1967), 1353–55, headings and notes on Revelation 2—3.

1 John

7. Eusebius, *Ecclesiastical History* 3.28, trans. Cruse, 103. It is said that there were some fifty varieties of Gnosticism. It is here proposed that 1 John was written not specifically against the particular kind that Cerinthus represented but simply against some form of that general approach.

8. Rudolf Bultmann writes that the source, at least, of certain discourses in the Fourth Gospel "is Gnostic in outlook." He recognizes that the Fourth Gospel is also anti-Gnostic, but one of its editors has used Gnostic language, he believes, in order to convert Gnostics (*The Gospel of John: A Commentary* [Philadelphia: Westminster Press, 1971]). It is certain that the Gnostics subsequently claimed John as one of their own. First John, therefore, may have been written in part to correct that kind of misunderstanding of the Gospel.

9. D. Moody Smith, *First, Second, and Third John* (Louisville, Ky.: Westminster/ John Knox Press, 1991), 7.

10. Irenaeus, *Against Heresies* 1.26, in Alexander Roberts and James Donaldson, eds., *The Ante-Nicene Fathers* (Grand Rapids: Wm. B. Eerdmans, 1956), 1:352.

11. For a very different interpretation of 1 John, see J. C. O'Neill, *The Puzzle of I John* (London: SPCK, 1966). O'Neill argues that the author was a member of a Jewish sect, many of whom had become Christians. His opponents are Jews who had not converted to Christianity. The book is outlined around a kind of liturgy. At this time, O'Neill has not been widely followed in this view.

2 John

12. Eusebius, *Ecclesiastical History* 3.39, trans. Cruse, 127.

3 John

13. *Didache* 12.1–5, in Cyril C. Richardson, trans. and ed., *Early Christian Fathers* (New York: Macmillan, 1970), 177.

14. Rudolf Bultmann, *The Johannine Epistles* (German ed., 1967; Philadelphia: Fortress Press, 1973), 101.

The Gospel according to John

15. James Sprunt, *These Are Written* (Richmond: Presbyterian Board of Publication, 1949), 7.

16. In the next few pages, there are a number of unacknowledged quotations from an earlier work by the present writer and his wife; see William M. Ramsay and DeVere M. Ramsay, *Written That You May Believe,* Teacher's Guide (Richmond: Board of Christian Education, Presbyterian Church in the United States, 1958).

17. Charles H. Talbert, *Reading John: A Literary and Theological Commentary on the Fourth Gospel and the Johannine Epistles* (New York: Crossroad, 1992), 64.

18. Clement, quoted by Eusebius, *Ecclesiastical History* 6.14, trans. Cruse.

19. So Norman Perrin, *The New Testament: An Introduction* (New York: Harcourt Brace Jovanovich, 1974), 245.

20. Floyd V. Filson, *The Gospel according to John,* Layman's Bible Commentary (Richmond: John Knox Press, 1963), 19:19–26.

21. For a defense of Johannine authorship, see Donald Guthrie, *New Testament Introduction* (Chicago: Inter-Varsity Press, 1962), 1:216–46.

22. Gerard S. Sloyan, *What Are They Saying about John?* (New York: Paulist Press, 1991), 20.

23. For example, Robert Tomson Fortner has actually attempted to reconstruct this signs source, which he believes to be the work of a Jewish-Christian convert (*The Gospel of Signs* [Cambridge: Cambridge University Press, 1970]). Compare Rudolf Bultmann, *The Gospel of John: A Commentary,* trans. G. R. Beasley-Murray et al., (Philadelphia: Westminster Press, 1971); and C. H. Dodd, *The Interpretation of the Fourth Gospel* (New York: Cambridge University Press, 1953).

24. The view that the Fourth Gospel was the product of more than one writer, perhaps of a kind of "Johannine school," is defended in various forms by such diverse scholars as the moderately conservative William Barclay, *The Gospel of John,* rev. ed. (Philadelphia: Westminster Press, 1975), 1:15–24; the somewhat radical Norman Perrin, *New Testament,* 223, 249; and the Roman Catholic scholar Raymond E. Brown, *The Gospel according to John,* Anchor Bible (Garden City, N.Y.: Doubleday, 1970), lxxxvii–cii. For a quite different view, holding that John is not only independent of the Synoptics but is, at times, a superior source of historical information; is based on accounts by an eyewitness; and may well have been written earlier than even Mark, see John A. T. Robinson, *The Priority of John* (Grand Rapids: Wm. B. Eerdmans, 1985). At this writing, Robinson's view has not been widely adopted.

25. R. Alan Culpepper, *Anatomy of the Fourth Gospel* (Philadelphia: Fortress Press, 1983).

26. Cleanthes, "Hymn to Zeus," quoted in Jason L. Saunders, ed., *Greek and Roman Philosophy after Aristotle* (New York: Free Press, 1966), 149.

27. See pp. 514–16, above.

28. As quoted in Perrin, *New Testament,* 230.

29. James H. Charlesworth, "Reinterpreting John: How the Dead Sea Scrolls Have Revolutionized Our Understanding of the Gospel of John," in *Bible Review* 9, 1 (Feb. 1993): 19–25, 54.

30. Richard J. Cassidy, *John's Gospel in New Perspective* (Maryknoll, N.Y.: Orbis Books, 1992).

31. *The Acts of John* 98–101, in Hennecke, *New Testament Apocrypha,* 233–34.

32. Both Charles H. Talbert and R. Alan Culpepper argue that the appendix is an integral part of the book.